Exploring Cognitive and Psychosocial Dynamics Across Childhood and Adolescence

Maria Sofologi
University of Ioannina, Greece

Dimitra Katsarou
University of the Aegean, Greece

Efthymia Efthymiou
Zayed University, UAE

A volume in the Advances in
Psychology, Mental Health, and
Behavioral Studies (APMHBS)
Book Series

Published in the United States of America by
    IGI Global
    Information Science Reference (an imprint of IGI Global)
    701 E. Chocolate Avenue
    Hershey PA, USA 17033
    Tel: 717-533-8845
    Fax: 717-533-8661
    E-mail: cust@igi-global.com
    Web site: http://www.igi-global.com

Library of Congress Cataloging-in-Publication Data

CIP DATA PENDING

ISBN13: 979-8-3693-4022-6
EISBN13: 979-8-3693-4023-3

British Cataloguing in Publication Data
A Cataloguing in Publication record for this book is available from the British Library.

All work contributed to this book is new, previously-unpublished material.
The views expressed in this book are those of the authors, but not necessarily of the publisher.

For electronic access to this publication, please contact: eresources@igi-global.com.

Table of Contents

    Alexandros Argyriadis, Frederick University, Cyprus
    Olga Drakopoulou, Hellenic Ministry of Education, Greece
    Agathi Argyriadi, Frederick University, Cyprus
    Evangelos Mantsos, University of Thessaly, Greece
    Dimitra V. Katsarou, University of the Aegean, Greece
    Asterios Patsiaouras, University of Thessaly, Greece

    Kalliopi Megari, Department of Psychology, CITY College, University
        of York Europe Campus, Thessaloniki, Greece
    Evanthia Smyrli, Department of Psychology, CITY College, University
        of York Europe Campus, Thessaloniki, Greece

    Christina Galanou, Panteion University, Greece

    Alexandros Argyriadis, Frederick University, Cyprus
    Efthymia Efthymiou, Zayed University, UAE
    Dimitra Katsarou, University of the Aegean, Greece
    Maria Sofologi, University of Ioannina, Greece
    Agathi Argyriadi, Frederick University, Cyprus

Detailed Table of Contents

    Alexandros Argyriadis, Frederick University, Cyprus
    Olga Drakopoulou, Hellenic Ministry of Education, Greece
    Agathi Argyriadi, Frederick University, Cyprus
    Evangelos Mantsos, University of Thessaly, Greece
    Dimitra V. Katsarou, University of the Aegean, Greece
    Asterios Patsiaouras, University of Thessaly, Greece

The aim of this literature review was to provide a comprehensive overview of these strategies and evaluate their effectiveness in promoting mental wellness. Utilizing a systematic literature review as primary method, this study examined peer-reviewed articles, clinical studies, and meta-analyses published over the past decade. It focused on identifying practices that support neurodiversity, such as tailored therapy modalities, inclusive educational practices, and workplace accommodations, alongside general mental health management strategies like mindfulness, cognitive-behavioral therapy (CBT), and community support initiatives. The results revealed that approaches which honor the individual's neurodiversity while addressing their mental health needs lead to improved outcomes, including enhanced self-esteem, better social integration, and increased productivity. Specifically, personalized interventions that consider the unique perspectives and needs of neurodiverse individuals were found to be more effective than traditional, one-size-fits-all approaches.

    Kalliopi Megari, Department of Psychology, CITY College, University
        of York Europe Campus, Thessaloniki, Greece
    Evanthia Smyrli, Department of Psychology, CITY College, University
        of York Europe Campus, Thessaloniki, Greece

According to Piaget's theory, there are four distinct neurodevelopment stages, each of which corresponds to a specific age group and is distinguished by a particular number of cognitive attainments. The stages are as follows: a) sensorimotor; b) preoperational; c) concrete operational; and d) formal operational. Four primary domains are used to track development from infancy to adolescence: a) speech and language; b) gross and fine motor abilities; c) social and emotional skills; and d) cognitive ability. By recognizing the normal growth milestones in every category, we may comprehend the variations linked to different abnormal developing patterns. In numerous cognitive domains, children with disabilities may have delays or deficits during childhood that may last into adulthood. Numerous studies have examined the changes in brain activity that corresponds with the acquisition of cognitive skills at each developmental stage. Some of these studies suggest that children with a variety of neuropsychological developmental disorders show neurocognitive deficits in areas like verbal communication, attention, memory, and specific executive functions, while language and visuospatial abilities vary.

    Christina Galanou, Panteion University, Greece

This chapter explores the prevalence and impact of psychosomatic symptoms in children and adolescents, emphasizing the crucial role of early intervention in mitigating their effects on overall well-being of youth. Drawing on recent evidence, the chapter aims to highlight the various psychosomatic symptoms observed in underage population and discusses the potential psychosocial consequences of untreated symptoms. Furthermore, it examines the importance of recognizing and addressing psychosomatic symptoms during the early stages of development and provides insights into effective intervention strategies. Lastly, it underscores the need for a holistic approach that promotes a non-binary perspective of the health of youth and involves collaboration among parents, educators, healthcare professionals, and mental health specialists.

Chapter 4

    Alexandros Argyriadis, Frederick University, Cyprus
    Efthymia Efthymiou, Zayed University, UAE
    Dimitra Katsarou, University of the Aegean, Greece
    Maria Sofologi, University of Ioannina, Greece
    Agathi Argyriadi, Frederick University, Cyprus

This chapter focuses on the critical examination of stress factors affecting adolescents and the effectiveness of various management techniques aimed at fostering resilience and promoting recovery. With the backdrop of escalating stress levels among adolescents driven by academic pressures, social dynamics, and digital media exposure, this chapter identifies emerging research trends that focus on both individual and systemic interventions designed to mitigate stress and enhance mental well-being. The results underscore the significant impact of multi-faceted stress management programs that combine psychological, physical, and social strategies. Techniques that promote mindfulness and emotional regulation, such as meditation and yoga, alongside CBT, were notably effective in enhancing adolescents' resilience to stress. In conclusion, the chapter highlights the imperative for a holistic approach to stress management among adolescents, emphasizing the need for interventions that are adaptable to diverse needs and contexts.

Antonia Stelianou, Independent Researcher, Greece
Evagelia Dalapera, Independent Researcher, Greece
Pineio Christodoulou, Department of Education, School of Education,
    University of Nicosia, Cyprus

The present study is a participatory action research entitled "I Learn, Play, and
Have Fun With Toys I Make," which was carried out in a kindergarten, with the
participation of the teachers and the preschool students who attended it. The aim
of this action research was to upgrade and enrich the educational material in a
playful way, by making improvised games, which facilitate and expand the teaching
process of the teachers and the learning process of the students. The action research
focused primarily on the active involvement of the participating kindergarten
students regarding the construction of improvised educational materials, primarily
with recyclable materials. As for the research tools, participatory observation, the
semi-structured interview, the questionnaire for parents and students, as well as the
diary of the participating teachers were selected and used as the most appropriate.
The results showed that the specific action research had many benefits for the
participating students. An effect on the all-round and balanced development of the
students' personalities was evident.

Assimina Tsibidaki, University of the Aegean, Greece
Vana Chiou, University of the Aegean, Greece

This study aims to explore the degree of loneliness of adolescents with LDs, and
the possible differences and correlations with the type of LDs, gender, and age. The
sample comprised 30 adolescences with LDs, 14 (46.7%) boys and 16 (53.3%) girls,
aged 12-15 years (M=13.60, Sd=.770). A self-report questionnaire and the children's
loneliness questionnaire (CLQ) were used for data collection. The findings of the
study indicated that all adolescents, regardless of the type of LDs, demonstrated
moderate to low levels of loneliness. There was no statistically significant difference
between students with MGLDs and students with SpLDs relating to feelings of
loneliness, although students with MGLDs experienced feelings of loneliness higher
compared to students with SLDs. As far as the gender, there was no significant
difference between girls and boys; however, the girls scored higher. Finally, there
was no correlation with age.

Aggressive behaviour in children and adolescents is a multifaceted problem with potentially severe consequences for individuals and society. The present chapter aims to provide a comprehensive literature review, examining the psychosocial dimensions of aggression that contribute to aggressive tendencies, highlighting the early onset and distinct developmental patterns during childhood and adolescence. It also emphasises the detrimental effects of factors such as difficult temperament, parenting style, bullying, social rejection, and hostile attribution bias. It explores the severe consequences of untreated aggression, including academic failure, social isolation, mental health problems, and increased risk of crime and violence. Finally, this chapter advocates evidence-based prevention strategies and interventions targeting individual, family, and social factors to reduce aggressive behaviour. Promising approaches include cognitive-behavioural therapy, parent education programs, and social skills training, fostering positive behaviour change for a safer society.

Autism is a neurobehavioral syndrome that significantly affects a person's social interaction, communication, and imagination. The term 'ASD' (autism spectrum disorders) refers to a group of neurodevelopmental disorders and is used to encompass and merge certain diagnoses. Disorders within this spectrum can be characterized as a continuum of ability levels that extends from mental retardation to intellectual intelligence. Moreover, they manifest themselves early in a person's life and profoundly affect the perception of oneself and the world, learning and adaptation to the demands of everyday life. This chapter aims to understand the nature of neurocognitive deficits in ASD with an emphasis on how this can influence the formulation of treatment goals at an educational and clinical level. It focuses on the definition of ASD and their description presenting the neurocognitive deficits and their behavioral manifestation, as well as the resulting goals.

The aim of the present chapter is to argue that educational strategies are not adequate on their own to promote inclusion for autistic individuals, because this holds only the individual responsible for their inclusion with no onus on the settings or other people involved; as a result, autistic individuals are facing challenges at school and in society throughout their lifespan. Therefore, for inclusion to be enacted, a change of attitudes, perceptions, and stereotypes about the education and development of autistic individuals considering a biopsychosocial bioecological model of disability is deemed critical. This chapter aims to discuss current conceptualization of autism, traditional models of disability in relation to autism and present an overarching framework that sheds light on overcoming existing tensions and challenges in the inclusion of autistic individuals as well as make suggestions for moving forward in promoting inclusion in the autism field.

Chapter 10

This study aimed to explore the cognitive abilities and executive functioning behaviors of students with ASD at an autism center in the UAE, employing the SB-5 and the teacher form of the BRIEF2. The findings provide important insights into the cognitive and executive function profiles of these students, highlighting the intricate relationships between various cognitive domains, executive function behaviors, and the impact of ASD severity and notable talents. The positive correlations observed between different SB-5 IQ measures (e.g., full-scale IQ, nonverbal IQ, verbal IQ, and working memory IQ) and the shift scale of the BRIEF are consistent with the findings of previous studies that highlight the link between cognitive flexibility and intelligence.

Chapter 11

Maria Theodoratou, Neapolis University Pafos, Cyprus
Georgios A. Kougioumtzis, National Kapodistrian University, Greece
Vasiliki Yotsidi, Panteion University, Greece
Panoraia Andriopoulou, University of Ioannina, Greece
Kalliopi Megari, City College, University of York, Europe Campus, Greece
Christiana Koundourou, Neapolis University Pafos, Cyprus
Zoi Siouti, National and Kapodistrian University, Greece
Marios Argyrides, Neapolis University Pafos, Cyprus

The co-occurrence of ADHD and ASD presents a complex diagnostic challenge due to overlapping symptoms, potentially leading to one condition being treated while the other is neglected. They are widely recognized psychiatric conditions in children and adolescents, with a solid hereditary, neurological, and biochemical basis. Effective intervention strategies must consider the distinct needs of both conditions, requiring a flexible, multidisciplinary approach integrating medication, behavioral therapies, educational supports, and family involvement. Increased awareness and education are essential to dispel misconceptions and foster supportive environments. Social and emotional support is crucial for individuals navigating life with both ADHD and ASD, addressing challenges in forming relationships, and managing anxiety. Future efforts should focus on developing sophisticated diagnostic tools, personalized treatment plans, and advocating for those affected by these conditions to enhance overall well-being and opportunities.

Kyriaki Tasiou, University of the Aegean, Greece
Eleni N. Nikolaou, University of the Aegean, Greece

Attention deficit hyperactivity disorder (ADHD) is a neurodevelopmental disorder
that affects people diagnosed with it and their families in many ways. The purpose
of this study was to evaluate possible determinants of parent wellbeing and to
examine the influence of having a child diagnosed with ADHD on the social and
emotional well-being of parents. The aim of the present study was also to add to the
existing literature information about intervention programs that have implemented
to parents of children with ADHD and examine their effectiveness on various
dimensions related to parental well-being and psychological well-being. These
programs, which are specially designed for the training of parents of children with
ADHD, are mainly based on the strengthening of mindfulness, self-care, guidance in
coping strategies and techniques for managing children's challenging behaviours, and
support and counseling of parents. The results obtained are encouraging regarding
the effectiveness of these programs.

Stergiani Giaouri, University of Western Macedonia, Greece

This chapter investigates theory of mind (ToM) development and performance on
fantasy-reality distinction tasks in children with intellectual disabilities (ID) of
different etiologies. ToM is crucial for understanding others' mental states, while the
ability to distinguish between fantasy and reality is essential for cognitive flexibility.
Children with ID often face challenges in these domains, impacting their social and
adaptive functioning. In this study, 106 children were examined: forty-two children
with typical development (TD), forty-one children with intellectual disability (ID)
of unknown etiology, and twenty-three children with Down syndrome (DS). A set of
fantasy-reality discrimination tasks was used. The findings contribute to advancing
our understanding of ToM development and the fantasy-reality distinction in children
with ID and DS, fostering inclusive education, and promoting social inclusion for
these individuals.

Early trauma is caused to increase disease among youth. It also has an adverse impact on brain development and impairs the various other facets of daily life functioning of youth. This chapter, thus, provides a systematic outline of physical manifestations of long-term psychological trauma and the somatization of psychological symptoms among youth. The summary of 50 research articles and book chapters are included in this chapter. A systematic method is employed to collect and synthesize information. The authors have screened open-sourced articles published in English available in the public domain which were published after 2000 using various keywords such as youth, psychological trauma, somatization, and childhood maltreatment. It supports the idea that prolonged exposure to trauma results in physical symptoms like exhaustion, fatigue, high blood pressure, and anxiety among youth. It may also be responsible for increasing various diseases like diabetes and abuse disorders among youth.

Violence in any of its forms is a common secret and an unseen wound that occurs behind closed doors in families whose members are reluctant to admit that they have been victimized because of the fear of renewed threats from the perpetrator and social stigmatization. Possible causes include inadequate psychological functioning of parents, the perpetrator's sense of receiving 'value' counterproductively, possible mental illness, controlling relationships, history of aggressive behavior, lack of trust and solidarity relationships, lack of meaningful communication, shaking of fundamentals, crisis of humanistic values and the institution of the family, etc. Dealing with such a multifactorial phenomenon requires the rallying of many institutions and organizations and systematic collective efforts to eliminate or at least reduce the phenomenon. Prevention focuses mainly on the cultivation of values such as social equality, justice, meritocracy, the cultivation of moral values and ideals, and the promotion of good role models.

Juvenile delinquency is considered as the act of engaging in any illegal behavior by a person under the legal age of majority. Individual characteristics, family, school, peer groups and society play a crucial role in the adoption of delinquent behavior by a minor. Some protective factors that limit criminal behavior of children and adolescents are the ability of the minor to both self-regulate their emotions and comprehend the consequences of their acts, a supportive family, an efficient parental supervision, commitment in school, and the development of friendships focused on values such as solidarity or empathy. Society plays a crucial role in the moulding of a minor's behavior. The policies/measures that can be taken have to be compatible with a number of dispositions on both national and international level. The proposed chapter seeks to both present the risk factors of juvenile delinquency and suggest techniques for the prevention and repression of criminality in minors.

Foreword

"Do not train a child to learn by force or harshness; but direct them to it by what amuses their minds, so that you may be better able to discover with accuracy the peculiar bent of the genius of each".

Plato
Greek Philosopher
427 – 328 BC

The intricate and multifaceted nature of cognitive, psychosocial, and developmental challenges presents opportunities and complexities for professionals working with affected individuals. In *Exploring Cognitive and Psychosocial Dynamics Across Childhood and Adolescence*, the editors and contributors offer a profound synthesis of contemporary research and evidence-based practices, addressing the nuanced needs of children and adolescents through their developmental stages.

United by their extensive expertise and practical insights, the editors and authors have crafted an informative and actionable volume. This book emerges at a pivotal time as our understanding of the various factors influencing cognitive and psychosocial development continues to evolve. In an era where technological advancements like Neuralink and brain-machine interfaces are beginning to transform our understanding of the brain's potential, the insights provided in this book could not be timelier. By exploring the cutting-edge intersection of technology, neuroscience, and psychosocial development, this volume lays the groundwork for future innovations that may one day reshape how we approach neurodevelopmental disorders and cognitive enhancement.

This book, which spans sixteen insightful chapters, explores diverse aspects of cognitive and psychosocial development. The initial chapters provide a foundation for understanding holistic wellness, mental health management, and neurodiversity. Subsequent chapters delve into neuropsychological development, psychosomatic issues in the digital age, and the significance of early intervention and stress management.

The volume further addresses the role of improvised play in preschool personality development, loneliness in students with learning disabilities, and strategies for managing aggressive behavior. It also examines the neurocognitive profiles of individuals with Autism Spectrum Disorder (ASD), educational strategies for promoting inclusion, and interventions for co-occurring conditions like ADHD and ASD.

Additional chapters review the well-being of parents raising children with ADHD, the theory of mind in children with intellectual disabilities, and the somatization of psychological symptoms. The book concludes with a focus on domestic and gender-based violence and juvenile delinquency, offering psychoeducational proposals and prevention techniques.

This comprehensive exploration not only enhances our current knowledge but also highlights areas in need of further research. On the brink of unprecedented advancements in neuroscience and biotechnology, understanding the complex interplay of genetic, neurological, and environmental factors becomes increasingly crucial. This book calls for future investigation and situates itself as a key resource in the evolving dialogue on how emerging technologies might one day offer new ideas for intervention and support. By unraveling the complex interplay of genetic, neurological, and environmental factors, this book paves the way for future investigation and practical application.

A notable strength of this volume is its emphasis on interdisciplinary collaboration. Integrating diverse perspectives and fostering a collaborative approach offers tailored interventions that can significantly improve outcomes for those affected by cognitive and psychosocial challenges.

I extend my deepest gratitude to the editors, Drs. Maria Sofologi, Dimitra Katsarou and Efthymia Efthymiou, for their exceptional contributions to this volume. Their dedication and expertise have been pivotal in creating a groundbreaking work that bridges the gap in existing literature. *Exploring Cognitive and Psychosocial Dynamics Across Childhood and Adolescence* offers a much-needed interdisciplinary perspective by integrating cutting-edge research from psycholinguistics, neuroscience, and developmental psychology. By synthesizing seminal works and highlighting innovative studies, Drs. Sofologi, Katsarou and Efthymiou have provided a holistic understanding of language development and emotional intelligence from preschool to adolescence. Their efforts not only advance our grasp of these critical issues but also deliver a vital resource for both professionals and families, enhancing the development of effective, evidence-based interventions and support strategies.

As we continue to navigate the evolving cognitive and psychosocial development landscape, we consider how future innovations, such as those inspired by neural technologies, might further influence our approaches. May this book inspire further exploration and dialogue and a forward-thinking vision that embraces the potential of tomorrow's breakthroughs. By embracing the strengths and experiences of those we aim to support, we can make a meaningful and lasting impact on their lives.

Marilena Mousoulidou

Neapolis University Pafos, Cyprus

Preface

In presenting *Exploring Cognitive and Psychosocial Dynamics Across Childhood and Adolescence*, we are not merely offering a collection of academic research; we are providing a transformative resource designed to influence both thought and practice in the fields of developmental psychology, psycholinguistics, and education. This book is crafted to meet the needs of a diverse audience, including researchers, clinicians, educators, and policymakers, all of whom are engaged in the critical work of shaping developmental outcomes for children and adolescents.

Our goal is to bridge the gap between cutting-edge research and practical application. By delving deeply into the cognitive and psychosocial factors that underpin language development and academic achievement, this volume provides a nuanced understanding that will have far-reaching implications for your work. Each chapter is structured to not only present the latest findings but also to offer actionable insights and evidence-based recommendations. Whether you are involved in diagnosing and treating developmental disorders, designing educational interventions, or formulating policy, this book equips you with the knowledge and tools needed to make informed, impactful decisions.

For researchers and scholars, this volume serves as a comprehensive reference that synthesizes current trends and emerging perspectives in the study of cognitive and psychosocial development. It presents a holistic view that integrates theory with practice, offering a platform for further investigation and discourse. The breadth of topics covered, from neuropsychological assessments to the integration of emotional intelligence in learning, ensures that you will find valuable resources to support and expand your research endeavors.

Clinicians will find this book to be a vital tool for understanding and addressing the complex interplay of cognitive and emotional factors in their practice. The detailed examinations of diagnostic tools and the latest advancements in neurolinguistics provide a solid foundation for accurate assessment and effective intervention strategies. By incorporating these insights into your clinical practice, you can enhance your ability to support and guide children and adolescents through their developmental challenges.

Educators and policymakers will benefit greatly from the practical strategies and recommendations presented in this book. The discussions on learning processes, school achievement, and educational strategies are designed to inform and inspire innovations in teaching and policy. The emphasis on inclusion and personalized approaches aligns with contemporary educational goals, offering guidance on how to create supportive learning environments that cater to the diverse needs of students.

In essence, *Exploring Cognitive and Psychosocial Dynamics Across Childhood and Adolescence* is more than a scholarly text; it is a catalyst for change. By integrating the latest research with practical applications, this book aims to empower its readers to drive advancements in developmental science and educational practice. It is our hope that the knowledge and insights provided will foster new ideas, inspire ongoing research, and contribute to the development of more effective, inclusive, and empathetic approaches to education and intervention.

We are excited to share this work with you and look forward to the impact it will undoubtedly have on advancing our understanding of cognitive and psychosocial development. May this book serve as a beacon of knowledge and a guide for those dedicated to making a meaningful difference in the lives of children and adolescents.

CHAPTER OVERVIEWS

Chapter 1: Towards Holistic Wellness: Strategies for Managing Mental Health and Embracing Neurodiversity

This chapter presents a thorough literature review on effective strategies for promoting mental wellness, particularly through the lens of neurodiversity. By synthesizing findings from peer-reviewed articles, clinical studies, and meta-analyses from the past decade, the chapter evaluates various practices that support neurodiverse individuals. It emphasizes the importance of personalized interventions, including tailored therapy modalities, inclusive educational practices, and workplace accommodations. The review highlights that approaches respecting neurodiversity and addressing mental health needs result in significant improvements in self-esteem, social integration, and productivity. It argues that personalized, nuanced interventions are more effective than traditional, uniform approaches, advocating for practices that recognize and cater to the unique needs of neurodiverse individuals.

Chapter 2: Neuropsychological Status From Preschool Age up to Adolescence: Evidence from Typical Children and Children with Disabilities

This chapter explores neuropsychological development from preschool through adolescence, focusing on both typical and atypical developmental trajectories. Based on Piaget's theory, it details the cognitive attainments across different developmental stages—sensorimotor, preoperational, concrete operational, and formal operational. It assesses development in speech and language, motor abilities, social-emotional skills, and cognitive functions. The chapter also examines how developmental disorders may impact these areas, noting that children with disabilities often exhibit delays or deficits that may persist into adulthood. It discusses the neurocognitive deficits observed in children with various developmental disorders, including verbal attention, memory, and executive functions.

Chapter 3: Psychosomatic Symptoms in Children and Adolescents in the Digital Era: The Importance of Early Intervention

Focusing on the prevalence and impact of psychosomatic symptoms among children and adolescents, this chapter underscores the critical role of early intervention. It reviews recent evidence on psychosomatic symptoms and their psychosocial consequences if left untreated. The chapter advocates for early recognition and intervention to mitigate the effects of these symptoms on youth well-being. It highlights the need for a holistic approach involving collaboration among parents, educators, healthcare professionals, and mental health specialists to address psychosomatic issues effectively and support overall developmental health.

Chapter 4: Resilience and Recovery: Effective Stress Management Techniques for Adolescents

This chapter examines the stress factors affecting adolescents and evaluates the effectiveness of various stress management techniques. Given the rising stress levels due to academic pressures, social dynamics, and digital media, the chapter reviews emerging research on individual and systemic interventions. It highlights the success of multi-faceted stress management programs that incorporate psychological, physical, and social strategies. Techniques such as mindfulness, meditation, yoga, and cognitive-behavioral therapy (CBT) are emphasized for their effectiveness in enhancing resilience and managing stress. The chapter concludes with a call for adaptable, holistic approaches to stress management that cater to diverse adolescent needs.

Chapter 5: The Contribution of Improvised Play to the Personality Development of Preschool Children

This participatory action research study investigates how improvised play contributes to the personality development of preschool children. Conducted in a kindergarten setting, the research involved teachers and students in creating educational materials from recyclable items. The study used participatory observation, semi-structured interviews, and questionnaires to gather data. Findings reveal that improvised play fosters all-around personality development in children, enhancing their learning experiences and contributing to a more engaging and effective educational environment.

Chapter 6: Students with Learning Disabilities and Feelings of Loneliness

This chapter explores the levels of loneliness among adolescents with learning disabilities (LDs) and examines correlations with LD types, gender, and age. Using self-report questionnaires and the Children's Loneliness Questionnaire (CLQ), the study finds that adolescents with LDs experience moderate to low levels of loneliness. There are no significant differences between types of LDs or genders in loneliness levels, though girls report slightly higher loneliness compared to boys. The study provides insights into the emotional experiences of students with LDs, highlighting the need for targeted support to address feelings of isolation.

Chapter 7: Psychosocial Development for Children and Adolescents Exhibiting Aggressive Behaviour

This chapter provides a comprehensive review of psychosocial factors contributing to aggressive behavior in children and adolescents. It examines the early onset of aggression, its developmental patterns, and the impact of factors such as temperament, parenting style, bullying, and social rejection. The chapter discusses the severe consequences of untreated aggression, including academic failure and social isolation, and advocates for evidence-based prevention strategies. It highlights cognitive-behavioral therapy, parent education programs, and social skills training as effective interventions to address aggressive behavior and promote positive change.

Chapter 8: Neurocognitive Profile in Autism Spectrum Disorder and Implementation of New Goals in Different Settings

This chapter delves into the neurocognitive deficits associated with Autism Spectrum Disorder (ASD) and their implications for setting educational and clinical goals. It describes the spectrum of ASD, from intellectual disability to high-functioning autism, and how these neurocognitive deficits impact learning and adaptation. The chapter provides insights into formulating treatment goals tailored to the specific needs of individuals with ASD, aiming to enhance their ability to navigate everyday life and achieve developmental milestones.

Chapter 9: Beyond Educational Strategies in Promoting Inclusion for Autistic Individuals: An Overarching Framework and the Way Forward

Arguing that educational strategies alone are insufficient for true inclusion of autistic individuals, this chapter proposes a broader framework that incorporates changes in attitudes, perceptions, and societal structures. It critiques traditional models of disability and emphasizes the need for a biopsychosocial approach. The chapter discusses current challenges in the inclusion of autistic individuals and offers recommendations for overcoming barriers to create more inclusive educational and social environments.

Chapter 10: Cognitive Abilities and Executive Functioning in Students with Autism Spectrum Disorder: Insights from the United Arab Emirates

This chapter investigates the cognitive abilities and executive functioning of students with ASD at an Autism Center in the UAE. Using tools like the SB-5 and the BRIEF2, the study provides insights into the cognitive and executive profiles of these students. It highlights the relationships between different cognitive domains and executive function behaviors, emphasizing the link between cognitive flexibility and intelligence. The findings contribute to a better understanding of how cognitive and executive functioning intersect with ASD severity and abilities.

Chapter 11: Clinical Neuropsychological Profile and Interventions for Co-occurrence of ADHD and ASD

Addressing the complexities of diagnosing and treating co-occurring ADHD and ASD, this chapter reviews the overlapping symptoms and challenges in managing both conditions simultaneously. It discusses the need for a multidisciplinary approach that includes medication, behavioral therapies, educational supports, and family involvement. The chapter advocates for increased awareness, sophisticated diagnostic tools, and personalized treatment plans to address the unique needs of individuals with both ADHD and ASD, aiming to improve their overall well-being and life opportunities.

Chapter 12: Well-being Among Parents Raising a Child Diagnosed with Attention Deficit Hyperactivity Disorder (ADHD) and Intervention Programs: A Literature Review

This literature review evaluates the impact of having a child with ADHD on parental well-being and examines intervention programs designed to support parents. The review identifies key factors affecting parental social and emotional well-being and assesses the effectiveness of programs focused on mindfulness, self-care, and coping strategies. The findings highlight the positive impact of these programs on parental well-being and offer insights into strategies for supporting families navigating the challenges of raising a child with ADHD.

Chapter 13: Theory of Mind and the Performance of Children with Intellectual Disability and Down Syndrome on Fantasy-Reality Distinction Tasks

This chapter explores Theory of Mind (ToM) development and the ability to distinguish between fantasy and reality in children with intellectual disabilities, including those with Down syndrome. By examining performance on fantasy-reality distinction tasks, the study enhances our understanding of cognitive flexibility and social functioning in these children. The findings contribute to inclusive education practices and promote social inclusion for children with intellectual disabilities and Down syndrome by addressing their unique cognitive and developmental needs.

Chapter 14: A Review-Based Theoretical Analysis on Somatization of Psychological Symptoms and Physical Manifestation of Trauma in Youth

Focusing on the physical manifestations of psychological trauma, this chapter provides a systematic review of research on somatization among youth. It outlines the long-term effects of trauma on physical health, including symptoms like fatigue, high blood pressure, and anxiety. The review synthesizes findings from various studies to illustrate how trauma can lead to increased disease prevalence and other health issues. This analysis underscores the need for addressing both psychological and physical aspects of trauma to support youth effectively.

Chapter 15: Domestic and Gender-Based Violence Data and Developmental Psychoeducational Proposals

This chapter addresses the hidden issue of domestic and gender-based violence, exploring its causes and impact on families. It highlights the need for comprehensive strategies to tackle this multifaceted problem, emphasizing the role of social values, education, and institutional efforts in prevention. The chapter proposes psychoeducational initiatives aimed at fostering social equality, justice, and moral values, and outlines steps for reducing violence and supporting affected individuals.

Chapter 16: Juvenile Delinquency: Risk Factors and Prevention Techniques

Examining juvenile delinquency, this chapter identifies key risk factors including individual traits, family dynamics, school environment, and societal influences. It also explores protective factors that can mitigate criminal behavior, such as emotional self-regulation, supportive family structures, and value-oriented friendships. The chapter discusses prevention techniques and policies necessary to address juvenile delinquency, emphasizing the need for interventions that are informed by both national and international frameworks to effectively reduce criminal behavior in minors.

Each chapter in this volume contributes to a comprehensive understanding of the cognitive and psychosocial dynamics influencing childhood and adolescence, offering valuable insights and practical strategies for professionals dedicated to fostering positive developmental outcomes.

As we reach the end of Exploring Cognitive and Psychosocial Dynamics Across Childhood and Adolescence, it is with great satisfaction that we reflect on the rich tapestry of insights and advancements presented in this volume. This book stands as a testament to the collective expertise and dedication of its contributors, each of whom has contributed to a deeper understanding of the myriad factors shaping the development of children and adolescents.

In our journey through this comprehensive collection, we have explored diverse dimensions of cognitive and psychosocial development. From holistic approaches to managing mental health and embracing neurodiversity, to understanding the intricate neuropsychological and psychosocial profiles of children with various developmental disorders, this volume offers a nuanced view of the challenges and opportunities present in developmental science.

The discussions on psychosomatic symptoms and stress management underscore the importance of early intervention and holistic support, advocating for collaborative approaches that involve families, educators, and mental health professionals. The insights into improvised play, learning disabilities, and aggressive behavior provide practical strategies for fostering positive developmental outcomes, while the exploration of Autism Spectrum Disorder and the co-occurrence of ADHD further highlights the need for tailored and multidisciplinary approaches.

Our examination of the impact of parental well-being, the importance of Theory of Mind, and the physical manifestations of psychological trauma reveals the complex interplay between psychological and physical health, calling for integrated support systems that address both dimensions. The chapters on domestic and gender-based violence, as well as juvenile delinquency, remind us of the broader social context and the critical role of preventive and psychoeducational strategies in promoting safety and well-being.

Ultimately, this volume is more than just a repository of knowledge; it is a catalyst for change. It bridges the gap between research and practice, offering actionable insights and evidence-based recommendations that have the potential to transform educational practices, clinical interventions, and policy-making. Our hope is that the knowledge contained within these pages will inspire continued research, foster innovation, and contribute to the development of more effective, inclusive, and compassionate approaches to supporting children and adolescents.

We extend our heartfelt thanks to the authors for their invaluable contributions and to our readers for their commitment to advancing the field. May this book serve as a guiding light for all those dedicated to understanding and nurturing the cognitive and psychosocial development of young people.

Chapter 1
Towards Holistic Wellness:
Strategies for Managing Mental Health and Embracing Neurodiversity

Alexandros Argyriadis
https://orcid.org/0000-0001-5754-4787

Frederick University, Cyprus

Olga Drakopoulou
Hellenic Ministry of Education, Greece

Agathi Argyriadi
Frederick University, Cyprus

Evangelos Mantsos
University of Thessaly, Greece

Dimitra V. Katsarou
https://orcid.org/0000-0001-8690-0314

University of the Aegean, Greece

Asterios Patsiaouras
https://orcid.org/0009-0005-3398-2885

University of Thessaly, Greece

ABSTRACT

The aim of this literature review was to provide a comprehensive overview of these strategies and evaluate their effectiveness in promoting mental wellness. Utilizing a systematic literature review as primary method, this study examined peer-reviewed articles, clinical studies, and meta-analyses published over the past decade. It focused on identifying practices that support neurodiversity, such as tailored therapy modalities, inclusive educational practices, and workplace accommodations, alongside general mental health management strategies like mindfulness, cognitive-behavioral therapy (CBT), and community support initiatives. The results revealed that approaches which honor the individual's neurodiversity while addressing their

DOI: 10.4018/979-8-3693-4022-6.ch001

1

mental health needs lead to improved outcomes, including enhanced self-esteem, better social integration, and increased productivity. Specifically, personalized interventions that consider the unique perspectives and needs of neurodiverse individuals were found to be more effective than traditional, one-size-fits-all approaches.

INTRODUCTION

The integration of neurodiverse individuals into mainstream mental health practices is increasingly recognized as essential for fostering an inclusive society. Neurodiversity, a term that encompasses a range of neurological conditions including autism, ADHD, dyslexia, and others, advocates for understanding and respecting these differences as variations in human functioning rather than deficiencies. Holistic wellness is an approach that considers the whole person, including their physical, emotional, social, and mental health needs. In the context of mental health, holistic strategies often incorporate practices such as mindfulness, yoga, and community support. These practices aim to enhance overall well-being rather than just treating specific symptoms. The literature indicates that such strategies can lead to improved mental health outcomes by fostering resilience and promoting self-care.

Recent research trends in the field of holistic wellness and neurodiversity reflect an increasing recognition of the need for inclusive and personalized approaches to mental health. Scholars and practitioners are moving away from one-size-fits-all models and towards strategies that honor individual differences, particularly those of neurodiverse populations. This shift is evident in several key areas of research (Argyriadis and Argyriadi, 2024).

One prominent trend is the development and implementation of personalized interventions tailored to the specific needs of neurodiverse individuals. For example, Cognitive Behavioral Therapy (CBT) has been adapted for individuals with Autism Spectrum Disorder (ASD) to include visual aids and concrete examples, making it more accessible and effective (Kozlowski et al., 2019). Similarly, mindfulness practices have been customized to help those with ADHD manage anxiety and enhance attention (Zylowska et al., 2008). These adaptations acknowledge that neurodiverse individuals require tailored therapeutic approaches that cater to their unique cognitive and emotional profiles.

Inclusive education is another critical area of focus. Research indicates that differentiated instruction and the use of assistive technology can significantly improve learning outcomes for neurodiverse students (Lindsay et al., 2019). For instance, speech-to-text software and visual schedules are increasingly being utilized to support students with dyslexia and ASD, respectively, enhancing both academic performance and social integration (Bakker et al., 2019). Inclusive educational practices are shown to not only facilitate better learning but also improve self-esteem and peer relationships among neurodiverse students (Ashburner et al., 2010).

In the realm of employment, there is growing evidence supporting the effectiveness of workplace accommodations for neurodiverse employees. Flexible working hours, quiet workspaces, and structured routines are examples of accommodations that help individuals with conditions like ASD and ADHD thrive in professional settings (Hendricks, 2010; Biederman et al., 2012). Studies have shown that such accommodations lead to higher job satisfaction, reduced turnover, and increased productivity (Scott et al., 2017). This trend highlights the importance of creating supportive work environments that recognize and leverage the strengths of neurodiverse individuals (Argyriadis et al., 2023).

The integration of technology into mental health and educational practices is another emerging trend. Assistive technologies, such as apps designed for mindfulness and cognitive training, are being developed to support neurodiverse individuals (Hartmann et al., 2012). Virtual reality (VR) and artificial intelligence (AI) are also being explored as tools for creating immersive and personalized therapeutic experiences (Parsons & Cobb, 2011). These technological advancements offer new avenues for providing support and enhancing the well-being of neurodiverse individuals.

Recent research also emphasizes the importance of holistic and multidisciplinary approaches to mental health and neurodiversity. Combining various therapeutic modalities, such as mindfulness, CBT, and physical activities like yoga, is shown to be effective in addressing the complex needs of neurodiverse individuals (Solloway et al., 2020). Multidisciplinary teams, including psychologists, educators, occupational therapists, and social workers, are increasingly collaborating to provide comprehensive care (Davidson et al., 2012). This holistic approach aims to support the overall well-being of individuals rather than focusing solely on symptom reduction.

Finally, there is a growing recognition of the need for culturally sensitive practices in supporting neurodiverse individuals. Research is beginning to explore how cultural contexts influence the effectiveness of interventions and how strategies can be adapted to be more inclusive of diverse populations (Walker, 2021). This trend is crucial for developing interventions that are not only effective but also respectful and relevant to individuals from various cultural backgrounds.

One significant research gap identified in the literature is the lack of longitudinal studies examining the long-term effects of holistic wellness strategies on mental health and neurodiversity. Most of the existing studies are cross-sectional or short-term, providing only a snapshot of the immediate outcomes. Longitudinal research is needed to understand how these strategies impact individuals over time, particularly in terms of sustained mental health improvements, social integration, and productivity.

Another gap is the insufficient exploration of how cultural contexts influence the effectiveness of holistic wellness strategies and neurodiversity accommodations. The majority of studies are conducted in Western countries, which may not be generalizable to other cultural settings. Research should be expanded to include diverse cultural backgrounds to understand how cultural differences affect the implementation and outcomes of these strategies. This would help in developing culturally sensitive interventions that are effective across various populations.

The review also highlights an underrepresentation of certain neurodiverse populations in the existing research. While there is a considerable focus on autism and ADHD, other conditions such as dyslexia, dyspraxia, and Tourette syndrome are less studied. Future research should aim to include a broader range of neurodiverse conditions to provide a more comprehensive understanding of how holistic wellness strategies can be tailored to meet diverse needs.

Although personalized interventions are recognized as more effective than generic approaches, there is a lack of detailed research on what constitutes effective personalization. More studies are needed to explore specific components and methodologies of personalized interventions, including how they can be customized based on individual preferences, strengths, and challenges. This includes investigating various therapy modalities, educational practices, and workplace accommodations in greater depth.

The role of technology in supporting holistic wellness and neurodiversity is another area that requires further exploration. While some studies mention the use of assistive technologies and digital tools, there is limited research on their long-term effectiveness and how they can be integrated into broader wellness strategies. Future research should focus on innovative technological solutions, such as apps, virtual reality, and artificial intelligence, to support mental health and neurodiversity.

Despite evidence supporting the benefits of holistic wellness strategies and inclusive practices, there is a gap in research on how these strategies are implemented in real-world settings. Studies often highlight successful interventions in controlled environments but fail to address the challenges and barriers faced in practical applications. Research should investigate the factors influencing the adoption and sustainability of these practices in educational institutions, workplaces, and community settings.

METHODS

Systematic Literature Review Approach

The primary methodology for this paper was a systematic literature review, which involved a comprehensive and structured approach to identifying, evaluating, and synthesizing relevant research. This method was chosen to provide a detailed and unbiased overview of the existing evidence regarding holistic wellness strategies and their effectiveness in promoting mental health and embracing neurodiversity.

Literature Search Strategy

The literature search was conducted using several electronic databases, including PubMed, PsycINFO, Scopus, and Web of Science. The search terms used were "holistic wellness," "mental health," "neurodiversity," "personalized interventions," "inclusive education," "workplace accommodations," "mindfulness," "cognitive-behavioral therapy," and "community support." Boolean operators (AND, OR) were utilized to combine keywords and refine the search results.

Inclusion and Exclusion Criteria

Inclusion criteria for selecting studies were as follows:

- Peer-reviewed articles published between January 2010 and December 2023.
- Studies focusing on holistic wellness strategies in mental health.
- Research addressing neurodiversity and personalized interventions.
- Articles discussing inclusive educational practices and workplace accommodations.
- Studies employing quantitative, qualitative, or mixed-methods research designs.

Exclusion criteria were:

- Articles not published in English.
- Studies that did not focus on mental health or neurodiversity.
- Review articles, opinion pieces, and editorials.
- Studies with insufficient methodological rigor or lacking relevant outcome measures.

DATA EXTRACTION AND SYNTHESIS

Data extraction was performed independently by two reviewers using a standardized extraction form. The extracted data included study characteristics (author, year, country), participant characteristics (sample size, age, gender, neurodiverse conditions), intervention details (type, duration, frequency), and outcomes (mental health measures, self-esteem, social integration, productivity). Discrepancies between reviewers were resolved through discussion or consultation with a third reviewer.

The extracted data were then synthesized using a narrative synthesis approach, which involves summarizing and explaining the findings of the included studies. This approach was chosen to accommodate the diversity of study designs and outcome measures. The synthesis focused on identifying common themes, patterns, and gaps in the literature.

QUALITY ASSESSMENT

The quality of the included studies was assessed using the Mixed Methods Appraisal Tool (MMAT), which allows for the evaluation of qualitative, quantitative, and mixed-methods studies. Each study was assessed on criteria such as the clarity of research questions, appropriateness of study design, methodological rigor, and relevance of findings. Studies were categorized as high, medium, or low quality based on their MMAT scores. Only studies rated as medium or high quality were included in the final synthesis to ensure the reliability and validity of the conclusions.

ETHICAL CONSIDERATIONS

As this study involved a systematic review of existing literature, it did not involve direct interaction with human participants and thus did not require ethical approval. However, ethical considerations included ensuring the accurate representation of findings, respecting intellectual property rights through proper citation, and avoiding plagiarism.

LIMITATIONS

The primary limitations of this systematic review include potential publication bias, as studies with positive findings are more likely to be published than those with negative or null results. Additionally, the reliance on English-language articles may have excluded relevant studies published in other languages. Despite these limitations, the systematic approach and rigorous quality assessment aimed to provide a comprehensive and reliable synthesis of the current evidence on holistic wellness strategies and neurodiversity.

RESULTS

A total of 39 peer-reviewed articles, clinical studies, and meta-analyses were included in this systematic review, encompassing research published between January 2010 and December 2023. These studies were selected based on their focus on holistic wellness strategies, neurodiversity, and personalized interventions in mental health, education, and workplace settings. The quality assessment using the Mixed Methods Appraisal Tool (MMAT) revealed that 33 studies were of high quality and 6 were of medium quality.

MENTAL HEALTH INTERVENTIONS

Cognitive Behavioral Therapy (CBT) has been extensively adapted to better serve individuals with Autism Spectrum Disorder (ASD), focusing on their specific needs and cognitive styles. Traditional CBT, which is highly verbal and abstract, can be challenging for individuals with ASD due to their often concrete and literal thinking patterns. Therefore, adaptations are necessary to make CBT more accessible and effective.

One notable adaptation involves incorporating visual aids and concrete examples into the therapy process. Visual supports, such as picture schedules, social stories, and visual organizers, help bridge the gap between abstract concepts and the concrete thinking style often observed in individuals with ASD. Kozlowski et al. (2019) demonstrated that these modifications led to significant improvements in managing anxiety and enhancing social skills. Visual supports enable individuals with ASD to better understand and apply therapeutic techniques by providing clear and consistent visual cues.

Additionally, therapists often use structured and predictable formats in CBT sessions for individuals with ASD. Predictability helps reduce anxiety and resistance to therapy. The use of clear, concrete language and step-by-step instructions further aids in comprehension and engagement. By breaking down complex concepts into smaller, manageable parts, therapists can help individuals with ASD understand and work through their thoughts and behaviors more effectively (Argyriadis et al., 2023).

Role-playing and modeling are also crucial components of adapted CBT for ASD. These techniques provide opportunities for individuals to observe and practice appropriate social interactions and coping strategies in a safe and controlled environment. For example, therapists might use role-playing to teach social skills, such as initiating conversations or responding to social cues. By practicing these skills in a supportive setting, individuals with ASD can build confidence and competence in real-life social situations.

Another adaptation involves the use of interests and strengths to motivate and engage individuals with ASD. Therapists can incorporate a person's special interests into therapy activities and discussions, making the sessions more engaging and relevant. This approach not only captures the individual's attention but also helps them apply therapeutic concepts to areas of personal significance. By leveraging their strengths and interests, therapists can create a more personalized and effective therapeutic experience (Lindsay et al. 2019).

Incorporating family members into the therapy process is another key adaptation. Family involvement can enhance the effectiveness of CBT by providing additional support and reinforcement outside of therapy sessions. Therapists can educate family members on the strategies and techniques used in CBT, enabling them to support the individual's progress at home. Family members can also provide valuable insights into the individual's behaviors and challenges, helping to tailor the therapy to their specific needs.

Furthermore, adapted CBT for individuals with ASD often includes a focus on emotional regulation. Individuals with ASD may have difficulty identifying and managing their emotions, leading to heightened anxiety and behavioral challenges. Therapists can use visual aids and concrete examples to teach emotional regulation skills, such as recognizing different emotions, understanding the causes of these emotions, and learning appropriate ways to express and cope with them. This focus on emotional regulation helps individuals with ASD develop greater self-awareness and emotional control.

Finally, therapists may use technology-based tools to enhance CBT for individuals with ASD. Computer programs and mobile apps can provide interactive and engaging ways to teach and reinforce therapeutic concepts. These tools can offer visual supports, step-by-step instructions, and opportunities for practice and feedback, making CBT more accessible and appealing to individuals with ASD. Technology-based interventions can also be tailored to the individual's specific needs and preferences, further enhancing their effectiveness.

Mindfulness-based interventions have shown promising results for individuals with Attention Deficit Hyperactivity Disorder (ADHD). These interventions are designed to help individuals manage anxiety and improve attention regulation through mindfulness practices tailored to their needs. Mindfulness involves paying attention to the present moment without judgment, which can help individuals with ADHD develop greater self-awareness and control over their attention.

Zylowska et al. (2008) reported significant improvements in psychological well-being and attention regulation among individuals with ADHD who participated in mindfulness-based programs. The practices helped participants develop greater self-awareness and control over their attention, leading to better overall functioning and reduced symptoms of anxiety and hyperactivity.

Mindfulness practices, such as meditation, breathing exercises, and mindful movement, can help individuals with ADHD calm their minds and focus their attention. These practices encourage a non-judgmental awareness of thoughts and feelings, which can reduce the tendency to become overwhelmed by distractions and impulses. By learning to observe their thoughts and feelings without reacting to them, individuals with ADHD can develop greater emotional regulation and impulse control.

One of the key benefits of mindfulness-based interventions is their emphasis on self-compassion and acceptance. Individuals with ADHD often struggle with feelings of frustration and self-criticism due to their difficulties with attention and hyperactivity. Mindfulness practices encourage a more compassionate and accepting attitude towards oneself, which can improve self-esteem and reduce stress. By fostering a kinder and more supportive relationship with themselves, individuals with ADHD can better manage their symptoms and overall well-being.

Mindfulness-based interventions can be delivered in various formats, including individual therapy, group programs, and online courses. Group programs, in particular, offer the added benefit of social support and shared experiences. Participants can learn from each other and develop a sense of community, which can be especially valuable for individuals with ADHD who may feel isolated or misunderstood.

In addition to traditional mindfulness practices, adapted mindfulness techniques can be tailored to the specific needs of individuals with ADHD. For example, shorter meditation sessions and more active forms of mindfulness, such as mindful walking or yoga, can be more suitable for individuals who find it challenging to sit still for extended periods. Therapists can also incorporate practical strategies for integrating mindfulness into daily activities, such as mindful eating or mindful listening, to make the practices more accessible and relevant to individuals with ADHD.

Furthermore, mindfulness-based interventions can be combined with other therapeutic approaches to enhance their effectiveness. For example, integrating mindfulness with Cognitive Behavioral Therapy (CBT) can provide a comprehensive approach to addressing the cognitive, emotional, and behavioral aspects of ADHD. This combined approach can help individuals with ADHD develop a more holistic set of skills for managing their symptoms and improving their quality of life.

The growing body of research on mindfulness-based interventions for ADHD underscores the potential of these practices to support the mental health and well-being of individuals with ADHD. As our understanding of mindfulness and its applications continues to evolve, it is likely that these interventions will become increasingly refined and tailored to meet the diverse needs of individuals with ADHD. By embracing mindfulness as a complementary approach to traditional therapies, mental health professionals can provide more comprehensive and effective support for individuals with ADHD.

EDUCATIONAL PRACTICES

Inclusive educational practices, such as differentiated instruction and the use of assistive technology, were shown to significantly improve learning outcomes for neurodiverse students. Lindsay et al. (2019) found that strategies like speech-to-text software and visual schedules enhanced both academic performance and social integration for students with dyslexia and ASD. Moreover, these inclusive practices were associated with improved self-esteem and peer relationships among neurodiverse students (Ashburner et al. 2010).

Beyond speech-to-text software and visual schedules, the use of personalized learning tools, such as adaptive learning software, has been particularly effective. These tools adjust the level of difficulty based on the student's progress, providing immediate feedback and targeted practice. This adaptive approach not only aids in keeping students engaged but also ensures they are working at a level that is appropriately challenging. Research by Pane et al. (2017) indicated that students using adaptive learning technologies showed significant gains in mathematics and reading comprehension compared to their peers using traditional methods.

Additionally, the implementation of Universal Design for Learning (UDL) principles has been instrumental in creating more inclusive educational environments. UDL emphasizes providing multiple means of representation, engagement, and expression to accommodate the diverse learning needs of all students. For example, offering information in various formats (text, audio, video) and allowing students to demonstrate their understanding through different modalities (written, oral, project-based) ensures that neurodiverse students can access and engage with the curriculum more effectively. Meyer et al. (2014) demonstrated that classrooms adhering to UDL principles saw enhanced participation and academic success among neurodiverse students.

Peer-mediated interventions, as previously noted, are also crucial in fostering an inclusive educational environment. When peers are trained to support and interact positively with neurodiverse students, the social dynamics within the classroom improve significantly. Kamps et al. (2015) found that peer-mediated interventions not only benefited neurodiverse students by enhancing their social skills and reducing isolation but also promoted empathy and understanding among neurotypical students. This inclusive atmosphere helps to break down social barriers and reduces bullying and stigma associated with neurodiversity.

Professional development for educators is another critical component of effective inclusive practices. Teachers who receive training on neurodiversity and inclusive teaching strategies are better equipped to meet the needs of all their students. Workshops and ongoing professional development programs that focus on differentiated instruction, the use of assistive technologies, and behavioral management techniques can significantly enhance the educational experience for neurodiverse students. A study by Roberts and Simpson (2016) highlighted that teachers who participated in comprehensive professional development programs reported increased confidence in their ability to support neurodiverse students, leading to more positive classroom outcomes.

Furthermore, involving parents and caregivers in the educational process is essential for reinforcing inclusive practices at home and ensuring continuity between school and home environments. Parent training programs that provide strategies for supporting learning and behavior at home can complement the efforts made in the classroom. Collaboration between teachers and parents helps to create a consistent and supportive learning environment for neurodiverse students. Research by Hornby and Witte (2010) suggests that strong home-school partnerships are associated with improved academic performance, better behavior, and higher levels of student engagement.

Inclusive practices also extend to extracurricular activities, which play a vital role in the overall development of neurodiverse students. Participation in sports, arts, and clubs provides opportunities for social interaction, skill development, and personal growth. Inclusive extracurricular programs that accommodate the needs of neurodiverse students ensure that they can fully participate and benefit from these activities. According to Shogren et al. (2018), students involved in inclusive extracurricular activities showed improved social skills, increased self-esteem, and greater school connectedness.

WORKPLACE ACCOMMODATIONS

Evidence supporting the effectiveness of workplace accommodations for neurodiverse employees was robust. Studies indicated that flexible working hours, quiet workspaces, and structured routines facilitated better job performance and satisfaction for individuals with ASD and ADHD (Hendricks 2010; Biederman et al. 2012). Scott et al. (2017) reported that such accommodations led to higher job satisfaction, reduced turnover, and increased productivity, underscoring the importance of supportive work environments.

Beyond these accommodations, the implementation of assistive technologies in the workplace has shown to further enhance the productivity and job satisfaction of neurodiverse employees. Tools such as noise-canceling headphones, speech-to-text software, and project management applications help individuals manage their work tasks more effectively. Research by Burgstahler and Doe (2006) highlighted that assistive technologies can significantly reduce the barriers faced by neurodiverse employees, enabling them to contribute fully to their roles.

Moreover, providing training for both neurodiverse employees and their coworkers on neurodiversity awareness and inclusion practices is critical. Such training fosters an inclusive culture that values diversity and promotes mutual respect and understanding. According to a study by Hagner and Cooney (2005), workplaces that invested in neurodiversity training reported improved team cohesion and communication, which are essential for a harmonious and productive work environment.

Mentorship programs tailored to support neurodiverse employees also play a crucial role. Having a mentor who understands the unique challenges and strengths of neurodiverse individuals can provide guidance, support, and advocacy within the workplace. A study by Smith et al. (2004) found that mentorship programs not only helped neurodiverse employees navigate their job roles more effectively but also contributed to their professional development and career advancement.

So, creating an inclusive workplace through accommodations, assistive technologies, training, and mentorship significantly enhances the job performance, satisfaction, and retention of neurodiverse employees. By fostering a supportive work environment, employers can leverage the unique strengths of neurodiverse individuals, leading to a more innovative and productive workforce.

TECHNOLOGICAL ADVANCEMENTS

The integration of technology into mental health and educational practices emerged as a significant trend. Assistive technologies, including apps designed for mindfulness and cognitive training, were shown to support neurodiverse individuals effectively. Hartmann et al. (2012) highlighted the potential of virtual reality (VR) and artificial intelligence (AI) in creating immersive and personalized therapeutic experiences, offering new avenues for enhancing well-being.

Furthermore, the use of wearable technology has gained traction in supporting neurodiverse individuals. Devices that monitor physiological signals, such as heart rate and skin conductance, can provide real-time feedback and alert users to impending stress or anxiety. This biofeedback can be instrumental in helping individuals manage their emotions proactively. A study by Picard et al. (2016) demonstrated that wearable devices effectively reduced anxiety levels in individuals with Autism Spectrum Disorder (ASD) by prompting timely relaxation exercises.

In the educational sphere, technology has been transformative in creating inclusive learning environments. Interactive whiteboards, educational software, and adaptive learning platforms cater to diverse learning styles, making education more accessible. For example, Kurzweil 3000, a text-to-speech software, supports students with dyslexia by providing auditory reinforcement alongside visual text, improving reading comprehension and retention. Research by Edyburn (2013) found that such technologies significantly enhanced academic outcomes for students with learning disabilities.

Moreover, online learning platforms and virtual classrooms have expanded educational opportunities for neurodiverse individuals who might struggle with traditional classroom settings. These platforms offer flexibility and a self-paced learning environment, accommodating various needs and preferences. A study by Smith et al. (2019) indicated that students with ADHD benefited from the structure and autonomy provided by online courses, leading to improved engagement and academic performance.

Incorporating AI in educational tools is also revolutionizing personalized learning. AI algorithms can analyze student performance data to tailor instructional content and provide personalized feedback. This approach not only addresses individual learning gaps but also promotes a more engaging and effective learning experience. A study by Luckin et al. (2016) showed that AI-driven educational tools significantly boosted learning outcomes for neurodiverse students by adapting to their unique learning needs.

In conclusion, the integration of technology into mental health and educational practices offers significant benefits for neurodiverse individuals. From wearable devices that assist in emotional regulation to AI-driven personalized learning tools, these technologies provide innovative solutions to enhance well-being and academic success. As technological advancements continue, their potential to support neurodiverse populations will undoubtedly grow, leading to more inclusive and effective practices in both mental health and education.

HOLISTIC AND MULTIDISCIPLINARY APPROACHES

Combining various therapeutic modalities, such as mindfulness, CBT, and physical activities like yoga, was found to be effective in addressing the complex needs of neurodiverse individuals. Solloway et al. (2020) demonstrated that multidisciplinary teams, including psychologists, educators, occupational therapists, and social workers, provided comprehensive care that supported overall well-being rather than focusing solely on symptom reduction.

CULTURALLY SENSITIVE PRACTICES

The review emphasized the necessity of culturally sensitive practices in supporting neurodiverse individuals. Walker (2021) suggested that understanding cultural contexts is crucial for developing effective and respectful interventions. This highlights the importance of tailoring strategies to be inclusive of diverse populations.

Culturally sensitive practices involve recognizing and respecting the unique cultural backgrounds, values, and beliefs of neurodiverse individuals and their families. This approach ensures that interventions are not only effective but also respectful and relevant to the individuals' cultural contexts. For instance, incorporating culturally specific examples and scenarios in therapeutic sessions can make interventions more relatable and impactful. According to Kohn-Wood and Hooper (2014), culturally adapted interventions have been shown to improve engagement and outcomes for individuals from diverse backgrounds.

Language is another critical component of culturally sensitive practices. Providing materials and conducting sessions in the individual's preferred language can significantly enhance understanding and participation. The use of bilingual therapists or translators can bridge communication gaps and ensure that neurodiverse individuals receive appropriate support. A study by Santiago-Rivera et al. (2002) found that language congruence between therapists and clients was associated with better therapeutic relationships and outcomes.

Furthermore, culturally sensitive practices involve understanding and addressing the stigma and misconceptions surrounding neurodiversity in different cultures. In some communities, neurodiverse conditions may be misunderstood or associated with negative stereotypes, which can hinder individuals from seeking or receiving support. Educating communities about neurodiversity and promoting positive attitudes can help reduce stigma and encourage more inclusive attitudes. Research by Corrigan and Watson (2002) indicated that community-based educational programs were effective in reducing stigma and improving acceptance of neurodiverse individuals.

Family involvement is also crucial in culturally sensitive practices. Engaging families in the therapeutic process and respecting their cultural values and traditions can enhance the effectiveness of interventions. This includes acknowledging the role of extended family members and community leaders who may have significant influence in certain cultures. According to Lynch and Hanson (2011), family-centered interventions that respect cultural values lead to better engagement and outcomes for neurodiverse individuals.

Culturally sensitive practices extend to educational settings as well. Schools can adopt culturally responsive teaching methods that reflect the diverse backgrounds of their students. This involves incorporating multicultural content into the curriculum and using teaching strategies that are inclusive of different learning styles and cultural perspectives. A study by Gay (2002) found that culturally responsive teaching improved academic performance and engagement among students from diverse backgrounds.

Additionally, involving community organizations and cultural groups in supporting neurodiverse individuals can enhance the reach and impact of interventions. Collaborating with community leaders and organizations that are trusted and respected within the culture can facilitate better access to services and resources. A study by Atkins et al. (2010) demonstrated that community-based partnerships were effective in reaching underserved populations and providing culturally relevant support.

In conclusion, culturally sensitive practices are essential in supporting neurodiverse individuals. By understanding and respecting cultural contexts, tailoring interventions to be inclusive and relevant, and engaging families and communities, practitioners can provide more effective and respectful support. Culturally sensitive approaches not only improve the engagement and outcomes of neurodiverse individuals but also promote a more inclusive and accepting society. As our understanding of neurodiversity continues to evolve, integrating cultural sensitivity into all aspects of support and intervention will remain crucial for fostering well-being and empowerment among neurodiverse populations.

CONCLUSION

This systematic review examined the current landscape of holistic wellness strategies aimed at promoting mental health and embracing neurodiversity. The findings underscore the critical importance of personalized and inclusive approaches that cater to the unique needs of neurodiverse individuals across various settings, including mental health interventions, educational practices, and workplace accommodations. The review highlighted the effectiveness of tailored interventions such as adapted Cognitive Behavioral Therapy (CBT) and mindfulness practices for individuals with Autism Spectrum Disorder (ASD) and Attention Deficit Hyperactivity Disorder (ADHD). These personalized approaches significantly improved mental health outcomes, demonstrating the necessity of considering individual cognitive and emotional profiles. Differentiated instruction and the use of assistive technologies were shown to enhance academic performance and social integration for neurodiverse students. These strategies not only support learning but also contribute to better self-esteem and peer relationships, emphasizing the value of inclusive education. Evidence strongly supports the implementation of workplace accommodations such as flexible working hours and structured routines. These adjustments lead to higher job satisfaction, reduced turnover, and increased productivity among neurodiverse employees, highlighting the importance of supportive and adaptable work environments. The integration of assistive technologies, virtual reality (VR), and artificial intelligence (AI) into therapeutic and educational practices offers promising new avenues for supporting neurodiverse individuals. These innovations facilitate personalized and immersive experiences that enhance overall well-being.Combining various therapeutic modalities, including mindfulness, CBT, and physical activities like yoga, was found to be effective in addressing the complex needs of neurodiverse individuals. Multidisciplinary teams provided comprehensive care that supported overall well-being, rather than focusing solely on symptom reduction. The necessity of culturally sensitive approaches was emphasized, with findings indicating that understanding cultural contexts is crucial for developing effective and respectful interventions. This highlights the importance of tailoring strategies to be inclusive of diverse populations.

FUTURE RESEARCH DIRECTIONS

While this systematic review has shed light on the current landscape of holistic wellness strategies for promoting mental health and embracing neurodiversity, several areas warrant further investigation to enhance our understanding and application of these approaches.

Future research should focus on longitudinal studies to examine the long-term effectiveness and sustainability of personalized interventions such as adapted CBT and mindfulness practices for individuals with ASD and ADHD. Long-term data would provide insights into how these interventions impact mental health, social skills, and overall quality of life over extended periods. The integration of assistive technologies, VR, and AI into therapeutic and educational practices presents promising avenues for supporting neurodiverse individuals. Future studies should explore the efficacy, accessibility, and user experience of these technologies. Research should also investigate the potential for these innovations to be tailored to individual needs, ensuring they are inclusive and effective across diverse neurodiverse populations. Combining various therapeutic modalities, such as mindfulness, CBT, and physical activities like yoga, has shown promise. However, more comparative studies are needed to identify which combinations are most effective for specific neurodiverse conditions and individual profiles. This research could guide the development of integrated therapeutic programs that optimize mental health outcomes.

LIMITATIONS

While this systematic review provides valuable insights into the current state of holistic wellness strategies for neurodiverse individuals, several limitations should be acknowledged.

The broad spectrum of neurodiverse conditions, including ASD and ADHD, presents a challenge in generalizing findings across different populations. The unique cognitive, emotional, and behavioral profiles of individuals with various neurodiverse conditions may require highly specific interventions, limiting the applicability of some findings. The effectiveness of interventions can vary significantly depending on how they are implemented. Differences in therapist training, intervention settings, and individual engagement levels can impact outcomes. This variability makes it challenging to draw definitive conclusions about the efficacy of specific interventions. Many of the studies reviewed focused on short-term outcomes, providing limited information on the long-term sustainability and impact of the interventions. Longitudinal studies are needed to understand how these strategies affect neurodiverse individuals over extended periods. The review highlights the importance of culturally sensitive approaches, yet there is limited research on how cultural factors influence the effectiveness of interventions for neurodiverse individuals. More studies are needed to explore the intersection of culture and neurodiversity to ensure that interventions are inclusive and effective for diverse populations. While assistive technologies, VR, and AI offer promising new avenues, accessibility remains a significant concern. Socioeconomic factors can limit access to these advanced technologies, potentially exacerbating existing disparities in support for neurodiverse individuals. Research should address issues of accessibility and equity to ensure that technological innovations benefit all individuals, regardless of their socioeconomic status.

REFERENCES

Argyriadis, A., & Argyriadi, A. (2024). Societal attitudes towards psychiatric patients, medication, and the antipsychiatric movement within the context of theoretical approaches and inclusion initiatives. The role of mental health professionals. *GSC Advanced Research and Reviews*, 18(2), 381–387. 10.30574/gscarr.2024.18.2.0075

Argyriadis, A., Efthymiou, E., & Argyriadi, A. (2023). Cultural Competence at Schools: The Effectiveness of Educational Leaders' Intervention Strategies. In *Inclusive Phygital Learning Approaches and Strategies for Students With Special Needs* (pp. 33-51). IGI Global.

Ashburner, J., Ziviani, J., & Rodger, S. (2010). Sensory processing and classroom emotional, behavioral, and educational outcomes in children with autism spectrum disorder. *American Journal of Occupational Therapy, 64*(3), 376-387. 10.5014/ajot.2010.09071

Atkins, M. S., Frazier, S. L., Adil, J. A., Talbott, E. M., Bettencourt, A. F., & Marinez-Lora, A. M. (2010). Adopting a model of partnership-based health services to urban schools: What do we need to know? *School Mental Health, 2*(3), 133-144. https://doi.org/10.1007/s12310-010-9035-6

Bakker, M., Heugten, C. M., & Verhey, F. R. (2019). Assistive technology in dementia care: A systematic review of effects and effectiveness. *Journal of the American Medical Directors Association*, 20(1), 71–81.

Baldwin, S., Costley, D., & Warren, A. (2014). Employment activities and experiences of adults with high-functioning autism and Asperger's Disorder. *Journal of Autism and Developmental Disorders*, 44(10), 2440–2449. 10.1007/s10803-014-2112-z24715257

Barkley, R. A. (2010). Differential diagnosis of adults with ADHD: The role of executive function and self-regulation. *The Journal of Clinical Psychiatry*, 71(1), e17. 10.4088/JCP.9066tx1c20667287

Biederman, J., Fried, R., Petty, C. R., Mahoney, L., & Faraone, S. V. (2012). The effects of ADHD on the functional outcomes of adults with ADHD. *Journal of Psychiatric Research*, 46(1), 73–78.

Bishop-Fitzpatrick, L., Minshew, N. J., & Eack, S. M. (2017). A systematic review of psychosocial interventions for adults with autism spectrum disorders. *Journal of Autism and Developmental Disorders, 43*(3), 687-694. 10.1007/s10803-012-1615-8

Brookman-Frazee, L., Stahmer, A., Baker-Ericzén, M., & Tsai, K. (2009). Parenting interventions for children with autism spectrum and disruptive behavior disorders: Opportunities for cross-fertilization. *Clinical Child and Family Psychology Review, 9*(3-4), 181-200. https://doi.org/10.1007/s10567-006-0006-4

Burgstahler, S., & Doe, T. (2006). Disability-related simulations: If, when, and how to use them in professional development. *Review of Disability Studies: An International Journal, 2*(2), 4-18.

Carter, E. W., Brock, M. E., & Trainor, A. A. (2016). Promoting inclusion, social connections, and learning through peer support arrangements. *Teaching Exceptional Children*, 48(3), 9–18.

Case-Smith, J., Weaver, L. L., & Fristad, M. A. (2015). A systematic review of sensory processing interventions for children with autism spectrum disorders. *Autism, 19*(2), 133-148. 10.1177/1362361313517762

Corrigan, P. W., & Watson, A. C. (2002). Understanding the impact of stigma on people with mental illness. *World Psychiatry, 1*(1), 16-20.

Davidson, L., Chinman, M., Sells, D., & Rowe, M. (2012). Peer support among adults with serious mental illness: A report from the field. *Schizophrenia Bulletin*, 32(3), 443–450. 10.1093/schbul/sbj04316461576

Dawson, G., Rogers, S., Munson, J., Smith, M., Winter, J., Greenson, J., & Varley, J. (2010). Randomized, controlled trial of an intervention for toddlers with autism: The Early Start Denver Model. *Pediatrics, 125*(1), e17-e23. 10.1542/peds.2009-0958

Edyburn, D. L. (2013). Inclusive technologies: Tools for helping diverse learners achieve academic success. *Practical Literacy: The Early & Primary Years, 18*(3), 34-36.

Gay, G. (2002). Preparing for culturally responsive teaching. *Journal of Teacher Education, 53*(2), 106-116. 10.1177/0022487102053002003

Goldberg, L., Stahl, S., & Castro, R. A. (2014). Yoga for pediatric ADHD: A pilot study. *Complementary Therapies in Clinical Practice, 20*(2), 123-126. https://doi.org/10.1016/j.ctcp.2014.01.003

Hagner, D., & Cooney, B. F. (2005). Building employer capacity to support employees with severe disabilities in the workplace. *Work, 25*(1), 111-120.

Hartmann, K., Hitz, K., & Guldimann, R. (2012). The potential of virtual reality for education and training. *Journal of Educational Technology & Society, 15*(2), 233-245.

Hehir, T., Schifter, L., Grindal, T., Ng, M., & Eidelman, H. (2016). *A summary of the evidence on inclusive education*. Abt Associates.

Hendricks, D. R. (2010). Employment and adults with autism spectrum disorders: Challengesand strategies for success. *Journal of Vocational Rehabilitation, 32*(2), 125-134. 10.3233/JVR-2010-0502

Hofmann, S. G., Asnaani, A., Vonk, I. J., Sawyer, A. T., & Fang, A. (2012). The efficacy of cognitive behavioral therapy: A review of meta-analyses. *Cognitive Therapy and Research*, 36(5), 427–440. 10.1007/s10608-012-9476-123459093

Hornby, G., & Witte, C. (2010). Parental involvement in inclusive education: Attitudes of parents of children with special educational needs. *European Journal of Special Needs Education, 25*(4), 345-358. 10.1080/08856257.2010.513550

Kabat-Zinn, J. (2003). Mindfulness-based interventions in context: Past, present, and future. *Clinical Psychology: Science and Practice, 10*(2), 144-156. 10.1093/clipsy/bpg016

Kabat-Zinn, J. (2003). Mindfulness-based interventions in context: Past, present, and future. *Clinical Psychology : a Publication of the Division of Clinical Psychology of the American Psychological Association*, 10(2), 144–156. 10.1093/clipsy.bpg016

Kapp, S. K., Gillespie-Lynch, K., Sherman, L. E., & Hutman, T. (2013). Deficit, difference, or both? Autism and neurodiversity. *Developmental Psychology*, 49(1), 59–71. 10.1037/a002835322545843

Ke, F., & Im, T. (2013). Virtual-reality-based social interaction training for children with high-functioning autism. *Journal of Educational Research, 106*(6), 441-451. 10.1080/00220671.2013.832999

Kohn-Wood, L. P., & Hooper, L. M. (2014). Cultural competence in applied psychology: We are not there yet. *Journal of Clinical Psychology, 70*(9), 829-843. 10.1002/jclp.22117

Kozlowski, A. M., Matson, J. L., & Belva, B. C. (2019). A review of social skills training and social skills interventions for children with autism spectrum disorders. *Behavior Modification, 36*(2), 317-335. https://doi.org/10.1177/0145445512443983

Kurth, J. A., & Mastergeorge, A. M. (2010). Individual education plan goals and services for adolescents with autism: Impact of age and educational setting. *Journal of Special Education, 44*(3), 146-160. 10.1177/0022466908329825

Lindsay, S., Cagliostro, E., Alcorn, A., Srikanthan, D., & Mortaji, N. (2019). A systematic review of the benefits of assistive technology for individuals with autism spectrum disorders. *Disability and Rehabilitation: Assistive Technology, 14*(7), 345-357. https://doi.org/10.1080/17483107.2018.1465137

Luckin, R., Holmes, W., Griffiths, M., & Forcier, L. B. (2016). *Intelligence unleashed: An argument for AI in education*. Pearson Education.

Lynch, E. W., & Hanson, M. J. (2011). *Developing cross-cultural competence: A guide for working with children and their families*. Brookes Publishing.

McCraty, R., & Childre, D. (2010). Coherence: Bridging personal, social, and global health. *Alternative Therapies in Health and Medicine*, 16(4), 10–24.20653292

Meyer, A., Rose, D. H., & Gordon, D. (2014). *Universal design for learning: Theory and practice*. CAST Professional Publishing.

Pane, J. F., Griffin, B. A., McCaffrey, D. F., & Karam, R. (2017). Effectiveness of cognitive tutor algebra I at scale. *Educational Evaluation and Policy Analysis, 36*(2), 127-144. 10.3102/0162373713507480

Picard, R. W., Vyzas, E., & Healey, J. (2016). Toward machine emotional intelligence: Analysis of affective physiological state. *IEEE Transactions on Pattern Analysis and Machine Intelligence, 23*(10), 1175-1191. 10.1109/34.954607

Roberts, J. M., & Simpson, K. (2016). A review of research into stakeholder perspectives on inclusion of students with autism in mainstream schools. *International Journal of Inclusive Education, 20*(10), 1084-1096. 10.1080/13603116.2016.1145267

Santiago-Rivera, A. L., Altarriba, J., Poll, N., Gonzalez-Miller, N., & Cragun, C. (2002). Therapists' views on working with bilingual Spanish-English speaking clients: A qualitative investigation. *Professional Psychology: Research and Practice, 33*(5), 435-442.

Schur, L. A., Kruse, D., Blanck, P., & Blanck, P. (2014). *People with disabilities: Sidelined or mainstreamed?* Cambridge University Press.

Scott, M., Falkmer, M., Girdler, S., & Falkmer, T. (2017). Viewpoints on factors for successful employment for adults with autism spectrum disorder. *PLoS One*, 12(12), e0187936.

Solloway, M. R., Taylor, S. L., Shekelle, P. G., Miake-Lye, I. M., Beroes, J. M., & Shanman, R. M. (2020). An evidence map of mindfulness. *Systematic Reviews*, 9(1), 67.32228696

Walker, N. (2021). *Neurodiversity: Some basic terms & definitions.* Autistic Self Advocacy Network.

Wood, J. J., Drahota, A., Sze, K., Har, K., Chiu, A., & Langer, D. A. (2009). Cognitive behavioral therapy for anxiety in children with autism spectrum disorders: A randomized, controlled trial. *Journal of Child Psychology and Psychiatry, and Allied Disciplines*, 50(3), 224–234. 10.1111/j.1469-7610.2008.01948.x19309326

Chapter 2
Neuropsychological Status From Preschool Age up to Adolescence:
Evidence From Typical Children and Children With Disabilities

Kalliopi Megari
https://orcid.org/0000-0002-5861-7199

Department of Psychology, CITY College, University of York Europe Campus, Thessaloniki, Greece

Evanthia Smyrli

Department of Psychology, CITY College, University of York Europe Campus, Thessaloniki, Greece

ABSTRACT

According to Piaget's theory, there are four distinct neurodevelopment stages, each of which corresponds to a specific age group and is distinguished by a particular number of cognitive attainments. The stages are as follows: a) sensorimotor; b) preoperational; c) concrete operational; and d) formal operational. Four primary domains are used to track development from infancy to adolescence: a) speech and language; b) gross and fine motor abilities; c) social and emotional skills; and d) cognitive ability. By recognizing the normal growth milestones in every category, we may comprehend the variations linked to different abnormal developing patterns. In numerous cognitive domains, children with disabilities may have delays or deficits during childhood that may last into adulthood. Numerous studies have examined the changes in brain activity that corresponds with the acquisition of cognitive skills at each developmental stage. Some of these studies suggest that children with a variety

DOI: 10.4018/979-8-3693-4022-6.ch002

of neuropsychological developmental disorders show neurocognitive deficits in areas like verbal communication, attention, memory, and specific executive functions, while language and visuospatial abilities vary.

NEUROPSYCHOLOGICAL DEVELOPMENT

Neuropsychological development from birth to adolescence is an ongoing process marked by significant changes in developmental, cognitive, linguistic, emotional, and behavioural areas (Berk, 2013; Hollister Sandberg & Spritz, 2010). Neurodevelopment proceeds in steps, with the diversity of its functions growing. For much of rapid evolution, the structure and function of the brain undergo significant alterations that correspond with the acquisition of motor, cognitive, academic, social-emotional, and sensory skills. This trek starts during pregnancy, when there may be prenatal indicators of either typical or disrupted development (Berk, 2013). Neurodevelopment can be influenced by risk factors both during infancy and during childhood development. In a similar vein, experiences, culture, trauma, and illness are important factors. Recognizing departures from expected behavior and skill acquisition requires a foundational understanding of the developmental trajectory of typical development.

This chapter looks at the stages of neuropsychological development of typical children from birth to adolescence outlined in Cognitive Development Theory (Piaget, 1936). It then outlines how the milestones of typical child development identified in cognitive development theory can be used to diagnose some prominent neuropsychological disorders, namely, autism spectrum disorder (ASD), attention-deficit/hyperactivity disorder (ADHD), and intellectual disabilities, including Down syndrome in 'atypical' children. The chapter then outlines key aspects to consider in relation to possible interventions to support 'atypical' children with neuropsychological disorders and which interventions may be appropriate.

Stages of Neuropsychological Development in Typical Children

Piaget (1936) introduced the Cognitive Development Theory, suggesting that children acquire milestone cognitive functions during specific periods in their lives, by actively exploring their environment through motor and perceptual activities. Piaget's theory outlined four distinct stages, each corresponding to a discrete age group, and characterised by a distinct number of cognitive attainments a) the sensorimotor stage, b) the preoperational stage, c) the concrete operational stage and, d) the formal operational stage (Mcleod, 2024). At each stage language development is one of several important areas.

During the sensorimotor stage, spanning from birth to around two years - Tuckman and Monetti (2011) suggest the duration lasts until the acquisition of language - the child makes sense of its surroundings through sensory experiences and by manipulating objects (Malik & Marwaha, 2023). The child develops object permanence, an understanding that things continue to exist when not seen, and a sense of separation from their environment (Cherry, 2023). Brain development is rapid. Myelination progresses enabling neural connections to grow rapidly, strengthening interaction between different parts of the brain, particularly those connected to language, memory and executive functions (Pujol et al, 2006).

In the preoperational stage (two to seven years), children advance in language acquisition and comprehension, attention, memory, development of emotions and executive functions and representational (mental representation of perceived objects) activities. Young children begin to comprehend sentences, acquire vocabulary and grammar, and engage in basic conversation (Cherry, 2022). Gross motor skills advance as children improve balance, coordination, and strength, enabling activities like running, jumping, climbing, while fine motor skills enable them to manipulate objects. In addition, this period is crucial for the development of self-regulation skills, which are further linked to school readiness and social skills (Blair & Raver, 2014).

The concrete operational stage (seven to 11 years) is a turning point in cognitive development and is characterised by the development of logical thought and an understanding of the reversibility of actions and of the concept of conservation where although things may change in appearance, certain properties remain the same (Cherry, 2023). The child advances in logical thinking, planning, organisation, prioritisation, problem-solving, and spatial reasoning, resembling the reasoning abilities of an adult (Börnert-Ringleb & Wilbert, 2018). Socially, the child become less egocentric and begins to think about how others feel, placing increasing importance on peer relationships and friendships. At this stage the child engages in cooperative activities and develops teamwork skills. Gross motor skills have developed to the extent where children can play various sports. Fine motor skills also progress, facilitating tasks such as drawing, writing, and manipulating small objects.

The formal operational stage begins at about age 12 and over. Cognitively, young people become capable of abstract thought, forming hypotheses with multiple solutions, and making predictions as adolescents develop deductive reasoning, applying logic to create specific conclusions from abstract concepts (Berk, 2013; Berger, 2014). Adolescents become more aware of their own thought processes, learning strategies, and cognitive strengths and weaknesses. Risk-taking behaviour and decision-making processes become more sophisticated, as adolescents weigh risks and benefits, anticipate consequences, and consider long-term goals and values (Malik & Marwaha, 2023).

Speech and language skills develop into more complex communication skills. Adolescents are capable of verbal expression, active listening, and nonverbal communication. Socially, adolescents explore and consolidate their gender, sexual and cultural identities, including values, beliefs, interests, and aspirations. Social connections with peers become increasingly important. They play a significant role in shaping behaviour, attitudes, and social norms, influencing decisions by providing social support and personal validation. Adolescents continue to develop emotional regulation skills, learning to manage intense emotions, cope with stress and navigate personal relationships. They also deepen their capacity for empathy and perspective-taking, enhancing their ability to understand and relate to others' emotions and experiences. They learn to resolve conflicts constructively, practicing negotiation, compromise, and assertiveness while respecting others' perspectives. By adolescence, motor skills have developed to enable young people to perform complex fine motor movements and navigate complex environments (Toto & Limone, 2021).

To fully appreciate the value and diversity of neuropsychological functions at any age of interest, neuropsychologists must have a thorough understanding of the developmental trajectories of these functions from conception to death. Environmental effects on growing brain systems and functions differ from those on mature brain functions. As a result, the framework and choices made for pediatric neuropsychological evaluation must take into account an understanding of the development of the brain and neural system as well as all of its particular influences. A synopsis of the key factors for child neuropsychological assessment is provided in this chapter (Vogt, & Heffelfinger, 2024).

Individual Differences in Neuropsychological Development in Typical Children

Although stages of neuropsychological development can be identified by certain characteristics at points in the life span, development is characterized by 'heterochronicity', as all functions do not evolve at the same pace or time (Roalf et al, 2014), and 'individual variability' (Voronova et al, 2015). Various biological, familial, socioeconomic, and psychological factors can lead to individual differences in neuropsychological development among typical children (Bush et al, 2020; Hackman et al, 2010).

Genetic variations may contribute to differences in intelligence, language skills, and susceptibility to certain neuropsychiatric conditions (Mollon et al, 2012). Some research suggests that around half of the variance in general cognition can be attributed to genetic factors (Haworth et al, 2010). Genetic variations can also influence attention (Fan et al, 2001) and working memory (Ando et al, 2001). There is also evidence that female children outperform male children on language tasks (Spironelli et al, 2010).

Early life experiences, including premature birth and extremely low birth weight (less than 1000 grams) (Anderson & Doyle, 2004), parenting styles, caregiver-child interactions, and family dynamics can also affect neuropsychological development (Beauregard et al, 2018). Supportive caregiving fosters secure attachment and promotes socio-emotional well-being. In contrast, harsh or inconsistent parenting may contribute to behavioural difficulties (Lunkenheimer et al, 2017). Similarly, prenatal exposure to toxins may also affect cognitive development (Landi et al, 2017).

There are various reasons why children are referred for neuropsychological evaluations, but the main objectives of these evaluations are to ascertain the general level of intellectual functioning, ascertain whether strengths and weaknesses in neuropsychology align with a neurobehavioral syndrome, and formulate treatment, educational, and intervention plans that are suitable. Assessments can be thorough, concise, customized, or re-evaluations (Vogt, & Heffelfinger, 2024).

Access to early childhood education plays a role in neuropsychological development. Children attending high-quality early childhood education benefit from enhanced cognitive and social-emotional development (Center on the Developing Child, 2007; Donoghue, 2017). Geoffroy et al (2007) found that early childcare giving could compensate for poorer economic environments in developing language skills. There is evidence that, while all children may benefit from high-quality early childhood education, children from low-income families are likely to derive more benefits than children from families with higher incomes (Yoshikawa et al, 2013). Social interaction with other children, enabled by early childhood education is also highly beneficial for developing critical social skills such as communication, cooperation, and empathy. Problematic peer relationships are indicative of lower cognitive competencies such as self-regulatory behaviour (Holmes et al, 2016).

Socioeconomic factors, such as family income, education level, and access to resources, influence neuropsychological development outcomes. Disadvantaged socio-economic status is associated with inferior performance across various cognitive skills (Beauregard et al, 2018), including language (Noble et al, 2007) and self-regulation as a mechanism for school readiness (Blair & Raver, 2014; Ansari & Winsler, 2012). Children from poorer homes are much less likely to attend preschool (McCartney et al, 2007) and have less exposure to learning materials (Fernald et al, 2013).

Cultural values, norms, and practices also affect neuropsychological development (Olson & Jacobson, 2015). Rosenqvist et al (2017) found that American children performed lower than European children on visuospatial, constructional, and fine-motor abilities. There is evidence that dual language learners enrolled in high-quality early childcare education make greater gains in cognitive skills, such as receptive language, maths, and executive functioning, compared to monolingual English speakers (Yazejian et al, 2015).

Development in 'Atypical' Children With Neuropsychological Disorders

Neurodiversity encompasses a range of neurodevelopmental differences. Neuropsychological disorders are a group of mental illnesses related to brain functioning and behaviour (Operto et al, 2021). They include autism spectrum disorder (ASD), attention-deficit/hyperactivity disorder (ADHD), and various intellectual disabilities, including Down syndrome.

These conditions are often associated with impairment of a child's cognitive, executive and adaptive functions (dealing with attention, memory, processing, planning, problem solving, and multitasking), language development, emotional regulation, and gross and fine motor skills. These impairments often inhibit a child's learning and present social problems in forming relationships and everyday living, which can cause emotional stress and even physical danger. Despite certain commonalities, like their 'typical' counterparts, 'atypical' children with neuropsychological disorders vary in their neurodevelopmental profiles due to type and degree of their disorder and their personal and social circumstances, which influence their abilities and the problems they face (Ogundele, 2018).

Neuropsychological/Neurodevelopmental disorders are clinically diagnosed by identifying atypical behaviours or delays in achieving the developmental milestones defined by Cognitive Development Theory, in comparison with typical children of the same demographic background (Straub et al, 2022). Neuropsychological tests and developmental assessment scales are used to assess the child's level of development against specific age-related milestones.

The 'heterochronicity' of individual development and the dynamic interactions between biological, cognitive, emotional, and social factors that shape individuals' identities, relationships, and behaviours that characterise the transition of typical children from childhood to adulthood can help us understand deviations associated with various atypical developments. Understanding development during childhood is highly relevant for both educators and clinicians working with children (Hollister Sandberg & Spritz, 2010) and allows for the establishment of pathways of atypical cognitive development for children in various clinical groups (Hughes & Leekam, 2004; Brown et al, 2020).

Many studies have looked at the ways in which cognitive skills are acquired during each developmental stage with their respective changes in brain activity. Some suggest that children with various neuropsychological developmental disorders demonstrate neurocognitive deficits in areas such as verbal communication, attention, memory, and specific executive functions, while language and visuospatial abilities are varied (Megari et al, 2023; Hamadelseed et al, 2023; Alsaedi et al, 2020). Top of Form. The characteristics of these different neuropsychological developments in relation to autism spectrum disorder, attention-deficit/ hyperactivity disorder, and learning disabilities, with specific reference to Down syndrome, are discussed below.

Neuropsychological Development in Children With Autism Spectrum Disorder (ASD)

Autism is a developmental disorder that affects information processing. Autism's symptoms vary greatly and hence the condition is referred to as autism spectrum disorder (ASD). Neuropsychological studies indicate abnormalities in the prefrontal cortex and its connections to other brain regions involved in executive functions like inhibitory control, working memory, and attentional processes (Demetriou et al, 2019). Children with ASD often exhibit unique neuropsychological developmental trajectories compared to typically developing children. The cognitive profile of children with ASD can vary widely, ranging from intellectual disability to average or above-average intelligence. Some children with ASD demonstrate exceptional abilities in specific areas, such as mathematics, music, or visual-spatial skills (Uddin, 2022).

Regarding the diversity of neuropathology in ASD, heterogeneity is seen in both baseline and comorbid features (Shkedy et al., 2019). The severity, developmental level, and concomitance with other medical or psychiatric diagnoses such mental retardation, epilepsy, and anxiety disorders all influence the symptoms (Zeidan et al., 2022). A person's personality, the environment, the calibre of social and familial stimuli, and speaking abilities are all significant factors that can contribute to varying levels of cognitive functioning (Megari, Frantzezou, Polyzopoulou, & Tzouni, 2024).

Problems with executive functioning (cognitive skills involved in self-regulation, problem-solving, planning, and organization) have been consistently found in school-age children, adolescents, and adults with ASD (Hughes et al, 1994; Pellicano, 2012). These can manifest as challenges in flexibility, attentional control, and impulse regulation. Bennie (2018), reports that some sources say that up to 80% of those with ASD suffer from executive function disorder, leading to difficulties managing time, and/or completing tasks. Many children with ASD also exhibit problems with adaptive functioning, struggling to independently perform daily activities necessary for personal and social sufficiency and making simple tasks complicated or seemingly impossible. Duncan & Bishop (2013) found half of teens with ASD had daily living skills that were "significantly below" expectations for someone of their age and IQ. Repetitive behaviours and restricted interests are features of ASD, which can manifest in various forms, including repetitive movements, such as hand-flapping, insistence on sameness, and intense interests in specific topics (Braconnier & Sipper, 2021),

Children with ASD often show deficits in social communication, interaction, including difficulties in understanding and using nonverbal cues such as facial expressions, gestures, and tone of voice. They may also struggle with initiating and maintaining conversations (Braconnier & Sipper, 2021). Language development in children with ASD is highly variable. Some children with ASD may exhibit delayed language acquisition or repeat words or phrases (echolalia), while others may develop fluent language but struggle with pragmatic aspects of communication (NIDCD, 2020).

Theory of Mind (ToM) concerns conceptualising the cognitive basis underlying social communication differences between individuals. Kristen & Sodian (2003) broadly defined ToM as a *"body of conceptual knowledge that underlies access to both one's own and others' mental states."* ToM includes the ability to understand implicit rules for personal interactions, such as reading body language. Children with ASD find it difficult to understand and read other people's intentions, thoughts, beliefs, desires, and emotions (Hutchins et al, 2015). It is also suggested, children with ASD show different patterns of ToM development to their neurotypical peers but continue to progress in ToM abilities during schooling (Williams, 2021).

Difficulties in emotional regulation are common among children with ASD. They may have challenges in identifying and expressing emotions appropriately, leading to meltdowns or behavioural dysregulation in response to stressors. Many children with ASD experience sensory processing difficulties, where they may be either hypo-sensitive or hyper-sensitive to sensory stimuli. This can impact their ability to modulate responses to sensory input and may lead to sensory seeking or avoidance behaviours. A study by Khalfa et al (2004) confirmed the presence of enhanced loudness perception in autism.

Understanding the neuropsychological development of children with ASD is crucial for tailoring interventions and support strategies to address their unique strengths and challenges. Early intervention programs that target social communication, cognitive flexibility, sensory regulation, and adaptive skills can significantly improve outcomes for children with ASD.

Neuropsychological Development in Children With Attention-Deficit/Hyperactivity Disorder (ADHD)

Neuropsychological studies of ADHD, (Attention-Deficit/Hyperactivity Disorder) indicate abnormalities in the prefrontal cortex (Gharamaleki et al, 2018; Vaidya, 2012; Arnsten, 2009). Presentation of ADHD can vary widely among children, and not all will experience the same challenges or exhibit the same symptoms. However, children with ADHD often exhibit distinct patterns of neuropsychological development compared to 'typical' children.

Those with ADHD often show problems with executive functions, struggling with planning, organization, and sustained attention, becoming distracted or forgetful (Yáñez-Téllez et al, 2012). In addition, children with ADHD may also show symptoms of hyperactivity and impulsivity, finding it difficult to sit still, wait their turn, or think before acting (Furman, 2005). They may also experience problems regulating their emotions and understanding social cues. Some children with ADHD may experience delays or problems with expressive or receptive language skills. They may also exhibit delays or difficulties in fine motor skills (such as writing or drawing) or gross motor skills (such as coordination and balance) (Tseng et al, 2004).

These characteristics pose problems for the social and emotional development of children with ADHD. They can undermine academic achievement and make children with ADHD more prone to behavioural problems such as aggression or defiance (Ek et al, 2010). Furthermore, they can lead to challenges in social interactions and maintaining friendships.

Neuropsychological Development in Children With Intellectual Disabilities, Including Down Syndrome

Neuropsychological development in children with intellectual disabilities can vary widely depending on the underlying cause, for example genetic parameters or exposure to toxins, and the severity of the disability, as well as the presence of co-conditions. Down syndrome, an intellectual disability is a genetic condition caused by the presence of an extra copy of chromosome 21 which can delay neuropsychological development compared to 'typical' children (Akhtar & Bokhari, 2023).

Like other children with intellectual disabilities, children with Down syndrome typically have intellectual disabilities ranging from mild to moderate. Development is characterised by delays in, cognitive and executive functions of memory, attention, and problem-solving (Pulina et al, 2019). Acquisition of language skills is also often delayed in children with Down syndrome. They may have difficulties with both expressive language skills, such as speaking and forming sentences and with receptive language skills, having difficulty understanding what they see and hear (Martin et al, 2009; Roberts et al, 2007). In the domains of communication, gross motor skills, fine motor skills, expressive language and language comprehension children with DS performed worse in comparison with other groups (ASD) (López Resa, & Moraleda Sepúlveda, 2024).

Emotionally, children with Down syndrome often exhibit strengths in empathy and sociability but may find it difficult to understand social cues and navigate social situations. Some children with Down syndrome may also struggle with regulating their emotions. This can lead to challenging behaviours, such as impulsivity, stubbornness, or difficulty with transitions (Jahromi et al, 2008). Some children with intellectual disabilities may also have sensory processing difficulties, having trouble processing and responding to sensory information from their environment. This can affect their ability to tolerate certain sensations (such as noise or textures) and may impact their overall functioning and behaviour. Research suggests that approximately 49% of individuals with Down syndrome experience sensory processing challenges, compared to about 5-16% of the general population (Down Syndrome Research Foundation, 2024).

Motor development, including gross motor skills (such as crawling, walking, and running) and fine motor skills (such as grasping objects and hand-eye coordination) can also be impaired in children with Down syndrome. These characteristics can lead to high rates of learning disabilities in children with Down syndrome, while many do manifest insight, creativity, and cleverness including strong visual awareness and visual learning skills (Down Syndrome International, 2022). Children with Down syndrome may also have difficult in making friends, but evidence of young adults with Down syndrome forming social relationships is positive. A small Australian study found that young adults with Down syndrome who had three or more positive social relationships outside of their immediate family tended to have a significantly better overall score on a quality-of-life assessment than those with two or fewer relationships (Haddad et al, 2018). Common developmental milestones or distinguishing features are present in various neurodevelopmental disorders (López Resa, & Moraleda Sepúlveda, 2024).

Interventions

While children with neuropsychological disorders and learning disabilities may face unique developmental challenges, with appropriate support and intervention, they can make significant progress and lead fulfilling lives. Understanding and addressing individual differences in neuropsychological development among typical children requires a holistic approach that considers the complex interplay of genetic, environmental, and socio-cultural factors influencing development.

Neuropsychological assessments can help identify specific strengths and weaknesses, guiding intervention strategies to support optimal development. A neuropsychological assessment measures in a quantitative standardized way complex aspects of human behaviour – attention, perception, memory, speech and language, building and drawing, reasoning, problem solving, judgement, planning and emotional processing (Lezak et al, 2012).

Neuropsychological assessments should consider all aspects of a child's life including social and cultural influences (Glozman, 2013), providing a neuropsychological profile of the child concerned. This profile, along with the evaluation of neurological clinical and social aspects will contribute to the diagnosis and help identify specific strengths and weaknesses, guiding and tailoring intervention strategies to support optimal development.

It is important to assess the specific impact of a neuropsychological disorder or disability on the child's development. Just like 'typical' children, 'atypical' children with neuropsychological disorders and disabilities will exhibit individual differences in their neuropsychological profiles The extent of the impact depends on various factors, including the type of disability, its severity, any associated conditions, and its various causes, including genetic factors, prenatal exposure to toxins, or perinatal complications.

Some atypical children may have strengths in certain areas despite their disorder or disability. Others may have more significant challenges across multiple cognitive, linguistic, behavioural and social domains. For example, children with ASD may have challenges with social interaction, communication, and repetitive behaviours, but also be highly intelligent. ADHD can vary widely among children, and not all children with ADHD will have the same symptoms or face the same challenges. Children with Down syndrome may have behavioural problems, but still be able to form social relationships. A child's physical condition may also affect their cognitive development and academic performance (Sommariva et al, 2020).

The brain has a remarkable ability (brain plasticity) to adapt and reorganize itself, known as neuroplasticity. This means that with appropriate interventions, children with disabilities can often make significant progress in their neuropsychological development (Hadders-Algra, 2022).

Given that neuropsychological disorders are often complex and difficult to diagnose and treat, the importance of assessment tools lies primarily in the early detection of neuropsychological disorders and disabilities, thus enabling timely and targeted therapeutic interventions (Costa et al, 2004). Early detection and intervention can help reduce the risks of further deterioration and improve the quality of life for those affected. Early intervention programmes, individualised education plans (IEPs), and multidisciplinary support teams can play crucial roles in promoting the optimal neuropsychological development of children, over the long-term, by addressing the specific needs of each child and providing support across various domains of development (Dawson et al, 2010; Papaeliou et al, 2011).

Intervention programmes may include a range of therapies that can be tailored to a child's individual needs, such as speech therapy to improve language skills and physical and occupational therapy to strengthen motor skills and coordination.

Other treatments may include behavioural therapy, psychotherapy, medications, or any combination of the above.

A supportive environment that caters to the individual needs of children with neuropsychological disorders and provides ongoing monitoring and support from family and caregivers, healthcare professionals, educators, and communities members are essential for promoting optimal development of 'atypical' children. Strong support networks provide emotional support, access to resources, and opportunities for social inclusion, while appropriate educational resources, assistive technologies, and accommodation adjustments can help 'atypical' children reach their full potential.

It is important to note that neuropsychological development is a lifelong process. 'Atypical' children with disabilities may continue to experience changes and challenges as they grow into adulthood. Continued support and intervention throughout their developmental years and into adulthood are important for optimizing their quality of life and independence (Megari, 2013).

CONCLUSION

The milestones of typical child development identified in Cognitive Development Theory can be used to diagnose some prominent neuropsychological disorders, such as autism spectrum disorder (ASD), attention-deficit/hyperactivity disorder (ADHD), and intellectual disabilities, including Down syndrome in 'atypical' children.

Extensive research on neuropsychological development from infancy to adolescence provides insights of typical development but also deviations that can be further linked to various disabilities. This allows early intervention and prevention planning, timely introduction of support services for optimising children's cognitive, emotional, academic, and social functioning. Furthermore, by addressing the unique needs and strengths of children with disabilities across the different developmental stages, researchers and practitioners can set up inclusive environments and ensure positive outcomes for all children (Braconnier & Siper, 2021).

The brain is flexible due to neurodevelopmental plasticity. Professionals can use their understanding of typical and atypical development to guide their practice; this includes clinical, counselling, and school psychologists. Interventions can focus on important window of time to maximize results. Even though children and adolescents are the subject of most research, neurodevelopmental changes persist into adulthood. Understanding the relationship between environmental factors and neural development enables professionals to advocate people of all ages (Papaeliou et al, 2011).

It is important to acknowledge that this research, although it contributes to the understanding on neuropsychological development in childhood, does not focus on age effects during typical neuropsychological development. Consequently, there are gaps in the literature on neuropsychological development. To date, understanding of atypical development is based on an understanding of typical development. The strength and nature of the relationship between abilities and achievement has been found to differ at different ages during childhood (Alloway & Passolunghi, 2011). The need for more research into typical neuropsychological development would aid understanding and provide a baseline of expected development. After all, the primary emphasis in neuropsychology is to assess functioning in a variety of domains to understand an individual's strengths and weaknesses (Baron, 2004).

Subsequent investigations will persist in transcending disciplinary lines, tackling inquiries pertaining to the interplay between neurobiological and contextual factors, individual variations in treatment reaction, and an augmented research foundation on severe instances, elderly individuals with disabilities, and particular domains like mathematical problem solving, reading comprehension, and written communication (Sommariva et al, 2020).

REFERENCES

Akhtar, F., & Bokhari, R. A. S. (2023). *Down Syndrome*. StatPearls. https://pubmed
.ncbi.nlm.nih.gov/30252272/

Alloway, T. P., & Passolunghi, M. C. (2011). The relationship between working
memory, IQ, and mathematical skills in children. *Learning and Individual Differences*, 21(1), 133–137. 10.1016/j.lindif.2010.09.013

Alsaedi, H. R., Carrington, S., & Watters, J. J. (2020). Behavioral and Neuropsychological Evaluation of Executive Functions in Children with Autism Spectrum
Disorder in the Gulf Region. *Brain Sciences*, 10(2), 120–141. 10.3390/brains-
ci1002012032098341

Anderson, P. J., & Doyle, L. W. (2004). Executive Functioning in School-Aged
Children Who Were Born Very Preterm or With Extremely Low Birth Weight in
the 1990s. *Pediatrics*, 114(1), 50–57. 10.1542/peds.114.1.5015231907

Ando, J., Ono, Y., & Wright, M. J. (2001, November). Genetic structure of
spatial and verbal working memory. *Behavior Genetics*, 31(6), 615–624.
10.1023/A:101335361359111838538

Ansari, A., & Winsler, A. (2012). School readiness among low-income, Latino children attending family childcare versus centre-based care. *Early Child Development
and Care*, 182(11), 1465–1485. 10.1080/03004430.2011.622755

Arnsten, F. T. A. (2009). The Emerging Neurobiology of Attention Deficit Hyperactivity Disorder: The Key Role of the Prefrontal Association Cortex. *The Journal
of Pediatrics*, 154(5), I-S43. 10.1016/j.jpeds.2009.01.01820596295

Baron, I. (2004a). Intelligence Testing: General Considerations. In *Neuropsychological Evaluation of the Child* (pp. 108–132). Oxford University Press.

Beauregard, J. L., Drews-Botsch, C., Sales, J. M., Flanders, W. D., & Kramer, M.
R. (2018, January). Preterm Birth, Poverty, and Cognitive Development. *Pediatrics*,
141(1), e20170509. 10.1542/peds.2017-050929242268

Bennie, M. (2018, March 19). *Executive function: what is it, and how do we support it in those with autism? Part I*. Autism Awareness Centre. https://autismaware
nesscentre.com/

Berger, K. S. (2014). *Invitation to the Life Span* (2nd ed.). Worth Publishers.

Berk, E. L. (2013). *Child Development* (9th ed.). Pearson.

Blair, C., & Raver, C. C. (2014). School Readiness and Self-Regulation: A Developmental Psychobiological Approach. *Annual Review of Psychology*, 66(1), 711–731. 10.1146/annurev-psych-010814-01522125148852

Börnert-Ringleb, M., & Wilbert, J. (2018). The Association of Strategy Use and Concrete-Operational Thinking in Primary School. *Frontiers in Education*, 3, 1–11. 10.3389/feduc.2018.00038

Braconnier, L. M., & Siper, M. P. (2021). Neuropsychological Assessment in Autism Spectrum Disorder. *Current Psychiatry Reports*, 23(10), 63. 10.1007/s11920-021-01277-134331144

Brown, A. K., Parikh, S., & Patel, R. D. (2020). Understanding basic concepts of developmental diagnosis in children. *Translational Pediatrics*, 9(1), 9–22. 10.21037/tp.2019.11.0432206580

Bush, R. N., Wakschlag, S. L., LeWinn, Z. K., Hertz-Picciotto, I., Nozadi, S. S., Pieper, S., Lewis, J., Biezonski, D., Blair, C., Deardorff, J., Neiderhiser, M. J., Leve, D. L., Elliott, J. A., Duarte, S. C., Lugo-Candelas, C., O'Shea, M. T., Avalos, A. L., Page, P. G., & Posner, J. (2020). Family Environment, Neurodevelopmental Risk, and the Environmental Influences on Child Health Outcomes (ECHO) Initiative: Looking Back and Moving Forward. *Frontiers in Psychiatry*, 11(547), 1–17. 10.3389/fpsyt.2020.0054732636769

Center on the Developing Child. (2017). *A science-based framework for early childhood policy*. Center on the Developing Child. www. developingchild.harvard.edu

Cherry, K. (2022, December 5). The Preoperational Stage of Cognitive Development. *Very Well Mind.* https://www.verywellmind.com/preoperational-stage-of-cognitive-development-2795461

Cherry, K. (2023, March 01). The Concrete Operational Stage of Cognitive Development. *Very Well Mind.* https://www.verywellmind.com/concrete-operational-stage-of-cognitive-development-2795458

Cherry, K. (2023, February 28). The Sensorimotor Stage of Cognitive Development. *Very Well Mind.* https://www.verywellmind.com/sensorimotor-stage-of-cognitive-development-2795462

Costa, I. D., Azambuja, S. L., Portuguez, W. M., & Costa, C. J. (2004). Neuropsychological assessment in children. *Jornal de Pediatria*, 80(2), 111–116. 10.2223/117515154079

Dawson, G., Rogers, S., Munson, J., Smith, M., Winter, J., Greenson, J., Donaldson, A., & Varley, J. (2009). Randomized, Controlled Trial of an Intervention for Toddlers With Autism: The Early Start Denver Model. *Pediatrics*, 125(1), 17–23. 10.1542/peds.2009-095819948568

Demetriou, A. E., DeMayo, M. M., & Guastella, J. A. (2019). Executive Function in Autism Spectrum Disorder: History, Theoretical Models, Empirical Findings, and Potential as an Endophenotype. *Frontiers in Psychiatry*, 10, 1–17. 10.3389/fpsyt.2019.0075331780959

Donoghue, E. A., Lieser, D., DelConte, B., Donoghue, E., Earls, M., Glassy, D., Mendelsohn, A., McFadden, T., Scholer, S., Takagishi, J., Vanderbilt, D., & Williams, P. G. (2017, August). Council on Early Childhood. Quality Early Education and Child Care From Birth to Kindergarten. *Pediatrics*, 140(2), e20171488. 10.1542/peds.2017-148828771418

Down Syndrome International. (2022, Sep 20). *Learning Profiles*. Down Syndrome International. https://www.ds-int.org/faqs/learning-profile

Down Syndrome Research Foundation. (2024). *Sensory Processing*. Down Syndrome Research Foundation. https://www.dsrf.org/resources/information/physical-skill-development/sensory-processing/

Duncan, A. W., & Bishop, S. L. (2013). Understanding the gap between cognitive abilities and daily living skills in adolescents with autism spectrum disorders with average intelligence. *Autism*.24275020

Ek, U., Westerlund, J., Holmberg, K., & Fernell, E. (2010). Academic performance of adolescents with ADHD and other behavioural and learning problems—A population-based longitudinal study. *Acta Paediatrica (Oslo, Norway)*, 100(3), 402–406. 10.1111/j.1651-2227.2010.02048.x21054512

Fan, J., Wu, Y., Fossella, J. A., Posner, M. I. (2001). Assessing the heritability of attentional networks. *BMC Neuroscience, 2*(14). 10.1186/1471-2202-2-14

Fernald, A., Marchman, V. A., & Weisleder, A. (2013, March). SES differences in language processing skill and vocabulary are evident at 18 months. *Developmental Science*, 16(2), 234–248. 10.1111/desc.1201923432833

Furman, L. (2005). What Is Attention-Deficit Hyperactivity Disorder (ADHD)? *Journal of Child Neurology*, 20(12), 994–1002. 10.1177/0883073805020012130116417850

Geoffroy, M.-C., Coté, S. M., Anne, I. H., Borge, A. I. H., Larouche, F., Jean, R., Séguin, J. R., & Rutter, M. (2007). Association between nonmaternal care in the first year of life and children's receptive language skills prior to school entry: The moderating role of socioeconomic status. *Journal of Child Psychology and Psychiatry, and Allied Disciplines*, 48(5), 490–497. 10.1111/j.1469-7610.2006.01704.x17501730

Gharamaleki, S. N., Roshan, R., Pourabdol, S., Saravani, S., & Ghaedi, H. G. (2018). A Comparison of Frontal Lobe Function Between Students with Attention-Deficit Hyperactivity Disorder and Normal Students. *Zahedan Journal of Researches in Medical Sciences*, 20(4), e64198. 10.5812/zjrms.64198

Glozman, J. (2013). *Developmental neuropsychology*. Routledge/Taylor & Francis Group.

Hackman, A. D., Farah, J. M., & Meaney, J. M. (2010). Socioeconomic status and the brain: Mechanistic insights from human and animal research. *Nature Reviews. Neuroscience*, 11(9), 651–659. 10.1038/nrn289720725096

Haddad, F., Bourke, J., Wong, K., & Leonard, H. (2018). An investigation of the determinants of quality of life in adolescents and young adults with Down syndrome. *PLoS One*, 13(6), e0197394. 10.1371/journal.pone.019739429897903

Hadders-Algra, M. (2022). *The developing brain: Challenges and opportunities to promote school readiness in young children at risk of neurodevelopmental disorders in low- and middle-income countries*.

Hamadelseed, O., Chan, K. S. M., Wong, B. F. M., & Skutella, T. (2023). Distinct neuroanatomical and neuropsychological features of Down syndrome compared to related neurodevelopmental disorders: A systematic review. *Frontiers in Neuroscience*, 17, 1–26. 10.3389/fnins.2023.122522837600012

Harmony, T. (2009). *Handbook of clinical child neuropsychology* (3rd ed.). Springer.

Haworth, C. M., Wright, M. J., Luciano, M., Martin, N. G., de Geus, E. J., van Beijsterveldt, C. E. M., Bartels, M., Posthuma, D., Boomsma, D. I., Davis, O. S., Kovas, Y., Corley, R. P., Defries, J. C., Hewitt, J. K., Olson, R. K., Rhea, S. A., Wadsworth, S. J., Iacono, W. G., McGue, M., & Plomin, R. (2010). The heritability of general cognitive ability increases linearly from childhood to young adulthood. *Molecular Psychiatry*, 15(11), 1112–1120. 10.1038/mp.2009.5519488046

Hollister Sandberg, E., & Spritz, L. B. (2010). *A Clinician's Guide to Normal Cognitive Development in Childhood*. Taylor & Francis.

Holmes, C. J., Kim-Spoon, J., & Deater-Deckard, K. (2016, January). Linking Executive Function and Peer Problems from Early Childhood Through Middle Adolescence. *Journal of Abnormal Child Psychology*, 44(1), 31–42. 10.1007/s10802-015-0044-526096194

Hughes, C., Russell, J., & Robbins, T. W. (1994). Evidence for executive dysfunction in autism. *Neuropsychologia, 32*(4), 477–492.

Hutchins, T. L., Prelock, P. A., Morris, H., Benner, J., LaVigne, T., & Hoza, B. (2016). Explicit vs. applied theory of mind competence: A comparison of typically developing males, males with ASD, and males with ADHD. *Research in Autism Spectrum Disorders*, 21, 94–108. 10.1016/j.rasd.2015.10.004

Jahromi, B. L., Gulsrud, A., & Kasari, C. (2008). Emotional competence in children with Down syndrome: Negativity and regulation. *American Journal of Mental Retardation*, 113(1), 32–43. 10.1352/0895-8017(2008)113[32:ECICWD]2.0.CO;218173298

Khalfa, S., Bruneau, N., Rogé, B., Georgieff, N., Veuillet, E., Adrien, J. L., Barthélémy, C., & Collet, L. (2004, December). Increased perception of loudness in autism. *Hearing Research*, 198(1-2), 87–92. 10.1016/j.heares.2004.07.00615617227

Kristen, S., & Sodian, B. (2014). Theory of mind (ToM) in early education: Developmental progression of early theory of mind skills, social developmental factors and the importance of ToM for learning. In Saracho, O. N. (Ed.), *Contemporary perspectives on research in theory of mind in early childhood education* (pp. 291–320). IAP Information Age Publishing.

Landi, N., Avery, T., Crowley, J. M., Wu, J., & Mayes, L. (2017). Prenatal Cocaine Exposure Impacts Language and Reading Into Late Adolescence: Behavioral and ERP Evidence. *Developmental Neuropsychology*, 42(6), 369–386. 10.1080/87565641.2017.136269828949778

Lezak, M. D., Howieson, D. B., Bigler, E. D., & Tranel, D. (2012). *Neuropsychological assessment* (5th ed.). Oxford University Press.

López Resa, P., & Moraleda Sepúlveda, E. (2024). Developmental Profile in Children Aged 3–6 Years: Down Syndrome vs. Autism Spectrum Disorder. *Behavioral Sciences (Basel, Switzerland)*, 14(5), 380. 10.3390/bs1405038038785871

Lunkenheimer, E., Ram, N., Skowron, E. A., & Yin, P. (2017, September). Harsh parenting, child behavior problems, and the dynamic coupling of parents' and children's positive behaviors. *Journal of Family Psychology*, 31(6), 689–698. 10.1037/fam000031028333490

Malik, F., & Marwaha, R. (2023, April 23). *Cognitive Development*. NCBI. https://www.ncbi.nlm.nih.gov/books/NBK537095/

Martin, E. G., Klusek, J., Estigarribia, B., & Roberts, E. J. (2009). Language Characteristics of Individuals with Down Syndrome. *Topics in Language Disorders*, 29(2), 112–132. 10.1097/TLD.0b013e3181a71fe120428477

McCartney, K., Dearing, E., Taylor, B. A., & Bub, K. L. (2007, September 1). Quality Child Care Supports the Achievement of Low-Income Children: Direct and Indirect Pathways Through Caregiving and the Home Environment. *Journal of Applied Developmental Psychology*, 28(5-6), 411–426. 10.1016/j.appdev.2007.06.01019578561

Mcleod, S. (2024, January 24) *Piaget's Theory And Stages Of Cognitive Development*. Simply Psychology. https://www.simplypsychology.org/piaget.html

Megari, K. (2013). Quality of life in chronic disease patients. *Health Psychology Research*, 1(3), 141–148. 10.4081/hpr.2013.93226973912

Megari, K., Frantzezou, C. K., Polyzopoulou, Z. A., & Tzouni, S. K. (2024). Neurocognitive features in childhood & adulthood in autism spectrum disorder: A Neurodiversity Approach. *International Journal of Developmental Neuroscience*, 1–29. 10.1002/jdn.1035638953464

Megari, K., Sofologi, M., Kougioumtzis, G., Thomaidou, E., Thomaidis, G., Katsarou, D., Yotsidi, V., & Theodoratou, M. (2024). Neurocognitive and psycho-emotional profile of children with disabilities. *Applied Neuropsychology. Child*, 4, 1–6. 10.1080/21622965.2024.230478138574392

Mollon, J., Knowles, E. E. M., Mathias, S. R., Gur, R., Peralta, J. M., Weiner, D. J., Robinson, E. B., Gur, R. E., Blangero, J., Almasy, L., & Glahn, D. C. (2021). Genetic influence on cognitive development between childhood and adulthood. *Molecular Psychiatry*, 26(2), 656–665. 10.1038/s41380-018-0277-030644433

NIDCD (National Institute on Deafness and Other Communication Disorders). (2020). *Autism Spectrum Disorder: Communication Problems in Children NIH Pub. No. 97–4315*. NIDCD.

Noble, K. G., McCandliss, B. D., & Farah, M. J. (2007). Socioeconomic gradients predict individual differences in neurocognitive abilities. *Developmental Science*, 10(4), 464–480. 10.1111/j.1467-7687.2007.00600.x17552936

Ogundele, O. M. (2018). Behavioural and emotional disorders in childhood: A brief overview for paediatricians. *World Journal of Clinical Pediatrics*, 7(1), 9–26. 10.5409/wjcp.v7.i1.929456928

Operto, F. F., Smirni, D., Scuoppo, C., Padovano, C., Vivenzio, V., Quatrosi, G., Carotenuto, M., Precenzano, F., & Pastorino, M. G. G. (2021). Neuropsychological Profile, Emotional/Behavioral Problems, and Parental Stress in Children with Neurodevelopmental Disorders. *Brain Sciences*, 11(5), 584–594. 10.3390/brainsci1105058433946388

Papaeliou, F. C., Fryssira, H., Kodakos, A., Kaila, M., Benaveli, E., Michaelides, K., Stroggilos, V., Vrettopoulou, M., & Polemikos, N. (2011). Nonverbal communication, play, and language in Greek young children with Williams syndrome. *Child Neuropsychology*, 17(3), 225–241. 10.1080/09297049.2010.52415121229406

Pellicano, E. (2012). The Development of Executive Function in Autism. *Autism Research and Treatment*, 146132, 1–8. 10.1155/2012/14613222934168

Piaget, J. (1936). *Origins of intelligence in the child*. Routledge & Kegan Paul.

Pujol, J., Soriano-Mas, C., Ortiz, H., & Galles, S. N. (2006). Myelination of language-related areas in the developing brain. *Neurology*, 66(3), 339–343. 10.1212/01.wnl.0000201049.66073.8d16476931

Pulina, F., Vianello, R., & Lanfranchi, S. (2019). Cognitive profiles in individuals with Down syndrome. In Lanfranchi, S. (Ed.), *International review of research in developmental disabilities: State of the art of research on Down syndrome* (pp. 67–92). Elsevier Academic Press. 10.1016/bs.irrdd.2019.06.002

Roberts, E. J., Price, J., & Malkin, C. (2007). Language and communication development in Down syndrome. *Mental Retardation and Developmental Disabilities Research Reviews*, 13(1), 26–35. 10.1002/mrdd.2013617326116

Rosenqvist, J., Lahti-Nuuttila, P., Urgesi, C., Holdnack, A. J., Kemp, S. L., & Laasonen, M. (2017). Neurocognitive Functions in 3- to 15-Year-Old Children: An International Comparison. *Journal of the International Neuropsychological Society*, 23(4), 1–14. 10.1017/S1355617716001193328143627

Sommariva, G., Zilli, T., Crescentini, C., Marini, A., Pilotto, C., Venchiarutti, M., Gortan, J. A., Fabbro, F., & Cogo, P. (2020). Toward a characterization of language development in children with congenital heart disease: A pilot study. *Child Neuropsychology*, 26(1), 1–14. 10.1080/09297049.2019.161726131120368

Spironelli, C., Penolazzi, B., & Angrilli, A. (2010). Gender Differences in Reading in School-Aged Children: An Early ERP Study. *Developmental Neuropsychology*, 35(4), 357–375. 10.1080/87565641.2010.48091320614355

Straub, L., Bateman, T. B., Hernandez-Diaz, S., York, C., Lester, B., Wisner, L. K., McDougle, J. C., Pennell, B. P., Gray, J. K., Zhu, Y., Suarez, A. E., Mogun, H., & Huybrechts, F. K. (2022). Neurodevelopmental Disorders Among Publicly or Privately Insured Children in the United States. *JAMA Psychiatry*, 79(3), 232–242. 10.1001/jamapsychiatry.2021.381534985527

Toto, A. G., & Limone, P. (2021). *The effect of motor development in adolescence on cognition: A cumulative literature review. Autumn Conferences of Sports Science*. Costa Blanca Sports Science Events., 10.14198/jhse.2021.16.Proc2.51

Tseng, H. M., Henderson, A., Chow, M. K. S., & Yao, C. (2004). Relationship between motor proficiency, attention, impulse, and activity in children with ADHD. *Developmental Medicine and Child Neurology*, 46(6), 381–388. 10.1017/S00121622040000062315174529

Tuckman, B. W., & Monetti, D. M. (2011). *Educational psychology* [International ed.]. Wadsworth Cengage Learning.

Uddin, L. Q. (2022, December). Exceptional abilities in autism: Theories and open questions. *Current Directions in Psychological Science*, 31(6), 509–517. 10.1177/09637214221113760 36776583

Vaidya, J. C. (2012). Neurodevelopmental Abnormalities in ADHD. *Current Topics in Behavioral Neurosciences*, 9, 49–66. 10.1007/7854_2011_13821541845

Vogt, E. M., & Heffelfinger, A. (2024). Pediatric assessment. In Parsons, M. W., & Braun, M. M. (Eds.), *Clinical neuropsychology: A pocket handbook for assessment* (4th ed., pp. 44–71). American Psychological Association., 10.1037/0000383-003

Voronova, N. M., Korneev, A. A., & Akhutina, V. T. (2015). Longitudinal Study of the Development of Higher Mental Functions in Primary School Children. *Journal of Russian & East European Psychology*, 52(3), 16–35. 10.1080/10610405.2015.1175833

Williams, G. L. (2021). Theory of autistic mind: A renewed relevance theoretic perspective on so-called autistic pragmatic "impairment.". *Journal of Pragmatics*, 180, 121–130. 10.1016/j.pragma.2021.04.032

Yáñez-Téllez, G., Romero-Romero, H., Rivera-García, L., Prieto-Corona, L., Bernal-Hernandez, J., Marosi-Holczberger, E., Guerrero-Juárez, V., Rodríguez-Camacho, M., & Silva-Pereyra, F. J. (2012). Cognitive and executive functions in ADHD. *Actas Españolas de Psiquiatría*, 40(6), 293–298.23165410

Yazejian, N., Bryant, D., Freel, K., Burchinal, M., & the Educare Learning Network (ELN) Investigative Team. (2015). High-quality early education: Age of entry and time in care differences in student outcomes for English-only and dual language learners. *Early Childhood Research Quarterly, 32,* 23-39. . ecresq.2015.02.002).10.1016/j

Yoshikawa, H., Weiland, C., Brooks-Gunn, J., Burchinal, M. R., Espinosa, L. M., Gormley, W. T., Ludwig, J., Magnuson, K., Phillips, D., & Zaslow, M. J. (2013). *Investing in our future: The evidence base on preschool education.* Society for Research in Child Development.

Chapter 3
Psychosomatic Symptoms in Children and Adolescents in the Digital Era:
The Importance of Early Intervention

Christina Galanou

Panteion University, Greece

ABSTRACT

This chapter explores the prevalence and impact of psychosomatic symptoms in children and adolescents, emphasizing the crucial role of early intervention in mitigating their effects on overall well-being of youth. Drawing on recent evidence, the chapter aims to highlight the various psychosomatic symptoms observed in underage population and discusses the potential psychosocial consequences of untreated symptoms. Furthermore, it examines the importance of recognizing and addressing psychosomatic symptoms during the early stages of development and provides insights into effective intervention strategies. Lastly, it underscores the need for a holistic approach that promotes a non-binary perspective of the health of youth and involves collaboration among parents, educators, healthcare professionals, and mental health specialists.

DOI: 10.4018/979-8-3693-4022-6.ch003

INTRODUCTION

The identification of psychosomatic phenomena involves recognizing that mental factors contribute to the symptomatology of a disease, despite the absence of any anatomical or physiological dysfunction or psychiatric signs. Although the concept of psychosomatics is relatively new, the understanding of the human species and disease as expressions of vital dynamism dates back centuries. Thus, the history of medicine encompasses the early roots of psychosomatic science. The ambiguity surrounding psychosomatics arises from the epistemological paradox of the human being's ontological unity and the dualism of its functions. To reconcile the mechanistic and moral-cultural models, the naturalistic approach emerged, aiming to resolve the longstanding soul-body dualism, leading to the development of modern psychosomatics.

Children and adolescents are in a critical stage of development, and psychosomatic factors can significantly influence their growth, behavior, and overall development. Early experiences and emotional well-being can have long-lasting effects on both mental and physical health. Children may not always have the vocabulary or emotional awareness to express their feelings verbally. Instead, they may manifest psychological distress through physical symptoms such as stomachaches, headaches, or changes in eating and sleeping patterns (Leonidou et al., 2019). Understanding these connections is vital for caregivers and healthcare professionals. Therefore, there has been a growing focus on adolescent mental health and well-being in many countries, with mental health problems now considered by the World Health Organization (2014) to be a major disease burden among adolescents. There is increasing concern that the current adolescent population is more at risk from mental health problems than previous generations. The potential increasing risk of mental health problems is problematic because these issues are universally recognized as having a detrimental effect on the well-being, development, academic performance, and social capital of adolescents (Li D et al., 2021).

Firstly, there is a need to address the definition of psychosomatic symptoms. These symptoms refer to physical manifestations of psychological distress and are increasingly recognized as a significant concern in children and adolescents (Vesterling et al., 2023). When the term "psychosomatic" is used, it indicates the undeniable relationship and interaction between the psychosocial and biological factors that contribute to the existence of psychosomatic health or the manifestation of a related disorder. The term "psychogenic" indicates that the source of a symptom is psychological. The term "psychosomatic disorder" indicates that psychological factors have a role in the occurrence of diseases. This term refers to physical disorders, which are caused or aggravated by psychological factors (Leonidou et al., 2019). Psychosomatic medicine is a relatively recent interdisciplinary field, which has been primarily influenced by psychoanalysis. It also incorporates theories from other approaches, with the aim of integrating the psychological, behavioral, and social dimensions of the individual and the physiology of the body (Vesterling et al., 2023).

PSYCHOSOMATICS THROUGH PSYCHOANALYSIS

Given that psychosomatic symptoms have a physical origin, this origin must be acknowledged, resulting in the mental organ's function being determined by the body's organic drives. Consequently, the body plays a dual role: as the material source of drives and as a formative influence, because psychoanalytic discourse is a biological and scientific discussion concerning the living body. Freud (1923) describes the ego as evolving from the body's interactions with external reality, serving as the interface of the mental organ by converting external energy into a will that feels personal. This indicates that the ego, though a derivative of the body, functions to connect mental processes and is distinct from the body itself, acting as the mental projection of the bodily surface or the consciousness of the body (Freud, 1923).

In psychoanalysis, the body does not feature prominently in terms of concepts like repulsion, libido, and transference, and it does not hold a significant role in Freud's key discoveries. Freud's work is a comprehensive effort to understand the human psyche through observable manifestations such as mental illness, dreams, delusions, and slips of the tongue. Epistemologically, Freud's path to psychoanalysis stemmed from a specific decoding of mental illness. The term "psychoanalysis" itself merges two seemingly opposing ideas: the soul, rich with spiritual and philosophical significance and associated with life and thought beyond the scientific realm, and analysis, which involves breaking down a whole into its parts. Therefore, the body does not occupy a central position in psychoanalysis because Freudian psychoanalysis focuses on the soul, making the lack of emphasis on the body understandable. Nonetheless, the body's function is studied in psychoanalysis and even dominates through the investigation of the mental organ (Freud, 1923).

According to Pierre Marty (1980), psychosomatic science encompasses knowledge from medicine, psychology, and biology, but it places special emphasis on the individual's unique evolving structure, economic organization, and operational dynamics. The Paris School of Psychosomatics (Marty, 1980) primarily focuses on the organization, disorganization, and reorganization of different personality types. For infants and young children, organization refers to their developmental state at the time of examination, while for adults, it signifies the completion of individual development. Disorganizations are counter-evolutionary events that disrupt an individual's structure temporarily or for extended periods. Reorganizations occur within complex systems that inhibit disorganization, and these systems correspond to fixation systems established at various developmental stages.

Individuals develop according to the general evolutionary patterns of their race and culture and their unique evolutionary traits. Hereditary issues or complications during pregnancy and birth can cause irreversible abnormalities in psychosomatic organization. Early difficulties in interactions with the mother, whether compounded by other issues, significantly impact the quality of developmental fixations, potentially disrupting the child's sensory-motor, perceptual, or digestive functions (Marty, 1980).

Key principles of somatization highlight that the newborn's condition is indicative of what Marty (1997) calls "the first mosaic," which encompasses the initial functions developing on different timelines. For instance, visceral functions develop quickly, vision by around the fifth year, motor functions by the twelfth year, and mental organization during adolescence. Functions that take longer to develop are more susceptible to fixations and regressions, which act as arrest stages before reorganization during disorganization phases. Functional organizations are influenced by interactions with the mother, who plays a crucial role in managing the child's stimulation systems and protection mechanisms against intense stimulation.

Each mother or caregiver addresses the child's reactivity, rhythmicity, and discharge style differently, which shapes the child's functional character. These characteristics are inherent in newborns and young children but evolve individually through interactions, especially with the mother. Reactivity, rhythmicity, and discharge style are complex at the mother's level, forming the framework of mother-child interactions at each stage of the child's functional development (Marty, 1997).

The Concept of Somatization

Somatization is central to psychosomatics but lacks a clear definition and consensus among different schools of thought. It refers to the production and manifestation of a physical disease or symptom due to or involving mental conditions. In psychoanalytic terms, somatization indicates the presence of a physical disorder that results from mental disorganization or deficits in mental functioning. Somatization expresses a mental deficit through a physical symptom that does not have a subjective symbolic meaning but rather signifies the disorganization of meaning processes (Marty 1980).

The Paris School of Psychosomatics, with Marty (1980) as a key representative, views psychosomatic illness as arising from significant depression, different from normal mourning, linked to a loss of pre-Oedipal object investment. These illnesses are often associated with periods of immune system decline and utilitarian life, reflecting a broader interplay between mental and physical health where somatization serves as an expression of underlying mental disorganization.

The School of Psychosomatics of Paris with Marty (1980) as its main representative accepts that a) mental development is a product of innate individual physical potentials which are later modified by the relationship with the mother. Also, immune functional bases may bring about new peculiarities in the mental structure (as happens, for example, with allergic structures) and b) the form of somatization depends on heredity, intrauterine life and conditions of birth, the psychosomatic history and external factors (e.g., stress factors) (Marty, 1997).

The release and maintenance of somatizations, which are often accompanied by the rupture of the subject with important invested objects, depend on unfavorable economic modifications in various homeostatic orders (e.g., the immune system). The rupture of these investments leads very quickly to the level of somatic pathology in behavioral neuroses, due to the inadequacy of the subjects' preconscious organization. These are borderline personalities in which the Oedipal organization has not been able to establish solid psychic defenses, resulting in a fragile ego that reacts to conflicts, losses, and injuries on a narcissistic and non-Oedipal level. It causes character neuroses, initially a mental disorganization - the so-called essential depression - in which fragile mental functioning is observed. When no regression system of mental or physical order protects against disorganization, the latter continues to endanger the body. It is therefore a progressive disorganization characterized by a succession of functional disconnections and anarchy (Marty, 1990).

Marty (1980) classified the processes of somatization into two categories: regressions and progressive disorganizations. An in-depth examination that takes into account the structure of the patients, allows, thanks to the concepts of regression and progressive disorganization, to illuminate the diagnosis, prognosis, and treatment of the disease, whatever its nature or form. Regressions have in common the cessation of disorganizing movements that stem from emotional injuries. More specifically, the concept of regression has qualities of a stage or intermediate phase that puts an end to the movement that resists growth. Once this stage of cessation of the disorganizing drive is active, the reconstruction of the individual is possible.

Marty (1991) separates regressions into full and partial for diagnostic and research purposes. He also speaks of straight adjacent lines when the physical development does not coincide with the mental, and of parallel lines when they do not correspond at all. Referring to regressions, Marty (1991) mentions hysterical somato-transformations, which he defines as partial regressions to the extent that the appearance of the somato-transformative symptoms only partially modifies the subject's mental organization.

If the repressed representations on which the symptom is based do indeed constitute a mute zone, the rest of the mental function remains most of the time compatible, "smooth," and not necessarily in a state of regression. Thanks to the verbalization of the repressed representations, the somatic symbolic and palindromic symptomatology disappears. Progressive disorganizations, the diagnosis, prognosis, and treatment of which differ in a given disease greatly from those of regressions, have in common the impossibility of arresting the movement that resists the growth which sustains them, since only the mechanisms of regression or physical mechanisms could cause said motion to cease. The absence of regressive mechanisms at the mental level and the accompanying absence of preconscious functioning point to substantial or significant depression and the useful life of the subjects.

Marty (1990) defined utilitarian thought as conscious thinking detached from imaginative activity, focused on reproducing and depicting actions within a limited time frame, sometimes preceding or following the action itself. This concept is central to the theoretical framework of the School of Paris and is linked to behavioral neuroses, significant depression, mental disorganization, and death drives.

Utilitarian Thought

Utilitarian thought refers to a mode of thinking and mental functioning that aligns with external reality. It features a logical, linear relationship between events and outcomes, often seen in individuals who are well-adjusted or professionally successful. This type of thinking is typically banal, lacks emotional involvement, and is devoid of daydreaming and imaginative activities. In speech, it corresponds to straightforward and unemotional communication (Marty, 1990).

Utilitarian thinking is connected to the good functioning of the preconscious. As preconscious, Marty (1980) defines the psychic space with the following features: a) the range according to the layers during development b) the flow of internal circulation between the different layers of representation c) the spontaneous availability at the time of said circulation When the above three properties work, the smooth functioning of the mental organ is certain. When their functioning is doubtful, the functioning of the mental organ is expected to be correspondingly precarious. When finally they disappear, the poor functioning of the mental organ is certain. Marty (1997) defined symptomatology at the phenomenological and clinical level as "behavioral neurosis".

In theory, the preconscious represents a site of functional connections of the most diverse orders that are assembled during development, like a reservoir, the contents of which are ready to overflow from consciousness. It manifests itself especially as a place of connection between sensuous mobility, which places the representations of things, and languages, which establish the representations of words. The preconscious is thus, a relatively layered world, the deep layers of which touch the unconscious, instincts, impulses, and the body, while the highest layers finally meet consciousness. The quality of the preconscious depends on the range of all its layers, on the internal mobility of the forms of representations it secures in its different layers, on its permanence, and finally on its function. The role of the functional quality of the preconscious is to inform at all times of the presence, absence, disappearance, and return of the psychosomatic functional hierarchy, which can change from one moment to another (Marty, 1997).

When utilitarian thinking predominates as the main mode of mental functioning, it forms what is known as utilitarian life. This concept is closely linked to alexithymia, and the term mechanistic thinking or lifestyle is also used. As Smadja (2007) notes, utilitarian thinking often acts as an anti-traumatic mechanism, developing after traumatic experiences to facilitate emotional processing and meaning making. The prevalence of this thinking can be temporary, due to the severity of a traumatic event, or more permanent, due to deeper psychological deficits. Elements of utilitarian thinking, detached from emotional and subjective traits, can be present in all personality types within the normal spectrum.

Fundamental Depression

The anti-traumatic and self-soothing effects of utilitarian thinking are limited due to the rigidity of mental functions. This limitation often leads to new traumatic experiences and losses, affecting the individual's narcissistic nature. The accumulation of these experiences can lead to fundamental depression, marked by the collapse of essential physical and mental elements. This type of depression features negative symptoms without positive symptoms like guilt, shame, worthlessness, or anxiety about loss (Green, 2002).

In terms of intrapsychic functioning, fundamental depression disrupts Ego functions, defense mechanisms, and preconscious functioning. This symptomatology increases the individual's vulnerability to subsequent traumatic experiences. Psychoanalytical psychosomatics posits that chronic fundamental depression creates a foundation for disorganization and the emergence of physical illnesses.

Defenses in Psychosomatics

The degree of mental organization and the structure of the mental organ, along with the nature of mental defenses in psychosomatic pathology, show considerable variation. Marty (1990) and the French school propose that each person develops a basic organizational style reflecting past injuries and deficits, leading to narcissistic pathology. This pathology and the resulting psychological impasses can activate defense mechanisms such as splitting or utilitarian thinking, while other personality aspects might use neurotic-type defenses.

In psychosomatic evaluations, it is crucial to assess the extent to which these defense mechanisms can support somatopsychic metabolism. A comprehensive psychodynamic history, including the ability to find meaning in various life situations (e.g., loss experiences, medical history, illness conditions), is essential for differential diagnosis. In psychosomatic pathology, the mental landscape often mirrors borderline disorders. However, when utilitarian thinking or fundamental depression prevails, there is a corresponding disorganization of the psyche and its dynamics (unconscious, conscious, preconscious – Ego, Id, Superego – Ideal Ego). Under the first local conditions, the preconscious's functioning is disrupted, while under the second local conditions, the Ego's functions, including meaning-making and emotional processing, are disorganized (Green, 2002).

BODY IMAGE AND PSYCHOSOMATICS

There is a connection between body image and psychosomatic symptoms. This connection underscores the importance of considering psychological factors in the assessment and treatment of physical health issues. Body image refers to how individuals perceive, think, and feel about their own bodies (Tarkhanova & Kholmogorova, 2011). By addressing body image concerns and promoting positive self-perception, healthcare providers can help individuals mitigate emotional distress and reduce the occurrence of psychosomatic symptoms.

Body image concerns can impact interpersonal relationships, including romantic partnerships, friendships, and family dynamics. Individuals may withdraw socially, experience difficulties in intimate relationships, or perceive social rejection due to their appearance (Martin et al., 2017). Social stressors, resulting from body image dissatisfaction, can further contribute to psychological distress and exacerbate psychosomatic symptoms. For example, social anxiety stemming from negative body image may lead to gastrointestinal symptoms or tension headaches in social situations.

Negative body image can trigger physiological responses in the body, such as increased muscle tension, changes in heart rate, and alterations in hormone levels. These physiological changes can contribute to the development and exacerbation of psychosomatic symptoms. For example, chronic stress resulting from negative body image can activate the body's stress response system, leading to physical symptoms such as gastrointestinal distress, fatigue, and headaches (Tarkhanova & Kholmogorova,. 2011).

Body image dissatisfaction can influence health behaviors and lifestyle choices. Individuals with negative body image may engage in unhealthy behaviors such as disordered eating, excessive exercise, substance abuse, or avoidance of healthcare services. These maladaptive behaviors can have direct physical consequences, contributing to the onset or exacerbation of psychosomatic symptoms (Thomson et al., 2002)

STRESS MECHANISM

Given that psychosomatic symptoms have a physical origin, this origin must be acknowledged, resulting in the mental organ's function being determined by the body's organic drives. Consequently, the body plays a dual role: as the material source of drives and as a formative influence, because psychoanalytic discourse is a biological and scientific discussion concerning the living body. Freud (1923) describes the ego as evolving from the body's interactions with external reality, serving as the interface of the mental organ by converting external energy into a will that feels personal. This indicates that the ego, though a derivative of the body, functions to connect mental processes and is distinct from the body itself, acting as the mental projection of the bodily surface or the consciousness of the body.

Historical work on stress represents another major current in research on psychosomatic disorders. Cannon (1929) elaborated a new theory of emotions taking as a starting point for his investigations the normal reactions of anger and fear. He showed that the organism reacts to critical situations with certain adaptive changes, with its entire economy. He also showed that emotional states activate physiological functions that prepare the organism for a state of which emotions are an indication, for example fear and anger stimulate the adrenal glands.

Selye 's (1935) pursuit was to delve into the concept of stress at a physiological level, which he defines as follows: the organism's response to any request made to it, to any physical or mental stimulus. The adaptation syndrome that causes stress develops in three phases according to Selye (1935): - acute alarm reaction (shock state or reaction to shock) continuous adaptation reaction, also called resistance or defense phase (psychological compensation) exhaustion phase during which the mechanisms fail and disorders appear.

In the face of a mental or physical attack that threatens the internal balance of the organism, it reacts by aiming to restore the disturbed balance. This reaction cannot be specified because it does not depend on the nature of the attacking agent. Dantzer (2003) according to this model, the conflict between the subject's expectations and reality sets in motion the reactive mechanisms which, due to their intensity, lead to illness.

Modern neuro-endocrine-immunology has examined many factors that contribute to the establishment of a stress condition in the organism, from the level of the cell to the set of systems and organs of the body, the hormonal system, the immune system, and of course the central, autonomic and the peripheral nervous system. In the context of these investigations, the presence of psychological stress or psychological traumatic experiences, especially that of early life, has been extensively examined. On the connection of traumatic situations and the appearance of physical diseases (Brudey et al., 2015; Sosa et al., 2014; Chida et al., 2008) or the disorder of basic immune, homeostatic, intracellular (Griffin et al., 2014) and histological (Brouwers et al., 2015) functions, there is extensive literature. Also, studies (Gawronski et al., 2014) show that the presence of "potentially traumatic factors and severe stress conditions is associated with an increase in visits and hospitalizations in primary and secondary care.

It is also reported that fibromyalgia exhibits similar neuro-endocrinological characteristics to psychiatric disorders, such as anxiety, depression, bipolar disorder, and post-traumatic stress disorder (Burke et al., 2016).

The impact of early trauma on neurobiological systems seems to concern functions such as reproductive performance and the development of infectious or cardio -metabolic diseases in later life (Konrad, Herpertz & Herpertz - Dahlmann, 2016). The impact of emotional arousal on the biological body has been highlighted in various studies, as acute and chronic stress causes structural and functional alterations in the prefrontal lobe, amygdala, and hypothalamus and by extension in the autonomic nervous system through changes in endocrinological and cellular function.

Keskin (2019) explored the close association between chronic stress and gastrointestinal disorders such as reflux, irritable bowel syndrome, Crohn 's disease and ulcerative colitis, and pointed out the overrepresentation of mental disorders such as anxiety and depression in patients with gastrointestinal disorders.

Sobański et al (2015) have also pointed out the close correlation between interpersonal difficulties and conflicts in adulthood (specifically in relationships with partner/parents) and the presence of gastrointestinal symptoms, such as irritable bowel syndrome, vomiting, functional dyspepsia, etc. Accordingly, Crosta et al. (2018) assessed the relationship between early trauma and resilience in a sample of patients with psoriasis and a control group without skin disorders. Psoriasis patients had a significant prevalence of childhood trauma and lower levels of mental resilience relative to the control group, while significant associations were also noted between early trauma, mental resilience, and quality of life in psoriasis patients (Crosta et al., 2018).

RECENT EVIDENCE

A thorough examination of the literature reveals a rising incidence of psychosomatic symptoms among children and adolescents. Common symptoms include headaches, stomachaches, fatigue, and sleep disturbances (Vesterling et al., 2023). Researchers attribute these symptoms to a range of factors, including academic stress, family dynamics, peer relationships, and exposure to trauma. Psychosomatic symptoms are very common at young ages. International surveys show that one in four children complain of physical symptoms, which lacks an organic cause at least once a week (Li D et al., 2021). In fact, it seems that almost 50% of visits to pediatric clinics concern psychosomatic symptoms and physical discomforts that are not linked to organic factors. In the general population 2–10% frequently complain of such physical complaints. Untreated psychosomatic symptoms can have profound implications for the overall well-being of children and adolescents. Academic performance may suffer, social relationships can become strained, and long-term mental health issues might emerge (Busch et al., 2020). Understanding the potential consequences underscores the urgency of addressing psychosomatic symptoms early on.

The most recent research about somatic complaints was conducted by WHO (2023). Researchers from countries among the world (Europe, central Asia and Canada) used the HBSC symptom checklist to assess nonclinical, subjective health complaints that have both physical and psychological origins. The instrument covers symptoms like headaches, stomach aches, back pain, feelings of depression, irritability, nervousness, sleep difficulties, and dizziness experienced over the last six months. The data reveals that psychological complaints are the most prevalent: nervousness (33%), irritability (33%), and sleep difficulties (29%), followed by feelings of depression (25%). Physical complaints include headaches (20%), back pain (17%), stomach aches (14%), and dizziness (15%). Among 13- and 15-year-olds, girls report higher rates of feeling low, headaches, and dizziness than boys, with nervousness being twice as common in girls. Girls aged 13 also report three times the rate of stomach aches compared to boys of the same age in 10 countries and regions, with this trend extending to 25 countries for 15-year-olds. Overall, individual health complaints peak at age 15, with gender influencing the type of complaints. For boys, the frequency of back pain, feeling low, irritability, and nervousness increases with age, while sleep difficulties, dizziness, headaches, and stomach aches remain stable across age groups. For girls, all health complaints rise significantly from ages 11 to 15 across nearly all countries and regions. Socioeconomic disparities in health complaints were found in less than half of the surveyed countries and regions. Where differences exist, adolescents from less affluent families generally report more frequent health complaints. However, in some countries, this pattern is reversed, with higher prevalence among adolescents from affluent families.

Multiple health complaints - defined as experiencing two or more symptoms more than once a week - were reported by 44% of adolescents. Older girls were most affected, with two-thirds of 15-year-olds reporting multiple complaints. Girls across all age groups reported higher prevalence than boys, with the gender gap widening with age. For example, at age 11, 31% of boys and 42% of girls reported multiple complaints; by age 15, these figures rose to 36% of boys and 66% of girls (WHO, 2023).

The prevalence of multiple health complaints varied widely between countries, from 16% among 11-year-old boys in Slovenia to 86% among 15-year-old girls in Italy. No significant difference in multiple health complaints was found between adolescents from high- and low-affluence families in most regions. However, higher prevalence was reported among less affluent adolescents in eight countries, while the reverse was observed in certain others. The prevalence of multiple health complaints has increased over the last three HBSC surveys, rising from 33% in 2014 to 44% in 2022, with a more pronounced increase among girls. The persistent and high prevalence of mental health difficulties, particularly among girls and adolescents from less affluent families, underscores the need for early intervention and comprehensive national strategies focused on adolescent well-being (WHO, 2023).

Results from a systematic review (Vesterling, et al., 2023) depicted the prevalence of somatoform symptoms setting and underscore the importance of school staff involvement. They suggest that school nurses and counselors undergo training to help them recognize somatoform symptoms and use screening tools as a preliminary measure. Additionally, their findings indicate that some children and adolescents may display somatoform symptoms without having been formally diagnosed, a point that healthcare professionals should consider.

CLINICAL PRACTICE

Modern life, characterized by fast-paced lifestyles, economic uncertainties, and global events (such as pandemics), has led to heightened levels of stress and mental health issues. The COVID-19 pandemic has significantly impacted mental health globally. The associated stress, anxiety, and depression have led to an increase in psychosomatic symptoms. Addressing these challenges requires a multi-faceted approach, including increasing public and professional awareness, improving education and training, integrating mental and physical health services, enhancing access to care, and conducting comprehensive research to inform evidence-based practices (Yasunobe et al., 2023).

There is a growing recognition of the need to integrate mental and physical health care. Addressing psychosomatic symptoms requires a holistic approach that considers both mental and physical aspects of health, promoting overall well-being. The current global context, characterized by heightened stress, advancements in medical science, and increasing healthcare costs, makes it imperative to focus on psychosomatic symptoms now. Doing so can lead to better health outcomes, more efficient healthcare systems, and improved quality of life for many individuals (Fava, 2023). Focusing on psychosomatic research can help develop cost-effective treatments and reduce the financial burden on healthcare systems. With increasing recognition of global health challenges such as chronic diseases and mental health disorders, addressing psychosomatic symptoms becomes part of a broader strategy to improve public health. Effective management of these symptoms can lead to better health outcomes on a global scale (Fava, 2023).

Clinical practice in psychosomatics involves a holistic approach to diagnosing and treating patients with psychosomatic symptoms. Effective clinical practice requires the integration of medical and psychological care to address the complex interplay between mind and body. A thorough medical history and physical examination are essential to rule out organic causes of symptoms. This includes reviewing the patient's past medical records, conducting a detailed interview about current symptoms, and performing necessary physical examinations (Botscheket et al., 2023).

Further on the assessment of psychological state of the patient using structured interviews and validated questionnaires, is needed. DSM 5 and ICD-10 have the criteria outlined for diagnosing somatic symptom disorder and related conditions, which can help differentiate psychosomatic disorders from other medical and psychiatric conditions. (Wise, 2014)

The use of a biopsychosocial approach is most useful in order to consider the biological, psychological, and social factors that may be contributing to the patient's symptoms. This comprehensive view helps in understanding the multifaceted nature of psychosomatic disorders. (Thabrew, de Sylva, Romans, 2012)

Diagnostic Tools

Diagnostic tools in psychosomatics are essential for accurately identifying and differentiating psychosomatic disorders from other medical conditions. Tools help clinicians assess the psychological and physical components of symptoms. Using diagnostic tools, clinicians can better understand the complexity of psychosomatic symptoms, leading to more accurate diagnoses and tailored treatment plans. Effective diagnosis involves not only identifying the presence of psychosomatic symptoms but also understanding the underlying psychological and social factors that contribute to these symptoms.

Few of the most used are:

Structured Clinical Interviews:

Structured Clinical Interview for DSM-5 (SCID-5): This is a comprehensive, standardized interview guide used to diagnose mental disorders based on DSM-5 criteria. It includes sections that can help identify somatic symptom disorders and related conditions (APA, 2013).

Mini International Neuropsychiatric Interview (MINI):

A brief structured diagnostic interview for major psychiatric disorders, including somatic symptom disorder. The MINI is a shorter and more efficient diagnostic tool compared to the DSM 5, suitable for both clinical and research settings (Sheehan et al., 1998).

Patient Health Questionnaire-15 (PHQ-15):

The PHQ-15 is a self-administered tool that assesses 15 common somatic symptoms. It helps identify individuals with significant somatic complaints that may be related to psychosomatic disorders (Kroenke, Spitzer & Williams, 2002)

Somatic Symptom Scale-8 (SSS-8):

This shorter tool focuses on the severity of eight key somatic symptoms, providing a quick assessment that can be used in various settings (Gierk et al., 2014)

Whiteley Index (WI):

The Whiteley Index helps identify individuals with excessive worry about their health, which can be a component of psychosomatic disorders (Speckens et al., 1196)

Somatosensory Amplification Scale (SSAS):

Evaluates the tendency to experience somatic sensations as intense and distressing. This scale measures how strongly individuals perceive and are bothered by physical sensations, which is relevant in diagnosing somatic symptom disorders (Barsky et al., 1983)

Illness Attitude Scales (IAS):

The IAS evaluates health anxiety, disease conviction, and related behaviors, providing insight into the cognitive aspects of psychosomatic symptoms (Stewart & Watt 2000).

General Health Questionnaire (GHQ):

Assesses overall mental health and includes items related to physical symptoms, aiding in the identification of psychosomatic issues (Montazeri et al., 2003)

Brief Symptom Inventory (BSI):

The BSI measures a range of psychological symptoms, including somatization, and helps identify individuals with significant distress (Derogatis, 1975).

Diagnostic Criteria for Psychosomatic Research (DCPR):

The DCPR includes detailed criteria for various psychosomatic syndromes such as health anxiety, functional somatic symptoms secondary to a psychiatric disorder, and persistent somatization. It complements standard diagnostic tools by focusing specifically on psychosomatic aspects (Fava et al., 1995).

Beck Depression Inventory (BDI): Assesses the severity of depression, which often coexists with psychosomatic disorders (Beck, 1996)

Beck Anxiety Inventory (BAI): Measures the severity of anxiety, another common co-occurring condition with psychosomatic symptoms (Beck, 1988).

Biopsychosocial Assessments:

Comprehensive assessments that consider biological, psychological, and social factors contributing to the patient's symptoms. These assessments often involve a combination of structured interviews, questionnaires, and clinical evaluations.

EARLY INTERVENTION

Early intervention is crucial in preventing the escalation of psychosomatic symptoms and their potential long-term effects. Recognizing the signs and providing timely support can significantly impact a child's ability to cope with stressors and build resilience (Habukawa, et al., 2021). This can have a lasting positive impact on their ability to handle future challenges and maintain mental health. However, early detection for prevention and improvement of adolescent mental health problems remains difficult.

Early intervention may involve collaboration between parents, educators, and mental health professionals to create a supportive environment. Several effective strategies exist for intervening early in the presence of psychosomatic symptoms (Richards et al., 2019). These include psychoeducation for parents and educators, implementing stress management programs in schools, and fostering open communication channels between children and trusted adults. Additionally, incorporating mental health education into school curricula can help destigmatize mental health discussions. The collaborative efforts of parents, educators, healthcare professionals and mental health specialists are essential for successful early intervention. Building a network of support ensures that children and adolescents receive comprehensive care that addresses both the physical and psychological aspects of their well-being (Richards et al., 2019).

Research evidence suggest that health researchers and professionals as well as health service institutions and governments must join forces to deliver integrated and multidisciplinary actions in mental health, especially in the early steps of the prevention chain (Richards et al., 2019). Mental health professionals have anyway the scientific, ethical, and moral responsibility to orient social, political, and overall health care actors involved in promotion and maintenance of mental health status (Kleszczewska et al., 2020).

Early identification and intervention for psychosomatic issues can be essential for preventing long-term mental health challenges. Providing children with coping skills, emotional support, and a nurturing environment can contribute to their overall resilience (Kleszczewska et al., 2020). Mind-body techniques, such as mindfulness and relaxation exercises, can be adapted for children to help them manage stress, anxiety, and emotional challenges. These techniques can be incorporated into school settings and at home to promote well-being. Open communication with children and adolescents about their emotions and physical health is crucial (Vesterling & Koglin, 2020). Educating them about the mind-body connection and helping them understand how emotions can impact their well-being can empower them to take an active role in their mental and physical health (Atzil et al., 2013)

Few intervention studies have been conducted in Greece, and most of them lack "robust" methodological approaches. In this sense there is an important need to investigate the effectiveness of interventions designed for the public sector. The most recent review highlighted the lack of nationally representative data for most mental health disorders, and therefore relied on regional data. This fact demonstrates the need to produce representative data (CAMHI, 2023). The research has revealed that mental health symptoms occur with alarming frequency in children and adolescents in Greece. However, simply measuring the frequency of these issues is not enough. We should also understand how young people experience and interpret these symptoms so that we can address the complex social and cultural factors that affect their well-being. In prioritizing the diverse perspectives of this population, we also need to consider the specific contexts and unique difficulties faced by populations with additional vulnerabilities, and work to create tailored interventions that will truly enhance their well-being. Furthermore, a pilot study was conducted in Greece – YES program-, in order to eliminate anxiety and stress. The program took place in school environments and the results showed that 63,5% of the adolescents believe that school requirements are the main reason of stress development. Although the program was designed and conducted by teachers, all of them mentioned that health professionals, that have the knowledge and expertise, are more needed than ever. This program was implemented within the school context, which is the core of children's and adolescents' difficulties, and at the same time the main source of questioning and answering each concern. This study focused as much on students as on teachers and school staff, resulting in future intervention programs (CAMHI, 2023).

CONCLUSION

There is still a significant stigma attached to psychosomatic symptoms, often viewed as "imaginary" or "not real." This misunderstanding can prevent individuals from seeking help and can also influence healthcare providers' attitudes, leading to inadequate care. Psychosomatic symptoms can mimic those of various physical illnesses, making diagnosis challenging. Differentiating between psychosomatic symptoms and symptoms of other medical conditions requires careful and comprehensive evaluation (Egger et al.,2017).

Integrating mental health care with general medical care remains a challenge. Many healthcare systems are still structured in a way that separates physical and mental health services, complicating comprehensive treatment approaches. Many healthcare providers lack adequate training in recognizing and treating psychosomatic symptoms. Enhancing education and training programs for physicians, nurses, and mental health professionals is essential. Access to mental health services is limited in many regions, particularly in low-income areas. This makes it difficult for individuals with psychosomatic symptoms to receive appropriate care and support (Sharma et al., 2016).

While there has been progress in understanding psychosomatic disorders, there are still significant gaps in research. More studies are needed to understand the underlying mechanisms, effective treatments, and long-term outcomes of these conditions. Patients might resist the idea that their physical symptoms have a psychological component, which can hinder treatment adherence and effectiveness. Building trust and educating patients about the mind-body connection is crucial. While technology offers new ways to monitor and treat psychosomatic symptoms, it also raises concerns about data privacy, the digital divide, and the potential for over-reliance on technology at the expense of personal interaction. Modern societal factors, including job insecurity, social isolation, and environmental stressors, contribute to chronic stress, which exacerbates psychosomatic symptoms. Addressing these broader societal issues is complex and requires coordinated efforts across multiple sectors (Fava, 2023).

As WHO (2023) refers countries should consider investing in national/regional programs to improve adolescent mental health, with attention to gender, age, and socioeconomic status. Schools should be the primary setting for mental health prevention and intervention programs, offering universal evidence-based programs, professional support, and connections to community services. Regular surveillance of adolescent mental health is vital to ensure positive mental well-being and to evaluate the effectiveness of support measures. Implementing targeted interventions and including mental health monitoring in school curricula are essential steps to improve overall adolescent mental health (WHO, 2023).

REFERENCES

American Psychiatric Association. (2013). *Diagnostic and Statistical Manual of Mental Disorders* (4th Edn. Text Revision). American Psychiatric Publishing.

American Psychiatric Association. (2013). *Diagnostic and Statistical Manual of Mental Disorders* (5th ed.). American Psychiatric Association.

Barsky, A. J. (1983). Overview: Hypochondriasis, bodily complaints, and somatic styles. *The American Journal of Psychiatry*.6338747

Beck, A., Steer, R., & Brown, G. (1996). Beck Depression Inventory (2nd ed.). E.U.: Psychological Corporation.

Beck, A. T., Epstein, N., Brown, G., & Steer, R. A. (1988). An inventory for measuring clinical anxiety: Psychometric properties. *Journal of Consulting and Clinical Psychology*, 56(6), 893–897. 10.1037/0022-006X.56.6.8933204199

Botschek, T., Monninger, M., Schäfer, D., Cevik, R., Memis, K., Müller, U., Monninger, M., & Brosig, B. (2023). Evaluation of multidimensional pediatric-psychosomatic inpatient therapy: A pilot study comparing two treatment modalities. *Frontiers in Psychology*, 14, 1022409. 10.3389/fpsyg.2023.102240937346420

Brudey, C., Park, J., Wiaderkiewicz, J., Kobayashi, I., Mellman, T., & Marvar, P. (2015). Autonomic and inflammatory consequences of posttraumatic stress disorder and the link to cardiovascular disease. *American Journal of Physiology. Regulatory, Integrative and Comparative Physiology*, 309(4), 315–321. 10.1152/ajpregu.00343.201426062635

Burke, N. N., Finn, D. P., McGuire, B. E., & Roche, M. (2016). Psychological stress in early life as a predisposing factor for the development of chronic pain: Clinical and preclinical evidence and neurobiological mechanisms. *Journal of Neuroscience Research*, 95(6), 1257–1270. 10.1002/jnr.2380227402412

Busch, , Moretti, F., Purgato, M., Barbui, C., Wu, A. W., & Rimondini, M. (2020). Psychological and Psychosomatic Symptoms of Second Victims of Adverse Events: A Systematic Review and Meta-Analysis. *Journal of Patient Safety*, 16(2), e61–e74. 10.1097/PTS.00000000000058930921046

CAMHI. (2023). *Ψυχική Υγεία Παιδιών και Εφήβων στην Ελλάδα: Ανάγκες και Προτεραιότητες. Συνοπτική Παρουσίαση μιας Ανάλυσης Πεδίου*. CAMHI.

CAMHI. (2023). *Πρόγραμμα Νεανικής Συμμετοχής YES (Youth Engagement Scheme) - Δράσεις στα Σχολεία*. CAMHI.

Cannon, W. B. (1929). *Bodily changes in Pain, Hunger, Fear and Rage*. New York, Appleton Century, Crofts Edit., Paris.

Chida, Y., Hamer, M., Wardle, J., & Steptoe, A. (2008). Do stress-related psychosocial factors contribute to cancer incidence and survival?'. *Nature Reviews. Clinical Oncology*, 5(8), 466–475. 10.1038/ncponc113418493231

Crosta, M. L., DeSimone, C., DiPietro, S., Acanfora, M., Caldarola, G., Moccia, L., Callea, A., Panaccione, I., Perris, K., Rinaldi, L., Janiri, L., & DiNicola, M. (2018). Childhood trauma and resilience in psoriatic patients: A preliminary report'. *Journal of Psychosomatic Research*, 106, 25–28. 10.1016/j.jpsychores.2018.01.00229455895

Dantzer, C., Swendsen, J., Maurice-Tison, S., & Salamon, R. (2003). Anxiety and depression in juvenile diabetes: A critical review. *Clinical Psychology Review*, 23(6), 787–800. 10.1016/S0272-7358(03)00069-214529698

Derogatis, L. R. (1975). *Brief Symptom Inventory*. Clinical Psychometric Research.

Egger, G., Binns, A., Rossner, S., & Saguer, M. (2017). *Lifestyle, the environment and preventive medicine in health and disease. Lifestyle Medicine* (3rd ed.). Elsevier.

Fava, G. A., Freyberger, H. J., Bech, P., Christodoulou, G., Sensky, T., Theorell, T., & Wise, T. N. (1995). Diagnostic criteria for use in psychosomatic research. *Psychotherapy and Psychosomatics*, 63(1), 1–8. 10.1159/0002889317740096

Freud, S. (1923): The Ego and the Id. Hogarth Press.

Gawronski, B., & De Houwer, J. (2014). Implicit measures in social and personality psychology. *Handbook of research methods in social and personality psychology*, 2, 283-310. 10.1007/978-3-319-08613-2_54-1

Gierk, B., Kohlmann, S., Kroenke, K., Spangenberg, L., Zenger, M., Brähler, E., & Löwe, B. (2014). The Somatic Symptom Scale-8 (SSS-8): A Brief Measure of Somatic Symptom Burden. *JAMA Internal Medicine*, 174(3), 399–407. 10.1001/jamainternmed.2013.1217924276929

Giovanni, A. (2023, May 31). Fava; Patients as Health Producers: The Psychosomatic Foundation of Lifestyle Medicine. *Psychotherapy and Psychosomatics*, 92(2), 81–86. 10.1159/00052995336958303

Green, A. (2002). *Key Ideas for a Contemporary Psychoanalysis. Misrecognition and Recognition of the Unconscious* [Trans. A. Weller]. Hove: Routledge, 2005.

Griffin, G., Charron, D., & Al-Daccak, R. (2014). Post-traumatic stress disorder: Revisiting adrenergics, glucocorticoids, immune system effects and homeostasis. *Clinical & Translational Immunology*, 3(11), e27. 10.1038/cti.2014.2625505957

Habukawa, C., Nagamitsu, S., Koyanagi, K., Nishikii, Y., Yanagimoto, Y., Yoshida, S., Suzuki, Y., & Murakami, K. (2021). Early intervention for psychosomatic symptoms of adolescents in school checkup. *Pediatrics International*, 64(1), e15117. 10.1111/ped.1511735616207

Keskin, D.B. (2019). Neoantigen vaccine generates intratumoral T cell responses in phase Ib glioblastoma trial. *Nature. Jan, 565*(7738), 234-239. .10.1038/s41586-018-0792-9

Kleszczewska, D., Mazur, J., Bucksch, J., Dzielska, A., Brindley, C., & Michalska, A. (2020). Active Transport to School May Reduce Psychosomatic Symptoms in School-Aged Children: Data from Nine Countries. *International Journal of Environmental Research and Public Health*, 17(23), 8709. 10.3390/ijerph1723870933255182

Konrad, K., Herpertz, S. C., & Herpertz-Dahlmann, B. (2016). Early trauma: Long lasting, difficult to treat and transmitted to the next generation'. *Journal of Neural Transmission (Vienna, Austria)*, 123(9), 1033–1035. 10.1007/s00702-016-1601-y27522500

Kroenke, K., Spitzer, R. L., & Williams, J. B. W. (2002). The PHQ-15: Validity of a new measure for evaluating the severity of somatic symptoms. *Psychosomatic Medicine*, 64(2), 258–266. 10.1097/00006842-200203000-0000811914441

Leonidou, C., Panayiotou, G., Bati, A., & Karekla, M. (2019). Coping with psychosomatic symptoms: The buffering role of psychological flexibility and impact on quality of life. *Journal of Health Psychology*, 24(2), 175–187. 10.1177/135910 531666665727596277

Li D., et al. (2021) Patterns of six behaviors and psychosomatic symptoms in adolescents: A six-province study in China. *Journal of Affective Disorders, 297*(2022), 593–601

Martin, L., Byrnes, M., McGarry, S., Rea, S., & Wood, F. (2017). Social challenges of visible scarring after severe burn: A qualitative analysis. Burns. *Burns*, 43(1), 76–83. 10.1016/j.burns.2016.07.02727576930

Marty, P. (1980). L'ordre psychosomatique: les mouvements individuels de vie et de mort: Vol. 2. *Désorganisation et régression [The Psychosomatic Order: Individual Life and Death Movements, vol 2. Disorganization and Regression]*. Payot.

Marty, P. (1990). *La psychosomatique de l'adulte[Adult Psychosomatics]*. Presses Universitaires de France.

Marty, P. (1991). Mentalisation et psychosomatique. *Les Empêcheurs de tourner en rond, Paris.*

Marty, P. (1997). Psychothérapie psychanalytique des troubles psychosomatiques [Psychoanalytic Psychotherapy of Psychosomatic Disorders]. *Revue Française de Psychosomatique*, 16, 195–204.

Montazeri A, Harirchi AM, Shariati M, Garmaroudi G, Ebadi M, Fateh A. (2003) The 12-item General Health Questionnaire (GHQ-12): translation and validation study of the Iranian version. *Health Qual Life Outcomes*. BMC. .10.1186/1477-7525-1-66

Richards, K., Austin, A., Allen, K., & Schmidt, U. (2019). Early intervention services for non-psychotic mental health disorders: A scoping review protocol. *BMJ Open*, 9(12), e033656. 10.1136/bmjopen-2019-03365631811012

Selye, H. (1994). *Stress sans détresse*. La Presse.

Sharma, A. E., Willard-Grace, R., Hessler, D., Bodenheimer, T., & Thom, D. H. (2016). What happens after health coaching? observational study 1 year following a randomized controlled trial. *Annals of Family Medicine*, 14(3), 200–207. 10.1370/afm.192427184989

Sheehan, D. V., Lecrubier, Y., Sheehan, K. H., Amorim, P., Janavs, J., Weiller, E., Hergueta, T., Baker, R., & Dunbar, G. C. (1998). The Mini-International Neuropsychiatric Interview (M.I.N.I.): The development and validation of a structured diagnostic psychiatric interview for DSM-IV and ICD-10. *The Journal of Clinical Psychiatry*, 59(Suppl 20), 22–33.9881538

Slonim, D. A., Shefler, G., Slonim, N., & Tishby, O. (2013). Adolescents in psychodynamic psychotherapy: Changes in internal representations of relationships with parents. *Psychotherapy Research*, 23(2), 201–217. 10.1080/10503307.2013.76599823577626

Smadja, C. (2007). L'impératif de retour au calme [The Imperative of Restoring a State of Calm]. *Revue Française de Psychosomatique*, 32(32), 71–79. 10.3917/rfps.032.0071

Sobański, J. A., Klasa, K., Mielimąka, M., Rutkowski, K., Dembińska, E., Müldner-Nieckowski, Ł., & Popiołek, L. (2015). The crossroads of gastroenterology and psychiatry – what benefits can psychiatry provide for the treatment of patients suffering from gastrointestinal symptoms. *Gastroenterology Research*, 4, 222–228.

Sosa, M., Bragado, P., & Aguirre-Ghiso, J. (2014). Mechanisms of disseminated cancer cell dormancy: An awakening field'. *Nature Reviews. Cancer*, 14(9), 611–622. 10.1038/nrc379325118602

Speckens, A. E., Spinhoven, P., Sloekers, P. P., Bolk, J. H., & van Hemert, A. M. (1996). A validation study of the Whitely Index, the illness attitude scales, and the somatosensory amplification scale in general medical and general practice patients. *Journal of Psychosomatic Research*, 40(1), 95–104. 10.1016/0022-3999(95)00561-78730649

Stewart, S.H. & Watt, M.C. (2000). Illness Attitudes Scale dimensions and their associations with anxiety-related constructs in a nonclinical sample. *Behav Res Ther., 38*(1), 83-99. . PMID: 10645026.10.1016/S0005-7967(98)00207-1

Tarkhanova, P. M., & Kholmogorova, A. B. (2011) Sotsial'nye i psikhologicheskie faktory fizicheskogo perfectionizma i unsatisfactoriness svoi telyu [Social and psychological factors of physical perfectionism and dissatisfaction with one's body]. -*PsyJournals.RU, (5),* 52-60.

Thabrew, H., de Sylva, S., & Romans, S. E. (2012). Evaluating childhood adversity. *Advances in Psychosomatic Medicine*, 32, 35–57. 10.1159/00033000222056897

Thomson, J. K. (2002). Measuring Body image attitudes among adolescents and adults / J.K. Thomson, P. Van den Berg. In Cash, T. F., & Pruzinsky, T. (Eds.), *Body Image: A Handbook of Theory, Research and Clinical Practice* (pp. 142–153). The Gilford Press.

Vesterling, C. (2023) Epidemiology of Somatoform Symptoms and Disorders in Childhood and Adolescence: A Systematic Review and Meta-Analysis. *Health & Social Care in the Community.* 10.1155/2023/6242678

Vesterling, C., & Koglin, U. (2020). The relationship between attachment and somatoform symptoms in children and adolescents: A systematic review and meta-analysis. *Journal of Psychosomatic Research*, 130, 109932. 10.1016/j.jpsychores.2020.10993231981896

Wise, T. N. (2014). Psychosomatics: Past, present and future. *Psychotherapy and Psychosomatics*, 83(2), 65–69. 10.1159/00035651824457983

World Health Organization. (2014). *Health for the World's Adolescents: A Second Chance in the Second Decade: Summary (Internet).* WHO Press.

World Health Organization. (2023). A focus on adolescent mental health and well-being in Europe, central Asia and Canada. *Health Behaviour in School-aged Children international report from the 2021/2022 survey.* WHO.

Yasunobe, Y., Akasaka, H., Yamamoto, K., Onishi, Y., Minami, T., Yoshida, S., & Rakugi, H. (2023). The relationship between changes in exercise habits and psychosomatic activities in older hypertensive patients during the COVID-19 pandemic. *Hypertension Research*, 46(1), 208–213. 10.1038/s41440-022-01043-736229528

Chapter 4
Resilience and Recovery:
Effective Stress Management Techniques for Adolescents

Alexandros Argyriadis
https://orcid.org/0000-0001-5754-4787
Frederick University, Cyprus

Efthymia Efthymiou
https://orcid.org/0000-0003-0411-1720
Zayed University, UAE

Dimitra Katsarou
https://orcid.org/0000-0001-8690-0314
University of the Aegean, Greece

Maria Sofologi
https://orcid.org/0000-0003-0380-2220
University of Ioannina, Greece

Agathi Argyriadi
Frederick University, Cyprus

ABSTRACT

This chapter focuses on the critical examination of stress factors affecting adolescents and the effectiveness of various management techniques aimed at fostering resilience and promoting recovery. With the backdrop of escalating stress levels among adolescents driven by academic pressures, social dynamics, and digital media exposure, this chapter identifies emerging research trends that focus on both individual and systemic interventions designed to mitigate stress and enhance mental well-being. The results underscore the significant impact of multi-faceted stress management

DOI: 10.4018/979-8-3693-4022-6.ch004

programs that combine psychological, physical, and social strategies. Techniques that promote mindfulness and emotional regulation, such as meditation and yoga, alongside CBT, were notably effective in enhancing adolescents' resilience to stress. In conclusion, the chapter highlights the imperative for a holistic approach to stress management among adolescents, emphasizing the need for interventions that are adaptable to diverse needs and contexts.

INTRODUCTION

Adolescence is a pivotal developmental stage marked by profound physical, emotional, and social transformations. During this period, individuals are particularly vulnerable to stress due to various internal and external pressures, including academic demands, social dynamics, and familial expectations. The adverse effects of stress on adolescents are well-documented, encompassing a range of psychological and physiological issues such as anxiety, depression, and compromised immune function (Reavley & Jorm, 2015). Consequently, the identification and implementation of effective stress management techniques for adolescents have become critical areas of focus in contemporary psychological research (Argyriadis and Argyriadi, 2024).

Recent studies have highlighted several promising approaches to mitigating stress in adolescents. Cognitive-behavioral therapy (CBT), a well-established modality in the treatment of anxiety and depression, has been adapted to address stress-related issues in this demographic (Argyriadi et al., 2023). By targeting dysfunctional thought patterns and behaviors, CBT helps adolescents develop healthier coping mechanisms, thereby reducing stress (Keles & Idsoe, 2018). Additionally, mindfulness-based interventions (MBIs), which emphasize present-moment awareness and emotional regulation, have shown significant efficacy in alleviating stress and improving overall psychological well-being (Zoogman, Goldberg, Hoyt, & Miller, 2015).

Physical activity and exercise are also recognized for their stress-relieving benefits. Engaging in regular physical activity can lead to the release of endorphins, which are natural mood enhancers, thereby reducing stress levels (Ahn & Fedewa, 2011). Social support from peers, family, and educational environments further contributes to stress management, as strong social networks provide emotional backing and a sense of belonging, which are crucial during the tumultuous adolescent years (Rueger, Malecki, Pyun, Aycock, & Coyle, 2016).

Moreover, educational and skills-based interventions delivered within school settings have proven effective in equipping adolescents with the tools necessary to navigate stress. Programs incorporating elements of CBT, mindfulness, and emotional regulation techniques foster resilience and enhance coping strategies (Shinde et al., 2018). In parallel, digital interventions leveraging mobile apps and online platforms offer accessible and scalable solutions for stress management, catering to the tech-savvy adolescent population (Flett, Hayne, Riordan, Thompson, & Conner, 2019).

Creative therapies, including art, music, and dance/movement therapy, provide alternative avenues for stress relief by allowing adolescents to express emotions creatively and non-verbally. These therapies have demonstrated significant reductions in stress and anxiety, contributing to improved emotional well-being (Utley & Garza, 2011; Goldbeck & Ellerkamp, 2012). Finally, family-based interventions that promote healthy communication and problem-solving skills are essential in creating supportive home environments, further aiding adolescents in managing stress (Compas et al., 2010).

Despite the substantial progress made in identifying effective stress management techniques for adolescents, several gaps remain in the existing literature that warrant further investigation. One significant gap lies in the understanding of how these interventions can be tailored to meet the diverse needs of adolescents from various cultural, socio-economic, and geographical backgrounds. Much of the current research predominantly reflects findings from Western contexts, leaving a knowledge gap regarding the applicability and effectiveness of these techniques in non-Western and underrepresented populations (Reavley & Jorm, 2015).

Additionally, while numerous studies have demonstrated the short-term efficacy of interventions such as CBT, mindfulness, and physical activity, there is a dearth of longitudinal research examining the long-term sustainability of these stress management techniques. It remains unclear how well adolescents maintain these practices over extended periods and how enduring the benefits are in mitigating stress-related symptoms as they transition into adulthood (Zoogman, Goldberg, Hoyt, & Miller, 2015).

The rapid advancement of technology has introduced digital interventions as promising tools for stress management. However, the field lacks comprehensive evaluations of the effectiveness of these digital tools compared to traditional, face-to-face interventions. More research is needed to understand the engagement levels, user adherence, and potential adverse effects of digital interventions among adolescents (Flett, Hayne, Riordan, Thompson, & Conner, 2019). Furthermore, the integration of digital and traditional methods remains underexplored, which could potentially enhance the efficacy of hybrid intervention models.

Another critical area requiring further exploration is the role of family dynamics and parental involvement in adolescent stress management. While family-based interventions have shown promise, more research is needed to identify the most effective components and strategies within these programs. Understanding the specific ways in which family interactions and parental support can be optimized to reduce stress in adolescents is essential for developing targeted and effective interventions (Compas et al., 2010).

Moreover, the impact of creative therapies, such as art, music, and dance/movement therapy, on adolescent stress management is an emerging area with limited empirical evidence. Although initial findings are promising, there is a need for more rigorous, large-scale studies to establish the effectiveness of these creative approaches and to understand the mechanisms through which they operate (Utley & Garza, 2011; Goldbeck & Ellerkamp, 2012).

Finally, while educational and skills-based interventions in schools have demonstrated positive outcomes, the variability in program implementation and the fidelity of these programs across different educational settings pose challenges. Research is needed to identify best practices for implementing these interventions in a consistent and effective manner, ensuring that all adolescents benefit equally regardless of their school environment (Shinde et al., 2018).

Addressing these research gaps is crucial for advancing the understanding of effective stress management techniques for adolescents. By expanding the scope of research to include diverse populations, examining long-term outcomes, evaluating digital interventions, exploring family dynamics, and rigorously testing creative therapies and educational programs, future studies can provide more comprehensive and inclusive strategies for supporting adolescents in managing stress.

METHODS

Research Design

This study employs a systematic literature review methodology to synthesize and evaluate existing research on effective stress management techniques for adolescents. The objective is to identify, appraise, and summarize the findings of relevant studies, providing a comprehensive understanding of the current state of knowledge and highlighting areas for future research.

Search Strategy

A systematic search was conducted using several electronic databases, including PubMed, PsycINFO, Web of Science, and Google Scholar. The search terms used included combinations of keywords such as "adolescent stress management," "cognitive-behavioral therapy," "mindfulness," "physical activity," "social support," "educational interventions," "digital interventions," "creative therapies," and "family-based interventions." Boolean operators (AND, OR) were employed to refine the search results and ensure the inclusion of relevant studies.

Inclusion and Exclusion Criteria

To ensure the relevance and quality of the included studies, specific inclusion and exclusion criteria were established:

Inclusion Criteria

- Studies published in peer-reviewed journals.
- Research focusing on stress management techniques specifically designed for adolescents (ages 10-19).
- Empirical studies, including randomized controlled trials (RCTs), quasi-experimental studies, longitudinal studies, and systematic reviews/meta-analyses.
- Studies published in English.
- Studies published within the last 5 years (2018-2023) to capture recent advancements in the field.

Exclusion Criteria

- Studies focusing on populations other than adolescents.
- Research not directly related to stress management (e.g., general mental health interventions without a specific focus on stress).
- Non-empirical studies, such as opinion pieces, commentaries, and editorials.
- Studies published in languages other than English.

Data Analysis

Data extraction was conducted using a standardized form to ensure consistency and comprehensiveness. The following information was extracted from each included study:

- Study characteristics: authors, year of publication, journal, country of origin.
- Participant characteristics: sample size, age range, gender distribution, socio-economic status, and other relevant demographics.
- Intervention details: type of intervention, duration, frequency, and delivery method.
- Outcome measures: specific stress-related outcomes assessed, measurement tools used, and main findings.
- Methodological quality: study design, randomization procedures, blinding, attrition rates, and potential biases.

The extracted data were systematically organized and analyzed to identify common themes, patterns, and gaps in the literature. The findings were then synthesized to provide a narrative summary of the evidence on effective stress management techniques for adolescents.

Quality Assessment

To assess the methodological quality of the included studies, the Cochrane Collaboration's Risk of Bias Tool for randomized trials and the Newcastle-Ottawa Scale (NOS) for observational studies were utilized. These tools evaluate various aspects of study quality, including selection bias, performance bias, detection bias, attrition bias, and reporting bias. Each study was rated as having low, moderate, or high risk of bias based on these criteria. The quality assessment helped to contextualize the findings and ensure that conclusions drawn from the review were based on robust evidence.

Data Synthesis

The synthesis of the included studies was conducted using a thematic analysis approach. This involved categorizing the studies into thematic groups based on the type of intervention (e.g., cognitive-behavioral techniques, mindfulness practices, physical activity, social support mechanisms, educational programs, digital tools, creative therapies, and family-based strategies). Within each category, the findings were compared and contrasted to identify consistent patterns, unique contributions, and areas of divergence.

Ethical Considerations

As this study is a literature review, it did not involve primary data collection and therefore did not require ethical approval. However, ethical considerations were observed by ensuring accurate representation of the reviewed studies and avoiding any form of plagiarism or misinterpretation of the original research findings.

RESULTS

The systematic literature review identified a total of 1,472 articles through the initial database search. After removing duplicates and screening titles and abstracts, 235 articles were selected for full-text review. Of these, 25 articles met the inclusion criteria and were included in the final synthesis. The results are organized into thematic categories based on the type of stress management intervention.

Cognitive-behavioral therapy (CBT) was the most extensively studied intervention in the research, with 7 articles meeting the inclusion criteria. The majority of these studies reported significant reductions in stress, anxiety, and depressive symptoms among adolescents who participated in CBT programs. For example, Reavley and Jorm (2015) conducted a meta-analysis that demonstrated the effectiveness of CBT in reducing symptoms of anxiety and depression, which are closely linked to stress. Another study by Keles and Idsoe (2018) found that group CBT was particularly effective in helping adolescents develop healthier coping mechanisms, leading to decreased stress levels.

CBT's widespread application and empirical support stem from its structured approach, which targets the interplay between thoughts, emotions, and behaviors. This therapeutic modality aims to identify and challenge maladaptive thought patterns, thus altering emotional responses and promoting more adaptive behaviors. Given the developmental changes and social pressures faced by adolescents, CBT's focus on cognitive restructuring and skill-building is particularly pertinent.

One critical aspect of CBT is its versatility and adaptability to various formats, including individual therapy, group sessions, and even digital platforms. Group CBT, as highlighted by Keles and Idsoe (2018), has shown particular promise. The group format not only provides therapeutic interventions but also fosters a sense of community and shared experiences among adolescents, which can be instrumental in reducing feelings of isolation and enhancing peer support. This format encourages participants to learn from one another and practice new skills in a safe environment, thereby reinforcing positive behavioral changes.

Additionally, studies have explored the integration of technology in delivering CBT to adolescents. For instance, online CBT programs have become increasingly popular, offering flexibility and accessibility to young individuals who might be reluctant or unable to attend in-person sessions. Research by Pennant et al. (2015) indicated that internet-based CBT could be as effective as traditional face-to-face therapy in reducing symptoms of anxiety and depression. This modality is particularly relevant in the digital age, where adolescents are adept at using technology, and it provides an avenue to reach those in remote or underserved areas.

The effectiveness of CBT in reducing stress, anxiety, and depressive symptoms can be attributed to several core components of the therapy. One such component is cognitive restructuring, which involves identifying and challenging irrational or maladaptive thoughts. Adolescents are guided to recognize negative thought patterns, evaluate their validity, and replace them with more realistic and positive alternatives. This process helps reduce the intensity and frequency of negative emotions, thereby alleviating stress and depressive symptoms.

Another crucial element of CBT is behavioral activation, which focuses on increasing engagement in positive and rewarding activities. Adolescents with depression often experience a decrease in motivation and withdrawal from enjoyable activities, which exacerbates their symptoms. By encouraging participation in such activities, CBT helps to break the cycle of depression and inactivity, promoting a sense of accomplishment and well-being.

CBT also emphasizes the development of coping skills and problem-solving strategies. Adolescents learn techniques such as relaxation exercises, mindfulness, and assertiveness training, which equip them with tools to manage stress and anxiety more effectively. These skills not only address current issues but also provide adolescents with a repertoire of strategies to handle future challenges, fostering resilience and emotional regulation.

Moreover, the structured nature of CBT sessions, typically involving goal setting and homework assignments, encourages active participation and accountability. This structure helps adolescents to stay engaged in the therapeutic process and apply the skills they learn in their daily lives. The collaborative relationship between the therapist and the adolescent further enhances motivation and commitment to the therapy.

In the context of anxiety disorders, CBT's focus on exposure therapy is particularly beneficial. Exposure therapy involves gradually confronting feared situations or stimuli in a controlled and systematic manner. This approach helps adolescents to reduce their avoidance behaviors and diminish the anxiety associated with specific triggers. For example, a study by Walkup et al. (2008) found that CBT with an emphasis on exposure therapy significantly reduced symptoms of obsessive-compulsive disorder in adolescents.

The empirical support for CBT extends beyond anxiety and depression to other psychological issues faced by adolescents. For instance, CBT has been effective in addressing post-traumatic stress disorder (PTSD) in young individuals. Research by Cohen et al. (2011) demonstrated that trauma-focused CBT significantly reduced PTSD symptoms in children and adolescents exposed to traumatic events. The structured and supportive environment of CBT allows for the safe processing of traumatic memories and the development of coping strategies to manage distress.

Furthermore, the benefits of CBT are not limited to clinical populations but extend to preventative interventions as well. School-based CBT programs have shown promise in promoting mental health and preventing the onset of anxiety and depression in adolescents. A study by Merry et al. (2011) found that a school-based CBT intervention significantly reduced the incidence of depression among high-risk adolescents. These findings highlight the potential of CBT as a proactive measure to enhance the mental well-being of young individuals in educational settings.

Despite the robust evidence supporting CBT, it is essential to consider the variability in individual responses to the therapy. Factors such as the severity of symptoms, comorbid conditions, and individual differences in cognitive and emotional processing can influence the outcomes of CBT. Therefore, personalized approaches and ongoing assessment are crucial to optimizing the effectiveness of the therapy.

In conclusion, the extensive body of research underscores the efficacy of cognitive-behavioral therapy in reducing stress, anxiety, and depressive symptoms among adolescents. The adaptability of CBT to various formats, including group and online therapy, enhances its accessibility and relevance to this demographic. The core components of CBT, such as cognitive restructuring, behavioral activation, and the development of coping skills, provide adolescents with practical tools to manage their mental health. The empirical support for CBT extends to various psychological issues and preventative interventions, highlighting its versatility and potential for promoting adolescent well-being. As mental health challenges continue to rise among young individuals, CBT stands out as a critical intervention to support their psychological resilience and overall development.

Mindfulness-based interventions (MBIs) were examined in 3 studies. These studies consistently showed that MBIs, including mindfulness meditation, mindful breathing, and body scans, led to significant reductions in perceived stress among adolescents. Zoogman et al. (2015) conducted a systematic review that highlighted the positive impact of MBIs on psychological outcomes, including stress reduction. Additionally, de Jong et al. (2012) reported that progressive muscle relaxation (PMR) and deep breathing exercises were effective in reducing stress and anxiety in adolescents.

The growing interest in MBIs for adolescents is driven by the increasing recognition of the unique stressors faced by this age group, such as academic pressures, social challenges, and the developmental changes associated with adolescence. Mindfulness practices, which emphasize present-moment awareness and non-judgmental acceptance of thoughts and feelings, offer a valuable approach to managing these stressors. The ability to cultivate mindfulness can help adolescents develop a more balanced and resilient response to their environment.

One significant aspect of MBIs is their focus on experiential learning and self-regulation. Mindfulness meditation, for example, involves paying attention to the breath or other focal points in a way that is calm and detached from evaluative thoughts. This practice helps adolescents become more aware of their thought patterns and emotional responses, enabling them to respond to stressors with greater equanimity. Research has shown that regular mindfulness meditation can lead to changes in brain regions associated with emotional regulation, such as the prefrontal cortex and amygdala, thereby enhancing an adolescent's ability to manage stress effectively.

Mindful breathing, another common MBI practice, involves focusing on the breath as a way to anchor the mind and reduce stress. This simple yet powerful technique can be easily taught and integrated into daily routines, making it accessible for adolescents. Studies have shown that mindful breathing can lower physiological markers of stress, such as cortisol levels, and improve heart rate variability, indicating a more relaxed state. For instance, a study by Biegel et al. (2009) demonstrated that adolescents who participated in a mindfulness-based stress reduction (MBSR) program exhibited significant reductions in stress and improvements in psychological well-being.

Body scans, a component of many MBI programs, involve systematically directing attention to different parts of the body to develop awareness and relaxation. This practice helps adolescents tune into bodily sensations and recognize areas of tension, promoting physical and mental relaxation. Body scans can also help adolescents become more attuned to their physical states and understand the connection between their mental and physical experiences. This heightened awareness can lead to better self-care and stress management strategies.

In addition to these mindfulness practices, progressive muscle relaxation (PMR) and deep breathing exercises have been identified as effective techniques for reducing stress and anxiety in adolescents. PMR involves tensing and then relaxing different muscle groups, which helps to release physical tension and promote relaxation. This technique can be particularly beneficial for adolescents who experience physical symptoms of stress, such as muscle tension and headaches. Deep breathing exercises, on the other hand, involve taking slow, deep breaths to activate the body's relaxation response. Both PMR and deep breathing are easy to learn and can be practiced anywhere, making them practical tools for stress management.

The effectiveness of MBIs in reducing stress and anxiety among adolescents is supported by a growing body of empirical research. For example, a study by Sibinga et al. (2016) found that a school-based mindfulness program led to significant reductions in perceived stress and improvements in emotional regulation among middle school students. The study also reported improvements in attention and classroom behavior, suggesting that MBIs can have a positive impact on academic performance and overall school experience.

Furthermore, MBIs have been shown to improve other psychological outcomes, such as depression and self-esteem. A study by Tan and Martin (2016) reported that adolescents who participated in a mindfulness-based cognitive therapy (MBCT) program exhibited significant reductions in depressive symptoms and increases in self-esteem. These findings highlight the potential of MBIs to address a range of mental health issues and promote overall psychological well-being in adolescents.

The mechanisms underlying the effectiveness of MBIs in reducing stress and anxiety are multifaceted. One key mechanism is the development of mindfulness skills, which enhance an adolescent's ability to observe their thoughts and feelings without becoming overwhelmed by them. This skill can lead to a greater sense of control over one's emotional responses and reduce the impact of stressors. Additionally, mindfulness practices can improve attentional control, allowing adolescents to focus more effectively on tasks and reduce rumination on negative thoughts.

Another important mechanism is the promotion of relaxation and the reduction of physiological arousal. Mindfulness practices such as meditation and deep breathing activate the body's parasympathetic nervous system, which counteracts the stress response and promotes relaxation. This physiological shift can lead to reductions in stress-related symptoms, such as increased heart rate and muscle tension.

Moreover, MBIs can enhance social and emotional learning by fostering greater empathy and compassion. Mindfulness practices encourage adolescents to adopt a non-judgmental and accepting attitude towards themselves and others, which can improve interpersonal relationships and reduce social stress. For example, a study by Bluth and Blanton (2015) found that mindfulness practices led to increased self-compassion and decreased perceived stress in adolescents, suggesting that cultivating a compassionate mindset can buffer against stress.

The integration of MBIs into school settings has shown particular promise in reaching a wide range of adolescents and promoting mental health on a broader scale. School-based mindfulness programs can be implemented as part of the regular curriculum or as extracurricular activities, providing students with regular opportunities to practice mindfulness skills. These programs can create a supportive and mindful school environment, which can enhance the overall well-being of students and staff.

Despite the demonstrated benefits of MBIs, there are several considerations and challenges in implementing these interventions with adolescents. One challenge is ensuring that mindfulness programs are developmentally appropriate and engaging for young people. Adolescents may have varying levels of interest and motivation for mindfulness practices, and it is important to tailor programs to meet their needs and preferences. Additionally, the training and experience of the facilitators can impact the effectiveness of mindfulness programs. Facilitators should be adequately trained in mindfulness practices and skilled in working with adolescents to create a supportive and effective learning environment.

Another consideration is the sustainability and scalability of mindfulness programs. While short-term interventions can provide immediate benefits, sustained practice is necessary to maintain and deepen the effects of mindfulness. Schools and community organizations should consider ways to integrate mindfulness practices into the daily routines and culture of the institution to ensure long-term impact.

In conclusion, mindfulness-based interventions (MBIs) offer a valuable and effective approach to reducing stress and anxiety among adolescents. The evidence from multiple studies highlights the significant benefits of mindfulness practices, including meditation, mindful breathing, body scans, progressive muscle relaxation, and deep breathing exercises. These practices not only reduce stress and anxiety but also promote overall psychological well-being and emotional regulation. As the interest in MBIs continues to grow, it is important to consider the best practices for implementing and sustaining these interventions to maximize their benefits for adolescents. By fostering mindfulness and self-regulation skills, MBIs can play a crucial role in supporting the mental health and resilience of young people.

Two studies focused on the impact of physical activity and exercise on adolescent stress. The findings indicated that regular physical activity, including aerobic exercises, yoga, and team sports, significantly reduced stress levels. Ahn and Fedewa (2011) found that physical activity interventions led to notable reductions in anxiety and stress among children and adolescents. The release of endorphins during exercise was cited as a key mechanism for these stress-relieving effects.

The variety of physical activities examined in these studies highlights the broad potential of exercise to alleviate stress among adolescents. Aerobic exercises, such as running, swimming, and cycling, have been particularly noted for their ability to reduce stress and improve mood. These activities elevate heart rate and promote cardiovascular health, which are beneficial not only for physical well-being but also for mental health. The physiological changes induced by aerobic exercise, such as increased oxygen flow to the brain and the release of endorphins, contribute to a reduction in stress and an enhancement of mood.

Yoga, another form of physical activity studied, combines physical postures, breathing exercises, and meditation to promote relaxation and mental clarity. The practice of yoga has been shown to reduce the physiological markers of stress, such as cortisol levels, and to enhance the body's parasympathetic response, which promotes relaxation. Research by Noggle et al. (2012) found that adolescents who participated in yoga classes reported significant reductions in stress and improvements in emotional regulation and resilience. The mindfulness component of yoga also helps adolescents develop a more present-focused awareness, which can mitigate the effects of stress.

Team sports, which provide both physical exercise and social interaction, have also been highlighted for their stress-reducing benefits. Participation in team sports can foster a sense of belonging and support among peers, which is crucial for adolescent development. The social aspect of team sports encourages teamwork, communication, and mutual support, all of which contribute to a reduction in stress. A study by Eime et al. (2013) found that adolescents who engaged in team sports experienced lower levels of stress and higher levels of psychological well-being compared to those who did not participate in such activities.

The underlying mechanisms that explain how physical activity reduces stress are multifaceted. One primary mechanism is the release of endorphins, which are chemicals in the brain that act as natural painkillers and mood elevators. Exercise-induced endorphin release can lead to feelings of euphoria and general well-being, commonly referred to as the "runner's high." This biochemical response helps counteract stress and anxiety, promoting a more positive mental state.

Moreover, regular physical activity can improve sleep quality, which is often disrupted by stress. Better sleep contributes to improved mood, cognitive function, and overall mental health. Exercise also helps to regulate the body's stress response systems, including the hypothalamic-pituitary-adrenal (HPA) axis, which controls the release of cortisol. By modulating the HPA axis, physical activity can reduce the physiological impact of stress and enhance resilience to stressors.

Additionally, physical activity can serve as a distraction from stressors, providing adolescents with a break from their worries and allowing them to focus on the physical sensations and enjoyment of the activity. This distraction can help to break the cycle of rumination and negative thinking that often accompanies stress and anxiety.

In conclusion, the evidence from the fourteen studies underscores the significant benefits of physical activity in reducing stress among adolescents. Aerobic exercises, yoga, and team sports all contribute to lower stress levels through various mechanisms, including the release of endorphins, improved sleep, and enhanced social support. As such, promoting regular physical activity should be a key component of strategies aimed at improving adolescent mental health and well-being. Schools, parents, and community organizations can play a crucial role in encouraging adolescents to engage in regular physical activities that they enjoy and find meaningful. By fostering an active lifestyle, we can help adolescents build resilience against stress and develop healthier coping mechanisms.

Social support emerged as a critical factor in stress management, as evidenced by 3 studies. Research by Rueger et al. (2016) demonstrated that adolescents with strong social support networks from friends, family, and teachers experienced lower levels of stress. These studies underscored the importance of fostering supportive environments both at home and in school to enhance adolescents' resilience to stress.

Four studies investigated the effectiveness of school-based programs aimed at teaching stress management skills. These programs often incorporated elements of CBT, mindfulness, and emotional regulation techniques. Shinde et al. (2018) highlighted that life skills education, which includes training in problem-solving, decision-making, and interpersonal skills, significantly reduced stress and improved coping mechanisms in adolescents.

Two studies explored the use of digital interventions, such as mobile apps and online platforms, for stress management. The findings indicated that digital tools could effectively reduce stress and improve mood among adolescents. Flett et al. (2019) reported that a mindfulness app significantly lowered perceived stress and enhanced overall mental health in adolescent users. However, the studies also noted variability in engagement and adherence to digital interventions.

Creative therapies were the focus of three studies. These studies provided evidence that art therapy, music therapy, and dance/movement therapy could significantly reduce stress and anxiety in adolescents. Utley and Garza (2011) found that art therapy allowed adolescents to express their emotions creatively, leading to decreased stress levels. Similarly, Goldbeck and Ellerkamp (2012) reported that music therapy had calming effects and improved emotional well-being.

One study examined the role of family-based interventions in managing adolescent stress. Compas et al. (2010) demonstrated that interventions focusing on enhancing family communication and problem-solving skills significantly reduced stress and improved mental health outcomes in adolescents. These studies emphasized the importance of a supportive family environment in helping adolescents cope with stress.

The synthesis of the included studies revealed the following:

Cognitive-behavioral techniques and mindfulness-based interventions are highly effective in reducing stress among adolescents, with numerous studies supporting their use.

Regular physical activity consistently reduces stress, with aerobic exercises, yoga, and team sports being particularly beneficial.

Strong social support networks from peers, family, and educational environments play a crucial role in mitigating stress.

Educational and skills-based interventions in schools are effective in teaching adolescents how to manage stress.

Digital tools offer accessible options for stress management, though user engagement and adherence vary.

Art, music, and dance/movement therapies provide alternative, effective methods for stress relief.

Family-focused strategies that improve communication and problem-solving skills are vital in reducing adolescent stress.

DISCUSSION

The findings from this systematic literature review provide a comprehensive overview of effective stress management techniques for adolescents, highlighting the multifaceted nature of stress mitigation in this demographic. The synthesis of

25 studies underscores the efficacy of various interventions, including cognitive-behavioral techniques, mindfulness practices, physical activity, social support, educational programs, digital tools, creative therapies, and family-based interventions. This discussion integrates these findings with the current literature and addresses the implications for practice and future research.

The review confirms the substantial body of evidence supporting cognitive-behavioral therapy (CBT) as a robust intervention for reducing stress among adolescents. The findings align with Reavley and Jorm (2015), who emphasized CBT's effectiveness in alleviating anxiety and depression, common correlates of stress. The focus on altering dysfunctional thought patterns and behaviors in CBT helps adolescents develop adaptive coping strategies, reinforcing the work of Keles and Idsoe (2018). These studies collectively suggest that CBT should remain a cornerstone of stress management programs for adolescents.

Mindfulness-based interventions (MBIs) have emerged as effective tools for stress reduction, echoing the findings of Zoogman et al. (2015). The significant reductions in perceived stress reported in this review highlight the utility of mindfulness practices such as meditation and breathing exercises. The physiological and psychological benefits of these practices support their inclusion in stress management curriculums for adolescents. Additionally, the efficacy of progressive muscle relaxation (PMR) and deep breathing exercises, as reported by de Jong et al. (2012), underscores the importance of incorporating relaxation techniques into adolescent stress management strategies.

The review corroborates the well-documented benefits of physical activity in stress reduction, consistent with the findings of Ahn and Fedewa (2011). Regular engagement in aerobic exercises, yoga, and team sports not only reduces stress through the release of endorphins but also enhances overall mental health and social interactions. These findings suggest that promoting physical activity should be a key component of holistic stress management programs for adolescents.

The critical role of social support in mitigating stress among adolescents is strongly supported by the literature. The findings from Rueger et al. (2016) indicate that strong social networks from peers, family, and teachers significantly reduce stress levels. This review reinforces the need for fostering supportive environments both at home and in educational settings. The positive impact of social support highlights the importance of interventions aimed at strengthening peer relationships and family dynamics.

School-based programs that teach stress management skills have shown considerable effectiveness, aligning with Shinde et al. (2018). These programs, which incorporate elements of CBT, mindfulness, and emotional regulation, equip adolescents with the necessary tools to navigate stress. The review suggests that integrating these programs into the school curriculum can enhance adolescents' resilience to stress, promoting better mental health and academic outcomes.

Digital tools for stress management present a promising avenue, especially given the increasing use of technology among adolescents. The findings from Flett et al. (2019) indicate that digital interventions, such as mindfulness apps, can effectively reduce stress. However, the variability in engagement and adherence points to the need for further research to optimize these tools. The integration of digital and traditional methods could potentially enhance the efficacy of stress management interventions, making them more accessible and appealing to adolescents.

The review highlights the benefits of creative therapies, such as art, music, and dance/movement therapy, in reducing stress among adolescents. These findings are consistent with the work of Utley and Garza (2011) and Goldbeck and Ellerkamp (2012), who demonstrated the therapeutic effects of creative expression. Creative therapies offer alternative, non-verbal methods for adolescents to process emotions and alleviate stress, suggesting their valuable role in comprehensive stress management programs.

The importance of family dynamics in adolescent stress management is well-supported by the literature. Compas et al. (2010) emphasize that interventions focusing on enhancing family communication and problem-solving skills can significantly reduce stress. This review underscores the necessity of involving families in stress management efforts, as supportive home environments are crucial for adolescent well-being.

CONCLUSION

The systematic literature review on effective stress management techniques for adolescents reveals a diverse array of interventions that have shown efficacy in reducing stress and improving mental health outcomes. Key interventions include cognitive-behavioral techniques, mindfulness practices, physical activity, social support mechanisms, educational and skills-based programs, digital tools, creative therapies, and family-based strategies. Each of these approaches contributes uniquely to the comprehensive management of stress among adolescents. CBT consistently demonstrates significant reductions in stress, anxiety, and depression among adolescents. This intervention helps adolescents develop adaptive coping strategies, making it a cornerstone of stress management programs. Mindfulness-based interventions (MBIs) and relaxation techniques like progressive muscle relaxation (PMR) and deep breathing exercises effectively reduce perceived stress. These practices promote emotional regulation and relaxation, which are crucial for stress relief. Regular physical activity, including aerobic exercises, yoga, and team sports, is effective in reducing stress through the release of endorphins and enhanced social interactions. Promoting physical activity should be a key component of adolescent stress management programs. Strong social support networks from peers, family, and educational environments play a critical role in mitigating stress. Interventions that strengthen these support systems are essential for fostering resilience among adolescents. School-based programs that incorporate CBT, mindfulness, and emotional regulation techniques are effective in teaching adolescents how to manage stress. These programs should be integrated into the school curriculum to enhance resilience and coping skills.

Digital tools, such as mobile apps and online platforms, offer accessible options for stress management. While these tools are effective, engagement and adherence vary, indicating a need for optimization and further research. Art, music, and dance/movement therapies provide alternative methods for stress relief through creative expression. These therapies are particularly beneficial for adolescents who may find traditional talk therapies challenging. Family-focused strategies that enhance communication and problem-solving skills significantly reduce stress. Involving families in stress management programs is crucial for creating supportive home environments.

FUTURE RESEARCH DIRECTIONS

Despite the progress made, several gaps remain in the literature. Future research should focus on the following. More studies are needed to understand how stress management techniques can be tailored to diverse cultural and socio-economic contexts. The current literature predominantly reflects findings from Western populations, and more inclusive research is necessary. There is a need for longitudinal studies to assess the long-term sustainability of stress management interventions and their effects as adolescents transition into adulthood.

LIMITATIONS

The findings of this review have several implications for practice. First, the integration of CBT and mindfulness practices into school-based programs can provide adolescents with essential skills to manage stress. Second, promoting physical activity and social support within school and community settings can further enhance stress resilience. Third, leveraging digital tools can make stress management interventions more accessible to adolescents, though efforts must be made to ensure sustained engagement. Finally, involving families in stress management programs can create supportive home environments that reinforce these efforts.

REFERENCES

Ahn, S., & Fedewa, A. L. (2011). A meta-analysis of the relationship between children's physical activity and mental health. *Journal of Pediatric Psychology*, 36(4), 385–397. 10.1093/jpepsy/jsq10721227908

Argyriadis, A., & Argyriadi, A. (2024). Societal attitudes towards psychiatric patients, medication, and the antipsychiatric movement within the context of theoretical approaches and inclusion initiatives. The role of mental health professionals. *GSC Advanced Research and Reviews*, 18(2), 381–387. 10.30574/gscarr.2024.18.2.0075

Biegel, G. M., Brown, K. W., Shapiro, S. L., & Schubert, C. M. (2009). Mindfulness-based stress reduction for the treatment of adolescent psychiatric outpatients: A randomized clinical trial. *Journal of Consulting and Clinical Psychology*, 77(5), 855-866. 10.1037/a0016241

Bluth, K., & Blanton, P. W. (2015). Mindfulness and self-compassion: Exploring pathways to adolescent emotional well-being. *Journal of Child and Family Studies*, 24(9), 2345-2356. https://doi.org/10.1007/s10826-014-0037-8

Cohen, J. A., Mannarino, A. P., & Deblinger, E. (2011). *Trauma-focused CBT for children and adolescents: Treatment applications*. Guilford Press.

Compas, B. E., Jaser, S. S., Dunbar, J. P., Watson, K. H., Bettis, A. H., Gruhn, M. A., & Williams, E. (2010). Coping and emotion regulation from childhood to early adulthood: Points of convergence and divergence. . *Australian Journal of Psychology*, 62(2), 95–107. 10.1080/00049530903567278 24895462

de Jong, R., Sportel, B. E., de Hullu, E., & Nauta, M. H. (2012). Cognitive behavioral therapy versus progressive relaxation in adolescents with social anxiety disorder: A randomized controlled trial. . *Behaviour Research and Therapy*, 50(1), 60–73. 10.1016/j.brat.2011.11.007

Eime, R. M., Young, J. A., Harvey, J. T., Charity, M. J., & Payne, W. R. (2013). A systematic review of the psychological and social benefits of participation in sport for children and adolescents: Informing development of a conceptual model of health through sport. *International Journal of Behavioral Nutrition and Physical Activity*, 10(98). 10.1186/1479-5868-10-98

Flett, J. A. M., Hayne, H., Riordan, B. C., Thompson, L. M., & Conner, T. S. (2019). Mobile mindfulness meditation: A randomised controlled trial of the effect of two popular apps on mental health. . *Mindfulness*, 10(5), 863–876. 10.1007/s12671-018-1050-9

Goldbeck, L., & Ellerkamp, T. (2012). A randomized controlled trial of multimodal music therapy for children with anxiety disorders. . *Journal of Music Therapy*, 49(4), 395–413. 10.1093/jmt/49.4.39523705344

Keles, F., & Idsoe, T. (2018). A meta-analysis of group cognitive behavioral therapy (CBT) for adolescents with depression. *Journal of Child Psychology and Psychiatry, 59*(3), 252-261. 10.1111/jcpp.12818

Merry, S. N., Hetrick, S. E., Cox, G. R., Brudevold-Iversen, T., Bir, J. J., & Mc-Dowell, H. (2011). The effectiveness of school-based mental health services for elementary-aged children: A meta-analysis. *Journal of the American Academy of Child & Adolescent Psychiatry, 50*(9), 865-878. 10.1016/j.jaac.2011.05.003

Noggle, J. J., Steiner, N. J., Minami, T., & Khalsa, S. B. (2012). Benefits of yoga for psychosocial well-being in a US high school curriculum: A preliminary randomized controlled trial. *Journal of Developmental & Behavioral Pediatrics, 33*(3), 193-201. 10.1097/DBP.0b013e31824afdc4

Pennant, M. E., Loucas, C. E., Whittington, C., Creswell, C., Fonagy, P., & Fuggle, P. (2015). Computerised therapies for anxiety and depression in children and young people: A systematic review and meta-analysis. *Behaviour Research and Therapy, 67*, 1-18. 10.1016/j.brat.2015.01.009

Reavley, N. J., & Jorm, A. F. (2015). The quality of mental health literacy in Australia: A national review. *BMC Public Health, 15*(1), 994. https://doi.org/10.1186/s12889-015-2333-9

Rueger, S. Y., Malecki, C. K., Pyun, Y., Aycock, C., & Coyle, S. (2016). A meta-analytic review of the association between perceived social support and depression in childhood and adolescence. . *Psychological Bulletin*, 142(10), 1017–1067. 10.1037/bul000005827504934

Shinde, S., Weiss, H. A., Khandeparkar, P., Pereira, B., Sharma, A., Gupta, R., & Patel, V. (2018). A multicomponent school-based intervention to reduce aggression, mental health problems, and improve psychosocial functioning among adolescents in India: A cluster-randomised controlled trial. . *Lancet*, 392(10154), 577–589. 10.1016/S0140-6736(18)31617-5

Sibinga, E. M., Webb, L., Ghazarian, S. R., & Ellen, J. M. (2016). School-based mindfulness instruction: An RCT. *Pediatrics, 137*(1), e20152532. 10.1542/peds.2015-2532

Tan, L. B., & Martin, G. (2016). Taming the adolescent mind: Preliminary development of a mindfulness-based psychological intervention for adolescents with clinical heterogeneity. *Cognitive and Behavioral Practice, 23*(3), 370-380. 10.1016/j.cbpra.2015.09.006

Utley, A., & Garza, Y. (2011). The therapeutic use of journaling with adolescents. . *Journal of Creativity in Mental Health, 6*(1), 29–41. 10.1080/15401383.2011.557312

Walkup, J. T., Albano, A. M., Piacentini, J., Birmaher, B., Compton, S. N., Sherrill, J. T., Ginsburg, G. S., Rynn, M. A., McCracken, J., Waslick, B., Iyengar, S., & March, J. S. (2008). Cognitive behavioral therapy, sertraline, or a combination in childhood anxiety. *The New England Journal of Medicine, 359*(26), 2753-2766. 10.1056/NEJMoa0804633

Zoogman, S., Goldberg, S. B., Hoyt, W. T., & Miller, L. (2015). Mindfulness interventions with youth: A meta-analysis. . *Mindfulness, 6*(2), 290–302. 10.1007/s12671-013-0260-4

APPENDIX

Table 1. Results

Intervention Type	Number of Studies	Key Findings
Cognitive-Behavioral Techniques	7	Significant reductions in stress, anxiety, and depression. CBT helps develop adaptive coping strategies.
Mindfulness and Relaxation Practices	3	Mindfulness practices lead to significant reductions in perceived stress. PMR and deep breathing also effective.
Physical Activity and Exercise	2	Regular physical activity reduces stress through endorphin release and improved social interactions.
Social Support and Peer Relationships	3	Strong social support networks from peers, family, and teachers significantly reduce stress levels.
Educational and Skills-Based Interventions	4	School-based programs incorporating CBT, mindfulness, and emotional regulation are effective.
Digital Interventions	2	Digital tools can effectively reduce stress, though engagement and adherence vary.
Art and Creative Therapies	3	Art, music, and dance/movement therapies reduce stress and anxiety through creative expression.
Family-Based Interventions	1	Family-focused strategies enhance communication and problem-solving, reducing stress.

Chapter 5
The Contribution of Improvised Play to the Personality Development of Preschool Children

Antonia Stelianou

Independent Researcher, Greece

Evagelia Dalapera

Independent Researcher, Greece

Pineio Christodoulou

Department of Education, School of Education, University of Nicosia, Cyprus

ABSTRACT

The present study is a participatory action research entitled "I Learn, Play, and Have Fun With Toys I Make," which was carried out in a kindergarten, with the participation of the teachers and the preschool students who attended it. The aim of this action research was to upgrade and enrich the educational material in a playful way, by making improvised games, which facilitate and expand the teaching process of the teachers and the learning process of the students. The action research focused primarily on the active involvement of the participating kindergarten students regarding the construction of improvised educational materials, primarily with recyclable materials. As for the research tools, participatory observation, the semi-structured interview, the questionnaire for parents and students, as well as the diary of the participating teachers were selected and used as the most appropriate. The results showed that the specific action research had many benefits for the participating students. An effect on the all-round and balanced development of

DOI: 10.4018/979-8-3693-4022-6.ch005

the students' personalities was evident.

INTRODUCTION

Action research is used internationally as a methodological tool to engage teachers in research processes, which focus on the systematic study of various aspects of teaching and learning in specific educational settings. In more detail, the application of action research in the school community aims to improve teaching and learning conditions, including all parameters that may affect the educational work. According to Elliot "action research is the study of a social situation with the aim of improving the quality within it".

Participatory action research, where all parties are actively involved in the design, implementation and evaluation of the research project, is a process that gives meaning to pedagogical practice. Educational researchers, as teachers conducting an action research are called, participate in all phases of the research process, from initial design to evaluation and redesign in a course of continuous overlapping research cycles (Altrichter et al., 2001).

More specifically, the main feature that differentiates participatory action research from other types of research is its collaborative nature that allows all those involved to participate equally and actively in the production of knowledge and in general the intended result/product. Compared to other types of research, participatory action research is research in education and not just research about education.

To sum up, the main goal of participatory educational action research is to connect theory with practice and for teachers to reflect on each project. The starting point of action research is a problematic situation, an issue that concerns teachers and needs improvement interventions (http://metavasis.edc.uoc.gr), as it also happened in this particular case.

Undoubtedly, the kindergarten space has a special pedagogical value, for this reason it must primarily be pleasant, attractive, arouse the interest of the children, and promote autonomy and at the same time cooperation both between the children and between the teacher and the children (Dafermou et al., 2006). In the realization of the above goal, the game plays a special role, as an activity, but also as a pedagogical material.

Play is considered a critical milestone for a child's well-being, learning, and development (Ginsburg et al., 2007), can be described as any activity that is spontaneously chosen, intrinsically motivated, and personally directed. It is a fact that play takes many forms, differing widely between cultures, and is therefore difficult to categorize. However, researchers have classified play into physical play, object play, symbolic play, pretend/sociodramatic play, and games with rules (Whitebread & O'Sullivan, 2012).

Research has shown that children learn through the natural process of exploring play, as anthropologists, developmental psychologists, and neuroscientists have extensively studied and documented this phenomenon (Whitebread et al., 2012). Through everyday play, young children are in position to acquire valuable life experiences, through a variety of roles that will support their development and ultimately be translated into necessary adulthood skills. According to research, play is essential for every aspect of a child's personality development, as all basic skills are experienced through the opportunities of play (Irvin, 2017).

Also, according to Parker and Thomsen (2019) playful pedagogical approaches can be more effective in enhancing social, emotional, physical, cognitive and creative skills, compared to "traditional" or more guided pedagogical approaches used in the classroom. Studies concluded that the advantages of these pedagogical approaches are many. More specifically, learning benefits were shown to be maintained over time (DeanJr., & Kuhn, 2007), transfer/generalization of acquired skills to new problem solving was shown (Purpura et al., 2016), knowledge recall acquired was more accurate and children's understanding of the concepts was deeper (Burke & Williams, 2012).

When students have the opportunity to practice making meaningful choices about their project or research topic and how they are undertaken, coupled with teacher support and facilitation, students demonstrate greater engagement, motivation and positive willingness to learning process (Parker & Thomsen, 2019).

Based on the literature, play is essential for the holistic and healthy development of a child (Bento & Dias 2017; Ginsburg 2007; Nijhofetal. 2018). Play is associated with the development of neural connections in the brain, social skills such as perspective taking, language skills, physical skills, problem solving skills and cognitive skills such as creative thinking, which lead to abstract thinking in the long run (Dankiwetal, 2020). It provides children with a framework to master many skills, such as literacy, problem solving, and impulse control skills (Xu, 2010).

At the same time, during the first years of childhood, play is the main means of physical activity for children (Prioreschi et al., 2020). Children develop and understand the rules of society through play which provides them with a safe context to explore these skills without fear of impending negative consequences (Hoffmann & Russ, 2016).

According to Dafermou, Koulouri & Basayianni (2006) every child in the game behaves like a creative writer, because he creates his own world or better, he adapts things to his world in a way that pleases him. The creative writer does the same as the child in the game. That is, he creates a fictional world that he takes seriously and in which he invests a great deal of emotion.

Montessori connects play with the development of the child's senses and special abilities, as well as with his motor, aesthetic and linguistic development (Tsiantzi, 1996). Montessori argues that for the child to be happy it is not enough to simply play but also to "work". He recognized the need for children to play, but rejected many forms of play, especially fantasy play because he believed that it did not correspond to real life (Yen & Spa, 2000). According to Montessori, children shape their personality through their individual effort - work and having the free choice of the activity they want to engage in according to their needs and interests. The role of the teacher in the educational process is limited and teaching turns into a game of interest between the teacher and the student (Hainstock, 1968, as cited by Hatzopoulou, 2020). According to Decroly, the game "constitutes a necessary preparation for future, serious engagement of the child and meets all his needs" (Kitsaras, 2001:199). "Play is a meaningful process in which children actively co-create their world with their peers and learn through interactions with their friends" (Avgitidou, 2001:172).

The game is directly related to the development of the child's imagination, creativity and sociability, through the possibilities it provides for cooperation with his peers, for undertaking specific tasks, but also for the fulfillment of common goals (Petkanopoulou, 2017).

The improvised play (board and non-board game) enables the teacher to observe the students' behavior in the context of the class, as well as the degree of their response to each activity. According to Bergeson et al. (2008) improvised play has proven to be a particularly effective method for recording student growth. At the same time, the teacher is given the opportunity for an empirical observation, which is the best method by which the teacher evaluates the qualitative parameters of the student's individuality (Haris, 1995). It also supports formative assessment as Assessment for Learning (Black & Wiliam, 2003; Broadfoot, 2008; Stiggins, 2002).

As mentioned above, the aim of this action research was the active involvement of the Kindergarten students regarding the enrichment and upgrading of the pedagogical material of their Kindergarten. The selection of the specific project was deemed necessary by the teachers and aimed at the emergence of new practices for the creation of educational material in a playful format and with the active participation of preschool students.

In particular, the selection of the specific action plan was based on the results of the systematic investigation of the needs of the school unit. A deficit was revealed in the school's educational material regarding the implementation and support of educational activities. It was deemed necessary by the teachers to highlight new practices for the creation of educational material in a playful form with the active participation of the students. Through the implementation of this project, it was expected, to support the relationships between students, between teachers and students, as well as to make a positive contribution to the better organization and coordination of school life.

In particular, the action plan was implemented in the two departments of the optional full-day program and the kindergarten integration department, where the responsible Kindergarten teachers adopted the improvised game as a tool to evolve the learning process into a continuous game. The guide of the transformation of the classroom into a playing classroom was the children's love, interest and enthusiasm for the improvised games, which they designed with the teachers and created by themselves during the implementation of the action plan, using recyclable materials.

Educators knowing well, that "any kind of recreation of the child's hands is characterized as a game" (Gougouli & Karakatsani, 2008), which can be either spontaneous activity based on imagination, or organized activity with defined rules.

Specifically, the fact that improvised play as an educational practice supports and enriches a creative learning environment, where imagination connects play with knowledge and contributes to the development of many mental and social skills, cooperation, planning, creativity, led the students on a creative journey of getting to know each other and making improvised games, table and floor, individual and group, which are played by children from the age of 4. Games designed on paper, or on the floor, with improvised dice, using recyclable materials are shown to be a valuable pedagogical means to reach knowledge to the child, and the child himself to knowledge in a natural, creative and effortless way.

Based on the aforementioned, the specific objectives of the present effort are summarized as follows:

- Strengthening the interest and participation of students in the construction of improvised games.
- The mobilization of teachers to participate in innovative practices.
- The development of strategies, mathematical thinking, computing skills, critical thinking and creativity.
- Cultivating a positive attitude and self-confidence.
- Engaging students by motivating them to engage in game-making activities that sharpen perception, promote mathematical thinking, practice memory, language skills, observation and inductive reasoning skills.
- The cultivation of environmental consciousness (use of recyclable/waste material).
- In addition, the goal was to cultivate their sociability, and cooperation in the exploration of new ideas.
    -Also, the main goal was to improve the performance of "All" children, including children with disabilities and special educational needs.

In terms of resources, all the available resources of the Kindergarten were used, as well as the required logistical equipment (PC, digital camera, printer, data storage devices, video, supervisory and pedagogical material, event room, etc.). The required financial resources were covered by the school unit.

METHODOLOGY

The choice of the participatory action research method was chosen for the following reasons:

- Presupposes participation and equal cooperation between all involved.
- It integrates teaching and research and links theory with practice.
- It offers a flexible implementation framework (the open circular-spiral process), through which participants act and reflect in order to understand, change and improve the everyday school reality.
- Presupposes and is organized based on the thoughtful and reflective process.
- Responds appropriately and is directly combined with the ecological-developmental model of transition.

Regarding the data collection methods with this particular method, teachers/researchers have the possibility to use both open and free techniques, as well as more strict and quantitative ones. The validity of the data collected is ensured to some extent by the method of "triangulation". It is about the cross-checking of the data either by using three different data collection methods, or by extracting the data from three different sources, which ensures the intersubjective control of the findings (retrieved from http://metavasis.edc.uoc.gr).

In particular, as mentioned above in the present effort regarding the research tools for the collection of information and data, participatory observation, the semi-structured interview, the questionnaire for parents and students, as well as the diary of the participating teachers were selected and used.

Regarding the participatory observation, an observation guide was used, in the form of keys, so that the recording of the observed interactions and behaviors is done in an organized and systematic way.

IMPLEMENTATION OF ACTION

The specific action research is divided into the following phases/stages:

1. Steps to prepare the action.
   -Recording needs.
   -Establishing an action group.

   - Submission of proposals by team members.
   - Coordinating the team to prepare the action and achieve common goals.

2. Action planning
   - Search for resources.
   - Gather material.
   - Informing parents and guardians about the action and their participation in ways that will be proposed by the action group (e.g. assistance in the collection of recyclable materials).
     -Planning and organizing activities that had an educational content, but at the same time a playful form and related to language, mathematics, fine motor skills and various other areas. The activities were consistent with the objectives; they were guided by the kindergarten's Interdisciplinary Unified Curriculum Frameworks and Detailed Curriculums, but also based on the interests of the children.
3. Implementation of action
   -Implementation of action in the all-day department and in the inclusion department of the school unit concerned (Construction of improvised games).

   - Monitoring and feedback of the action where necessary and always according to the needs of the participating students.
   - Formative assessment - readjustment of the current action, so as to improve the achievements of the students in relation to the teaching objectives that were set.

   -Presentation and application of the action results of the participants in the departmental action, in the plenary session of the other departments of the school.
   -Monitoring and feedback of the action with observation and summary recording of the results of the approach of the action to the plenary session of the students of all application departments.

4.   Final action evaluation

The final evaluation was carried out on the basis of the success criteria, which were defined in the initial phase, i.e. during the planning of the specific project.
In more detail, the distinct levels of the action plan are summarized as follows:

- Collection, classification, grouping of recyclable materials by type (plastic, paper, fabric, etc.) and their processing by the students (cutting - dyeing).
- Construction of improvised games with the corresponding materials.
- Teaching each game to the full department.
- Game in the "pedagogical material corner".
- Connection with the pedagogical and educational process in the integration department.

Below are some illustrative examples related to the above levels:

a)   Example of teaching in the plenary session: As soon as the construction of an improvised game was completed, it was presented to the plenary session of the department. Kindergarten teachers explained:
- The materials from which it was made,
- The symbols, features and concepts of the game,
- The rules and instructions for use of the game.

The children then played the game in plenary. Finally, the kindergarten teachers placed each game in the "pedagogical corner", prompting the children through probing questions (e.g.: How would you like to play each game? What are the rules of each game? Would you like to add or remove some rules?) for children to play individually or in small groups in an effective way.

b)   Example of interface with the pedagogical process in kindergarten:

Taking into account the philosophy of Universal Design, the improvised toys were also adapted to the needs of children with disabilities or special educational needs, in order for the material to be accessible for "All" kindergarten children. More specifically, within the framework of inclusive education, emphasis was placed primarily on the cultivation of fine motor skills, the development of oral and written language, the construction of mathematical concepts, the development of communication skills, the development of the concepts of space and time, as well as the cultivation of the skills that are generally related to School Readiness for the smooth transition from kindergarten to the first grade of primary school.

Also, the final product was used in a structured or spontaneous way during the educational process, under the framework of the implementation of the respective goals.

After the implementation of the specific action, some actions followed, aimed at disseminating the results, which are listed below.

- Presentation of improvised games in all sections of the basic Compulsory program.
- Presentation of improvised games at the neighboring primary school.
- Game construction activity together with the students of the 1st grade of primary school, of the relevant school within the framework of the smooth Transition Program.
- Opening the school to the local community with the main action being the organization of an exhibition of improvised games in the school's event hall, open to the public.
- Online presentation of the Action Plan to parents.

Regarding the evaluation of this project, it should be noted that the course of development of the specific action was assessed each time by the reactions, feelings, attitudes and behaviors of the participating students, which were recorded by the teachers during the implementation of the action. At regular intervals there were reflection and feedback meetings of the teachers with evaluation of the recording data. In the event that it was judged that some modification or revision was needed, the corresponding adjustment was carried out, as well as the required changes in relation to the original design, so that all the success criteria of the action were utilized. After the completion of the aforementioned action plan, a special meeting was planned, where the results obtained from the active participation and cooperation of all involved were presented. The final evaluation was carried out after presenting the results to all the school's students and parents.

Regarding the evaluation methods and in particular the collection of the final data, the method of semi-structured interview, questionnaire and participatory observation was used and then a comparison was made of the data before the implementation of the action plan and after its implementation.

In conclusion, after the end of the implementation of the specific action plan, the degree of achievement of the goals that had been set was evaluated. An assessment was made of the reasons that led to the achievement of the objectives, as well as reference to the factors/parameters that facilitated the achievement of the objective.

In addition, reference was made to the difficulties that arose during the implementation of the planned actions. The degree of achievement of the objectives, under the framework of the implementation of this action plan, was captured by the use of an evaluation rubric.

RESULTS

The action was implemented according to the original timetable and flexibly led the participating students on a journey of creating improvised games through teamwork and collaboration, upgrading the playful form of the school's educational material and emphasizing the all-round and balanced development of the students' personality, through improvised game (table and floor).

Below are indicatively some of the toys made by the young students, primarily with the use of waste/recyclable material:

- "I play and learn with Akis the hedgehog" (Figures - The meaning of numbers 1-20).
- "The Colorful Clown" (Color Matching).
- "Company with the Alphabet" (Fine motor exercise - Sequencing alphabet letters - creative writing with caps).
- "I write in magic dust" (Sensory writing game - Hand eye coordination - Development of fine motor skills - Activating concentration).
- "Lovely shapes and worked hands" (Fine mobility).
- "Time bar" (Time sequence).
- "Creative egg cases and plastic cups" (Patterns-numbers-tens-colors).
- "The box of addition" (practice logical-mathematical thinking).
- "How do you feel; - What do you feel?" (Emotional therapy).
- "Playing with the elephant" (Physical Education).
- "I'm buttoning, unbuttoning, the little hands are getting stronger!" (Development of fine motor skills for the child's normal development and self-care).
- "Shoes in a row" (Motive release game for inside the class or group).
- "Rolls of rope routes" (Education of logical thinking and development of motor skills).
- "Colored caps in Action" (Strengthening concentration skills and speed).
- "Image reconstruction, color puzzle" (Improve concentration and speed skills).

- "Pinball, my friend" (Development of attention and concentration on the final goal and at the same time strengthening coordination of movements with visual discrimination and observation).
- "I create with tongue depressors, toothpicks and cotton" (Multi-skill games).
- Several multi-skill floor games were also manufactured, e.g. "Theseus and the Minotaur", "Our friends the animals", "I play, learn, create on the floor I walk on".

The activities, the climate of the class, the organization of the recyclable material, the processing of it by the class students, the way of communication and cooperation of the toddlers played an important role in the development of a more general ecological culture, but also triggers for a discovery/investigative and at the same time experiential learning. Particular emphasis was placed on actions that highlight and cultivate skills such as critical thinking, collaboration, communication and creativity, and the results were as expected.

A key criterion for the success of this action was its contribution to the all-round and balanced development of the students' personality, through the improvised game.

In particular, the action's success criteria are summarized as follows:

- The material of improvised games to motivate students for creative work.
- To provide opportunities for exploratory/investigative learning.
- To strengthen the students' self-activity and teamwork experience.
- The games that will be made respond to the interests and needs of the students.
- To make use of the students' previous experiences and knowledge in the teaching of a new subject.
- To gradually guide students towards independent learning.
- To organize assessment activities that offer feedback to the student.
- Contribute to the active participation of students in the knowledge building process, in an experiential way.

In any case, the construction of the games is very important to ensure an active role for the student, to constantly give him opportunities to use his thinking, to look for solutions, to problematize him and not to offer him ready-made solutions and answers.

In conclusion, the action plan is considered a success, as the objectives set during its planning phase were achieved to the greatest extent possible.

From the results it emerged that the construction and engagement with the improvised game had many benefits for the participating students. Through the improvised game, an effect on the all-round and balanced development of the students' personality was evident. After all, it is no coincidence that "the pedagogical use of the playful form of teaching emerged as a fundamental teaching principle and the function of play as the basis of education and training was highlighted (Diakogeorgiou, 1995). Play is a key characteristic of preschool children. The child's nature is connected to playing and through play both his organic and psychological needs are satisfied (Kitsara, 2001, Kotsalidou, 2010).

The results showed that the participating children were able to develop initiatives regarding the effective construction of improvised educational material. They were pleased and happy that thanks to their own efforts the existing game material of the school was enriched. They felt the joy of creation and with their own contribution the pedagogical and psychological climate of the class was significantly strengthened. From the results, it became clear that the redesign of the space and the enrichment of the pedagogical material with the participation of the children, using methodologies that allow their active action, expand communication within the context of the group.

Thus the students managed to:

- To develop their initiative, ingenuity, imagination,
- Their independence, their responsibility, their ability to cooperate,
- Gain self-confidence and develop positive self-esteem.
- They were helped to realize that they should not get frustrated and angry when they lose in the game, but try again and experiment with different strategies.
- To know themselves better in relation to all their socio-emotional and mental capacities and skills.
- To discuss, explain, argue, support the group's decisions and cooperate harmoniously for their implementation.
- Cultivate the oral language, producing speeches with structure, coherence and communicative orientation while simultaneously enriching their vocabulary through the feelings of joy they feel when they play.
- To gain new experiences.
- Cultivate their social skills.
- To cultivate logic-mathematical thinking, but also critical thinking.

In conclusion, children through improvised play gain many benefits. In particular, by interacting, they transform their experiences based on their knowledge and characteristics and reorganize their mental structures (Shunk, 2010). Within the classroom with the various phases of designing, creating, playing, presenting or changing the rules of the improvised game, micro-environments are formed, where ideal conditions for meaningful and active interaction are created, based on the activities that the children undertake.

DISCUSSION

Action research, in order to reach some conclusions, is based on the teacher's experiences and reflective practice. In this research activity, reflection is the key component of the teacher's actions.

From the philosophy of action research presented above, as well as from the epigrammatically presented example, it is clear that the role of the modern teacher is diversifying and expanding. He does not only care about the acquisition of knowledge by his students. But at the same time, he is also the co-researcher who, together with his students, will reflect on the nature of knowledge and teaching, will face any difficulties in an effective way, will use every circumstance in a creative and flexible way and will adopt "forms" that transform the theoretical knowledge in practice inside and outside the classroom (Xochellis, 2005).

Action Research is a modern form of self-evaluation, as it is primarily based on the notion that development and innovation are an essential element of professional practice, where the teacher takes an active role. Thus, on the one hand, theory and practice are combined and on the other hand, it is directly connected to the theoretical background of the problematic situation under investigation. It is a learning process, with various benefits, that leads to the acquisition of new knowledge, skills, attitudes, as well as to the qualitative improvement of the previous ones (McNiff et al, 2003; Katsarou & Tsafos, 2003; Vergidis, 2003).

Improvised board games are offered for simple free empirical observation, formative assessment, differentiated teaching, education of bilingual children and children with special educational needs and contribute to the pursuit of the goals set by the current Analytical Curriculum of kindergarten.

In addition, the harmonious interconnection of play with teaching gives alternative outlets to the teacher who, through the process of play, discovers, invents, innovates, selects, organizes, studies, coordinates and adapts the goals, content and characteristics of the game, so that this to be completely understandable to the target group, attractive, and ultimately effective in terms of knowledge, socialization, and adoption of values, perceptions and behaviors. In this context, the teacher through the game attempts to fully respond to the multiple goals of education, in order to achieve the all-round and balanced development of the students' personality. At the same time, he himself becomes a co-creator and teammate with the children, experiencing a guiding role, particularly interesting.

Teachers also have the ability to more accurately and objectively assess the "zone of imminent development" recorded each time, which is defined as the distance between the child's current developmental level, as determined by independent problem solving, and the level of potential development, as determined through problem solving under adult guidance or in collaboration with more capable peers (Vygotsky, 1978).

On the basis of the above, the factors that contributed to the achievement of the objectives of this project were the adoption of strategies such as the realization of regular meetings of the action group during the implementation, in the context of the continuous evaluation of its progress following the reflective process. The "reflective process" was an important element of the participants' discussions in order to have an active interaction between the teachers who participated in this effort.

In the above context, discussions and collaborative practices took place regarding the design of new activities, in order to enrich the already existing ones and to improve the educational process with any interventions and adjustments to the original design. Also, the creation of groups of toddlers and the implementation of prioritized and clearly targeted activities in the sections of the optional full-day program of the kindergarten and in the integration section contributed positively.

Particular emphasis should be placed on the role of participating teachers and students. During the implementation of the action plan, the educators had mainly a coordinating and less guiding role. They supported and enhanced student work while promoting discovery/investigative learning. The students had an active role in the whole process, on the one hand, co-deciding on the constructions and on the other hand, helping in the design of the games, but also in their construction.

At the same time, experiential actions were implemented to inform and raise the awareness of toddlers, as well as their parents, regarding the understanding of the role of play in preschool age, but also highlighting the necessity of improvised play in the modern inclusive school. As Garry Landreth (1991) very aptly points out, "Birds fly, fish swim and children play." Arguably, play is in the child's nature and is the way to live. The game is a fundamental pedagogical means of learning and development of students, especially preschoolers.

In conclusion, this action research contributed to the cognitive, physical, emotional, social development of children, the development of their imagination and creativity, but also to environmental awareness and the formation of ecological consciousness.

REFERENCES

Altrichter, H., Posch, P., & Somekh, B. (2001). *Teachers research their work. An introduction to the methods of action research* (Deligiannis, M., Trans.). Metaichmio.

Avgitidou, S. (2001). Children's Play: exploring children's collaborative world-building in early childhood education. In Avgitidou, S. (Ed.), *The Game. Contemporary Research and Teaching Approaches* (pp. 159–174). Typothito-G. Dardanus.

Avgitidou, S., Tzekaki, M., & Tsafos, V. (2016). *Enhancing children's learning: Signification and play in Pre-service teachers observe, intervene and reflect.* Gutenberg.

Bento, G., & Dias, G. (2017). The importance of outdoor play for young children's healthy development. *Porto Biomedical Journal*, 2(5), 157–160. 10.1016/j.pbj.2017.03.00332258612

Bergeson, T., Davidson, C., Mueller, M., & Williams-Appleton, D. (2008). *A Guide to Assessment in Early Childhood: Infancy to Age Eight.* Washington State Office of Superintendent of Public Instruction.

Black, P., & Wiliam, D. (1998). Assessment and classroom learning. *Assessment in Education: Principles, Policy & Practice*, 5(1), 7–74. 10.1080/0969595980050102

Broadfoot, P. M., Daugherty, R., Gardner, J., Gipps, C. V., Harlen, W., James, M., & Stobart, G. (1999). *Assessment for learning: beyond the black box.* University of Cambridge School of Education.

Burke, L. A., & Williams, J. M. (2012). The impact of a thinking skills intervention on children's concepts of intelligence. *Thinking Skills and Creativity*, 7(3), 145–152. 10.1016/j.tsc.2012.01.001

Crowther, J., Hamilton, M., & Tett, L. (2001). Powerful literacies: an introduction. In Crowther, J., Hamilton, M., & Tett, L. (Eds.), *Powerful Literacies* (pp. 1–9). NIACE.

Dafermou, X., Koulouri, P., & Basayianni, E. (2006). *Kindergarten Teacher's Guide: Instructional Designs, Creative Learning Environments.* OEDB.

Dankiw, K. A., Tsiros, M. D., Baldock, K. L., & Kumar, S. (2020). The impacts of unstructured nature play on health in early childhood development: A systematic review. *PLoS One*, 15(2), 1–22. 10.1371/journal.pone.022900632053683

Dean, D.Jr, & Kuhn, D. (2007). Direct instruction vs. discovery: The long view. *Science Education*, 91(3), 384–397. 10.1002/sce.20194

Diakogeorgiou, G. (1995). The child and the game, *Antitetradio of education*, issue 34-3 Dankiw, K.A., Tsiros, M.D., Baldock, K.L. & Kumar, S., (2020), 'The impacts of unstructured nature play on health in early childhood development: A systematic review'. *PLoS One*, 15(2), 1–22.

Efstathiou, M. (2007). *Supporting teaching interventions in mixed classes through action research.*

Elliot, J. (1991). Action Research for Educational Change. Milton Keynes: Open University.

Gougoulis, K., & Karakatsani, D. (Eds.). (2008). *The Greek game. Routes in the history of* (1st ed.). MIET.

Haris, T. (1995). *The Adventure of Assessment in Schools.* Kodika.

Hoffmann, J. D., & Russ, S. W. (2016). Fostering pretend play skills and creativity in elementary school girls: A group play intervention. *Psychology of Aesthetics, Creativity, and the Arts*, 10(1), 114–125. 10.1037/aca0000039

Irvin, M. (2017). *The Importance of Play in Early Childhood Education.* North-western College- Orange City.

Katsarou, E., & Tsafos, B. (2003). *From Research to Teaching: Educational action research.* Savvalas.

Kitsaras, G. (2001). *Preschool Pedagogy.* GSAR Publishers.

Kotsalidou, D. (2010). *Interdisciplinary work proposals for kindergarten and elementary school: Theory and practice.* Kastaniotis.

Kyriazopoulou – Valinaki, P. (1997). Kindergarten. *Vlassi, 3*, 236.

Landreth, G. L. (1991). *Play therapy: The art of the relationship.* Accelerated Development.

McNiff, J. (1999). *Action Research: Principles and Practices.* Routledge.

McNiff, J., Lomax, P., & Whitehead, J. (2003). *You and your action research project.* Routledge Falmer.

Nevo, D. (2001). School evaluation: Internal or external? *Studies in Educational Evaluation*, 27(2), 95–106. 10.1016/S0191-491X(01)00016-5

Nijhof, S. L., Vinkers, C. H., Van Geelen, S. M., Duijff, S. N., Achterberg, E. J. M., Van der Net, J., Veltkamp, R. C., Grootenhuis, M. A., van de Putte, E. M., Hillegers, M. H. J., van der Brug, A. W., Wierenga, C. J., Benders, M. J. N. L., Engels, R. C. M. E., van der Ent, C. K., Vanderschuren, L. J. M. J., & Lesscher, H. M. B. (2018). Healthy play, better coping: The importance of play for the development of children in health and disease. *Neuroscience and Biobehavioral Reviews*, 95(September), 421–429. 10.1016/j.neubiorev.2018.09.02430273634

Pantazis, S. (2004). *Pedagogy and play - a target object of the kindergarten.* Gutenberg.

Parker, R., & Thomsen, B. S. (2019). *Learning through play at school: A study of playful integrated pedagogies that foster children's holistic skills development in the primary school classroom.* Billund: LEGOFoundation.

Petkanopoulou, M. (2017). *The improvised board game as a "supporting tool" for teaching in preschool age",* [Master thesis, University of Western Macedonia]. https://dspace.uowm.gr/xmlui/bitstream/handle/123456789/919/Maria%20Petkanopoulou.pdf?sequence=1&isAllowed=y

Prioreschi, A., Wrottesley, S. V., Slemming, W., Cohen, E., & Norris, S. A. (2020). A qualitative study reporting maternal perceptions of the importance of play for healthy growth and development in the first two years of life. *BMC Pediatrics*, 20(1), 1–11. 10.1186/s12887-020-02321-432907550

Purpura, D., Baroody, A., Eiland, M., & Reid, E. (2016). Fostering first graders' reasoning strategies with basic sums: The value of guided instruction. *The Elementary School Journal*, 117(1), 72–100. 10.1086/687809

Stiggins, R. J. (2002). Assessment crisis: The absence of assessment for learning. *Phi Delta Kappan*, 83(10), 758–765. 10.1177/003172170208301010

Vergidis, D. (2003). The contribution of assessment to the implementation of integrated adult education programs. In Vergidis, D. (Ed.), *Adult Education. Contribution to the specialization of executives and trainers.* Greek Letters.

Vygotsky, L. (1978). *Mind in Society: The Development of Higher Psychological Processes.* Harvard University Press.

Whitebread, D., Basilio, M., Kuvalja, M., & Verma, M. (2012). *The Importance of Play.* Toy Industries of Europe.

Whitebread, D., & O'Sullivan, L. (2012). Preschool children's social pretend play: Supporting the development of metacommunication, metacognition and self regulation. *International Journal of Play*, 1(2), 197–213. 10.1080/21594937.2012.693384

Xochellis, P. (2005). *Education in the modern world*. Typothito.

Xu, Y. (2010). Children's social play sequence: Parten's classic theory revisited'. *Early Child Development and Care*, 180(4), 489–498. 10.1080/03004430802090430

Yen, S. C., & Spa, J. M. (2000). Children's Temperament and Behavior in Montessori and Contructivist Early Childhood Programms. *Early Education and Development*, 11(2), 171–186. 10.1207/s15566935eed1102_3

Chapter 6
Students With Learning Disabilities and Feelings of Loneliness

Assimina Tsibidaki
University of the Aegean, Greece

Vana Chiou
University of the Aegean, Greece

ABSTRACT

This study aims to explore the degree of loneliness of adolescents with LDs, and the possible differences and correlations with the type of LDs, gender, and age. The sample comprised 30 adolescences with LDs, 14 (46.7%) boys and 16 (53.3%) girls, aged 12-15 years (M=13.60, Sd=.770). A self-report questionnaire and the children's loneliness questionnaire (CLQ) were used for data collection. The findings of the study indicated that all adolescents, regardless of the type of LDs, demonstrated moderate to low levels of loneliness. There was no statistically significant difference between students with MGLDs and students with SpLDs relating to feelings of loneliness, although students with MGLDs experienced feelings of loneliness higher compared to students with SLDs. As far as the gender, there was no significant difference between girls and boys; however, the girls scored higher. Finally, there was no correlation with age.

DOI: 10.4018/979-8-3693-4022-6.ch006

INTRODUCTION

Learning disabilities (LDs) are a general term for a special education need and disabilities (SEND) that has an impact on different learning domains. The term "General learning disabilities" (GLDs) refers to a situation in which a child's or young person's cognitive challenges have an influence on all aspects of the school curriculum and frequently also on extracurricular activities. Specific Learning Disabilities (SpLDs) are where the impact of the child's or young person's cognitive difficulties is seen in a particular area of learning, such as reading, writing, spelling, or mathematics (SchoolsWeb, 2022). There are different types of LDs, which can be mild, moderate, severe, or profound. According to the DSM-5, 5 to 15 percent of school-age children across different cultures are affected by a learning disorder that limits them in reading, writing, or mathematics (American Psychiatric Association, 2013).

Students with LDs are experiencing challenges in academic work, mainly reading, writing, and/or calculation difficulties (American Psychiatric Association, 2013). Although students with LDs are often regarded as a heterogeneous group, they are situated in specific social surroundings, such as schools and families, with which they interact dynamically every day (Yu et al., 2005).

Various studies have highlighted a number of issues related to the emotional and social aspects of the education of students with LDs (Schiff & Joshi, 2016). Students with LDs may encounter many difficulties in their education, such as issues related to peer group acceptance, friendship, and social isolation, low self-efficacy and self-esteem, and externalized and internalized behavior problems (Cavioni et al., 2017). Moreover, students with LDs also face social obstacles at school, including more active rejection and detachment from their classmates (Wagner et al., 2007) and more feelings of loneliness (Margalit, 2010).

Loneliness is the emotional and mental distress or unease that comes from being alone or feeling alone (APA, 2024). It is defined as involving the cognitive awareness of a deficiency in one's social and personal relationships and the ensuing affective reactions of sadness, emptiness, or longing (Asher & Paquette, 2003). It reflects a global indicator of dissatisfaction with the quality and/or quantity of individuals' social relationships (Asher et al., 1990).

Psychological theory and research provide numerous perspectives. Social psychology focuses on the emotional distress caused by unmet needs for intimacy and companionship, while cognitive psychology emphasizes on the unsettling experience resulting from a perceived discrepancy between desired and actual social relationships. Psychologists following existential or humanistic viewpoints view loneliness as an unavoidable and distressing part of being human, which can lead to heightened self-awareness and renewal (APA, 2024).

Moreover, feelings of loneliness are defined as a painful emotion that appears when a person is rejected, feels alienated, or is misunderstood by others (Al-Yagon & Margalit, 2016). Feelings of loneliness can have many consequences for an individual's health, both physically and mentally. Feelings of loneliness early in life may affect a child's development and learning abilities, in addition to the physical and mental health consequences (Kwan et al., 2020).

Children with LDs have personal characteristics that not only increase the likelihood that they will be lonely but may also make it more difficult for them to cope with the feelings that accompany loneliness (Margalit & Al-Yagon, 2002). Research on the relationship between loneliness and LDs is often associated with the construct of peer acceptance (Yu et al., 2005). Students with LDs report having fewer friends and feeling less popular than other students (Sentenac et al., 2012). They also report feeling lonelier than their peers (Margalit & Al-Yagon, 2002). Moreover, the comparisons of specific academic self-efficacies, general academic self-efficacy, loneliness, and effort investment revealed significant differences between groups of students with and without LDs (Lackaye & Margalit, 2008).

In addition, research demonstrates the relationship of the loneliness experience to a wide range of sociodemographic aspects, such as age, gender, and cultural difference (Barreto et al., 2021). Literature refers that LDs occur in different groups of students belonging to different cultures, different races, and different socioeconomic statuses in boys and girls. This latest definition displays a dynamic ecological multidimensional model that recognizes the existence of different levels of various SEND, and combines an observation into social, emotional, and cultural factors (Margalit, 2014 as cited in Tarabia & Abu-Rabia, 2016). Moreover, loneliness is more common in adolescence than in all other age groups (Heinrich & Gullone, 2006).

Effective approaches to helping children and adolescents with LD overcome loneliness require both a carefully structured social environment and close attention to each child's particular social skills and challenges. With the overarching goal of empowering the child and the adolescent with LD to improve his/her social relations with peers, successful interventions rely on a combination of approaches (Margalit & Al-Yagon, 2002). Professionals' and specialists' awareness as well as psychoeducational programs could be tailor-made to enhance hopeful beliefs and reduce loneliness (Icekson et al., 2021).

The Present Study

Many studies have supported that students with LGs feel that school is their main factor of frustration and reflects on their social reputations, isolation, and socio-relational discomfort. However, the role of LDs in psychosocial outcomes in adolescence is still unclear (Musetti et al., 2019). The present study aims to explore the degree of loneliness of adolescents with LDs, and the possible differences and correlations with the type of LDs, gender, and age.

METHODOLOGY

The study presents the pilot findings of a large-scale survey.

Participants

The sample comprised 30 adolescents with LDs, 14 (46.7%) boys and 16 (53.3%) girls, aged 12-15 years (M=13.60, Sd=.770). Moreover, 14 (46.7%) students were diagnosed with "Mild generalised learning disabilities (MGLDs)" and 16 (53.3%) with "Specific learning disabilities (SpLDs)" (M=1.53, Sd=2.0). All of them were students at a mainstream public secondary school and they followed inclusive classes (IC) for the subjects of language and math. Table 1 shows the students' demographics.

Table 1. The demographics of students with LDs (n=30)

Students' demographics	
Age	12-15 years (M=13.60, Sd=.770)
Gender	
Boy	20 (66.7%)
Girl	10 (33.3%)
School classroom	
1st grade	12 (23.3%)
2nd grade	4 (13.3%)
3rd grade	9 (30%)
LDs type	
MGLDs	6 (20%) boys and 8 (26.7%) girls
SLDs	8 (26.7%) boys and 8 (26.7%) girls

Instruments

A self-report questionnaire and the Children's Loneliness Questionnaire (CLQ) were used for data collection.

1) Child demographic form. The questionnaire is composed of ten questions aiming to derive information relating to the following axes: sex, age, birth order, school class, etc.

2) Children's Loneliness Questionnaire (CLQ) (Asher & Wheeler, 1985). This test evaluates the feelings of loneliness of children over 8 years old. The CLQ includes 16 primary items focused on children's feelings of loneliness, social adequacy versus inadequacy, and subjective estimations of peer status. Eight "filler" items that ask about children's hobbies and other activities are included to help children feel more relaxed and open about expressing their feelings. CLQ has excellent internal consistency, with an alpha of 0.90 for the 16 primary items. A one-year test/retest correlation of 0.55 suggests good long-term stability.

Procedure and Data Analysis

Data collection was conducted between January and March 2023. For data analysis, normality tests, descriptive statistics (percentages, mean, and standard deviation), t-tests for independent samples, and Pearson's r coefficient were implemented.

Findings

Regarding the normality test, the ratio of the kurtosis for its standard error and the ratio of the skewness for its standard error are between -2 and 2, so the distribution of the CLQ mean variable is approximately normal and there is no normality problem for our sample.

Correlation Between Type of Learning Disability and Feelings of Loneliness

From the descriptive data, we observed that students with MGLDs experienced feelings of loneliness more than students with SpLDs (Table 2).

Table 2. Descriptive statistics of CLQ

Type of LDs		N	M	Sd
CLQ	MGLDs	14	42.21	11.801
	SpLDs	16	36.81	9.425

The t-test showed that there was no statistically significant difference between students with GLDs and students with SpLDs in terms of feeling lonely $t(28)=1.393$, $p=.175>0.05$.

The lowest score with which the feelings of loneliness can be assessed is 16 and the highest is 80. Therefore, the median between the scores 16 and 80 was 48. Students with MGLDs presented a mean score of 42.21 and those with SLDs had a mean score of 36.61. Therefore, all students, regardless of the type of LDs, experienced moderate to low levels of loneliness.

Correlations Between Gender and Feelings of Loneliness

Descriptive data showed that girls experience the feeling of loneliness more than boys. The t-test results indicated that there was no statistically significant difference between girls and boys in terms of the feelings of loneliness $t(28)= -1,480$, $p=.150>0.05$.

As mentioned above, the lowest score with which the feelings of loneliness can be assessed is 16 and the highest is 80. Therefore, the median between the scores 16 and 80 was 48. We observed that the girls showed a mean score of 42.00 and the boys had a mean score of 36.29. Therefore, all students, regardless of their gender, experienced moderate to low levels of feelings of loneliness.

Correlations Between Age and Feelings of Loneliness

Aiming to examine the association between students' age and their feelings of loneliness, Pearson's r coefficient was applied. The results showed that the two variables mentioned above did not have a linear correlation $r.=-,354, p=.055>0.5$.

DISCUSSION

The current study aimed to study the degree of loneliness among adolescents with LDs, and the possible differences and correlations with the type of LDs, gender, and age.

According to the findings of the study, all adolescents, regardless of the type of LDs, demonstrated moderate to low levels of loneliness. This finding is in line with a variety of research that suggests loneliness reveals a unique picture (Lackaye & Margalit, 2008). More specifically, Lackaye and Margalit, 2008 found that the level of loneliness for students with LDs was lower in high school than in middle school, and perhaps the move to high school, which may be seen in many ways as a continuation of the pressures of middle school, was less threatening to students with LDs, who had experienced increased stresses at an earlier stage. On the other hand, this finding is not consistent with those research findings suggesting that most children with LDs report higher levels of loneliness than their peers and that this increases during the transition from childhood to adolescence (Eboli & Corsano, 2017; Kwan et al., 2020; Margalit & Al-Yagon, 2002).

Regarding the sociodemographics, our study found that although there were not statistically significant differences between the degree of loneliness and the type of LDs, gender, and age, students with MGLDs experienced feelings of loneliness higher compared to students with SpLDs, and girls scored higher than boys in the loneliness test. This finding is in line with research findings that argue for the relationship of the loneliness experience to a wide range of sociodemographic aspects (Barreto et al., 2021).

More specifically, in terms of the type of LDs, students with MGLDs experienced feelings of loneliness higher compared to students with SpLDs. This finding was to be expected because students with more severe types of SEND, such as MGLDs compared to SpLDs, experience loneliness to a greater extent. Literature reports that students with chronic academic difficulties often report higher levels of loneliness (Emerson & Hatton, 2009). Furthermore, our study suggests that girls scored higher than boys in the loneliness test. This finding is consistent with other studies' findings, which show that girls are more likely than boys to feel lonely (Huntington & Bender, 1993). Furthermore, research examining gender differences in adulthood loneliness shows that women are more likely to report higher rates of loneliness and depression relative to men (Borys & Perlman, 1985 as cited in Goosby et al., 2013), although this pattern is not consistently found among adolescents (Goosby et al., 2013). In terms of age, there was no correlation between the feelings of loneliness and the participants ages of 12 to 15 years old. As all students belonged to the same age group, adolescence (Griffin, 2010) argue that there are no significant age differences in loneliness, though various studies (Barreto et al., 2021) report that loneliness is particularly prevalent among older people, but research does not support that proposition.

Implications for Practice

The results focused awareness on the feelings of loneliness that adolescents with LDs may experience. Providing academic support and helping to meet the academic needs of students with LDs is only a partial response.

Educators, schools, and professionals have to look at the learning profiles of students with LDs in relation to their social and emotional functioning. Moreover, curriculum and instruction must be carefully modified to help students with LDs reach their potential in areas such as resilience and inclusion.

Limitations

This study has certain limitations that should be mentioned. First, the sample was small and located outside of Greece. A comparative study between the study's sample and others in the capital would be most helpful to see other possible personality components. Second, the sample inclusion criteria of the study suggested that all adolescents with LDs attended inclusive settings; results may differ if the adolescents attended different educational settings. Third, a comparison of different degrees and types of LDs would be desirable. Finally, additional alternative qualitative methods for collecting data (e.g., interviews) could be used (on adolescents as well as educators or parents).

CONCLUSION

The findings of the study indicated that all adolescents, regardless of the type of LDs, demonstrated moderate to low levels of loneliness. Moreover, there was no statistically significant difference between students with MGLDs and students with SpLDs relating to feelings of loneliness, although students with MGLDs experienced feelings of loneliness higher than students with SpLDs. As far as gender, there was no significant difference between girls and boys, however, the girls scored higher. Finally, there was no correlation with age.

REFERENCES

Al-Yagon, M., & Margalit, M. (2016). Specific learning disorder. In Levesque, R. J. R. (Ed.), *Encyclopedia of Adolescence* (pp. 1–6). Springer International Publishing. 10.1007/978-3-319-32132-5_806-1

American Psychiatric Association. (2013). *Diagnostic and statistical manual of mental disorders (DSM-5)*. American Psychiatric Association Publishing.

American Psychiatric Association. (2024). *APA dictionary of psychology*. American Psychological Association. https://dictionary.apa.org/

Asher, S. R., & Paquette, J. A. (2003). Loneliness and peer relations in childhood. *Current Directions in Psychological Science*, 12(3), 75–78. 10.1111/1467-8721.01233

Asher, S. R., Parkhurst, J. T., Hymel, S., & Williams, G. A. (1990). Peer rejection and loneliness in childhood. In Asher, S. R., & Coie, J. D. (Eds.), *Peer rejection in childhood* (pp. 253–273). Cambridge University Press.

Asher, S. R., & Wheeler, V. A. (1985). Children's loneliness: A comparison of rejected and neglected peer status. *Journal of Consulting and Clinical Psychology*, 53(4), 500–505. 10.1037/0022-006X.53.4.5004031205

Barreto, M., Victor, C., Hammond, C., Eccles, A., Richins, M. T., & Qualter, P. (2021). Loneliness around the world: Age, gender, and cultural differences in loneliness. *Personality and Individual Differences*, 169, 110066. 10.1016/j.paid.2020.11006633536694

Cavioni, V., Grazzani, I., & Ornaghi, V. (2017). Social and emotional learning for children with learning disability: Implications for inclusion. *The International Journal of Emotional Education*, 9(2), 100–109. https://files.eric.ed.gov/fulltext/EJ1162075.pdf

Eboli, G., & Corsano, P. (2017). Loneliness in children and adolescents with Learning Disabilities: A review. *Psicologia Clinica dello Sviluppo*, 21(1), 25–50. 10.1449/86184

Emerson, E., & Hatton, C. (2009). Chapter 4 socioeconomic position, poverty, and family research. *International Review of Research in Mental Retardation*, 37, 97–129. 10.1016/S0074-7750(09)37004-4

Goosby, B. J., Bellatorre, A., Walsemann, K. M., & Cheadle, J. E. (2013). Adolescent loneliness and health in early adulthood. *Sociological Inquiry*, 83(4), 505–536. 10.1111/soin.1201824187387

Griffin, J. (2010). *The lonely society?* Social Welfare Foundation. https://www.bl .uk/collection-items/lonely-society

Heinrich, L. M., & Gullone, E. (2006). The clinical significance of loneliness: A literature review. *Clinical Psychology Review*, 26(6), 695–718. 10.1016/j. cpr.2006.04.00216952717

Huntington, D. D., & Bender, W. N. (1993). Adolescents with learning disabilities at risk? Emotional well-being, depression, suicide. *Journal of Learning Disabilities*, 26(3), 159–166. 10.1177/002221949302600303848693

Ickson, T., Begerano, O. D., Levinson, M., Savariego, J., & Margalit, M. (2021). Learning difficulties and loneliness in college and beyond: The mediating role of self-efficacy, proactive coping, and hope. *International Journal of Environmental Research and Public Health*, 18(19), 10508. 10.3390/ijerph18191050834639809

Kwan, C., Gitimoghaddam, M., & Collet, J.-P. (2020). Effects of social isolation and loneliness in children with neurodevelopmental disabilities: A scoping review. *Brain Sciences*, 10(11), 786. 10.3390/brainsci1011078633126519

Lackaye, T., & Margalit, M. (2008). Self-efficacy, loneliness, effort, and hope: Developmental differences in the experiences of students with learning disabilities and their non-learning disabled peers at two age groups. Learning Disabilities. *Learning Disabilities (Weston, Mass.)*, 6(2), 1–20. https://files.eric.ed.gov/fulltext/ EJ804508.pdf

Margalit, M. (2010). *Lonely children and adolescents: Self perceptions, social exclusion and hope*. Springer. 10.1007/978-1-4419-6284-3

Margalit, M., & Al-Yagon, M. (2002). The loneliness experience of children with learning disabilities. In Wong, B. Y. L., & Donahue, M. L. (Eds.), *The social dimensions of learning disabilities: Essays in honor of Tanis Bryan* (pp. 53–75). Lawrence Erlbaum Associates Publishers.

Musetti, A., Eboli, G., Cavallini, F., & Corsano, P. (2019). Social relationships, self-esteem, and loneliness in adolescents with learning disabilities. *Clinical Neuropsychiatry, 16*(4), 165–172. https://doi.org/PMID: 34908952.

Schiff, R., & Joshi, R. M. (2016). *Interventions in learning disabilities: A handbook on systematic training programs for individuals with learning disabilities*. Springer. 10.1007/978-3-319-31235-4

SchoolsWeb. (2022). *General learning difficulties*. SchoolsWeb. https://schoolsweb .buckscc.gov.uk/ send-and-inclusion/sen-support-toolkit/supporting-presenting- needs/cognition-a n d-learning/general-learning-difficulties/

Sentenac, M., Arnaud, C., Gavin, A., Molcho, M., Gabhainn, S. N., & Godeau, E. (2012). Peer victimization among school-aged children with chronic conditions. *Epidemiologic Reviews*, 34(1), 120–128. 10.1093/epirev/mxr02422130095

Tarabia, E., & Abu-Rabia, S. (2016). Social competency, sense of loneliness and self-image among reading disabled (RD) Arab adolescents. *Creative Education*, 7(9), 1292–1313. 10.4236/ce.2016.79135

Wagner, M., Newman, L., Cameto, R., Levine, P., Marder, C., & Malouf, D. (2007). *Perceptions and expectations of youth with disabilities. A special topic report of findings from the National Longitudinal Transition Study-2 (NLTS2) (NCSER 2007-3006)*. SRI International.

Yu, G., Zhang, Y., & Yan, R. (2005). Loneliness, peer acceptance, and family functioning of Chinese children with learning disabilities: Characteristics and relationships. *Psychology in the Schools*, 42(3), 325–331. 10.1002/pits.20083

Chapter 7
Psychosocial Development for Children and Adolescents Exhibiting Aggressive Behaviour

Marilena Mousoulidou
https://orcid.org/0000-0002-3549-2522
Neapolis University Pafos, Cyprus

Andri Christodoulou
https://orcid.org/0000-0002-3281-3327
Neapolis University Pafos, Cyprus

Theodoros Goutoglou
https://orcid.org/0009-0008-9888-0814
Neapolis University Pafos, Cyprus

ABSTRACT

Aggressive behaviour in children and adolescents is a multifaceted problem with potentially severe consequences for individuals and society. The present chapter aims to provide a comprehensive literature review, examining the psychosocial dimensions of aggression that contribute to aggressive tendencies, highlighting the early onset and distinct developmental patterns during childhood and adolescence. It also emphasises the detrimental effects of factors such as difficult temperament, parenting style, bullying, social rejection, and hostile attribution bias. It explores the severe consequences of untreated aggression, including academic failure, social

DOI: 10.4018/979-8-3693-4022-6.ch007

isolation, mental health problems, and increased risk of crime and violence. Finally, this chapter advocates evidence-based prevention strategies and interventions targeting individual, family, and social factors to reduce aggressive behaviour. Promising approaches include cognitive-behavioural therapy, parent education programs, and social skills training, fostering positive behaviour change for a safer society.

INTRODUCTION

Aggressive behaviour is a complex and pervasive issue with devastating consequences for both children and adolescents themselves, those around them, and wider society; it is considered a phenomenon that manifests itself in a variety of forms, from verbal abuse to physical violence (Murray-Close et al., 2010). While a degree of aggression, particularly in early childhood, is considered normal, its persistence in middle childhood and escalation into adolescence can lead to significant harm (Krahé and Busching 2014). This chapter delves into the psychosocial dimensions of aggressive behaviour in children and adolescents, exploring the complex interplay of age, individual, family, and cognitive factors contributing to its development and maintenance.

Research reveals that aggression often emerges in early childhood and follows distinct patterns throughout development. For instance, a coercive cycle within the family environment can reinforce aggressive behaviours, setting the stage for future aggression (Smith et al., 2014). Numerous psychosocial factors influence aggression, including individual characteristics like temperament and emotion regulation difficulties (Hu et al., 2023). Family dynamics, particularly parenting styles and conflict resolution strategies, play a pivotal role. Authoritarian and permissive parenting styles are associated with increased aggression, while authoritative parenting fosters prosocial behaviour (Baumrind, 1991).

Peer relations is another crucial area. Bullying and social rejection, as Juvonen and Graham (2014) point out, can trigger and exacerbate aggressive tendencies in vulnerable individuals. Moreover, cognitive processes such as hostile attribution bias, where ambiguous social cues are interpreted as hostile, can contribute to a cycle of aggression (Hiemstra et al., 2018). The consequences of untreated aggression are dire, leading to academic failure, social isolation, mental health problems, and increased risk of delinquency and violence (Liu, 2011).

Below, presents a comprehensive exploration of the psychosocial dimensions of aggressive behaviour in children and adolescents, recognizing the complex interplay of age, individual, family, and cognitive factors contributing to its development and maintenance. At the same time, perspectives from developmental, cognitive, and behavioural psychology are incorporated, seeking to elucidate the underlying mechanisms that fuel and perpetuate aggressive tendencies, providing information for the development of effective prevention and intervention strategies.

Psychosocial Influences in Early Childhood (Ages 2-5 Years Old)

With the interplay of personal, environmental, and family characteristics having a significant impact on a child's path to aggression, "Early Childhood" is a fundamental period where the seeds of aggressive behaviour can be sown covering the ages of 2 to 5 years (Feldman, 2016; Tarsha & Narvaez, 2019).

Personal Characteristics

With temperament and biologically based individual differences in reactivity and self-regulation playing a crucial role, children with a difficult temperament, characterized by high reactivity, negative emotionality, and low effortful control, are more prone to aggressive outbursts (Rothbart & Bates, 2007). In addition, they are likely to have difficulty managing frustration and exhibit impulsive reactions, thus increasing the likelihood of aggressive behaviour (Muris & Ollendick, 2005; Rothbart & Bates, 2007).

In addition, the attachment style, the emotional bond that is formed between a child and their primary caregiver, also shapes social-emotional development. Insecure attachment, and particularly disorganized attachment, has been linked to increased aggression in early childhood. Children with insecure attachment may lack trust in their caregivers and the world around them, leading to emotional dysregulation and difficulty forming positive peer relationships (Cassidy et al., 2013).

Finally, emotion regulation, the ability to manage and express emotions in a socially acceptable way, is another critical personal characteristic. Young children with limited emotion regulation skills may resort to aggression to express frustration or anger and are likely to have difficulty recognising and labelling their emotions, leading to impulsive reactions and challenges in peacefully resolving conflicts (Graziano et al., 2007)

Environmental Characteristics

Family characteristics significantly influence a child's development. Parenting styles, specifically harsh, inconsistent, or neglectful parenting, can create a breeding ground for aggression. Children who experience harsh discipline, physical punishment, or emotional abuse may learn that aggression is an acceptable way to resolve conflict. Inconsistent parenting, where rules and expectations constantly change, can lead to confusion and frustration in children, increasing the likelihood of aggressive outbursts (Lanjekar et al., 2022).

Moreover, socioeconomic status (SES) also plays a role, with children from low-SES families facing a higher risk of exposure to violence and stress, which can contribute to aggressive behaviour. Limited access to resources, such as quality childcare and educational opportunities, can exacerbate these challenges (Zilanawala & Pilkauskas, 2012).

Furthermore, social characteristics, such as peer interactions and the preschool environment, also shape early aggression. Exposure to aggressive peers or witnessing aggression in the preschool setting can normalize aggressive behavior and provide children with models for aggression (Bandura et al., 1961).

Risk Factors

Several risk factors increase the likelihood of aggression in early childhood. Witnessing aggression, whether at home or in the community, can desensitize children to violence and make them more likely to resort to aggression themselves. Harsh discipline and inconsistent parenting, as discussed earlier, also contribute to aggression. Additionally, children with certain temperamental traits, such as high reactivity and low effortful control, may be more susceptible to developing aggressive behaviour in the face of these risk factors (Liu, 2011).

Aspects of Development in Early Childhood (Ages 2-5 Years Old)

Early childhood is a period of rapid development across multiple domains, including biological, cognitive, social-emotional, and personality development. Understanding how these aspects interact is crucial for comprehending the emergence of aggressive behaviour (Belsky, 2019; Feldman, 2016).

Biological Development

The brain undergoes significant maturation during early childhood, particularly in areas responsible for emotional regulation and impulse control. The prefrontal cortex, crucial for executive functions such as planning, decision-making, and inhibiting impulsive behaviours, still develops in young children. This immaturity can contribute to difficulties in managing emotions and controlling aggressive impulses (Belsky, 2019; Feldman, 2016).

Additionally, hormonal changes also play a role, with testosterone linked to increased aggression in both boys and girls (Welker et al., 2017). While genetics contribute to temperament and predisposition to aggression, it is essential to note that genes interact with environmental factors to shape behaviour (Tuvblad & Beaver, 2013).

Cognitive Development

According to Piaget's (1952) theory of cognitive development, young children are in the sensorimotor and preoperational stages. During the sensorimotor stage (birth to 2 years), children learn about the world through sensory experiences and motor actions. In the preoperational stage (2 to 7 years), they develop symbolic thinking and language but still struggle with logical reasoning and understanding others' perspectives.

According to Piaget's theory (1952), egocentric thinking can contribute to aggression. Young children may have difficulty understanding how their actions affect others. They may also misinterpret social cues, leading to conflicts and aggressive behaviour.

Social-Emotional Development

Early childhood is a critical period for social-emotional development. Young children learn to express emotions, develop empathy, and engage in social play. However, emotional understanding and expression limitations can lead to frustration and aggression (Belsky, 2019; Feldman, 2016; Malik & Marwaha, 2022).

Also, empathy, the ability to understand and share the feelings of others, is still developing in early childhood. Young children may struggle to recognize and respond to the emotional cues of others, increasing the likelihood of misinterpreting social situations and resorting to aggression (Eisenberg et al., 2010).

Furthermore, while important for learning social skills and cooperation, social play can also be a source of conflict. Children with limited social skills may struggle to initiate and maintain positive peer interactions, leading to frustration and aggression (Rubin et al., 2009).

Personality

Early childhood is a time of developing self-concept and self-esteem. Children begin to form a sense of who they are based on their interactions with others and their experiences in the world. A negative self-concept or low self-esteem can contribute to aggression, as children may use aggression to compensate for feelings of inadequacy or to gain a sense of control (Raburu, 2015).

Psychosocial Influences in Middle Childhood (Ages 6-12 Years Old)

Middle childhood, encompassing ages 6 to 12, is a period of significant social and emotional growth where the roots of aggressive behaviour can either strengthen or weaken. Personal characteristics, environmental factors, and their interplay, profoundly influence a child's propensity for aggression during this stage (Belsky, 2019; Feldman, 2016).

Personal Characteristics

Self-concept, the individual's beliefs and evaluations about themselves, is crucial in shaping behaviour. Children with a negative self-concept or low self-esteem may be more likely to engage in aggression to compensate for feelings of inadequacy or to gain a sense of power. They may also be more susceptible to peer pressure and engage in aggressive behaviour to gain peer acceptance or approval (Donnellan et al., 2005; Jankowski et al., 2021).

Additionally, peer relationships become increasingly important during middle childhood. Children who struggle to form positive peer relationships or experience peer rejection are at a higher risk of developing aggressive behaviour. Rejected children may lack social skills, have difficulty understanding social cues, or exhibit aggressive behaviours that further alienate them from peers. This can lead to a vicious cycle where social rejection reinforces aggressive tendencies (Feldman, 2016; Lynn Mulvey et al., 2017).

School experiences also significantly impact aggression in middle childhood. Academic difficulties, such as learning disabilities or poor academic performance, can lead to frustration and a sense of failure, which can manifest as aggression towards peers or teachers. Additionally, an adverse school climate characterized by bullying and a lack of support can contribute to aggressive behaviour (Bierman et al., 2013).

Environmental Characteristics

Family characteristics continue to play a vital role in shaping aggression during middle childhood. Parental involvement, particularly warm and supportive parenting, can buffer against the development of aggressive behaviour. Conversely, parental rejection, harsh discipline, or inconsistent parenting can increase the risk of aggression (Feldman, 2016; Labella & Masten, 2018).

Sibling dynamics also contribute to aggression. Sibling conflict and rivalry can provide a training ground for aggressive behaviour, as children may learn to use aggression to resolve disputes with siblings (Song et al., 2016).

Moreover, family stressors, such as financial difficulties, parental mental health problems, or marital conflict, can create a stressful home environment that increases the likelihood of aggression in children. Children may model aggressive behaviour witnessed in their families or use aggression to cope with stress and anxiety (Masarik & Conger, 2017).

Furthermore, the social environment outside the family also influences aggression in middle childhood. The school environment, as mentioned earlier, plays a crucial role. Bullying, both as a victim and a perpetrator, is a significant risk factor for aggressive behaviour. Children who are bullied may develop aggressive tendencies to protect themselves or retaliate against bullies. Conversely, children who bully others may reinforce their aggressive behaviour through the power and control they gain over their victims (Badger et al., 2023).

Finally, extracurricular activities, such as sports or clubs, can provide children with positive social experiences, opportunities for skill development, and a sense of belonging. This can buffer against the development of aggression by providing children with alternative outlets for their energy and emotions (Bundick, 2011).

Risk Factors

Several risk factors increase the likelihood of aggression in middle childhood. Academic difficulties, peer rejection, and exposure to violence are key concerns. Children who struggle academically may experience frustration and a sense of failure, leading to aggression (Ettekal & Ladd, 2014). Peer rejection can leave children feeling isolated and lonely, increasing the risk of developing aggressive tendencies to cope with social pain (Gazelle & Druhen, 2009). Exposure to violence, whether through media or real-life experiences, can desensitize children to violence and make them more likely to resort to aggression themselves (Anderson et al., 2010; Gentile & Bushman, 2012).

Aspects of Development in Middle Childhood (Ages 6-12 Years Old)

Middle childhood marks a period of significant transformation across multiple domains of development, including biological, cognitive, social-emotional, and personality development. These changes interact in complex ways to shape a child's behaviour, including their propensity for aggression (Belsky, 2019; Feldman, 2016; Del Giudice, 2014).

Biological Development

While puberty's most dramatic physical changes occur in adolescence, some children may experience early pubertal changes during middle childhood. These hormonal fluctuations can affect mood and behaviour, potentially contributing to increased aggression (Belsky, 2019; Feldman, 2016; Smith, 2013).

Cognitive Development

According to Piaget's theory (1952), children in middle childhood enter the concrete operational stage, characterized by logical thinking and the ability to understand concrete concepts. However, they still struggle with abstract reasoning and hypothetical thinking.

Regarding information processing, children in this stage show improvements in attention, memory, and problem-solving skills. These cognitive advancements allow for a greater understanding of social situations and the consequences of actions, potentially mitigating aggressive impulses. However, children with cognitive deficits or difficulties in social information processing may be more prone to misinterpreting social cues and resorting to aggression (Coffman et al., 2018; De Castro, 2004).

Social-Emotional Development

Middle childhood is a crucial period for social-emotional development, marked by forming friendships, developing a sense of self and identity, and the continued refinement of emotional regulation skills. Friendships provide opportunities for social learning, emotional support, and the development of social skills. Children who lack close friendships may experience loneliness and isolation, increasing the risk of aggression (Belsky, 2019; Feldman, 2016).

Also, identity formation, the process of developing a sense of self and one's place in the world, begins in earnest during middle childhood. Children grapple with questions about who they are, what they value, and what they want to become. A positive sense of identity can serve as a protective factor against aggression, while a negative or confused identity can increase the risk (Feldman, 2016).

Furthermore, emotional regulation continues to develop throughout middle childhood, with children becoming more adept at managing their emotions and expressing them in socially acceptable ways. However, children who struggle with emotional regulation may still resort to aggression to cope with frustration or anger (Abtahi & Kerns, 2017).

Personality

Middle childhood is a time of consolidating personality traits and developing values. While some children may exhibit aggressive tendencies due to temperamental or environmental factors, others may develop prosocial traits such as empathy, kindness, and cooperation. The values instilled by parents and other significant figures and the child's experiences in school and social settings play a role in shaping these traits (Kotelnikova et al., 2013).

Psychosocial Influences in Adolescence (Ages 13-19 Years Old)

The transition from childhood to adolescence, which includes the ages 13 to 19, is a period of enormous change and upheaval. During adolescence, personal characteristics such as identity exploration, the pursuit of autonomy, and sensitivity to peer influence play a key role in shaping aggressive behaviour. Understanding these influences is crucial to elucidate the complex dynamics contributing to aggression at this developmental stage (Belsky, 2019; Feldman, 2016).

Personal Characteristics

Adolescence is marked by a profound quest for identity, a process of self-discovery and exploration of values, beliefs, and aspirations. This journey often involves experimenting with different roles and identities, seeking feedback from peers and adults, and integrating personal experiences into a coherent sense of self (Zhang & Qin, 2023).

However, the path to identity formation can be fraught with challenges. Adolescents who struggle to develop a clear sense of self may experience identity confusion, leading to feelings of insecurity and a lack of direction. This internal turmoil can manifest as aggression, as adolescents may lash out in frustration or seek validation through antisocial behaviour (Mitchell et al., 2021).

Pursuing autonomy, the desire for independence and self-governance, is another hallmark of adolescence. Adolescents strive to make their own decisions, challenge authority, and establish a sense of control over their lives. While this process is essential for healthy development, conflicts with parents and authority figures can escalate into aggression (Belsky, 2019; Feldman, 2016).

Finally, peer influence also reaches its peak during adolescence. Adolescents are highly susceptible to the opinions and behaviours of their peers, often seeking acceptance and validation through conformity. This susceptibility can lead to risky behaviours, including aggression, as adolescents may engage in antisocial activities to gain approval or avoid rejection from their peers (Laursen & Veenstra, 2021).

Environmental Characteristics

Family relationships undergo significant transformations during adolescence. Parent-adolescent relationships become increasingly complex as adolescents seek more independence and challenge parental authority. Effective communication and parental monitoring are crucial for maintaining healthy relationships and reducing the risk of aggression. Adolescents who feel heard and understood by their parents are less likely to resort to aggression to express frustration or rebellion (Belsky, 2019; Feldman, 2016; Kerr et al., 2003).

Family communication patterns also play a role. Open and supportive communication can foster trust and understanding between parents and adolescents, reducing conflict and promoting healthy problem-solving skills. Conversely, poor communication, characterized by criticism, hostility, or lack of emotional support, can contribute to aggression (Belsky, 2019; Feldman, 2016).

Social characteristics outside the family also shape adolescent behaviour. Peer pressure can be a powerful force, leading adolescents to engage in risky behaviours, including aggression, to fit in with their peers. Social media platforms, while providing opportunities for connection and self-expression, can also amplify peer pressure and expose adolescents to cyberbullying and online aggression (Libisch et al., 2022).

Romantic relationships, another significant aspect of adolescent social life, can be a source of joy and conflict. Relationship problems, such as jealousy, infidelity, or breakups, can trigger intense emotions and lead to aggression in some adolescents (Giordano et al., 2010).

Risk Factors

Several risk factors increase the likelihood of aggression in adolescence. Substance use, particularly alcohol and drug abuse, can impair judgment and impulse control, leading to aggressive behaviour. Delinquency, involving antisocial behaviours such as theft, vandalism, or assault, is also strongly associated with aggression (Shahzad & Yasmin, 2015).

Exposure to violence, whether through direct victimization, witnessing violence in the community, or exposure to media violence, can desensitize adolescents to violence and make them more likely to resort to aggression themselves (Mrug et al., 2015).

Aspects of Development in Adolescence (Ages 13-19 Years Old)

Adolescence is a period of continued development across multiple domains. Biological, cognitive, social-emotional, and personality development interact in complex ways, shaping an adolescent's behaviour, identity, and relationships (Belsky, 2019; Feldman, 2016).

Biological Development

The adolescent brain undergoes significant changes, particularly in the prefrontal cortex, the area responsible for decision-making, impulse control, and emotional regulation. This ongoing development can contribute to risk-taking behaviours, including aggression, as adolescents may struggle to assess consequences and control impulses (Arain et al., 2013; Belsky, 2019).

Hormonal fluctuations associated with puberty can also influence mood and behaviour. Increased levels of testosterone, particularly in boys, have been linked to increased aggression. However, it is essential to note that hormones interact with environmental and social factors to shape behaviour (Laube et al., 2020).

Cognitive Development

According to Piaget's theory (1952), adolescence marks the attainment of formal operational thinking, the ability to engage in abstract reasoning, hypothetical thinking, and systematic problem-solving. This cognitive development allows adolescents to consider multiple perspectives, anticipate consequences, and engage in more sophisticated moral reasoning. However, this newfound cognitive ability can also justify aggressive behaviour, as adolescents may rationalize their actions or blame others for their problems.

Metacognition, the ability to think about one's thinking, also develops during adolescence. Adolescents become more aware of their cognitive processes, allowing them to monitor and evaluate their thoughts and behaviours. This awareness can be harnessed to promote self-regulation and reduce impulsive aggression (Weil et al., 2013)

Social-Emotional Development

Adolescence can be considered a stage of identity or role confusion. Adolescents grapple with questions of who they are, what they believe in, and where they are headed in life. This process involves exploring different identities, values, and beliefs and integrating them into a coherent sense of self (Erikson 1968, as cited in Knight, 2017).

Moreover, failure to resolve this identity crisis can lead to role confusion, characterized by a lack of direction, insecurity, and a susceptibility to negative peer influence. This can increase the risk of aggression as adolescents may engage in antisocial behaviour to gain a sense of belonging or identity (Knight, 2017).

Emotional autonomy, the ability to regulate emotions independently from parents, also develops during adolescence. Adolescents learn to manage their emotions, cope with stress, and make decisions based on their values and beliefs. This emotional independence can reduce the likelihood of aggressive outbursts triggered by parental conflict or disapproval (Xiao, 2023).

Finally, peer support plays a crucial role in adolescent development. Positive peer relationships can provide a sense of belonging, validation, and support, buffering against stress and promoting healthy emotional development. Conversely, negative peer influences can lead to risky behaviours, including aggression (Belsky, 2019; Feldman, 2016).

Personality

Adolescence is a time of identity consolidation, solidifying a sense of self and establishing a stable identity. This process involves integrating personal values, beliefs, and experiences into a coherent narrative about who they are and where they are going. Adolescents who successfully consolidate their identity tend to be more resilient, less susceptible to negative peer influence, and less likely to engage in aggressive behaviour (Marcia, 1980, as cited in Feldman, 2016).

Future orientation, the ability to plan and set goals for the future, also develops during adolescence. Adolescents begin to think about their future careers, relationships, and life goals. This focus on the future can motivate them to make positive choices and avoid behaviours that may jeopardize their prospects (Feldman, 2016).

CONCLUSION

In early childhood (2-5 years old), aggressive behaviour is often rooted in temperament, attachment style, emotional regulation difficulties, and exposure to negative family and social environments. Addressing aggression at this stage by fostering secure attachments, teaching emotional regulation skills, and providing positive parenting strategies to prevent aggressive patterns from solidifying is crucial.

As children progress into middle childhood (6-12 years old), their self-concept, peer relationships, and school experiences become central influences on aggressive behaviour. Promoting healthy self-esteem, facilitating positive peer interactions, and addressing academic difficulties are essential for preventing aggression from escalating during this phase. Additionally, supportive family environments and effective parental involvement are vital for buffering children against stressors and promoting prosocial behaviour.

Adolescence (13-19 years old) is a time of identity exploration, the quest for autonomy, and peer influence that significantly impacts aggressive behaviour. Encouraging open communication, fostering healthy parent-adolescent relationships, and providing guidance on navigating peer pressure are critical for preventing aggression. Understanding the adolescent brain's development and addressing risk factors like substance use and delinquency are also crucial.

Finally, addressing aggressive behaviour across all stages of psychosocial development is paramount for fostering healthy individuals and creating a harmonious society. By recognizing the unique challenges and vulnerabilities at each age, implementing tailored interventions, and promoting positive social-emotional development, we can equip children and adolescents with the skills and resilience needed to navigate conflicts peacefully and build fulfilling relationships. Early intervention and prevention efforts are vital to mitigating the long-term consequences of aggression and paving the way for a brighter future.

PREVENTION AND INTERVENTION PROGRAMS

By understanding the complex interaction of personal characteristics, environmental influences, and developmental processes, we can gain valuable insights into the factors contributing to aggression from early childhood through adolescence. By addressing these factors through early prevention and intervention programs, we can mitigate the risk of aggression, equipping children with the social-emotional skills needed to successfully navigate through all developmental stages, thereby reducing, if not eliminating, the risk.

Building Empathy

Empathy education focuses on helping children recognize and understand their own and others' feelings. Programs such as "Roots of Empathy" in early childhood use infant visits to teach young children emotional cues and empathy through observation and discussion. This helps develop emotional intelligence and promotes pro-social behaviour, reducing the likelihood of aggression (Nader, 2012).

In middle childhood, empathy education can be integrated into the school curriculum through role-playing activities, stories, and discussions about different perspectives. Programs such as "Making Caring Common" encourage students to practice empathy in real-life situations and consider the impact of their actions on others (Montero, 2022).

Conversely, adolescents can benefit from more sophisticated empathy education that addresses social issues and moral dilemmas. Community service or volunteering programs can help adolescents connect with others and develop a deeper understanding of different perspectives, enhancing empathy and reducing aggressive tendencies (Scott & Graham, 2015).

Building Emotional Regulation

Additionally, emotional regulation programs for children in early childhood focus on teaching them to recognize and label their emotions and providing coping strategies for managing difficult emotions such as anger and frustration. These programs often use games, stories, and playful activities to engage children and make learning fun (Thümmler et al. 2022)

For middle childhood children, emotional regulation programs often include cognitive-behavioural techniques, such as teaching children to identify triggers for their anger, identify calming thoughts, and practice relaxation techniques such as deep breathing or progressive muscle relaxation (Rohlf & Krahé, 2015).

Adolescents can benefit from programs that combine cognitive-behavioural techniques with mindfulness practices. These practices help them become more aware of their emotions and bodily sensations, allowing them to respond to stressors more mindfully and less reactively (Perry-Parrish et al., 2016).

Building Conflict Resolution

Moreover, teaching young children basic conflict resolution skills involves modelling appropriate behaviour, using simple language to explain how to share and take turns, and encouraging them to use words to express their feelings instead of resorting to physical aggression (see Chen 2003 for a review).

Conflict resolution programs for children in middle childhood, often involve more structured activities, such as role-playing different conflict scenarios and practicing active listening and compromise skills. These programs may also address issues like bullying and peer mediation (Levi-Keren et al., 2021).

For teenagers, conflict resolution programs may focus on communication skills, negotiation strategies, and understanding the underlying causes of conflict. These programs can also address issues like dating violence and gang-related conflict (Hettler & Johnston, 2009).

Building Resilience

Still, building resilience in young children involves creating a safe and supportive environment, fostering secure attachments, and providing opportunities for play and exploration. Parents and caregivers can also help young children develop coping skills by teaching them to label their emotions, identify sources of comfort, and practice relaxation techniques like deep breathing (see Lynch et al. 2004 for a discussion).

Resilience-building programs for middle-aged children often focus on developing a growth mindset, encouraging children to see challenges as opportunities for learning and growth. These programs may also teach problem-solving skills, stress management techniques, and coping strategies for dealing with adversity (see Lynch et al. 2004 for a discussion).

Conversely, adolescents can benefit from programs that focus on developing self-efficacy, the belief in one's ability to succeed. These programs may also teach coping skills for managing stress, anxiety, and depression, as well as strategies for building supportive relationships and seeking help when needed (see Lynch et al. 2004 for a discussion).

Building Teamwork and Collaboration

Furthermore, encouraging teamwork and collaboration in young children involves creating opportunities for cooperative play, such as building blocks together or playing group games. These activities help children learn to share, take turns, and work together towards a common goal (Ramani & Brownell, 2013).

Teamwork and cooperation in middle childhood can be promoted through teamwork, team sports, and other extracurricular activities. These experiences help children develop communication skills, learn to negotiate, and compromise, and build positive relationships with their peers (Kao, 2019).

Adolescents can benefit from programs encouraging them to participate in community projects, volunteer work, or other group activities involving working towards a shared goal. These experiences can foster a sense of belonging, purpose, and social responsibility, reducing the risk of aggression (Moorfoot et al., 2015).

In conclusion, by implementing these evidence-based prevention and intervention programs, it is possible to equip children and adolescents with the skills and resources they need to manage their emotions, peacefully resolve conflicts, and build positive relationships, ultimately reducing the frequency and impact of aggressive behaviour.

REFERENCES

Abtahi, M. M., & Kerns, K. A. (2017). Attachment and emotion regulation in middle childhood: Changes in affect and vagal tone during a social stress task. *Attachment & Human Development*, 19(3), 221–242. 10.1080/14616734.2017.129169628277093

Anderson, C. A., Shibuya, A., Ihori, N., Swing, E. L., Bushman, B. J., Sakamoto, A., Rothstein, H. R., & Saleem, M. (2010). Violent video game effects on aggression, empathy, and prosocial behavior in Eastern and Western countries: A meta-analytic review. *Psychological Bulletin*, 136(2), 151–173. 10.1037/a001825120192553

Arain, M., Haque, M., Johal, L., Mathur, P., Nel, W., Rais, A., Sandhu, R., & Sharma, S. (2013). Maturation of the adolescent brain. *Neuropsychiatric Disease and Treatment*, 449, 449. 10.2147/NDT.S3977623579318

Badger, J. R., Zaneva, M., Hastings, R. P., Broome, M. R., Hayes, R., Patterson, P., Rose, N., Clarkson, S., Hutchings, J., & Bowes, L. (2023). Associations between School-Level Disadvantage, Bullying Involvement and Children's Mental Health. *Children (Basel, Switzerland)*, 10(12), 1852. 10.3390/children1012185238136054

Bandura, A., Ross, D., & Ross, S. A. (1961). Transmission of aggression through imitation of aggressive models. *Journal of Abnormal and Social Psychology*, 63(3), 575–582. 10.1037/h004592513864605

Baumrind, D. (1991). The influence of parenting style on adolescent competence and substance use. *The Journal of Early Adolescence*, 11(1), 56–95. 10.1177/0272431691111004

Belsky, J. (2019). *Experiencing the Lifespan* (5th ed.). Worth.

Bierman, K. L., Coie, J., Dodge, K., Greenberg, M., Lochman, J., McMohan, R., & Pinderhughes, E. (2013). School Outcomes of Aggressive-Disruptive Children: Prediction from Kindergarten risk factors and impact of the Fast Track Prevention Program. *Aggressive Behavior*, 39(2), 114–130. 10.1002/ab.2146723386568

Bundick, M. J. (2011). Extracurricular activities, positive youth development, and the role of meaningfulness of engagement. *The Journal of Positive Psychology*, 6(1), 57–74. 10.1080/17439760.2010.536775

Cassidy, J., Jones, J. D., & Shaver, P. R. (2013). Contributions of attachment theory and research: A framework for future research, translation, and policy. *Development and Psychopathology*, 25(4pt2), 1415–1434. 10.1017/S095457941300069224342848

Chen, D. W. (2003). Preventing Violence by Promoting the Development of Competent Conflict Resolution Skills: Exploring Roles and Responsibilities. *Early Childhood Education Journal*, 30(4), 203–208. 10.1023/A:1023379306124

Coffman, J. L., Grammer, J. K., Hudson, K. N., Thomas, T. E., Villwock, D., & Ornstein, P. A. (2018). Relating children's early elementary classroom experiences to later skilled remembering and study skills. *Journal of Cognition and Development*, 20(2), 203–221. 10.1080/15248372.2018.147097631372098

De Castro, B. O. (2004). The development of social information processing and aggressive behaviour: Current issues. *European Journal of Developmental Psychology*, 1(1), 87–102. 10.1080/17405620444000058

Del Giudice, M. (2014). Middle Childhood: An Evolutionary-Developmental Synthesis. *Child Development Perspectives*, 8(4), 193–200. 10.1111/cdep.12084

Donnellan, M. B., Trzesniewski, K. H., Robins, R. W., Moffitt, T. E., & Caspi, A. (2005). Low Self-Esteem is related to aggression, antisocial behavior, and delinquency. *Psychological Science*, 16(4), 328–335. 10.1111/j.0956-7976.2005.01535.x15828981

Eisenberg, N., Eggum, N. D., & Di Giunta, L. (2010). Empathy-Related Responding: Associations with Prosocial Behavior, Aggression, and Intergroup Relations. *Social Issues and Policy Review*, 4(1), 143–180. 10.1111/j.1751-2409.2010.01020.x21221410

Ettekal, I., & Ladd, G. W. (2014). Developmental pathways from childhood Aggression–Disruptiveness, chronic peer rejection, and deviant friendships to Early-Adolescent rule breaking. *Child Development*, 86(2), 614–631. 10.1111/cdev.1232125403544

Feldman, R. (2016). *Development Across the Life Span* (8th ed.).

Gazelle, H., & Druhen, M. J. (2009). Anxious solitude and peer exclusion predict social helplessness, upset affect, and vagal regulation in response to behavioral rejection by a friend. *Developmental Psychology*, 45(4), 1077–1096. 10.1037/a001616519586181

Gentile, D. A., & Bushman, B. J. (2012). Reassessing media violence effects using a risk and resilience approach to understanding aggression. *Psychology of Popular Media Culture*, 1(3), 138–151. 10.1037/a0028481

Giordano, P. C., Soto, D. A., Manning, W. D., & Longmore, M. A. (2010). The characteristics of romantic relationships associated with teen dating violence. *Social Science Research*, 39(6), 863–874. 10.1016/j.ssresearch.2010.03.00921037934

Graziano, P. A., Reavis, R. D., Keane, S. P., & Calkins, S. D. (2007). The role of emotion regulation in children's early academic success. *Journal of School Psychology*, 45(1), 3–19. 10.1016/j.jsp.2006.09.00221179384

Hettler, S., & Johnston, L. M. (2009). Living peace: An exploration of experiential peace education, conflict resolution and violence prevention programs for youth. *Journal of Peace Education*, 6(1), 101–118. 10.1080/17400200802658340

Hiemstra, W., De Castro, B. O., & Thomaes, S. (2018). Reducing Aggressive Children's Hostile Attributions: A Cognitive Bias Modification procedure. *Cognitive Therapy and Research*, 43(2), 387–398. 10.1007/s10608-018-9958-x

Hu, Y., Cai, Y., Wang, R., Gan, Y., & He, N. (2023). The relationship between self-esteem and aggressive behavior among Chinese adolescents: A moderated chain mediation model. *Frontiers in Psychology*, 14, 1191134. 10.3389/fpsyg.2023.119113437377697

Jankowski, T., Bak, W., & Miciuk, Ł. (2021). Adaptive self-concept: Identifying the basic dimensions of self-beliefs. *Self and Identity*, 21(7), 739–774. 10.1080/15298868.2021.1997796

Juvonen, J., & Graham, S. (2014). Bullying in schools: The power of bullies and the plight of victims. *Annual Review of Psychology*, 65(1), 159–185. 10.1146/annurev-psych-010213-11503023937767

Kao, C. (2019). Development of Team Cohesion and Sustained Collaboration Skills with the Sport Education Model. *Sustainability (Basel)*, 11(8), 2348. 10.3390/su11082348

Kerr, M., Stattin, H., Biesecker, G., & Ferrer-Wreder, L. (2003). Handbook of Psychology: Vol. 395–419. *Relationships with parents and peers in adolescence.*, 10.1002/0471264385.wei0616

Knight, Z. G. (2017). A proposed model of psychodynamic psychotherapy linked to Erik Erikson's eight stages of psychosocial development. *Clinical Psychology & Psychotherapy*. *Clinical Psychology & Psychotherapy*, 24(5), 1047–1058. 10.1002/cpp.206628124459

Kotelnikova, Y., Olino, T. M., Mackrell, S. V., Jordan, P. L., & Hayden, E. P. (2013). Structure of observed temperament in middle childhood. *Journal of Research in Personality*, 47(5), 524–532. 10.1016/j.jrp.2013.04.01324293740

Krahé, B., & Busching, R. (2014). Interplay of normative beliefs and behavior in developmental patterns of physical and relational aggression in adolescence: A four-wave longitudinal study. *Frontiers in Psychology*, 5. 10.3389/fpsyg.2014.0114625360124

Labella, M. H., & Masten, A. S. (2018). Family influences on the development of aggression and violence. *Current Opinion in Psychology*, 19, 11–16. 10.1016/j. copsyc.2017.03.02829279207

Lanjekar, P. D., Joshi, S. H., Lanjekar, P. D., & Wagh, V. (2022). The Effect of Parenting and the Parent-Child Relationship on a Child's Cognitive Development: A literature review. *Cureus*. 10.7759/cureus.3057436420245

Laube, C., Lorenz, R., & Van Den Bos, W. (2020). Pubertal testosterone correlates with adolescent impatience and dorsal striatal activity. *Developmental Cognitive Neuroscience*, 42, 100749. 10.1016/j.dcn.2019.10074931942858

Laursen, B., & Veenstra, R. (2021). Toward understanding the functions of peer influence: A summary and synthesis of recent empirical research. *Journal of Research on Adolescence*, 31(4), 889–907. 10.1111/jora.1260634820944

Levi-Keren, M., Godeano-Barr, S., & Levinas, S. (2021). Mind the conflict: Empathy when coping with conflicts in the education sphere. *Cogent Education*, 9(1), 2013395. Advance online publication. 10.1080/2331186X.2021.2013395

Libisch, C. A., Marsiglia, F., Kulis, S., Cutrín, O., Gómez-Fraguela, J. A., & Ruiz, P. (2022). *The role of peer pressure in adolescents' risky behaviors*. Springer. 10.1007/978-3-031-06908-6_8

Liu, J. (2011). Early health risk factors for violence: Conceptualization, evidence, and implications. *Aggression and Violent Behavior*, 16(1), 63–73. 10.1016/j. avb.2010.12.00321399727

Lynch, K. B., Geller, S. R., & Schmidt, M. G. (2004). Multi-Year Evaluation of the Effectiveness of a Resilience-Based Prevention Program for Young Children. *The Journal of Primary Prevention*, 24(3), 335–353. 10.1023/B:JOPP.0000018052.12488.d1

Lynn Mulvey, K., Boswell, C., & Zheng, J. (2017). Causes and Consequences of Social Exclusion and Peer Rejection Among Children and Adolescents. *PubMed, 17*(3), 30100820. https://pubmed.ncbi.nlm.nih.gov/30100820/

Malik, F., & Marwaha, R. (2022, September 18). *Developmental stages of social emotional development in children*. StatPearls - NCBI Bookshelf. https://www.ncbi .nlm.nih.gov/books/nbk534819/

Masarik, A. S., & Conger, R. D. (2017). Stress and child development: A review of the Family Stress Model. *Current Opinion in Psychology*, 13, 85–90. 10.1016/j. copsyc.2016.05.00828813301

Mitchell, L. L., Lodi-Smith, J., Baranski, E. N., & Whitbourne, S. K. (2021). Implications of identity resolution in emerging adulthood for intimacy, generativity, and integrity across the adult lifespan. *Psychology and Aging*, 36(5), 545–556. 10.1037/pag000053734197138

Montero, J. (2022). Developing empathy through design thinking in elementary art education. *The International Journal of Art & Design Education. International Journal of Art & Design Education*, 42(1), 155–171. 10.1111/jade.12445

Moorfoot, N., Leung, R. K., Toumbourou, J. W., & Catalano, R. F. (2015). The longitudinal effects of adolescent volunteering on secondary school completion and adult volunteering. *International Journal of Developmental Science*, 9(3,4), 115–123. 10.3233/DEV-14014827458548

Mrug, S., Madan, A., & Windle, M. (2015). Emotional desensitization to violence contributes to adolescents' violent behavior. *Journal of Abnormal Child Psychology*, 44(1), 75–86. 10.1007/s10802-015-9986-x25684447

Muris, P., & Ollendick, T. H. (2005). The role of Temperament in the etiology of Child Psychopathology. *Clinical Child and Family Psychology Review*, 8(4), 271–289. 10.1007/s10567-005-8809-y16362256

Murray-Close, D., Ostrov, J. M., Nelson, D. A., Crick, N. R., & Coccaro, E. F. (2010). Proactive, reactive, and romantic relational aggression in adulthood: Measurement, predictive validity, gender differences, and association with Intermittent Explosive Disorder. *Journal of Psychiatric Research*, 44(6), 393–404. 10.1016/j.jpsychires.2009.09.00519822329

Nader, K. (2012). School shootings and other youth problems: The need for early preventive interventions. In K. Nader (Ed.), *School rampage shootings and other youth disturbances: Early preventative interventions* (pp. 3–32). Routledge/Taylor & Francis Group.

Perry-Parrish, C., Copeland-Linder, N., Webb, L., Shields, A. H., & Sibinga, E. M. (2016). Improving self-regulation in adolescents: Current evidence for the role of mindfulness-based cognitive therapy. *Adolescent Health, Medicine and Therapeutics*, 7, 101–108. 10.2147/AHMT.S6582027695378

Piaget, J. (1952). *The origins of intelligence in children*. W W Norton & Co., 10.1037/11494-000

Raburu, P. A. (2015). The Self- Who Am I?: Children's Identity and Development through Early Childhood Education. *Journal of Educational and Social Research*. 10.5901/jesr.2015.v5n1p95

Ramani, G. B., & Brownell, C. A. (2014). Preschoolers' cooperative problem solving: Integrating play and problem solving. *Journal of Early Childhood Research*, 12(1), 92–108. 10.1177/1476718X13498337

Rohlf, H. L., & Krahé, B. (2015). Assessing anger regulation in middle childhood: Development and validation of a behavioral observation measure. *Frontiers in Psychology*, 6. 10.3389/fpsyg.2015.0045325964767

Rothbart, M. K., & Bates, J. E. (2007). Temperament. In Eisenberg, N., Damon, W., & Lerner, R. M. (Eds.), *Social, emotional, and personality development* (6th ed., pp. 99–166). Handbook of child psychology. John Wiley & Sons, Inc.

Rubin, K. H., Coplan, R. J., & Bowker, J. C. (2009). Social withdrawal in childhood. *Annual Review of Psychology*, 60(1), 141–171. 10.1146/annurev.psych.60.110707.16364218851686

Scott, K. E., & Graham, J. A. (2015). Service-Learning. *Journal of Experiential Education*, 38(4), 354–372. 10.1177/1053825915592889

Shahzad, S., & Yasmin, S. (2015). Aggression as risk for delinquency and substance abuse in adolescents. *International Journal of Prevention and Treatment*, 1(3–4), 106. 10.4038/ijptsud.v1i3-4.7842

Smith, J. D., Dishion, T. J., Shaw, D. S., Wilson, M. N., Winter, C. C., & Patterson, G. R. (2014). Coercive family process and early-onset conduct problems from age 2 to school entry. *Development and Psychopathology*, 26(4pt1), 917–932. 10.1017/S0954579414000016924690305

Smith, S. S. (2013). The influence of stress at puberty on mood and learning: Role of the $\alpha_4\beta\delta$ GABA$_A$ receptor. *Neuroscience*, 249, 192–213. 10.1016/j.neuroscience.2012.09.06523079628

Song, J., Volling, B. L., Lane, J. D., & Wellman, H. M. (2016). Aggression, Sibling Antagonism, and Theory of Mind during the first Year of Siblinghood: A Developmental cascade model. *Child Development*, 87(4), 1250–1263. 10.1111/cdev.1253027096923

Tarsha, M. S., & Narvaez, D. (2019). Early life experience and aggression. *Peace Review*, 31(1), 14–23. 10.1080/10402659.2019.1613591

Thümmler, R., Engel, E.-M., & Bartz, J. (2022). Strengthening Emotional Development and Emotion Regulation in Childhood—As a Key Task in Early Childhood Education. *International Journal of Environmental Research and Public Health*, 19(7), 3978. 10.3390/ijerph1907397835409661

Tuvblad, C., & Beaver, K. M. (2013). Genetic and environmental influences on antisocial behavior. *Journal of Criminal Justice*, 41(5), 273–276. 10.1016/j.jcrimjus.2013.07.00724526799

Weil, L. G., Fleming, S. M., Dumontheil, I., Kilford, E. J., Weil, R. S., Rees, G., Dolan, R. J., & Blakemore, S. (2013). The development of metacognitive ability in adolescence. *Consciousness and Cognition*, 22(1), 264–271. 10.1016/j.concog.2013.01.00423376348

Welker, K. M., Norman, R. E., Goetz, S., Moreau, B. J., Kitayama, S., & Carré, J. M. (2017). Preliminary evidence that testosterone's association with aggression depends on self-construal. *Hormones and Behavior*, 92, 117–127. 10.1016/j.yhbeh.2016.10.01427816624

Xiao, S. (2023). Development of Emotional Autonomy of Adolescents in the Context of Family Relations and Academic Performance in Middle School. *Polish Psychological Bulletin*, 54(1), 58–64. 10.24425/ppb.2023.144884

Zhang, Y., & Qin, P. (2023). Comprehensive Review: Understanding Adolescent Identity. *Studies in Psychological Science*, 1(2), 17–31. 10.56397/SPS.2023.09.02

Zilanawala, A., & Pilkauskas, N. V. (2012). Material hardship and child socioemotional behaviors: Differences by types of hardship, timing, and duration. *Children and Youth Services Review*, 34(4), 814–825. 10.1016/j.childyouth.2012.01.00822408284

Chapter 8
Neurocognitive Profile in Autism Spectrum Disorder and Implementation of New Goals in Different Settings

Dimitra V. Katsarou
https://orcid.org/0000-0001-8690-0314
University of the Aegean, Greece

ABSTRACT

Autism is a neurobehavioral syndrome that significantly affects a person's social interaction, communication, and imagination. The term 'ASD' (autism spectrum disorders) refers to a group of neurodevelopmental disorders and is used to encompass and merge certain diagnoses. Disorders within this spectrum can be characterized as a continuum of ability levels that extends from mental retardation to intellectual intelligence. Moreover, they manifest themselves early in a person's life and profoundly affect the perception of oneself and the world, learning and adaptation to the demands of everyday life. This chapter aims to understand the nature of neurocognitive deficits in ASD with an emphasis on how this can influence the formulation of treatment goals at an educational and clinical level. It focuses on the definition of ASD and their description presenting the neurocognitive deficits and their behavioral manifestation, as well as the resulting goals.

DOI: 10.4018/979-8-3693-4022-6.ch008

INTRODUCTION

Autism Spectrum Disorders (ASD) is a neurodevelopmental syndrome of genetic or epigenetic origin with unclear etiology and diverse behavioral manifestations. It presents with deficits in communication, social interaction and imagination, with frequent occurrence of repetitive behaviors. It is a syndrome with coexisting subtypes and varying degrees of severity ranging between mental retardation and high intelligence (Chia, 2012; Karr et al., 2018). According to Treffert (2009) the autistic savant, which he calls the savant syndrome, is a rare condition where people with severe intellectual disorders, such as autistic disorder, have some islands of intelligence (eg lightning calculation, design, etc) that are in contrast to the deficits they present. The objectives of this chapter are, in a first stage, to present the neurocognitive deficits of individuals with ASD and to link them to specific behavioral manifestations. Then, after the presentation of these deficits and the recording of the behavior resulting from them, to emerge proposed goals related to these weaknesses of children that can be utilized in a clinical and educational context (Glahn et al., 2014).

Beginning the listing of neurocognitive deficits, a first deficit experienced by children with ASD concerns weak central coherence. According to the Weak Central Coherence theoretical model, individuals with ASD show a weakness in processing an overall task and instead focus on its details (Barkley, 2003; Braaten et al., 2020; Happe & Vital, 2009). This tendency of children, according to Happe and Vital (2009), to focus on individual projects, due to a cognitive inability to see them globally, is also the characteristic that leads these children to the development of specific talents. As a result of the above deficit, children seek uniformity and display repetitive and limited behaviors, avoiding engaging in more general projects (Burton et al., 2019; Happe & Vital, 2009). They show difficulties in generalizing their knowledge and also in connecting rules of behavior to the respective context.

Continuing, a second neurocognitive deficit of children with ASD is, according to the theory of mind, their inability at a social level to understand the way of thinking and feelings of others (Crooke et al., 2016; Happe & Vital, 2009). Due to the reduced social influence and also the reduced concern they have for others this deficit, as well as the weak central coherence, leads to the emergence of special talents for people with ASD (Buti et al., 2011; Happe & Vital, 2009). According to Bishop (1993) this deficit is linked to the dysfunction of the frontal lobe and in particular the prefrontal cortex and its connections with the limbic system while according to Ozonoff et al. (1991) and Crooke et al. (2016) the specific deficits are linked to the dysfunction of executive functions. As a consequence of these deficits at the behavioral level, difficulties in communication and social interaction are due to reduced social mental representations, but also the appearance of a stereotypical behavior due to their inability to guide it (Brookman-Frazee et al., 2018; Joseph & Tager-Flusberg, 2004).

In addition, deficits shown by children with ASD are related to difficulties in executive cognitive functions (Kaur, & Pany, 2020). According to Corbett et al. (2009) the term executive functions is broad and refers to neuropsychological processes that include cognitive, physical and emotional control of ourselves (Corbett et al., 2009). Based on the executive cognitive dysfunction approach, the deficits that appear in the frontal lobe of children with ASD (Carter Leno et al., 2018; Happe, 1999) lead to weaknesses in cognitive flexibility, organization and planning projects (Hill, 2004) but also increased working memory skills (Happe & Vital, 2009). More specifically, when talking about cognitive flexibility we mean the ability to switch their thinking in different projects while planning is related to the ability to organize their behavior in a context to achieve a goal (Chevrier, & Schachar, 2020). A consequence of the deficits in the above executive functions is the appearance of a repetitive behavior and the absence of connection of thoughts and actions in relation to the conditions and the context of a project which are attributed to the autism spectrum regardless of the IQ level of the children (Chang et al., 2020; Pooragha et al., 2013). People with ASD have difficulty switching from one task to another (cognitive flexibility), organizing their actions, and planning strategies that help them perform various tasks (Lam, 2013; Ozonoff et al., 2004). According to Kenworthy et al (2010), the deficits associated with organizational and planning strategies make the context of social learning and their interaction difficult (Cho & Ahn, 2016). Cognitive flexibility and planning are also associated with processes of monitoring, evaluating and informing action, therefore difficulties in these functions affect children's attention in terms of maintaining or shifting it (Antshel & Russo, 2019; Craig et al., 2015; Salimpoor & Desrocher, 2006).

Regarding working memory in people with ASD, many researchers identify possibilities but also difficulties. By working memory we mean the non-conscious preservation of useful information during the processing and completion of a cognitive task (Psoma & Vlachos, 2018). The different performances of children in working memory tasks are related to the form of the stimulus and its connection with different mechanisms (verbal or visuospatial) (Williams et al., 2005). However, other approaches question the connection of working memory deficits with the stimulus and state that the difficulties are encountered in situations that require the representation of information, the holistic approach of the task, its planning and organization (Happe & Frith, 2006). According to Steele et al (2007) deficits appear in complex and demanding projects. Working memory is linked to executive functions at the level of neurons and specifically due to prefrontal dysfunction (Barendse et al., 2013) As a result of deficits in working memory, linked to executive functions, is the inability to solve problems as they have difficulty retaining information (Meyer & Minshew, 2002; Williams et al., 2005).

An additional deficit of individuals with ASD related to executive functions is inhibitory control. Inhibitory control is related to a person's ability to block out stimuli unrelated to the task to be performed and pay attention only to that information that is important to him, interacting satisfactorily with the environment (Chevrier & Schachar, 2020; Salimpoor & Desrocher, 2006; Wheelright et al., 2006). Findings regarding deficits in inhibitory control in children with ASD are equivocal. According to Christ et al (2007), this is due to different cognitive processes (stimulus selection, reaction selection, reaction execution), some of which are underfunctioning. Such executive deficits in inhibitory control are associated with difficulties in controlling reactions (inability to inhibit inappropriate behaviors and actions) and difficulty in self-control (Kenworthy et al., 2010).

The executive deficits observed in people with ASD are characteristic of the symptoms of autism spectrum disorder and are observed throughout childhood, without affecting the IQ or the level of verbal ability of the individuals (Robinson et al., 2009). The varied findings resulting from the research are due to the diversity of the population, co-morbidity with other disorders, the focus on different cognitive processes and the different assessment tools used (Geurts et al., 2004).

The cognitive deficits of people with ASD are also linked to the Enhanced Perceptual Function approach. According to Mottron et al (2006) individuals with autism unlike typically developing individuals can have competent access to lower level processes that are difficult to perceive for processing. This may be due to either an increased function of brain regions associated with basic perceptual functions or a hypofunction of cognitive mechanisms associated with high-level cognitive processes (Joshi et al., 2017). Perception plays a different role in autistic cognition and it is difficult to explain why most of the cognitive functions performed by individuals with autism differ from those of typically developing individuals (Albajara Sáenz et al., 2020; Mottron et al., 2006). However, this increased perceptual ability derived from the hyperfunction of brain regions may be related to the development of special abilities (savant syndrome) for individuals with autism and also explain their perceptual endophenotype (Bauman & Kemper, 2005; Boedhoe et al., 2020; Mottron et al., 2006). At the behavioral level, individuals with autism show limited and specific interests associated with those projects that have the possibility of practice (special talents/savant syndrome) (Albaugh et al., 2017; Bolte & Poustka, 2004; Mottron, Dawson, & Soulieres, 2009). That is, they show obsession and intense interest in specific skills, e.g. mathematics, avoiding engagement with more general projects.

Neurocognitive deficits experienced by individuals with ASD include a lack of empathy and a tendency to systematize (Baron-Cohen, 2002; Cascia & Barr, 2020; Lawson et al., 2004; Wakabayashi et al., 2006). More specifically, the inability to empathize is linked to the difficulties of people with ASD to perceive the thoughts and feelings of other people (theory of mind) but also the inability to develop feelings and react in an appropriate way to the emotional states of other people so that to achieve social interaction between them (Baron-Cohen, 2002; Liss et al., 2001). On the other hand, there is a strong tendency towards systematization, i.e. an emphasis on the analysis, prediction and control of systems based on specific rules (Baron-Cohen, 2002; Megari et al., 2024). People with autism treat each task as a system in which they seek to identify the elements that repeat within it (Minshew & Goldstein, 2001; Mottron et al., 2009). As a result of the above theory at the behavioral level is the obsessive engagement with specific projects/stereotypes, focusing their attention on the details of a project but also the display of special abilities and interests (Chia, 2012). They seek uniformity/routine and have difficulty in social interaction due to a lack of empathy (Hill & Frith, 2003).

Taking into account the deficits in weak central cohesion, the following objectives arise:

- Strengthen their weak central coherence with attention games and sequencing activities.
- Connecting their stereotyped behavior and obsession with some objects with a multitude of activities, eg the obsession with coins to be utilized in mathematics. Expanding the obsession, not eliminating it.
- Use of visual aids and images linked to their interests where they will gradually expand to other broader activities.
- Inclusion in the daily schedule of activities related to their areas of special interest (SIE) to avoid stress and emotional breakdowns (Heward, 2011).

Based on deficits in theory of mind, the following goals are proposed:

- The creation of activities (eg role plays) to develop social interaction skills. Guided activities with feedback with the ultimate goal of maintaining and generalizing the skills children learn (Heward, 2011)
- The development of structured social interaction activities, at an initial stage, one to one (therapist/teacher - child) and then more natural interaction within regular classrooms with other children (Sandbank et al., 2020)
- Creating activities to develop imitation skills through play that will help relationships with others (Heward, 2011)

- The systematic use of social stories with pictures in the classroom with the aim of improving and managing their behavior (eg aggression) but also connecting a behavior with the result (eg if I hit someone they will cry)
- The presentation of activities in a planned manner. Creating opportunities to develop new skills in different contexts with different materials and different people according to applied behavior analysis (EA) (Heward, 2011)
- Positive reinforcement for creating social relationships, recording desired behaviors and rewards in cases of good behavior (eg stickers, treats)
- The implementation of Cognitive Behavioral Therapy / CBT programs, Peers method. With training in psychology, the application of cognitive strategies, with behavioral exercises, feedback on their performance, the extension of work and at home with the participation of parents will lead to the improvement of their social skills and interaction (Laugeson & Park, 2014). They will learn to control their behavior, to manage situations such as angry outbursts, they will improve their self-esteem (Alderson et al., 2008).

Taking into account the deficits in executive functions, the following objectives result:

- Creation of activities based on the TEACCH program (Treatment and Education of Autistic and related Communication-Handicapped Children). Implementation of activities in a structured environment with planned work routines and use of visual images. The TEACCH program presents what activity the student has to complete, how much work is to be completed, how the work is completed, and what will happen after it is completed. TEACCH systems classrooms have minimal distractions, specific activities, and extensive use of visual schedules and assist student self-monitoring and self-management (Sandbank et al., 2020).
- Apply activities in a playful way and of increasing difficulty related to organizational and planning skills. The activities have a functional use and relate to real life (eg how to choose the ingredients for a sandwich, find the way out of a maze by overcoming the obstacles that appear, choose from a suitcase the clothes they need for their vacation summer, based on instructions to locate a route on a map, etc. (Escolano-Pérez et al., 2019).
- Creating social stories both for controlling their reactions and changing those behaviors that are problematic (eg angry outbursts) and for transitioning from one task to another (cognitive flexibility) (Richman, 2001)
- Develop simple activities and avoid complex and difficult tasks that strain working memory. Transition from simple to more complex depending on the children's level of understanding (Anderson et al., 1996).

- Creating a structured, predictable and stable environment in which the child will feel safe. Avoiding sudden changes in the environment that can cause anxiety and strong reactions (Katsarou et al., 2023).
- The implementation of Cognitive Behavioral Therapy / CBT programs, with the Peers method. Tasks using computers that will lead to improved performance regarding processing speed on executive functions (Siffredi et al., 2021), increasing their confidence and self-esteem.

Based on the Enhanced Perceptual Functional approach, we have the following goals:

- Utilizing the child's strengths in order to teach new skills. Creating new activities based on their interests is a stressful process for children with autism.
- Creating activities through organized play in which children develop special talents. The combination of activities with music, especially for children who show more verbal communication problems can be very beneficial for their psychology.
- Using pictures and visual support for activities in the classroom to enhance their independence and improve their special abilities.

In the context of the deficits of empathy and the tendency to systematize (choose closed systems) the following goals arise:

- The creation of appropriate social-emotional activities so that through organized play the child can perceive the emotions of others (eg anger) and connect these emotions with various social situations (eg I am angry because my toy was taken away)
- Creating activities (eg role plays) to manage social situations in an appropriate and socially acceptable way (eg I don't squeal when I'm anxious and want something but I ask for it with speech).
- The use of social stories and visual images that connect emotion with behavior and the best way to manage it.
- Use of play (play-therapy) in order for the child to explore his emotional world and understand what he is experiencing. Through the game he will express his feelings in a natural way which many times he cannot express verbally. Play therapy works as a psychological therapy for all children and especially for people with ASD.
- Building a stable environment in which the child will feel self-esteem and self-confidence so that he can learn to express his feelings and manage them in the best way.

- The inclusion of the computer and multimedia (image / sound) in the children's education program due to their tendency to systematize. Self-directed children are asked using pictures or words from a notebook to perform activities as they are presented in sequence on the computer. Practice a variety of skills (functional, communicative, social, cognitive) (Stromer et al., 2006)
- Positive reinforcement for personal engagement with the computer and multimedia that promotes student independence and self-direction in learning and creating an engaging environment free of distracting information.

CONCLUSION

In conclusion, we see that individuals with ASD show deficits linked to the domains of communication, social interaction and imagination in the presence of many stereotypical patterns. These are neurocognitive deficits due to weak central coherence, in theory of mind, deficits in executive functions, cognitive deficits associated with increased perceptual function, empathic deficits and a tendency towards closed systems avoiding wider social situations (Demetriou et al., 2018). The above difficulties faced by these individuals lead to specific behaviors which present a range depending on the severity of the symptoms and the general cognitive ability of the individual.

Based on the above deficits, a distinct cognitive endophenotype of individuals with ASD is presented, showing the particular way in which they receive and process environmental stimuli. These characteristics are reflected in specific behavioral ways such as the search for uniformity, stereotypical behaviors and constant repetitions, difficulties in the social field to control their reactions, the development of special talents, etc (Finkel & Pedersen 2014; Ghirardi et al., 2019).

In conclusion, in the context of the above deficits, goals emerge that can be exploited at an educational and clinical level. Positive reinforcement and the formation of a stable and structured environment in which sudden changes are avoided are considered important so that the child can relieve his anxiety. In an educational context, interventions using various methods (eg TEACCH program, social stories, etc.) depending on the deficits and cognitive needs presented by people with ASD can contribute to improving their performance.

REFERENCES

Albajara Sáenz, A., Septier, M., Van Schuerbeek, P., Baijot, S., Deconinck, N., Defresne, P., Delvenne, V., Passeri, G., Raeymaekers, H., Salvesen, L., Victoor, L., Villemonteix, T., Willaye, E., Peigneux, P., & Massat, I. (2020). ADHD and ASD: Distinct brain patterns of inhibition-related activation? *Translational Psychiatry*, 10(1), 24. 10.1038/s41398-020-0707-z32066671

Albaugh, M. D., Orr, C., Chaarani, B., Althoff, R. R., Allgaier, N., D'Alberto, N., Hudson, K., Mackey, S., Spechler, P. A., Banaschewski, T., Brühl, R., Bokde, A. L. W., Bromberg, U., Büchel, C., Cattrell, A., Conrod, P. J., Desrivières, S., Flor, H., Frouin, V., & Potter, A. S. (2017). Inattention and Reaction Time Variability Are Linked to Ventromedial Prefrontal Volume in Adolescents. *Biological Psychiatry*, 82(9), 660–668. 10.1016/j.biopsych.2017.01.00328237458

Alderson, R. M., Rapport, M. D., Sarver, D. E., & Kofler, M. J. (2008). ADHD and behavioral inhibition: A re-examination of the stop-signal task. *Journal of Abnormal Child Psychology*, 36(7), 989–998. 10.1007/s10802-008-9230-z18461439

American Psychiatry Association. (2013). Diagnostic and Statistical Manual of Mental Disorders, (5th Edition). DSM-V, Washington: DC.

Anderson, S., Taras, M., & Cannon, B. (1996). Teaching new skills to young children with autism. In C. Maurice, G. Green, S. Luce (Eds), *Behavioral intervention for young children with autism: A manual for parents and professionals* (pp. 181-194) Austin, TX: pro-ed publications.

Antshel, K. M., & Russo, N. (2019). Autism Spectrum Disorders and ADHD: Overlapping Phenomenology, Diagnostic Issues, and Treatment Considerations. *Current Psychiatry Reports*, 21(5), 34. 10.1007/s11920-019-1020-530903299

Barends, E. M., Hendriks, M. P. H., Jansen, J., Backers, W., & Hofman, P. (2013). Working memory deficits in high functioning adolescents with autism spectrum disorders: Neuropsychological and neuroimaging correlates. *Journal of Neurodevelopmental Disorders*, 14(1), 1–11. 10.1186/1866-1955-5-14

Barkley, R. A. (2003). Attention-Deficit / Hyperactivity Disorder. In Mash, E. J., & Barkley, R. A. (Eds.), *Child Psychopathology* (2nd ed., pp. 75–143). The Guilford Press.

Baron-Cohen, S. (2002). The extreme male brain theory of autism. *Trends in Cognitive Sciences*, 6(6), 248–254. 10.1016/S1364-6613(02)01904-612039606

Baron-Cohen, S. (2006). The hyper-systemizing, assortative mating theory of autism. *Progress in Neuro-Psychopharmacology & Biological Psychiatry*, 30(5), 865–872. 10.1016/j.pnpbp.2006.01.01016519981

Bauman, M. L., & Kemper, T. L. (Eds.). (2005). *The neurobiology of autism* (2nd ed.). Johns Hopkins University Press.

Bishop, D. (1993). Annotation: Autism, Executive Functions and Theory of Mind: A Neuropsychological Perspective. *Journal of Child Psychology and Psychiatry, and Allied Disciplines*, 34(3), 279–293. 10.1111/j.1469-7610.1993.tb00992.x8463368

Boedhoe, P. S. W., van Rooij, D., Hoogman, M., Twisk, J. W. R., Schmaal, L., Abe, Y., Alonso, P., Ameis, S. H., Anikin, A., Anticevic, A., Arango, C., Arnold, P. D., Asherson, P., Assogna, F., Auzias, G., Banaschewski, T., Baranov, A., Batistuzzo, M. C., Baumeister, S., & van den Heuvel, O. A. (2020). Subcortical brain volume, regional cortical thickness, and cortical surface area across disorders: Findings from the ENIGMA ADHD, ASD, and OCD working groups. *The American Journal of Psychiatry*, 177(9), 834–843. 10.1176/appi.ajp.2020.19030331132539527

Bolte, S., & Poustka, F. (2004). Comparing the Intelligence Profiles of Savant and Nonsavant Individuals with Autistic Disorder. *Intelligence*, 32(2), 121–131. 10.1016/j.intell.2003.11.002

Braaten, E. B., Ward, A. K., Forchelli, G., Vuijk, P. J., Cook, N. E., McGuinness, P., Lee, B. A., Samkavitz, A., Lind, H., O'Keefe, S. M., & Doyle, A. E. (2020). Characteristics of child psychiatric outpatients with slow processing speed and potential mechanisms of academic impact. *European Child & Adolescent Psychiatry*, 29(10), 1453–1464. 10.1007/s00787-019-01455-w31980930

Brookman-Frazee, L., Stadnick, N., Chlebowski, C., Baker-Ericzén, M., & Ganger, W. (2018). Characterizing psychiatric comorbidity in children with autism spectrum disorder receiving publicly funded mental health services. *Autism*, 22(8), 938–952. 10.1177/136236131771265028914082

Burton, C. L., Wright, L., Shan, J., Xiao, B., Dupuis, A., Goodale, T., Shaheen, S.-M., Corfield, E. C., Arnold, P. D., Schachar, R. J., & Crosbie, J. (2019). SWAN scale for ADHD trait-based genetic research: a validity and polygenic risk study. *Journal of Child Psychology and Psychiatry and Allied Disciplines, 60*(9). https://doi.org/10.1111/jcpp.13032

Buti, J., Glenny, A.-M., Worthington, H. V., Nieri, M., & Baccini, M. (2011). Network meta-analysis of randomised controlled trials: Direct and indirect treatment comparisons. *European Journal of Oral Implantology*, 4(1), 55–62.21594220

Carter Leno, V., Chandler, S., White, P., Pickles, A., Baird, G., Hobson, C., Smith, A. B., Charman, T., Rubia, K., & Simonoff, E. (2018). Testing the specificity of executive functioning impairments in adolescents with ADHD, ODD/CD and ASD. *European Child & Adolescent Psychiatry*, 27(7), 899–908. 10.1007/s00787-017-1089-529224173

Cascia, J., & Barr, J. J. (2020). Associations among parent and teacher ratings of systemizing, vocabulary and executive function in children with autism spectrum disorder. *Research in Developmental Disabilities*, 106, 1–11. 10.1016/j.ridd.2020.10377932947163

Chan, P. C., Chen, C. T., Feng, H., Lee, Y. C., & Chen, K. L. (2016). Theory of Mind Deficit Is Associated with Pretend Play Performance, but Not Playfulness, in Children with Autism Spectrum Disorder. *Hong Kong Journal of Occupational Therapy*, 28(1), 43–52. 10.1016/j.hkjot.2016.09.00230186066

Chang, S., Yang, L., Wang, Y., & Faraone, S. V. (2020). Shared polygenic risk for ADHD, executive dysfunction and other psychiatric disorders. *Translational Psychiatry*, 10(1), 182. 10.1038/s41398-020-00872-932518222

Chevrier, A., & Schachar, R. J. (2020). BOLD differences normally attributed to inhibitory control predict symptoms, not task-directed inhibitory control in ADHD. *Journal of Neurodevelopmental Disorders*, 12(1), 1–12. 10.1186/s11689-020-09311-832085698

Chia, N. K. H. (2012). Autism enigma: The need to include savant and crypto-savant in the current definition. *Academic Research International*, 2(2), 234.

Chia, N. K. H. (2012). The Need to Include Savant and Crypto-savant in the Current Definition. *Academic Research International*, 2, 234–240.

Cho, S. J., & Ahn, D. H. (2016). Socially Assistive Robotics in Autism Spectrum Disorder. *Hanyang Medical Reviews*, 36(1), 17–26. 10.7599/hmr.2016.36.1.17

Christ, S. E., Holt, D., White, D., & Green, L. (2007). Inhibitory control in children with autism spectrum disorder. *Journal of Autism and Developmental Disorders*, 37(6), 1155–1165. 10.1007/s10803-006-0259-y17066307

Corbett, B. A., Constantine, L. J., Hendren, R., Rocke, D., & Ozonoff, S. (2009). Examining executive functioning in children with autism spectrum disorder, attention deficit hyperactivity disorder and typical development. *Psychiatry Research*, 166(2-3), 210–222. 10.1016/j.psychres.2008.02.00519285351

Craig, F., Lamanna, A. L., Margari, F., Matera, E., Simone, M., & Margari, L. (2015). Overlap Between Autism Spectrum Disorders and Attention Deficit Hyperactivity Disorder: Searching for Distinctive/Common Clinical Features. *Autism Research*, 8(3), 328–337. 10.1002/aur.144925604000

Crooke, P. J., Winner, M. G., & Olswang, L. B. (2016). Thinking socially. *Topics in Language Disorders*, 36(3), 284–298. 10.1097/TLD.0000000000000094

Demetriou, E. A., Lampit, A., Quintana, D. S., Naismith, S. L., Song, Y. J. C., Pye, J. E., Hickie, I., & Guastella, A. J. (2018). Autism spectrum disorders: A meta analysis of executive function. *Molecular Psychiatry*, 23(5), 1198–1204. 10.1038/mp.2017.7528439105

Escolano-Pérez, E., Acero-Ferrero, M., & Herrero-Nivela, M. (2019). Improvement of planning skills in children with autism spectrum disorder after an educational intervention: A study from a mixed methods approach. *Frontiers in Psychology*, 10, 2824. 10.3389/fpsyg.2019.0282431920859

Finkel, D., & Pedersen, N. L. (2014). Genetic and environmental contributions to the associations between intraindividual variability in reaction time and cognitive function. *Neuropsychology, Development, and Cognition. Section B, Aging, Neuropsychology and Cognition*, 21(6), 746–764. 10.1080/13825585.2013.87452324400992

Frith, U. (2003). *Autism: Explaining the Enigma* (2nd ed.). Blackwell.

Geurts, H. M., Verte, S., Oosterlaan, J., Roeyers, H., & Sergeant, J. (2004). How specific are executive functioning deficits in attention deficit hyperactivity disorder and autism? *Journal of Child Psychology and Psychiatry, and Allied Disciplines*, 45(4), 836–854. 10.1111/j.1469-7610.2004.00276.x15056314

Ghirardi, L., Pettersson, E., Taylor, M. J., Freitag, C. M., Franke, B., Asherson, P., Larsson, H., & Kuja-Halkola, R. (2019). Genetic and environmental contribution to the overlap between ADHD and ASD trait dimensions in young adults: A twin study. *Psychological Medicine*, 49(10), 1713–1721. 10.1017/S003329171800243X30191778

Glahn, D. C., Knowles, E. E. M., Mckay, D. R., Sprooten, E., Raventós, H., Blangero, J., Gottesman, I. I., & Almasy, L. (2014). Arguments for the sake of endophenotypes: Examining common misconceptions about the use of endophenotypes in psychiatric genetics. *American Journal of Medical Genetics. Part B, Neuropsychiatric Genetic. American Journal of Medical Genetics. Part B, Neuropsychiatric Genetics*, 165(2), 122–130. 10.1002/ajmg.b.3222124464604

Happe, F. (1999). Autism: Cognitive deficit or cognitive style? *Trends in Cognitive Sciences*, 3(6), 216–222. 10.1016/S1364-6613(99)01318-210354574

Happe, F., & Firth, U. (2006, January). (1006). The weak central coherence account: Detailed focused cognitive style in Autism Spectrum Disorders. *Journal of Autism and Developmental Disorders*, 36(1), 5–25. 10.1007/s10803-005-0039-016450045

Happé, F., & Vital, P. (2009). What aspects of autism predispose to talent? *Philosophical Transactions of the Royal Society of London. Series B, Biological Sciences*, 364(1522), 1369–1375. 10.1098/rstb.2008.033219528019

Heward, W. L. (2011). *Children with special needs. An introduction to Special Education*. Topos.

Hill, E. L. (2004). Executive Dysfunction in autism. *Trends in Cognitive Sciences*, 8(1), 26–32. 10.1016/j.tics.2003.11.00314697400

Hill, E. L., & Frith, U. (2003). Understanding Autism: Insights from mind and brain. In Frith, U., & Hill, E. (Eds.), *Autism: Mind and brain* (pp. 1–19). Oxford University Press.

Joseph, R. M., & Tager–Flusberg, H. E. L. E. N. (2004). The relationship of theory of mind and executive functions to symptom type and severity in children with autism. *Development and Psychopathology*, 16(1), 137–155. 10.1017/S095457940404444X15115068

Joshi, G., Faraone, S. V., Wozniak, J., Tarko, L., Fried, R., Galdo, M., Furtak, S. L., & Biederman, J. (2017). Symptom Profile of ADHD in Youth With High Functioning Autism Spectrum Disorder: A Comparative Study in Psychiatrically Referred Populations. *Journal of Attention Disorders*, 21(10), 846–855. 10.1177/1 08705471454336825085653

Karr, J. E., Areshenkoff, C. N., Rast, P., Hofer, S. M., Iverson, G. L., & Garcia-Barrera, M. A. (2018). The unity and diversity of executive functions: A systematic review and re-analysis of latent variable studies. *Psychological Bulletin*, 144(11), 1147–1185. 10.1037/bul000016030080055

Katsarou, D., Nikolaou, E., & Stamatis, P. (2023). Is coteaching an effective way of including children with autism? The Greek parallel coteaching as an example: Issues and Concerns. In Efthymiou, E. (Ed.), *Inclusive Phygital Learning Approaches and Strategies For Students with Special Needs* (pp. 189–197). IGI Global. 10.4018/978-1-6684-8504-0.ch009

Kaur, K., & Pany, S. (2020). Executive function profiles of autism spectrum disorder using the executive function performance based tasks: A systematic review. *Journal of Critical Reviews*, 7(19), 8395–8403.

Kenworthy, L. E., Black, D. O., Wallace, G. L., Ahluvalia, T., Wagner, A. E., & Sirian, L. M. (2010). Disorganization: The forgotten executive dysfunction in high-functioning autism (HFA) spectrum disorders. *Developmental Neuropsychology*, 28(3), 809–827. 10.1207/s15326942dn2803_416266250

Lam, Y. G. (2013). Re-examining the cognitive phenotype in autism: a study with young Chinese children. *Research in Developmental Disabilities, 34*(12), 4591-4598. 10.1016/j.ridd.2013.09.039

Laugeson, E. A., & Park, M. N. (2014). Using a CBT approach to teach social skills to adolescents with autism spectrum disorder and other social challenges: The PEERS® method. *Journal of Rational-Emotive & Cognitive-Behavior Therapy*, 32(1), 84–97. 10.1007/s10942-014-0181-8

Lawson, J., Baron-Cohen, S., & Wheelwright, S. (2004). Empathising and Systemising in Adults with and without Asperger Syndrome. *Journal of Autism and Developmental Disorders*, 34(3), 301–310. 10.1023/B:JADD.0000029552.42724.1b15264498

Liss, M., Fein, D., Allen, D., Dunn, M., Feinstein, C., Morris, R., Waterhouse, L., & Rapin, I. (2001). Executive functioning in high-functioning children with autism. *Journal of Child Psychology and Psychiatry, and Allied Disciplines*, 42(2), 261–270. 10.1111/1469-7610.0071711280422

Megari, K., Sofologi, M., Kougioumtzis, G., Thomaidou, E., Katsarou, D., Yotsidi, V., & Theodoraotu, M. (2024). Neurocognitive and psychoemotional profile of children with disabilities. *Applied Neuropsychology. Child*, 1–6. 10.1080/21622965.2024.230478138574392

Meyer, J. A., & Minshew, N. J. (2002). An Update on Neurocognitive Profiles in Asperger Syndrome and High- Functioning Autism. *Focus on Autism and Other Developmental Disabilities*, 17(3), 152–160. 10.1177/10883576020170030501

Minshew, N. G., & Goldstein, G. (2001). The Pattern of Intact and Impaired Memory Functions in Autism. *Journal of Child Psychology and Psychiatry, and Allied Disciplines*, 42(8), 1095–1101. 10.1111/1469-7610.0080811806691

Mottron, L., Dawson, M., & Soulières, I. (2009). Enhanced perception in savant syndrome: Patterns, structure and creativity. *Philosophical Transactions of the Royal Society of London. Series B, Biological Sciences*, 364(1522), 1385–1391. 10.1098/rstb.2008.033319528021

Mottron, L., Dawson, M., Soulieres, I., Hubert, B., & Burack, J. (2006). Enhanced perceptual functioning in autism: An update, and eight principles of autistic perception. *Journal of Autism and Developmental Disorders*, 36(1), 27–43. 10.1007/s10803-005-0040-716453071

Ozonoff, S., Pennington, B. F., & Rogers, S. I. (1991). Executive function deficits in high-functioning autistic children: Relationship to theory of mind. *Journal of Child Psychology and Psychiatry, and Allied Disciplines*, 32(7), 1081–1105. 10.1111/j.1469-7610.1991.tb00351.x1787138

Pooragha, F., Kafi, S. M., & Sotodeh, S. O. (2013). Comparing response inhibition and flexibility for two components of executive functioning in children with autism spectrum disorder and normal children. *Iranian Journal of Pediatrics*, 23(3), 309.23795254

Psoma, M., & Vlahos, F. (2018). Neurocognitive Approaches to Autism Spectrum Disorders. In Vlachos, F. (Ed.), *Brain, learning and special education* (pp. 395–425). Gutenberg.

Richman, S. (2001). *Raising a Child with Autism: A Guide to Applied Behavior Analysis for Parents*. Jessica Kingsley Publishers.

Robinson, S., Goddard, L., Dritschel, B., Wisley, M., & Howlin, P. (2009). Executive functions in children with Autism Spectrum Disorders. *Brain and Cognition*, 71(3), 362–368. 10.1016/j.bandc.2009.06.00719628325

Salimpoor, V. N., & Desrocher, M. (2006). Increasing the Utility of EF Assessment of Executive Function in Children. *Developmental Disabilities Bulletin*, 34, 15–42.

Sandbank, M., Bottema-Beutel, K., Crowley, S., Cassidy, M., Dunham, K., Feldman, J., Crank, J., Albarran, S., Raj, S., Mahbub, P., & Woynaroski, T. (2020). Project AIM. *Psychological Bulletin*, 146(1), 1–29. 10.1037/bul000021531763860

Siffredi, V., Liverani, M. C., Hüppi, P. S., Freitas, L. G., De Albuquerque, J., Gimbert, F., & Borradori Tolsa, C. (2021). The effect of a mindfulness- based intervention on executive, behavioural and socio-emotional competencies in very preterm young adolescents. *Scientific Reports*, 11(1), 1–12. 10.1038/s41598-021-98608-234615893

Steele, S.D., Minshew, N.J., Luna, B. & Sweeney, J.A. (2007). Spatial working memory deficits in autism. *Journal of Autism and Developmental Disorders, 37*. 10.1007/s10803-006-0202-2

Stromer, R., Kimball, J. W., Kinney, E. M., & Taylor, B. A. (2006). Activity schedules, computer technology, and teaching children with autism spectrum disorders. *Focus on Autism and Other Developmental Disabilities, 21*(1). 10.1177/10883576060210010301

Treffert, D. (1009). The savant syndrome: an extraordinary condition. A synopsis: Past, Present, Future. *Philosophical Transactions of the Royal Society V, 364*, 1351-1357. 10.1098/rstb.2008.0326

Wakabayashi, A., Baron-Cohen, S., Wheelright, S., Goldenfeld, N., Delaney, J., Fine, D., Smith, R., & Weil, L. (2006). Development of short forms of the Empathy Quotient (EQ-Short) and the Systemizing Quotient (SQ-Short). *Personality and Individual Differences*, 41(5), 929–940. 10.1016/j.paid.2006.03.017

Wheelright, S., Baron-Cohen, S., Goldenfeld, N., Delaney, J., Fine, D., Smith, R., Weil, L., & Wakabayashi, A. (2006). Predicting Autism Spectrum Quotient (AQ) from the Systemizing Quotient-Revised (SQ-R) and Empathy Quotient (EQ). *Brain Research*, 1079(1), 47–56. 10.1016/j.brainres.2006.01.01216473340

Williams, D. L., Goldstein, G., Carpenter, P. A., & Minshew, N. J. (2005). Verbal and spatial working memory in autism. *Journal of Autism and Developmental Disorders*, 35(6), 747–756. 10.1007/s10803-005-0021-x16267641

Chapter 9
Beyond Educational Strategies in Promoting Inclusion for Autistic Individuals:
An Overarching Framework and the Way Forward

Despina Papoudi
https://orcid.org/0000-0002-1079-5471
University of Thessaly, Greece

Lia Tsermidou
National and Kapodistrian University of Athens, Greece

Prithvi Perepa
https://orcid.org/0000-0003-3130-9193
University of Birmingham, UK

ABSTRACT

The aim of the present chapter is to argue that educational strategies are not adequate on their own to promote inclusion for autistic individuals, because this holds only the individual responsible for their inclusion with no onus on the settings or other people involved; as a result, autistic individuals are facing challenges at school and in society throughout their lifespan. Therefore, for inclusion to be enacted, a change of attitudes, perceptions, and stereotypes about the education and development of autistic individuals considering a biopsychosocial bioecological model of disability is deemed critical. This chapter aims to discuss current conceptualization of autism,

DOI: 10.4018/979-8-3693-4022-6.ch009

traditional models of disability in relation to autism and present an overarching framework that sheds light on overcoming existing tensions and challenges in the inclusion of autistic individuals as well as make suggestions for moving forward in promoting inclusion in the autism field.

INTRODUCTION

Autism has been understood and viewed from different perspectives since its identification as a discrete disability. These views have been formalized into specific models such as the medical model, social model, or critical autism studies model, to explain their distinct differences in conceptualization of autism. This chapter will focus on these various theoretical models to argue for a need to use a biopsychosocial bioecological model of disability. This model acknowledges that while current perspectives are all valid, none of them provide a comprehensive view that accounts for the individual experiences of autistic individuals, and how these are formed by the social attitude and perceptions, as well as structural barriers. This chapter argues that when inclusive education does not consider this comprehensive picture, then strategies put in place may not necessarily achieve inclusion.

CURRENT CONCEPTUALIZATION OF AUTISM

Autism is a lifelong developmental condition that affects how individuals perceive the world and interact with other people. Autistic individuals have persistent difficulties in social communication and social interaction including those who have language abilities. They may also have restricted and repetitive patterns of behaviors, activities or interests and sensory sensitivities including over-sensitivity or under-sensitivity to sounds, light, colors etc. (APA, 2022). Some autistic individuals also have intellectual disabilities, mental health issues and high support needs contributing to autism being widely accepted as a heterogeneous condition (Masi et al., 2017). The heterogeneity seen in autistic individuals is reflected in the use of the term autism spectrum and the medical term autism spectrum disorder as introduced by the American Psychiatric Association in DSM V (APA, 2013).

According to recent reports, autism has been increasing dramatically in recent years with reports as high as 1 in 36 (2.8%) 8-year-old children (CDC, 2023). These trends have resulted in the widening of heterogeneity in autism and the investigation of the phenomenon through new dimensions by introducing the concept of chronogeny. Chronogeny has been informed as a concept by long-term studies and clinical experience, which show that autistic individuals present a different developmental course. Based on the concept of chronogeny, the underlying differences in autistic individuals are related with the nature of autism and are manifested during the cognitive, social, and emotional development of each individual (Georgiades et al., 2017).

MODELS OF DISABILITY: TOWARDS AN OVERARCHING FRAMEWORK

The understanding of autism has undergone significant changes over the years, and autism is viewed as a specific psychiatric disorder as well as part of a broader spectrum condition. This transition has been influenced by critical re-evaluations of historical standpoints such as those pioneered by Leo Kanner (1943), which initially framed autism as a uniform and distinct disorder. Contemporary perspectives, informed by the principles of neurodiversity and the social construction of disability, advocate for a more inclusive view, asserting that autism should be considered a natural part of human diversity rather than a deficit to be remedied (Donvan & Zucker, 2016; Silberman, 2015). These contemporary views challenge the earlier, narrow interpretations that often resulted in stigmatizing and pathologizing autistic individuals and emphasize the complexity and variation within the autism spectrum, moving beyond simplistic views of autism as a medical diagnosis to understanding it as an integral part of human diversity (Grinker, 2007).

Discussing the Medical Model of Disability Within the Autism Field Through a Critical Lens

Historically, the medical model considered autism a neurodevelopmental disorder, heavily defined by behavioral symptoms and various genetic factors, emphasizing the necessity for diagnosis and the need for treatment. The medical model prioritizes aligning autistic behaviors with typical developmental milestones, often encouraging interventions that aim to 'normalize' these behaviors (Lord et al., 2020), a practice that has attracted significant criticism for failing to recognize the unique developmental trajectories of autistic individuals. This can impose unrealistic expectations and pressures on both the individuals and their families, which can be detrimental rather than supportive (Milton, 2012). Moreover, the prevailing interventions often center on normalizing autistic behaviors to align with established developmental milestones. This focus, while rooted in a desire to aid integration, has been increasingly criticized for not accommodating the nuanced needs of autistic individuals. As Davidson and Orsini (2013) highlight, such approaches frequently overlook the subjective experiences and individuality of autistic people, potentially resulting in interventions that misalign with their actual needs or life contexts.

The medical model pathologizes autism by presenting it as a disorder in need of correction, which can lead to stigmatization and exclusion. This approach often overlooks the strengths of autistic people. In contrast, the social model, which underpins inclusive education, focuses on removing societal barriers and creating supportive environments. It celebrates diversity and adapts educational practices to meet the needs of all students, ensuring that every learner can thrive. In addition, the medical model is often viewed as diminishing the inherent value and potential of neurodiverse persons, promoting a view of autistic differences as deficits and deficiencies (Timimi et al., 2010) and its focus on genetic processes and standardized behaviors frequently leads to overlooking the significant environmental, cultural, and psychological factors that also profoundly affect autistic individuals' lives (Pellicano & Stears, 2011). It also neglects the perspectives and lived experiences of autistic individuals themselves, with a predominant focus on external assessments and evaluations by professionals, which can potentially result to a misalignment between recommended interventions and the actual needs of the autistic community (Davidson & Orsini, 2013).

Recent empirical studies raised significant concerns about the effectiveness of some clinical interventions and therapies. Masi et al. (2017) reported that despite advances in understanding the biological underpinnings of autism, many existing therapies have failed to consistently demonstrate efficacy in improving the core aspects of autism across diverse populations. This inconsistency in outcomes shows the limitations of a one-size-fits-all approach and highlights the need for interventions that are more personalized and attuned to the specific contexts of individuals with autism. Furthermore, the pharmacological treatment of autism spectrum disorder is complex, given the condition's heterogeneity. These treatments primarily aim to manage specific symptoms rather than addressing the core aspects of the autism spectrum, such as difficulties in communication, social interaction, and repetitive behaviors. Research often points to the limited efficacy of these interventions, highlighting a gap between expected outcomes and actual improvements in core symptoms. Additionally, concerns about the side effects of long-term use of these medications emphasize the need for more holistic and individualized approaches (King & Bearman, 2009; Coury et al., 2012).

The above criticisms highlight the necessity for a paradigm shift toward integrating socio-cultural insights and human bioecology with clinical practices, advocating for frameworks that recognize and respect the diversity and richness of autistic experiences; such an integrated approach would promote more compassionate, person-centered interventions that honor the complexity of autism beyond its medicalization, supporting autistic people in ways that affirm their individuality and potential contributions to society.

In conclusion, while the medical model has historically framed the treatment and understanding of autism, there is a compelling call nowadays within the scholarly community to adopt a more integrated perspective that recognizes the complex interplay of biological, psychological, and social factors. This approach can foster environments that truly support autistic individuals and enable them to thrive and lead fulfilling lives by acknowledging their potential and contributions as integral to the collective social fabric. Therefore, it is argued that there is a need to shift from a purely medical model that seeks to 'normalize' autism towards approaches that embrace the full spectrum of neurodiversity. Such a paradigm shift would advocate for interventions that not only address biological factors but also incorporate the rich tapestry of social, cultural, and personal dimensions integral to the lives of autistic individuals.

Recontextualizing Autism Within the Social Model of Disability

The social model of disability, significantly shaped by the Union of the Physically Impaired Against Segregation (UPIAS, 1976), challenges the dominant medical model narrative by positing that society itself constructs disability through the limitations it imposes. This model of disability directly confronts traditional definitions, such as those of the World Health Organization (2023), by emphasizing that societal structures, rather than individual impairments, are often the primary barriers that limit inclusion and accessibility for disabled people (Campbell & Oliver, 1996; Oliver, 1990) as well as autistic individuals (Chapman, 2020; Woods, 2017). Therefore, within the context of the social model of disability, autism is not merely viewed as a neurological divergence but a characteristic that society must accommodate, not stigmatize, or seek to cure. This repositioning is crucial to understanding how environments can be restructured to better support the autistic individuals (Woods, 2017), emphasizing that barriers in public infrastructure, education, and policy often hinder full participation (Thomas & Woods, 2008; Turnock et al., 2022).

Moreover, the theoretical foundation of the social model offers a robust critique of the normative standards that define public and private spaces (Finkelstein, 2001; Barnes & Sheldon, 2010), which can stigmatize, exclude, or marginalize autistic individuals from active societal participation (Turnock et al., 2022). It advocates for a re-evaluation of how society can implement inclusive designs that cater to a spectrum of neurodiverse needs, thus promoting a more democratic and accessible community. For example, Priestley (1998) elaborates on two key approaches within the social model that enhance our understanding of autism: the social-materialistic and the social-idealist positions. The social-materialistic view considers disability as a product of social power dynamics and historical conditions, which aligns with disability activism that seeks to dismantle exclusionary practices and foster societal change. This perspective is particularly resonant in the autism community, where activism often focuses on transforming policies and practices to better accommodate diverse neurological states. Conversely, the social-idealist approach views disability, including autism, as a cultural construct, influenced by societal perceptions and the cultural framework within which diversity is either accepted or rejected. This stance highlights how autism is variously constructed across different cultures and stresses the role of cultural imperialism in defining what is considered 'normal' or 'abnormal' (Priestley, 1998).

Furthermore, the application of the social model in autism research focuses on exploring how autistic individuals navigate barriers in education, employment, and social engagement. Such studies aim to expose and address the systemic oppressions that autistic individuals face, advocating for structural changes to enhance their autonomy and inclusion (Turnock et al., 2022; Chapman, 2020). Research in this area also emphasizes the importance of societal restructuring, particularly in times of economic crisis, to ensure that policies reflect and support the diverse needs of all citizens, including those who are neurodiverse.

This expanded understanding of the social model, when applied to autism, not only critiques the pathologizing perspective of the medical model but also promotes a more nuanced appreciation of autism as an integral aspect of human diversity. It calls for a multi-dimensional approach to disability that recognizes the complex interplay between individual characteristics and societal structures, advocating for a society that does not merely accommodate but actively includes and values neurodiverse individuals. In essence, rethinking autism through the social model encourages a shift from viewing autistic individuals as needing to adapt to society, to reforming society itself to embrace and support neurodiversity as a valuable form of human variation. This paradigm shift is essential for building a more inclusive society where the rights and contributions of autistic individuals are fully recognized and valued.

Reframing Autism Through Critical Autism Studies

Critical Autism Studies is an offshoot of the social model of disability and delves into the impact of viewing autism through multidimensional lenses that integrate critical psychiatry, social psychology, and the broader social sciences and challenge the traditional medical and biological models. Critical scholars argue that autism should not be viewed solely through the lens of pathology and that a deeper appreciation for the diverse manifestations of autism should be acknowledged to promote a shift towards recognizing variations as natural and integral aspects of human diversity rather than anomalies to be corrected (Davidson & Orsini, 2013;

Milton & Ryan, 2023). The approach of Critical Autism Studies, by bringing together academic and non-academic discourses, provides a platform where a variety of voices and approaches are not only heard but also integrated into a coherent narrative that shifts the focus from deficit to diversity and from exclusion to inclusion. This integration is observed in the emphasis on emancipatory methodologies that aim to reposition power from the researcher to the community being researched, which is a critical aspect in fostering an inclusive society where autistic individuals can thrive (Connolly, 2023, as cited by Milton & Ryan, 2023, p.16).

In addition, the neurodiversity movement, and the concept of neurodiversity within Critical Autism Studies significantly redefine autism, proposing that autism should not be viewed as a disorder but as a variation in human brain function that is as natural as any other human difference. This perspective aligns with the social model of disability, which sees autism through the lens of diversity rather than deficiency. Advocates like Judy Singer (2017) promote the notion of neurodiversity to emphasize that autistic individuals should be accepted and integrated into society as they are, not forced to conform to traditional expectations of normality (Singer, 2017; den Houting, 2019).

In sum, Critical Autism Studies not only challenge the existing paradigms in autism research but also contribute to a more inclusive understanding of autism recognising that autistic identity should be embraced as part of the rich tapestry of human diversity and integral aspect of human variation.

TOWARDS AN OVERARCHING FRAMEWORK: THE BIOPSYCHOSOCIAL BIOECOLOGICAL MODEL OF DISABILITY

It appears that the existing models of disability are antithetical and fragmented. The medical model of disability gives emphasis on diagnosis and treatment viewing the autistic individual as the source of his/her condition, the social model of disability focuses on the role of society for the construction of disability, and critical autism studies embraces neurodiversity and advocate for the rights of autistic individuals. Therefore, a more holistic approach is needed to incorporate all aspects of human development and a comprehensive model is required. It is proposed that a biopsychosocial bioecological model of disability could serve as an overarching framework in the autism field and on this basis a comprehensive framework could be constructed that allows for a nuanced understanding accommodating both the biological aspects of development and its socio-cultural implications for autistic individuals.

Bronfenbrenner (Bronfenbrenner & Morris, 2006) proposed the bioecological model of development and organized the differing external factors that interact and influence human development to microsystem (e.g. family, parents, siblings, school, teachers peers), mesosystem (the interaction between the microsystems), exosystem (extended family, community and school resources, mass media), macrosystem (policies, social norms, cultural values, political and economic system) and the chronosystem (change over time) with the individual being at the center of his/her own development. Bronfenbrenner also suggested that these interactions are reciprocal and therefore there is a need to focus on the person, context, and developmental outcome, as the way people are affected by these processes during development differs (Bronfenbrenner & Evans, 2000).

Sameroff (2010) extended Bronfenbrenner's views and suggested the biopsychosocial ecological model of human development. He argued that there is a dialectical process and interconnection between the contextual systems described in Bronfenbrenner's bioecological model with the self being at the center of human development and formulated by interacting psychological (e.g., cognition, mental health, identity etc.) and biological processes (e.g., genetics, epigenetics, neuropsychology, physiology etc.). According to Sameroff (2010), this biopsychological self-system interacts with the other interacting systems in society that relate to social ecology (e.g., family, school, community, etc.).

Such a framework based on the biopsychosocial factors and the bioecology of human development not only helps in addressing the immediate needs of autistic individuals but also in structuring environments that support their well-being and full participation in society (Lehman et al., 2017; Pinder-Amaker, 2014). Furthermore, the biopsychosocial bioecological model of disability offers a holistic framework for understanding autism by recognizing the dynamic interactions among biological, psychological, and social factors. By embracing this model, the discourse around autism moves beyond the deficit-focused narratives to highlight the strengths and challenges faced by autistic individuals, advocating for a balanced approach that respects the complexity in autism and fosters inclusion of autistic individuals in all aspects of society (Lehman et al., 2017). Autistic individuals differ from one another, and their development is influenced by multiple factors and therefore educational strategies should be individualized and personalized considering these biopsychosocial influences and the bioecology of the development. This view is further supported by Kranzler et al. (2020) who proposed the use of the biopsychosocial ecological model as an overarching framework within the field of educational/ school psychology arguing that the research focus in this field should not be "one size fits all" school-wide interventions. In this vein, the focus needs to be on the acceptance of diversity, breaking down stereotypes with the aim of educational and social inclusion of autistic people throughout their lifespan. Last but not least, the biopsychosocial bioecological model of disability underscores the importance of viewing autistic individuals not just in terms of biological or psychological characteristics but accepts them as active participants in a social context that shapes and is shaped by their experiences (Milton & Ryan, 2023).

CHALLENGES IN THE INCLUSION OF AUTISTIC INDIVIDUALS AND THE WAY FORWARD

The United Nations sustainable goals (UN, 2015) clearly state that all countries should aim for inclusive and equitable education for all. However, there are various ways that different scholars and countries have defined inclusion, often referring to access to regular or mainstream schools as inclusion (for example UNESCO Salamanca Statement, 1994). This suggests that inclusion is only related to being present in a mainstream setting and does not necessarily involve any other factors such as a sense of belonging.

The varying definitions makes it difficult to understand what is referred to as inclusion and whether this is the responsibility of the education setting alone or whether inclusion as a concept is applicable to wider society as well. The UNESCO's guidelines (2005) state that inclusion involves not only being present within a setting (such as being in a regular school) but having opportunities to participate in the activities provided in the setting and with other individuals in the setting. It should also include an opportunity for the child or young person to achieve success within that context. Taking this view, UNESCO argues that the process of creating an inclusive environment involves an active emphasis on factors that create barriers in achieving the above objectives. This view is closer to the above mentioned biopsychosocial bioecological model of disability. It can also be argued that that description of inclusion suggests that it is not bound to a specific location, such as mainstream schools only.

If this definition is used, then it can be argued that children on the autism spectrum experience exclusion not only in educational contexts, but also in wider society because their opportunities for participating and achieving are often curtailed. Even though educational inclusion has been included in legislations of many countries, research evidence suggests that formal and informal exclusion of students on the autism spectrum takes place even in high-resource countries (Adams, 2022; Guldberg et al., 2021; Martin-Denham, 2022). For example, in their research in the UK, Guldberg et al. (2021) have found that students on the autism spectrum are twice as likely to be excluded from schools compared to children without autism.

The causes for exclusion seem to be a combination of factors, such as schools being unable to accommodate the needs of autistic students because of lack of resources, as well as structural barriers such as rigid curriculum and school structures (Gray et al., 2023; Timpson review, 2019). Lack of staff understanding and their attitude towards including autistic students has been mentioned in some studies (Guldberg et al., 2021; Martin-Denham, 2022). The nature of autism could mean that some autistic students may find it difficult to navigate the social expectations within a school setting (Brede et al., 2017; Sedgewick et al., 2016) and may have difficulties in organizing themselves due to their weak executive functioning skills (Keen et al., 2016). This can lead to frustration and behaviors which are then considered as inappropriate or challenging and lead to exclusions. At a social level, students on the autism spectrum have often reported social isolation and bullying as their experiences within a school setting (Aube et al., 2020; Goodall, 2020).

Perepa et al. (2023) found that rates of exclusion are also related to a child's ethnicity, gender, and social class; with boys, children belonging to families from lower economic status, and those from minority ethnic communities being more likely to be excluded. Papoudi et al. (2021) conducted a systematic review and reported that parents belonging to minority ethnic communities also experience exclusion as they often feel stigmatized because of their child's autism, and their ethnicity. Stigma can be experienced by families within their own communities because of lack of autism awareness, and in the majority community because of lack of understanding and acceptance of cultural diversities. Studies such as these highlight the importance of considering multiple factors that can contribute to further marginalization of autistic children and families and emphasizing the need for a model that acknowledges these issues, such as the above suggested model of disability.

Exclusion and marginalization can have a negative impact on the mental well-being of the child (Lu et al., 2022) and their family members (Perepa et al., 2023). Therefore, it is important to work towards inclusion not only in educational contexts but also in wider society. Research around stigma and bullying suggests these mainly occur due to prejudice. Using this as a basis for intervention, two separate studies, one conducted by Cook et al. (2020) and another by Nistor and Dumitru (2021) found that when neurotypical children were exposed to their autistic peers and opportunities for personal interaction and contact were facilitated, this has led to change of attitudes. Therefore, it is important that opportunities for contact and understanding are created within educational settings as well as wider society. Such opportunities could also reduce discrimination that happens on multiple levels along with autism, such as ethnicity, gender, sexuality, or social class.

It is noteworthy that limited research has explored how inclusive attitudes and an inclusive philosophy and ethos can be developed amongst professionals. However, it can be argued that using similar strategies of exposure and interaction could be beneficial for professionals working in the field of autism as well. Professionals will need to reflect on their own personal bias and take active measures to not let these impact their interactions with the child or their family. It is important that cultural appropriateness of the assessment procedures and strategies being used is considered while working with individuals belonging to minority ethnic communities (Papoudi et al., 2021).

In addition, there is a need to develop professionals' understanding of autism. This should draw their attention to the findings from studies with children and family members (Brede et al., 2017; Goodall, 2020; Perepa et al., 2023) which suggest that listening to the child and their family is important for professionals aiming to create an inclusive environment. This could then enable developing trust and can lead to an open dialogue. Understanding the experiences, needs and aspirations of the child and their family can help professionals to understand the barriers for inclusion for that individual or their family and encourage them to consider the changes that are required at a strategic level such as considering the environment, the activities provided and the nature of support that is offered.

To illustrate the challenges in the inclusion of autistic individuals and to provide an example of how a holistic approach adopting a biopsychosocial bioecological model of disability we describe below the case study of Yusuf who is a 13-year-old boy diagnosed with autism and attends a secondary school in England. Yusuf often gets into trouble for his behaviour with the teaching staff and his peers and the school excludes him on a regular basis ('exclusions' is the process followed in the UK where a student is not allowed to come to the school for a short period or on a permanent basis). According to the biopsychosocial bioecological model of disability, Yusuf's condition is associated with the biological explanation of autism, his behaviour with the psychological explanation, and the school's reaction with the social environment.

Positive practices that adhere to the biopsychosocial bioecological model of disability were followed taking into consideration all systems encountered and interacting in a child's development and schooling (the individual, the family, the peers, the teachers, the school, the wider community). His parents reached out to a parent advocacy group for support, the parent advocate facilitated a meeting with the school staff, Yusuf and his parents. During the discussions Yusuf shared that other students in his class make fun of him and ostracize him because of his autism, religion and ethnicity. He also felt that the teachers seem to favour the White students and unfairly punish him when he is trying to defend himself. The school Special Educational Needs Coordinator (SENCO) devised a plan along with Yusuf, his parents and the parent advocate whereby the approach to reduce his exclusions has three aspects. First, all the school staff were offered training in autism and unconscious bias. Secondly, the school developed a plan for raising peer awareness of diversity. This was done by having school assemblies and lessons where diversity issues were explored. They also implemented a peer mentoring system for all the students that normalized that every student has some strengths that they can share but will also need support. Finally, Yusuf was provided some strategies for anger management and strategies for interacting with peers and adults. He was also provided support in developing a positive self-identity which included his autistic, ethnic and religious identities. Taking a holistic approach to Yusuf's school exclusions has started showing positive results where Yusuf is engaging more with his peers and his exclusions have reduced.

CONCLUSION

Autism is complex, variable and is manifested beyond the borders of clinical categories (Bussu et al., 2021) and therefore many challenges are presented in the inclusion of autistic individuals. Inclusion is a wider term and applies not only to inclusion into the school environment but also to inclusion in society, equality of opportunities and social justice. Therefore, educational strategies should be individualized and personalized considering the biopsychosocial influences and the bioecology of development. According to the European Society's of Child and Adolescent Psychiatry (ESCAP) practice guidance for autism (Fuentes et al., 2019, p. 974) "there are no specific interventions that can be recommended for all individuals" and the focus should be on making the environment more autism friendly, on providing opportunities during the day to facilitate progress and access to full and effective participation and inclusion within all contexts in society. Yet, although there are several approaches and interventions developed for autistic people these are mainly focusing on the child rather than addressing society's attitudes and changes in the environment. There is a need to get a balance between providing autistic individuals with required skills, but also changing the environment and others' views.

Therefore, inclusion demands change of attitudes, perceptions, and stereotypes about the education of autistic individuals considering a biopsychosocial bioecological model of disability. To foster inclusion for autistic people and their families within society and at the workplace, greater awareness, understanding, and acceptance is needed for removing existing barriers. In doing so, participatory research paradigms with the inclusion of autistic people and their families in the research design and the analysis of the data could enlighten our understanding of autistic experiences (Nicolaidis et al., 2019).

"...right from the start, from the time someone came up with the word 'autism', the condition has been judged from the outside, by its appearances, and not from the inside according to how it is experienced" (Williams, 1996, p. 14).

Last but not least, by giving more emphasis on the rights of autistic people, on approaches that foster their wellbeing and quality of life and considering expected outcomes as proposed by the autistic community, we could move to a more inclusive paradigm showing compassion to our fellow neurodiverse human beings.

REFERENCES

Adams, D. (2022). Child and parental mental health as correlates of school non-attendance and school refusal in children on the autism spectrum. *Journal of Autism and Developmental Disorders*, 52(8), 2253–3365. 10.1007/s10803-021-05211-534331173

American Psychiatric Association. (2013). *Diagnostic and statistical manual of mental disorders: DSM-5* (*Vol. 5*, No. 5). American psychiatric association.

American Psychiatric Association. (2022). *Diagnostic and statistical manual of mental disorders* (5th ed., text rev.). APA. 10.1176/appi.books.9780890425787

Aubé, B., Follenfant, A., Goudeau, S., & Derguy, C. (2020). Public stigma of autism spectrum disorder at school: Implicit attitudes matter. *Journal of Autism and Developmental Disorders*, 51(5), 1584–1597. 10.1007/s10803-020-04635-932780195

Barnes, C., & Sheldon, A. (2010). *Rethinking disability policy*. Longman.

Brede, J., Remington, A., Kenny, L., Warren, K., & Pellicano, E. (2017). Excluded from school: Autistic students' experiences of school exclusion and subsequent re-integration into school. *Autism & Developmental Language Impairments*, 2, 1–20. 10.1177/2396941517737511

Bronfenbrenner, U., & Evans, G. W. (2000). Developmental science in the 21st century: Emerging questions, theoretical models, research designs and empirical findings. *Social Development*, 9(1), 115–125. 10.1111/1467-9507.00114

Bronfenbrenner, U., & Morris, P. (2006). The bioecological model of human development. In Damon, W., & Lerner, R. (Eds.), (pp. 793–828). Handbook of child psychology. John Wiley & Sons.

Bussu, G., Llera, A., Jones, E. J., Tye, C., Charman, T., Johnson, M. H., Beckmann, C. F., & Buitelaar, J. K. (2021). Uncovering neurodevelopmental paths to autism spectrum disorder through an integrated analysis of developmental measures and neural sensitivity to faces. *Journal of Psychiatry & Neuroscience*, 46(1), E34–E43. 10.1503/jpn.19014833009904

Campbell, J., & Oliver, M. (2013). *Disability politics: Understanding our past, changing our future*. Routledge. 10.4324/9780203410639

CDC. (2023). *Centers for Disease Control and Prevention*. CDC. https://www.cdc.gov/media/releases/2023/p0323-autism.html

Chapman, R. (2020). The reality of autism: On the metaphysics of disorder and diversity. *Philosophical Psychology*, 33(6), 799–819. 10.1080/09515089.2020.1751103

Cook, A., Ogden, J., & Winstone, N. (2020). The effect of school exposure and personal contact on attitudes towards bullying and autism in schools: A cohort study with a control group. *Autism*, 24(8), 2178–2189. 10.1177/13623613209370 8832668954

Coury, D. L., Ashwood, P., Fasano, A., Fuchs, G., Geraghty, M., Kaul, A., Mawe, G., Patterson, P., & Jones, N. E. (2012). Gastrointestinal conditions in children with autism spectrum disorder: Developing a research agenda. *Pediatrics*, 130(Suppl 2), S160–S168. 10.1542/peds.2012-0900N23118247

Davidson, J., & Orsini, M. (2013). *Worlds of autism: Across the spectrum of neurological difference*. University of Minnesota Press. 10.5749/minnesota/9780816688883.001.0001

den Houting, J. (2019). Neurodiversity: An insider's perspective. *Autism*, 23(2), 271–273. 10.1177/136236131882076230556743

Donvan, J., & Zucker, C. (2016). *In a different key: The story of autism*. Crown.

Finkelstein, V. (2001). A personal journey into disability politics. *Social Policy and Administration*, 35(5), 602–616.

Fuentes, J., Hervás, A., & Howlin, P. (2021). ESCAP practice guidance for autism: A summary of evidence-based recommendations for diagnosis and treatment. *European Child & Adolescent Psychiatry*, 30(6), 961–984. 10.1007/s00787-020-01587-432666205

Georgiades, S., Bishop, S. L., & Frazier, T. (2017). Editorial Perspective: Longitudinal research in autism–introducing the concept of 'chronogeneity'. *Journal of Child Psychology and Psychiatry, and Allied Disciplines*, 58(5), 634–636. 10.1111/jcpp.1269028414862

Goodall, C. (2020). Inclusion is a feeling, not a place: A qualitative study exploring autistic young people's conceptualisations of inclusion. *International Journal of Inclusive Education*, 24(12), 1285–1310. 10.1080/13603116.2018.1523475

Gray, L., Hill, V., & Pellicano, E. (2023). "He's shouting so loud but nobody's hearing him": A multi-informant study of autistic pupils' experiences of school non-attendance and exclusion. *Autism & Developmental Language Impairments*, 8, 23969415231207816. 10.1177/23969415231207816637860824

Grinker, R. R. (2007). *Unstrange minds: Remapping the world of autism*. Basic Books.

Guldberg, G., Wallace, S., Bradley, R., Perepa, P., Ellis, L., & MacLeod, A. (2021). *Investigation of the causes and implications of exclusion for autistic children and young people.* University of Birmingham. https://www.birmingham.ac.uk/documents/college-social-sciences/education/reports/causes-and-implications-of-exclusion-for-autistic-children-and-young-people.pdf

Kanner, L. (1943). Autistic disturbances of affective contact. *Nervous Child*, 2(3), 217–250.

Keen, D., Webster, A., & Ridley, G. (2016). How well are children with autism spectrum disorder doing academically at school? An overview of the literature. *Autism*, 20(3), 276–294. 10.1177/13623613155809622594 8598

King, M., & Bearman, P. (2009). Diagnostic change and the increased prevalence of autism. *International Journal of Epidemiology*, 38(5), 1224–1234. 10.1093/ije/dyp26119737791

Kranzler, J. H., Floyd, R. G., Bray, M. A., & Demaray, M. K. (2020). Past, present, and future of research in school psychology: The biopsychosocial ecological model as an overarching framework. *School Psychology*, 35(6), 419–427. 10.1037/spq000040133444055

Lehman, B. J., David, D. M., & Gruber, J. A. (2017). Rethinking the biopsychosocial model of health: Understanding health as a dynamic system. *Social and Personality Psychology Compass*, 11(8), e12328. 10.1111/spc3.12328

Lord, C., Brugha, T. S., Charman, T., Cusack, J., Dumas, G., Frazier, T., Jones, J. H. E., Jones, M. R., Pickles, A., State, W. M., Taylor, L. J., & Veenstra-VanderWeele, J. (2020). Autism spectrum disorder. *Nature Reviews. Disease Primers*, 6(1), 1–23. 10.1038/s41572-019-0138-431949163

Lu, H., Chen, D., & Chou, A. (2022). The school environment and bullying victimization among seventh grades with autism spectrum disorder: A cohort study. *Child and Adolescent Psychiatry and Mental Health*, 16(22), 22. 10.1186/s13034-022-00456-z35292070

Martin-Denham, S. (2022). Marginalization, autism and school exclusion: Caregivers' perspectives. *Support for Learning*, 37(1), 108–143. 10.1111/1467-9604.12398

Masi, A., DeMayo, M. M., Glozier, N., & Guastella, A. J. (2017). An overview of autism spectrum disorder, heterogeneity and treatment options. *Neuroscience Bulletin*, 33(2), 183–193. 10.1007/s12264-017-0100-y28213805

Milton, D. (2012). On the ontological status of autism: The 'double empathy problem'. *Disability & Society*, 27(6), 883–887. 10.1080/09687599.2012.710008

Milton, D., & Ryan, S. (Eds.). (2023). *The routledge international handbook of critical autism studies*. Routledge.

Nicolaidis, C., Raymaker, D., Kapp, S. K., Baggs, A., Ashkenazy, E., McDonald, K., Weiner, M., Maslak, J., Hunter, M., & Joyce, A. (2019). The AASPIRE practice-based guidelines for the inclusion of autistic adults in research as co-researchers and study participants. *Autism*, 23(8), 2007–2019. 10.1177/1362361319830523 30939892

Nistor, G., & Dumitru, C.-L. (2021). Preventing school exclusion of students with autism spectrum disorder (ASD) through reducing discrimination: Sustainable integration through contact-based education sessions. *Sustainability (Basel)*, 13(13), 7056. 10.3390/su13137056

Oliver, M. (1990). *The politics of disablement*. Macmillan. 10.1007/978-1-349-20895-1

Papoudi, D., Jørgensen, C. R., Guldberg, K., & Meadan, H. (2021). Perceptions, experiences, and needs of parents of culturally and linguistically diverse children with autism: A scoping review. *Review Journal of Autism and Developmental Disorders*, 8(2), 195–212. 10.1007/s40489-020-00210-1

Pellicano, E., & Stears, M. (2011). Bridging autism, science and society: Moving toward an ethically informed approach to autism research. *Autism Research*, 4(4), 271–282. 10.1002/aur.20121567986

Perepa, P., Wallace, S., & Guldberg, G. (2023). *The experiences of marginalized families with autistic children*. University of Birmingham., https://www.birmingham.ac.uk/documents/college-social-sciences/education/publications/marginalised-families-with-autistic-children.pdf.pdf

Pinder-Amaker, S. (2014). Identifying the unmet needs of college students on the autism spectrum. *Harvard Review of Psychiatry*, 22(2), 125–137. 10.1097/HRP.00000000000003224 614767

Priestley, M. (1998). Constructions and creations: Idealism, materialism and disability theory. *Disability & Society*, 13(1), 75–94. 10.1080/09687599826920

Sameroff, A. (2010). A unified theory of development: A dialectic integration of nature and nurture. *Child Development*, 81(1), 6–22. 10.1111/j.1467-8624.2009.01378.x 20331651

Sedgewick, F., Hill, V., Yates, R., Pickering, L., & Pellicano, E. (2016). Gender differences in the social motivation and friendship experiences of autistic and non-autistic adolescents. *Journal of Autism and Developmental Disorders*, 46(4), 1297–1306. 10.1007/s10803-015-2669-1 26695137

Silberman, S. (2015). *NeuroTribes: The legacy of autism and the future of neuro-diversity*. Avery.

Singer, J. (2017). *Neurodiversity: The birth of an idea*. Singer Books.

Thomas, C., & Woods, H. (2008). The medical model of disability: A sociological critique. *Disability & Society*, 23(2), 209–222.

Timimi, S., Gardner, N., & McCabe, B. (2010). *The myth of autism: Medicalising men's and boys' social and emotional competence*. Palgrave Macmillan. 10.1007/978-1-137-05773-0

Turnock, A., Langley, K., & Jones, C. (2022). Understanding stigma in autism: A narrative review and theoretical model. *Autism in Adulthood: Challenges and Management*, 4(1), 76–91. 10.1089/aut.2021.000536605561

UN. (2015). *Sustainable Development Goal 4*. United Nations. https://www.un.org/sustainabledevelopment/education/

UNESCO. (1994). *The Salamanca Statement and framework for action on special needs*. UNESCO. https://unesdoc.unesco.org/ark:/48223/pf0000098427

UNESCO. (2005). *Guidelines for inclusion*. UNESCO.

UPIAS. (1976). *Fundamental Principles of Disability*. Union of the Physically Impaired Against Segregation.

Williams, D. (1996). *Autism: An inside-out approach*. Jessica Kingsley Publishers.

Woods, R. (2017). Exploring how the social model of disability can be re-invigorated for autism: In response to Jonathan Levitt. *Disability & Society*, 32(7), 1090–1095. 10.1080/09687599.2017.1328157

World Health Organization. (2023). *Disability*. WHO. https://www.who.int/news-room/fact-sheets/detail/disability

Chapter 10
Cognitive Abilities and Executive Functioning in Students With Autism Spectrum Disorder:
Insights From the United Arab Emirates

Shamsa Almarzooqi

Al Ain Autism Center, Zayed Higher Organisation, Al Ain, UAE

Ahmed Mohamed

https://orcid.org/0000-0002-8225-2310

College of Education, United Arab Emirates University, Al Ain, UAE

ABSTRACT

This study aimed to explore the cognitive abilities and executive functioning behaviors of students with ASD at an autism center in the UAE, employing the SB-5 and the teacher form of the BRIEF2. The findings provide important insights into the cognitive and executive function profiles of these students, highlighting the intricate relationships between various cognitive domains, executive function behaviors, and the impact of ASD severity and notable talents. The positive correlations observed between different SB-5 IQ measures (e.g., full-scale IQ, nonverbal IQ, verbal IQ, and working memory IQ) and the shift scale of the BRIEF are consistent with the findings of previous studies that highlight the link between cognitive flexibility and intelligence.

DOI: 10.4018/979-8-3693-4022-6.ch010

AUTISM SPECTRUM DISORDER

Autism Spectrum Disorder (ASD) is a complex, lifelong developmental condition characterized by difficulties in social communication and interaction alongside restricted and repetitive behaviors, interests, or activities (American Psychiatric Association [APA], 2013). The diagnosis of ASD focuses on impairments in social communication and the presence of restricted/repetitive behaviors (Sharma et al., 2018). Recent advances include the development of deep learning models that have significantly improved the accuracy of diagnosing ASD. These models use advanced algorithms to analyze patterns in data, achieving an impressive 93.41% accuracy in detecting and classifying autism (Sharma & Tanwar, 2024). The prevalence of ASD has been increasing significantly in recent years (McConkey, 2019). Research indicates that both genetic and environmental factors contribute to its etiology (Lyall et al., 2017). Genetic factors include mutations and variations in certain genes that are linked to ASD, while environmental factors can include prenatal exposures to certain chemicals, maternal infections during pregnancy, and other stressors (Beversdorf et al., 2018; Hecht et al., 2016; Ornoy et al., 2015). ASD often co-occurs with other psychiatric conditions, such as Attention-Deficit/Hyperactivity Disorder (ADHD), anxiety, and depression. Studies have shown that individuals with ASD are at a higher risk for these comorbidities compared to the general population (Casseus et al., 2023; Gordon-Lipkin et al., 2018; Kirsch et al., 2020). ADHD is commonly observed in ASD, affecting executive function and leading to attention and hyperactivity issues (Leitner, 2014). Anxiety disorders, including generalized anxiety and social anxiety, are prevalent and can exacerbate social and communication difficulties inherent to ASD (Factor et al., 2022). Depression is also frequently seen in ASD, particularly in adolescents and adults, contributing to a complex clinical picture that requires comprehensive treatment approaches (DeFilippis, 2018). Both pharmacological and non-pharmacological treatments are used to manage ASD symptoms. Behavioral therapies, such as Applied Behavior Analysis (ABA), speech therapy, and occupational therapy, are critical components of treatment, focusing on improving communication, social skills, and daily living abilities (Castellanos et al., 2022; Makrygianni et al., 2018; Ranjan & Pradhan, 2022; Vitomska, 2021). Medications like antipsychotics (e.g., risperidone and aripiprazole) and antidepressants are also commonly prescribed to manage symptoms like irritability, aggression, and anxiety (Alsayouf et al., 2021; Persico et al., 2021; Stigler, 2014). These medications help reduce disruptive behaviors, making behavioral therapies more effective.

INTELLIGENCE QUOTIENT AND EXECUTIVE FUNCTION

Intelligence Quotient (IQ) and executive function are critical areas of focus in understanding ASD. Research indicates that individuals with autism exhibit a wide range of IQ scores, from intellectual disability to above-average intelligence (Rommelse et al., 2015). Recent studies show that approximately 31% of children with ASD have an IQ below 70, 25% fall in the borderline range (IQ 71-85), and 44% have an IQ in the average to above-average range. This diversity in IQ profiles underscores the heterogeneous nature of ASD (Wolff et al., 2022). Current research by Wilson (2024) reveals that children and adults with ASD generally perform within the typical range for verbal and nonverbal reasoning. However, they score about one standard deviation below the mean in processing speed and have slightly lower scores in working memory. This supports the idea of a 'spiky' cognitive profile in autism (Wilson, 2024).

Executive function (EF), which includes skills such as working memory, cognitive flexibility, and inhibitory control, often presents distinct challenges for individuals with ASD (Hill, 2004; Lopez et al., 2005). These EF deficits are linked to difficulties in daily functioning and social interactions. Braverman et al. (2024) found that the cognitive-adaptive gap, which refers to the discrepancy between cognitive abilities and adaptive functioning, is more pronounced in school-age children (7-12 years) compared to preschool children (2-4 years). Poor EF, especially deficits in emotional control, is significantly associated with a greater cognitive-adaptive gap (Braverman et al., 2024).

Research suggests that impaired executive function in individuals with ASD can lead to increased rigidity in thought processes, difficulties in adapting to new situations, and challenges in managing goal-directed behaviors (Leung et al., 2015; Vogan et al., 2018). The heterogeneity in EF performance among individuals with ASD highlights the need for tailored diagnostic and intervention strategies to address these specific cognitive challenges (Demetriou et al., 2019; Gentil-Gutiérrez et al., 2022). For instance, the development of programs such as the Emotional Recognition Memory Training Program (ERMTP) shows promise in improving social cognition in children with ASD by using computer-based learning activities (Paulra et al., 2024).

The correlation between IQ and EF in children with ASD is complex and multifaceted. Studies indicate that while there is a relationship between IQ and EF in typically developing children, this correlation is not as straightforward in children with autism. For instance, children with ASD often exhibit significant impairments in executive functions such as working memory, cognitive flexibility, and inhibitory control, regardless of their IQ levels (McLean et al., 2014; Merchán-Naranjo et al., 2016; Van Eylen et al., 2015). Research suggests that executive functioning deficits in children with autism can persist even when controlling for IQ, highlighting that these deficits are not merely a byproduct of intellectual capabilities but rather intrinsic to the disorder (Liss et al., 2001).

In some cases, specific executive function deficits, such as difficulties with cognitive flexibility and planning, are found to be independent of IQ in children with ASD (Robinson et al., 2009). This indicates that while IQ can influence certain cognitive processes, executive dysfunction in autism is a distinct and pervasive issue. Furthermore, children with high-functioning autism (those with average or above-average IQ) still show pronounced executive function deficits compared to their typically developing peers, which affects their daily living and adaptive behaviors (McLean et al., 2014).

ASSESSMENT TOOLS: STANFORD-BINET INTELLIGENCE SCALES AND BRIEF2

Stanford-Binet Intelligence Scales

The Stanford-Binet Intelligence Scales has been a fundamental tool in the assessment of intelligence since its inception in 1905 by Alfred Binet and Theodore Simon (Kamphaus & Juechter, 2010). Originally designed to identify children with mental retardation, the scales have undergone multiple revisions to improve their accuracy and theoretical grounding (Roid & Barram, 2004). The fifth edition, known as SB-5, aligns with the Cattell-Horn-Carroll (CHC) theoretical model of cognitive abilities, offering refined measures across verbal and nonverbal domains (Janzen et al., 2004). This edition also introduced significant changes in item content, administration format, and standardization procedures to better capture the multifaceted nature of intelligence (DiStefano & Dombrowski, 2006). The SB-5 is recognized for its robustness in both general and special populations, providing reliable assessments of cognitive profiles (Coolican et al., 2007). Throughout its iterations, the Stanford-Binet scales have maintained their status as a comprehensive and reliable measure of intelligence (Kamphaus & Juechter, 2010). The SB-5 has been widely adopted in various settings, including clinical, educational, and research environments, due to its comprehensive approach to measuring intelligence (Dale et al., 2014). One of the notable features of the SB-5 is its use of hierarchical models to assess broad and narrow cognitive abilities, which allows for a nuanced understanding of an individual's cognitive strengths and weaknesses (Janzen et al., 2004). The test is divided into five factors: Fluid Reasoning, Knowledge, Quantitative Reasoning, Visual-Spatial Processing, and Working Memory, each contributing to an overall Full-Scale IQ score (Roid & Barram, 2004). These factors align closely with the

CHC model, providing a theoretical basis that supports the interpretation of test results in a meaningful way (Keith et al., 2001). Moreover, the SB-5's standardization process involved a large and diverse sample, enhancing the test's validity across different demographic groups (Janzen et al., 2004). This comprehensive standardization ensures that the test results are reflective of the broader population, thereby increasing the test's applicability and fairness. Additionally, the SB-5 incorporates adaptive testing techniques, which adjust the difficulty of questions based on the test-taker's performance, making the assessment more efficient and tailored to the individual's ability level (Roid & Barram, 2004).

Behavior Rating Inventory of Executive Function

The Behavior Rating Inventory of Executive Function, Second Edition (BRIEF2), is an extensively used tool designed to assess executive function behaviors in children and adolescents in both home and school environments (Gioia et al., 2015). The BRIEF2 is structured into three indexes: Behavioral Regulation, Emotional Regulation, and Cognitive Regulation, encompassing nine scales including Inhibit, Shift, Self-Monitor, Emotional Control, Initiate, Working Memory, Plan/Organize, Organization of Materials, and Task-Monitor. It is recognized for its comprehensive evaluation capabilities, allowing clinicians to gather data from multiple informants, including parents, teachers, and the individuals themselves. The BRIEF2 has demonstrated strong psychometric properties, such as high reliability and validity across different cultures and populations. The BRIEF2 has demonstrated strong psychometric properties, such as high reliability and validity, in multiple countries. For instance, it has been validated in Persian for assessing Iranian children with ADHD, confirming its reliability and utility (Parhoon et al., 2021). In Russia, the BRIEF2 has been validated for use with both typically developing children and those with a history of institutional care, emphasizing the importance of cultural adaptation in psychological testing (Gavrilova et al., 2023). Additionally, the BRIEF2 has been validated in the Netherlands, further demonstrating its applicability and reliability across different European populations (Huizinga et al., 2023). The BRIEF2's robustness as a clinical tool for evaluating executive functions in children and adolescents is well-supported by these diverse cultural validations. Additionally, the BRIEF2 is effective in differentiating between various diagnostic groups, as shown in research involving typically developing children and those with ADHD, where it provided valuable insights into executive dysfunction (Dodzik, 2017). The instrument's multidimensional nature, capturing behavioral regulation, metacognition, and emotional regulation, further enhances its utility in clinical and educational settings, supporting detailed and context-specific evaluations of executive functions (Mcauley et al.,

2010). The BRIEF2's broad applicability and robust psychometric backing make it a crucial tool for practitioners assessing executive function in various populations.

AIMS AND RESEARCH QUESTIONS

This study focuses on a group of students at an Autism Center in the United Arab Emirates (UAE), aiming to provide a comprehensive evaluation of their cognitive and executive profiles. The SB-5, and the BRIEF2, were employed to assess these dimensions. By examining the correlation between cognitive abilities and executive functioning behaviors, as well as the impact of ASD severity and notable talents, this research seeks to contribute valuable insights for tailored educational and therapeutic interventions.

The study aims to:

- To assess the cognitive abilities of students with ASD at an Autism Center in the UAE using the SB-5.
- Evaluate the executive functioning behaviors of these students using the Teacher Form of the BRIEF2.
- To explore the relationship between cognitive abilities and executive functioning behaviors in students with ASD.
- To investigate the impact of the severity of ASD on cognitive abilities and executive functioning.
- To examine the differences in cognitive and executive functioning between students with and without notable talents.

The study questions are:

- What are the cognitive abilities of students with ASD as measured by the SB-5?
- How do the executive functioning behaviors of students with ASD manifest according to the Teacher Form of the BRIEF2 assessments?
- Is there a correlation between cognitive abilities and executive functioning behaviors in students with ASD?
- How does the severity of ASD influence the cognitive abilities and executive functioning behaviors of these students?
- Are there significant differences in cognitive and executive functioning between students with ASD who have notable talents and those who do not?

METHODOLOGY

Participants

This study includes several students enrolled at the Autism Center in a region of the UAE. The Autism Center specializes in providing tailored educational and therapeutic support for individuals with ASD. Table 1 presents the demographic characteristics of the students.

Table 1. Demographic characteristics of the students

Name	Gender	Age	Diagnosis	Level of Severity	Level of Support Needed	Comorbidities	Therapeutic Services	Medication	Medical Problems	Talented
Salem	Male	15y-6m	ASD	Mild	Minimal support	Language disorder	None	None	Asthma Obesity	Yes
Ahmed	Male	17y-7m	ASD	Mild	Minimal support	Language disorder	None	None	None	Yes
Ali	Male	16y-7m	ASD	Mild	Minimal support	Language disorder, OCD	None	None	Obesity	No
Abdulla	Male	16y-4m	ASD	Mild	Minimal support	None	None	None	None	No
Mohammed	Male	14y-9m	ASD	Moderate	Moderate support	Language disorder, ADHD	Occupational, Speech Therapy	Risperdal	None	No
Humaid	Male	11y-4m	ASD	Moderate	Moderate support	Language disorder, ADHD, Anxiety	Occupational, Behavioral, Speech Therapy	Compify	None	No

OCD: Obsessive-Compulsive Disorder, ASD: Autism Spectrum Disorder, ADHD: Attention-Deficit/Hyperactivity Disorder

Profile: Salem

One of the participants is Salem, a 15-year-and-6-month-old male student diagnosed with autism. Salem's autism is classified as mild, and he exhibits a talent for technology, particularly in using Microsoft applications such as Word and PowerPoint. His interests include music, playing PlayStation, reading the Holy Quran, and participating in sports. Salem is known for his polite demeanor and consistently follows his teachers' instructions.

Despite his proficiency in using two-word sentences, Salem has a communication disorder characterized by a language disorder and direct echolalia. However, he remains sociable and enjoys interacting and playing with his peers.

Profile: Ahmed

Another participant is Ahmed, a 17-year-and-7-month-old male diagnosed with autism, classified as mild. Ahmed has demonstrated exceptional talent in reading the Holy Quran, having participated in numerous competitions and winning many awards within the region. His skills extend to creating handicrafts such as carpets, accessories, and Hair clip, which he sells through various initiatives.

Ahmed is also an accomplished athlete, having participated in several sports tournaments, including bowling, where he has won awards. Additionally, he has a knack for assembling puzzles and actively engages in volunteer work.

Ahmed communicates using clear sentences; however, he often provides direct responses and tends to repeat what others say. Despite this, he is very sociable, enjoys interacting with others, and is known for his constant smile.

Profile: Ali

Ali is a 16-year-and-7-month-old male diagnosed with autism, classified as mild. Despite having a language disorder that makes speaking difficult, Ali has made significant progress in reading the Holy Quran through continuous practice and teacher support.

He can read simple words and answer basic questions after hearing a story. Ali is able to follow simple and clear commands, although it sometimes takes him a bit longer to understand them. With patience and clear instructions, Ali successfully engages in various activities and demonstrates a dedication to overcoming his communication challenges.

Ali is a quiet student who often keeps to himself and does not frequently communicate with his peers. He tends to engage in solitary activities and prefers spending time alone.

Profile: Abdulla

Abdulla is a 16-year-and-4-month-old male diagnosed with autism, classified as mild. He speaks fluently and demonstrates good social interaction skills. Abdulla is able to follow commands and instructions effectively, making him a reliable assistant to the teacher in the classroom.

His role as a classroom assistant showcases his ability to engage with both teachers and peers, contributing positively to the learning environment. Abdulla's communication skills and willingness to help make him an integral part of the classroom dynamics.

Profile: Mohammed

Mohammed is a 14-year-and-9-month-old male diagnosed with autism, classified as moderate. While he can speak, he experiences speech delays and exhibits direct echolalia. Mohammed faces several behavioral challenges; he often tries to provoke those around him, waiting for their reactions. He has a tendency to hurt others and sometimes resorts to hitting to elicit a response.

To manage his excessive movements, reactions, stereotypical behaviors, and sensory interests, Mohammed takes medications that help mitigate these symptoms. Despite these challenges, continuous support and intervention are crucial to help him navigate his behavioral issues and improve his interactions with others.

Profile: Humaid

Humaid is an 11-year-and-4-month-old male diagnosed with autism, classified as moderate. Humaid has communication disorders; he can speak by using sentences of two words and has direct echolalia. He has always preferred to be silent rather than speak. He requires assistance with daily activities and is accompanied by a nanny when attending the center.

Humaid's diet is highly restricted due to extreme sensitivity to the texture and smell of foods, limiting him to consuming only milk. He experiences several sensory processing issues, including an aversion to loud sounds, which necessitates the use of headphones to mitigate his discomfort. These sensory sensitivities also impact his movement; he often walks in an unusual manner and prefers to remain stationary, avoiding tasks that require physical activity.

To manage his behaviors and symptoms associated with autism, Humaid takes medication. Despite these challenges, continuous support and tailored interventions are crucial to help him navigate daily life and enhance his overall well-being.

PROCEDURES

Approval was obtained from the center where the students receive their education and rehabilitative services. Six students were nominated, representing a range of abilities. This group included two students with mild autism who possess special talents, two students with mild autism without notable talents, and two students with moderate autism spectrum disorder. Consent was obtained from all parents after the selection process.

To measure cognitive abilities, the SB-5 was administered. This test was translated and standardized for the Gulf environment (Saudi Arabia) and is culturally relevant to the UAE context. Both the verbal and non-verbal sections of the test were administered to all students.

Additionally, the Behavior Rating Inventory of Executive Function, Second Edition (BRIEF-2), a teacher form designed for children aged 5 to 18 years, was utilized. This form includes 63 items that assess various aspects of executive functioning. The BRIEF-2 teacher version was distributed to all the students' teachers, who completed the questionnaire to provide detailed insights into each student's executive functioning.

RESULTS

Stanford-Binet Intelligence Scales, Fifth Edition (SB-5) Assessment Scores

Table 2 presents each student's detailed SB-5 assessment scores. This table provides a comprehensive view of cognitive abilities across various domains, such as Full-Scale IQ, Nonverbal IQ, Verbal IQ, Abbreviated IQ, Fluid Reasoning, Knowledge, Quantitative Reasoning, Visual-Spatial, and Working Memory.

Behavior Rating Inventory of Executive Function (BRIEF) T-Scores

Table 3 displays the Teacher Form of the BRIEF2 T-scores and the percentile rank for each student. The BRIEF2 scores cover various executive function domains such as Inhibit, Self-Monitor, Behavior Regulation Index, Shift, Emotional Control, Emotion Regulation Index, Initiate, Working Memory, Plan/Organize, Task Monitor, Organization of Materials, Cognitive Regulation Index, and Global Executive Composite.

Descriptive Statistics for Students' SB-5 Measures and BRIEF2 Indices

Table 4 presents the descriptive statistics for students' SB-5 measures and BRIEF indices derived from a sample of six students. The Full-Scale IQ scores ranged from 46 to 65, with a mean of 53.50 and a standard deviation of 7.0, indicating some variability within the sample. Nonverbal IQ had a higher mean score of 62.6 and showed greater variability (SD = 10.6), with scores ranging between 52 and 78. In contrast, Verbal IQ scores were more consistent, ranging from 45 to 53, and exhibited a lower mean of 48.0 and a smaller standard deviation of 3.8. Other IQ measures, such as Fluid Reasoning IQ, and Visual Spatial IQ, showed diverse ranges and variability, reflecting distinct cognitive strengths and weaknesses within the sample. The BRIEF indices, which assess various aspects of executive functioning, also displayed a wide range of scores. The Behavior Regulation Index (BRI) had scores between 46 and 72, with a mean of 57.67 and a standard deviation of 9.8, while the Emotion Regulation Index (ERI) and the Cognitive Regulation Index (CRI) had means of 60.5 and 57.3, respectively. The Global Executive Composite (GEC) reflected overall executive functioning with scores ranging from 52 to 66, a mean of 58.8, and a standard deviation of 5.6.

Correlation Between SB-5 and Behavior Rating Inventory of Executive Function

The data in Table 5 represents the correlation coefficients between various subscales of the SB-5 and the BRIEF-2:

FULL-SCALE IQ

FSIQ demonstrated a moderate positive correlation with the Shift scale ($r = 0.637$), suggesting that higher overall intelligence is associated with better cognitive flexibility.

There were weak negative correlations with Emotional Control ($r = -0.372$) and Emotional Regulation Index ($r = -0.223$), indicating that higher IQ scores might be associated with fewer difficulties in emotional control and regulation.

Other correlations with BRIEF scales were generally weak and negative, suggesting minimal relationship between FSIQ and these executive function behaviors.

NONVERBAL IQ

NVIQ showed a moderate positive correlation with the Shift scale (r = 0.572), similar to FSIQ, implying a link between nonverbal reasoning abilities and cognitive flexibility.

Weak negative correlations were observed with Emotional Control (r = -0.416) and Emotional Regulation Index (r = -0.301), reinforcing the pattern seen with FSIQ.

VERBAL IQ

VIQ exhibited a strong positive correlation with Shift (r = 0.707) and moderate positive correlations with Inhibit (r = 0.568), Self-Monitor (r = 0.649), and Behavior Regulation Index (r = 0.596). This suggests that verbal intelligence is strongly related to various aspects of executive function, particularly cognitive flexibility and behavior regulation.

There were moderate negative correlations with Emotional Control (r = -0.384) and Organization of Materials (r = -0.397), indicating that higher verbal IQ might correspond with fewer difficulties in emotional control and organization.

ABBREVIATED IQ

ABIQ had a moderate positive correlation with Shift (r = 0.530) and moderate negative correlations with Emotional Control (r = -0.601) and Emotional Regulation Index (r = -0.501). This pattern suggests that abbreviated measures of intelligence similarly relate to cognitive flexibility and emotional regulation.

FLUID REASONING IQ

FRIQ was moderately positively correlated with Shift (r = 0.598), indicating a relationship between fluid reasoning abilities and cognitive flexibility.

There were weak negative correlations with Emotional Control (r = -0.329) and Emotional Regulation Index (r = -0.190), consistent with the general trend of higher cognitive abilities being associated with better emotional regulation.

KNOWLEDGE IQ

KNIQ had a very strong positive correlation with Shift (r = 0.942), indicating that acquired knowledge significantly predicts cognitive flexibility.

Weak to moderate negative correlations were found with Emotional Control (r = -0.462) and Emotional Regulation Index (r = -0.173), maintaining the observed pattern across other IQ measures.

Quantitative Reasoning IQ

QRIQ showed moderate to strong negative correlations with Inhibit (r = -0.514), Self-Monitor (r = -0.604), and Behavior Regulation Index (r = -0.590), suggesting that higher quantitative reasoning abilities might be associated with fewer inhibitory control and self-monitoring problems.

A moderate positive correlation was observed with Working Memory (r = 0.446), indicating a link between quantitative reasoning and working memory abilities.

VISUAL-SPATIAL IQ

VSIQ had strong negative correlations with Inhibit (r = -0.564), Self-Monitor (r = -0.628), and Behavior Regulation Index (r = -0.620), suggesting that higher visual-spatial abilities are associated with fewer issues in inhibitory control and self-monitoring.

Moderate positive correlations were observed with Shift (r = 0.336) and moderate negative with Emotional Regulation Index (r = -0.314), highlighting a complex relationship between visual-spatial skills and various executive functions.

WORKING MEMORY IQ

WMIQ exhibited strong positive correlations with Shift (r = 0.676) and moderate positive correlations with Inhibit (r = 0.426) and Self-Monitor (r = 0.347), suggesting a strong link between working memory and cognitive flexibility as well as inhibitory control.

Moderate negative correlations with Emotional Control (r = -0.591) and Emotional Regulation Index (r = -0.402) were observed, in line with the general pattern.

IMPACT OF SEVERITY LEVELS ON COGNITIVE AND EXECUTIVE FUNCTIONING: A MANN-WHITNEY U ANALYSIS

Table 6 presents the results of the Mann-Whitney U test, which compares the distribution of scores on cognitive (SB-5) and executive function (BRIEF-2) measures between mild and moderate severity levels of ASD.

The Mann-Whitney U test results indicate a statistically significant difference in the "Emotional Control ERI BRIEF" variable between individuals with mild and moderate severity levels, with a p-value of 0.049. This finding suggests that individuals with moderate severity exhibit significantly poorer emotional control compared to those with mild severity. This difference underscores the importance of addressing emotional regulation in therapeutic interventions for individuals with higher severity levels to potentially improve their emotional control capabilities.

Moreover, the variables "Full-Scale IQ" (p = 0.064) and "Nonverbal IQ" (p = 0.064) demonstrated near-significant differences between the severity levels. The trend suggests that individuals with moderate severity tend to have lower scores in these areas, indicating a possible decline in overall cognitive functioning and nonverbal reasoning abilities as severity increases. Similarly, "Abbreviated IQ" (p = 0.060) showed a near-significant difference, reinforcing the potential impact of severity on general cognitive performance.

The "Working Memory IQ" variable, with a p-value of 0.095, also approached significance, suggesting that working memory might be affected by the severity level. Although not statistically significant, the observed trend highlights a possible decline in working memory abilities with increasing severity, warranting further investigation.

The lack of statistically significant differences in the remaining variables, such as "Verbal IQ," "Fluid Reasoning IQ," and various BRIEF scales, might be attributed to the small sample size, which limits the power to detect more subtle differences.

IMPACT OF TALENT LEVELS ON COGNITIVE AND EXECUTIVE FUNCTIONING: A MANN-WHITNEY U ANALYSIS

Table 7 presents the results of the Mann-Whitney U test, which compares the distribution of scores on cognitive (SB-5) and executive function (BRIEF-2) measures between students with and without notable talents.

Full-Scale IQ, Nonverbal IQ, Verbal IQ, and Abbreviated IQ: The p-values for these variables (0.355, 0.355, 0.333, and 0.348, respectively) are greater than 0.05, indicating no statistically significant differences in these cognitive measures between students with and without notable talents.

Fluid Reasoning IQ, Knowledge IQ, Visual-Spatial IQ, and Working Memory IQ: These variables show high p-values (ranging from 0.814 to 1.000), suggesting no significant differences between the talent levels.

Quantitative Reasoning IQ: This variable has a p-value of 0.057, which is close to the significance threshold of 0.05, indicating a trend towards significance. This suggests a potential difference in quantitative reasoning abilities between the talent levels, although it is not statistically significant in this sample.

Inhibit, Self-Monitor, Behavior Regulation Index, Shift, Emotional Control, and other BRIEF scales: The p-values for these variables are all greater than 0.05, indicating no significant differences in executive function measures between the talent levels.

The analysis reveals no significant differences in most cognitive and executive functioning measures across different talent levels. The exception is a trend towards significance in quantitative reasoning IQ, suggesting further investigation with a larger sample may be warranted to determine if talent levels impact this cognitive domain.

Table 2. SB-5 standard scores of students

Students	Full-Scale IQ	Nonverbal IQ	Verbal IQ	Abbreviated battery IQ	Fluid Reasoning	Knowledge	Quantitative Reasoning	Visual-Spatial	Working Memory
Salem	57	71	45	62	61	58	66	73	56
Ahmed	55	66	46	62	61	52	66	71	58
Ali	50	56	53	56	50	56	53	56	58
Abdulla	65	78	53	68	81	60	59	83	68
Mohammed	46	52	45	53	53	52	56	61	56
Humaid	48	53	46	50	50	52	56	73	51

40-54: Moderate intellectual disability, 55-69: Mild intellectual disability, 70-79: Borderline intellectual functioning, 80-89: Low average intelligence, 90- 109 Average intelligence.

Table 3. Teacher form of the BRIEF2 T-scores and the percentile rank for each student

Students	Inhibit Scale	%ile	Self-Monitor Scale	%ile	Behavior Regulation Index	%ile	Shift Scale	%ile
Salem	52	78	55	80	53	80	65	93
Ahmed	49	73	51	75	50	72	58	87
Ali	66	92	80	98	72	95	65	93
Abdulla	58	87	63	92	60	89	69	96
Mohammed	62	90	67	94	65	92	61	86

continued on following page

Table 3. Continued

Students	Emotional Control Scale	%ile	Emotion Regulation Index	%ile	Initiate Scale	%ile		
Humaid	44	45	47	52	46	47	61	87
Salem	53	85	59	90	62	92		
Ahmed	53	85	56	85	62	92		
Ali	49	83	58	87	67	94		
Abdulla	53	85	61	91	53	74		
Mohammed	55	84	59	83	60	91		
Humaid	75	94	70	93	50	55		

Students	Working Memory Scale	%ile	Plan/Organize Scale	%ile	Task-Monitor Scale	%ile		
Salem	77	98	73	96	70	95		
Ahmed	59	86	47	60	45	56		
Ali	59	86	55	75	54	71		
Abdulla	43	52	55	75	57	78		
Mohammed	62	88	64	92	64	92		
Humaid	52	64	48	53	54	75		

Students	Organization of Materials Scale	%ile	Cognitive Regulation Index	%ile	Global Executive Composite	%ile		
Salem	63	91	72	96	66	91		
Ahmed	44	61	51	67	52	71		
Ali	44	61	56	77	61	90		
Abdulla	49	74	52	69	56	81		
Mohammed	58	80	64	90	64	88		
Humaid	41	36	49	51	54	62		

%ile: Percentile
The percentile rank (%ile) indicates how a student's score compares to a normative sample.

Table 4. Descriptive statistics for the student's SB-5 IQ and BRIEF-2 scores

Variable	Minimum	Maximum	Mean	Std. Deviation
Full-Scale IQ	46	65	53.5	7.0
Nonverbal IQ	52	78	62.6	10.6
Verbal IQ	45	53	48.0	3.8
Abbreviated IQ	50	68	58.5	6.6

continued on following page

Table 4. Continued

Variable	Minimum	Maximum	Mean	Std. Deviation
Fluid Reasoning IQ	50	81	59.3	11.7
Knowledge IQ	52	60	55.0	3.5
Quantitative Reasoning IQ	53	66	59.3	5.5
Visual-Spatial IQ	56	83	69.5	9.6
Working Memory IQ	51	68	57.8	5.6
Inhibit (BRI)	44	66	55.1	8.3
Self-Monitor (BRI)	47	80	60.5	12.0
Behavior Regulation Index (BRI)	46	72	57.6	9.8
Shift (ERI)	58	69	63.1	3.9
Emotional Control (ERI)	49	75	56.3	9.3
Emotion Regulation Index (ERI)	56	70	60.5	4.9
Initiate (CRI)	50	67	59.0	6.3
Working Memory (CRI)	43	77	58.6	11.2
Plan Organize (CRI)	47	73	57.0	9.9
Task Monitor (CRI)	45	70	57.3	8.7
Organization of Materials (CRI)	41	63	49.8	8.7
Cognitive Regulation Index (CRI)	49	72	57.3	8.9
Global Executive Composite (GEC)	52	66	58.8	5.6

Table 5. Correlation between SB-5 and the BRIEF-2

SB-5 Measures	Inhibit	SM	BRI	Shift	EC	ERI	Initiate	WM	PO	TM	OM	CRI	GEC
Full-Scale IQ	-0.053	-0.112	-0.122	0.637	-0.372	-0.223	-0.181	-0.265	0.063	0.007	0.115	-0.061	-0.189
Nonverbal IQ	-0.092	-0.168	-0.172	0.572	-0.416	-0.301	-0.101	-0.099	0.179	0.092	0.245	0.079	-0.097
Verbal IQ	0.568	0.649	0.596	0.707	-0.384	-0.114	0.081	-0.586	0.263	0.265	0.397	0.390	0.154
Abbreviated IQ	0.088	0.004	0.006	0.530	-0.601	-0.501	0.071	-0.122	0.135	-0.007	0.213	0.054	-0.098
Fluid Reasoning IQ	0.012	-0.096	-0.072	0.598	-0.329	-0.190	-0.315	-0.408	0.043	0.026	0.154	-0.102	-0.206
Knowledge IQ	0.321	0.305	0.278	0.942**	-0.462	-0.173	0.018	-0.070	0.411	0.391	0.316	0.254	0.290
Quantitative Reasoning IQ	-0.514	-0.604	-0.590	-0.198	-0.212	-0.376	0.103	0.446	0.219	0.051	0.365	0.290	-0.075

continued on following page

Table 5. Continued

SB-5 Measures	Inhibit	SM	BRI	Shift	EC	ERI	Initiate	WM	PO	TM	OM	CRI	GEC
Visual-Spatial IQ	-0.564	-0.628	-0.620	0.336	0.253	-0.314	-0.703	-0.373	-0.104	-0.005	0.011	-0.228	-0.416
Working Memory IQ	0.426	0.347	0.363	0.676	-0.591	-0.402	-0.028	-0.485	-0.011	-0.077	0.044	-0.151	-0.121

Correlation between SB-5 and BRIEF:

SM: Self-Monitor, EC: Emotional Control, ERI: Emotion Regulation Index, WM: Working Memory, PO: Plan Organize, TM: Task Monitor, OM: Organization of Materials, GEC: Global Executive Composite, CRI: Cognitive Regulation Index, BRI: Behavior Regulation Index

Table 6. Assessing the impact of severity levels of ASD on cognitive (SB-5) and executive functioning (BRIEF-2): A Mann-Whitney U test analysis

Variable	Mann-Whitney U	Z Value	Asymp. Sig. (2-tailed)
Full-Scale IQ	0.0	-1.852	0.064
Nonverbal IQ	0.0	-1.852	0.064
Verbal IQ	2.0	-0.968	0.333
Abbreviated IQ	0.0	-1.879	0.06
Fluid Reasoning IQ	1.5	-1.192	0.233
Knowledge IQ	1.0	-1.476	0.14
Quantitative Reasoning IQ	2.0	-0.953	0.34
Visual-Spatial IQ	3.5	-0.235	0.814
Working Memory IQ	0.5	-1.669	0.095
Inhibit (BRI)	3.0	-0.463	0.643
Self-Monitor BRI	3.0	-0.463	0.643
Behavior Regulation Index BRI	3.0	-0.463	0.643
Shift (ERI)	2.0	-0.953	0.34
Emotional Control (ERI)	0.0	-1.967	0.049
Emotion Regulation Index (ERI)	1.5	-1.174	0.24
Initiate (CRI)	1.0	-1.409	0.159
Working Memory (CRI)	4.0	0.0	1.0
Plan Organize (CRI)	4.0	0.0	1.0
Task Monitor (CRI)	3.5	-0.235	0.814
Organization of Materials (CRI)	3.0	-0.47	0.639
Cognitive Regulation Index (CRI)	3.0	-0.463	0.643
Global Executive Composite (GEC)	4.0	0.0	1.0

Table 7. Assessing the differences in cognitive (SB-5) and executive functioning (BRIEF-2) across talent levels: A Mann-Whitney U test analysis

Variable	Mann-Whitney U	Z Value	Asymp. Sig. (2-tailed)
Full-Scale IQ	2.0	-0.926	0.355
Nonverbal IQ	2.0	-0.926	0.355
Verbal IQ	2.0	-0.968	0.333
Abbreviated IQ	2.0	-0.939	0.348
Fluid Reasoning IQ	4.0	-0.953	0.931
Knowledge IQ	4.0	-1.000	1.000
Quantitative Reasoning IQ	3.5	-1.907	0.057
Visual-Spatial IQ	4.0	-0.235	0.814
Working Memory IQ	4.0	-1.000	0.931
Inhibit (BRI)	2.0	-0.926	0.355
Self-Monitor BRI	2.0	-0.926	0.355
Behavior Regulation Index BRI	2.0	-0.926	0.355
Shift (ERI)	2.0	-0.715	0.533
Emotional Control (ERI)	2.5	-0.492	0.623
Emotion Regulation Index (ERI)	3.0	-1.174	0.240
Initiate (CRI)	2.0	-0.939	0.348
Working Memory (CRI)	2.0	-0.705	0.933
Plan Organize (CRI)	2.0	-1.174	0.240
Task Monitor (CRI)	4.0	-0.235	0.814
Organization of Materials (CRI)	4.0	-0.481	0.933
Cognitive Regulation Index (CRI)	3.0	-0.463	0.800
Global Executive Composite (GEC)	4.0	0.0	1.000

DISCUSSION

This study aimed to explore the cognitive abilities and executive functioning behaviors of students with ASD at an Autism Center in the UAE, employing the SB-5 and the Teacher Form of the BRIEF2. The findings provide important insights into the cognitive and executive function profiles of these students, highlighting the intricate relationships between various cognitive domains, executive function behaviors, and the impact of ASD severity and notable talents. The positive correlations observed between different SB-5 IQ measures (e.g., Full-Scale IQ, Nonverbal IQ, Verbal IQ, and Working Memory IQ) and the Shift scale of the BRIEF are consistent with the findings of previous studies that highlight the link between cognitive flexibility and intelligence. Cognitive flexibility, a critical component of executive function, has been shown to be influenced by overall cognitive abilities. Similar studies, such as those by Tschida and Yerys (2021), have demonstrated the importance of cognitive flexibility in ASD and its association with general intelligence measures. Additionally, the negative correlations between IQ measures (e.g., Full-Scale IQ, Nonverbal IQ, and Verbal IQ) and the Emotional Control and Emotional Regulation Indexes of the BRIEF are in line with research that indicates higher cognitive abilities are associated with better emotional regulation. Studies have shown that children with higher IQs tend to have fewer difficulties in managing their emotions, which is crucial for adaptive functioning. This pattern is supported by findings from Blijd-Hoogewys et al. (2014), which suggest a strong link between emotional regulation and cognitive processes in ASD. Also, the article by Matthews et al. (2015) supports the statement regarding the strong positive correlations between Verbal IQ and various executive function scales. It highlights the significant role of verbal intelligence in executive functioning and corroborates earlier studies emphasizing the impact of verbal skills on executive functions, particularly in ASD. For example, it discusses the interaction between intellectual ability and SB-5 subtests, illustrating how verbal abilities influence cognitive profiles among individuals with ASD (Matthews et al., 2015).

The meta-analysis by Wilson (2024) supports these findings, highlighting that autistic individuals often show strengths in verbal and nonverbal reasoning but have weaknesses in processing speed and working memory. This evidence of a "spiky" cognitive profile in autism aligns with our observation of cognitive flexibility's dependency on overall cognitive abilities (Wilson, 2024). The study by Braverman et al. (2024) further supports these findings by demonstrating that poor EF, particularly deficits in emotional control, is associated with a greater cognitive-adaptive gap in individuals with ASD. This aligns with our observation of significant negative correlations between IQ measures and emotional regulation indexes. The results of the meta-analysis by Wilson (2024) also support the association of higher cognitive abilities with better emotional regulation, emphasizing the impact of processing speed and working memory on emotional control in ASD.

While our results are largely in agreement with existing literature, some contrasts were observed. The moderate to strong negative correlations between Quantitative Reasoning IQ and executive function scales such as Inhibit and Self-Monitor contrast with some studies that found minimal relationships between these domains. For example, Tsai et al. (2021) reported less consistent correlations between quantitative reasoning and executive behaviors, suggesting variability in how these relationships manifest in different samples of individuals with ASD. The strong negative correlations between visual-spatial IQ and inhibitory control/self-monitoring contradict some research that suggests weaker associations between visual-spatial skills and executive functions. For instance, Coolican et al. (2008) found that visual-spatial abilities were not as strongly linked to executive function deficits in ASD, highlighting potential differences in sample characteristics or assessment methods. The results of our study highlight significant differences in cognitive and executive functioning between individuals with mild and moderate severity levels of ASD, providing valuable insights into how severity impacts these domains. Specifically, the findings from the Mann-Whitney U test suggest that certain cognitive and executive functions are more adversely affected in individuals with moderate-severity ASD. One of the key findings is the statistically significant difference in the "Emotional Control ERI BRIEF" variable, with individuals having moderate severity levels displaying significantly poorer emotional control compared to those with mild severity ($p = 0.049$). This aligns with previous research that has identified emotional regulation as a critical area of difficulty in more severe cases of ASD (Mazefsky et al., 2013). Additionally, while the differences in "Full-Scale IQ," "Nonverbal IQ," and "Abbreviated IQ" were not statistically significant, the near-significant p-values (all around 0.06) indicate a trend where individuals with moderate severity ASD tend to have lower cognitive scores. This trend is supported by other studies that have shown a decline in cognitive functioning as the severity of ASD increases (Charman et al., 2011). These findings suggest that the cognitive challenges in ASD become more pronounced with increased severity, impacting areas such as nonverbal reasoning and overall cognitive performance.

Furthermore, the results from the Mann-Whitney U test indicated that cognitive and executive functioning measures did not significantly differ based on talent levels. The study found no significant differences in Full-Scale IQ, Nonverbal IQ, Verbal IQ, and Abbreviated IQ among students with ASD based on their talent levels. These findings align with previous research suggesting that intellectual functioning in children with ASD is not necessarily linked to the presence of special talents (Howlin et al., 2009). Similarly, no significant differences were observed in Fluid Reasoning IQ, Knowledge IQ, Visual-Spatial IQ, and Working Memory IQ. These results are consistent with studies that have shown the heterogeneous nature of cognitive abilities in individuals with ASD, irrespective of their talents (Estes et al., 2011; Troyb et al., 2014). Additionally, the executive functioning measures, including Inhibit, Self-Monitor, Behavior Regulation Index, Shift, and Emotional Control, did not show significant differences across talent levels. This is in line with existing research that suggests executive dysfunction is a common characteristic in ASD but does not necessarily correlate with the presence of savant abilities (Hill, 2004; Kenworthy et al., 2008). The consistency of our findings with these studies reinforces the understanding that executive function deficits in ASD are pervasive and not moderated by the presence of special talents.

LIMITATIONS

This study has several limitations that need to be considered for a comprehensive understanding of the findings. Firstly, the small sample size of only six students limits the generalizability of the results. A larger sample size would provide more robust data and allow for more definitive conclusions. Additionally, the sample homogeneity, with all participants drawn from a single Autism Center in the UAE, may not represent the broader ASD population, limiting the applicability of the findings to other regions or cultural contexts. Another significant limitation is the reliance on the SB-5 and the BRIEF2. While these tools are widely recognized and validated, they have inherent limitations. The BRIEF2, for example, depends on teacher reports, which may introduce subjectivity and potential bias. Moreover, the SB-5 was translated and standardized for the Gulf environment, but cultural differences could still impact the validity of the assessments in the UAE context. The study's cross-sectional design is another limitation, as it only provides a snapshot of cognitive and executive function at one point in time. Longitudinal studies are needed to understand developmental changes and how cognitive and executive functions evolve over time in individuals with ASD. The absence of a control group is also a notable limitation. Without a comparison group of typically developing children or children with other developmental disorders, it is challenging to determine whether the observed profiles are unique to ASD or if they share similarities with other conditions. Lastly, while the study explores the relationship between cognitive abilities, executive functioning, ASD severity, and notable talents, it does not account for other potential confounding variables, such as socioeconomic status, educational background, or family support, which could influence the outcomes.

IMPLICATIONS

The findings of this study highlight crucial implications for educational practices, therapeutic interventions, and policy development for students with ASD. Firstly, the strong correlation between cognitive flexibility and various intelligence measures underscores the importance of integrating activities and curricula that enhance cognitive flexibility in educational settings, thereby potentially improving academic outcomes for students with ASD. Additionally, the significant relationship between higher cognitive abilities and better emotional regulation suggests that interventions aimed at boosting cognitive skills may also enhance emotional control. For therapeutic interventions, the study indicates a need for intensified and individualized therapy for individuals with moderate to severe ASD, focusing on behavioral and emotional regulation strategies. Policymakers should advocate for comprehensive and regular assessments of both cognitive abilities and executive functions in schools and therapeutic centers to ensure targeted and effective interventions. Furthermore, continuous professional development for educators and therapists in evidence-based practices is essential. Future research should involve larger, diverse samples and explore the underlying mechanisms linking cognitive abilities with executive functions, as well as the influence of socioeconomic and familial factors. Finally, adapting and validating assessment tools for different cultural contexts remains vital to ensure the accuracy and relevance of findings across diverse populations.

CONCLUSION

This study examined the cognitive abilities and executive functioning behaviors of students with ASD at an Autism Center in the UAE, using the SB-5 and the BRIEF2. The findings demonstrate strong correlations between cognitive flexibility and various SB-5 IQ measures, emphasizing the importance of cognitive flexibility in ASD profiles. Higher cognitive abilities were generally linked to better emotional regulation. The severity of ASD significantly impacted cognitive and executive functions, with moderate severity associated with poorer emotional control and lower cognitive performance. Interestingly, the presence of special talents did not significantly affect cognitive and executive functioning measures, suggesting that intellectual functioning in ASD is diverse and independent of talents.

REFERENCES

Alsayouf, H. A., Talo, H., Biddappa, M. L., & De Los Reyes, E. (2021). Risperidone or aripiprazole can resolve autism core signs and symptoms in young Children: Case study. *Children (Basel, Switzerland)*, 8(5), 318. DOI:10.3390/children8050318 PMID:33921933

American Psychiatric Association, DSM-5 Task Force. (2013). *Diagnostic and statistical manual of mental disorders: DSM-5* (5th ed.). American Psychiatric Publishing, Inc., DOI:10.1176/appi.books.9780890425596

Beversdorf, D. Q., Stevens, H. E., & Jones, K. L. (2018). Prenatal stress, maternal immune dysregulation, and their association with autism spectrum disorders. *Current Psycchiatry Reports. Current Psychiatry Reports*, 20(9), 76. DOI:10.1007/s11920-018-0945-4 PMID:30094645

Blijd-Hoogewys, E. M. A., Bezemer, M. L., & Van Geert, P. L. C. (2014). Executive Functioning in Children with ASD: An Analysis of the BRIEF. *Journal of Autism and Developmental Disorders*, 44(12), 3089–3100. DOI:10.1007/s10803-014-2176-9 PMID:24996868

Braverman, Y., Edmunds, S. R., Hastedt, I., & Faja, S. (2024). Mind the Gap: Executive Function Is Associated with the Discrepancy Between Cognitive and Adaptive Functioning in Autistic Children Without Cognitive Delay. *Journal of Autism and Developmental Disorders*. DOI:10.1007/s10803-024-06354-x PMID:38778001

Casseus, M., Kim, W. J., & Horton, D. B. (2023). Prevalence and treatment of mental, behavioral, and developmental disorders in children with co-occurring autism spectrum disorder and attention-deficit/hyperactivity disorder: A population-based study. *Autism Research*, 16(4), 855–867. DOI:10.1002/aur.2894 PMID:36644987

Castellanos, A. E. O., Liu, C., & Shi, C. (2022). Deep Mobile Linguistic Therapy for Patients with ASD. *International Journal of Environmental Research and Public Health. International Journal of Environmental Research and Public Health*, 19(19), 12857. DOI:10.3390/ijerph191912857 PMID:36232157

Charman, T., Pickles, A., Simonoff, E., Chandler, S., Loucas, T., & Baird, G. (2010). IQ in children with autism spectrum disorders: Data from the Special Needs and Autism Project (SNAP). *Psychological Medicine*, 41(3), 619–627. DOI:10.1017/S0033291710000991 PMID:21272389

Coolican, J., Bryson, S. E., & Zwaigenbaum, L. (2007). Brief Report: Data on the Stanford–Binet Intelligence Scales (5th ed.) in Children with Autism Spectrum Disorder. *Journal of Autism and Developmental Disorders, 38*(1), 190–197. DOI:10.1007/s10803-007-0368-2

Dale, B. A., Finch, M. H., Mcintosh, D. E., Rothlisberg, B. A., & Finch, W. H. (2014). UTILITY OF THE STANFORD–BINET INTELLIGENCE SCALES, FIFTH EDITION, WITH ETHNICALLY DIVERSE PRESCHOOLERS. *Psychology in the Schools*, 51(6), 581–590. DOI:10.1002/pits.21766

DeFilippis, M. (2018). Depression in Children and Adolescents with Autism Spectrum Disorder. *Children (Basel, Switzerland)*, 5(9), 112. DOI:10.3390/children5090112 PMID:30134542

Demetriou, E. A., DeMayo, M. M., & Guastella, A. J. (2019). Executive function in autism spectrum Disorder: History, theoretical models, empirical findings, and potential as an endophenotype. *Frontiers in Psychiatry*, 10, 753. DOI:10.3389/fpsyt.2019.00753 PMID:31780959

DiStefano, C., & Dombrowski, S. C. (2006). Investigating the theoretical structure of the Stanford-Binet-Fifth Edition. *Journal of Psychoeducational Assessment*, 24(2), 123–136. DOI:10.1177/0734282905285244

Dodzik, P. (2017). Behavior Rating Inventory of Executive Function, Second edition Gerard A. Gioia, Peter K. Isquith, Steven C. Guy, and Lauren Kenworthy. *Journal of Pediatric Neuropsychology, 3*(3–4), 227–231. DOI:10.1007/s40817-017-0044-1

Estes, A., Rivera, V., Bryan, M., Cali, P., & Dawson, G. (2011). Discrepancies Between Academic Achievement and Intellectual Ability in Higher-Functioning School-Aged Children with Autism Spectrum Disorder. *Journal of Autism and Developmental Disorders*, 41(8), 1044–1052. DOI:10.1007/s10803-010-1127-3 PMID:21042871

Factor, R. S., Moody, C. T., Sung, K. Y., & Laugeson, E. A. (2022). Improving Social Anxiety and Social Responsiveness in Autism Spectrum Disorder through PEERS®. *Evidence-Based Practice in Child and Adolescent Mental Health*, 7(1), 142–159. DOI:10.1080/23794925.2021.2013138

Gavrilova, M., Aslanova, M., Tarasova, K., & Zinchenko, Y. (2023). Russian version of BRIEF2 Teacher Forms: Validation study in typically developing children aged 5 to 7 years old. *Frontiers in Psychology*, 14, 1260107. DOI:10.3389/fpsyg.2023.1260107 PMID:38078211

Gentil-Gutiérrez, A., Santamaría-Peláez, M., Mínguez-Mínguez, L. A., Fernández-Solana, J., González-Bernal, J. J., González-Santos, J., & Obregón-Cuesta, A. I. (2022). Executive Functions in Children and Adolescents with Autism Spectrum Disorder in Family and School Environment. *International Journal of Environmental Research and Public Health. International Journal of Environmental Research and Public Health*, 19(13), 7834. DOI:10.3390/ijerph19137834 PMID:35805490

Gioia, G. A., Isquith, P. K., Guy, S. C., & Kenworthy, L. (2015). *Behavior Rating Inventory of Executive Function* (2nd ed.). PAR. https://www.parinc.com/Products/Pkey/24

Gordon-Lipkin, E., Marvin, A. R., Law, J. K., & Lipkin, P. H. (2018). Anxiety and mood disorder in children with autism spectrum disorder and ADHD. *Pediatrics*, 141(4), e20171377. DOI:10.1542/peds.2017-1377 PMID:29602900

Hecht, P. M., Hudson, M., Connors, S. L., Tilley, M. R., Liu, X., & Beversdorf, D. Q. (2016). Maternal serotonin transporter genotype affects risk for ASD with exposure to prenatal stress. *Autism Research*, 9(11), 1151–1160. DOI:10.1002/aur.1629 PMID:27091118

Hill, E. L. (2004). Evaluating the theory of executive dysfunction in autism. *Developmental Review*, 24(2), 189–233. DOI:10.1016/j.dr.2004.01.001

Howlin, P., Goode, S., Hutton, J., & Rutter, M. (2009). Savant Skills in Autism: Psychometric Approaches and Parental Reports. *Philosophical Transactions of the Royal Society of London. Series B, Biological Sciences*, 364(1522), 1359–1367. https://www.jstor.org/stable/40485907. DOI:10.1098/rstb.2008.0328 PMID:19528018

Huizinga, M., Smidts, D. P., Baeyens, D., & Kan, K. (2023). The Dutch version of the Behavior Rating Inventory of Executive Function-2 (BRIEF-2). *Psychological Test Adaptation and Development*, 4(1), 97–115. DOI:10.1027/2698-1866/a000038

Janzen, H. L., Obrzut, J. E., & Marusiak, C. W. (2004). Test Review: Roid, G. H. (2003). Stanford-Binet Intelligence Scales, fifth Edition (SB:V). Itasca, IL: Riverside Publishing. *Canadian Journal of School Psychology, 19*(1–2), 235–244. DOI:10.1177/082957350401900113

Kamphaus, R. W., & Juechter, J. I. (2010). Stanford-Binet Intelligence scales. *The Corsini Encyclopedia of Psychology*, 1–2. DOI:10.1002/9780470479216.corpsy0941

Keith, T. Z., Kranzler, J. H., & Flanagan, D. P. (2001). What does the Cognitive Assessment System (CAS) measure? Joint Confirmatory Factor Analysis of the CAS and the Woodcock-Johnson Tests of Cognitive Ability (3rd Edition). *School Psychology Review, 30*(1), 89–119. DOI:10.1080/02796015.2001.12086102

Kenworthy, L., Yerys, B. E., Anthony, L. G., & Wallace, G. L. (2008). Understanding executive control in autism spectrum disorders in the lab and in the real world. *Neuropsychology Review*, 18(4), 320–338. DOI:10.1007/s11065-008-9077-7 PMID:18956239

Kirsch, A. C., Huebner, A. R. S., Mehta, S. Q., Howie, F. R., Weaver, A. L., Myers, S. M., Voigt, R. G., & Katusic, S. K. (2020). Association of comorbid mood and anxiety disorders with autism spectrum disorder. *JAMA Pediatrics*, 174(1), 63. DOI:10.1001/jamapediatrics.2019.4368 PMID:31790555

Leitner, Y. (2014). The Co-Occurrence of Autism and Attention Deficit Hyperactivity Disorder in Children â€" What Do We Know? *Frontiers in Human Neuroscience*, 8. Advance online publication. DOI:10.3389/fnhum.2014.00268 PMID:24808851

Leung, R. C., Vogan, V. M., Powell, T. L., Anagnostou, E., & Taylor, M. J. (2015). The role of executive functions in social impairment in Autism Spectrum Disorder. *Child Neuropsychology/Neuropsychology, Development, and Cognition. Section C. Child Neuropsychology*, 22(3), 336–344. DOI:10.1080/09297049.2015.1005066 PMID:25731979

Liss, M., Fein, D., Allen, D., Dunn, M., Feinstein, C., Morris, R., Waterhouse, L., & Rapin, I. (2001). Executive Functioning in High-functioning Children with Autism. *Journal of Child Psychology and Psychiatry, and Allied Disciplines*, 42(2), 261–270. DOI:10.1111/1469-7610.00717 PMID:11280422

Lopez, B. R., Lincoln, A. J., Ozonoff, S. J., & Lai, Z. (2005). Examining the Relationship between Executive Functions and Restricted, Repetitive Symptoms of Autistic Disorder. *Journal of Autism and Developmental Disorders*, 35(4), 445–460. DOI:10.1007/s10803-005-5035-x PMID:16134030

Lyall, K., Croen, L., Daniels, J., Fallin, M. D., Ladd-Acosta, C., Lee, B. K., Park, B. Y., Snyder, N. W., Schendel, D., Volk, H., Windham, G. C., & Newschaffer, C. (2017). The changing epidemiology of autism spectrum disorders. *Annual Review of Public Health*, 38(1), 81–102. DOI:10.1146/annurev-publhealth-031816-044318 PMID:28068486

Makrygianni, M. K., Gena, A., Katoudi, S., & Galanis, P. (2018). The effectiveness of applied behavior analytic interventions for children with Autism Spectrum Disorder: A meta-analytic study. *Research in Autism Spectrum Disorders*, 51, 18–31. DOI:10.1016/j.rasd.2018.03.006

Matthews, N. L., Pollard, E., Ober-Reynolds, S., Kirwan, J., Malligo, A., & Smith, C. J. (2015). Revisiting Cognitive and Adaptive Functioning in Children and Adolescents with Autism Spectrum Disorder. *Journal of Autism and Developmental Disorders*, 45(1), 138–156. DOI:10.1007/s10803-014-2200-0 PMID:25117583

Mazefsky, C. A., Herrington, J., Siegel, M., Scarpa, A., Maddox, B. B., Scahill, L., & White, S. W. (2013). The role of emotion regulation in autism spectrum Disorder. *Journal of the American Academy of Child and Adolescent Psychiatry*, 52(7), 679–688. DOI:10.1016/j.jaac.2013.05.006 PMID:23800481

Mcauley, T., Chen, S., Goos, L., Schachar, R., & Crosbie, J. (2010). Is the behavior rating inventory of executive function more strongly associated with measures of impairment or executive function? *Journal of the International Neuropsychological Society*, 16(3), 495–505. DOI:10.1017/S1355617710000093 PMID:20188014

McConkey, R. (2019). The increasing prevalence of school pupils with ASD: Insights from Northern Ireland. *European Journal of Special Needs Education*, 35(3), 414–424. DOI:10.1080/08856257.2019.1683686

McLean, R. L., Harrison, A. J., Zimak, E., Joseph, R. M., & Morrow, E. M. (2014). Executive function in probands with autism with average IQ and their unaffected First-Degree relatives. *Journal of the American Academy of Child and Adolescent Psychiatry*, 53(9), 1001–1009. DOI:10.1016/j.jaac.2014.05.019 PMID:25151423

Merchán-Naranjo, J., Boada, L., Del Rey-Mejías, Á., Mayoral, M., Llorente, C., Arango, C., & Parellada, M. (2016). La función ejecutiva está alterada en los trastornos del espectro autista, pero esta no correlaciona con la inteligencia. *Revista de Psiquiatría y Salud Mental*, 9(1), 39–50. DOI:10.1016/j.rpsm.2015.10.005 PMID:26724269

Ornoy, A., Weinstein-Fudim, L., & Ergaz, Z. (2015). Prenatal factors associated with autism spectrum disorder (ASD). *Reproductive Toxicology (Elmsford, N.Y.)*, 56, 155–169. DOI:10.1016/j.reprotox.2015.05.007 PMID:26021712

Parhoon, K., Moradi, A., Alizadeh, H., Parhoon, H., Sadaphal, D. P., & Coolidge, F. L. (2021). *Psychometric properties of the behavior rating inventory of executive function,* second edition (BRIEF2) in a sample of children with ADHD in Iran. *Child Neuropsychology/Neuropsychology, Development, and Cognition. Section C, Child Neuropsychology, 28*(4), 427–436. DOI:10.1080/09297049.2021.1975669

Paulra, S. J. P. V., Chinchai, S., Munkhetvit, P., & Sriphetcharawut, S. (2024). The development and content validity of the emotional recognition memory training program (ERMTP) for children with autism spectrum disorder: A trial phase. *Journal of Associated Medical Sciences*, 57(1), 177–189. DOI:10.12982/JAMS.2024.020

Persico, A. M., Ricciardello, A., Lamberti, M., Turriziani, L., Cucinotta, F., Brogna, C., Vitiello, B., & Arango, C. (2021). The pediatric psychopharmacology of autism spectrum disorder: A systematic review - Part I: The past and the present. *Progress in Neuro-Psychopharmacology & Biological Psychiatry*, 110, 110326. DOI:10.1016/j.pnpbp.2021.110326 PMID:33857522

Ranjan, R., & Pradhan, K. R. (2022). Social Interaction Skills Development in Children with ASD: A Group-Based Comparative Study. *International Journal of Science and Healthcare Research*, 7(2), 450–456. DOI:10.52403/ijshr.20220463

Robinson, S., Goddard, L., Dritschel, B., Wisley, M., & Howlin, P. (2009). Executive functions in children with Autism Spectrum Disorders. *Brain and Cognition*, 71(3), 362–368. DOI:10.1016/j.bandc.2009.06.007 PMID:19628325

Roid, G. H., & Barram, R. A. (2004). *Essentials of Stanford-Binet Intelligence Scales (SB5) assessment*. John Wiley & Sons.

Rommelse, N., Langerak, I., Van Der Meer, J., De Bruijn, Y., Staal, W., Oerlemans, A., & Buitelaar, J. (2015). Intelligence May Moderate the Cognitive Profile of Patients with ASD. *PLoS One*, 10(10), e0138698. DOI:10.1371/journal.pone.0138698 PMID:26444877

Sharma, A., & Tanwar, P. (2024). Model for autism disorder detection using deep learning. *IAES International Journal of Artificial Intelligence*, 13(1), 391. DOI:10.11591/ijai.v13.i1.pp391-398

Sharma, S. R., Gonda, X., & Tarazi, F. I. (2018). Autism Spectrum Disorder: Classification, diagnosis and therapy. *Pharmacology & Therapeutics*, 190, 91–104. DOI:10.1016/j.pharmthera.2018.05.007 PMID:29763648

Stigler, K. A. (2014). Psychopharmacologic Management of Serious Behavioral disturbance in ASD. *Child and Adolescent Psychiatric Clinics of North America*, 23(1), 73–82. DOI:10.1016/j.chc.2013.07.005 PMID:24231168

Troyb, E., Orinstein, A., Tyson, K., Helt, M., Eigsti, I., Stevens, M., & Fein, D. (2014). Academic abilities in children and adolescents with a history of autism spectrum disorders who have achieved optimal outcomes. *Autism*, 18(3), 233–243. DOI:10.1177/1362361312473519 PMID:24096312

Tschida, J. E., & Yerys, B. E. (2021). Real-world executive functioning for autistic children in school and home settings. *Autism*, 26(5), 1095–1107. DOI:10.1177/13623613211041189 PMID:34465230

Van Eylen, L., Boets, B., Steyaert, J., Wagemans, J., & Noens, I. (2015). Executive functioning in autism spectrum disorders: Influence of task and sample characteristics and relation to symptom severity. *European Child & Adolescent Psychiatry*, 24(11), 1399–1417. DOI:10.1007/s00787-015-0689-1 PMID:25697266

Vitomska, M. V. (2021). Modern Approaches to Occupational Therapy of Children with Authistic Spectric Disorders. *Ukraïns kij Žurnal Medicini. Bìologìï Ta Sportu*, 6(2), 7–12. DOI:10.26693/jmbs06.02.007

Vogan, V. M., Leung, R. C., Safar, K., Martinussen, R., Smith, M. L., & Taylor, M. J. (2018). Longitudinal examination of everyday executive functioning in children with ASD: Relations with social, emotional, and behavioral functioning over time. *Frontiers in Psychology*, 9, 1774. DOI:10.3389/fpsyg.2018.01774 PMID:30364134

Wilson, A. C. (2024). Cognitive Profile in Autism and ADHD: A Meta-Analysis of Performance on the WAIS-IV and WISC-V. *Archives of Clinical Neuropsychology*, 39(4), 498–515. DOI:10.1093/arclin/acad073 PMID:37779387

Wolff, N., Stroth, S., Kamp-Becker, I., Roepke, S., & Roessner, V. (2022). Autism spectrum disorder and IQ – a complex interplay. *Frontiers in Psychiatry*, 13, 856084. DOI:10.3389/fpsyt.2022.856084 PMID:35509885

Chapter 11
Clinical Neuropsychological Profile and Interventions for Co–Occurrence of ADHD and ASD

Maria Theodoratou

https://orcid.org/0000-0003-4200-4643

Neapolis University Pafos, Cyprus

Georgios A. Kougioumtzis

https://orcid.org/0000-0002-2362-2094

National Kapodistrian University, Greece

Vasiliki Yotsidi

https://orcid.org/0000-0001-7242-2948

Panteion University, Greece

Panoraia Andriopoulou

University of Ioannina, Greece

Kalliopi Megari

https://orcid.org/0000-0002-5861-7199

City College, University of York, Europe Campus, Greece

Christiana Koundourou

https://orcid.org/0009-0005-4050-0493

Neapolis University Pafos, Cyprus

Zoi Siouti

https://orcid.org/0000-0002-8316-7505

National and Kapodistrian University, Greece

Marios Argyrides

https://orcid.org/0000-0002-9936-7229

Neapolis University Pafos, Cyprus

DOI: 10.4018/979-8-3693-4022-6.ch011

ABSTRACT

The co-occurrence of ADHD and ASD presents a complex diagnostic challenge due to overlapping symptoms, potentially leading to one condition being treated while the other is neglected. They are widely recognized psychiatric conditions in children and adolescents, with a solid hereditary, neurological, and biochemical basis. Effective intervention strategies must consider the distinct needs of both conditions, requiring a flexible, multidisciplinary approach integrating medication, behavioral therapies, educational supports, and family involvement. Increased awareness and education are essential to dispel misconceptions and foster supportive environments. Social and emotional support is crucial for individuals navigating life with both ADHD and ASD, addressing challenges in forming relationships, and managing anxiety. Future efforts should focus on developing sophisticated diagnostic tools, personalized treatment plans, and advocating for those affected by these conditions to enhance overall well-being and opportunities.

INTRODUCTION

Numerous research studies have delved into Attention Deficit Hyperactivity Disorder (ADHD) and its underlying factors, as defined in DSM-V (Swanson et al., 2009). However, despite the abundance of research, ADHD remains inadequately recognized or understood by the general public, primarily due to the numerous controversies, discriminations, and misunderstandings surrounding the disorder (Mueller et al., 2012). Consequently, ADHD remains a contentious subject in children's and adolescents' mental health. Additionally, ADHD often co-occurs with autism spectrum disorders (ASD), further complicating diagnosis and management.

ADHD and ASD are widely recognized psychiatric conditions in children and adolescents, with a solid hereditary, neurological, and biochemical basis (Drechsler et al., 2020). Characterized by signs of inattentiveness and/or impulsiveness and hyperactivity, ADHD significantly affects individuals' behavior and performance at school and home (Purper-Ouakil, 2011). Symptoms frequently persist into adulthood in the majority of patients (Sibley et al., 2017), correlating with functional impairment and increased risks of depression and antisocial behavior (Biederman, 2021). Overall, ADHD profoundly impacts children, parents, and siblings' quality of life, generates substantial economic costs, and leaves lasting effects on families and society (Sciberras et al., 2020).

Children with ADHD commonly face academic challenges, putting them at a disadvantage upon starting school. Research by DuPaul et al. (2001) reveals that compared to their peers without ADHD, they often struggle with basic math and pre-reading skills in their first year of school, a disadvantage extending to preschoolers with ADHD (Vlachakis & Kougioumtzis, 2016). Moreover, their disruptive behavior frequently elicits adverse reactions from parents, teachers, and peers, leading to correction, punishment, reprimand, and criticism, particularly from teachers. They are also at higher risk of suspension or expulsion from school, particularly if ADHD co-occurs with ASD. For those with ASD, social difficulties prevail due to a fundamental inability to understand social norms and interpret nonverbal cues. Alongside academic hurdles, children with ADHD and ASD often encounter difficulties in forming social relationships, being less well-liked, having fewer friends, and facing rejection compared to their peers (Mc Vey et al., 2018).

The purpose of this chapter is to depict the main clinical and neuropsychological characteristics of this co-occurrence. In addition, it aims to highlighting diagnostic challenges, as well as genetic and environmental factors related to these disorders. Finally, evidence- based treatment and interventions are presented.

METHODS

The literature review for this chapter synthesizes existing research on Attention Deficit Hyperactivity Disorder (ADHD), particularly its co-occurrence with Autism Spectrum Disorders (ASD), along with aspects of diagnosis and interventions. A comprehensive search was conducted using multiple academic databases, including PubMed, PsycINFO, and Google Scholar, with keywords such as "ADHD," "Autism Spectrum Disorders," "comorbidity," "children," "adolescents," "diagnosis," and "interventions." The review focused on peer-reviewed journal articles and high-impact conference papers published between 2000 and 2023. Inclusion criteria comprised studies published in English involving children and adolescents aged 3-18 years, addressing ADHD, ASD, or the comorbidity of ADHD and ASD, and focusing on diagnosis and interventions for ADHD. Articles focusing exclusively on adults, those not available in full text, and non-peer-reviewed sources such as editorials and opinion pieces were excluded. Relevant data were extracted from the selected articles, including study design, sample size, population characteristics, key findings, and conclusions. They were organized into thematic categories related to co-occurrence, diagnosis, and interventions. The analysis identified common themes, trends, and gaps in the literature, mainly focusing on the interplay between ADHD and ASD and how their co-occurrence affects diagnosis and treatment outcomes. Additionally, the review explored the efficacy of various intervention strategies, including pharmacological, behavioral, and educational approaches. The findings are presented to provide a comprehensive overview of the current state of research on the co-occurrence of ADHD and ASD, diagnostic challenges, and effective interventions.

RESULTS

Diagnosis

Diagnosing comorbidities in individuals with Attention Deficit Hyperactivity Disorder (ADHD) is crucial as they significantly influence the management and treatment of the disorder. One of the most common and impactful comorbidities is Autism Spectrum Disorder (ASD). Conditions such as ASD, along with learning disabilities, anxiety, depression, and sleep-wake disorders, can worsen ADHD symptoms and impair patient functioning (Chan et al., 2016; American Psychiatric Association, 2013).

ADHD frequently co-occurs with other disorders, notably ASD. According to the DSM-V, a dual diagnosis of ADHD and ASD is permissible if the diagnostic criteria for both disorders are met. Recent studies have shown that the comorbidity rate of ADHD and ASD is around 59%. ADHD is linked to an earlier diagnosis of ASD and other difficulties such as anger management, insomnia, learning difficulties, obsessive-compulsive disorder (OCD), mood disorders, and self-injurious behavior.

Recognizing and addressing ASD as a comorbid condition with ADHD is essential to ensure that individuals receive optimal treatment (Wolraich et al., 2019; NICE, 2018). The presence of ASD can sometimes mask ADHD symptoms, leading to misdiagnosis or delayed diagnosis. Therefore, clinicians need to be vigilant about the presence of ASD and conduct thorough evaluations to identify this coexisting condition. Treating ADHD and ASD together can be complex, and clinicians must prioritize treatment goals to develop the most effective treatment plans for each individual (Coghill et al., 2021).

In summary, diagnosing ASD as a comorbidity in individuals with ADHD is vital for optimal treatment and management. Failure to recognize and address ASD can result in poor treatment outcomes and reduced quality of life for individuals with ADHD.

ADHD Overview

Challenges with attention, impulsivity, and hyperactivity typify Attention Deficit Hyperactivity Disorder (ADHD). Individuals with ADHD may have trouble focusing, completing tasks, organizing activities, and staying still when required.

They often exhibit impulsive behaviors, such as interrupting others and finding it difficult to wait their turn.

Asperger's Syndrome / Autism Spectrum Disorder (ASD) Overview

Previously classified as a distinct condition, Asperger's Syndrome is now recognized under the broader category of Autism Spectrum Disorder (ASD). It is marked by significant challenges in social interaction and nonverbal communication, as well as restrictive and repetitive behaviors and interests. Those with ASD, including individuals with Asperger's profiles, generally possess strong language and cognitive skills but struggle with social communication and often display repetitive behaviors or intense, narrowly focused interests (Sofologi et al., 2020).

Overlapping Symptoms

ADHD and ASD share several symptoms, including difficulties with social interactions, executive functioning (such as planning, organizing, and prioritizing), and sustaining attention. Despite these similarities, the underlying causes and specific manifestations of these symptoms can vary:

- Social Interaction: For individuals with ADHD, social challenges often arise from impulsivity and inattention (e.g., interrupting others, missing social cues due to distraction). Conversely, for those with ASD, social difficulties are primarily due to a fundamental inability to understand social norms and interpret nonverbal cues.

Tools for Assessing ADHD and Comorbidities in Children Aged 6-18

Tools for Diagnosis of ADHD
Several widely recognized tools facilitate the evaluation of ADHD and its comorbidities in children aged 6-18. The Vanderbilt Assessment Scales, the Swanson, Nolan, and Pelham Questionnaire (SNAP), and the Conners 3rd Edition are among the most commonly employed.

-Vanderbilt Assessment Scales: These scales are free and available in parent and teacher versions, specifically designed for children aged 6-12. They are comprehensive tools that help in assessing ADHD symptoms as well as comorbid conditions (Wolraich et al., 2003).

- Swanson, Nolan, and Pelham Questionnaire (SNAP): The SNAP questionnaire aligns with the DSM criteria for ADHD and Oppositional Defiant Disorder (ODD). While it is freely accessible, it lacks specific versions for adolescents and normative data, which can limit its applicability in certain age groups (Markowitz, 2020).
- Conners 3rd Edition: This tool offers separate forms for parents, teachers, and self-report versions for children aged 8-18. Despite its thoroughness and detailed structure, it is not freely available (Conners et al., 2011).

These tools are essential for accurately diagnosing ADHD and identifying co-occurring disorders in children, thus ensuring appropriate and effective intervention strategies (Theodoratou et al., 2024).

Tools for Diagnosis of Comorbid Conditions

In addition to ADHD-specific tools, several diagnostic instruments are available for assessing other common comorbid conditions:

- Autism Spectrum Disorder (ASD):

Autism Diagnostic Observation Schedule (ADOS): This is a standardized tool used to assess communication, social interaction, and play through a series of structured activities and observations (Lord et al., 2000).
Autism Diagnostic Interview-Revised (ADI-R): This is a semi-structured interview that evaluates developmental history and current behaviors, focusing on social interaction, communication, and repetitive behaviors (Rutter et al.M, 2003; Lebersfeld et al.,2021).

- Learning Disabilities:
- Wechsler Intelligence Scale for Children (WISC) and Woodcock-Johnson Tests of Achievement: These tools assess cognitive abilities and academic achievement, respectively, to diagnose learning disabilities (Wechsler, 2003; Schrank & Wendling, 2018).

By utilizing these diagnostic tools, clinicians can achieve a comprehensive understanding of a child's condition, facilitating targeted interventions and improving outcomes for children with ADHD and comorbidities.

- Focus and Attention: ADHD and ASD can involve an intense focus on particular interests (Theodoratou, Gkintoni, & Farmakopoulou, 2023). However, in ADHD, this focus is typically more variable and inconsistent, whereas individuals with ASD often exhibit a more intense and sustained focus on specific interests.

Etiology

Attention-Deficit/Hyperactivity Disorder (ADHD) is a complex condition resulting from various developmental and causative factors. The etiology of ADHD involves a multifaceted interplay between genetic predispositions and environmental influences (Tarver et al., 2014). While ADHD has a strong hereditary component, environmental factors also contribute significantly, including prenatal exposure to toxins, childbirth complications such as low birth weight, adverse early childhood experiences, illnesses during childhood, and brain injuries.

Genetic Factors

ADHD exhibits a significant familial component, with first-degree relatives of individuals with ADHD having a two to four-fold increased risk of the disorder. Twin and adoption studies indicate that ADHD is highly heritable, accounting for 36% to 81% of the variance (Faraone & Larsson, 2019). Nonshared environmental factors exert a modest to small effect, while shared environmental factors have minimal impact. The concordance rate for ADHD among monozygotic twins is approximately 80%, underscoring the substantial genetic influence. ADHD has a more robust genetic basis than several other disorders, including schizophrenia, breast cancer, and asthma.

Research in molecular genetics has aimed to identify specific genes associated with ADHD. Genome-wide scans seek to pinpoint chromosomal regions linked to the disorder, though large sample sizes are required, and findings are often complex. One region of interest is 5p13, which has been associated with both ADHD and Autism Spectrum Disorder (ASD). This region houses the dopamine transporter gene, influencing dopamine reuptake in the synapse. Studies have linked specific alleles, such as the 10-repeat and 7-repeat variants of tandem repeat polymorphisms in this gene, to ADHD. Dopamine receptor genes, particularly the D4 receptor, have also been implicated. These genetic findings suggest that ADHD has a robust genetic foundation, with specific genes and neurotransmitter systems playing crucial roles in its development.

Neurobiological Pathways

Sonuga-Barke (2003) proposed that the dual-pathway model posits that ADHD arises from dysfunctions in two biological pathways: the dopaminergic mesocortical and mesolimbic systems. Dysregulation in the mesocortical pathway is thought to result in inhibitory dysfunction, affecting the self-regulation of thoughts and actions. Conversely, dysfunction in the mesolimbic pathway may lead to a delay-averse motivational style characterized by a preference for immediate rewards and a tendency to discount future rewards. Social factors can moderate this immediate preference. Both pathways contribute to ADHD symptoms and impairments in task engagement. In 2010, a third pathway involving temporal processing deficits was added to this model, highlighting difficulties with timing, time discrimination, and time reproduction as additional contributors to ADHD (Sonuga-Barke et al.,2010).

Comorbidity of ADHD and ASD

The comorbidity of ADHD and Autism Spectrum Disorder (ASD) is well-documented, with studies showing that a significant number of individuals with ADHD also meet the criteria for ASD and vice versa (Hours et al., 2022; Young et al., 2020). According to scientific literature, 50 to 70% of individuals with autism spectrum disorder (ASD) also exhibit comorbid attention deficit hyperactivity disorder (ADHD) (Young et al., 2020). Clinically, this high rate of comorbidity is significant, prompting an investigation into the true nature of this dual diagnosis. It raises the question of whether ADHD is continuously present or if the attentional impairments seen in ASD patients are distinct traits of ASD, such as impaired joint attention. Additionally, the agitation observed in these individuals might stem from joint attention impairment or a different form of physical restlessness rather than typical ADHD-related agitation. The neurobiological reality of ASD-ADHD comorbidity remains debated, and amphetamine-based treatments can have paradoxical or undesirable effects in the ASD population. Consequently, the dual diagnosis of ASD with ADHD, despite being frequently discussed in the literature, can obscure our understanding of the main physiopathological issues related to ASD. Additionally, it complicates the etiological landscape by implying overlapping genetic and environmental factors.

Genetic Overlap

Both ADHD and ASD have strong genetic components, with shared genetic factors contributing to their co-occurrence. Molecular genetic studies have identified common genetic variants that increase the risk for both disorders. For instance, the chromosomal region 5p13, which includes the dopamine transporter gene, has been linked to both ADHD and ASD (Thapar & Stergioulaki, 2008). This shared genetic vulnerability indicates that there may be common neurobiological pathways underlying both conditions.

Neurobiological Mechanisms

The neurobiological mechanisms that contribute to the comorbidity of ADHD and ASD include abnormalities in brain structure and function that affect multiple cognitive and behavioral processes (Cundari et al., 2023; Theodoratou et al., 2023). Dysfunction in the dopaminergic system, which is implicated in ADHD, also plays a role in the social and communicative deficits seen in ASD. Additionally, both disorders involve impairments in executive function, attention regulation, and reward processing, further highlighting their interconnected nature.

Neuropsychological Aspects

The neuropsychological profiles of individuals with ADHD and ASD are heterogeneous, reflecting diverse underlying neurobiological pathways (de Silva et al., 2023). Attempts to categorize patients based on selective performance profiles have yielded inconclusive results (Drechsler et al., 2020). The identified neuropsychological deficit profiles are not exclusive to ADHD; they are also present in the general population, albeit with more extreme values in children with ADHD. In comparison to typically developing controls, individuals with ADHD exhibit significant impairments across nearly every neuropsychological domain. However, the effect sizes are often relatively small. These consistent impairments span multiple domains and may be related to deficiencies in top-down cognitive control, strategic processing, and primary processing deficits.

Overall, a better understanding of the etiological and neuropsychological underpinnings of ADHD and its comorbidity with ASD is essential in order to develop effective diagnostic and intervention strategies, as outlined in the work of Theodoratou and Farmakopoulou (2021). This comprehensive approach helps to address the multifaceted nature of these disorders and to improve outcomes for affected individuals.

Environmental Factors

Environmental factors that contribute to the comorbidity of ADHD and ASD include prenatal and perinatal complications, such as maternal stress, exposure to toxins, and birth complications (Ronald et al., 2011; Yuan et al., 2024; Carlson et al., 2021). These factors can exacerbate genetic vulnerabilities and contribute to the development of both disorders. Furthermore, early childhood experiences, including social interactions and learning environments, also play a role in shaping the symptomatology of ADHD and ASD.

TREATMENT AND INTERVENTIONS

The development of efficacious intervention strategies for individuals with co-occurring ADHD and ASD presents a significant challenge. It is possible that interventions beneficial for ADHD may not address the core symptoms of ASD, and vice versa. Consequently, a multidisciplinary approach that integrates medication, behavioral therapies, educational support, and family involvement is essential to meet the complex needs of individuals with both conditions. It is imperative that this approach remain flexible in order to adapt to the individual's evolving needs.

Psychopharmacological Treatment: The optimal treatment approach for children with a dual diagnosis of ADHD and autism spectrum disorder (ASD) remains unclear. The efficacy of ADHD medications can vary significantly, even among children who do not have ASD (Research Units on Pediatric Psychopharmacology Autism Network, 2005). In addition, children with ASD may exhibit a diminished response or greater difficulty in tolerating these drugs (Aman et al., 2004). Consequently, it is of the utmost importance to gain a comprehensive understanding of effective interventions and their optimal duration. A key challenge in this field is to identify the most effective combined treatments.

Efforts to enhance treatment methodologies and early detection have been advanced through various studies. One objective was to identify early indicators of ADHD in children with ASD in order to minimise delays in ASD diagnosis for those displaying ADHD symptoms (Dawson et al., 2010). The objective of these studies was to compare patterns of brain activity, attention, and behavior across different groups of children. Furthermore, studies were conducted to examine the potential efficacy of stimulant medications in augmenting early behavioral interventions for children diagnosed with both ASD and ADHD.

Medication Management: Stimulant and non-stimulant medications commonly used for ADHD may require adjustment or combination with other treatments to address ASD symptoms (Rommelse et al., 2018; RUPP, 2002, 2005; The MTA Group, 1999). Collaboration between psychiatrists, pediatricians, and neurologists is essential.

Behavioral Therapies: Applied Behavior Analysis (ABA), Cognitive Behavioral Therapy (CBT), and social skills training can be adapted to address the unique needs of individuals with dual diagnoses (You et al., 2024). These therapies can help manage behavioral issues, improve social interactions, and enhance emotional regulation.

Educational Supports: The co-occurrence of ADHD and ASD presents unique challenges in educational settings, emphasizing the need for integrated neuroscience-based approaches that address both conditions (Farmakopoulou et al., 2023). Individualized Education Programs (IEPs) and plans should be designed to accommodate both ADHD and ASD symptoms (DuPaul et al., 2019). It is imperative that special education teachers, school psychologists, and counselors collaborate to create a supportive learning environment (Siouti et al., 2023, 2024, Katsarou et al., 2023).

Family Involvement: Family therapy and parental training programs can equip families with strategies to manage daily challenges, improve communication, and support their child's development (Dai et al., 2018; Bjornstad & Montgomery, 2005). Furthermore, integrating psychoeducation into the treatment plans for autism and ADHD may enhance outcomes, as suggested by its demonstrated efficacy in many conditions (Puri & Theodoratou, 2022). Providing resources and support for families is essential in creating a consistent and nurturing environment (Katsarou, 2018).

Social and Emotional Support: The social and emotional implications of living with ADHD and ASD simultaneously cannot be understated. Individuals may experience difficulties in forming and maintaining relationships, face challenges in academic and occupational settings, and experience heightened anxiety and frustration. Providing social and emotional support, including therapy and peer support groups, is vital for addressing these aspects of co-occurring conditions (Kalra et al., 2023; Megari et al., 2024). Programs that focus on developing social competencies can assist individuals with ADHD and ASD in learning how to navigate social interactions, understand social cues, and build meaningful relationships.

Academic and Occupational Guidance: Career counseling and job coaching can assist individuals in finding and maintaining employment that aligns with their strengths and interests (Fong et al., 2021). Academic support services like tutoring and mentoring can help them achieve their educational goals. Encouraging participation in community activities, clubs, and organizations can provide a sense of belonging and purpose. Creating inclusive and accommodating environments within the community is essential for fostering social connections and reducing isolation.

By addressing treatment, intervention strategies, and the social and emotional impact, a comprehensive and holistic approach can be developed to support individuals with co-occurring ADHD and ASD, promoting their overall well-being and quality of life.

CONCLUSION

A nuanced understanding of the distinct and overlapping characteristics of ADHD and ASD is critical to the effective treatment and support of individuals with these conditions. For individuals with comorbid ADHD and ASD, it is essential to provide a comprehensive, multidisciplinary approach that addresses the wide range of symptoms and challenges presented by both disorders (Theodoratou, Gkintoni, & Farmakopoulou, 2023). Collaboration among health care providers, educators, families, and the individuals themselves is essential in developing and implementing strategies that promote holistic development and well-being (Sofologi et al., 2022). Such interdisciplinary approaches are critical to creating an integrated support system that effectively addresses the complex needs of individuals with these neurodevelopmental disorders.

REFERENCES

Al Ghamdi, K., & AlMusailhi, J. (2024). Attention-deficit Hyperactivity Disorder and Autism Spectrum Disorder: Towards Better Diagnosis and Management. *Medical archives (Sarajevo, Bosnia and Herzegovina), 78*(2), 159–163. https://doi.org/10.5455/medarh.2024.78.159-163

Aman, M. G., Novotny, S., Samango-Sprouse, C., Lecavalier, L., Leonard, E., Gadow, K. D., King, B. H., Pearson, D. A., Gernsbacher, M. A., & Chez, M. (2004). Outcome measures for clinical drug trials in autism. *CNS Spectrums*, 9(1), 36–47. 10.1017/S109285290000834814999174

Bjornstad, G. J., & Montgomery, P. (2005). Family therapy for attention-deficit disorder or attention-deficit/hyperactivity disorder in children and adolescents. *Cochrane Database of Systematic Reviews*. 10.1002/14651858.CD005042.pub215846741

Carlsson, T., Molander, F., Taylor, M. J., Jonsson, U., & Bölte, S. (2021). Early environmental risk factors for neurodevelopmental disorders—A systematic review of twin and sibling studies. *Development and Psychopathology*, 33(4), 1448–1495. 10.1017/S095457942000062032703331

Chan, E., Fogler, J. M., & Hammerness, P. G. (2016). Treatment of attention-deficit/hyperactivity disorder in adolescents: A systematic review. *Journal of the American Medical Association*, 315(18), 1997–2008. 10.1001/jama.2016.545327163988

Chung, K. M., Chung, E., & Lee, H. (2024). Behavioral Interventions for Autism Spectrum Disorder: A Brief Review and Guidelines with a Specific Focus on Applied Behavior Analysis. *Journal of the Korean Academy of Child and Adolescent Psychiatry*, 35(1), 29–38. 10.5765/jkacap.23001938204739

Dai, Y. G., Brennan, L., Como, A., Hughes-Lika, J., Dumont-Mathieu, T., Carcani-Rathwell, I., Minxhozi, O., Aliaj, B., & Fein, D. A. (2018). A video parent-training program for families of children with autism spectrum disorder in Albania. *Research in Autism Spectrum Disorders*, 56, 36–49. 10.1016/j.rasd.2018.08.00831275428

Dawson, G., Rogers, S., Munson, J., Smith, M., Winter, J., Greenson, J., Donaldson, A., & Varley, J. (2010). Randomized, controlled trial of an intervention for toddlers with autism: The Early Start Denver Model. *Pediatrics*, 125(1), e17–e23. 10.1542/peds.2009-095819948568

Drechsler, R., Brem, S., Brandeis, D., Grünblatt, E., Berger, G., & Walitza, S. (2020). ADHD: Current concepts and treatments in children and adolescents. *Neuropediatrics*, 51(5), 315–335. 10.1055/s-0040-170165832559806

DuPaul, G. J., Chronis-Tuscano, A., Danielson, M. L., & Visser, S. N. (2018). Predictors of receipt of school services in a national sample of youth with ADHD. *Journal of Attention Disorders*, 23(11), 1303–1319. 10.1177/108705471881616930526188

Farmakopoulou, I., Theodoratou, M., & Gkintoni, E. (2023). Neuroscience as a component in educational setting: An interpretive overview. *Technium Education and Humanities*, 4, 1–7. 10.47577/teh.v4i.8236

Fong, C. J., Taylor, J., Berdyyeva, A., McClelland, A. M., Murphy, K. M., & Westbrook, J. D. (2021). Interventions for improving employment outcomes for persons with autism spectrum disorders: A systematic review update. *Campbell Systematic Reviews*, 17(3), e1185. 10.1002/cl2.118537052419

Handen, B. L., Aman, M. G., Arnold, L. E., Hyman, S. L., Tumuluru, R. V., Lecavalier, L., Corbett-Dick, P., Pan, X., Hollway, J. A., Buchan-Page, K. A., Silverman, L. B., Brown, N. V., Rice, R. R.Jr, Hellings, J., Mruzek, D. W., McAuliffe-Bellin, S., Hurt, E. A., Ryan, M. M., Levato, L., & Smith, T. (2015). Atomoxetine, parent training, and their combination in children with autism spectrum disorder and attention-deficit/hyperactivity disorder. *Journal of the American Academy of Child and Adolescent Psychiatry*, 54(11), 905–915. 10.1016/j.jaac.2015.08.01326506581

Hours, C., Recasens, C., & Baleyte, J. M. (2022). ASD and ADHD comorbidity: What are we talking about? *Frontiers in Psychiatry*, 13, 837424. 10.3389/fpsyt.2022.83742435295773

Kalra, R., Gupta, M., & Sharma, P. (2023). Recent advancement in interventions for autism spectrum disorder: A review. *Journal of Neurorestoratology*, 11(3), 100068. 10.1016/j.jnrt.2023.100068

Katsarou, D. (2018). Emotional state differences of parents with children diagnosed with autism. *International Journal of Current Innovation Research*, 4(4), 1177–1183.

Katsarou, D., Nikolaou, E., & Stamatis, P. (2023). Is coteaching an effective way of including children with autism? The Greek parallel coteaching as an example: Issues and Concerns. In Efthymiou, E. (Ed.), *Inclusive Phygital Learning Approaches and Strategies For Students with Special Needs* (pp. 189–197). IGI Global. 10.4018/978-1-6684-8504-0.ch009

Kollins, S. H., Childress, A., Heusser, A. C., & Lutz, J. (2021). Effectiveness of a digital therapeutic as adjunct to treatment with medication in pediatric ADHD. *NPJ Digital Medicine*, 4(1), 58. 10.1038/s41746-021-00429-033772095

Lebersfeld, J. B., Swanson, M., Clesi, C. D., & O'Kelley, S. E. (2021). Systematic Review and Meta-Analysis of the Clinical Utility of the ADOS-2 and the ADI-R in Diagnosing Autism Spectrum Disorders in Children. *Journal of Autism and Developmental Disorders*, 51(11), 4101–4114. 10.1007/s10803-020-04839-z33475930

Lord, C., Risi, S., Lambrecht, L., Cook, E. H.Jr, Leventhal, B. L., DiLavore, P. C., Pickles, A., & Rutter, M. (2000). The autism diagnostic observation schedule-generic: A standard measure of social and communication deficits associated with the spectrum of autism. *Journal of Autism and Developmental Disorders*, 30(3), 205–223. 10.1023/A:100559240194711055457

McVey, A. J., Schiltz, H. K., Haendel, A. D., Dolan, B. K., Willar, K. S., Pleiss, S. S., Karst, J. S., Carlson, M., Krueger, W., Murphy, C. C., Casnar, C. L., Yund, B., & Van Hecke, A. V. (2018). Social difficulties in youth with autism with and without anxiety and ADHD symptoms. *Autism research: official journal of the International Society for Autism Research, 11*(12), 1679–1689. 10.1002/aur.2039

Megari, K., Sofologi, M., Kougioumtzis, G., Thomaidou, E., Thomaidis, G., Katsarou, D., Yotsidi, V., & Theodoratou, M. (2024). Neurocognitive and psycho-emotional profile of children with disabilities. *Applied Neuropsychology. Child*, 1–6. 10.108 0/21622965.2024.230478138574392

Mueller, A. K., Fuermaier, A. B., Koerts, J., & Tucha, L. (2012). Stigma in attention deficit hyperactivity disorder. *Attention Deficit and Hyperactivity Disorders*, 4(3), 101–114. 10.1007/s12402-012-0085-322773377

Puri, B. K., & Theodoratou, M. (2023). The efficacy of psychoeducation in managing low back pain: A systematic review. *Psychiatrike = Psychiatriki, 34*(3), 231–242. 10.22365/jpsych.2022.104

Purper-Ouakil, D., Ramoz, N., Lepagnol-Bestel, A. M., & Simonneau, M. (2011). Neurobiology of attention deficit/hyperactivity disorder. *Pediatric Research*, 69(5 Part 2), 69–76. 10.1203/PDR.0b013e318212b40f21289544

Research Units on Pediatric Psychopharmacology (RUPP) Autism Network. (2005). Randomized, controlled, crossover trial of methylphenidate in pervasive developmental disorders with hyperactivity. *Archives of General Psychiatry*, 62(11), 1266–1274. 10.1001/archpsyc.62.11.126616275814

Rommelse, N., Visser, J., & Hartman, C. (2018). Differentiating between ADHD and ASD in childhood: Some directions for practitioners. *European Child & Adolescent Psychiatry*, 27(6), 679–681. 10.1007/s00787-018-1165-529754280

Ronald, A., Pennell, C. E., & Whitehouse, A. J. O. (2011). Prenatal Maternal Stress Associated with ADHD and Autistic Traits in early Childhood. *Frontiers in Psychology*, 1. 10.3389/fpsyg.2010.0022321833278

Rutter, M., LeCouteur, A., & Lord, C. (2003). *Autism Diagnostic Interview-Revised (ADI-R)*. Western Psychological Services.

Schrank, F. A., & Wendling, B. J. (2018). The Woodcock–Johnson IV: Tests of cognitive abilities, tests of oral language, tests of achievement. In Flanagan, D. P., & McDonough, E. M. (Eds.), *Contemporary intellectual assessment: Theories, tests, and issues* (4th ed., pp. 383–451). The Guilford Press.

Sibley, M. H., Swanson, J. M., Arnold, L. E., Hechtman, L. T., Owens, E. B., Stehli, A., Abikoff, H., Hinshaw, S. P., Molina, B. S. G., Mitchell, J. T., Jensen, P. S., Howard, A. L., Lakes, K. D., & Pelham, W. E.MTA Cooperative Group. (2017). Defining ADHD symptom persistence in adulthood: Optimizing sensitivity and specificity. *Journal of Child Psychology and Psychiatry, and Allied Disciplines*, 58(6), 655–662. 10.1111/jcpp.1262027642116

Siouti, Z., Kougioumtzis, G. A., Kaltsouda, A., & Theodoratou, M. (2023). The role of support networks for children and adolescents with language developmental problems. In Katsarou, D. (Ed.), *Childhood Developmental Language Disorders* (pp. 149–158). IGI Global. 10.4018/979-8-3693-1982-6.ch010

Siouti, Z., Kougioumtzis, G. A., Kaltsouda, A., Theodoratou, M., Yotsidi, V., & Mitraras, A. (2024). Stress Management, Clinical Interventions, and Social Support of Students With Learning Disabilities. In Sofologi, M., Kougioumtzis, G., & Koundourou, C. (Eds.), *Perspectives of Cognitive, Psychosocial, and Learning Difficulties From Childhood to Adulthood: Practical Counseling Strategies*. IGI Global. 10.4018/978-1-6684-8203

Sofologi, M., Markou, E., Kougioumtzis, G. A., Kamari, A., Theofyllidis, A., & Bonti, E. (2020). Emphasizing on the Neurobiological Basis of Autism Spectrum Disorder: A Closer look to a Different Brain. *Dual Diagnosis Open Access, 5*(1, 2). http://hdl.handle.net/11728/12137

Sofologi, M., Pliogou, V., Bonti, E., Efstratopoulou, M., Kougioumtzis, G. A., Papatzikis, E., Ntritsos, G., Moraitou, D., & Papantoniou, G. (2022). An investigation of working memory profile and fluid intelligence in children with neurodevelopmental difficulties. *Frontiers in Psychology, 6657*. 10.3389/fpsyg.2021.773732

Sonuga-Barke, E., Bitsakou, P., & Thompson, M. (2010). Beyond the dual pathway model: Evidence for the dissociation of timing, inhibitory, and delay-related impairments in attention-deficit/hyperactivity disorder. *Journal of the American Academy of Child and Adolescent Psychiatry*, 49(4), 345–355. 10.1097/00004583-201004000-0000920410727

Sonuga-Barke, E. J. (2003). The dual pathway model of ADHD: An elaboration of neuro-developmental characteristics. *Neuroscience and Biobehavioral Reviews*, 27(7), 593–604. 10.1016/j.neubiorev.2003.08.00514624804

Swanson, J. M., Wigal, T., & Lakes, K. (2009). DSM-V and the future diagnosis of attention-deficit/hyperactivity disorder. *Current Psychiatry Reports*, 11(5), 399–406. 10.1007/s11920-009-0060-719785982

The MTA Cooperative Group. (1999). A 14-month randomized clinical trial of treatment strategies for attention-deficit/hyperactivity disorder. *Archives of General Psychiatry*, 56(12), 1073–1086. 10.1001/archpsyc.56.12.107310591283

Theodoratou, M., & Farmakopoulou, I. (2021). Comorbidity Issues between Autism Spectrum Disorders and Internet Addiction. Diagnosis and Treatment Implications. *EC Neurology*, 13, 10–17.

Theodoratou, M., Farmakopoulou, I., & Gkintoni, E. (2023). ADHD, Comorbidities, and Multimodal Treatment: Case Study Vignette. *Perspectives of Cognitive, Psychosocial, and Learning Difficulties From Childhood to Adulthood: Practical Counseling Strategies*, 245-278. IGI Global.

Theodoratou, M., Gkintoni, E., & Farmakopoulou, I. (2023). Executive Functions and Quality of Life in Neurodevelopmental Spectrum. An Outline. *Technium Social Sciences Journal*, 39(1), 430–439. 10.47577/tssj.v39i1.8231

Theodoratou, M., Kougioumtzis, G. A., Kaltsouda, A., Katsarou, D., Siouti, Z., Sofologi, M., Tsitsas, G., & Flora, K. (2023). Neuropsychological Aspects and Interventions for Internet Addiction in Adolescents with Asperger's Syndrome-Narrative Review. *Neurology & Neuroscience*, 4(3), 1–9. 10.33425/2692-7918.1052

Theodoratou, M., Ralli, M., Mylonaki, T., & Bekou, H. (2024). Screening for ADHD Traits in University Students: Prevalence, Traits and Departmental Variations. *Journal of Behavioral Sciences*, 34(1).

Velarde, M., & Cárdenas, A. (2022). Trastornos del espectro autista y trastornos por déficit de atención con hiperactividad: Desafíos en el diagnóstico y tratamiento [Autism spectrum disorder and attention-deficit/hyperactivity disorder: Challenge in diagnosis and treatment]. *Medicina*, 82(Suppl 3), 67–70.36054861

Vlachakis, I., & Kougioumtzis, G. A. (2016). ADHD and Teachers' Counseling. *Journal of Regional Socio-Economic Issues, 6*(2).

Wechsler, D. (2003). Wechsler Intelligence Scale for Children, *Fourth Edition (WISC-IV)* [Database record]. APA PsycTests. 10.1037/t15174-000

Wolraich, M., Lambert, W., Doffing, M., Bickman, L., Simmons, T., & Worley, K. (2003). Psychometric Properties of the Vanderbilt ADHD Diagnostic Parent Rating Scale in a Referred Population. *Journal of Pediatric Psychology*, 28(8), 559–568. 10.1093/jpepsy/jsg04614602846

You, X.-R., Gong, X.-R., Guo, M.-R., & Ma, B.-X. (2024). Cognitive behavioural therapy to improve social skills in children and adolescents with autism spectrum disorder: A meta-analysis of randomised controlled trials. [Αρχή φόρμας]. *Journal of Affective Disorders*, 344, 8–17. 10.1016/j.jad.2023.10.00837802322

Young, S., Hollingdale, J., Absoud, M., Bolton, P., Branney, P., Colley, W., Craze, E., Dave, M., Deeley, Q., Farrag, E., Gudjonsson, G., Hill, P., Liang, H. L., Murphy, C., Mackintosh, P., Murin, M., O'Regan, F., Ougrin, D., Rios, P., & Woodhouse, E. (2020). Guidance for identification and treatment of individuals with attention deficit/ hyperactivity disorder and autism spectrum disorder based upon expert consensus. *BMC Medicine*, 18(1), 146. 10.1186/s12916-020-01585-y32448170

Yuan, J. J., Zhao, Y. N., Lan, X. Y., Zhang, Y., & Zhang, R. (2024). Prenatal, perinatal and parental risk factors for autism spectrum disorder in China: A case- control study. *BMC Psychiatry*, 24(1), 219. 10.1186/s12888-024-05643-038509469

Chapter 12
Well–Being Among Parents Raising a Child Diagnosed With Attention Deficit Hyperactivity Disorder (ADHD) and Intervention Programs:
A Literature Review

Kyriaki Tasiou
https://orcid.org/0000-0001-8144-8090
University of the Aegean, Greece

Eleni N. Nikolaou
https://orcid.org/0000-0003-1840-3433
University of the Aegean, Greece

ABSTRACT

Attention deficit hyperactivity disorder (ADHD) is a neurodevelopmental disorder that affects people diagnosed with it and their families in many ways. The purpose of this study was to evaluate possible determinants of parent wellbeing and to examine the influence of having a child diagnosed with ADHD on the social and emotional well-being of parents. The aim of the present study was also to add to the existing literature information about intervention programs that have implemented to parents of children with ADHD and examine their effectiveness on various dimensions related to parental well-being and psychological well-being. These programs, which

DOI: 10.4018/979-8-3693-4022-6.ch012

are specially designed for the training of parents of children with ADHD, are mainly based on the strengthening of mindfulness, self-care, guidance in coping strategies and techniques for managing children's challenging behaviours, and support and counseling of parents. The results obtained are encouraging regarding the effectiveness of these programs.

INTRODUCTION

Neurodevelopmental disorders are common in the school population and present a variety of symptoms (Katsarou & Zerva, 2024). Attention Deficit Hyperactivity Disorder (ADHD), is a type of neurodevelopmental condition that affects approximately 5-7% of children worldwide (APA, 2013). Children diagnosed with this disorder may exhibit symptoms of inattention, hyperactivity or a combination of both, and symptoms may persist or disappear during adulthood (Sadock & Sadock, 2014). Children may also exhibit inadequate impulse control, self-regulation difficulties, emotional outbursts, lack of motivation, low self-esteem, difficulty in solving problems, inadequate inhibition. All of the above make it difficult for parents to manage such behaviours (Aberson et al., 2007; Barkley, 2005; Rief, 2005). Children with ADHD may, in addition to behavioural problems, display emotional dysfunction (Shaw et al., 2015), mental disorders (self-harm, anti-social behaviour, disruptive and oppositional behaviour) and low academic achievement (Sayal et al., 2018).

It has been suggested that parents of children with ADHD describe experiencing more anxiety about their parenting role and less psychological well-being compared to parents of neurotypical children (Theule et al., 2013). Assessing the extent of the impact of having a child with ADHD in the family on the well-being of parents/caregivers is of paramount importance for clinical practice, service professionals and policy makers (Peasgood et al., 2016).

The aim of this literature review is to understand the difficulties and challenges faced by parents caring for a child with ADHD. Assessing their overall well-being makes it imperative to implement intervention programs to enhance this. Following an extensive review, specific intervention programs are reported and the evaluation of their effectiveness is described.

WELL-BEING: PARENTS OF CHILDREN WITH ADHD

Well-being is a subjective feeling and describes the way in which a person evaluates life and himself or herself (Sørensen et al., 1996). Psychological well-being has until recently been considered to be the absence of illness or other diseases. In recent years, and according to the positive approach, psychological well-being can be experienced by a person rather than an illness, when he or she is possessed of positive emotions, such as life satisfaction and happiness, which may reduce the level of anxiety due to the illness (Park, 2004).

According to the multidimensional model described by Ryff (2014), psychological well-being consists of six different dimensions: self-acceptance, positive relationships with others, autonomy, mastery of the environment, purpose in life and personal growth.

From the perspective of positive psychology, the ability to optimize an individual's abilities to claim their happiness makes it possible to optimize subjective well-being in clinical settings (Duckworth & Quinn, 2009). The development of feelings of happiness and positive emotions in general, a sense of meaning in order to cope with the effects of pain or disorder are key goals of positive psychology (Seligman et al., 2004).

Overall well-being essentially describes the interaction of all those elements that lead the individual to consider his/her life meaningful and is related to the balanced coexistence of the individual in all areas (psychological, social, physical, community, economic, occupational). Oversaturation or neglect of one domain may have negative effects on the individual (Beetham, & Okhai, 2017).

Attention Deficit Hyperactivity Disorder, is one of the most common disorders in childhood, and if appropriate accommodations are not made, it can negatively affect the psychological and social development of children (Dogangun & Yavuz, 2011). The difficulties experienced by children with ADHD affect their academic performance, interpersonal relationships, internal functioning and communication with parents, teachers and peers (Powell et al., 2010). Parenting a child with ADHD is a complex and difficult situation that requires inner strength to cope with daily challenges (Moen et al, 2011). Some of the difficulties faced by parents of children with ADHD are related to discipline, giving instructions, assistance in practicing daily routines, transportation to public places, family gatherings. It has even been suggested about mothers of children with ADHD that they face difficulties due to low social status, poor health, social stigma and also because of relationship problems (Ogundele, 2018). In addition, low paternal involvement and inconsistent paternal discipline have been associated with increased maternal stress, making it imperative that fathers be involved in the management of the child's disorder (Ellis & Nigg, 2009).

It has even been reported that due to the difficulties in parent-child interaction and the inability to handle a child with ADHD who also has difficulty following instructions, the mother's self-efficacy is disrupted, thus affecting her psychological well-being (Abidin, 1992). Social support has been found to be a determinant factor, which influences stress, well-being and quality of life (Zeng et al., 2020).

Also, support from community health services is considered important for families with children with ADHD (Moen, et al., 2011; 2014).

The difficulty in controlling the child's behaviours resulting from the disorder can lead parents to increased stress, despite the healthy physical and mental development they may be experiencing (Nuri et. al., 2019). Parents' well-being is affected by stress as their balance is disrupted. Indeed, the adverse effects of the presence of ADHD in the family have been identified and documented, specifically on parents' stress levels, quality of life and psychological well-being (Cappe et al, 2017; Craig et al, 2016; Muñoz-Silva et al, 2017). The chronic nature of the disorder may affect the lives of both children and their parents (Mousavi, 2015), however the mental burnout of parents due to raising and supporting a child with these difficulties is often overlooked (Dianasari & Dianasari, 2023). The existence of a positive family environment is instrumental in promoting children's emotional and behavioural well-being and can help normalise behaviours due to ADHD (Mulligan et al. 2011).

Discussions about well-being or health mostly focus on the psychopathological aspect of a person, the development of treatment strategies and preventive programs (Hapsari et al., 2020). There are few studies on the well-being of parents themselves who have a child diagnosed with ADHD.

Hallberg et al. (2008) in a qualitative study of 12 parents of adolescent girls concluded that parents are stretched to their limits as they have sole parenting responsibility, struggle for professional support, work long hours and try to resolve family conflicts. Parents described the emotional, physical and psychological burden they experience and the negative impact of raising a child with ADHD on their well-being.

Nuri et al. (2019) in their quantitative study of 110 mothers and 90 fathers of children with ADHD in northern Cyprus, found that mothers scored higher emotional well-being scores than fathers. The researchers explain this difference by the fact that childcare is primarily a mother's concern. It was also shown from the results that family interaction, child rearing, nature of disability, physical/mental well-being are related to support and emotional well-being while poor self-efficacy is a predictor of these.

A study by Neff (2010) examined the extent to which the impact of child's ADHD, problem behaviour, drug use and fathers' social support influence their sense of wellbeing. Interviews were conducted with 145 fathers of children diagnosed with ADHD and 2,635 fathers of children without ADHD. Social or emotional differences between fathers were also assessed. Regarding the emotional and social burden associated with raising a child with ADHD, few differences were found between fathers of children with and without ADHD. Fathers of children with ADHD reported significantly greater emotional well-being, as the disorder and its characteristics did not appear to have a detrimental impact on their personal and social resources. Also, no differences were found in the social support received by fathers of children with and without the disorder. In addition, social support and the child's disorder status were found to be positively associated with fathers' emotional well-being. Children appeared to have a significant impact on fathers' sense of well-being, and they appeared to be well equipped to cope with the challenges associated with raising their children with ADHD.

On the opposite side, Peasgood et al. (2016) found significant negative effects of childhood ADHD on parent/caregiver work hours, sleep quality, leisure satisfaction and health-related quality of life. More specifically, they observed a decrease in life satisfaction, mental well-being and relationship satisfaction. Similarly, in a study by Angeline et al. (2023) among 131 mothers of children with ADHD, a negative correlation was observed between mothers' anxiety and their psychological well-being, while the mediating role of their perceived social support in this relationship was found. In a qualitative study aimed at identifying the factors affecting the subjective well-being of mothers caring for children with hyperactivity, it was found that lack of social support (family and environment), low knowledge of the disorder, time management problems, and the mother's physical condition contribute negatively to maternal subjective well-being. This well-being is also negatively affected by the child's hyperactive behaviour, high levels of difficulty, denial of the child's symptoms and the mother's particular problems (anxiety, depression)(Nayla, 2024). Lam, Hong, & Shum (2024) found in their research that children's disorder symptoms and adjustment significantly predicted their emotional dysfunction, resulting in parental anxiety, emotional dysfunction, and parental mental health problems.

In their survey of 264 parents of children with ADHD, Moen et al. (2016) answered questions about psychological distress, sense of family cohesion and family functioning. Mothers reported more psychological distress compared to fathers, as mothers of children with ADHD take on more responsibilities related to childrearing and daily life (Moen et al., 2011; Peters & Jackson, 2009). In addition, parents of children with ADHD reported greater psychological distress, weaker well-being and sense of family cohesion, and less favorable family functioning compared to parents of children without ADHD. Parents' well-being and psychological distress seem to have a greater impact on family functioning; on the other hand, the determinant role of the child's behaviour with ADHD and support from community health services was also highlighted.

Dianasari & Dianasari (2023), in an online survey, assessed the well-being of 65 caregivers of children with ADHD in Indonesia, as well as their levels of anxiety and depression. Of these, only 20 had a well-being score of 60 or higher (out of 100), while 45 participants had a score below 60, indicating lower well-being. Finally, 62% reported experiencing symptoms of depression, ranging from mild to very severe.

Similarly, in Peters & Jackson's (2009) qualitative study with a sample of mothers of children with ADHD, it was reported that the functional impairments in different areas of life (social, academic, emotional) due to the disorder make parenting a demanding process and the challenges that arise may negatively affect mothers' mental and emotional well-being (Peters & Jackson, 2009).

Finally, for Sundarall et al. (2016) parents of children with ADHD in South Africa experience a decline in functioning resulting in a negative impact on their well-being.

INTERVENTIONS

Some of the difficulties experienced by children with ADHD are related to executive functions such as cognitive flexibility, inhibition, self-regulation, self-control, working memory, problem solving, reasoning and planning (Barkley, 2015). It is important to seek psychosocial interventions that target the well-being of the whole family (Lo et al., 2020). Inclusive education should be based on cooperation, commitment and innovation (Efthymiou & Katsarou, 2024). Interventions that target the mental well-being of parents and lead to the mitigation of problems and problematic behaviours of children with ADHD, may be a form of alternative intervention for families of children with ADHD that can have positive outcomes (Chan et al., 2018). Interventions to educate parents of children with ADHD to enhance their psychological wellbeing have been conducted from time to time and their effectiveness has been evaluated. According to several practitioners, it has been argued that training parents in self-care techniques and stress management skills contributes to the development of healthy relationships with their children (Rodrigo et al., 2004; Betta Olivares, 2007).

It is a common assumption in the research literature that there are three effective treatments: medication (Abikoff et al., 2004), behaviour management therapy (Dopfner, et al., 2004; DuPaul & Eckert, 1997) and a combination of the two (MTA, 2004; Pelham et al., 2005).

Parent education is a form of therapeutic behaviour management and is considered more effective by parents, compared to the exclusive use of medication (MTA, 1999). Parent education (Danforth, 1998) and parent counselling and support (Blackman, 1999; Davis & Spurr, 1998) are two of the most popular approaches. The role of parent education has been shown to be crucial in the management of ADHD (Anastopoulos et al., 1993). In education, parents are informed about ADHD and about behavioral strategies for increasing attention, organizing behavior, and reducing challenging and difficult behaviors (Sonuga-Barke et al., 2001). Three well-known parent training programs were designed by Barkley (1987), Patterson and Reid (1973), as well as Forehand and McMahon (1981) to improve parental behavior management skills. In these programs parents may be taught the application of reinforcement or punishment following acceptable or unacceptable behaviours (Mash & Barkley, 1998), where it is suggested that these techniques can be applied at home by parents to manage behaviour problems associated with ADHD. Parent counselling on the other hand has been reported as more helpful in managing children's behavioural problems (Pelham et al., 1998).

Parenting behaviour management training and cognitive-behavioural therapy (CBT) for ADHD are some common non-pharmacological interventions for children with ADHD. However, it has been suggested that parents who are self-diagnosed with ADHD do not respond adequately to behavior management training (Zeng et al., 2020).

Behavioral Parent Training (BPT) is an intervention used quite frequently with parents to train them to avoid anxiety when interacting with their children. It is primarily based on behaviour modification techniques, however it is questioned as to the sustainability and longevity of its effects without ongoing supervision and monitoring by qualified professionals (Lee et al., 2012).

On the other hand, self-care and enhancing one's well-being through mindfulness training helps to address anxiety. This training may include practices of focused attention on a stimulus or open monitoring practices by shifting attention to thoughts or emotions that concern the individual in the present situation (Hervás et al., 2016). That is, individuals are trained to "verbalize" their thoughts, making them mere observers. Such mindfulness and self-care parenting training techniques may be beneficial to parents whose child has been diagnosed with ADHD, as it may help to manage unpleasant emotions (Van der Oord et al., 2012), improve parent-child relationships and develop attentional skills with children. The contribution of these practices in enhancing well-being, self-care and satisfaction in parenting on the part of parents has also been reported (Harnett, 2012).

A key goal of mindfulness training is to cultivate awareness through teaching participants to focus on the present without judgement (Martel et al., 2011). Mindfulness training can help children with ADHD to regulate their attention and executive functions, with a direct consequence on parents' self-regulation when they are called upon to respond to challenging behaviors of their child due to ADHD, contributing to changing dysfunctional patterns that may occur in parental parenting practices (Bögels et al, 2010; Shapiro, et al., 2006). Mindfulness may therefore benefit the family through enhancing the strengths of its members. The value of mindfulness in enhancing parental self-management, reducing parental anxiety and increasing psychological well-being has been research-proven (Lo et al., 2016).

Some of the formal practices included in mindfulness enhancement programs include walking meditation, sitting meditation, mindful eating, mindful movements and body scanning (Kabat-Zinn, 2013). Participants practice focusing their attention on the experience of emotions, thoughts, bodily sensations and sounds, as well as noticing when these surface or subside (Keng et al., 2011).

The research of Salgado et al. (2020) evaluated the effectiveness of a mindfulness program on various dimensions related to well-being and psychological flexibility in parents of children with ADHD. More specifically, stress reduction protocols based on mindfulness and cognitive therapy were examined, through self-compassion and self-care exercises. The group intervention program, consisting of 12 weekly training sessions in self-awareness and self-care skills, was applied to 22 parents of children and adolescents diagnosed with ADHD, and its effects on parents' psychological flexibility, cognitive fusion, mindfulness, adaptation and self-compassion were evaluated. The results showed a significant increase in mindfulness skills, psychological flexibility, self-compassion, improvement in attention focus skills, conscious and not impulsive reaction in dealing with situations and the use of humor as a strategy to deal with problematic situations.

Lo et al. (2016), in their evaluation of a six-week mindfulness-based training (FBMI) program for 100 children with ADHD, found that the family mindfulness intervention was effective based on the children's positive outcomes. Themes of the program for parents included: stress of parenting, automatic responses, conscientious responding to children, quality parenting, coping with difficulties with kindness, and parental self-care. In families receiving intervention, a reduction in their children's symptoms of inattention and hyperactivity was evident, making FBMI a treatment option for ADHD. In fact, the improvement in problem behaviors due to ADHD demonstrates the effectiveness of the intervention toward reducing children's internalizing and externalizing problems. The effectiveness of the program was also found in other applications of the intervention with parents of children with ADHD (van der Oord et al., 2012) as improvements in parental anxiety and parental hyperactivity were found.

The research by Sonuga-Barke et al. (2001) evaluated the effectiveness of two different treatments, parent training in child management techniques as well as counselling and support. Child and maternal symptoms and well-being were measured before and after the intervention over a 15-week period, and an increase in mothers' sense of well-being and a decrease in children's ADHD symptoms were observed in families who received parent education compared to the other two groups (control group, group receiving counselling and support).

Ghadampour et al. (2016) examined the effectiveness of mindfulness training and its impact on the psychological well-being of 30 mothers of children with ADHD. Eight two-hour sessions of mindfulness training were conducted, and it was shown that mothers' psychological well-being increased significantly.

Siebelink et al. (2022) wanted to examine the effects of MindChamp, in the context of a pre-registered randomised controlled trial comparing the effects of a mindfulness-based family intervention "MYmind", alongside usual care, lasting 8 weeks. MYmind is a protocol of a mindfulness-based family intervention implemented over eight weekly 90-minute group sessions and includes a booster session eight weeks later. The children and parents may meet and homework is often assigned approximately 30-45 minutes/day for parents and 15 minutes/day for children. The researchers found that compared to outcomes in exclusive care families, significant improvements were seen in families who received an intervention regarding their own ADHD symptoms, well-being and conscientious parenting of their children.

Shimabukuro et al. (2024) examined the effectiveness of the Well Parent Japan (WPJ) intervention in improving the psychological well-being of mothers. It is a 13-session program aimed at improving parents' knowledge about ADHD, to improve their psychological wellbeing in order to prepare them to support their children with ADHD (Treacy et al., 2005). It includes psychoeducation about ADHD, sessions related to mothers' psychological wellbeing (stress management, cognitive restructuring, problem-solving and communication skills) and behaviour management sessions (Shimabukuro et al, 2017). They observed significant effects of the WPJ intervention on parenting practices, parenting efficacy, family tension, mothers' self-reported well-being and family adjustment.

DISCUSSION

Raising a child with Attention Deficit Hyperactivity Disorder can be a stressful process for parents (Tasiou & Nikolaou, 2023; 2024). Symptoms and behaviours resulting from hyperactivity, impulsivity and/or inattention can affect home and school. Families raising a child with ADHD report a lower quality of life compared to those without children with ADHD (Klassen et al., 2004). Although ADHD is one of the most common mental disorders in early childhood, existing treatments appear to be limited, resulting in families of children with ADHD experiencing high levels of anxiety with direct effects and burdens on school systems and the community. Incorrect handling of the child's behavior management and difficulties in family relationships result in increased chances of comorbidity with other psychopathological conditions such as Oppositional Defiant Disorder, behavioral disorders in children and symptoms of depressive disorder in adult caregivers. It is therefore necessary to search for effective treatments that contribute to improving family functioning and quality of life (Lo, 2016).

Parents' views on their children's strengths and challenges are often a guide to better understanding the needs of both children and parents (Ralli, Alexandri, & Sofologi, 2024). Interventions aimed at supporting the well-being of caregivers are of research interest as an element of great importance in the therapeutic process. Intervention that emphasizes mindful parenting has been shown according to emerging research evidence to contribute towards improving the well-being of caregivers of young children with ADHD. Conscientious parenting involves intentional, non-judgmental awareness of the parenting experience, aims to regulate parental responses, enhances the capacity to respond with knowledge and presence, and to be aware of and accept the child's unique nature, feelings and needs. Such interventions may help to reduce caregiver burnout and enhance parents' effectiveness in managing the symptoms of their child's disorder (Kurahashi & Reichert, 2020).

REFERENCES

Aberson, B., Shure, M. B., & Goldstein, S. (2007). Social problem-solving intervention can help children with ADHD. *Journal of Attention Disorders*, 12(5), 391–393. 10.1177/108705470729940917606767

Abidin, R. R. (1992). The determinants of parenting behavior. *Journal of Clinical Child Psychology*, 21(4), 407–412. 10.1207/s15374424jccp2104_12

Abikoff, H., Hechtman, L., Klein, R., Weiss, G., Fleiss, K., Etcovitch, J., Cousins, L., Greenfield, B., Martin, D., & Pollack, S. (2004). Symptomatic improvement in children with ADHD treated with long-term methylphenidate and multimodal psychosocial treatment. *Journal of the American Academy of Child and Adolescent Psychiatry*, 43(7), 802–811. 10.1097/01.chi.0000128791.10014.ac15213581

American Psychiatric Association. (2013). *Diagnostic and statistical manual of mental disorders* (5th ed.). American Psychiatric Association.

Anastopoulos, A. D., Shelton, T. L., DuPaul, G. J., & Guevremont, D. C. (1993). Parent training for attention-deficit hyperactivity disorder: Its impact on parent functioning. *Journal of Abnormal Child Psychology*, 21(5), 581–596. 10.1007/BF009163208294653

Angeline, J., Rathnasabapathy, M., & Taylor, G. (2023). Role of Perceived Social Support in the Relationship between Parenting Stress and Psychological Well-Being of Mothers of Children with ADHD: A Mediation Model. *Universal Journal of Public Health*, 11(6), 838–844. 10.13189/ujph.2023.110607

Barkley, R. (2005). *Taking Charge of AD/HD: The complete, authoritative guide for parents* (Rev.ed.). Guilford.

Barkley, R. A. (2015). Executive functioning and self-regulation viewed as an extended phenotype: Implications of the theory for ADHD and its treatment. In Barkley, R. A. (Ed.), *Attention deficit hyperactivity disorder: A handbook for diagnosis and treatment* (4th ed., pp. 405–434). Guilford.

Barkley, R. B. (1987). *Defiant children: A clinician manual for parent training*. Guilford Press.

Beetham, J., & Okhai, L. (2017). Workplace Dyslexia & Specific Learning Difficulties-Productivity, Engagement and Well-Being. *Open Journal of Social Sciences*, 5(6), 56–78. 10.4236/jss.2017.56007

Betta Olivares, R., Morales Messerer, G., Rodríguez Ureta, K., & Guerra Vio, C. (2007). La frecuencia de emisión de conductas de autocuidado y su relación con los niveles de estrés traumático secundario y de depresión en psicólogos clínicos. *Pensam. Psicológico, 3.*

Blackman, J. A. (1999). Attention-deficit/hyperactivity disorder in preschoolers: Does it exist and should we treat it? *Pediatric Clinics of North America*, 46(5), 1011–1025. 10.1016/S0031-3955(05)70169-310570702

Bögels, S. M., Lehtonen, A., & Restifo, K. (2010). Mindful parenting in mental health care. *Mindfulness*, 1(2), 107–120. 10.1007/s12671-010-0014-521125026

Cappe, E., Bolduc, M., Rougé, M. C., Saiag, M. C., & Delorme, R. (2017). Quality of life, psychological characteristics, and adjustment in parents of children with Attention-Deficit/Hyperactivity Disorder. *Quality of Life Research: An International Journal of Quality of Life Aspects of Treatment, Care and Rehabilitation*, 26(5), 1283–1294. 10.1007/s11136-016-1446-827798755

Chan, S.K.C., Zhang, D., Bögels, S.M., Chan, C.S., Lai, K.Y.C., Lo, H.H.M., Yip, B.H.K., Lau, E.N.S, Gao, T.T., & Wong, S.Y.S. (2018). Effects of a mindfulness-based intervention (MYmind) for children with ADHD and their parents: protocol for a randomised controlled trial. *BMJ Open, 12*(11), e022514.

Craig, F., Operto, F. F., De Giacomo, A., Margari, L., Frolli, A., Conson, M., Ivagnes, S., Monaco, M., & Margari, F. (2016). Parenting stress among parents of children with Neurodevelopmental Disorders. *Psychiatry Research*, 242, 121–129. 10.1016/j.psychres.2016.05.01627280521

Danforth, J. S. (1998). The Outcome of Parent lraining Using the Behavior Management Flow Chart with Mothers and Their Children with Oppositional Defiant Disorder and Attention-Deficit Hyperactivity Disorder. *Behavior Modification*, 22(4), 443–473. 10.1177/0145445598022400197556446

Davis, H., & Spurr, P. (1998). Parent counselling: An evaluation of a community child mental health service. *Journal of Child Psychology and Psychiatry, and Allied Disciplines*, 39(3), 365–376. 10.1111/1469-7610.003329670092

Dianasari, & Dianasari. (2023). Level Stress, Anxiety, Depression, and Well-being among Parents of Children with ADHD in Indonesia. *International Conference on Sustainable Health Promotion, 3(*1), 142-147.

Dogangun, B., & Yavuz, M. (2011). Attention Deficit Hyperactivity Disorder. *Turkish Psychiatry Archive*, 46, 25–28.

Dopfner, M., Breuer, D., Schurmann, S., Wolff Metternich, T., Rademacher, C., & Lehmkuhl, G. (2004). Effectiveness of an adaptive multimodal treatment in children with attention-deficit hyperactivity disorder-global outcome. *European Child & Adolescent Psychiatry*, 13(1), 117–129.

Duckworth, A. L., Quinn, P. D., & Seligman, M. E. P. (2009). Positive predictors of teacher effectiveness. *The Journal of Positive Psychology*, 4(6), 540–547. 10.1080/17439760903157232

DuPaul, G., & Eckert, T. (1997). The effects of school-based interventions for Attention Deficit Hyperactivity Disorder: A meta-analysis. *School Psychology Review*, 26(1), 5–27. 10.1080/02796015.1997.12085845

Efthymiou, E., & Katsarou, D. V. (2024). Fostering Inclusive Education: Collaborative Strategies, Emerging Technologies, and Parental Engagement for Children With Language Disorders. In *Childhood Developmental Language Disorders: Role of Inclusion, Families, and Professionals* (pp. 65-84). IGI Global.

Ellis, B., & Nigg, J. (2009). Parenting practices and attention- deficit/hyperactivity disorder: New findings suggest partial specificity of effects. *Journal of the American Academy of Child and Adolescent Psychiatry*, 48(2), 146–154. 10.1097/CHI.0b013e31819176d019065110

Forehand, R. L., & McMahon, R. J. (1981). *Helping the noncompliant child. A clinician's guide to parent training*. Guilford Press.

Ghadampour, E., Shirazi, A., & Tehrani, M. A. (2016). Effectiveness of training of mindfulness-based stress reduction on psychological well-being of ADHD children's mothers. *Journal of Exceptional Children*, 16(3), 35–48.

Hallberg, U., Klingberg, G., Reichenberg, K., & Möller, A. (2008). Living at the edge of one's capability: Experiences of parents of teenage daughters diagnosed with ADHD. *International Journal of Qualitative Studies on Health and Well-being*, 3(1), 52–58. 10.1080/17482620701705523

Hapsari, I. I., Iskandarsyah, A., Joefiani, P., & Siregar, J. R. (2020). Parents' Perceptions of Subjective Well-Being in Children with ADHD. *Journal of Psychology and Instruction*, 4(2), 44–51. 10.23887/jpai.v4i2.32437

Harnett, P. H., & Dawe, S. (2012). The contribution of mindfulness-based therapies for children and families and proposed conceptual integration. *Child and Adolescent Mental Health*, 17(4), 195–208. 10.1111/j.1475-3588.2011.00643.x32847274

Hervás, G., Cebolla, A., & Soler, J. (2016). Intervenciones psicológicas basadas en mindfulness y sus beneficios: Estado actual de la cuestión. *Cliníca y Salud*, 27(3), 115–124. 10.1016/j.clysa.2016.09.002

Kabat-Zinn, J. (2013). *Full Catastrophe living: Using the wisdom of your body and mind to face stress, pain, and illness* (Revised and Updated ed.). New York, NY: Bantam.

Katsarou, D., & Zerva, E. (2024). Writing disorders in specific reading disorder (dyslexia) and attention deficit hyperactivity disorder: The clinical continuum between the two neurodevelopmental disorders. *Archives of Hellenic Medicine*, 41(3), 339–345.

Keng, S. L., Smoski, M. J., & Robins, C. J. (2011). Effects of mindfulness on psychological health: A review of empirical studies. *Clinical Psychology Review*, 31(6), 1041–1056. 10.1016/j.cpr.2011.04.00621802619

Klassen, A. F., Miller, A., & Fine, S. (2004). Health-related quality of life in children and adolescents who have a diagnosis of attention-deficit/hyperactivity disorder. *Pediatrics*, 114(5), e541–e547. 10.1542/peds.2004-084415520087

Kurahashi, M., & Reichert, E. (2020). How Mindful Parenting Can Support Caregivers In Managing Their Young Children With ADHD. *Journal of the American Academy of Child & Adolescent Psychiatry, 59*(10). 10.1016/j.jaac.2020.07.458

Lam, I. K. Y., Hong, J., & Shum, K. K. M. (2024, July). Mediating role of emotion regulation between ADHD children's adjustment and parents' well-being. In *33rd International Congress of Psychology*, Prague.

Lee, P. C., Niew, W. I., Yang, H. J., Chen, V. C. H., & Lin, K. C. (2012). A meta-analysis of behavioral parent training for children with attention deficit hyperactivity disorder. *Research in Developmental Disabilities*, 33(6), 2040–2049. 10.1016/j.ridd.2012.05.01122750360

Lo, H. H., Wong, S. W., Wong, J. Y., Yeung, J. W., Snel, E., & Wong, S. Y. (2020). The effects of family-based mindfulness intervention on ADHD symptomology in young children and their parents: A randomized control trial. *Journal of Attention Disorders*, 24(5), 667–680. 10.1177/108705471774333029185375

Lo, H. H. M., Wong, S., Wong, J., Wong, S., & Yeung, J. (2016). The effect of a family-based mindfulness intervention on children with attention deficit and hyperactivity symptoms and their parents: Design and rationale for a randomized, controlled clinical trial (Study protocol). *BMC Psychiatry*, 16(1), 65. 10.1186/s12888-016-0773-126980323

Martel, M. M., Nikolas, M., Jernigan, K., Friderici, K., Waldman, I., & Nigg, J. T. (2011). The dopamine receptor D4 gene (DRD4) moderates family environmental effects on ADHD. *Journal of Abnormal Child Psychology*, 39(1), 1–10. 10.1007/s10802-010-9439-520644990

Mash, E., & Barkley, R. (1998). Treatment of childhood disorders. New York: The Guilford Press MTA Cooperative Group. (1999). A 14-month randomized clinical trial of treatment strategies for Attention-Deficit/Hyperactivity Disorder. *Archives of General Psychiatry*, 56, 1073–1086.

Moen, Ø. & Hedelin, B. & Hall-Lord, M. (2016). Family Functioning, Psychological Distress, and Well-Being in Parents with a Child Having ADHD. *SAGE Open. 6.* 1-10.1177/2158244015626767.

Moen, Ø. L., Hall-Lord, M. L., & Hedelin, B. (2011). Contending and adapting every day: Norwegian parents' lived experience of having a child with ADHD. *Journal of Family Nursing*, 17(4), 441–462. 10.1177/10748407114239242422084482

Moen, Ø. L., Hall-Lord, M. L., & Hedelin, B. (2014). Living in a family with a child with attention deficit hyperactivity disorder: A phenomenographic study. *Journal of Clinical Nursing*, 23(21-22), 3166–3176. 10.1111/jocn.1255925453121

Mousavi, S., Pahlavanzadeh, S., & Maghsoudi, J. (2019). Evaluating the effect of a need-based program for caregivers on the stress, anxiety, depression, and the burden of care in families of children with attention deficit-hyperactive disorder. *Iranian Journal of Nursing and Midwifery Research*, 24(2), 96–101. 10.4103/ijnmr. IJNMR_11_1730820219

MTA Cooperative Group. (1999). A 14-month randomized clinical trial of treatment strategies for Attention-Deficit/Hyperactivity Disorder. *Archives of General Psychiatry*, 56(12), 1073–1086. 10.1001/archpsyc.56.12.107310591283

MTA Cooperative Group. (2004). National institute of mental health multimodal treatment study of ADHD follow-up: 24-month outcomes of treatment strategies for Attention-Deficit/Hyperactivity Disorder. *Pediatrics*, 113(4), 754–761. 10.1542/peds.113.4.75415060224

Mulligan, A., Anney, R., Butler, L., O'Regan, M., Richardson, T., Tulewicz, E. M., Fitzgerald, M., & Gill, M. (2011). Home environment: Association with hyperactivity/impulsivity in children with ADHD and their non-ADHD siblings. *Child: Care, Health and Development*, 39(2), 202–212. 10.1111/j.1365-2214.2011.01345.x22168816

Muñoz-Silva, A., Lago-Urbano, R., Sanchez-Garcia, M., & Carmona-Márquez, J. (2017). Child/adolescent's ADHD and parenting stress: The mediating role of family impact and conduct problems. *Frontiers in Psychology*, 8, 300021. 10.3389/fpsyg.2017.0225229312090

Nayla, M. R. (2024). Factors Influencing The Subjective Well-Being Of Mothers Who Have Hyperactive Children. *JHSS*, 8(1), 216–220.

Neff, P. E. (2010). Fathering an ADHD Child: An Examination of Paternal Well-being and Social Support*. *Sociological Inquiry*, 80(4), 531–553. 10.1111/j.1475-682X.2010.00348.x20879176

Nuri, C., Akçamete, G., & Direktör, C. (2019). The Quality Of Life And Stress Levels In Parents Of Children With Attention Deficit Hyperactivity Disorder. *European Journal Of Special Education Research, 4*(3).

Ogundele, M. O. (2018). Behavioural and emotional disorders in childhood: A brief overview for paediatricians. *World Journal of Clinical Pediatrics*, 7(1), 9–26. 10.5409/wjcp.v7.i1.929456928

Park, N. (2004). The Role of Subjective Well-Being in Positive Youth Development. *The Annals of the American Academy of Political and Social Science*, 2004(591), 25–39. 10.1177/0002716203260078

Patterson, G. R., & Reid, J. B. (1973). Intervention for families of aggressive boys: A replication study. *Behaviour Research and Therapy*, 11(4), 383–394. 10.1016/0005-7967(73)90096-X4777636

Peasgood, T., Bhardwaj, A., Biggs, K., Brazier, J. E., Coghill, D., Cooper, C. L., Daley, D., De Silva, C., Harpin, V., Hodgkins, P., Nadkarni, A., Setyawan, J., & Sonuga-Barke, E. J. (2016). The impact of ADHD on the health and well-being of ADHD children and their siblings. *European Child & Adolescent Psychiatry*, 25(11), 1217–1231. 10.1007/s00787-016-0841-627037707

Pelham, W., Burrows-MacLean, L., Gnagy, E., Fabiano, G., Coles, E., Tresco, K., Wymbs, B., Wienke, A., Walker, K., & Hoffman, M. (2005). Transdermal methylphenidate, behavioral, and combined treatment for children with ADHD. *Experimental and Clinical Psychopharmacology*, 13(2), 111–126. 10.1037/1064-1297.13.2.11115943544

Pelham, W. E.Jr, Wheeler, T., & Chronis, A. (1998). Empirically supported psychosocial treatments for attention deficit hyperactivity disorder. *Journal of Clinical Child Psychology*, 27(2), 190–205. 10.1207/s15374424jccp2702_69648036

Peters, K., & Jackson, D. (2009). Mothers' experiences of parenting a child with attention deficit hyperactivity disorder. *Journal of Advanced Nursing*, 65(1), 62–71. 10.1111/j.1365-2648.2008.04853.x19120583

Powell, D. R., Son, S. H., File, N., & San Juan, R. R. (2010). Parent–school relationships and children's academic and social outcomes in public school pre-kindergarten. *Journal of School Psychology*, 48(4), 269–292. 10.1016/j.jsp.2010.03.00220609850

Ralli, A. M., Alexandri, M., & Sofologi, M. (2024). Language, Socio-Emotional Skills, and School Performance of Children and Adolescents With Developmental Language Disorder According to Parents' Perceptions. In *Childhood Developmental Language Disorders: Role of Inclusion, Families, and Professionals* (pp. 85-101). IGI Global.

Rief, S. F. (2005). *How to reach and teach children with ADD/ADHD: Practical Techniques, strategies and interventions* (2nd ed.). Jossey-Bass.

Rodrigo, M. J., Máiquez, M. L., García, M., Mendoza, R., Rubio, A., Martínez, A., & Martín, J. C. (2004). Relaciones padres-hijos y estilos de vida en la adolescencia. *Psicothema*, 16, 203–210.

Ryff, C. D. (2013). Psychological well-being revisited: Advances in the science and practice of eudaimonia. *Psychotherapy and Psychosomatics*, 83(1), 10–28. 10.1159/00035326324281296

Sadock, B. J., & Sadock, V. A. (2014). *Synopsis of Psychiatry: Behavioural Sciences/Clinical Psychiatry*. NIH.

Salgado, C., Martín Antón, L., & Carbonero, M. (2020). Impact of a Mindfulness and Self-Care Program on the Psychological Flexibility and Well-Being of Parents with Children Diagnosed with ADHD. *Sustainability (Basel)*, 12(18), 7487. 10.3390/su12187487

Sayal, K., Prasad, V., Daley, D., Ford, T., & Coghill, D. (2018). ADHD in children and young people: Prevalence, care pathways, and service provision. *The Lancet. Psychiatry*, 5(2), 175–186. 10.1016/S2215-0366(17)30167-029033005

Seligman, M. E. P., Parks, A. C., & Steen, T. (2004). A balanced psychology and a full life. *Philosophical Transactions of the Royal Society of London. Series B, Biological Sciences*, 359(1449), 1379–1381. 10.1098/rstb.2004.151315347529

Shapiro, S. L., Carlson, L., Astin, J., & Freedman, B. (2006). Mechanisms of mindfulness. *Journal of Clinical Psychology*, 62(3), 373–386. 10.1002/jclp.2023716385481

Shaw, P., Stringaris, A., Nigg, J., & Leibenluft, E. (2014). Emotion dysregulation in attention deficit hyperactivity disorder. *The American Journal of Psychiatry*, 171(3), 276–293. 10.1176/appi.ajp.2013.1307096624480998

Shimabukuro, S., Daley, D., Thompson, M. J., Laver-Bradbury, C., Nakanishi, E., & Tripp, G. (2017). Supporting Japanese mothers of children with ADHD: Cultural adaptation of the new Forest parent training Programme. *The Japanese Psychological Research*, 59(1), 35–48. 10.1111/jpr.12140

Shimabukuro, S., Oshio, T., Endo, T., Harada, S., Yamashita, Y., Tomoda, A., Guo, B., Goto, Y., Ishii, A., Izumi, M., Nakahara, Y., Yamamoto, K., Daley, D., & Tripp, G. (2024). A pragmatic randomised controlled trial of the effectiveness and cost-effectiveness of Well Parent Japan in routine care in Japan: The training and nurturing support for mothers (TRANSFORM) study. *Journal of Child Psychology and Psychiatry, and Allied Disciplines*, jcpp.14007. 10.1111/jcpp.1400738831654

Siebelink, N. M., Bögels, S. M., Speckens, A. E., Dammers, J. T., Wolfers, T., Buitelaar, J. K., & Greven, C. U. (2022). A randomised controlled trial (Mind-Champ) of a mindfulness-based intervention for children with ADHD and their parents. *Journal of Child Psychology and Psychiatry, and Allied Disciplines*, 63(2), 165–177. 10.1111/jcpp.1343034030214

Sonuga-Barke, E. J., Daley, D., Thompson, M., Laver-Bradbury, C., & Weeks, A. (2001). Parent-based therapies for preschool attention-deficit/hyperactivity disorder: A randomized, controlled trial with a community sample. *Journal of the American Academy of Child and Adolescent Psychiatry*, 40(4), 402–408. 10.1097/00004583-200104000-0000811314565

Sørensen, T., & Næss, S. (1996). To measure quality of life: Relevance and use in the psychiatric domain. *Nordic Journal of Psychiatry*, 50(sup37, Suppl. 37), 29–39. 10.3109/08039489609099728

Tasiou, K., & Nikolaou, E. N. (2023). Psychological resilience of families of children with Attention Deficit Hyperactivity Disorder. In *New trends and approaches in child and adult psychopathology and mental health* (pp. 99–121). Gutenberg.

Tasiou, K., & Nikolaou, E. N. (2024). A Family's Experiences of Raising a Child Diagnosed With ADHD: Family Functioning and Organization, Sources of Support and Quality of Life–A Case Study. In *Childhood Developmental Language Disorders: Role of Inclusion, Families, and Professionals* (pp. 116-133). IGI Global.

Theule, J., Wiener, J., Tannock, R., & Jenkins, J. M. (2013). Parenting stress in families of children with ADHD: A meta-analysis. *Journal of Emotional and Behavioral Disorders*, 21(1), 3–17. 10.1177/1063426610387433

Treacy, L., Tripp, G., & Baird, A. (2005). Parent stress management training for attention-deficit/hyperactivity disorder. *Behavior Therapy*, 36(3), 223–233. 10.1016/S0005-7894(05)80071-1

Vago, D. R., & Silbersweig, D. A. (2012). Self-awareness, self-regulation, and self-transcendence (S-ART): A framework for understanding the neurobiological mechanisms of mindfulness. *Frontiers in Human Neuroscience*, 6, 296. 10.3389/fnhum.2012.0029623112770

Van der Oord, S., Bögels, S. M., & Peijnenburg, D. (2012). The effectiveness of mindfulness training for children with ADHD and mindful parenting for their parents. *Journal of Child and Family Studies*, 21(1), 139–147. 10.1007/s10826-011-9457-022347788

Zeng, S., Hu, X., Zhao, H., & Stone-MacDonald, A. K. (2020). Examining the relationships of parental stress, family support and family quality of life: A structural equation modeling approach. *Research in Developmental Disabilities*, 96, 103523. 10.1016/j.ridd.2019.10352331785472

Chapter 13
Theory of Mind and the Performance of Children With Intellectual Disability and Down Syndrome on Fantasy–Reality Distinction Tasks

Stergiani Giaouri
https://orcid.org/0000-0002-2280-9172
University of Western Macedonia, Greece

ABSTRACT

This chapter investigates theory of mind (ToM) development and performance on fantasy-reality distinction tasks in children with intellectual disabilities (ID) of different etiologies. ToM is crucial for understanding others' mental states, while the ability to distinguish between fantasy and reality is essential for cognitive flexibility. Children with ID often face challenges in these domains, impacting their social and adaptive functioning. In this study, 106 children were examined: forty-two children with typical development (TD), forty-one children with intellectual disability (ID) of unknown etiology, and twenty-three children with Down syndrome (DS). A set of fantasy-reality discrimination tasks was used. The findings contribute to advancing our understanding of ToM development and the fantasy-reality distinction in children with ID and DS, fostering inclusive education, and promoting social inclusion for these individuals.

DOI: 10.4018/979-8-3693-4022-6.ch013

INTRODUCTION

Theory of mind (ToM), the ability to infer mental states to oneself and others, has been a pervasive research theme across many disciplines, including developmental, educational, neuro- and social psychology, and speech therapy. Specifically, ToM refers to the ability to understand and attribute mental states, such as beliefs, desires, intentions, and emotions to oneself and others. It plays a crucial role in social interactions, perspective-taking, empathy, and moral reasoning (Wellman, Cross, & Watson, 2011). This ability is important for successful social interaction and is typically acquired during early childhood (Perner, Leekam, & Wimmer, 1987). ToM abilities have been consistently linked to markers of social adaptation and have been shown to be affected by a broad range of clinical conditions (Beaudoin et al., 2020).

Additionally, the study of the understanding of imaginary states has provided us with important insights into the development of theory of mind in children. The distinction between fantasy and reality is basic to human cognition, reflecting a fundamental ontological divide between the non-real and the real. The ability to differentiate between fantasy and reality is also essential for cognitive flexibility, problem-solving, and imaginative play (Harris et al., 1991). Research has shown that, from the third year of age onwards, children begin to understand: pretend, indeed demonstrating exceptional imaginative capacity in these tasks (Harris et al., 1991; Sobel & Lillard, 2001); fantasy, especially in tasks that are emotionally neutral (Sharon & Woolley, 2004); and dream (Woolley & Wellman, 1992), as mental states whose contents differ from external reality.

In a review, Woolley (1997) highlighted the continuing debate over children's understanding of the distinction between fantasy and reality. Her basic thesis supposes that children and adults do not differ fundamentally in their propensity to fantasy-reality confusion; nevertheless, there are aspects of children's understanding of fantasy that require further investigation. In the past, it has often been claimed that young children fail to distinguish systematically between mental phenomena and real phenomena. For example, Piaget (1929) claimed that young children cannot distinguish a real entity from a dream or image of that entity. However, Wellman and Estes (1986) found that even 3-year-olds can use behavioral-sensory criteria to distinguish between real objects (e.g., a balloon) and mental objects (e.g., an imagined balloon). Additionally, Estes, Wellman, and Woolley (1989) have shown that children as young as 3 years of age can distinguish between mental entities such as an image or dream of an object and a real object. At about this same age, children in their everyday talk discuss the contrasts between toys and reality, pictures and reality, and pretense and reality (Wolley & Wellman, 1990). They can track real and pretend transformations concurrently (Harris & Kavanaugh, 1993) and, when their pretend play is interrupted, are able to flexibly step out of the pretense mode and then return to it (Davis et al., 2002; Golomb & Kuersten, 1996; Sharon & Woolley, 2004).

To find out what conception children have of such imaginary creatures, 4- and 6-year-olds were questioned about three types of items: real items (e.g., a cup), ordinary imagined items (e.g., an image of a cup), and supernatural imagined items (e.g., an image of a monster) in the research of Harris et al. (1991). In two experiments, both age groups sharply differentiated the real items from both types of imagined items. Despite this apparently firm grasp of the distinction between fantasy and reality, two further experiments showed that 4- and 6-year-olds are not always certain that a creature that they have imagined cannot become real. Having imagined a creature inside a box, they show apprehension or curiosity about what is inside the box and often admit to wondering whether the creature is inside. The experiments suggest that children systematically distinguish fantasy from reality but are tempted to believe in the existence of what they have merely imagined. These observations raise the possibility that young children have a firm understanding of the fantasy-reality distinction, but only with respect to common, everyday objects. Young children also appreciate some of the special qualities of mental entities, for example, that they may be non-existent, impossible entities (e.g., pigs that fly). A very young child may initially be somewhat unsure about attributing human-like properties to various entities. With experience, children acquire increasing knowledge about everything in their world—both about real entities and their properties and about such socially supported myths as Santa Claus. Thus, rather than having misplaced the boundary between real and fantastical entities, young children are still in the process of actively constructing it (Sharon & Woolley, 2004).

Nevertheless, children often show a persistent fear of imaginary creatures, particularly monsters (Jersild, 1943). Children might be less sure of the imaginary status of more supernatural, exotic creatures, such as monsters. This would provide a plausible explanation of their fear of such creatures (Harris et al., 1991; Johnson & Harris, 1994; Sharon & Woolley, 2004). Recent experiments suggest that fantasy-reality confusions may, for some children, persist well into middle childhood (Bourchier & Davis, 2010). Similarly, some children, but not all, remain fearful of imaginary creatures long after they have started school. Consequently, thinking only in terms of how children come to adopt a skeptical stance (i.e., to cast off their child-like beliefs in fantasy figures like Santa Claus) will therefore provide only part of the story. To complement our current knowledge base, we must begin to unpack the factors associated with children's naïve skepticism and document the factors that lead children to relax their biases toward that stance and eventually find a comfortable balance between acceptance and doubt (Woolley & Ghossainy, 2013).

Especially in the field of theory of mind studies, initial research (Baron-Cohen et al., 1985; Flavell et al., 1990; Hala et al., 1991) dealt with the classical experimental tasks of theory of mind (e.g., false belief performance, deception, unexpected movement, etc.) and has been of great research interest, particularly in the study of children with autism spectrum disorder compared to children with intellectual disabilities (Charman et al., 1998). The findings of these studies mainly support the idea that individuals with intellectual disabilities also have difficulties in their performance on their respective tasks, but their difficulties are not as severe as those of individuals with autism. In other studies, as well (Baron-Cohen et al., 1985; Yirmiya et al., 1996; Yirmiya et al., 1998; Zelazo et al., 1996), it was found that individuals with intellectual disabilities of unknown etiology and Down syndrome have difficulty with mainly false belief and theory of mind deception tasks, compared to typically developing children, equalized in terms of their overall mental age.

ToM development in children with intellectual disabilities and Down syndrome can be understood through various theoretical frameworks, such as cognitive and socio-emotional perspectives. Cognitive theories suggest that ToM development is influenced by cognitive processes such as memory, attention, and executive functions (Beauchamp, 2017). Socio-emotional theories, on the other hand, emphasize the role of social experiences and interactions in shaping TOM development (Beauchamp & Anderson, 2010). The developmental trajectory of ToM in these populations may differ from that of typically developing children, with some acquiring ToM skills at a later age or demonstrating persistent challenges in specific aspects, such as understanding false beliefs or sarcasm.

The study also by Yirmiya, Solomonica-Levi, Shulman, and Pilowsky (1996) found no statistically significant differences in performance on false belief and theory of mind deception tasks between adults with intellectual disabilities of unknown cause and Down syndrome. It is quite possible, of course, as the researchers themselves claim, that the differences between these two clinical groups are more pronounced at younger ages than at older ages.

Most contemporary studies (Amadó et al., 2022; Baurain & Nader-Grosbois, 2013; Beauchamp & Anderson, 2010; Cebula et al., 2017; Comblain & Schmetz, 2020; de Rosnay & Hughes, 2006; Giaouri et al., 2010; Thirion-Marissiaux & Nader-Grosbois, 2008) have used as comparison groups diverse clinical groups with different etiologies, such as individuals with Down syndrome, individuals with autism and intellectual disability, individuals with intellectual disability of unknown etiology, and individuals with general learning disabilities. However, all these individual groups of people show different developmental patterns of abilities and weaknesses. Thus, the existing heterogeneity of these clinical cases often makes it difficult to interpret the data from these studies. Findings may also differ because the studies also use different tasks of theory of mind, and some may be related to differently important environmental factors. Further analysis of the resulting correlations with a variety of cognitive, social, and affective factors is therefore required, as is, of course, better selection of the sample of individuals compared each time (Cicchetti & Beeghly, 1990; Hodapp et al., 1990).

However, many studies have attempted to define comparison groups more precisely by selecting specific subgroups of individuals with intellectual disabilities, such as those with genetic syndromes (Abbeduto & Murphy, 2004; Alevriadou & Giaouri, 2011; Amadó et al., 2022; Lewis et al., 2006; Yirmiya et al., 1998). In these studies, similarities and differences in performance on theory of mind tasks emerged between these different clinical groups, which appear to be mainly related to the linguistic, social, and cognitive abilities of these individuals, especially on false belief performance tasks of theory of mind.

Initially, previous research showed a significant correlation between chronological age, verbal and practical abilities, and theory of mind ability, but these findings were not consistent. More specifically, chronological age was found to be correlated with theory of mind ability in some studies (Baron-Cohen, 1992), but not in others of these (Leekman & Perner, 1991). Happe's (1995) studies found a correlation between chronological age and theory of mind ability in people with intellectual disabilities. Older individuals performed lower than younger individuals, but this finding was considered erroneous and was attributed to the sample effect. Some researchers had found a correlation between verbal mental age and theory of mind ability (Eisenmajer et al., 1998; Happe´, 1995). Practical mental age was not found to be related to the theory of mind ability (Charman & Baron-Cohen, 1992; Leekman & Perner, 1991). Earlier research did not show correlations between language and performance on false belief performance tasks, but because they examined the language factor, mainly considering the general verbal cognitive age of people with intellectual disabilities rather than the different dimensions of language (Sullivan et al., 1994; Yirmiya et al., 1998).

Data from a series of studies over the last twenty years or so (Abbeduto et al., 2004; Alevriadou & Giaouri, 2011; Amadó et al., 2022; Astington & Baird, 2005; Giaouri et al., 2010) confirm that it is the verbal and executive demands of theory of mind tasks that appear to significantly influence and differentiate the performance of children with intellectual disabilities of different etiologies. Research shows that language, especially its narrative skill and theory of mind ability, seems to be related in children mainly with autism spectrum disorders (Happe´, 1995), in people with intellectual disabilities during childhood (Abbeduto et al., 2004; Fisher et al., 2005), and in people with intellectual disabilities of genetic etiology (Amadó et al., 2022; Lorusso et al., 2007).

For children with intellectual disabilities, it was also found that their general practical mental age is related to their performance in deception tasks (Yirmiya et al., 1996) and false beliefs about the theory of mind (Yirmiya & Shulman, 1996). In line with earlier findings by Happé´ (1995), although she studied mainly verbal mental age, Yirmiya, Solomonica-Levi, Shulman, and Pilowsky (1996) did not find consistently significant associations between general performance on theory of mind tasks and cognitive abilities measured by the WISC-R intelligence test scales (Wechsler, 1974) in individuals with intellectual disability of unknown cause and Down syndrome.

More specifically, some studies (Amadó et al., 2022; de Rosnay & Hughes, 2006; Giaouri et al., 2010; Hughes et al., 2007; Thirion-Marissiaux & Nader-Grosbois, 2008) found that these clinical groups of children mainly follow different developmental trajectories and perform differently on theory of mind tasks, but not necessarily on all tasks differently from those of typically developing children. It seems, however, that the different types and variety of content of the tasks, which assess different aspects of theory of mind with different levels of difficulty, play an important role here. These are tasks that require abilities such as switching visual perspective, understanding deception, metacognition, and executive functions including working memory, control, and attention, in which generally people with intellectual disabilities have difficulties (Burack et al., 2001; Hodapp & Fidler, 2016; Tsakiridou & Alevriadou, 2017; van der Molen et al., 2007; Zagaria et al., 2021).

In addition, other studies (Cornish et al., 2005; Giaouri et al., 2010; Tager-Flusberg & Sullivan, 2000) in the field of intellectual disability of different genetic etiologies (e.g., Down syndrome, fragile X chromosome syndrome, Williams syndrome, and Prader-Will syndrome) are trying to investigate the relationship between visual perception and theory of mind. Their data yield significant qualitative differences in individuals' performance on the types of mainly phenomenology-reality error tasks as well as false belief tasks of theory of mind. These variations go beyond the pattern of intellectual disability with cognitive deficits, emphasizing mainly the weaknesses and abilities of these individuals. As also mentioned, the distinction between the phenomenological perception of objects or events and reality is like the distinction between false beliefs and reality, as well as the distinction between two different perspectives from different observers. These types of distinctions tend to develop together, i.e., young children who succeed or fail on phenomenology-reality tasks also perform similarly on false belief theory-of-mind tasks.

Research also by Cornish, Burack, Rahman, Munir, Russo, and Grant (2005) on false belief theory of mind tasks (e.g., unexpected movement and in phenomenology-reality distinction tasks: color, size, material, and object identity) among children from different clinical groups of intellectual disability such as fragile X syndrome and Down syndrome yields significant qualitative differences in the types of errors in phenomenology-reality tasks. More specifically, children with Down syndrome showed a propensity for phenomenological errors (Giaouri et al., 2010).

Children's engagement in fantasy worlds has been found to be related to their ToM development in a short-term longitudinal study (Richert & Smith, 2011). This relationship suggests that tasks that involve the fantasy-reality distinction may be useful in assessing ToM abilities in children with intellectual disabilities and Down syndrome. These tasks can help identify the specific areas where these children may struggle and inform targeted interventions to support their development. Fantasy-reality distinction tasks assess individuals' ability to differentiate between imagined scenarios and real events. These tasks often involve storytelling, role-playing, pretend play, or hypothetical situations. Children with ID and DS may encounter challenges in these tasks due to difficulties in abstract reasoning, imagination, symbolic representation, and understanding the boundaries between reality and fiction. These challenges can affect their engagement in imaginative play, comprehension of narratives, and interpretation of social situations.

Some studies have investigated the relationship between ToM and fantasy-reality distinction tasks in children with intellectual disabilities and Down syndrome. For example, Payne, Porter, Pride, and North (2016) examined the ToM abilities of children with neurofibromatosis type 1, a genetic condition associated with intellectual disability, and found that these children performed significantly worse on ToM tasks compared to typically developing children. Similarly, Baurain and Nader-Grosbois (2013) found that children with intellectual disabilities and typically developing children differed in their performance on tasks that required understanding of false beliefs and socio-emotional problem-solving.

Due to the limited previous research in the field of fantasy-reality distinction in children with intellectual disabilities, this study is original and tries to investigate possible differences and similarities in the development of imagination-reality distinction in theory of mind tasks between children with typical development and intellectual disability of unknown etiology and Down syndrome. Therefore, three questions were investigated in the present study: (a) "Do children with intellectual disability-ID (non-specific ID and Down syndrome-DS) differ in their performance on imagination-reality distinction tasks when compared with typically developing-TD children matched on their mental age-MA?" (b) "Do children with ID (non-specific ID and DS) have similar or different strengths and weaknesses in these ToM tasks?" and (c) "Which verbal and performance abilities, as assessed with the WISC-III, are associated with performance on the ToM tasks for each one of the groups?"

METHOD

Participants

The present study involved two clinical groups of participants: 23 children with Down syndrome (DS) and 41 children with non-specific intellectual disability (ID). The control group consisted of 42 typical development (TD) children. The sex ratio in these three groups was approximately 1:1 (male: female). The mean chronological age (CA) in the DS group (mean (M) = 10,18 years, standard deviation (SD) = 0,49) and the mean CA in the non-specific ID group (M = 9,77 years, S.D. = 0,49) were significantly higher than in the TD group (M = 6,49 years, S.D. = 0,33) (F2,103 = 812, p <.001). The participants were matched on overall mental age (MA) as revealed by the Wechsler Intelligence Scale for Children (WISC-III-GR) (Georgas et al., 1997). The mean MA did not differ among the ID groups [(DS group: M = 6,60 years, S.D. = 0,38), (ID group: M = 6,83 years, S.D. = 0,60)] and the TD group (M = 6,83 years, S.D. = 0,41), (F2,103 =1,98, p =.14, p >.10). All children with ID had mild ID (IQ: 55–70) and were receiving special education support in inclusive general schools. Furthermore, none of the children in any of the groups had sensory impairments, including hearing difficulties, and decreased visual acuity. Finally, none of the children were on drugs.

Most studies in people with ID use a mental age comparison group, as it is still the best available choice to investigate if a specific ability is delayed compared with general cognitive ability (Giaouri et al., 2011; Messer et al., 2021).

Materials

A set of four works of fiction-reality distinction was presented. In this category of tasks, the child is required to distinguish fantasy from reality in himself and in others. Four stories were selected, two of which were given in combination as verbal story scripts with parallel color scene-visuals on the H/Y, and the other two as action works with questions at the end. The tasks were presented in random order. The first two verbal and visual scripts refer to fantasy-reality distinction tasks, and variants of the tasks were used: a) a variant of Wellman and Estes' (1986) classic task with the imaginary cookies; and b) a variant of Woolley and Phels' (1994) classic task with the imaginary box.

In the *imaginary box task*, the examiner presented the children with a verbal script with corresponding visual scenes on the H/Y, in which there were three boxes, which he had named 'real', 'empty', and 'imaginary' boxes, and a girl, the protagonist Helen. Helen opened the boxes one by one, saw what was inside, and then closed them. Only the "real" box contained one object (a watch). The other two boxes were empty. When Helen opened the "imaginary" box and discovered that it was empty, the examiner encouraged the children to imagine that it contained an object, specifically a pencil. Then an adult, Helen's teacher, appeared in the next visual scene and begged Helen to give him a pencil to write with. The imagination-reality distinction question the examiner asked the children was, "What will Helen do?". The control question was: "What is inside each box?" (Comprehension of the story was tested.) If the examinee gave the wrong answer to the control question, then the examiner did not give the child any additional help and continued the procedure only to reinforce motivation, but without marking the performance. If the child answered the control question and the fantasy-reality distinction question correctly, the examiner would give 1 point (the correct answer was that Mary does not have a pencil to give him) and 0 points if he answered incorrectly (the incorrect answer was that Mary will give him the pencil).

In the *imaginary biscuit task*, the examiner presented the children with a verbal script with corresponding visual scenes on the H/Y, in which there were two boys sitting at a table, John and Nick. John was hungry, and his mother gave him biscuits to eat. Nikos was also very hungry, and out of his hunger, he began to imagine eating biscuits. The imagination-reality distinction question that the examiner asked the children was: "Which child can eat the cookies?" In this test, there was a control question, and it was: "Which child did Mommy give cookies to?" (comprehension of the story is tested). If the child answered the control question and the fantasy-reality distinction question correctly, the examiner gave 1 point (the correct answer was that John could eat the cookies) and 0 points if the child answered incorrectly.

The other two fantasy-reality distinction tasks were given as action tasks and presented in random order. Specifically, the following were used: a) the two black boxes task by Harris, Brown, Marriot, Whittall, and Harmer (1991); and b) the balloon task by Estes, Wellman, and Woolley (1989).

For example, in the two *black boxes task*, the examiner showed the children two large black boxes, the top of which had a small hole the size of a finger. The children were first asked to imagine that one of them contained a bunny rabbit and the other a monster. Then, observe the children's reactions (e.g., whether they headed without hesitation or whether they expressed emotions, e.g., joy for the bunny and fear for the monster) when prompted to approach each box and put their finger inside. In this test, there were no control questions, and the examiner gave 1 mark if the children put their finger in both holes and 0 marks if they hesitated to put their finger in both holes and only in one of them. Observations of children's responses were recorded separately for further analysis and interpretation.

Finally, in the *balloon task,* the examiner asked each child if they liked balloons and asked them to imagine a balloon of a particular color. Then the examiner asked the child the imagination question: "Can you change the color of the balloon with your imagination?" and then the examiner showed the child a real inflated balloon that was red in color and asked the child the control question, "Can you change the color?". If the examinee gave the wrong answer to the control question, then the examiner did not give the child any additional help and continued the procedure only for motivational reinforcement, but without scoring the child's performance. If the child answered the control question and the fantasy-reality distinction question correctly, the examiner gave 1 point if the child answered correctly and 0 points if the child answered incorrectly.

The time allowed for each child to answer was 1 minute. If this answer time limit was exceeded and the child continued to think, the examiner did not stop the child, and no extra point was given for speed of recognition of each piece. According to the above data, the overall minimum, and maximum scores for this category of projects were 0-4.

Finally, the sum of the total scores derived from the above four general categories of the theory of mind tasks resulted in an overall score for this category of tasks with a total minimum and maximum score of 0-26.

Procedure

All participants were tested at school. Total administration time varied from participant to participant but was required from 1.30 to 2 hours across two sessions for each participant (during 40–60 minutes according to the participant's attention). WISC-III was administered before the theory of mind tasks. The session took place in a quiet and familiar room. Children's participation was completely voluntary, and their families approved the informed consent process for children's participation in this study. The study was conducted according to the Declaration of Helsinki with written informed consent obtained from the legal representatives of all participants.

RESULTS

All statistical analyses were performed using IBM SPSS Statistics 22. To test for differences in the category of fantasy-reality discriminating projects of theory of mind and gender, factor analysis of variance 3 (groups) x 2 (gender) was used. Comparisons of the group of children with typical development to the groups of children with intellectual disability of unknown cause and Down syndrome, with gender as the second factor and the dependent variables being the children's performance in the category of fantasy-reality distinction tasks of theory of mind, showed that the group effect was statistically significant [F $(5,100)$ =10.99 p<. 001], but there was no effect of gender [F (5,100) =1.39 p=.24, p>.10], and no interaction between group and gender [F (5,100) =0.14 p=.86, p>.10].

In the post-hoc tests of multiple comparisons, based on Bonferroni's criterion, children with typical development performed best with a statistically significant difference (p<.05) compared to the other groups. There were no differences (p > 0.05) between children with intellectual disabilities of unknown cause and those with Down syndrome. Table 3.1 below shows the means and standard deviations of performance in the fantasy-reality category of theory of mind distinction tasks for children with TD, ID of unknown etiology, and Down syndrome, by gender.

Table 1. Means and standard deviations of performance in the category of fantasy-reality distinction tasks of theory of mind for children with TD, ID of unknown etiology, and Down syndrome

Performance in the category of fantasy-reality distinction tasks of theory of mind				
Groups	Means		Standard deviations	
	Boys	Girls	Boys	Girls
TD	3,05	2,90	0,59	0,62
ID	2,30	2,19	0,92	1,03
SD	2,33	2	0,77	0,89
Total	2,60	2,43	0,84	0,93

No correlations were found between the chronological age and gender of children in all three groups and their performance in the category of fantasy-reality distinction of theory of mind tasks. Additionally, to determine the effect of cognitive parameters on the performance of children in all three groups on the theory of mind tasks, stepwise regressions were conducted with the category of theory of mind tasks as the dependent variable and the cognitive factors (i.e., the WISC-III verbal and practical intelligence scores) and participant group as independent variables. Regression analysis showed that the proportion of variance explained by the independent variables (verbal and practical intelligence quotients, group) accounted for 21% of the variance [F (9,96) =2.84 p<.001] in the variable of fantasy-reality distinction theory of mind tasks. Of the independent variables, only the verbal intelligence quotient contributed statistically significantly to explaining the variability of the fantasy-reality distinction tasks of the theory of mind for all groups (β =.022, Beta =.531, t = 2.092, p =.039).

DISCUSSION

Because there was no previous empirical data, the existence of differences in performance between children with typical development and children with intellectual disabilities of different etiologies was investigated without prior prediction. The data are original and showed that children with typical development differed statistically significantly only from children with Down syndrome and not from children with intellectual disabilities of unknown etiology, whereas the performance of the two groups of children with intellectual disabilities did not differ.

As already stated, the understanding of imagined situations not only requires biological maturation but is also influenced by verbal, emotional, and other behavioral factors, which seemed to have a greater impact on children with intellectual disabilities. According to the qualitative observations, children of typical development also had greater flexibility and adaptation in approaching the above tasks. According to the qualitative observations as well, children with intellectual disabilities glossed over off-task more often, had difficulty suppressing irrelevant information, and then showed limited ability to process and organize information. These difficulties increase as tasks involve disruptive information and require much of children's attention ((Merrill et al., 1996; van der Molen et al., 2007), as well as more complex strategies (Zagaria et al., 2021).

However, it would be one-sided to interpret the difference between these two groups if it were limited to cognitive level alone. Almost all people with intellectual disabilities have some difficulties with language comprehension and expression. The exact type of difficulty depends largely on the etiology of their cognitive disability (Abbeduto et al., 2006). Children with intellectual disabilities, because they have difficulty identifying the demands of tasks, retaining the required information, and typically using inefficient processing strategies without flexibility (Wehmeyer et al., 2008), fail more often in problem-solving tasks. They have significant difficulties in applying cognitive and metacognitive strategies to problem-solving processes, although not all children present the same cognitive limitations (Dermitzaki et al., 2008; Ferretti, 2019). However, they develop a strong sense of failure known as "learned helplessness," which increases with age (Weisz, 1979) and is due to the accumulation of experiences of failure and frustration.

In the fantasy-reality distinction tasks as well, other factors such as emotional reactions (Harris et al., 1991) seem to have played an important role, according to qualitative observations, rather than the children's inability to understand fantasy as a mental state (Harris et al., 1991). The low performance of children with intellectual disabilities in the category of fantasy-reality discrimination tasks, even at this mental age of 6 years, may not reflect a genuine inability of children to understand fantasy objects as states of mind, both their own and other people's. But instead, they may be the result of intense emotional reactions (e.g., fear) triggered by the stimulus they were supposed to imagine (monster or rabbit). These reactions can also be found in adults (Rozin et al., 1986).

Also, considering their cognitive pattern, children with Down syndrome have some difficulties in auditory processing, auditory-motor pathway, and generally slow auditory information processing, as well as verbal short-term memory (Alevriadou & Giaouri, 2013; Amadó et al., 2022; Giaouri, 2010; Frenkel & Bourdin, 2009; Lafranchi et al., 2015). The key behavioral characteristics of children with Down syndrome that appear to have affected their performance are a) the use of cognitive avoidance strategies when faced with difficult learning situations; b) inadequate use of existing problem-solving skills; c) difficulty consolidating newly acquired cognitive skills in their repertoire; and d) an increasing reluctance to take initiative in learning.

According to Gibson (1991), the metacognitive difficulties experienced by individuals with Down syndrome are related to knowledge acquisition and executive functions. More specifically, they show reduced perseveration, difficulty in cognitive sequencing, retention of incorrect answers, and less (or different) motivation when performing problem-solving tasks. Research by Pitcairn and Wishart (1994) and Kasari and Freeman (2001) found that children with Down syndrome spent a lot of time trying to perform the task while engaging in many task-irrelevant behaviors. For example, using their good communication skills, they would stare at the examiner for a long time, shout, laugh, and try to distract the examiner from the task they had to perform.

Therefore, it is the type and level of difficulty of the subtests of the tasks that differentiate the performance of children with intellectual disabilities from that of children with typical development. In addition, it is the cognitive and behavioral patterns of children with intellectual disabilities that differentiate their performance from that of children with typical development, not solely the existence of cognitive difficulties.

Understanding the cognitive profiles of children with ID and DS is crucial for designing effective intervention strategies and support mechanisms. Interventions targeting ToM skills, such as social skills training, narrative therapy, perspective-taking exercises, and video modeling, have shown promise in enhancing social competence and adaptive functioning in these populations (Baragash et al., 2020; Park et al., 2020). Similarly, interventions focusing on enhancing fantasy-reality distinction abilities through structured activities, visual supports, and cognitive-behavioral techniques may improve cognitive flexibility, problem-solving skills, and imaginative play.

CONCLUSION

The limitations of the present study could include the small sample of children with intellectual disabilities of different etiologies. The data collection for the study was synchronic rather than longitudinal. However, the longitudinal method allows for multiple assessments of children during the developmental period, which could provide more reliable conclusions regarding the development of cognitive skills in children with intellectual disabilities. In addition, further study of children with intellectual disabilities of different etiologies could be done by equating children in groups of lower and higher mental age, with the aim of investigating whether increasing mental age increases the probability of significant differences in favor of typically developing children in other cognitive abilities (executive functions, mental imagery, attention, memory, self-regulation, etc.). This will provide a more complete picture of the developmental rates and the trajectory of the strengths and weaknesses of children with intellectual disabilities of different etiologies.

From the results of our study and considering that the intervention in children with intellectual disabilities is aimed at improving their quality of life and their social relationships, we suggest that early childhood cognitive enrichment programs are an important element for developing the theory of mind. With experience, children acquire increasing knowledge about everything in their world. Beliefs are not directly caused by current reality, and reality is not directly influenced by fantasy. Thus, there is an interaction between individual and developmental differences in the effects of increased cognitive availability on children's beliefs about the fantasy-reality distinction. Such a finding would have extensive implications for the ways trainers could interact with groups of people with intellectual disabilities to develop theories of mind understanding and empower them to use this type of thinking in their everyday lives (Amadó et al., 2022).

Future research should continue to explore the complexities of ToM development and the fantasy-reality distinction in children with ID and DS, considering individual differences, developmental trajectories, and cultural factors. Longitudinal studies, intervention trials, and neuroimaging research can provide further insights into the underlying mechanisms and effective strategies for supporting cognitive and social functioning in these populations. By advancing our understanding of the ToM and fantasy-reality distinctions, we can promote inclusive education, social inclusion, and quality of life for children with ID and DS.

ETHICS APPROVAL AND CONSENT TO PARTICIPATE

Children's participation was completely voluntary, and their families approved the informed consent process for children's participation in this study.

DISCLOSURE STATEMENT

I have no conflicts of interest to declare. In addition, I have not been granted APC funds from my institution.

DATA AVAILABILITY STATEMENT

The data I've collected during my research is available on demand.

REFERENCES

Abbeduto, L., Keller-Bell, Y., Richmond, E., & Murphy, M. M. (2006). Research on language development and mental retardation: History, theories, findings, and future directions. *International Review of Research in Mental Retardation*, 32, 1–39. 10.1016/S0074-7750(06)32001-0

Abbeduto, L., & Murphy, M. M. (2004). Language, social cognition, maladaptive behavior, and communication in Down syndrome and fragile X syndrome. In Rice, M. L., & Warren, S. F. (Eds.), *Developmental language disorders: From phenotypes to etiologies* (pp. 77–97). Lawrence Erlbaum Associates Publishers.

Alevriadou, A., & Giaouri, S. (2011). Second-order Mental State Attribution in Children with Intellectual Disability: Cognitive Functioning and Some Educational Planning Challenges. *Journal of Educational and Developmental Psychology, 1*(1), 146-153. https://doi:. v1n1p14610.5539/jedp

Amadó, A., Sidera, F., & Serrat, E. (2022). Affective and cognitive theory of mind in children with Down syndrome: A brief report. *International Journal of Disability Development and Education*. 10.1080/1034912X.2022.2095355

Astington, J. W., & Baird, J. A. (Eds.). (2005). *Why language matters for theory of mind*. Oxford University Press. 10.1093/acprof:oso/9780195159912.001.0001

Baragash, R. S., Al-Samarraie, H., Alzahrani, A. I., & Alfarraj, O. (2020). Augmented reality in special education: A meta-analysis of single-subject design studies. *European Journal of Special Needs Education*, 35(3), 382–397. 10.1080/08856257.2019.1703548

Baron-Cohen, S. (1992). Out of sight or out of mind? Another look at deception in autism. *Journal of Child Psychology and Psychiatry, and Allied Disciplines*, 33(7), 1141–1155. 10.1111/j.1469-7610.1992.tb00934.x1400697

Baron-Cohen, S., Leslie, A. M., & Frith, U. (1985). Does the autistic child have a "theory of mind"? *Cognition*, 21(1), 37–46. 10.1016/0010-0277(85)90022-82934210

Baron-Cohen, S., O'Riordan, M., Stone, V., Jones, R., & Plaisted, K. (1999). Recognition of faux pas by normally developing children and children with Asperger syndrome or high-functioning autism. *Journal of Autism and Developmental Disorders*, 29(5), 407–418. 10.1023/A:102303501243610587887

Bartsch, K., & Wellman, H. (1989). Young children's attribution of action to beliefs and desires. *Child Development*, 60(4), 946–964. 10.2307/11310352758888

Battacchi, M. W., Celani, G., & Bertocchi, A. (1997). The influence of personal involvement on the performance in a false belief task: A structural analysis. *International Journal of Behavioral Development*, 21(2), 313–329. 10.1080/016502597384893

Baurain, C., & Nader-Grosbois, N. (2013). Theory of mind, socio-emotional problem-solving, socio-emotional regulation in children with intellectual disability and in typically developing children. *Journal of Autism and Developmental Disorders*, 43(5), 1080–1097. 10.1007/s10803-012-1651-422965300

Beauchamp, H. M. (2017). Neuropsychology's social landscape: Common ground with social neuroscience. *Neuropsychology*, 31(8), 981–1002. 10.1037/neu000039529376673

Beauchamp, H. M., & Anderson, V. (2010). SOCIAL: An integrative framework for the development of social skills. *Psychological Bulletin*, 136(1), 39–64. 10.1037/a001776820063925

Beaudoin, C., Leblanc, É., Gagner, C., & Beauchamp, M. H. (2020). Systematic review and inventory of theory of mind measures for young children. *Frontiers in Psychology*, 10, 2905. 10.3389/fpsyg.2019.0290532010013

Bellagamba, F., Laghi, F., Lonigro, A., Pace, C. S., & Longobardi, E. (2014). Concurrent relations between inhibitory control, sarcasm, and advanced theory of mind understanding in children and adults with prelingual deafness. *Developmental Psychology*, 50(7), 1862–1877. 10.1037/a0036654

Bourchier, A., & Davis, A. (2010). Individual and developmental differences in children's understanding of the fantasy-reality distinction. *British Journal of Developmental Psychology*, 18(3), 353–368. 10.1348/026151000165742

Burack, J. A., Evans, D. W., Klaiman, C., & Larocci, G. (2001). The mysterious myth of attention deficits and other defect stories: Contemporary issues in the developmental approach to mental retardation. *International Review of Research in Mental Retardation*, 24, 299–320. 10.1016/S0074-7750(01)80012-4

Cebula, K., Wishart, J., Willis, D., & Pitcairn, T. (2017). Emotion recognition in children with Down syndrome: Influence of emotion label and expression intensity. *American Journal on Intellectual and Developmental Disabilities*, 122(2), 138–155. 10.1352/1944-7558-122.2.13828257244

Charman, T., & Baron-Cohen, S. (1992). Understanding drawings and beliefs: A further test of the metarepresentation theory of autism: A research note. *Journal of Child Psychology and Psychiatry, and Allied Disciplines*, 33(6), 1105–1112. 10.1111/j.1469-7610.1992.tb00929.x1400691

Charman, T., Swettenham, J., Baron-Cohen, S., Cox, A., Baird, G., & Drew, A. (1998). An experimental investigation of social-cognitive abilities in infants with autism: Clinical implications. *Infant Mental Health Journal*, 19(2), 260–275. 10.1002/(SICI)1097-0355(199822)19:2<260::AID-IMHJ12>3.0.CO;2-W

Cicchetti, D., & Beeghly, M. (1990). *Children with Down syndrome: A developmental perspective*. Cambridge University Press. 10.1017/CBO9780511581786

Comblain, A., & Schmetz, C. (2020). Improving theory of mind skills in down syndrome? A pilot study. *Journal of Cognitive Education and Psychology*, 19(1), 20–31. 10.1891/JCEP-D-18-00034

Cornish, K., Burack, J. A., Rahman, A., Munir, F., Russo, N., & Grant, C. (2005). Theory of mind deficits in children with fragile X syndrome. *Journal of Intellectual Disability Research*, 49(5), 372–378. 10.1111/j.1365-2788.2005.00678.x15817054

Davis, D. L., Woolley, J. D., & Bruell, M. (2002). Young children's understanding of the roles of knowledge and thinking in pretense. *British Journal of Developmental Psychology*, 20(1), 25–45. 10.1348/026151002166307

de Rosnay, M., & Hughes, C. (2006). Conversation and theory of mind: Do children talk their way to socio-cognitive understanding? *British Journal of Developmental Psychology*, 24(1), 7–37. 10.1348/026151005X82901

Dermitzaki, I., Stavroussi, P., Bandi, M., & Nisiotou, I. (2008). Investigating ongoing strategic behaviour of students with mild mental retardation: Implementation and relations to performance in a problem-solving situation. *Evaluation and Research in Education*, 21(2), 96–110. 10.1080/09500790802152175

Eisenmajer, R., Prior, M., Leekam, S., Wing, L., Ong, B., Gould, J., & Welham, M. (1998). Delayed language onset as a predictor of clinical symptoms in pervasive developmental disorders. *Journal of Autism and Developmental Disorders*, 28(6), 527–533. 10.1023/A:10260042123759932239

Estes, D., Wellman, H. M., & Woolley, J. D. (1989). Children's understanding of mental phenomena. In Reese, H. W. (Ed.), *Advances in Child Development and Behavior*. Academic Press.

Ferretti, R. (2019). Problem-solving and working memory in people with intellectual disabilities: An historical perspective. In Matson, J. (Ed.), *Handbook of Intellectual Disabilities: Integrating Theory, Research, and Practice* (pp. 61–70). Springer. 10.1007/978-3-030-20843-1_4

Fisher, N., Happé, F., & Dunn, J. (2005). The relationship between vocabulary, grammar, and false belief task performance in children with autistic spectrum disorders and children with moderate learning difficulties. *Journal of Child Psychology and Psychiatry, 46,* 409-419. https://doi.org/10.1111/j.1469-7610.2004.00371.x

Flavell, J., Flavell, E., Green, F., & Moses, L. (1990). Young children's understanding of fact beliefs versus value beliefs. *Child Development*, 61(4), 915–928. 10.2307/11308652209196

Frenkel, S., & Bourdin, B. (2009). Verbal, visual, and spatio-sequential short-term memory: Assessment of the storage capacities of children and teenagers with Down's syndrome. *Journal of Intellectual Disability Research*, 53(2), 152–160. 10.1111/j.1365-2788.2008.01139.x19077148

Georgas, D. D., Paraskevopoulos, I. N., Bezevegis, H. G., & Giannitsas, N. D. (1997). *Greek version of Wechsler intelligence scale for children, WISC-III.* Ellinika Grammata.

Giaouri, S., Alevriadou, A., & Lang, L. (2011). Ambiguous figures perception and theory of mind understanding in children with intellectual disabilities: An empirical study with some educational implications. *International Journal of Academic Research*, 3(1), 396–400.

Giaouri, S., Alevriadou, A., & Tsakiridou, E. (2010). Theory of mind abilities in children with Down syndrome and non-specific intellectual disabilities: An empirical study with some educational implications. *Procedia: Social and Behavioral Sciences*, 2(2), 3883–3887. 10.1016/j.sbspro.2010.03.609

Gibson, D. (1991). Down syndrome and cognitive enhancement: Not like the others. In Marfo, K. (Ed.), *Early intervention in transition: Current perspectives in programs for handicapped children* (pp. 61–90). Praeger.

Golomb, C., & Kuersten, R. (1996). On the transition from pretence play to reality: What are the rules of the game? *British Journal of Developmental Psychology*, 14(2), 203–217. 10.1111/j.2044-835X.1996.tb00702.x

Hala, S., Chandler, M., & Fritz, A. S. (1991). Fledgling theories of mind: Deception as a marker of three-year-olds' understanding of false belief. *Child Development*, 62(1), 83–97. 10.2307/1130706

Happé, F. G. E. (1995). The role of age and verbal ability in the theory of mind task performance of subjects with autism. *Child Development*, 66(3), 843–855. 10.2307/11319547789204

Harris, P. L., Brown, E., Marriott, C., Whittall, S., & Harmer, S. (1991). Monsters, ghosts, and witches: Testing the limits of the fantasy-reality distinction in young children. *British Journal of Developmental Psychology*, 9(1), 105–123. 10.1111/j.2044-835X.1991.tb00865.x

Harris, P. L., & Kavanaugh, R. D. (1993). Young children's understanding of pretense. *Monographs of the Society for Research in Child Development, 58*(1)[231], v–92. 10.2307/1166074

Hodapp, R. (1990). One road or many? Issues in the similar sequence hypothesis. In Hodapp, R., Burack, J., & Zigler, E. (Eds.), *Issues in the developmental approach to mental retardation* (pp. 49–70). Cambridge University Press. 10.1017/CBO9780511582325.004

Hodapp, R., & Fidler, D. (2016). *International review of research in developmental disabilities*. Elsevier Academic Press.

Hughes, C., Lecce, S., & Wilson, C. (2007). Do you know what I want? Preschoolers' talk about desires, thoughts, and feelings in their conversations with sibs and friends. *Cognition and Emotion*, 21(2), 330–350. 10.1080/02699930600551691

Jersild, A. T. (1943). Studies of children's fears. In Barker, R. G., Kounin, J. S., & Wright, H. F. (Eds.), *Child Behavior and Development*. McGraw-Hill. 10.1037/10786-019

Johnson, C. N., & Harris, P. L. (1994). Magic: Special but not excluded. *British Journal of Developmental Psychology*, 12(1), 35–51. 10.1111/j.2044-835X.1994.tb00617.x

Kasari, C., & Freeman, S. (2001). Task-related social behavior in children with Down syndrome. *American Journal of Mental Retardation*, 106(3), 253–264. 10.1352/0895-8017(2001)106<0253:TRSBIC>2.0.CO;211389666

Lanfranchi, S., Cornoldi, C., & Vianello, R. (2015). Verbal and visuospatial working memory deficits in children with Down syndrome. *American journal of mental retardation. American Journal of Mental Retardation*, 109(6), 456–466. 10.1352/0895-8017(2004)109<456:VAVWMD>2.0.CO;215471512

Leekam, S. R., & Perner, J. (1991). Does the autistic child have a metarepresentational deficit? *Cognition*, 40(3), 203–218. 10.1016/0010-0277(91)90025-Y1786675

Lewis, P., Abbeduto, L., Murphy, M., Richmond, E., Giles, N., Bruno, L., & Schroeder, S. (2006). Cognitive, language and social skills of individuals with fragile X syndrome with and without autism. *Journal of Intellectual Disability Research*, 50(7), 532–545. 10.1111/j.1365-2788.2006.00803.x16774638

Lorusso, L., Galli, R., Libera, L., Gagliardi, C., Borgatti, R., & Hollebrandse, B. (2007). Indicators of theory of mind in narrative production: A comparison between individuals with genetic syndromes and typically developing children. *Clinical Linguistics & Phonetics*, 21(1), 37–53. 10.1080/02699200600565587117364616

Merrill, E., Goodwwyn, E., & Gooding, H. (1996). Mental Retardation and the Acquisition of Automatic Processing. *American Journal of Mental Retardation*, 101, 49–62.8827251

Messer, D. J., Henry, L. A., & Danielsson, H. (2021). Children with intellectual and developmental disabilities: Issues about matching, recruitment, and group comparisons. *Manuscript.*

Park, J., Bouck, E. C., & Duenas, A. (2020). Using video modeling to teach social skills for employment to youth with intellectual disability. *Career Development and Transition for Exceptional Individuals*, 43(1), 40–52. 10.1177/2165143418810671

Piaget, J. (1929). *The Child's Conception of the World*. Routledge & Kegan Paul.

Pitcairn, T., & Wishart, J. (1994). Reactions of young children with Down' syndrome to an impossible task. *British Journal of Developmental Psychology*, 12(4), 485–489. 10.1111/j.2044-835X.1994.tb00649.x

Rozin, P., Millman, L., & Nemeroff, C. (1986). Operation of the laws of sympathetic magic in disgust and other domains. *Journal of Personality and Social Psychology*, 50(4), 703–712. 10.1037/0022-3514.50.4.703

Sharon, T., & Woolley, J. D. (2004). Do monsters dream? Young children's understanding of the fantasy/reality distinction. *British Journal of Developmental Psychology*, 22(2), 293–310. 10.1348/026151004323044627

Sobel, D., & Lillard, A. (2001). The impact of fantasy and action on young children's understanding of presence. *British Journal of Developmental Psychology*, 19(1), 85–98. 10.1348/026151001165976

Sullivan, K., Zaitchik, D., & Tager-Flusberg, H. (1994). Preschoolers can attribute second-order beliefs. *Developmental Psychology*, 30(3), 395–402. 10.1037/0012-1649.30.3.395

Tager-Flusberg, H., & Sullivan, K. (2000). A componential view of theory of mind: Evidence from Williams syndrome. *Cognition*, 76(1), 59–89. 10.1016/S0010-0277(00)00069-X10822043

Thirion-Marissiaux, A., & Nader-Grosbois, N. (2008). Theory of mind "beliefs", developmental characteristics and social understanding in children and adolescents with intellectual disabilities. *Research in Developmental Disabilities*, 29(6), 547–566. 10.1016/j.ridd.2007.09.00418023323

Tsakiridou, E., & Alevriadou, A. (2017). A challenging approach concerning the cognitive strategies in problem solving situations by boys with and without intellectual disabilities using Markov chains. In Colombus, A. (Ed.), *Advances in Psychology Research* (Vol. 127). Nova Press.

Van der Molen, M. J., Van Luit, J. E., Jongmans, M. J., & Van der Molen, M. W. (2007). Verbal working memory in children with mild intellectual disabilities. *Journal of Intellectual Disability Research*, 51(2), 162–169. 10.1111/j.1365-2788.2006.00863.x17217480

Wechsler, D. (1974). *Selected papers of David Wechsler*. Academic Press.

Wehmeyer, M., Buntinx, W., Lachapelle, Y., Luckasson, R., Schalock, R., Verdugo, M., Borthwick-Duffy, S., Bradley, V., Craig, E. M., Coulter, D. L., Gomez, S. C., Reeve, A., Shogren, K. A., Snell, M. E., Spreat, S., Tassé, M. J., Thompson, J. R., & Yeager, M. H. (2008). The intellectual disability. Construct and its relation to human functioning. *Intellectual and Developmental Disabilities*, 46(4), 311–318. 10.1352/1934-9556(2008)46[311:TIDCAI]2.0.CO;218671445

Weisz, J. R. (1979). Perceived control and learned helplessness among retarded and nonretarded children: A developmental analysis. *Developmental Psychology*, 15(3), 311–319. 10.1037/0012-1649.15.3.311

Wellman, H. M., & Estes, D. (1986). Early understanding of mental entities: A reexamination of childhood realism. *Child Development*, 57(4), 910–923. 10.2307/11303673757609

Woolley, J. D. (1997). Thinking about fantasy: Are children fundamentally different thinkers and believers from adults? *Child Development*, 68(6), 991–1011. 10.2307/11322829418217

Woolley, J. D. (2000). The development of beliefs about mental-physical causality in imagination, magic, and religion. In Rosengren, K., Johnson, C., & Harris, P. (Eds.), *Imagining the impossible: Magical, scientific, and religious thinking in children*. Cambridge University Press. 10.1017/CBO9780511571381.005

Woolley, J. D., & Ghossainy, M. E. (2013). Revisiting the fantasy-reality distinction: Children as naïve skeptics. *Child Development*, 84(5), 1496–1510. 10.1111/cdev.1208123496765

Woolley, J. D., & Phelps, K. E. (1994). Young children's practical reasoning about imagination. *British Journal of Developmental Psychology*, 12(1), 53–67. 10.1111/j.2044-835X.1994.tb00618.x

Woolley, J. D., & Wellman, H. M. (1990). Young children's understanding of realities, nonrealities, and appearances. *Child Development*, 61(4), 946–961. 10.2307/11308672209198

Woolley, J. D., & Wellman, H. M. (1992). Children's conceptions of dreams. *Cognitive Development*, 7(3), 365–380. 10.1016/0885-2014(92)90022-J

Yirmiya, N., Erel, O., Shaked, M., & Solomonica-Levi, D. (1998). Meta-analysis comparing theory of mind abilities of individuals with autism, individuals with mental retardation, and normally developing individuals. *Psychological Bulletin*, 124(3), 283–307. 10.1037/0033-2909.124.3.2839849110

Yirmiya, N., & Shulman, C. (1996). Seriation, conservation, and theory of mind abilities in individuals with autism, individuals with mental retardation, and normally developing children. *Child Development*, 67(5), 2045–2059. 10.2307/11316089022228

Yirmiya, N., Solomonica-Levi, D., Shulman, C., & Pilowsky, T. (1996). Theory of mind abilities in individuals with autism, Down syndrome, and mental retardation of unknown etiology: The role of age and intelligence. *Journal of Child Psychology and Psychiatry, and Allied Disciplines*, 37(8), 1003–1014. 10.1111/j.1469-7610.1996.tb01497.x9119934

Zagaria, T., Antonucci, G., Buono, S., Recupero, M., & Zoccolotti, P. (2021). Executive Functions and Attention Processes in Adolescents and Young Adults with Intellectual Disability. *Brain Sciences*, 11(1), 42. 10.3390/brainsci1101004233401550

Zelazo, P. D., Burack, J. A., Benedetto, E., & Frye, D. (1996). Theory of mind and rule use in individuals with Down's syndrome: A test of the uniqueness and specificity claims. *Journal of Child Psychology and Psychiatry, and Allied Disciplines*, 37(4), 479–484. 10.1111/j.1469-7610.1996.tb01429.x8735448

Chapter 14
A Review–Based Theoretical Analysis on Somatization of Psychological Symptoms and Physical Manifestation of Trauma in Youths

Aastha Singh

Department of Humanities and Social Sciences, Graphic Era University (Deemed), Dehradun, India

Ravindra Singh
https://orcid.org/0000-0003-3062-1812

Department of Psychology, Magadh University, Bodh Gaya, India

Ajay Kumar Singh
https://orcid.org/0000-0003-0429-0925

Department of Humanities and Social Sciences, Graphic Era University (Deemed), Dehradun, India

ABSTRACT

Early trauma is caused to increase disease among youth. It also has an adverse impact on brain development and impairs the various other facets of daily life functioning of youth. This chapter, thus, provides a systematic outline of physical

DOI: 10.4018/979-8-3693-4022-6.ch014

manifestations of long-term psychological trauma and the somatization of psychological symptoms among youth. The summary of 50 research articles and book chapters are included in this chapter. A systematic method is employed to collect and synthesize information. The authors have screened open-sourced articles published in English available in the public domain which were published after 2000 using various keywords such as youth, psychological trauma, somatization, and childhood maltreatment. It supports the idea that prolonged exposure to trauma results in physical symptoms like exhaustion, fatigue, high blood pressure, and anxiety among youth. It may also be responsible for increasing various diseases like diabetes and abuse disorders among youth.

INTRODUCTION

A child undergoes several changes in terms of intellectual, cognitive, and physical development until adolescence. Therefore, stated indicators depend on various internal and external activities. There are many other social-economic activities like parent-child relationship, parent's awareness towards their children, etc. that have significant impact on child's development. For instance, family background, education level of parents and relatives, geographical location, culture, availability of physical resources, income of parents, and social interaction of family are crucial determinants to increase the intellectual, cognitive, physical and mental development of adolescence. The climatic conditions also have a significant reflection on development of children and youths. Teacher and student's relationship also reduce the multiple obstacles among the children. While, early interactions and experiences of a child's life create foundations for learning and personality development later in their life. Although genetics determine the initial development, everyday relationships and experiences significantly affect a child's brain and mind.

Accordingly, children are active to cope with many psychological problems in their life. Furthermore, there are certain other psychological variables like happiness in the family, social interaction, mother and father relationship, social ethics and internal conflict in the family which also have a significant influence on a child's brain. Unfortunately, all children do not get positive experiences from their family or relatives or neighbours. Children, therefore, face childhood trauma in all societies which is a major psychosocial and medical problem that has serious long-term consequences throughout the life of children. Trauma for a child in childhood has severe negative implications on mental and psychological development of child (Colich et al., 2020; Greenman et al., 2024). Childhood trauma is a public health risk and it reduces the physical health of children (Eilers et al., 2023). Sexual, physical and emotional abuse are responsible for increasing complex trauma (Greenman et al., 2024). Trauma also has an adverse impact on the body and increases eagerness among the children (Colich et al., 2020). While, in developing countries, the share of physical abuse of children is significantly high due to low literacy, low income, low child care opportunities, low income etc. Low per capita income, low social inclusion, low child care practices and lack of financial resources also create the trauma in the children in most developing countries.

Furthermore, most families are unable to give proper time to their child during childhood. Therefore, most children undergo trauma. Hence, the child faces several shocks during their initial stage of physical and mental growth. According to the National Crime Records Bureau (2020), an average 31 children died every day due to commitment of suicide in India, whereas contribution of family problems was reported as 35 percent (Nation, 2021). The issue of childhood trauma is increasing all across the world. Childhood trauma has several negative impacts on the mental and social life of children. For instance, family problems and clashes have increased during COVID-19 pandemic in developed and developing countries. It could happen due to change in social-economic and implementation of social distancing to overcome the stress of COVID-19 (Singh et al., 2022).

Early childhood experiences of maltreatment and trauma are related to psychological disorder, borderline personality disorder (Berenz et al., 2013), antisocial behavior, and developed negative personality traits (Allen & Lauterbach, 2007). Depending upon the perception, these experiences may affect a person differently due to diversity in social-economic structure within family, across families and communities (Allen & Lauterbach, 2007). The occurrence of childhood trauma is also increased due to the education level of parents and their poor behaviour with the children. Further, environmental factors (Baldo et al., 2007), biological factors (Bolton, 1902) and cultural factors (Korbin, 1991; Wong et al., 2009) may also contribute towards personality development of children. Sudden changes in climatic factors also increase the prevalence of childhood trauma. High variability in climatic and environmental conditions may lead to an increase in multiple diseases among the youth and children (Singh & Singh, 2020).

Also, eastern and western culture showed differences in parenting perception and involvement and independent and interdependent selves of the child. In addition, most of earlier studies were conducted on (i) school going students or (ii) clinical setting and (iii) persons suffering with any kind of personality disorder or/and psychological disorders. Moreover, bodies hold past memories of a negative nature which affect behavior and act as a seed of transformation of mental health issues into ailments of a physical nature. Events or circumstances that are physically or emotionally experienced as adverse by an individual which result in long-lasting negative effects are regarded as traumatic events (Greenman et al., 2024). Experiences that cannot be assumed within the usual cognitive and emotional schemes of an individual are considered "trauma". Traumatic experiences challenge the limits of a person's physical and mental capacity. Events like these cause a strong stress reaction which may act as an antecedent for serious psychological and physical illnesses (North, 2002).

Long-term trauma exposure leads to increased development of a variety of psychological and physical symptoms in the youth. Further, these have negative implications on mental and physical growth of the children. The development of symptoms that have no organic cause is known as somatization (Elklit & Christiansen, 2009). Somatization straddles the interface between physical and psychological health of the children. A majority of trauma survivors report unexplained symptoms, along with causing a great amount of psychological distress. Further, psychological distress hampers the development of the children in the long-run. These symptoms are also called somatoforms which are also highly disabling, anxiety and mood disorders. Anxiety and mood disorder may also lead to increased chronic depression among the children. Further, these are also good predictors of somatization (Thomson et al., 2014). Intense and poorly differentiated affective states marked with a tendency to feel overwhelmed are associated with somatization (Breslau et al., 1998). Traumatic experiences have a direct link with somatoform symptoms among the children and youth. Victims of trauma score higher on self-reports of somatic complaints as compared to controls. Adverse childhood experience also led to increased somatic inflictions, obesity cancers and health diseases among the youths (Greenman et al., 2024). Somatic illness also has adverse impacts on somatic symptoms (Sardesai et al., 2023). Somatic symptoms are also induced by stress, anxiety and depression (Sperling et al., 2023).

The previous research specified somatization among youth. It is relatively common among children and adolescents, below age 18 with different prevalence rates (Gander et al., 2020). While the age of youth under 18 years is significant to increase the personal and mental development and skill development of youth. Hence, the children require more care under the age of 18. Somatization can be understood as the process of reflecting distress via physical symptoms (Sardesai et al., 2023). It is a partially unanswered, and complex phenomenon among youth (Greenberg, 2014). Somatization of unobserved psychological symptoms and its physical manifestation of trauma in children and youth is a complex interplay of biological, psychological, genetic, and psycho-social factors (Haugland et al., 2021). In addition, with the previous finding it was found that trauma and adverse childhood experiences are closely linked with stress and emotional response in children within the age of 18 years (Haugland et al., 2021).

Childhood trauma, such as physical and verbal abuse, emotional neglect, and exposure to domestic or school violence, is a significant predictor of somatization among children (Sadeghi et al., 2017; Korhonen et al., 2018). Understanding the relationship between trauma and somatization is a critical step for effective treatment strategies for the psychologists and psychiatrists. Most studies suggested that a significant number of the children population report recurrent physical complaints which may have underlying psychological issues (Haugland et al., 2021). Moreover, for the reporting purpose, Children may express continuous emotional distress through physical symptoms. The root cause of this is not reporting clearly and it has several limitations of emotional vocabulary, social stigmas, and mental health levelling. It may be due to the learned behavior from caregivers. Children observe and learn how to respond more to physical complaints than emotional ones (North, 2002).

A decent number of neurobiological studies also reported that trauma can also affect brain regions involved in stress regulation. Hypothalamic-pituitary-adrenal (HPA) axis is one of the potential regions leading to somatic symptoms in children (Haugland et al., 2021). Headaches are also associated with somatic symptoms along with other factors such as dissociative symptoms (Kratzer et al., 2022). Furthermore, it is also found that frequent exposure to traumatic episodes negatively contributed to mental and physical health (Greenman et al., 2024). Thus, it also led to increased worsening consequences of trans-diagnostically symptom level. However, strong support between physiological recurrence and pain symptoms could give detailed insight for treatment prioritization (Kratzer et al., 2022). Post-traumatic stress disorder (PTSD) has emerged as the best predictor of somatization in trauma (Elklit & Christiansen, 2009). Moreover, arousal was the only PTSD symptom cluster to significantly predict somatization in children (Elklit & Christiansen, 2009). McFarlane (1992) reported that the intrusion subscale analysis is significant when it is used with the different PTSD clusters to predict somatization.

Symptoms for post-traumatic stress disorder (PTSD) diagnosis, according to DSM IV, somatoform symptoms and dissociation were originally combined in the concept of hysteria (Elklit & Christiansen, 2009). From a psychoanalytic view, it is considered to be linked with trauma among the children and youth. According to past research, individuals who experienced childhood trauma, such as physical or sexual abuse, frequently exhibit dissociation and physically inexplicable symptoms (Sadeghi et al., 2017; Greenman et al., 2024). Oginyi et al. (2024) also investigated childhood sexual abuse among undergraduates' personality trait, substance abuse and loneliness in Ebonyi state University, Ababkaliki. It claimed that extraversion, personality and substance abuse as responsible for increasing childhood sexual abuse (Eilers et al., 2023). After a stressful occurrence, new somatoform symptoms were shown to be unrelated to gender, injuries, or property damage. However, there is no correlation between the quantity of physical symptoms and the degree of trauma exposure (Kirmayer et al., 1994). Physical symptoms are caused to increase somatic symptom disorder (Sardesai et al., 2023). Trauma is strongly linked with post-traumatic re-experiencing, active avoidance, hyperarousal, and numbing. Somatic symptoms are found to be associated with substance use. A common mental state that arises in response to a possible threat is anxiety. Unsuitable or excessive anxiety might develop into multiple mental and health diseases (Kirmayer et al., 1994).

Early developmental pathways may have a role in an adult's vulnerability to anxiety. An organism's propensity to exhibit anxiety under specific circumstances is determined by developmental pathways that are influenced by both hereditary (Beesdo et al., 2009). Somatoform symptoms and traumatic exposure have consistently been linked with anxiety (Kratzer et al., 2022). Somatization can also occur when trauma leads to poorer health behaviors, an increase in physiological arousal, and alterations in the nervous system. Additionally, somatization may also have a connection to anxiety and depression which are the consequences of trauma. Because medical systems are unable to identify the physical origin of symptoms that cause significant anguish to individuals, trauma survivors are often disregarded. Such patients should be given appropriate care and respect, and their suffering should be valued (Kratzer et al., 2022).

It is also seen that a high level of anxiety transforms itself into somatic symptoms. Somatic symptoms include body pain, fatigue, joint pain, etc. Self-efficacy and self-esteem have an indirect impact on this relationship. Somatic disorder is also caused to increase the quality of life of children (Renzi et al., 2024). High levels of self-esteem and self-efficacy lower the chances of the development of severe anxiety and subsequent somatization. The chances of somatization due to a high level of anxiety increase due to a low level of self-esteem and somatization (Renzi et al., 2024). There is reported a positive correlation between child somatic symptoms and anxiety (Renzi et al., 2024). The result of the study might highlight the importance of concepts like self-esteem and self-efficacy in moderating anxiety and somatic symptoms in individuals. It attempts to emphasize the importance of building a positive self-concept in the area of self-efficacy and self-esteem. Interventions tackling mental health disorders like anxiety and somatic symptoms should be made to reduce childhood trauma.

The objective of this research is to investigate the effect of self-efficacy and self-esteem on the somatic manifestation along with the level of anxiety. It also examines how low and high levels of self-esteem and self-efficacy in individuals change the somatic presentation of anxiety and its severity? Further, this chapter intends to educate and throw light on the possible somatization of long-term trauma among youth. It also attempts to spread awareness about the possibility of somatoform symptoms among youths. Previous studies have focused majorly on early life experiences as an antecedent of anxiety and further developed somatic symptoms. The present study aims to answer the following questions:

· What is the long-term effect of trauma among youth?

· What is the connection between psychological health and physical health?
· How does the body cope with trauma and stress?
· How do somatic symptoms develop in traumatized people?
· How can we reduce childhood trauma?

RESEARCH METHOD

A thorough and methodical examination of the available literature was conducted to obtain a deep comprehension of the subject. Research articles and journals pertinent to the title and objectives of this chapter were found by using keywords such as "Physical trauma," and "Child abuse." "Psychological trauma," and "somatization." For accurate, up-to-date information, publications from the year 2000 to till date were finalized. To locate pertinent materials, the research papers' bibliographies were also consulted. A total of 50 articles are included for final review work to ensure that the final results only included high-quality research papers and publications. The study was able to show how psychological trauma can have long-term consequences that manifest as physical problems.

REVIEW OF LITERATURE

According to recent estimates, 6.7% of the general population have gone through at least one unpleasant event throughout their childhood (Mirzaei et al., 2019). In Australia, due to nurturing home environments, a majority of children experience trauma through abuse or neglect. Children reported physical abuse (8.9%), sexual abuse (8.6%), emotional abuse (8.7%), and neglect (2.4%) (Mathews et al., 2023). Similar findings are also reported by Oginyi et al. (2024). This finding seems underreported as measurements of such experiences are difficult to quantify through academic research. All tougher around 8.7% of persons (or more) are reported going through traumatic experiences during their early years. Child maltreatment is also caused to increase destruction of childhood trauma. Traumatic early life events are also linked to increased rates of smoking, using illegal substances, attempting suicide, engaging in numerous sexual orientations, and developing depression in later life (Korhonen et al., 2018).

Highly apprehensive thoughts of a negative nature are also known as anxious thoughts. Excessive anxious thoughts lead to increased development of somatic symptoms i.e., physical symptoms present without a physiological basis (Beaumont, 2024). Along with anxiety, mood disorders are the second-best predictors of somatization. Intense and poorly differentiated affective states marked with a tendency to feel overwhelmed are associated with somatization (Carmassi et al., 2021). Anxiety and despair are accompanied by physical issues in about 2-5% of patients in intensive care units. An estimated 400 million clinic visits in the USA are attributed to physical symptoms (Joellenbeck et al., 1999). Physical symptoms account for more than half of all outpatient complaints (Kroenke, 2014). Among these, one-third have no established medical cause; they also result in functional impairments and are closely linked to psychiatric disorders and quality of life (Creed, 2023).

Childhood trauma is also negatively associated with the functioning of the health of children. It is also reported by the existing studies that self-esteem and self-efficacy are two of the most important components of an individual's self-concept and play a moderating role in the relationship of anxiety and somatization (Mercader-Rubio et al., 2023). High levels of Self-esteem and self-efficacy work to reduce the level of anxiety in an individual and the subsequent somatization by countering negative thoughts (Mercader-Rubio et al., 2023). persistently present during anxiety whereas a lower level of self-esteem and self-efficacy acts as an antecedent for heightened anxiety and greater Somatization. The development of symptoms that have no organic cause is known as somatization (Kallivayalil & Punnoose, 2010). A majority of trauma survivors report these unexplained symptoms, along with causing a great amount of psychological distress these symptoms called somatoforms are also highly disabling.

Intense and poorly differentiated affective states marked with a tendency to feel overwhelmed are associated with somatization (Lipowski, 1987). Somatization straddles the interface between physical and psychological health. Anxiety and somatization are directly linked to each other. Anxiety and mood disorders are good predictors of somatization. Anxiety typically presents as bodily symptoms, and this population is known to need medical services more frequently than others (Bandelow & Michaelis, 2015). If the physical symptoms are the somatic expressions of anxiety, this may lead to self-reflection and fear-driven selective perception, which in turn may increase anxiety and cause somatic symptoms to arise. Having great self-esteem means appreciating and believing in oneself. According to Sedikides and Gregg (2003); Sharma and Agarwala (2015), self-esteem encompasses an individual's subjective judgment of self-worth, emotions of self-respect and confidence, and their positive or negative self-perception.

The association between exposure to trauma and symptoms of somatization is partially mediated by post-traumatic stress disorder. According to Morina et al. (2018), BMC Psychiatry, there is a strong indirect positive effect of post-traumatic stress symptoms via hyperarousal and a large indirect negative effect of somatization symptoms via active avoidance. Numerous research investigations in the field of mental epidemiology have demonstrated that the quality-of-life declines as the number of physical symptoms and maladaptive thoughts, feelings, and behaviors increase (Dimsdale et al., 2013). The best indicators of the severity of somatic symptoms are emotional neglect and the length of the trauma (Sadeghi et al., 2017). More women than males have reported experiencing somatic symptoms (Barsky et al., 2001). Gender and trauma do not significantly interact with somatic symptom intensity in models where the possible intervening variables are taken into account collectively. Somatic symptoms are caused to increase fatigue and emotional distress.

The severity of somatic symptoms is related with depression and substance addiction in males and depression in women (Barsky et al., 2001). Men have more direct pathways from trauma experience to the effects on their mental health (Barsky at al., 2001). Greenman et al. (2024) also reported the childhood traumatic experience is harmful for physical and mental health of children during their lifespan. Unravelling experiences also have a negative impact on mental health, physical health and trust of children. According to earlier research, conversion symptoms can be brought on by both bad experiences early in life and later in life (Roelofs et al., 2005). Adolescents with traumatic early life experiences are more likely to take drugs and have poor mental and physical health. As adults, further long-term exposure to trauma which makes an individual experience high levels of stress, fear, anxiety, and negative emotions has a lasting effect on the neurobiology of the individual (Sherin & Nemeroff, 2011). Psychological trauma manifests itself as physical symptoms that have no identifiable organic cause, patients might report having joint pains, stiffness, anxiety, hypertension, weakness, muscle aches, fatigue, and abdominal issues like constipation (Trivedi, 2004).

This transformation of psychological symptoms into physical symptoms is often dismissed by healthcare professionals leaving the patients distressed. Furthermore, psychological trauma experienced especially in childhood makes the individual more susceptible to developing physical health conditions later in life like diabetes, hypertension, and substance use disorder. Although somatic examination is insufficient to diagnose the illness, patients typically present with persistent physical problems (Konnopka et al., 2013). The results of primary and community care research on specific symptoms that have not been medically suggested that these symptoms may increase the likelihood of developing later diseases like anxiety and depression. The high prevalence of pain symptoms and excruciating medical diseases associated with childhood abuse and trauma has been explained by a number of ideas (Sachs-Ericsson et al., 2007). Many researchers proposed that underlying destructive elements that connect all forms of abuse and neglect should be referred to as the term psychological maltreatment.

A number of findings suggested that many individuals who cope well during traumatic experiences tend to become unwell afterward (McFarlane, 2010). At least one traumatic event is experienced by nearly 80% of patients seen in community mental health clinics across countries. Somatoform symptoms in primary care patients are associated with traumatic experiences like migration stress, war-related experiences, refugee status, and lack of acculturation (Waitzkin & Magana, 1997; Hazer & Gredebäck, 2023; Lopez, 2024). War has an adverse impact on psychological behaviour of children (Lopez, 2024). Hazer and v (2023) explained the psychological development of refugee children due to war. The degree of a traumatic event and the degree of threat to self-determines the severity and frequency of traumatic symptoms. The physical consequences of trauma amplify with an increase in environmental exposure as well as with psychiatric distress. The body's systems are adversely affected by trauma. There is a significant disruption to the musculoskeletal system, gastrointestinal functioning, immunological functioning, cardiovascular system, neuroendocrine functioning, reproductive system, and finally brain structure and functioning. In addition to this, the risk factors for the development of future medical disease are exponentially greater following exposure to trauma.

These events influence the life span development of individuals and are causal factors for a number of diagnoses later, most notably posttraumatic stress disorder (Lopez-Martinez et al., 2018). Psychopathology lacks a model to explain this impact of adversity which is delayed and lingering in nature. Two scenarios occur in the physical manifestation of trauma. In the first scenario, there is a clear manifestation of psychiatric distress most commonly PTSD, anxiety, and depression. In this, due to trauma, there is a sensitivity generation to triggers that reactivate stress continuously creating a number of stressors that are acute in nature that occur together. This scenario is parallel to the allostatic load models of chronic stress. Second scenario, no report of any psychological or physical distress. Likewise, research suggests further 2l pathways to health problems following exposure to trauma (McFarlane, 2010).

The body's stress response is chronically elevated by conscious or nonconscious reactivity to triggered reminders. A physical strain is generated by suppressive emotion management techniques which elevates the body's stress response chronically. Further, physical neuroendocrine reactions to trauma are also evident through the stress response system of the hypothalamic–pituitary–adrenocortical axis (HPA) which due to exposure to violence and trauma may become dysregulated (D'Andrea et al., 2011). The key component of the phenomenological response to traumatic events is the repeated recollection of traumatic memories. According to Freud Traumatic memories were extremely important, suggesting that these were "agents still at work" which played an essential role in symptom onset and maintenance. Subsequently, modelling in epidemiological sample modelling highlighted how the relationship between exposure to traumatic events and the symptoms of hyperarousal and avoidance are accounted for by traumatic memories (McFarlane, 1992).

A high-risk group for trauma exposure is toddlers, preschoolers, and young children (Christina et al., 2016). Approximately 7 months of age, the affective, perceptual, social, and behavioral capacities required for the manifestation of trauma emerge (Substance Abuse and Mental Health Services Administration (US), 2014). Young children often resort to avoidance behavior as an effort to avoid situations, people, places, and objects that remind them of their trauma. They might subtly turn their head, divert their gaze or actively engage in stimulus avoidance by crying (Substance Abuse and Mental Health Services Administration (US), 2014). Social withdrawal from family and friends may manifest because of emotional numbing. Due to the limited coping skills, dependency, and expectation for a protective shield from the primary caregiver along with the rapid early childhood social, emotional, physical, and neurological development (Haugland et al., 2021).

The belief that children are resistant to developing severe psychological distress along with the lack of assessment and diagnostic challenges for this age group makes this population extremely neglected. Further, research suggests childhood trauma fosters insecure adult attachment which in turn influences adult somatization levels for women, childhood trauma influences adult levels of somatization by fostering insecure adult attachment (Liu et al., 2011). In the case of men, findings are suggestive that two important independent predictors of adult somatization are trauma and attachment. The connection between somatic symptoms and trauma have been proposed by several theories. For example, hypersensitivity and hyperarousal in response to bodily sensations are perpetuated by arousal in the context of trauma, and dissociation (Salmon et al., 2003; Waller et al., 2011; Kugler et al., 2012).

An interaction at the time of a traumatic event between the individual's psychophysical reactivity, distress, and neurohormonal response is caused by the process of sensitization to the reminders of previously experienced trauma memories and possible future traumatic events. Individual's reactivity to minor cues acts as an antecedent in exacerbating and increasing the reactivity of dysfunctional individuals (McFarlane, 2010). Research findings suggest that irrespective of whether there was permanent tissue damage, physical symptoms are common after severe or recurrent traumatic stress and/or if there were physical sensations at the time of the stressor. Tissue damage and physiological hyperactivity after a traumatic experience may result in somatic symptoms (Ford, 1997; Waldinger et al., 2006). Somatic symptoms are also significantly associated with mental ill-health among the students (Sperling et al., 2023). Physiological symptoms may be responsible for increasing mental illness (Beaumont, 2024). The most commonly reported traumas are interpersonal forms of trauma. They are more likely to damage well-being when compared with non-interpersonal forms.

There also exists a strong association between interpersonal trauma and general physical health issues and somatoform symptoms (Lopez-Martinez et al., 2018). Stressors and mediators regulate trauma pathways (Lopez-Martinez et al., 2018). In addition, some findings have suggested a strong association between interpersonal victimization and negative physical and psychological status in adults who report chronic medical illness. Research findings also suggested that an increase in health practices is associated with a history of trauma exposure. Risk of substance use disorders and an increased engagement is more adverse with a history of trauma. Chances of physical illness are increased in traumatized individuals.

RESULTS AND DISCUSSION

Trauma is experiences that challenge an individual's physical and mental capacity, leading to stress reactions and causing serious psychological and physical illnesses (Elklit & Christiansen, 2009). Long-term trauma exposure results in somatoform symptoms, which are often unexplained and disabling (North, 2002). Victims of trauma score higher on self-reports of somatic complaints and symptoms for PTSD diagnosis are linked to trauma (Kuhfuß et al., 2021). Active avoidance and hyperarousal symptoms seem to play a key role in traumatized people suffering from somatic symptoms (Morina et al., 2018). Childhood trauma is a significant issue, with 6.7% of the general population experiencing unpleasant events and 8.7% experiencing traumatic experiences (Kuhfuß et al., 2021). Somatization can occur when trauma leads to poorer health behaviors, an increase in physiological arousal, and alterations in the nervous system.

Somatoform symptoms like hyperarousal, dizziness, chest pain, and traumatic exposure have consistently been linked (Elklit & Christiansen, 2009; Lopez, 2024). Persistent physical problems are common in patients, and these symptoms may increase the likelihood of developing diseases later in life such as hypertension and diabetes along with increased rates of smoking, substance abuse, suicide, and depression (Colich et al., 2020; Carmassi et al., 2021). The quality-of-life declines with the number of physical symptoms and maladaptive thoughts, feelings, and behaviors (Kuhfuß et al., 2021). The study could be able to show how psychological trauma can have long-term consequences that manifest as physical problems. Psychological trauma can manifest as physical symptoms, such as joint pain, palpitation, fatigue, shortness of breath, and hypertension. Somatic symptoms are influenced by emotional neglect and trauma duration. (Elklit & Christiansen, 2009). Men are more likely to experience these symptoms than women. (Carmassi et al., 2021). It also increases back pain, neck pain and sleeping disorder (Sperling et al., 2023).

Childhood trauma increases susceptibility to physical health conditions like diabetes and substance use disorder (Colich et al., 2020). Somatic symptoms are commonly noticed in substance users (Elklit & Christiansen, 2009). A lower sense of self-esteem and self-efficacy can increase the likelihood of an individual developing a higher and more severe form of anxiety which can further present itself as somatic symptoms. A positive and higher sense of self-efficacy and self-esteem in an individual can make them less susceptible to developing severe forms of anxiety and protect them from further developing somatic symptoms. Early identification of these symptoms and their integration into treatment approaches are essential for addressing these issues. The treatment outcome is highly dependent upon the early intervention for affected children and adolescents (Gander et al., 2020). Further, future researchers must take possible necessary initiatives to enhance understanding of trauma and create a support system for this vulnerable population.

CONCLUSION

The paper was successful in demonstrating the positive association between long-term traumatic experiences and the somatic symptoms experienced. The studies showed the effects trauma has on the physical aspects of health and the various factors that contribute to symptomatology. This study successfully highlighted the role of self-esteem and self-efficacy in the development of anxiety and somatic symptoms. It aims to analyse self-esteem and self-efficacy both as an antecedent as well as moderators in the severity of anxiety and somatization. Additionally, attempts to shed light upon the coexistence and interdependence of physical health and mental health and the effect of their relationship on an individual. The present study considers self-esteem and self-efficacy being the two determinants of anxiety and somatization and attempts to examine the effect of their levels on an individual's level of anxiety and further presented somatic symptoms. The study aims to bridge the gap between mental health and physical health symptoms by throwing light on the effect of covert concepts like self-esteem and self-efficacy and their possible effect on anxiety and physical health through somatic symptoms. It attempts to contribute to the literature by highlighting psychological symptoms and Physical Manifestations as an antecedent of anxiety and somatic disorders.

POLICY IMPLICATIONS

The parents and relative should avoid emotional abuse, physical abuses, sexual abuse trauma, emotional neglect trauma and physical neglect trauma to increase agreeableness. Childhood trauma also leads to an increase in other symptoms of diseases among the children (Eilers et al., 2023). These suggestions will be positive to increase the mental development of adolescents. Emotional abuse must be avoided by the parents to increase conscientiousness of children (Renzi et al., 2024). Avoiding their children by parents is also responsible for increasing physical and mental health of their children (Renzi et al., 2024). The findings of the present study are helpful for policy makers to understand the role of globalization on parenting and personality development of the children. Also, it would be beneficial to reduce the mental illness crisis in children in India and other developing countries. Furthermore, the findings may be helpful to identify the development of negative personality in children (Gander et al., 2020). Accordingly, policy makers and child development thinkers can reduce the negative impact of various psychological variables on mental development of children in India and other countries. The school administration should deem it necessary to understand substance abuser and personality traits of an individual that are vulnerable to childhood sexual abuse (Oginyi et al., 2024).

LIMITATIONS AND SCOPE FOR FUTURE RESEARCH

Even though the aim of the research is to add valuable insights, the data being self-reported may pose a possible limitation due to factors like social desirability. Further research can be done tackling these factors and using a larger more diverse data set and focusing on factors besides self-esteem and self-efficacy as sole moderators or antecedents of anxiety and somatic symptoms keeping in mind the social and cultural context. Although, there are several other factors which could be associated with childhood trauma. Childhood trauma is also responsible for increased personality disorder. Accordingly, the mental and psychological development of children may be nurtured appropriately. Further study, therefore, can be conducted including more personality factors using a large sample size of children from different locations of India. This would be highly effective to check the consistency of descriptive and empirical findings of the present research. Accordingly, clinical phycologists, medical practitioners, teachers and parents can make effective plans to increase mental and psychological development of adolescents in India. The existing researchers and scientists can formulate questionnaires considering most characteristics and all the norms of psychology.

REFERENCES

Allen, B., & Lauterbach, D. (2007). Personality characteristics of adult survivors of childhood trauma. *Journal of Traumatic Stress*, 20(4), 587–595. 10.1002/jts.2019517721954

Baldo, M. V., Cravo, A. M., & Haddad, H. (2007). The time of perception and the other way around. *The Spanish Journal of Psychology*, 10(2), 258–265. 10.1017/S1138741600006521 17992952

Bandelow, B., & Michaelis, S. (2015). Epidemiology of anxiety disorders in the 21st century. *Dialogues in Clinical Neuroscience*, 17(3), 327–335. 10.31887/DCNS.2015.17.3/bbandelow 26487813

Barsky, A. J., Peekna, H. M., & Borus, J. F. (2001). Somatic symptom reporting in women and men. *Journal of General Internal Medicine*, 16(4), 266–275. 10.1046/j.1525-1497.2001.016004266.x 11318929

Beaumont, S. (2024). *Correlation of adverse childhood experiences and somatic symptoms in adolescents.* [Thesis, CSUSB]. Electronic Theses, Projects, and Dissertations. https://scholarworks.lib.csusb.edu/etd/1964

Beesdo, K., Knappe, S., & Pine, D. S. (2009). Anxiety and anxiety disorders in children and adolescents: Developmental issues and implications for DSM-V. *Psychiatria Clinica*, 32(3), 483–524. 10.1016/j.psc.2009.06.002 19716988

Berenz, E. C., Amstadter, A. B., Aggen, S. H., Knudsen, G. P., Reichborn-Kjennerud, T., Gardner, C. O., & Kendler, K. S. (2013). Childhood trauma and personality disorder criterion counts: A co-twin control analysis. *Journal of Abnormal Psychology*, 122(4), 1070–1076. 10.1037/a0034238 24364608

Bolton, T. L. (1902). A biological view of perception. *Psychological Review*, 9(6), 537–548. 10.1037/h0071504

Breslau, N., Kessler, R. C., Chilcoat, H. D., Schultz, L. R., Davis, G. C., & Andreski, P. (1998). Trauma and posttraumatic stress disorder in the community: The 1996 detroit area survey of trauma. *Archives of General Psychiatry*, 55(7), 626–632. 10.1001/archpsyc.55.7.626 9672053

Carmassi, C., Dell'Oste, V., Barberi, F. M., Pedrinelli, V., Cordone, A., Cappelli, A., Cremone, I. M., Rossi, R., Bertelloni, C. A., & Dell'Osso, L. (2021). Do somatic symptoms relate to PTSD and gender after earthquake exposure? A cross-sectional study on young adult survivors in Italy. *CNS Spectrums*, 26(3), 268–274. 10.1017/S1092852920000097 32248878

Christina, C., Yvonne, R., Frank, S., Jordan, P., Michael, S., & Cindy, C. (2016). The assessment of early trauma exposure on social-emotional health of young children. *Children and Youth Services Review*, 71(1), 308–314. 10.1016/j. childyouth.2016.11.004

Colich, N. L., Williams, E. S., Rosen, M. L., & McLaughlin, K. A. (2020). Childhood trauma and accelerated biological aging: Evidence from a meta-analysis. *Psychological Bulletin*, 146(9), 721–743. 10.1037/bul000027032744840

Creed, F. (2023). Psychiatric disorders comorbid with general medical illnesses and functional somatic disorders: The lifelines cohort study. *PLoS One*, 18(5), 1–23. 10.1371/journal.pone.028641037253033

D'Andrea, W., Sharma, R., Zelechoski, A. D., & Spinazzola, J. (2011). Physical health problems after single trauma exposure: When stress takes root in the body. *Journal of the American Psychiatric Nurses Association*, 17(6), 378–392. 10.1177 /107839031142518722142975

Dimsdale, J. E., Creed, F., Escobar, J., Sharpe, M., Wulsin, L., Barsky, A., Lee, S., Irwin, M. R., & Levenson, J. (2013). Somatic symptom disorder: An important change in DSM. *Journal of Psychosomatic Research*, 75(3), 223–228. 10.1016/j. jpsychores.2013.06.03323972410

Eilers, H., Rot, M. A. H., & Jeronimus, B. F. (2023). Childhood trauma and adult somatic symptoms. *Psychosomatic Medicine*, 85(5), 408–416. 10.1097/ PSY.00000000000120837097117

Elklit, A., & Christiansen, D. M. (2009). Predictive factors for somatization in a trauma sample. *Clinical Practice and Epidemiology in Mental Health*, 5(1), 1–8. 10.1186/1745-0179-5-119126224

Ford, C. V. (1997). Somatic symptoms, somatization, and traumatic stress: An overview. *Nordic Journal of Psychiatry*, 51(1), 5–13. 10.3109/08039489709109078

Gander, M., Buchheim, A., Bock, A., Steppan, M., Sevecke, K., & Goth, K. (2020). Unresolved attachment mediates the relationship between childhood trauma and impaired personality functioning in adolescence. *Journal of Personality Disorders*, 34(2, Supplement B), 84–103. 10.1521/pedi_2020_34_46831990614

Greenberg, T. M. (2014). Abnormal Illness behaviors. *Encyclopedia of the Neurological Sciences, 21*(1), 7-10. 10.1016/B978-0-12-385157-4.01072-1

Greenman, P. S., Renzi, A., Monaco, S., Luciani, F., & Trani, M. D. (2024). How does trauma make you sick the role of attachment in explaining somatic symptoms of survivors of childhood trauma. *Health Care*, 12(2), 1–10. 10.3390/healthcare1202020338255090

Haugland, S. H., Dovran, A., Albaek, A. U., & Sivertsen, B. (2021). Adverse childhood experiences among 28,047 Norwegian adults from a general population. *Frontiers in Public Health*, 9(1), 1–8. 10.3389/fpubh.2021.71134434381754

Hazer, L., & Gredebäck, G. (2023). The effects of war, displacement, and trauma on child development. *Humanities & Social Sciences Communications*, 10(909), 1–7. 10.1057/s41599-023-02438-8

Joellenbeck, L. M., Russell, P. K., & Guze, S. B. (1999). Strategies to Protect the Health of Deployed U.S. Forces: Medical Surveillance, Record Keeping, and Risk Reduction. Institute of Medicine (US) Medical Follow-Up Agency, National Academies Press (US), USA. 10.17226/9711

Kallivayalil, R. A., & Punnoose, V. P. (2010). Understanding and managing somatoform disorders: Making sense of non-sense. *Indian Journal of Psychiatry*, 52(7, 11), 240–245. 10.4103/0019-5545.6923921836685

Kirmayer, L. J., Robbins, J. M., & Paris, J. (1994). Somatoform disorders: Personality and the social matrix of somatic distress. *Journal of Abnormal Psychology*, 103(1), 125–136. 10.1037/0021-843X.103.1.1258040474

Konnopka, A., Kaufmann, C., König, H. H., Heider, D., Wild, B., Szecsenyi, J., Herzog, W., Heinrich, S., & Schaefert, R. (2013). Association of costs with somatic symptom severity in patients with medically unexplained symptoms. *Journal of Psychosomatic Research*, 75(4), 370–375. 10.1016/j.jpsychores.2013.08.01124119945

Korbin, J. E. (1991). Cross-cultural perspectives and research directions for the 21st century. *Child Abuse & Neglect*, 15(1), 67–77. 10.1016/0145-2134(91)90010-B2032129

Korhonen, T., Sihvola, E., Latvala, A., Dick, D. M., Pulkkinen, L., Nurnberger, J., Rose, R., & Kaprio, J. (2018). Early-onset tobacco use and suicide-related behavior–A prospective study from adolescence to young adulthood. *Addictive Behaviors*, 79(1), 32–38. 10.1016/j.addbeh.2017.12.00829245024

Kratzer, L., Knefel, M., Haselgruber, A., Heinz, P., Schennach, R., & Karatzias, T. (2022). Co-occurrence of severe PTSD, somatic symptoms and dissociation in a large sample of childhood trauma inpatients: A network analysis. *European Archives of Psychiatry and Clinical Neuroscience*, 272(5), 897–908. 10.1007/s00406-021-01342-z34635928

Kroenke, K. (2014). A practical and evidence-based approach to common symptoms: A narrative review. *Annals of Internal Medicine*, 161(8), 579–586. 10.7326/M14-046125329205

Kugler, B. B., Bloom, M., Kaercher, L. B., Truax, T. V., & Storch, E. A. (2012). Somatic symptoms in traumatized children and adolescents. *Child Psychiatry and Human Development*, 43(5), 661–673. 10.1007/s10578-012-0289-y22395849

Kuhfuß, M., Maldei, T., Hetmanek, A., & Baumann, N. (2021). Somatic experiencing–effectiveness and key factors of a body-oriented trauma therapy: A scoping literature review. *European Journal of Psychotraumatology*, 12(1), 1–7. 10.1080/20008198 .2021.192902334912501

Lipowski, Z. J. (1987). Somatization: The experience and communication of psychological distress as somatic symptoms. *Psychotherapy and Psychosomatics*, 47(3-4), 160–167. 10.1159/0002880133333284

Liu, L., Cohen, S., Schulz, M. S., & Waldinger, R. J. (2011). Sources of somatization: Exploring the roles of insecurity in relationships and styles of anger experience and expression. *Social Science & Medicine*, 73(9), 1436–1443. 10.1016/j. socscimed.2011.07.03421907475

Lopez, M. A. (2024). Scars unseen: the enduring effects of war on children's mental health. *Psychiatry Advisor*. https://www.psychiatryadvisor.com/features/psychological-effects-of-war-on-children/

Lopez-Martinez, A. E., Serrano-Ibanez, E. R., Ruiz-Parraga, G. T., Gomez-Perez, L., Ramirez-Maestre, C., & Esteve, R. (2018). Physical health consequences of interpersonal trauma: A systematic review of the role of psychological variables. *Trauma, Violence & Abuse*, 19(3), 305–322. 10.1177/15248380166594882745613

Mathews, B., Pacella, R., Scott, J. G., Finkelhor, D., Meinck, F., Higgins, D. J., Erskine, H. E., Thomas, H. J., Lawrence, D. M., Haslam, D. M., Malacova, E., & Dunne, M. P. (2023). The prevalence of child maltreatment in Australia: Findings from a national survey. *The Medical Journal of Australia*, 218(1), 13–18. 10.5694/mja2.5187337004184

McFarlane, A. C. (1992). Avoidance and intrusion in posttraumatic stress disorder. *The Journal of Nervous and Mental Disease*, 180(7), 439–445. 10.1097/00005053-199207000-000061624925

McFarlane, A. C. (2010). The long-term costs of traumatic stress: Intertwined physical and psychological consequences. *World Psychiatry; Official Journal of the World Psychiatric Association (WPA)*, 9(1), 3–10. 10.1002/j.2051-5545.2010.tb00254.x20148146

Mercader-Rubio, I., Ángel, N. G., Silva, S., & Brito-Costa, S. (2023). Levels of somatic anxiety, cognitive anxiety, and self-efficacy in university athletes from a Spanish public university and their relationship with basic psychological needs. *International Journal of Environmental Research and Public Health*, 20(5), 44–52. 10.3390/ijerph2003241536767781

Mirzaei, M., Ardekani, S. M. Y., Mirzaei, M., & Dehghani, A. (2019). Prevalence of depression, anxiety and stress among adult population: Results of Yazd health study. *Iranian Journal of Psychiatry*, 14(2), 137–146. https://pubmed.ncbi.nlm.nih.gov/31440295/. 10.18502/ijps.v14i2.99331440295

Morina, N., Schnyder, U., Klaghofer, R., Müller, J., & Martin-Soelch, C. (2018). Trauma exposure and the mediating role of posttraumatic stress on somatic symptoms in civilian war victims. *BMC Psychiatry*, 18(92), 1–7. 10.1186/s12888-018-1680-429631551

Nation. (2021). India saw 31 kids die by suicide every day in 2020; experts say COVID upped trauma. *Daccan Chronicle*. https://www.deccanchronicle.com/nation/in-other-news/311021/india-saw-31-kids-die-by-suicide-every-day-in-2020-experts-say-covid.html

National Crime Records Bureau. (2020). *Crime in India, 2020*. NCRB. https://ruralindiaonline.org/en/library/resource/crime-in-india-2020-volume-iii/

North, C. S. (2002). Somatization in survivors of catastrophic trauma: A methodological review. *Environmental Health Perspectives*, 4(4, suppl 4), 637–640. 10.1289/ehp.02110s463712194899

Oginyi, C., Nwoye, E., Ude, U., & Okeke, N. (2024). Childhood sexual abuse among undergraduates: Personality trait, substance abuse, and loneliness as predictor variables. *The Japanese Psychological Research*, 48(2), 123–136. https://ebsu-jssh.com/index.php/EBSUJSSH/article/view/148

Renzi, A., Lionetti, F., Bruni, O., Parisi, P., & Galli, F. (2024). Somatization in children and adolescents with headache: The role of attachment to parents. *Current Psychology (New Brunswick, N.J.)*, 43(1), 14358–14366. 10.1007/s12144-023-05466-4

Roelofs, K., Spinhoven, P., Sandijck, P., Moene, F. C., & Hoogduin, K. A. (2005). The impact of early trauma and recent life-events on symptom severity in patients with conversion disorder. *The Journal of Nervous and Mental Disease*, 193(8), 508–514. 10.1097/01.nmd.0000172472.60197.4d16082294

Sachs-Ericsson, N., Kendall-Tackett, K., & Hernandez, A. (2007). Childhood abuse, chronic pain, and depression in the National Comorbidity survey. *Child Abuse & Neglect*, 31(5), 531–547. 10.1016/j.chiabu.2006.12.00717537506

Sadeghi, S., Dolatshahi, B., Pourshahbaz, A., Zarei, M., & Kami, M. (2017). Relationship between traumatic experiences and somatic symptoms severity in students. *Practice in Clinical Psychology*, 5(3), 211–216. https://jpcp.uswr.ac.ir/article-1-465-en.html. 10.18869/acadpub.jpcp.5.3.211

Salmon, P., Skaife, K., & Rhodes, J. (2003). Abuse, dissociation, and somatization in irritable bowel syndrome: Towards an explanatory model. *Journal of Behavioral Medicine*, 26(1), 1–18. 10.1023/A:102171830463312690943

Sardesai, A., Muneshwar, K. N., Bhardwaj, M., & Goel, D. B. (2023). The importance of early diagnosis of somatic symptom disorder: A case report. *Cureus*, 15(9), 1–17. 10.7759/cureus.4455437790046

Sedikides, C., & Gregg, A. P. (2003). Portraits of the self. In Hogg, M., & Cooper, J. (Eds.), *The SAGE Handbook of Social Psychology* (pp. 110–138). SAGE Publications. 10.4135/9781848608221.n5

Sharma, S., & Agarwala, S. (2015). Self-esteem and collective self-esteem among adolescents: An interventional approach. *Psychological Thought*, 8(1), 105–113. 10.5964/psyct.v8i1.121

Sherin, J. E., & Nemeroff, C. B. (2011). Post-traumatic stress disorder: The neurobiological impact of psychological trauma. *Dialogues in Clinical Neuroscience*, 13(3), 263–278. 10.31887/DCNS.2011.13.2/jsherin22034143

Singh, A. K., Kumar, S., & Jyoti, B. (2022). Impact of the COVID-19 on food security and sustainable development goals in India: Evidence from existing literature. *GNOSI: An Interdisciplinary Journal of Human Theory and Praxis* 5(2), 94-109. http://gnosijournal.com/index.php/gnosi/article/view/196/225

Singh, A. K., & Singh, B. J. (2020). Assessing the infectious diseases of students in different weather seasons in DIT University Dehradun, Uttarakhand (India). *Asian Journal of Multidimensional Research*, 9(3), 34–48. 10.5958/2278-4853.2020.00055.5

Sperling, E. L., Hulett, J. M., Sherwin, L. B., Thompson, S., & Betterncourt, B. A. (2023). Prevalence, characteristics and measurement of somatic symptoms related to mental health in medical students: A scoping review. *Annals of Medicine*, 55(2), 1–13. 10.1080/07853890.2023.224278137552776

Thomson, K., Randall, E., Ibeziako, P., & Bujoreanu, I. S. (2014). Somatoform disorders and trauma in medically-admitted children, adolescents, and young adults: Prevalence rates and psychosocial characteristics. *Psychosomatics*, 55(6), 630–639. 10.1016/j.psym.2014.05.00625262040

Trivedi, M. H. (2004). The link between depression and physical symptoms. *Primary Care Companion to the Journal of Clinical Psychiatry*, 6(1), 12. https://www.ncbi.nlm.nih.gov/pmc/articles/PMC486942/16001092

Waitzkin, H., & Magana, H. (1997). The black box in somatization: Unexplained physical symptoms, culture, and narratives of trauma. *Social Science & Medicine*, 45(6), 811–825. 10.1016/S0277-9536(96)00422-49255914

Waldinger, R. J., Schulz, M. S., Barsky, A. J., & Ahern, D. K. (2006). Mapping the road from childhood trauma to adult somatization: The role of attachment. *Psychosomatic Medicine*, 68(1), 129–135. 10.1097/01.psy.0000195834.37094.a416449423

Waller, G., Hamilton, K., Elliott, P., Lewendon, J., Stopa, L., Waters, A., Kennedy, F., Lee, G., Pearson, D., Kennerey, H., Hargreaves, I., Bashford, V., & Chalkley, J. (2001). Somatoform dissociation, psychological dissociation, and specific forms of trauma. *Journal of Trauma & Dissociation*, 1(4), 81–98. 10.1300/J229v01n04_05

Wong, W. C. W., Leung, P. W. S., Tang, C. S. K., Chen, W. Q., Lee, A., & Ling, D. C. (2009). To unfold a hidden epidemic: Prevalence of child maltreatment and its health implications among high school students in Guangzhou, China. *Child Abuse & Neglect*, 33(1), 441–450. 10.1016/j.chiabu.2008.02.01019586660

Chapter 15
Domestic and Gender–Based Violence Data and Developmental Psychoeducational Proposals

Eleonora Papaleontiou Louca
https://orcid.org/0000-0001-8690-0314
European University Cyprus, Cyprus

Eleonora Papaleontiou Louca
https://orcid.org/0000-0001-9300-6150
European University of Cyprus, Cyprus

ABSTRACT

Violence in any of its forms is a common secret and an unseen wound that occurs behind closed doors in families whose members are reluctant to admit that they have been victimized because of the fear of renewed threats from the perpetrator and social stigmatization. Possible causes include inadequate psychological functioning of parents, the perpetrator's sense of receiving 'value' counterproductively, possible mental illness, controlling relationships, history of aggressive behavior, lack of trust and solidarity relationships, lack of meaningful communication, shaking of fundamentals, crisis of humanistic values and the institution of the family, etc. Dealing with such a multifactorial phenomenon requires the rallying of many institutions and organizations and systematic collective efforts to eliminate or at least reduce the phenomenon. Prevention focuses mainly on the cultivation of values such as social equality, justice, meritocracy, the cultivation of moral values and ideals, and

DOI: 10.4018/979-8-3693-4022-6.ch015

the promotion of good role models.

INTRODUCTION

Violence is born in the womb of society and domestic violence is its most common and essential form. Its main victims are women and children (Hornor, 2005; Rodriquez et al., 1999). It is a social scourge that affects people from all socio-economic strata and educational levels and brings about many psychological and physical consequences.

The term 'domestic violence' is a negative experience of abuse in the home and refers to any act or behavior that is intended to cause some form of harm to another family member, and which is used to coerce, dominate, or isolate.

Known as domestic abuse, it refers to a pattern of abusive behavior, where one person tries to exert power and control over the other. It is using any form of power imposed on the individual to maintain control of the relationship and of the victim's behavior. It is a clear violation of human rights and is severely punishable by law [PTA, Section 3 of *Act 119*(1)2000].

It is a widespread and serious social problem that affects people of all genders, ages, races, and socio-economic backgrounds, and it can have devastating consequences not only for victims and perpetrators but also for children exposed to these behaviors.

Violence against children in particular still plays a leading role among the forms of domestic violence. Unfortunately, throughout human history, children have been subjected to all kinds of abuse, such as child abuse and neglect, abandonment, exploitation, and even murder by their parents and caregivers, etc.

All of these negative childhood experiences constitute serious traumatic events that can have profound, harmful, and long-term effects on children's lives. As a consequence, children's later social and emotional development and overall health (physical and mental) are at high risk of developing severe impairments and a variety of psychological problems such as low self-esteem, anxiety, depression, behavioral problems, educational difficulties, and distorted social relationships.

Indeed, several studies have shown that child abuse/neglect is associated with a range of harmful effects that can persist well during lifespan, including physical and mental health problems, serious illness, anxiety, depression, and suicidality (Holman et al, 2016; Sheffler et al., 2020; Thompson et al., 2019), while long-term abuse can extend negative health effects often across the lifespan (Kong et al., 2021). Although the problem of child abuse/neglect is not a new phenomenon, it is only in the last fifty years or so that researchers have focused on studying it more systematically, and the implementation of effective interventions to prevent abuse seems relatively new.

Types of violence can include physical, emotional/psychological, verbal, sexual, economic, economic, spiritual, social, religious, political, legal, racist, neglect, etc.

In particular, we describe and explain below the most common types of violence:

Verbal violence: Involves the use of offensive words or tone/tone of voice to humiliate, belittle, threaten, or manipulate another person. It can take many forms, including insulting name-calling, belittling and ridiculing, threats and intimidation, accusations and slander, shouting and swearing, silencing (ignoring or refusing to communicate with someone as a means of control or punishment), gaslighting (i.e. manipulating someone to challenge their perceptions, memory or reasoning) - degrading and belittling comments, criticism and belittling, sarcasm, etc.

Physical violence: This is any form of physical harm, such as hitting, slapping, punching, kicking, or using weapons to harm the victim.

Emotional and psychological violence: Includes tactics such as intimidation, threats, isolation, humiliation, and controlling behavior intended to manipulate and erode the victim's self-esteem.

Emotional violence includes cases of humiliation such as calling you names and/or criticizing you); "isolation" (restriction of social contact: e.g., trying to keep you from doing something you want, such as going out with friends or going to meetings); "intimidation" (frightening with actions or gestures: e.g., gave you angry stares or look); "male privileges" (compliance demanded based on male entitlement: e.g., ended a discussion with you and made the decision himself) etc. (Winstok & Sowan-Basheer, 2015).

Patrick-Hoffman (1982) defined psychological abuse as a behavior that is sufficiently threatening to limit the capacity to work, family and social interactions, and the enjoyment of good physical or mental health can be as damaging to women as physical abuse.

Sexual violence: It is the extreme form of gender-based violence, often accompanied by the other types of violence and usually (but not always) affecting women. It is one of the most common and most severe forms of violence conducted either by intimate or non-intimate partners. It includes cases such as non-consensual sexual acts, coercion, or sexual exploitation in the context of an intimate relationship, as well as trafficking, forced prostitution, exploitation of labour, physical and sexual violence against prostitutes, sex-selective abortion, female infanticide, deliberate neglect of girls, and rape in war (Tavara, 2006).

Despite many efforts to enact legislation to protect women, statistics show a dramatic increase in cases of sexual violence. One possible reason is the focus on punishing perpetrators rather than prevention (Ningrum, 2024).

Though it is difficult to determine the exact dimensions of the problem, it is estimated that this type of violence affects at least one-third of women at some time in their life. It has multiple effects on women's physical and gynaecological health, and these depend greatly on the quality of care that women receive immediately after the assault (Tavara, 2006).

Economic violence: This occurs when the abuser controls the victim's financial resources, restricts access to money, or prevents the victim from working or making financial decisions.

Social violence: Refers to the arbitrary deprivation of liberty whether this occurs in public or private life. It involves complete control and interference in the victim's relationships with other people.

Racist violence: Refers to Stereotypes, Prejudice, and Discrimination based on race/ethnicity.

Gender-based violence or violence against women refers to any act of gender-based violence that (potentially) results in harm or suffering to women. It mainly stems from traditional perceptions that perceive women as subordinate and inferior to men, and/or give the former the right to use violence to control women.

The World Health Organization identifies violence against women and sexual violence (in intimate relations) as a major public health problem (WHO, 2021). They estimate that globally 30% of women have been experienced either physical or sexual violence in their lifetime. Violence can negatively affect women's physical, mental, sexual, and reproductive health, and can lead to femicide and increased risk of suicide (Chopra et al, 2022, Houghton et al, 2024).

Women in Asia and the Middle East are killed in the name of honor. Girls in West Africa undergo genital mutilation in the name of custom. Migrant and refugee women in Western Europe are attacked for not accepting the social mores of their host community. Young girls in southern Africa are raped and infected with HIV/AIDs because the perpetrators believe that sex with virgins will cure them of their disease. And in the richest, most developed countries of the world, women are battered to death by their partners (*Amnesty International, 2004*, p. iii-iv).

The focus on gender-based violence against women does not mean that women do not perpetrate violence against men. Rates and forms of violence, including intimate partner violence, vary widely across cultures (Kishor & Johnson, 2004). Indeed, research findings have reported that both women and men commonly commit acts of violence such as reported common acts of violence such as pushing, punching and throwing objects. Furthermore, little difference was reported between men and women in the prevalence of such acts (Archer, 2000). There was little difference in the prevalence of such acts by gender (Archer, 2000, 2002; Brush, 1990, 2005; Frieze & McHugh, 2005; Mettugh, 2005).

Gender shapes the meaning of acts of violence differently for women and men, though the meaning varies greatly depending on the context and cultural background. For example, the seriousness of a particular physical act is evaluated differently depending on whether the perpetrator is male or female (Marshall, 1992).

In order to fully understand gender-based violence, it is necessary not only to focus on gender differences in rates and evaluations of specific actions, but also to consider various factors such as how women behavior towards their partners and generally, how gender affects violence and shapes the determinants, the dynamics and consequences of violence (Russo & Pirlott, 2006).

Gender-based violence is experienced as both stigmatizing and shameful (Buchbinder & Eilsikovits, 2003). This very feeling of shame has been identified as a factor that traps women inhibiting them from talking to other people about their traumatic experiences and having a pervasive influence on them and their relationships. It is experienced as an emotional abuse, and becomes an obstacle in quitting violence and seeking help (Giles-Sims, 1998). Shame has been also found as a key predictor for the relation between psychological violence and PTSD (Street & Arias, 2001).

Interdisciplinary research, needs to be conducted at multiple levels makes an important contribution to the examination of the psychological meaning of actions and experiences. The psychological meaning of actions and experiences for perpetrators, victims and external observers reflects situational, structural, cultural and social factors. The situational, structural and cultural context needs to be examined as well as gender differences (especially related to the social and economic status, the objectification of women and the sexual gender-based violence). For this reason, a more complex and multi-layered approach is needed to the study of how such violence is experienced in women's lives (Russo & Pirlott, 2006).

Neglect: It constitutes the inadequacy in providing care corresponding to each age stage of the child. It is divided into Physical, Educational, Emotional, and Medical (Precate & Yiotakos, 2006).

According to the WHO (2006) "Neglect includes both isolated incidents, as well as a pattern of failure over time on the part of a parent or other family member to provide for the development and well-being of the child – where the parent is in a position to do so – in one or more of the following areas: health; education; emotional development; nutrition; shelter and safe living conditions. The parents of neglected children are not necessarily poor. They may equally be financially well-off" and the Centres for Disease and Control Prevention, (2022) state that "Neglect is the failure to meet a child's basic physical and emotional needs. These needs include housing, food, clothing, education, access to medical care, and having feelings validated and appropriately responded to." An actively abusive caregiver is indeed a traumatic condition. This is because he/she, who should be the primary source of safety and care, is also the source of an active or aggressive abuse. Because he/she, who is supposed to be the primary source of safety and care, is at the same time a source of active or passive threat (Massullo et al, 2023).

THE CYCLE OF VIOLENCE

Domestic violence often follows a cycle, including a tension-building phase, an explosive phase where the abuse occurs, and a honeymoon phase where the abuser may apologize and promise to change. This cycle may repeat itself over time.

Causes of Violence

Possible causes of domestic violence include inadequate parental psychological functioning, the perpetrator's sense of receiving 'value' counterproductively, possible mental illness and/or disturbed personality, confusional/proprietary/controlling relationships, history of aggressive behavior (perpetrators who have been victims or witnesses themselves), lack of trust and solidarity, lack of dialogue and effective communication, breakdown of fundamental values of the democratic state such as justice, law and order, security, crisis of humanitarian values, violation of human rights, crisis of the family institution, etc.

A study on the "Psychological Characteristics of Adults Who Have Experienced Sexual Violence in Childhood or Adolescence" (Tukhtaeva & Lukovtseva, 2024) revealed that low /unstable self-esteem, depression and anxiety, as well as the psychological alienation of the past, and the negative perception of relationships with parents are some possible factors that make the victims more vulnerable to sexual violence. Other factors related to sexual violence include the emotional-protective role of the mnestic-attentive decrease and our relationships with others. Of course, we need more studies including victims of different gender, age and nosological affiliation, so as to compare their characteristics to those of victims who did not seek professional help.

Impact on Victims

Domestic violence can have serious physical and emotional consequences for victims. Some of its multiple traumatic effects include, in addition to physical injuries, post-traumatic stress disorder, trauma, anxiety, depression, low self-esteem/

self-confidence, depression, sleep disorders, phobias, aggression, substance abuse, suicidal tendencies, and even death.

Research using imaging methods (MRI scanning) to see which brain regions are activated when someone experiences social rejection and abandonment and which are activated when someone experiences physical pain (Kross et al, 2011) has shown that in both forms of pain (psychological & physical) the same neural circuits are activated, in such a way that one could say that "literally, rejection hurts...". In addition, the electrical activity of the brain of abused individuals is reduced (Pollak et al, 2000; Pollak & Sinha, 2002). In particular, there is reduced volume of the medulla oblongata and hippocampus, with a potential reduction in the individual's functioning.

These alterations in brain structures are associated with higher rates of psychopathology in adulthood (Teichera et al., 2010).

Children who witness domestic violence may also experience lasting emotional and psychological consequences, so it is advisable to consult a mental health professional, as we will see below.

Many victims unfortunately face significant barriers to reporting domestic violence, such as fear of retaliation, financial dependence on the perpetrator, shame, cultural factors, and lack of support.

TACKLING VIOLENCE

Tackling such a complex and multifactorial phenomenon requires the involvement of many institutions and organizations and systematic collective efforts to eliminate or at least reduce the phenomenon.

Indicative (short-term) ways of coping include e.g. the immediate removal of the victim from the abuser (with an action/escape plan), immediate help from the family environment (relatives, friends, neighbours), help from Mental Health Specialists (psychologists, psychiatrists, counsellors), immediate action from state agencies such as the police, help from a doctor, recourse to Support Centres and Social Welfare Centres.

At the same time, long-term ways of dealing with the phenomenon include proper education (proper education of students, educational/ intervention programs for prevention and response, development of programs for cultivating skills of effective communication, psychoeducation of parents), education (general population and special groups/intervention and empowerment programs for victims of violence/information and awareness-raising activities for the general public, early intervention, criminal sanctions, compliance with legislation, social changes (e.g., shaping of social values, removal of stereotypes), the contribution of the Church (humanitarian services, assistance programs, cultivation of universal values, respect for the human person) Mental Health Services / Counselling Services (Psychotherapy - Psychologists / Psychiatrists), Psychological Empowerment (e.g. self-respect, self-care, learning anger control techniques, developing self-esteem, improving communication skills).

As long as women are kept away from education, information, work, and intellectual cultivation, they will remain dependent and victims of an obscurantist regime.

For, let us not forget, education and spiritual cultivation open windows to the mind and heart!

And what certainly locks them tightly is fanaticism, racism, prejudice, and illiteracy.

PREVENTION AND EDUCATION

Prevention focuses mainly on the cultivation of values such as social equality, justice, meritocracy, the cultivation of moral values and ideals, and the promotion of good role models - values that should be cultivated primarily in the context of the family and school, but also of education in a broader sense. The proper education of young people in the family and at school, and the proper use of leisure time, so that young people's energy can be channelled into something creative, are actions that act preventively and effectively against the phenomenon of violence and other social problems.

Efforts to prevent domestic violence often include public awareness campaigns, educational programs in schools, and intervention programs at a community basis, so as to support to change social attitudes, and patterns that contribute to violence. An example of such a successful intervention program is the " Lilac Programme", which invites parents who experienced childhood sexual abuse, and offers them structured support and a healing experience tailored to their unique needs (Houghton et al, 2024).

It is important to understand that domestic violence is never the fault of the victim and that no one deserves to be abused. If you or someone you know is experiencing domestic violence, it is vital to seek help and support from professionals, friends, or organizations dedicated to helping survivors of domestic abuse.

In addition, society and the state must enact measures such as addressing unemployment and creating new jobs.

LEGAL PROTECTION

Laws and legal protections for victims of domestic violence vary by country and jurisdiction. They often include restraining orders, shelters, and remedies that help protect victims and hold perpetrators accountable.

SUPPORT AND RESOURCES

There are numerous organizations, hotlines, and shelters available to help victims of domestic violence. These organizations offer counseling, legal assistance, and resources to help individuals escape abusive situations.

CONCLUSION

It is therefore extremely important that individuals experiencing violence be persuaded to seek help from a person they trust or to turn to a competent agency. Forms of psychotherapy appropriate for addressing this phenomenon are varied such as individual/couple/group or a combination of the above and dominant approaches taken to issues such as this include Cognitive-Behavioural (involving a change in beliefs and patterns), Systemic Counselling (change in system dysfunction) and problem-solving to make the problem functional (Tura & Licoze, 2019).

Finally, of great importance is the fact that only when victims of violence find someone they can trust and connect with lovingly, can they manage to reach the point where the experience of trauma no longer has the power it once did, and the trauma no longer controls and defines their lives (Lappas, 2023).

Violence is not a private, personal, or family affair, but a social problem that affects us all.

For this reason, we highlight the need for awareness, research, and targeted interventions, urging a multidimensional and collaborative approach (Houghton et al, 2024) and inviting all involved parts (policy makers, schools, teachers, church, psychologists, social workers, lawyers, parents, etc) to work together towards this end.

As long as a child/person is suffering from violence, then we are all responsible too! If we are not part of the solution, then we are part of the problem!

REFERENCES

Amnesty International. (2004). *It's in our hands: Stop violence against women.* Alden Press.

Archer, J. (2000). Sex differences in aggression between heterosexual partners: A meta-analytic review. *Psychological Bulletin*, 126(5), 651–680. 10.1037/0033-2909.126.5.65110989615

Archer, J. (2002). Sex differences in physically aggressive acts between heterosexual partners: A meta- analytic review. *Aggression and Violent Behavior*, 7(4), 313–351. 10.1016/S1359-1789(01)00061-1

Buchbinder, E., & Eisikovits, Z. (2003). Battered women's entrapment in shame: A phenomenological study. *The American Journal of Orthopsychiatry*, 73(4), 355–366. 10.1037/0002-9432.73.4.35514609398

Chopra, J., Sambrook, L., McLoughlin, S., Randles, R., Palace, M., & Blinkhorn, V. (2022). Risk factors for intimate partner homicide in England and Wales. *Health & Social Care in the Community*, 30(5), 3086–3095. 10.1111/hsc.1375335178829

Farina, B., Liotti, M., & Imperatori, C. (2019). The role of attachment trauma and disintegrative pathogenic processes in the traumatic-dissociative dimension. *Frontiers in Psychology*, 10, 933. 10.3389/fpsyg.2019.0093331080430

Frieze, I. H., & Mchugh, M. (Eds.). (2005). Female violence against intimate partners. *Psychology of Women Quarterly, 29*(3).

Giles-Sims, J. (1998). The aftermath of partner violence. In Jasinski, J. L., & Williams, L. M. (Eds.), *Partner violence: A comprehensive review of 20 years of research* (pp. 44–72). Sage.

Holman, D. H., Ports, K. A., Buchanan, N. D., Hawkins, N. A., Merrick, M. T., Metzler, M., & Trivers, K. F. (2016). The association between adverse childhood experiences and risk of cancer in adulthood: A systematic review of the literature. *Pediatrics*, 138(Supplement_1), S81–S91. 10.1542/peds.2015-4268L27940981

Hornor, G. (2005). Domestic violence and children. *Journal of Pediatric Health Care*, 19(4), 206–212. 10.1016/j.pedhc.2005.02.00216010259

Houghton, F., Rourke Scott, L., Moran Stritch, J., Larkin, H. K., & Heinz, L. (2024). Sexual, Domestic, and Gender-based Abuse: A collection of experience and opinion. *JGPOH*, 2023. 10.61034/JGPOH-2024-2

Kong, J., Martire, L. M., Liu, Y., & Almeida, D. M. (2021). Effects of parental childhood abuse on daily stress processes in adulthood. *Journal of Interpersonal Violence*, 36(19-20), 9580–9599. 10.1177/0886260519869906831423882

Kross E, Berman MG, Mischel W, Smith EE, & Wager TD. (2011). Social rejection shares somatosensory representations with physical pain. *Proc Natl Acad. Science 12, 108*(15), 6270-5.10.1073/pnas.1102693108

Lappas, A. (Λάππας, A.) (2023). *Κακοποίηση Παιδιών από Κακοποιημένες Μητέρες*. Προφορική Ανακοίνωση στο Ινστιτούτο ΠροςΟψη. [Video]. Youtube. https://www.youtube.com/watch?v=ybIGqTKPN0Q

Marshall, L. L. (1992). Development of the severity of violence against women scales. *Journal of Family Violence*, 7(2), 103–121. 10.1007/BF00978700

Massullo, C., De Rossi, E., Carbone, G. A., Imperatori, C., Ardito, R. B., Adenzato, M., & Farina, B. (2023). Child maltreatment, abuse, and neglect: An umbrella review of their prevalence and definitions. *Clinical Neuropsychiatry: Journal of Treatment Evaluation*, 20(2), 72–99.37250758

McHugh, M. C. (2005). Understanding gender and intimate partner abuse. *Sex Roles*, 52(11-12), 717–724. 10.1007/s11199-005-4194-8

Ningrum, I. T. K. (2024). Legal Political Review of The Protection of Sexual Violence Victims In the Perspective of Law Number 12 of 2022 Concerning Sexual Violence Crimes. *Journal Equitable*, 9(2), 156–168.

Patrick-Hoffman, P. (1982). *Psychological abuse of women by spouses and live-in lovers*. [Unpublished doctoral dissertation, Union for Experimenting Colleges and Universities].

Pollak, S. D., Cicchetti, D., Hornung, K., & Reed, A. (2000). Recognizing Emotion in Faces: Developmental Effects of Child Abuse and Neglect. *Developmental Psychology*, 36(5), 679–688. 10.1037/0012-1649.36.5.67910976606

Pollak, S. D., & Sinha, P. (2002). Effects of early experience on children's recognition of facial displays of emotion. *Developmental Psychology*, 38(5), 784–791. 10.1037/0012-1649.38.5.78412220055

Precate, B., & Yiotakos, O. (2006). *Σεξουαλική κακοποίηση: Μυστικό; Όχι πια*. Ελληνικά Γράμματα.

Rodriguez, M. A., Bauer, H. M., McLoughlin, E., & Grumbach, K. (1999). Screening and Intervention for Intimate Partner Abuse: Practices and Attitudes of Primary Care Physicians. *Journal of the American Medical Association*, 282(5), 468–474. 10.1001/jama.282.5.46810442663

Russo, N. F., & Pirlott, A. (2006). Gender-based violence: Concepts, methods, and findings. In Denmark, F. L., Krauss, H. H., Halpern, E., & Sechzer, J. A. (Eds.), *Violence and exploitation against women and girls* (pp. 178–205). Blackwell Publishing.

Sheffler, J. L., Stanley, I., & Sachs-Ericsson, N. (2020). Chpt. 4 - ACEs and mental health outcomes. In: Asmundson GJG, Afifi TO, (eds.) *Adverse childhood experiences.* Academic Press.

Street, A. E., & Arias, I. (2001). Psychological abuse and posttraumatic stress disorder in battered women: Examining the role of shame and guilt. *Violence and Victims*, 16(1), 65–78. 10.1891/0886-6708.16.1.6511281225

Tavara, L. (2006). Sexual Abuse. *Best Practice & Research Clinical Obstetrics and Gynaecology, 20,* 3, 395e408. http://www.sciencedirect.com10.1016/j.bpobgyn.2006.01.011

Teixeira, A. L., Barbosa, I. G., Diniz, B. S., & Kummer, A. (2010). Circulating levels of brain-derived neurotrophic factor: Correlation with mood, cognition, and motor function. *Biomarkers in Medicine*, 4(6), 871–887. 10.2217/bmm.10.11121133708

Thompson, M. P., Kingree, J. B., & Lamis, D. (2019). Associations of adverse childhood experiences and suicidal behaviors in adulthood in a U.S. nationally representative sample. *Child: Care, Health and Development*, 45(1), 121–128. 10.1111/cch.1261730175459

Tukhtaeva D.A. & Lukovtseva Z.V. (2024). Psychological Characteristics of Adults Who Have Experienced Sexual Violence in Childhood or Adolescence. Psikhologiya i pravo = *Psychology and Law, 14,* 1, 33–52. 10.17759/psylaw.2024140103

Tura, H., & Licoze, A. (2019). Women's experience of intimate partner violence and uptake of antenatal care in sofala, mozambique. *PLoS One*, 14(5), e0217407. 10.1371/journal.pone.0217407311253370

WHO. (2021). *Violence against women Prevalence Estimates 2018. Violence Global, regional and national prevalence estimates for intimate partner violence against women and global and regional prevalence estimates for non-partner sexual violence against women.* World Health Organisation.

Winstok, Z., & Sowan-Basheer, W. (2015). Does psychological violence contribute to partner violence research? A historical, conceptual and critical review. *Aggression and Violent Behavior*, 21, 5–16. 10.1016/j.avb.2015.01.003

Chapter 16
Juvenile Delinquency:
Risk Factors and Prevention Techniques

Zoi Siouti
https://orcid.org/0000-0002-8316
-7505

*National and Kapodistrian University
of Athens, Greece*

Evangelos Tolis

*National and Kapodistrian University
of Athens, Greece*

Maria Theodoratou
https://orcid.org/0000-0003-4200
-4643

Hellenic Open University, Greece

Anna Kaltsouda

University of Ioannina, Greece

Kalliopi Megari
https://orcid.org/0000-0002-5861
-7199

City College, University of York, Greece

Georgios A. Kougioumtzis
https://orcid.org/0000-0002-2362
-2094

*National and Kapodistrian University
of Athens, Greece*

ABSTRACT

Juvenile delinquency is considered as the act of engaging in any illegal behavior by a person under the legal age of majority. Individual characteristics, family, school, peer groups and society play a crucial role in the adoption of delinquent behavior by a minor. Some protective factors that limit criminal behavior of children and adolescents are the ability of the minor to both self-regulate their emotions and comprehend the consequences of their acts, a supportive family, an efficient parental supervision, commitment in school, and the development of friendships focused on values such as solidarity or empathy. Society plays a crucial role in the moulding of a minor's behavior. The policies/measures that can be taken have to be compatible with a number of dispositions on both national and international level. The proposed chapter seeks to both present the risk factors of juvenile delinquency

DOI: 10.4018/979-8-3693-4022-6.ch016

and suggest techniques for the prevention and repression of criminality in minors.

INTRODUCTION

It is evident that children can commit crimes. As a matter of fact, juvenile delinquency can be categorized as the situation "when a kid acts like a grown-up" (Singh & Goyat, 2020), referring to violations of criminal law committed by minors (Brezina & Agnew, 2015). Delinquency can be described as a kind of abnormality or as a deviation from the course of normal social life (Venktachalam & Aravidan, 2014). According to greek law, an offender is considered "juvenile" when his age is between twelve and eighteen years old (article 121 par. 1 of the Greek Criminal Code-Law n. 4619/2019). Juvenile offenders are either subjected to reformative and therapeutic measures or confined in special juvenile detention facilities (article 121 par. 2 of the greek Criminal Code).

Behaviors that can be characterized as juvenile delinquency include crimes related to drugs, property crimes or white collar as well as violent crimes. Juvenile delinquency can be categorized into four major groups (Venktachalam & Aravidan, 2014): (a) Individual delinquency. In this case, a minor may commit crimes by its own and without the help of another person. This type of criminal behavior occurs from existing psychological issues that prevent the minor offender from complying with the rules set by society. It is evident that children consider their parents or caregivers as "role models". Hence any potential aggressive behavior by a parent or caregiver may affect child's development and behavior. A potential lack of support from the family may as well cause the child to develop an antisocial behavior. Poverty, insufficient education, use of drugs, alcohol abuse and any potential criminal background of a parent or caregiver are considered as the main risk factors that lead a child to adopt a criminal behavior. (b) Group-supported criminality is considered as the criminal behavior that a child adopts by being a member of a group that resembles a gang. Each group adopts its own unique style. Minors that form part of this team also adopt their gang's behavior in their personal life. Nevertheless, an adolescent is prone to a delinquent behavior because of its lack of intellectual maturity. As a matter of fact, any minor is eager to participate in any delinquent act in order to be accepted by its peers. When a minor starts to follow the criminal way of living and behavior, that some of its peers follow, setting aside its parents' or caregivers' advices, its behavior cannot be easily controlled. Inequalities that exist in the contemporary society force a person to become member of delinquent subgroups in order to achieve its goals. (c) Organized criminality. This type of delinquent behavior occurs when a minor is part of a group that resembles a criminal organization, hence having a certain hierarchical structure as well as a continuous activity. (d) Situational criminality.

In contrast to criminality at the individual level, group criminality and organized criminality, situational criminality is easier to control. Every individual has its own criminal tendencies. Nevertheless, those criminal tendencies are suppressed by social norms. In situational criminality, even though the child knows the norms as well as all the rules, it succumbs to crime on account of temptations.

This chapter studies the risk factors of juvenile delinquency, as well as the prevention and intervention techniques that can be used in order to control and limit this antisocial behavior.

NATURE AND LEGAL TREATMENT OF JUVENILE OFFENDERS

According to article 121 par. 1 of the Greek Criminal Code, an individual is characterized as a "juvenile" if his age is between 12 and 18 years old. Juveniles are subjected to therapeutic and reformative measures or are incarcerated in special corrective facilities for juveniles (article 121 par. 2). Juvenile offenders under the age of 12 years old are not legally responsible for their crimes, because they are a matter of interest for social services and not for justice (Explanatory Statement of law n. 4609/2019). Juveniles between ages of 12 and 15 years old are subjected to a special procedural treatment. According to article 126 of the Greek Criminal Code, juveniles aged between 12 and 15 years old are considered as "penally irresponsible". Thus, the court's verdict concerning such a case is not that "the defendant is found guilty" but rather "the defendant has committed the crime" (Supreme Court 621/2019, Supreme Court 58/2010). It should be noted that the basic principles concerning the treatment of juvenile offenders are the following (Kosmatos & Martinis, 2021): (a) The crime is evaluated in combination with the personality of the concerned juvenile offender. (b) Informal rather than formal sanctions are preferred. (c) Therapeutic or reformative measures are preferred instead of incarceration. (d) The principle of education in applied. Juveniles are being trialed by special juvenile courts (article 121 of the Greek Code of Criminal Procedure). The peculiarity of cases involving juvenile offenders imposes the establishment of a mediator between the juvenile offender and the court. This role is played by the juvenile probation officer (article 7 of the Law n. 4689/2020).

At an international level, the General Assembly of the United Nations adopted, in 1959, the Declaration of the Rights of the Child. Also, in 1989, world leaders adopted the United Nations Convention on the Rights of the Child. In 2000, the United Nations General Assembly adopted an Optional Protocol to the above mentioned Convention, thus strengthening prohibitions and penalties concerning the sale of children, child prostitution and child pornography.

RISK FACTORS OF JUVENILE DELINQUENCY

Trying to answer the question concerning the risk factors of juvenile delinquency, some theories were developed: Strain theory (Agnew, 2007) suggests that a number of pre-existing strains (or stressors) may increase the possibility for a juvenile to commit a crime. "Strains" are identified as events or conditions that cause negative emotions to individuals; those factors can be categorized in three groups. The first group of strains includes individual's inability to achieve goals, the second includes the loss of positive stimuli, such as the loss of a romantic relationship or material possessions and the third group consists of a priori negative stimuli, such as verbal or physical abuse. According to strain theory, children who experience parental rejection, erratic, excessive or harsh supervision or discipline, abuse, neglect, law grades, peer abuse, discrimination or economic problems are more likely to violate the rules (Annor et al., 2024; Childs et al., 2020; Brezina & Agnew, 2015; Nisar et al, 2015).

On the other hand, social learning theory states that delinquency can be taught (Akers, 1998; Akers & Sellers 2012). As a matter of fact, individuals can learn delinquent behaviors by their environment such as abusive parents, social media, and delinquent peers. Criminality can be taught in three ways: Reinforcement (approval by their peers), exposition (that results in imitation) and beliefs (for example the impression that a certain "street code" exists- c.f. Anderson, 1999).

Control theories focus on the factors that restrain juveniles from criminal behaviors. According to control theories, individuals are motivated to break the law because by this behavior it is easier to obtain what they want. For example, given the fact that it is easier to steal money than to work for it, individuals are strongly motivated to become thieves. Hence, kids don't violate the law and they do not commit crimes when certain compensating factors exist. Those compensating factors include direct control by family or school, the existence of a strong stake in conformity (individual has a lot to lose if he commits a crime) and when an individual is taught how to exercise self-control (Britt & Gottfredson, 2003). It should also be noted that changes in family structure are associated with behavior problems in children (Hadfield et al., 2018; Magnuson & Berger, 2009) as well as with juvenile delinquency (Boccio & Beaver, 2017). As a matter of fact, single-parent households are more criminogenic that two-parent households (Jacobsen & Zaatut, 2020; Song, Benin & Glick, 2012).

Labeling theories focus merely on the reaction of society vis-à-vis the delinquent individual. As a matter of fact, since society views delinquents as "evil" and "dangerous" people, criminal offenders are treated negatively. This negative treatment by society can lead an individual to commit more (and sometimes even more serious) crimes (Farrington & Murray, 2013).

Situational action theory defines crime as "acts that break moral rules of conduct stated by law". The above mentioned theory states that social disadvantages, affecting the emergence of crime propensity and criminogenic conditions of the environment, are not the causes of juvenile delinquency but rather the "causes of causes" (Wikström, 2006, 2009; Wikström et al., 2012, Schepers, 2016).

Other theories focus on the individual traits of the delinquent, that can be categorized in three general traits: low self-control, irritability and low IQ, especially verbal IQ (as a matter of fact, delinquent individuals often lack factual knowledge, abstract thinking, social comprehension and judgment) (Brezina & Agnew, 2015). For example, a study has shown a correlation between ADHD symptoms and criminal behavior (Margari et al., 2015).

Furthermore, environment plays a crucial role in the development of a potential delinquent behavior vis-à-vis a number of categorized "causes" of delinquency. Kraus has conducted a study (2000) that aimed to investigate what juvenile delinquents and non-delinquents perceive as "causes" of delinquency. The sample was originated by the metropolitan area of Sydney, and it consisted of 106 boys from a low delinquency area and 110 boys from a high delinquency area (50 of them were incarcerated in a state corrective institution for juveniles). Identified causes of delinquency were parental inadequacy, peer influence, thrill seeking, proving oneself, boredom, material gain, monetary gain, personal inadequacy, "dared" by peers, parental discipline, other social reasons, anti-social character, hostility, locality, and society attitudes. Boys from the area with low crime rates identified parental inadequacy (58,5), peer influence (34,9) and thrill seeking as the three mere causes of delinquency. Boys from the area with high crime rates identified parental inadequacy (42,7), proving oneself (32,7) and material gain (30,9) as the three major causes of delinquency. Finally, incarcerated delinquents suggested peer influence (56,0), parental inadequacy (42,0) and boredom (42,0) as the three most contributing factors to criminal behavior (Kraus, 2000).

PREVENTION

It is evident that juvenile delinquency is an important social problem, affecting with negative consequences individuals, communities as well as society by itself as a whole (Vries et al., 2015; Rathinabalan & Naaraayan, 2017). Prevention of a delinquent behavior may occur in two different levels: First, the prevention stricto sensu which exists when the individual hasn't yet committed any crime. This type of prevention is realized via the application of certain prevention programs. The second type of prevention is deterrence. Deterrence occurs when a crime is already committed and the goal is both, to limit its consequences as well as to prevent the commission of other crimes (deVries et al., 2015).

In order for a prevention program to be effective, it should be intensive (lasting for several months) and it should employ techniques that aim to change juveniles, focusing on the cognitive-behavioral approach (Brezina & Agnew, 2015). Treatment format depends on the program, varying from one-on-one, family, group or multimodal. Also, the main type of intervention is not standard and it can be short-term behavioral intervention, moral reasoning, community-based program, family group conferencing, coaching, mentoring and skill training, school-based program and other types of interventions (de Vries et al., 2015). An effective program for the prevention of juvenile delinquency is focused on causes such as low self-control, family problems, school problems, drug use and the amelioration of the child's environment. Examples of such programs include mentoring programs (Big Brothers/Big Sisters), programs in which parents are taught effective parenting techniques (these programs also ameliorate the bonds between family members) and programs that aim at the prevention of domestic violence and bullying. It should also be noted that each and every program should be focused on the individual concerned (Brezina & Agnew, 2015). Other programs that were proven effective follow certain components such as behavioral modeling, conflict resolution, community service, rewarding appropriate behavior and self-efficacy (de Vries et al., 2015).

Any penal law consists of two parts: on the one hand, the description of the crime, on the other hand, the sanction. The type of sanction (incarceration, fine, detention) depends on the gravity of the committed crime as well as on the characteristics of the criminal. Even though sanction was considered as society's pay-back to the criminal, nowadays sanction is imposed in order to achieve deterrence (Jacobs, 2010). As a matter of fact, deterrence is distinguished in: (a) specific deterrence (referring to the concept that the punishment of an offender deters him from the commission of new crimes) and (b) general deterrence (referring to the concept that the punishment of another individual deters any other member of the society from conducting a similar crime) (Jacobs, 2010). The concept of deterrence is closely linked to "risk calculation" by the offender. As it is well stated, "if an individual's relative immunity to the threat of sanctions while filing out his income tax return is attributable to a personality characteristic, the same characteristic could determine his reaction to the temptation to steal of to exceed speed limit" (Jacobs, 2010). Hence, the notion of deterrence is closely linked to repression, considering that the imposition of a sanction pre requires the commitment of a crime. In U.S.A., a Scared-Straight-type prevention program is available; this program aims to achieve prevention by applying a general deterrence technique. As a matter of fact, in these programs juveniles visit real prisons where interviewed prisoners describe the "harsh" and "dangerous" prison life (Brezina & Agnew, 2015).

REPRESSION

Punishment by itself is not considered as an effective way of dealing with juvenile delinquency. Neither punishing children as adults, nor increasing the severity of the punishment is considered as an effective solution (Brezina & Agnew, 2015). After all, there are cases of juvenile delinquents who are not afraid of their crimes' consequences because they have nothing to lose. In our opinion, the most effective programs for the repression of juvenile delinquency are rehabilitation programs and restorative justice.

Rehabilitation programs focus on the reintegration of the offender to the society. It is evident that an individual who has committed a crime can be socially labeled as "criminal". This situation causes discrimination against the former offender which results to less opportunities and alienation. Less opportunities, discrimination and labeling can lead the individual to commit other crimes (Farrington & Murray, 2013). One of the main purposes of rehabilitation programs is to minimize the effects of labeling. Generally speaking, rehabilitation programs should also be intensive and they should employ techniques focusing on the cognitive-behavioral approach (Brezina & Agnew, 2015).

It is a widely accepted principle of criminal law that individuals convicted for crimes are often incarcerated (Apel & Diller, 2017). However contemporary criminal justice tends to introduce new forms of restitution for the offense that was created because of the committed crime. Hence, restorative justice has appeared. Broadly defined, restorative justice is described by a system of procedures based in peacemaking practices and guiding to the reparation of harm. In theory, restorative justice promotes society's well-being (Pavlacic, Kellum & Schulenberg, 2021). The above mentioned term encompasses a wide range of programs whose goal is to both restore the harm cause by the crime as well as to eliminate the possibility of future criminal activity (Bergseth & Bouffard, 2012). In greek penal system, forms of restorative justice exist inter alia: (a) in the form of "penal mediation" according to article 12 of the law against domestic violence (law n. 3500/2006); (b) in the form of plea-bargain according to article 302 of the Greek Code of Criminal Procedure; (c) in the form of mediation between the juvenile offender and its victim for the amicable resolution of the case according to article 122 par. 1 el. e of the Greek Criminal Code; (d) in the form of compensation according to article 122 par. 1 el. st of the Greek Criminal Code.

Concerning the effectiveness of restorative justice programs some studies have shown that these programs are effective (Bonta et al., 2002; Bradshaw & Roseborough, 2005; Latimer, Dowden, & Muise, 2001, 2005; Nugent, Williams, & Umbreit, 2003, 2004), while other studies prove that restorative justice is less effective (McCold & Wachtel, 1998; Niemeyer & Shichor, 1996; Roy, 1993; Umbreit, 1994)

315

DISCUSSION

Considering the fact that children are the future of our society, juvenile delinquency threatens not only the victims and the offenders but rather the society in general.

The existing risk factors for juvenile delinquency are relevant to the developmental phase of the child concerned (Gupta, Mohapatra & Mahanta, 2022). Specifically, in the initial phase (during pregnancy to infancy period) the risk factors are linked to the child (complications during pregnancy, exposure to neurotoxins, early childhood serious diseases, impulsivity / Hyperactivity) and its family (alcohol and drug abuse, smoking by mother during pregnancy, parents' poor education). During the toddler phase, the risk factors are linked to the child (aggressive or impulsive behavior, persistent attention seeking, lack of empathy), its family (harsh, abusive, erratic discipline, lack of supervision, neglect) and the community (violent television shows, violent neighbors). During middle childhood period, the risk factors are related to the child (disruptive behavior, involving in criminal activities, substance abuse, hyperactivity, poor attention, antisocial behavior), its family (lack of parental supervision, parental conflict, deprivation of basic need in the family), school (poor academic performance, negative attitude towards schools), its peer groups (rejection by peers, association with gang members deviant peers and siblings) and community (residence in a disorganized neighborhood, availability of arms/weapons and drugs/substances, poverty, neighbors' involvement in criminal activities). During adolescent period, the risk factors are linked to the adolescent (psychological conditions, personality, physical disabilities, involvement in any illegal activity), its family (poor family management, low levels of parental supervision, family conflict or poor bonding, child misbehave or maltreatment), its school (school dropout, low attachment with teachers), peer groups (involving in a gang) and community (community disorganization, poverty, drugs and other substances availability) (Gupta et al., 2022).

The prevention of juvenile delinquency can be achieved by both the development of certain programs and the functioning of the penal system by its self. Some juvenile delinquency prevention programs are available, including parental guidance, family therapy, individual therapy, group therapy, educational support and change of peer group (May, Osmond & Billick, 2014). In other words, the programs that aim at the prevention of juvenile delinquency try to minimize the risk factors. On the other hand, the functioning of the penal system by itself achieves deterrence. Contemporary penal systems do not aim at punishing the criminal, but rather at the amelioration of the offender's behavior and at his restitution in the society as a vital and healthy part of it. Hence, the imposition of a sanction is not considered as "society's revenge over the criminal". If a juvenile has already committed a crime, the available programs aim at offender's rehabilitation. This can be also achieved via amicable resolution procedures, hence the role of restorative justice is crucial.

Juvenile delinquency is a critical issue in modern society and its treatment pre requires the cooperation of numerous scientists and professionals such as psychologists, teachers or judges.

REFERENCES

Agnew, R. (2007). *Pressured Into Crime: An Overview of General Strain Theory*. University Press.

Akers, R. L. (1998). *Social Learning and Social Structure: A General Theory of Crime*. Northeastern University Press.

Akers, R. L., & Sellers, C. S. (2012). *Criminological Theories*. Oxford University Press.

Anderson, E. (1999). *Code of the Street*. W.W. Norton.

Annor, F. B., Amene, E. W., Zhu, L., Stamatakis, C., Picchetti, V., Matthews, S., Miedema, S. S., Brown, C., Thorsen, V. C., Manuel, P., Gilbert, L. K., Kambona, C., Coomer, R., Trika, J., Kamuingona, R., Dube, S. R., & Massetti, G. M. (2024). Parental absence as an adverse childhood experience among young adults in sub-Saharan Africa. *Child Abuse & Neglect*, 150, 106556. 10.1016/j.chiabu.2023.10655637993366

Apel, A. B., & Diller, J. W. (2017). Prison as punishment: A behavior- analytic evaluation of incarceration. *The Behavior Analyst*, 40(1), 243–256. 10.1007/s40614-016-0081-631976937

Bergeth, K. J., & Bouffard, J. A. (2007). The long-term impact of restorative justice programming for juvenile offenders. *Journal of Criminal Justice*, 35(4), 433–451. 10.1016/j.jcrimjus.2007.05.006

Bergseth, K. J., & Bouffard, J. A. (2012). Examining the Effectiveness of a Restorative Justice Program for Various Types of Juvenile Offenders. *International Journal of Offender Therapy and Comparative Criminology*, 57(9), 1054–1075. 10.1177/030 6624X1245355122811474

Boccio, C. M., & Beaver, K. M. (2017). The Influence of Family Structure on Delinquent Behavior. *Youth Violence and Juvenile Justice*, XX(X), 1–19.

Bonta, J., Wallace-Capretta, S., Rooney, J., & McAnoy, K. (2002). An outcome evaluation of a restorative justice alternative to incarceration. *Contemporary Justice Review*, 5(4), 319–338. 10.1080/10282580214772

Bradshaw, W., & Roseborough, D. (2005). Restorative justice dialogue: The impact of mediation and conferencing on juvenile recidivism. *Federal Probation*, 69(2), 15–21.

Brezina, T., & Agnew, R. (2015). *Juvenile Delinquency. Its Nature, Causes, and Control*. In E. Goode, (ed.) *The Handbook of Deviance*. Wiley.

Britt, C. L., & Gottfredson, M. R. (Eds.). (2003). *Control Theories of Crime and Delinquency*. Transaction.

Childs, K. K., Brady, C. M., Cameron, A. L. J., & Kaukinen, C. (2020). The Role of Family Structure and Family Process on Adolescent Problem Behavior. *Deviant Behavior*, 43(1), 1–16. 10.1080/01639625.2020.1771128

de Vries, S. L. A., Hoeve, M., Assink, M., Stams, G. J. M., & Asscher, J. J. (2015). Practitioner Review: Effective ingredients of prevention programs for youth at risk of persistent juvenile delinquency-recommendations for clinical practice. *Journal of Child Psychology and Psychiatry, and Allied Disciplines*, 56(2), 108–121. 10.1111/jcpp.1232025143121

Farrington, D. P., & Murray, J. (Eds.). (2013). *Labeling Theory: Empirical Tests*. Transaction.

Gupta, M. K., Mohapatra, S., & Mahanta, P. K. (2022). Juvenile's Delinquent Behavior, Risk Factors, and Quantitative Assessment Approach: A Systematic Review. *Indian Journal of Community Medicine*, 47(4), 483–490. 10.4103/ijcm.ijcm_1061_2136742966

Hadfield, K., Amos, M., Ungar, M., Gosselin, J., & Ganong, L. (2018). Do Changes to Family Structure Affect Child and Family Outcomes? A Systematic Review of the Instability Hypothesis. *Journal of Family Theory & Review*, 10(1), 87–110. 10.1111/jftr.12243

Jacobs, B. A. (2010). Deterrence and deterrability. *Criminology*, 48(2), 417–441. 10.1111/j.1745-9125.2010.00191.x

Jacobsen, S. K., & Zaatut, A. (2020). Quantity or Quality? Assessing the Role of Household Structure and Parent-Child Relationship in Juvenile Delinquency. *Deviant Behavior*, 43(1), 30–43. 10.1080/01639625.2020.1774241

Kosmatos, K., & Martinis, M. (2021). Article 121. In: Charalabakis, A. *The New Criminal Code* (law N. 4609/2019), 991-1003.

Kraus, J. (2000). Causes of Delinquency as Perceived by Juveniles. *International Journal of Offender Therapy and Comparative Criminology*, 79–86.

Latimer, J., Dowden, C., & Muise, D. (2005). The effectiveness of restorative justice practices: A meta-analysis. *The Prison Journal*, 85(2), 127–144. 10.1177/0032885505276969

Latimer, J., & Kleinknecht, S. (2000). *The effects of restorative justice programming: A review of the empirical research.* Department of Justice Canada, Research and Statistics Division.

Magnuson, K., & Berger, L. M. (2009). Family structure states and transitions: Associations with children's well-being during middle childhood. *Journal of Marriage and Family*, 71(3), 575–591. 10.1111/j.1741-3737.2009.00620.x20228952

Margari, F., Craig, F., Margari, L., Matera, E., Lamanna, A. L., Lecce, P. A., La Tegola, D., & Carabellese, F. (2015). Psychopathology, symptoms of attention-deficit/hyperactivity disorder, and risk factors in juvenile offenders. *Neuropsychiatric Disease and Treatment*, 11, 343–352. 10.2147/NDT.S7594225709458

May, J., Osmond, K., & Billick, St. (2014). Juvenile Delinquency Treatment and Prevention: A Litterature Review. *The Psychiatric Quarterly*, 85(3), 295–301. 10.1007/s11126-014-9296-424610601

McCold, P., & Wachtel, B. (1998). *Restorative policing experiment: The Bethlehem Pennsylvania, Police Family Group Conferencing Project.* Community Service Foundation.

Mwangangi, R. M. (2019). The Role of Family in Dealing with Juvenile Delinquency. *Journal of Social Sciences*, 7, 52–63.

Niemeyer, M., & Shichor, D. (1996). A preliminary study of a large victim/offender reconciliation program. *Federal Probation*, 60, 30–34.

Nisar, M., Ullah, S., Ali, M., & Alam, S. (2015). Juvenile Delinquency: The Influence of Family, Peer and Economic Factors of Juvenile Delinquents. *Applied Scientific Research*, 9(1), 37–48.

Nugent, W., Williams, M., & Umbreit, M. (2003). Participation in victim-offender mediation and the prevalence and severity of subsequent delinquent behavior: A meta-analysis. *Utah Law Review*, 137(1), 137–166.

Nugent, W., Williams, M., & Umbreit, M. (2004). Participation in victim-offender mediation and the prevalence of subsequent delinquent behavior: A meta-analysis. *Research on Social Work Practice*, 14(6), 408–416. 10.1177/1049731504265831

Pavlacic, J. M., Kellum, K. K., & Schulenberg, St. E. (2021). Advocating for the Use of Restorative Justice Practices: Examining the Overlap between Restorative Justice and Behavior Analysis. *Behavior Analysis in Practice*, 1–10.34457213

Rathinabalan, I., & Naaraayan, S. A. (2017). Effect of family factors on juvenile delinquency. *International Journal of Contemporary Pediatrics*, 4(6), 2079–2082. 10.18203/2349-3291.ijcp20174735

Roy, S. (1993). Two types of juvenile restitution programs in two Midwestern counties: A comparative study. *Federal Probation*, 57, 48–53.

Schepers, D. (2016). Causes of the causes of juvenile delinquency: Social disadvantages in the context of Situational Action Theory. *European Journal of Criminology*, 1–17.

Song, C., Benin, M., & Glick, J. (2012). Dropping Out of High School: The Effects of Family Structure and Family Transitions. *Journal of Divorce & Remarriage*, 53(1), 18–33. 10.1080/10502556.2012.635964

Wikström, P.-O. (2006). Individuals, settings, and acts of crime: Situational mechanisms and the explanation of crime. In Wikström, P.-O., & Sampson, R. J. (Eds.), *The Explanation of Crime* (pp. 61–108). Cambridge University Press. 10.1017/CBO9780511489341.004

Wikström, P.-O. (2009). Crime propensity, criminogenic exposure and crime involvement in early to mid-adolescence. *Monatsschrift fur Kriminologie und Strafrechtsreform*, 92(2-3), 253–266. 10.1515/mks-2009-922-312

Wikström, P.-O., Oberwittler, D., Treiber, K., & Hardie, B. (2012). *Breaking Rules. The Social and Situational Dynamics of Young People's Urban Crime*. Oxford University Press.

Compilation of References

Abbeduto, L., Keller-Bell, Y., Richmond, E., & Murphy, M. M. (2006). Research on language development and mental retardation: History, theories, findings, and future directions. *International Review of Research in Mental Retardation*, 32, 1–39. DOI:10.1016/S0074-7750(06)32001-0

Abbeduto, L., & Murphy, M. M. (2004). Language, social cognition, maladaptive behavior, and communication in Down syndrome and fragile X syndrome. In Rice, M. L., & Warren, S. F. (Eds.), *Developmental language disorders: From phenotypes to etiologies* (pp. 77–97). Lawrence Erlbaum Associates Publishers.

Aberson, B., Shure, M. B., & Goldstein, S. (2007). Social problem-solving intervention can help children with ADHD. *Journal of Attention Disorders*, 12(5), 391–393. DOI:10.1177/1087054707299409 PMID:17606767

Abidin, R. R. (1992). The determinants of parenting behavior. *Journal of Clinical Child Psychology*, 21(4), 407–412. DOI:10.1207/s15374424jccp2104_12

Abikoff, H., Hechtman, L., Klein, R., Weiss, G., Fleiss, K., Etcovitch, J., Cousins, L., Greenfield, B., Martin, D., & Pollack, S. (2004). Symptomatic improvement in children with ADHD treated with long-term methylphenidate and multimodal psychosocial treatment. *Journal of the American Academy of Child and Adolescent Psychiatry*, 43(7), 802–811. DOI:10.1097/01.chi.0000128791.10014.ac PMID:15213581

Abtahi, M. M., & Kerns, K. A. (2017). Attachment and emotion regulation in middle childhood: Changes in affect and vagal tone during a social stress task. *Attachment & Human Development*, 19(3), 221–242. DOI:10.1080/14616734.2017.1291696 PMID:28277093

Adams, D. (2022). Child and parental mental health as correlates of school non-attendance and school refusal in children on the autism spectrum. *Journal of Autism and Developmental Disorders*, 52(8), 2253–3365. DOI:10.1007/s10803-021-05211-5 PMID:34331173

Agnew, R. (2007). *Pressured Into Crime: An Overview of General Strain Theory*. University Press.

Ahn, S., & Fedewa, A. L. (2011). A meta-analysis of the relationship between children's physical activity and mental health. *Journal of Pediatric Psychology*, 36(4), 385–397. DOI:10.1093/jpepsy/jsq107 PMID:21227908

Akers, R. L. (1998). *Social Learning and Social Structure: A General Theory of Crime*. Northeastern University Press.

Akers, R. L., & Sellers, C. S. (2012). *Criminological Theories*. Oxford University Press.

Akhtar, F., & Bokhari, R. A. S. (2023). *Down Syndrome*. StatPearls. https://pubmed.ncbi.nlm.nih.gov/30252272/

Al Ghamdi, K., & AlMusailhi, J. (2024). Attention-deficit Hyperactivity Disorder and Autism Spectrum Disorder: Towards Better Diagnosis and Management. *Medical archives (Sarajevo, Bosnia and Herzegovina), 78*(2), 159–163. https://doi.org/DOI: 10.5455/medarh.2024.78.159-163

Albajara Sáenz, A., Septier, M., Van Schuerbeek, P., Baijot, S., Deconinck, N., Defresne, P., Delvenne, V., Passeri, G., Raeymaekers, H., Salvesen, L., Victoor, L., Villemonteix, T., Willaye, E., Peigneux, P., & Massat, I. (2020). ADHD and ASD: Distinct brain patterns of inhibition-related activation? *Translational Psychiatry*, 10(1), 24. DOI:10.1038/s41398-020-0707-z PMID:32066671

Albaugh, M. D., Orr, C., Chaarani, B., Althoff, R. R., Allgaier, N., D'Alberto, N., Hudson, K., Mackey, S., Spechler, P. A., Banaschewski, T., Brühl, R., Bokde, A. L. W., Bromberg, U., Büchel, C., Cattrell, A., Conrod, P. J., Desrivières, S., Flor, H., Frouin, V., & Potter, A. S. (2017). Inattention and Reaction Time Variability Are Linked to Ventromedial Prefrontal Volume in Adolescents. *Biological Psychiatry*, 82(9), 660–668. DOI:10.1016/j.biopsych.2017.01.003 PMID:28237458

Alderson, R. M., Rapport, M. D., Sarver, D. E., & Kofler, M. J. (2008). ADHD and behavioral inhibition: A re-examination of the stop-signal task. *Journal of Abnormal Child Psychology*, 36(7), 989–998. DOI:10.1007/s10802-008-9230-z PMID:18461439

Alevriadou, A., & Giaouri, S. (2011). Second-order Mental State Attribution in Children with Intellectual Disability: Cognitive Functioning and Some Educational Planning Challenges. *Journal of Educational and Developmental Psychology, 1*(1), 146-153. https://doi:. v1n1p146DOI:10.5539/jedp

Allen, B., & Lauterbach, D. (2007). Personality characteristics of adult survivors of childhood trauma. *Journal of Traumatic Stress*, 20(4), 587–595. DOI:10.1002/jts.20195 PMID:17721954

Alloway, T. P., & Passolunghi, M. C. (2011). The relationship between working memory, IQ, and mathematical skills in children. *Learning and Individual Differences*, 21(1), 133–137. DOI:10.1016/j.lindif.2010.09.013

Alsaedi, H. R., Carrington, S., & Watters, J. J. (2020). Behavioral and Neuropsychological Evaluation of Executive Functions in Children with Autism Spectrum Disorder in the Gulf Region. *Brain Sciences*, 10(2), 120–141. DOI:10.3390/brainsci10020120 PMID:32098341

Alsayouf, H. A., Talo, H., Biddappa, M. L., & De Los Reyes, E. (2021). Risperidone or aripiprazole can resolve autism core signs and symptoms in young Children: Case study. *Children (Basel, Switzerland)*, 8(5), 318. DOI:10.3390/children8050318 PMID:33921933

Altrichter, H., Posch, P., & Somekh, B. (2001). *Teachers research their work. An introduction to the methods of action research* (Deligiannis, M., Trans.). Metaichmio.

Al-Yagon, M., & Margalit, M. (2016). Specific learning disorder. In Levesque, R. J. R. (Ed.), *Encyclopedia of Adolescence* (pp. 1–6). Springer International Publishing. DOI:10.1007/978-3-319-32132-5_806-1

Amadó, A., Sidera, F., & Serrat, E. (2022). Affective and cognitive theory of mind in children with Down syndrome: A brief report. *International Journal of Disability Development and Education*. DOI:10.1080/1034912X.2022.2095355

Aman, M. G., Novotny, S., Samango-Sprouse, C., Lecavalier, L., Leonard, E., Gadow, K. D., King, B. H., Pearson, D. A., Gernsbacher, M. A., & Chez, M. (2004). Outcome measures for clinical drug trials in autism. *CNS Spectrums*, 9(1), 36–47. DOI:10.1017/S1092852900008348 PMID:14999174

American Psychiatric Association, DSM-5 Task Force. (2013). *Diagnostic and statistical manual of mental disorders: DSM-5* (5th ed.). American Psychiatric Publishing, Inc., DOI:10.1176/appi.books.9780890425596

American Psychiatric Association. (2013). *Diagnostic and Statistical Manual of Mental Disorders* (4th Edn. Text Revision). American Psychiatric Publishing.

American Psychiatric Association. (2013). *Diagnostic and statistical manual of mental disorders (DSM-5)*. American Psychiatric Association Publishing.

American Psychiatric Association. (2013). *Diagnostic and statistical manual of mental disorders: DSM-5* (*Vol. 5*, No. 5). American psychiatric association.

American Psychiatric Association. (2022). *Diagnostic and statistical manual of mental disorders* (5th ed., text rev.). APA. DOI:10.1176/appi.books.9780890425787

American Psychiatric Association. (2024). *APA dictionary of psychology*. American Psychological Association. https://dictionary.apa.org/

American Psychiatry Association. (2013). Diagnostic and Statistical Manual of Mental Disorders, (5th Edition). DSM-V, Washington: DC.

Amnesty International. (2004). *It's in our hands: Stop violence against women.* Alden Press.

Anastopoulos, A. D., Shelton, T. L., DuPaul, G. J., & Guevremont, D. C. (1993). Parent training for attention-deficit hyperactivity disorder: Its impact on parent functioning. *Journal of Abnormal Child Psychology*, 21(5), 581–596. DOI:10.1007/BF00916320 PMID:8294653

Anderson, S., Taras, M., & Cannon, B. (1996). Teaching new skills to young children with autism. In C. Maurice, G. Green, S. Luce (Eds), *Behavioral intervention for young children with autism: A manual for parents and professionals* (pp. 181-194) Austin, TX: pro-ed publications.

Anderson, C. A., Shibuya, A., Ihori, N., Swing, E. L., Bushman, B. J., Sakamoto, A., Rothstein, H. R., & Saleem, M. (2010). Violent video game effects on aggression, empathy, and prosocial behavior in Eastern and Western countries: A meta-analytic review. *Psychological Bulletin*, 136(2), 151–173. DOI:10.1037/a0018251 PMID:20192553

Anderson, E. (1999). *Code of the Street*. W.W. Norton.

Anderson, P. J., & Doyle, L. W. (2004). Executive Functioning in School-Aged Children Who Were Born Very Preterm or With Extremely Low Birth Weight in the 1990s. *Pediatrics*, 114(1), 50–57. DOI:10.1542/peds.114.1.50 PMID:15231907

Ando, J., Ono, Y., & Wright, M. J. (2001, November). Genetic structure of spatial and verbal working memory. *Behavior Genetics*, 31(6), 615–624. DOI:10.1023/A:1013353613591 PMID:11838538

Angeline, J., Rathnasabapathy, M., & Taylor, G. (2023). Role of Perceived Social Support in the Relationship between Parenting Stress and Psychological Well-Being of Mothers of Children with ADHD: A Mediation Model. *Universal Journal of Public Health*, 11(6), 838–844. DOI:10.13189/ujph.2023.110607

Annor, F. B., Amene, E. W., Zhu, L., Stamatakis, C., Picchetti, V., Matthews, S., Miedema, S. S., Brown, C., Thorsen, V. C., Manuel, P., Gilbert, L. K., Kambona, C., Coomer, R., Trika, J., Kamuingona, R., Dube, S. R., & Massetti, G. M. (2024). Parental absence as an adverse childhood experience among young adults in sub-Saharan Africa. *Child Abuse & Neglect*, 150, 106556. DOI:10.1016/j.chiabu.2023.106556 PMID:37993366

Ansari, A., & Winsler, A. (2012). School readiness among low-income, Latino children attending family childcare versus centre-based care. *Early Child Development and Care*, 182(11), 1465–1485. DOI:10.1080/03004430.2011.622755

Antshel, K. M., & Russo, N. (2019). Autism Spectrum Disorders and ADHD: Overlapping Phenomenology, Diagnostic Issues, and Treatment Considerations. *Current Psychiatry Reports*, 21(5), 34. DOI:10.1007/s11920-019-1020-5 PMID:30903299

Apel, A. B., & Diller, J. W. (2017). Prison as punishment: A behavior- analytic evaluation of incarceration. *The Behavior Analyst*, 40(1), 243–256. DOI:10.1007/s40614-016-0081-6 PMID:31976937

Arain, M., Haque, M., Johal, L., Mathur, P., Nel, W., Rais, A., Sandhu, R., & Sharma, S. (2013). Maturation of the adolescent brain. *Neuropsychiatric Disease and Treatment*, 449, 449. DOI:10.2147/NDT.S39776 PMID:23579318

Archer, J. (2000). Sex differences in aggression between heterosexual partners: A meta-analytic review. *Psychological Bulletin*, 126(5), 651–680. DOI:10.1037/0033-2909.126.5.651 PMID:10989615

Archer, J. (2002). Sex differences in physically aggressive acts between heterosexual partners: A meta- analytic review. *Aggression and Violent Behavior*, 7(4), 313–351. DOI:10.1016/S1359-1789(01)00061-1

Argyriadis, A., Efthymiou, E., & Argyriadi, A. (2023). Cultural Competence at Schools: The Effectiveness of Educational Leaders' Intervention Strategies. In *Inclusive Phygital Learning Approaches and Strategies for Students With Special Needs* (pp. 33-51). IGI Global.

Argyriadis, A., & Argyriadi, A. (2024). Societal attitudes towards psychiatric patients, medication, and the antipsychiatric movement within the context of theoretical approaches and inclusion initiatives. The role of mental health professionals. *GSC Advanced Research and Reviews*, 18(2), 381–387. DOI:10.30574/gscarr.2024.18.2.0075

Arnsten, F. T. A. (2009). The Emerging Neurobiology of Attention Deficit Hyperactivity Disorder: The Key Role of the Prefrontal Association Cortex. *The Journal of Pediatrics*, 154(5), I-S43. DOI:10.1016/j.jpeds.2009.01.018 PMID:20596295

Ashburner, J., Ziviani, J., & Rodger, S. (2010). Sensory processing and classroom emotional, behavioral, and educational outcomes in children with autism spectrum disorder. *American Journal of Occupational Therapy, 64*(3), 376-387. DOI:10.5014/ajot.2010.09071

Asher, S. R., & Paquette, J. A. (2003). Loneliness and peer relations in childhood. *Current Directions in Psychological Science*, 12(3), 75–78. DOI:10.1111/1467-8721.01233

Asher, S. R., Parkhurst, J. T., Hymel, S., & Williams, G. A. (1990). Peer rejection and loneliness in childhood. In Asher, S. R., & Coie, J. D. (Eds.), *Peer rejection in childhood* (pp. 253–273). Cambridge University Press.

Asher, S. R., & Wheeler, V. A. (1985). Children's loneliness: A comparison of rejected and neglected peer status. *Journal of Consulting and Clinical Psychology*, 53(4), 500–505. DOI:10.1037/0022-006X.53.4.500 PMID:4031205

Astington, J. W., & Baird, J. A. (Eds.). (2005). *Why language matters for theory of mind*. Oxford University Press. DOI:10.1093/acprof:oso/9780195159912.001.0001

Atkins, M. S., Frazier, S. L., Adil, J. A., Talbott, E. M., Bettencourt, A. F., & Marinez-Lora, A. M. (2010). Adopting a model of partnership-based health services to urban schools: What do we need to know? *School Mental Health, 2*(3), 133-144. https://doi.org/DOI:10.1007/s12310-010-9035-6

Aubé, B., Follenfant, A., Goudeau, S., & Derguy, C. (2020). Public stigma of autism spectrum disorder at school: Implicit attitudes matter. *Journal of Autism and Developmental Disorders*, 51(5), 1584–1597. DOI:10.1007/s10803-020-04635-9 PMID:32780195

Avgitidou, S. (2001). Children's Play: exploring children's collaborative world-building in early childhood education. In Avgitidou, S. (Ed.), *The Game. Contemporary Research and Teaching Approaches* (pp. 159–174). Typothito-G. Dardanus.

Avgitidou, S., Tzekaki, M., & Tsafos, V. (2016). *Enhancing children's learning: Signification and play in Pre-service teachers observe, intervene and reflect*. Gutenberg.

Badger, J. R., Zaneva, M., Hastings, R. P., Broome, M. R., Hayes, R., Patterson, P., Rose, N., Clarkson, S., Hutchings, J., & Bowes, L. (2023). Associations between School-Level Disadvantage, Bullying Involvement and Children's Mental Health. *Children (Basel, Switzerland)*, 10(12), 1852. DOI:10.3390/children10121852 PMID:38136054

Bakker, M., Heugten, C. M., & Verhey, F. R. (2019). Assistive technology in dementia care: A systematic review of effects and effectiveness. *Journal of the American Medical Directors Association*, 20(1), 71–81.

Baldo, M. V., Cravo, A. M., & Haddad, H. (2007). The time of perception and the other way around. *The Spanish Journal of Psychology*, 10(2), 258–265. DOI:10.1017/S1138741600006521 PMID:17992952

Baldwin, S., Costley, D., & Warren, A. (2014). Employment activities and experiences of adults with high-functioning autism and Asperger's Disorder. *Journal of Autism and Developmental Disorders*, 44(10), 2440–2449. DOI:10.1007/s10803-014-2112-z PMID:24715257

Bandelow, B., & Michaelis, S. (2015). Epidemiology of anxiety disorders in the 21st century. *Dialogues in Clinical Neuroscience*, 17(3), 327–335. DOI:10.31887/DCNS.2015.17.3/bbandelow PMID:26487813

Bandura, A., Ross, D., & Ross, S. A. (1961). Transmission of aggression through imitation of aggressive models. *Journal of Abnormal and Social Psychology*, 63(3), 575–582. DOI:10.1037/h0045925 PMID:13864605

Baragash, R. S., Al-Samarraie, H., Alzahrani, A. I., & Alfarraj, O. (2020). Augmented reality in special education: A meta-analysis of single-subject design studies. *European Journal of Special Needs Education*, 35(3), 382–397. DOI:10.1080/08856257.2019.1703548

Barends, E. M., Hendriks, M. P. H., Jansen, J., Backers, W., & Hofman, P. (2013). Working memory deficits in high functioning adolescents with autism spectrum disorders: Neuropsychological and neuroimaging correlates. *Journal of Neurodevelopmental Disorders*, 14(1), 1–11. DOI:10.1186/1866-1955-5-14

Barkley, R. (2005). *Taking Charge of AD/HD: The complete, authoritative guide for parents* (Rev.ed.). Guilford.

Barkley, R. A. (2003). Attention-Deficit / Hyperactivity Disorder. In Mash, E. J., & Barkley, R. A. (Eds.), *Child Psychopathology* (2nd ed., pp. 75–143). The Guilford Press.

Barkley, R. A. (2010). Differential diagnosis of adults with ADHD: The role of executive function and self-regulation. *The Journal of Clinical Psychiatry*, 71(1), e17. DOI:10.4088/JCP.9066tx1c PMID:20667287

Barkley, R. A. (2015). Executive functioning and self-regulation viewed as an extended phenotype: Implications of the theory for ADHD and its treatment. In Barkley, R. A. (Ed.), *Attention deficit hyperactivity disorder: A handbook for diagnosis and treatment* (4th ed., pp. 405–434). Guilford.

Barkley, R. B. (1987). *Defiant children: A clinician manual for parent training*. Guilford Press.

Barnes, C., & Sheldon, A. (2010). *Rethinking disability policy*. Longman.

Baron-Cohen, S. (1992). Out of sight or out of mind? Another look at deception in autism. *Journal of Child Psychology and Psychiatry, and Allied Disciplines*, 33(7), 1141–1155. DOI:10.1111/j.1469-7610.1992.tb00934.x PMID:1400697

Baron-Cohen, S. (2002). The extreme male brain theory of autism. *Trends in Cognitive Sciences*, 6(6), 248–254. DOI:10.1016/S1364-6613(02)01904-6 PMID:12039606

Baron-Cohen, S. (2006). The hyper-systemizing, assortative mating theory of autism. *Progress in Neuro-Psychopharmacology & Biological Psychiatry*, 30(5), 865–872. DOI:10.1016/j.pnpbp.2006.01.010 PMID:16519981

Baron-Cohen, S., Leslie, A. M., & Frith, U. (1985). Does the autistic child have a "theory of mind"? *Cognition*, 21(1), 37–46. DOI:10.1016/0010-0277(85)90022-8 PMID:2934210

Baron-Cohen, S., O'Riordan, M., Stone, V., Jones, R., & Plaisted, K. (1999). Recognition of faux pas by normally developing children and children with Asperger syndrome or high-functioning autism. *Journal of Autism and Developmental Disorders*, 29(5), 407–418. DOI:10.1023/A:1023035012436 PMID:10587887

Baron, I. (2004a). Intelligence Testing: General Considerations. In *Neuropsychological Evaluation of the Child* (pp. 108–132). Oxford University Press.

Barreto, M., Victor, C., Hammond, C., Eccles, A., Richins, M. T., & Qualter, P. (2021). Loneliness around the world: Age, gender, and cultural differences in loneliness. *Personality and Individual Differences*, 169, 110066. DOI:10.1016/j.paid.2020.110066 PMID:33536694

Barsky, A. J. (1983). Overview: Hypochondriasis, bodily complaints, and somatic styles. *The American Journal of Psychiatry*. PMID:6338747

Barsky, A. J., Peekna, H. M., & Borus, J. F. (2001). Somatic symptom reporting in women and men. *Journal of General Internal Medicine*, 16(4), 266–275. DOI:10.1046/j.1525-1497.2001.016004266.x PMID:11318929

Bartsch, K., & Wellman, H. (1989). Young children's attribution of action to beliefs and desires. *Child Development*, 60(4), 946–964. DOI:10.2307/1131035 PMID:2758888

Battacchi, M. W., Celani, G., & Bertocchi, A. (1997). The influence of personal involvement on the performance in a false belief task: A structural analysis. *International Journal of Behavioral Development*, 21(2), 313–329. DOI:10.1080/016502597384893

Bauman, M. L., & Kemper, T. L. (Eds.). (2005). *The neurobiology of autism* (2nd ed.). Johns Hopkins University Press.

Baumrind, D. (1991). The influence of parenting style on adolescent competence and substance use. *The Journal of Early Adolescence*, 11(1), 56–95. DOI:10.1177/0272431691111004

Baurain, C., & Nader-Grosbois, N. (2013). Theory of mind, socio-emotional problem-solving, socio-emotional regulation in children with intellectual disability and in typically developing children. *Journal of Autism and Developmental Disorders*, 43(5), 1080–1097. DOI:10.1007/s10803-012-1651-4 PMID:22965300

Beauchamp, H. M. (2017). Neuropsychology's social landscape: Common ground with social neuroscience. *Neuropsychology*, 31(8), 981–1002. DOI:10.1037/neu0000395 PMID:29376673

Beauchamp, H. M., & Anderson, V. (2010). SOCIAL: An integrative framework for the development of social skills. *Psychological Bulletin*, 136(1), 39–64. DOI:10.1037/a0017768 PMID:20063925

Beaudoin, C., Leblanc, É., Gagner, C., & Beauchamp, M. H. (2020). Systematic review and inventory of theory of mind measures for young children. *Frontiers in Psychology*, 10, 2905. DOI:10.3389/fpsyg.2019.02905 PMID:32010013

Beaumont, S. (2024). *Correlation of adverse childhood experiences and somatic symptoms in adolescents.* [Thesis, CSUSB]. Electronic Theses, Projects, and Dissertations. https://scholarworks.lib.csusb.edu/etd/1964

Beauregard, J. L., Drews-Botsch, C., Sales, J. M., Flanders, W. D., & Kramer, M. R. (2018, January). Preterm Birth, Poverty, and Cognitive Development. *Pediatrics*, 141(1), e20170509. DOI:10.1542/peds.2017-0509 PMID:29242268

Beck, A., Steer, R., & Brown, G. (1996). Beck Depression Inventory (2nd ed.). E.U.: Psychological Corporation.

Beck, A. T., Epstein, N., Brown, G., & Steer, R. A. (1988). An inventory for measuring clinical anxiety: Psychometric properties. *Journal of Consulting and Clinical Psychology*, 56(6), 893–897. DOI:10.1037/0022-006X.56.6.893 PMID:3204199

Beesdo, K., Knappe, S., & Pine, D. S. (2009). Anxiety and anxiety disorders in children and adolescents: Developmental issues and implications for DSM-V. *Psychiatria Clinica*, 32(3), 483–524. DOI:10.1016/j.psc.2009.06.002 PMID:19716988

Beetham, J., & Okhai, L. (2017). Workplace Dyslexia & Specific Learning Difficulties-Productivity, Engagement and Well-Being. *Open Journal of Social Sciences*, 5(6), 56–78. DOI:10.4236/jss.2017.56007

Bellagamba, F., Laghi, F., Lonigro, A., Pace, C. S., & Longobardi, E. (2014). Concurrent relations between inhibitory control, sarcasm, and advanced theory of mind understanding in children and adults with prelingual deafness. *Developmental Psychology*, 50(7), 1862–1877. DOI:10.1037/a0036654

Belsky, J. (2019). *Experiencing the Lifespan* (5th ed.). Worth.

Bennie, M. (2018, March 19). *Executive function: what is it, and how do we support it in those with autism? Part I.* Autism Awareness Centre. https://autismawarenesscentre.com/

Bento, G., & Dias, G. (2017). The importance of outdoor play for young children's healthy development. *Porto Biomedical Journal*, 2(5), 157–160. DOI:10.1016/j.pbj.2017.03.003 PMID:32258612

Berenz, E. C., Amstadter, A. B., Aggen, S. H., Knudsen, G. P., Reichborn-Kjennerud, T., Gardner, C. O., & Kendler, K. S. (2013). Childhood trauma and personality disorder criterion counts: A co-twin control analysis. *Journal of Abnormal Psychology*, 122(4), 1070–1076. DOI:10.1037/a0034238 PMID:24364608

Berger, K. S. (2014). *Invitation to the Life Span* (2nd ed.). Worth Publishers.

Bergeson, T., Davidson, C., Mueller, M., & Williams-Appleton, D. (2008). *A Guide to Assessment in Early Childhood: Infancy to Age Eight*. Washington State Office of Superintendent of Public Instruction.

Bergeth, K. J., & Bouffard, J. A. (2007). The long-term impact of restorative justice programming for juvenile offenders. *Journal of Criminal Justice*, 35(4), 433–451. DOI:10.1016/j.jcrimjus.2007.05.006

Bergseth, K. J., & Bouffard, J. A. (2012). Examining the Effectiveness of a Restorative Justice Program for Various Types of Juvenile Offenders. *International Journal of Offender Therapy and Comparative Criminology*, 57(9), 1054–1075. DOI:10.1177/0306624X12453551 PMID:22811474

Berk, E. L. (2013). *Child Development* (9th ed.). Pearson.

Betta Olivares, R., Morales Messerer, G., Rodríguez Ureta, K., & Guerra Vio, C. (2007). La frecuencia de emisión de conductas de autocuidado y su relación con los niveles de estrés traumático secundario y de depresión en psicólogos clínicos. *Pensam. Psicológico, 3.*

Beversdorf, D. Q., Stevens, H. E., & Jones, K. L. (2018). Prenatal stress, maternal immune dysregulation, and their association with autism spectrum disorders. *Current Psycchiatry Reports. Current Psychiatry Reports*, 20(9), 76. DOI:10.1007/s11920-018-0945-4 PMID:30094645

Biederman, J., Fried, R., Petty, C. R., Mahoney, L., & Faraone, S. V. (2012). The effects of ADHD on the functional outcomes of adults with ADHD. *Journal of Psychiatric Research*, 46(1), 73–78.

Biegel, G. M., Brown, K. W., Shapiro, S. L., & Schubert, C. M. (2009). Mindfulness-based stress reduction for the treatment of adolescent psychiatric outpatients: A randomized clinical trial. *Journal of Consulting and Clinical Psychology, 77*(5), 855-866. DOI:10.1037/a0016241

Bierman, K. L., Coie, J., Dodge, K., Greenberg, M., Lochman, J., McMohan, R., & Pinderhughes, E. (2013). School Outcomes of Aggressive-Disruptive Children: Prediction from Kindergarten risk factors and impact of the Fast Track Prevention Program. *Aggressive Behavior*, 39(2), 114–130. DOI:10.1002/ab.21467 PMID:23386568

Bishop, D. (1993). Annotation: Autism, Executive Functions and Theory of Mind: A Neuropsychological Perspective. *Journal of Child Psychology and Psychiatry, and Allied Disciplines*, 34(3), 279–293. DOI:10.1111/j.1469-7610.1993.tb00992.x PMID:8463368

Bishop-Fitzpatrick, L., Minshew, N. J., & Eack, S. M. (2017). A systematic review of psychosocial interventions for adults with autism spectrum disorders. *Journal of Autism and Developmental Disorders, 43*(3), 687-694. DOI:10.1007/s10803-012-1615-8

Bjornstad, G. J., & Montgomery, P. (2005). Family therapy for attention-deficit disorder or attention-deficit/hyperactivity disorder in children and adolescents. *Cochrane Database of Systematic Reviews.* DOI:10.1002/14651858.CD005042.pub2 PMID:15846741

Blackman, J. A. (1999). Attention-deficit/hyperactivity disorder in preschoolers: Does it exist and should we treat it? *Pediatric Clinics of North America*, 46(5), 1011–1025. DOI:10.1016/S0031-3955(05)70169-3 PMID:10570702

Black, P., & Wiliam, D. (1998). Assessment and classroom learning. *Assessment in Education: Principles, Policy & Practice*, 5(1), 7–74. DOI:10.1080/0969595980050102

Blair, C., & Raver, C. C. (2014). School Readiness and Self-Regulation: A Developmental Psychobiological Approach. *Annual Review of Psychology*, 66(1), 711–731. DOI:10.1146/annurev-psych-010814-015221 PMID:25148852

Blijd-Hoogewys, E. M. A., Bezemer, M. L., & Van Geert, P. L. C. (2014). Executive Functioning in Children with ASD: An Analysis of the BRIEF. *Journal of Autism and Developmental Disorders*, 44(12), 3089–3100. DOI:10.1007/s10803-014-2176-9 PMID:24996868

Bluth, K., & Blanton, P. W. (2015). Mindfulness and self-compassion: Exploring pathways to adolescent emotional well-being. *Journal of Child and Family Studies, 24*(9), 2345-2356. https://doi.org/DOI:10.1007/s10826-014-0037-8

Boccio, C. M., & Beaver, K. M. (2017). The Influence of Family Structure on Delinquent Behavior. *Youth Violence and Juvenile Justice*, XX(X), 1–19.

Boedhoe, P. S. W., van Rooij, D., Hoogman, M., Twisk, J. W. R., Schmaal, L., Abe, Y., Alonso, P., Ameis, S. H., Anikin, A., Anticevic, A., Arango, C., Arnold, P. D., Asherson, P., Assogna, F., Auzias, G., Banaschewski, T., Baranov, A., Batistuzzo, M. C., Baumeister, S., & van den Heuvel, O. A. (2020). Subcortical brain volume, regional cortical thickness, and cortical surface area across disorders: Findings from the ENIGMA ADHD, ASD, and OCD working groups. *The American Journal of Psychiatry*, 177(9), 834–843. DOI:10.1176/appi.ajp.2020.19030331 PMID:32539527

Bögels, S. M., Lehtonen, A., & Restifo, K. (2010). Mindful parenting in mental health care. *Mindfulness*, 1(2), 107–120. DOI:10.1007/s12671-010-0014-5 PMID:21125026

Bolte, S., & Poustka, F. (2004). Comparing the Intelligence Profiles of Savant and Nonsavant Individuals with Autistic Disorder. *Intelligence*, 32(2), 121–131. DOI:10.1016/j.intell.2003.11.002

Bolton, T. L. (1902). A biological view of perception. *Psychological Review*, 9(6), 537–548. DOI:10.1037/h0071504

Bonta, J., Wallace-Capretta, S., Rooney, J., & McAnoy, K. (2002). An outcome evaluation of a restorative justice alternative to incarceration. *Contemporary Justice Review*, 5(4), 319–338. DOI:10.1080/10282580214772

Börnert-Ringleb, M., & Wilbert, J. (2018). The Association of Strategy Use and Concrete-Operational Thinking in Primary School. *Frontiers in Education*, 3, 1–11. DOI:10.3389/feduc.2018.00038

Botschek, T., Monninger, M., Schäfer, D., Cevik, R., Memis, K., Müller, U., Monninger, M., & Brosig, B. (2023). Evaluation of multidimensional pediatric-psychosomatic inpatient therapy: A pilot study comparing two treatment modalities. *Frontiers in Psychology*, 14, 1022409. DOI:10.3389/fpsyg.2023.1022409 PMID:37346420

Bourchier, A., & Davis, A. (2010). Individual and developmental differences in children's understanding of the fantasy-reality distinction. *British Journal of Developmental Psychology*, 18(3), 353–368. DOI:10.1348/026151000165742

Braaten, E. B., Ward, A. K., Forchelli, G., Vuijk, P. J., Cook, N. E., McGuinness, P., Lee, B. A., Samkavitz, A., Lind, H., O'Keefe, S. M., & Doyle, A. E. (2020). Characteristics of child psychiatric outpatients with slow processing speed and potential mechanisms of academic impact. *European Child & Adolescent Psychiatry*, 29(10), 1453–1464. DOI:10.1007/s00787-019-01455-w PMID:31980930

Braconnier, L. M., & Siper, M. P. (2021). Neuropsychological Assessment in Autism Spectrum Disorder. *Current Psychiatry Reports*, 23(10), 63. DOI:10.1007/s11920-021-01277-1 PMID:34331144

Bradshaw, W., & Roseborough, D. (2005). Restorative justice dialogue: The impact of mediation and conferencing on juvenile recidivism. *Federal Probation*, 69(2), 15–21.

Braverman, Y., Edmunds, S. R., Hastedt, I., & Faja, S. (2024). Mind the Gap: Executive Function Is Associated with the Discrepancy Between Cognitive and Adaptive Functioning in Autistic Children Without Cognitive Delay. *Journal of Autism and Developmental Disorders*. DOI:10.1007/s10803-024-06354-x PMID:38778001

Brede, J., Remington, A., Kenny, L., Warren, K., & Pellicano, E. (2017). Excluded from school: Autistic students' experiences of school exclusion and subsequent re-integration into school. *Autism & Developmental Language Impairments*, 2, 1–20. DOI:10.1177/2396941517737511

Breslau, N., Kessler, R. C., Chilcoat, H. D., Schultz, L. R., Davis, G. C., & Andreski, P. (1998). Trauma and posttraumatic stress disorder in the community: The 1996 detroit area survey of trauma. *Archives of General Psychiatry*, 55(7), 626–632. DOI:10.1001/archpsyc.55.7.626 PMID:9672053

Brezina, T., & Agnew, R. (2015). *Juvenile Delinquency. Its Nature, Causes, and Control*. In E. Goode, (ed.) *The Handbook of Deviance*. Wiley.

Britt, C. L., & Gottfredson, M. R. (Eds.). (2003). *Control Theories of Crime and Delinquency*. Transaction.

Broadfoot, P. M., Daugherty, R., Gardner, J., Gipps, C. V., Harlen, W., James, M., & Stobart, G. (1999). *Assessment for learning: beyond the black box*. University of Cambridge School of Education.

Bronfenbrenner, U., & Evans, G. W. (2000). Developmental science in the 21st century: Emerging questions, theoretical models, research designs and empirical findings. *Social Development*, 9(1), 115–125. DOI:10.1111/1467-9507.00114

Bronfenbrenner, U., & Morris, P. (2006). The bioecological model of human development. In Damon, W., & Lerner, R. (Eds.), (pp. 793–828). Handbook of child psychology. John Wiley & Sons.

Brookman-Frazee, L., Stahmer, A., Baker-Ericzén, M., & Tsai, K. (2009). Parenting interventions for children with autism spectrum and disruptive behavior disorders: Opportunities for cross-fertilization. *Clinical Child and Family Psychology Review,* 9(3-4), 181-200. https://doi.org/DOI:10.1007/s10567-006-0006-4

Brookman-Frazee, L., Stadnick, N., Chlebowski, C., Baker-Ericzén, M., & Ganger, W. (2018). Characterizing psychiatric comorbidity in children with autism spectrum disorder receiving publicly funded mental health services. *Autism*, 22(8), 938–952. DOI:10.1177/1362361317712650 PMID:28914082

Brown, A. K., Parikh, S., & Patel, R. D. (2020). Understanding basic concepts of developmental diagnosis in children. *Translational Pediatrics*, 9(1), 9–22. DOI:10.21037/tp.2019.11.04 PMID:32206580

Brudey, C., Park, J., Wiaderkiewicz, J., Kobayashi, I., Mellman, T., & Marvar, P. (2015). Autonomic and inflammatory consequences of posttraumatic stress disorder and the link to cardiovascular disease. *American Journal of Physiology. Regulatory, Integrative and Comparative Physiology*, 309(4), 315–321. DOI:10.1152/ajpregu.00343.2014 PMID:26062635

Buchbinder, E., & Eisikovits, Z. (2003). Battered women's entrapment in shame: A phenomenological study. *The American Journal of Orthopsychiatry*, 73(4), 355–366. DOI:10.1037/0002-9432.73.4.355 PMID:14609398

Bundick, M. J. (2011). Extracurricular activities, positive youth development, and the role of meaningfulness of engagement. *The Journal of Positive Psychology*, 6(1), 57–74. DOI:10.1080/17439760.2010.536775

Burack, J. A., Evans, D. W., Klaiman, C., & Larocci, G. (2001). The mysterious myth of attention deficits and other defect stories: Contemporary issues in the developmental approach to mental retardation. *International Review of Research in Mental Retardation*, 24, 299–320. DOI:10.1016/S0074-7750(01)80012-4

Burgstahler, S., & Doe, T. (2006). Disability-related simulations: If, when, and how to use them in professional development. *Review of Disability Studies: An International Journal, 2*(2), 4-18.

Burke, L. A., & Williams, J. M. (2012). The impact of a thinking skills intervention on children's concepts of intelligence. *Thinking Skills and Creativity*, 7(3), 145–152. DOI:10.1016/j.tsc.2012.01.001

Burke, N. N., Finn, D. P., McGuire, B. E., & Roche, M. (2016). Psychological stress in early life as a predisposing factor for the development of chronic pain: Clinical and preclinical evidence and neurobiological mechanisms. *Journal of Neuroscience Research*, 95(6), 1257–1270. DOI:10.1002/jnr.23802 PMID:27402412

Burton, C. L., Wright, L., Shan, J., Xiao, B., Dupuis, A., Goodale, T., Shaheen, S.-M., Corfield, E. C., Arnold, P. D., Schachar, R. J., & Crosbie, J. (2019). SWAN scale for ADHD trait-based genetic research: a validity and polygenic risk study. *Journal of Child Psychology and Psychiatry and Allied Disciplines, 60*(9). https://doi.org/DOI:10.1111/jcpp.13032

Busch, , Moretti, F., Purgato, M., Barbui, C., Wu, A. W., & Rimondini, M. (2020). Psychological and Psychosomatic Symptoms of Second Victims of Adverse Events: A Systematic Review and Meta-Analysis. *Journal of Patient Safety*, 16(2), e61–e74. DOI:10.1097/PTS.0000000000000589 PMID:30921046

Bush, R. N., Wakschlag, S. L., LeWinn, Z. K., Hertz-Picciotto, I., Nozadi, S. S., Pieper, S., Lewis, J., Biezonski, D., Blair, C., Deardorff, J., Neiderhiser, M. J., Leve, D. L., Elliott, J. A., Duarte, S. C., Lugo-Candelas, C., O'Shea, M. T., Avalos, A. L., Page, P. G., & Posner, J. (2020). Family Environment, Neurodevelopmental Risk, and the Environmental Influences on Child Health Outcomes (ECHO) Initiative: Looking Back and Moving Forward. *Frontiers in Psychiatry*, 11(547), 1–17. DOI:10.3389/fpsyt.2020.00547 PMID:32636769

Bussu, G., Llera, A., Jones, E. J., Tye, C., Charman, T., Johnson, M. H., Beckmann, C. F., & Buitelaar, J. K. (2021). Uncovering neurodevelopmental paths to autism spectrum disorder through an integrated analysis of developmental measures and neural sensitivity to faces. *Journal of Psychiatry & Neuroscience*, 46(1), E34–E43. DOI:10.1503/jpn.190148 PMID:33009904

Buti, J., Glenny, A.-M., Worthington, H. V., Nieri, M., & Baccini, M. (2011). Network meta-analysis of randomised controlled trials: Direct and indirect treatment comparisons. *European Journal of Oral Implantology*, 4(1), 55–62. PMID:21594220

CAMHI. (2023). *Πρόγραμμα Νεανικής Συμμετοχής YES (Youth Engagement Scheme) - Δράσεις στα Σχολεία*. CAMHI.

CAMHI. (2023). *Ψυχική Υγεία Παιδιών και Εφήβων στην Ελλάδα: Ανάγκες και Προτεραιότητες. Συνοπτική Παρουσίαση μιας Ανάλυσης Πεδίου*. CAMHI.

Campbell, J., & Oliver, M. (2013). *Disability politics: Understanding our past, changing our future*. Routledge. DOI:10.4324/9780203410639

Cannon, W. B. (1929). *Bodily changes in Pain, Hunger, Fear and Rage*. New York, Appleton Century, Crofts Edit., Paris.

Cappe, E., Bolduc, M., Rougé, M. C., Saiag, M. C., & Delorme, R. (2017). Quality of life, psychological characteristics, and adjustment in parents of children with Attention-Deficit/Hyperactivity Disorder. *Quality of Life Research: An International Journal of Quality of Life Aspects of Treatment, Care and Rehabilitation*, 26(5), 1283–1294. DOI:10.1007/s11136-016-1446-8 PMID:27798755

Carlsson, T., Molander, F., Taylor, M. J., Jonsson, U., & Bölte, S. (2021). Early environmental risk factors for neurodevelopmental disorders—A systematic review of twin and sibling studies. *Development and Psychopathology*, 33(4), 1448–1495. DOI:10.1017/S0954579420000620 PMID:32703331

Carmassi, C., Dell'Oste, V., Barberi, F. M., Pedrinelli, V., Cordone, A., Cappelli, A., Cremone, I. M., Rossi, R., Bertelloni, C. A., & Dell'Osso, L. (2021). Do somatic symptoms relate to PTSD and gender after earthquake exposure? A cross-sectional study on young adult survivors in Italy. *CNS Spectrums*, 26(3), 268–274. DOI:10.1017/S1092852920000097 PMID:32248878

Carter Leno, V., Chandler, S., White, P., Pickles, A., Baird, G., Hobson, C., Smith, A. B., Charman, T., Rubia, K., & Simonoff, E. (2018). Testing the specificity of executive functioning impairments in adolescents with ADHD, ODD/CD and ASD. *European Child & Adolescent Psychiatry*, 27(7), 899–908. DOI:10.1007/s00787-017-1089-5 PMID:29224173

Carter, E. W., Brock, M. E., & Trainor, A. A. (2016). Promoting inclusion, social connections, and learning through peer support arrangements. *Teaching Exceptional Children*, 48(3), 9–18.

Cascia, J., & Barr, J. J. (2020). Associations among parent and teacher ratings of systemizing, vocabulary and executive function in children with autism spectrum disorder. *Research in Developmental Disabilities*, 106, 1–11. DOI:10.1016/j.ridd.2020.103779 PMID:32947163

Case-Smith, J., Weaver, L. L., & Fristad, M. A. (2015). A systematic review of sensory processing interventions for children with autism spectrum disorders. *Autism*, 19(2), 133-148. DOI:10.1177/1362361313517762

Casseus, M., Kim, W. J., & Horton, D. B. (2023). Prevalence and treatment of mental, behavioral, and developmental disorders in children with co-occurring autism spectrum disorder and attention-deficit/hyperactivity disorder: A population-based study. *Autism Research*, 16(4), 855–867. DOI:10.1002/aur.2894 PMID:36644987

Cassidy, J., Jones, J. D., & Shaver, P. R. (2013). Contributions of attachment theory and research: A framework for future research, translation, and policy. *Development and Psychopathology*, 25(4pt2), 1415–1434. DOI:10.1017/S0954579413000692 PMID:24342848

Castellanos, A. E. O., Liu, C., & Shi, C. (2022). Deep Mobile Linguistic Therapy for Patients with ASD. *International Journal of Environmental Research and Public Health. International Journal of Environmental Research and Public Health*, 19(19), 12857. DOI:10.3390/ijerph191912857 PMID:36232157

Cavioni, V., Grazzani, I., & Ornaghi, V. (2017). Social and emotional learning for children with learning disability: Implications for inclusion. *The International Journal of Emotional Education*, 9(2), 100–109. https://files.eric.ed.gov/fulltext/EJ1162075.pdf

CDC. (2023). *Centers for Disease Control and Prevention*. CDC. https://www.cdc.gov/media/releases/2023/p0323-autism.html

Cebula, K., Wishart, J., Willis, D., & Pitcairn, T. (2017). Emotion recognition in children with Down syndrome: Influence of emotion label and expression intensity. *American Journal on Intellectual and Developmental Disabilities*, 122(2), 138–155. DOI:10.1352/1944-7558-122.2.138 PMID:28257244

Center on the Developing Child. (2017). *A science-based framework for early childhood policy*. Center on the Developing Child. www. developingchild.harvard.edu

Chan, S.K.C., Zhang, D., Bögels, S.M., Chan, C.S., Lai, K.Y.C., Lo, H.H.M., Yip, B.H.K., Lau, E.N.S, Gao, T.T., & Wong, S.Y.S. (2018). Effects of a mindfulness-based intervention (MYmind) for children with ADHD and their parents: protocol for a randomised controlled trial. *BMJ Open, 12*(11), e022514.

Chan, E., Fogler, J. M., & Hammerness, P. G. (2016). Treatment of attention-deficit/hyperactivity disorder in adolescents: A systematic review. *Journal of the American Medical Association*, 315(18), 1997–2008. DOI:10.1001/jama.2016.5453 PMID:27163988

Chang, S., Yang, L., Wang, Y., & Faraone, S. V. (2020). Shared polygenic risk for ADHD, executive dysfunction and other psychiatric disorders. *Translational Psychiatry*, 10(1), 182. DOI:10.1038/s41398-020-00872-9 PMID:32518222

Chan, P. C., Chen, C. T., Feng, H., Lee, Y. C., & Chen, K. L. (2016). Theory of Mind Deficit Is Associated with Pretend Play Performance, but Not Playfulness, in Children with Autism Spectrum Disorder. *Hong Kong Journal of Occupational Therapy*, 28(1), 43–52. DOI:10.1016/j.hkjot.2016.09.002 PMID:30186066

Chapman, R. (2020). The reality of autism: On the metaphysics of disorder and diversity. *Philosophical Psychology*, 33(6), 799–819. DOI:10.1080/09515089.2020.1751103

Charman, T., & Baron-Cohen, S. (1992). Understanding drawings and beliefs: A further test of the metarepresentation theory of autism: A research note. *Journal of Child Psychology and Psychiatry, and Allied Disciplines*, 33(6), 1105–1112. DOI:10.1111/j.1469-7610.1992.tb00929.x PMID:1400691

Charman, T., Pickles, A., Simonoff, E., Chandler, S., Loucas, T., & Baird, G. (2010). IQ in children with autism spectrum disorders: Data from the Special Needs and Autism Project (SNAP). *Psychological Medicine*, 41(3), 619–627. DOI:10.1017/S0033291710000991 PMID:21272389

Charman, T., Swettenham, J., Baron-Cohen, S., Cox, A., Baird, G., & Drew, A. (1998). An experimental investigation of social-cognitive abilities in infants with autism: Clinical implications. *Infant Mental Health Journal*, 19(2), 260–275. DOI:10.1002/(SICI)1097-0355(199822)19:2<260::AID-IMHJ12>3.0.CO;2-W

Chen, D. W. (2003). Preventing Violence by Promoting the Development of Competent Conflict Resolution Skills: Exploring Roles and Responsibilities. *Early Childhood Education Journal*, 30(4), 203–208. DOI:10.1023/A:1023379306124

Cherry, K. (2022, December 5). The Preoperational Stage of Cognitive Development. *Very Well Mind*.https://www.verywellmind.com/preoperational-stage-of-cognitive-development-2795461

Cherry, K. (2023, February 28). The Sensorimotor Stage of Cognitive Development. *Very Well Mind*. https://www.verywellmind.com/sensorimotor-stage-of-cognitive-development-2795462

Cherry, K. (2023, March 01). The Concrete Operational Stage of Cognitive Development. *Very Well Mind*. https://www.verywellmind.com/concrete-operational-stage-of-cognitive-development-2795458

Chevrier, A., & Schachar, R. J. (2020). BOLD differences normally attributed to inhibitory control predict symptoms, not task-directed inhibitory control in ADHD. *Journal of Neurodevelopmental Disorders*, 12(1), 1–12. DOI:10.1186/s11689-020-09311-8 PMID:32085698

Chia, N. K. H. (2012). Autism enigma: The need to include savant and crypto-savant in the current definition. *Academic Research International*, 2(2), 234.

Chia, N. K. H. (2012). The Need to Include Savant and Crypto-savant in the Current Definition. *Academic Research International*, 2, 234–240.

Chida, Y., Hamer, M., Wardle, J., & Steptoe, A. (2008). Do stress-related psychosocial factors contribute to cancer incidence and survival?'. *Nature Reviews. Clinical Oncology*, 5(8), 466–475. DOI:10.1038/ncponc1134 PMID:18493231

Childs, K. K., Brady, C. M., Cameron, A. L. J., & Kaukinen, C. (2020). The Role of Family Structure and Family Process on Adolescent Problem Behavior. *Deviant Behavior*, 43(1), 1–16. DOI:10.1080/01639625.2020.1771128

Chopra, J., Sambrook, L., McLoughlin, S., Randles, R., Palace, M., & Blinkhorn, V. (2022). Risk factors for intimate partner homicide in England and Wales. *Health & Social Care in the Community*, 30(5), 3086–3095. DOI:10.1111/hsc.13753 PMID:35178829

Cho, S. J., & Ahn, D. H. (2016). Socially Assistive Robotics in Autism Spectrum Disorder. *Hanyang Medical Reviews*, 36(1), 17–26. DOI:10.7599/hmr.2016.36.1.17

Christina, C., Yvonne, R., Frank, S., Jordan, P., Michael, S., & Cindy, C. (2016). The assessment of early trauma exposure on social-emotional health of young children. *Children and Youth Services Review*, 71(1), 308–314. DOI:10.1016/j.childyouth.2016.11.004

Christ, S. E., Holt, D., White, D., & Green, L. (2007). Inhibitory control in children with autism spectrum disorder. *Journal of Autism and Developmental Disorders*, 37(6), 1155–1165. DOI:10.1007/s10803-006-0259-y PMID:17066307

Chung, K. M., Chung, E., & Lee, H. (2024). Behavioral Interventions for Autism Spectrum Disorder: A Brief Review and Guidelines with a Specific Focus on Applied Behavior Analysis. *Journal of the Korean Academy of Child and Adolescent Psychiatry*, 35(1), 29–38. DOI:10.5765/jkacap.230019 PMID:38204739

Cicchetti, D., & Beeghly, M. (1990). *Children with Down syndrome: A developmental perspective*. Cambridge University Press. DOI:10.1017/CBO9780511581786

Coffman, J. L., Grammer, J. K., Hudson, K. N., Thomas, T. E., Villwock, D., & Ornstein, P. A. (2018). Relating children's early elementary classroom experiences to later skilled remembering and study skills. *Journal of Cognition and Development*, 20(2), 203–221. DOI:10.1080/15248372.2018.1470976 PMID:31372098

Cohen, J. A., Mannarino, A. P., & Deblinger, E. (2011). *Trauma-focused CBT for children and adolescents: Treatment applications*. Guilford Press.

Colich, N. L., Williams, E. S., Rosen, M. L., & McLaughlin, K. A. (2020). Childhood trauma and accelerated biological aging: Evidence from a meta-analysis. *Psychological Bulletin*, 146(9), 721–743. DOI:10.1037/bul0000270 PMID:32744840

Comblain, A., & Schmetz, C. (2020). Improving theory of mind skills in down syndrome? A pilot study. *Journal of Cognitive Education and Psychology*, 19(1), 20–31. DOI:10.1891/JCEP-D-18-00034

Compas, B. E., Jaser, S. S., Dunbar, J. P., Watson, K. H., Bettis, A. H., Gruhn, M. A., & Williams, E. (2010). Coping and emotion regulation from childhood to early adulthood: Points of convergence and divergence. .*Australian Journal of Psychology*, 62(2), 95–107. DOI:10.1080/00049530903567278 PMID:24895462

Cook, A., Ogden, J., & Winstone, N. (2020). The effect of school exposure and personal contact on attitudes towards bullying and autism in schools: A cohort study with a control group. *Autism*, 24(8), 2178–2189. DOI:10.1177/1362361320937088 PMID:32668954

Coolican, J., Bryson, S. E., & Zwaigenbaum, L. (2007). Brief Report: Data on the Stanford–Binet Intelligence Scales (5th ed.) in Children with Autism Spectrum Disorder. *Journal of Autism and Developmental Disorders, 38*(1), 190–197. DOI:10.1007/s10803-007-0368-2

Corbett, B. A., Constantine, L. J., Hendren, R., Rocke, D., & Ozonoff, S. (2009). Examining executive functioning in children with autism spectrum disorder, attention deficit hyperactivity disorder and typical development. *Psychiatry Research*, 166(2-3), 210–222. DOI:10.1016/j.psychres.2008.02.005 PMID:19285351

Cornish, K., Burack, J. A., Rahman, A., Munir, F., Russo, N., & Grant, C. (2005). Theory of mind deficits in children with fragile X syndrome. *Journal of Intellectual Disability Research*, 49(5), 372–378. DOI:10.1111/j.1365-2788.2005.00678.x PMID:15817054

Corrigan, P. W., & Watson, A. C. (2002). Understanding the impact of stigma on people with mental illness. *World Psychiatry, 1*(1), 16-20.

Costa, I. D., Azambuja, S. L., Portuguez, W. M., & Costa, C. J. (2004). Neuropsychological assessment in children. *Jornal de Pediatria*, 80(2), 111–116. DOI:10.2223/1175 PMID:15154079

Coury, D. L., Ashwood, P., Fasano, A., Fuchs, G., Geraghty, M., Kaul, A., Mawe, G., Patterson, P., & Jones, N. E. (2012). Gastrointestinal conditions in children with autism spectrum disorder: Developing a research agenda. *Pediatrics*, 130(Suppl 2), S160–S168. DOI:10.1542/peds.2012-0900N PMID:23118247

Craig, F., Lamanna, A. L., Margari, F., Matera, E., Simone, M., & Margari, L. (2015). Overlap Between Autism Spectrum Disorders and Attention Deficit Hyperactivity Disorder: Searching for Distinctive/Common Clinical Features. *Autism Research*, 8(3), 328–337. DOI:10.1002/aur.1449 PMID:25604000

Craig, F., Operto, F. F., De Giacomo, A., Margari, L., Frolli, A., Conson, M., Ivagnes, S., Monaco, M., & Margari, F. (2016). Parenting stress among parents of children with Neurodevelopmental Disorders. *Psychiatry Research*, 242, 121–129. DOI:10.1016/j.psychres.2016.05.016 PMID:27280521

Creed, F. (2023). Psychiatric disorders comorbid with general medical illnesses and functional somatic disorders: The lifelines cohort study. *PLoS One*, 18(5), 1–23. DOI:10.1371/journal.pone.0286410 PMID:37253033

Crooke, P. J., Winner, M. G., & Olswang, L. B. (2016). Thinking socially. *Topics in Language Disorders*, 36(3), 284–298. DOI:10.1097/TLD.0000000000000094

Crosta, M. L., DeSimone, C., DiPietro, S., Acanfora, M., Caldarola, G., Moccia, L., Callea, A., Panaccione, I., Perris, K., Rinaldi, L., Janiri, L., & DiNicola, M. (2018). Childhood trauma and resilience in psoriatic patients: A preliminary report'. *Journal of Psychosomatic Research*, 106, 25–28. DOI:10.1016/j.jpsychores.2018.01.002 PMID:29455895

Crowther, J., Hamilton, M., & Tett, L. (2001). Powerful literacies: an introduction. In Crowther, J., Hamilton, M., & Tett, L. (Eds.), *Powerful Literacies* (pp. 1–9). NIACE.

D'Andrea, W., Sharma, R., Zelechoski, A. D., & Spinazzola, J. (2011). Physical health problems after single trauma exposure: When stress takes root in the body. *Journal of the American Psychiatric Nurses Association*, 17(6), 378–392. DOI:10.1177/1078390311425187 PMID:22142975

Dafermou, X., Koulouri, P., & Basayianni, E. (2006). *Kindergarten Teacher's Guide: Instructional Designs, Creative Learning Environments*. OEDB.

Dai, Y. G., Brennan, L., Como, A., Hughes-Lika, J., Dumont-Mathieu, T., Carcani-Rathwell, I., Minxhozi, O., Aliaj, B., & Fein, D. A. (2018). A video parent-training program for families of children with autism spectrum disorder in Albania. *Research in Autism Spectrum Disorders*, 56, 36–49. DOI:10.1016/j.rasd.2018.08.008 PMID:31275428

Dale, B. A., Finch, M. H., Mcintosh, D. E., Rothlisberg, B. A., & Finch, W. H. (2014). UTILITY OF THE STANFORD–BINET INTELLIGENCE SCALES, FIFTH EDITION, WITH ETHNICALLY DIVERSE PRESCHOOLERS. *Psychology in the Schools*, 51(6), 581–590. DOI:10.1002/pits.21766

Danforth, J. S. (1998). The Outcome of Parent lraining Using the Behavior Management Flow Chart with Mothers and Their Children with Oppositional Defiant Disorder and Attention-Deficit Hyperactivity Disorder. *Behavior Modification*, 22(4), 443–473. DOI:10.1177/01454455980224001 PMID:9755646

Dankiw, K. A., Tsiros, M. D., Baldock, K. L., & Kumar, S. (2020). The impacts of unstructured nature play on health in early childhood development: A systematic review. *PLoS One*, 15(2), 1–22. DOI:10.1371/journal.pone.0229006 PMID:32053683

Dantzer, C., Swendsen, J., Maurice-Tison, S., & Salamon, R. (2003). Anxiety and depression in juvenile diabetes: A critical review. *Clinical Psychology Review*, 23(6), 787–800. DOI:10.1016/S0272-7358(03)00069-2 PMID:14529698

Davidson, J., & Orsini, M. (2013). *Worlds of autism: Across the spectrum of neurological difference*. University of Minnesota Press. DOI:10.5749/minnesota/9780816688883.001.0001

Davidson, L., Chinman, M., Sells, D., & Rowe, M. (2012). Peer support among adults with serious mental illness: A report from the field. *Schizophrenia Bulletin*, 32(3), 443–450. DOI:10.1093/schbul/sbj043 PMID:16461576

Davis, D. L., Woolley, J. D., & Bruell, M. (2002). Young children's understanding of the roles of knowledge and thinking in pretense. *British Journal of Developmental Psychology*, 20(1), 25–45. DOI:10.1348/026151002166307

Davis, H., & Spurr, P. (1998). Parent counselling: An evaluation of a community child mental health service. *Journal of Child Psychology and Psychiatry, and Allied Disciplines*, 39(3), 365–376. DOI:10.1111/1469-7610.00332 PMID:9670092

Dawson, G., Rogers, S., Munson, J., Smith, M., Winter, J., Greenson, J., & Varley, J. (2010). Randomized, controlled trial of an intervention for toddlers with autism: The Early Start Denver Model. *Pediatrics, 125*(1), e17-e23. DOI:10.1542/peds.2009-0958

De Castro, B. O. (2004). The development of social information processing and aggressive behaviour: Current issues. *European Journal of Developmental Psychology*, 1(1), 87–102. DOI:10.1080/17405620444000058 de Jong, R., Sportel, B. E., de Hullu, E., & Nauta, M. H. (2012). Cognitive behavioral therapy versus progressive relaxation in adolescents with social anxiety disorder: A randomized controlled trial. . *Behaviour Research and Therapy*, 50(1), 60–73. DOI:10.1016/j.brat.2011.11.007

de Rosnay, M., & Hughes, C. (2006). Conversation and theory of mind: Do children talk their way to socio-cognitive understanding? *British Journal of Developmental Psychology*, 24(1), 7–37. DOI:10.1348/026151005X82901

de Vries, S. L. A., Hoeve, M., Assink, M., Stams, G. J. M., & Asscher, J. J. (2015). Practitioner Review: Effective ingredients of prevention programs for youth at risk of persistent juvenile delinquency-recommendations for clinical practice. *Journal of Child Psychology and Psychiatry, and Allied Disciplines*, 56(2), 108–121. DOI:10.1111/jcpp.12320 PMID:25143121

Dean, D.Jr, & Kuhn, D. (2007). Direct instruction vs. discovery: The long view. *Science Education*, 91(3), 384–397. DOI:10.1002/sce.20194

DeFilippis, M. (2018). Depression in Children and Adolescents with Autism Spectrum Disorder. *Children (Basel, Switzerland)*, 5(9), 112. DOI:10.3390/children5090112 PMID:30134542

Del Giudice, M. (2014). Middle Childhood: An Evolutionary-Developmental Synthesis. *Child Development Perspectives*, 8(4), 193–200. DOI:10.1111/cdep.12084

Demetriou, A. E., DeMayo, M. M., & Guastella, J. A. (2019). Executive Function in Autism Spectrum Disorder: History, Theoretical Models, Empirical Findings, and Potential as an Endophenotype. *Frontiers in Psychiatry*, 10, 1–17. DOI:10.3389/fpsyt.2019.00753 PMID:31780959

Demetriou, E. A., Lampit, A., Quintana, D. S., Naismith, S. L., Song, Y. J. C., Pye, J. E., Hickie, I., & Guastella, A. J. (2018). Autism spectrum disorders: A meta analysis of executive function. *Molecular Psychiatry*, 23(5), 1198–1204. DOI:10.1038/mp.2017.75 PMID:28439105

den Houting, J. (2019). Neurodiversity: An insider's perspective. *Autism*, 23(2), 271–273. DOI:10.1177/1362361318820762 PMID:30556743

Dermitzaki, I., Stavroussi, P., Bandi, M., & Nisiotou, I. (2008). Investigating ongoing strategic behaviour of students with mild mental retardation: Implementation and relations to performance in a problem-solving situation. *Evaluation and Research in Education*, 21(2), 96–110. DOI:10.1080/09500790802152175

Derogatis, L. R. (1975). *Brief Symptom Inventory*. Clinical Psychometric Research.

Diakogeorgiou, G. (1995). The child and the game, *Antitetradio of education*, issue 34-3 Dankiw, K.A., Tsiros, M.D., Baldock, K.L. & Kumar, S., (2020), 'The impacts of unstructured nature play on health in early childhood development: A systematic review'. *PLoS One*, 15(2), 1–22.

Dianasari, & Dianasari. (2023). Level Stress, Anxiety, Depression, and Well-being among Parents of Children with ADHD in Indonesia. *International Conference on Sustainable Health Promotion, 3(*1), 142-147.

Dimsdale, J. E., Creed, F., Escobar, J., Sharpe, M., Wulsin, L., Barsky, A., Lee, S., Irwin, M. R., & Levenson, J. (2013). Somatic symptom disorder: An important change in DSM. *Journal of Psychosomatic Research*, 75(3), 223–228. DOI:10.1016/j.jpsychores.2013.06.033 PMID:23972410

DiStefano, C., & Dombrowski, S. C. (2006). Investigating the theoretical structure of the Stanford-Binet-Fifth Edition. *Journal of Psychoeducational Assessment*, 24(2), 123–136. DOI:10.1177/0734282905285244

Dodzik, P. (2017). Behavior Rating Inventory of Executive Function, Second edition Gerard A. Gioia, Peter K. Isquith, Steven C. Guy, and Lauren Kenworthy. *Journal of Pediatric Neuropsychology, 3*(3–4), 227–231. DOI:10.1007/s40817-017-0044-1

Dogangun, B., & Yavuz, M. (2011). Attention Deficit Hyperactivity Disorder. *Turkish Psychiatry Archive*, 46, 25–28.

Donnellan, M. B., Trzesniewski, K. H., Robins, R. W., Moffitt, T. E., & Caspi, A. (2005). Low Self-Esteem is related to aggression, antisocial behavior, and delinquency. *Psychological Science*, 16(4), 328–335. DOI:10.1111/j.0956-7976.2005.01535.x PMID:15828981

Donoghue, E. A., Lieser, D., DelConte, B., Donoghue, E., Earls, M., Glassy, D., Mendelsohn, A., McFadden, T., Scholer, S., Takagishi, J., Vanderbilt, D., & Williams, P. G. (2017, August). Council on Early Childhood. Quality Early Education and Child Care From Birth to Kindergarten. *Pediatrics*, 140(2), e20171488. DOI:10.1542/peds.2017-1488 PMID:28771418

Donvan, J., & Zucker, C. (2016). *In a different key: The story of autism*. Crown.

Dopfner, M., Breuer, D., Schurmann, S., Wolff Metternich, T., Rademacher, C., & Lehmkuhl, G. (2004). Effectiveness of an adaptive multimodal treatment in children with attention-deficit hyperactivity disorder-global outcome. *European Child & Adolescent Psychiatry*, 13(1), 117–129.

Down Syndrome International. (2022, Sep 20). *Learning Profiles*. Down Syndrome International. https://www.ds-int.org/faqs/learning-profile

Down Syndrome Research Foundation. (2024). *Sensory Processing.* Down Syndrome Research Foundation. https://www.dsrf.org/resources/information/physical-skill-development/sensory-processing/

Drechsler, R., Brem, S., Brandeis, D., Grünblatt, E., Berger, G., & Walitza, S. (2020). ADHD: Current concepts and treatments in children and adolescents. *Neuropediatrics*, 51(5), 315–335. DOI:10.1055/s-0040-1701658 PMID:32559806

Duckworth, A. L., Quinn, P. D., & Seligman, M. E. P. (2009). Positive predictors of teacher effectiveness. *The Journal of Positive Psychology*, 4(6), 540–547. DOI:10.1080/17439760903157232

Duncan, A. W., & Bishop, S. L. (2013). Understanding the gap between cognitive abilities and daily living skills in adolescents with autism spectrum disorders with average intelligence. *Autism.* PMID:24275020

DuPaul, G. J., Chronis-Tuscano, A., Danielson, M. L., & Visser, S. N. (2018). Predictors of receipt of school services in a national sample of youth with ADHD. *Journal of Attention Disorders*, 23(11), 1303–1319. DOI:10.1177/1087054718816169 PMID:30526188

DuPaul, G., & Eckert, T. (1997). The effects of school-based interventions for Attention Deficit Hyperactivity Disorder: A meta-analysis. *School Psychology Review*, 26(1), 5–27. DOI:10.1080/02796015.1997.12085845

Eboli, G., & Corsano, P. (2017). Loneliness in children and adolescents with Learning Disabilities: A review. *Psicologia Clinica dello Sviluppo*, 21(1), 25–50. DOI:10.1449/86184

Edyburn, D. L. (2013). Inclusive technologies: Tools for helping diverse learners achieve academic success. *Practical Literacy: The Early & Primary Years, 18*(3), 34-36.

Efstathiou, M. (2007). *Supporting teaching interventions in mixed classes through action research.*

Efthymiou, E., & Katsarou, D. V. (2024). Fostering Inclusive Education: Collaborative Strategies, Emerging Technologies, and Parental Engagement for Children With Language Disorders. In *Childhood Developmental Language Disorders: Role of Inclusion, Families, and Professionals* (pp. 65-84). IGI Global.

Egger, G., Binns, A., Rossner, S., & Saguer, M. (2017). *Lifestyle, the environment and preventive medicine in health and disease. Lifestyle Medicine* (3rd ed.). Elsevier.

Eilers, H., Rot, M. A. H., & Jeronimus, B. F. (2023). Childhood trauma and adult somatic symptoms. *Psychosomatic Medicine*, 85(5), 408–416. DOI:10.1097/PSY.0000000000001208 PMID:37097117

Eime, R. M., Young, J. A., Harvey, J. T., Charity, M. J., & Payne, W. R. (2013). A systematic review of the psychological and social benefits of participation in sport for children and adolescents: Informing development of a conceptual model of health through sport. *International Journal of Behavioral Nutrition and Physical Activity, 10*(98). DOI:10.1186/1479-5868-10-98

Eisenberg, N., Eggum, N. D., & Di Giunta, L. (2010). Empathy-Related Responding: Associations with Prosocial Behavior, Aggression, and Intergroup Relations. *Social Issues and Policy Review*, 4(1), 143–180. DOI:10.1111/j.1751-2409.2010.01020.x PMID:21221410

Eisenmajer, R., Prior, M., Leekam, S., Wing, L., Ong, B., Gould, J., & Welham, M. (1998). Delayed language onset as a predictor of clinical symptoms in pervasive developmental disorders. *Journal of Autism and Developmental Disorders*, 28(6), 527–533. DOI:10.1023/A:1026004212375 PMID:9932239

Ek, U., Westerlund, J., Holmberg, K., & Fernell, E. (2010). Academic performance of adolescents with ADHD and other behavioural and learning problems—A population-based longitudinal study. *Acta Paediatrica (Oslo, Norway)*, 100(3), 402–406. DOI:10.1111/j.1651-2227.2010.02048.x PMID:21054512

Elklit, A., & Christiansen, D. M. (2009). Predictive factors for somatization in a trauma sample. *Clinical Practice and Epidemiology in Mental Health*, 5(1), 1–8. DOI:10.1186/1745-0179-5-1 PMID:19126224

Elliot, J. (1991). Action Research for Educational Change. Milton Keynes: Open University.

Ellis, B., & Nigg, J. (2009). Parenting practices and attention- deficit/hyperactivity disorder: New findings suggest partial specificity of effects. *Journal of the American Academy of Child and Adolescent Psychiatry*, 48(2), 146–154. DOI:10.1097/CHI.0b013e31819176d0 PMID:19065110

Emerson, E., & Hatton, C. (2009). Chapter 4 socioeconomic position, poverty, and family research. *International Review of Research in Mental Retardation*, 37, 97–129. DOI:10.1016/S0074-7750(09)37004-4

Escolano-Pérez, E., Acero-Ferrero, M., & Herrero-Nivela, M. (2019). Improvement of planning skills in children with autism spectrum disorder after an educational intervention: A study from a mixed methods approach. *Frontiers in Psychology*, 10, 2824. DOI:10.3389/fpsyg.2019.02824 PMID:31920859

Estes, A., Rivera, V., Bryan, M., Cali, P., & Dawson, G. (2011). Discrepancies Between Academic Achievement and Intellectual Ability in Higher-Functioning School-Aged Children with Autism Spectrum Disorder. *Journal of Autism and Developmental Disorders*, 41(8), 1044–1052. DOI:10.1007/s10803-010-1127-3 PMID:21042871

Estes, D., Wellman, H. M., & Woolley, J. D. (1989). Children's understanding of mental phenomena. In Reese, H. W. (Ed.), *Advances in Child Development and Behavior*. Academic Press.

Ettekal, I., & Ladd, G. W. (2014). Developmental pathways from childhood Aggression–Disruptiveness, chronic peer rejection, and deviant friendships to Early-Adolescent rule breaking. *Child Development*, 86(2), 614–631. DOI:10.1111/cdev.12321 PMID:25403544

Factor, R. S., Moody, C. T., Sung, K. Y., & Laugeson, E. A. (2022). Improving Social Anxiety and Social Responsiveness in Autism Spectrum Disorder through PEERS®. *Evidence-Based Practice in Child and Adolescent Mental Health*, 7(1), 142–159. DOI:10.1080/23794925.2021.2013138

Fan, J., Wu, Y., Fossella, J. A., Posner, M. I. (2001). Assessing the heritability of attentional networks. *BMC Neuroscience, 2*(14). DOI:10.1186/1471-2202-2-14

Farina, B., Liotti, M., & Imperatori, C. (2019). The role of attachment trauma and disintegrative pathogenic processes in the traumatic-dissociative dimension. *Frontiers in Psychology*, 10, 933. DOI:10.3389/fpsyg.2019.00933 PMID:31080430

Farmakopoulou, I., Theodoratou, M., & Gkintoni, E. (2023). Neuroscience as a component in educational setting: An interpretive overview. *Technium Education and Humanities*, 4, 1–7. DOI:10.47577/teh.v4i.8236

Farrington, D. P., & Murray, J. (Eds.). (2013). *Labeling Theory: Empirical Tests*. Transaction.

Fava, G. A., Freyberger, H. J., Bech, P., Christodoulou, G., Sensky, T., Theorell, T., & Wise, T. N. (1995). Diagnostic criteria for use in psychosomatic research. *Psychotherapy and Psychosomatics*, 63(1), 1–8. DOI:10.1159/000288931 PMID:7740096

Feldman, R. (2016). *Development Across the Life Span* (8th ed.).

Fernald, A., Marchman, V. A., & Weisleder, A. (2013, March). SES differences in language processing skill and vocabulary are evident at 18 months. *Developmental Science*, 16(2), 234–248. DOI:10.1111/desc.12019 PMID:23432833

Ferretti, R. (2019). Problem-solving and working memory in people with intellectual disabilities: An historical perspective. In Matson, J. (Ed.), *Handbook of Intellectual Disabilities: Integrating Theory, Research, and Practice* (pp. 61–70). Springer. DOI:10.1007/978-3-030-20843-1_4

Finkel, D., & Pedersen, N. L. (2014). Genetic and environmental contributions to the associations between intraindividual variability in reaction time and cognitive function. *Neuropsychology, Development, and Cognition. Section B, Aging, Neuropsychology and Cognition*, 21(6), 746–764. DOI:10.1080/13825585.2013.874523 PMID:24400992

Finkelstein, V. (2001). A personal journey into disability politics. *Social Policy and Administration*, 35(5), 602–616.

Fisher, N., Happé, F., & Dunn, J. (2005). The relationship between vocabulary, grammar, and false belief task performance in children with autistic spectrum disorders and children with moderate learning difficulties. *Journal of Child Psychology and Psychiatry, 46,* 409-419. https://doi.org/1DOI:0.1111/j.1469-7610.2004.00371.x

Flavell, J., Flavell, E., Green, F., & Moses, L. (1990). Young children's understanding of fact beliefs versus value beliefs. *Child Development*, 61(4), 915–928. DOI:10.2307/1130865 PMID:2209196

Flett, J. A. M., Hayne, H., Riordan, B. C., Thompson, L. M., & Conner, T. S. (2019). Mobile mindfulness meditation: A randomised controlled trial of the effect of two popular apps on mental health. . *Mindfulness*, 10(5), 863–876. DOI:10.1007/s12671-018-1050-9

Fong, C. J., Taylor, J., Berdyyeva, A., McClelland, A. M., Murphy, K. M., & Westbrook, J. D. (2021). Interventions for improving employment outcomes for persons with autism spectrum disorders: A systematic review update. *Campbell Systematic Reviews*, 17(3), e1185. DOI:10.1002/cl2.1185 PMID:37052419

Ford, C. V. (1997). Somatic symptoms, somatization, and traumatic stress: An overview. *Nordic Journal of Psychiatry*, 51(1), 5–13. DOI:10.3109/08039489709109078

Forehand, R. L., & McMahon, R. J. (1981). *Helping the noncompliant child. A clinician's guide to parent training*. Guilford Press.

Frenkel, S., & Bourdin, B. (2009). Verbal, visual, and spatio-sequential short-term memory: Assessment of the storage capacities of children and teenagers with Down's syndrome. *Journal of Intellectual Disability Research*, 53(2), 152–160. DOI:10.1111/j.1365-2788.2008.01139.x PMID:19077148

Freud, S. (1923): The Ego and the Id. Hogarth Press.

Frieze, I. H., & Mchugh, M. (Eds.). (2005). Female violence against intimate partners. *Psychology of Women Quarterly, 29*(3).

Frith, U. (2003). *Autism: Explaining the Enigma* (2nd ed.). Blackwell.

Fuentes, J., Hervás, A., & Howlin, P. (2021). ESCAP practice guidance for autism: A summary of evidence-based recommendations for diagnosis and treatment. *European Child & Adolescent Psychiatry*, 30(6), 961–984. DOI:10.1007/s00787-020-01587-4 PMID:32666205

Furman, L. (2005). What Is Attention-Deficit Hyperactivity Disorder (ADHD)? *Journal of Child Neurology*, 20(12), 994–1002. DOI:10.1177/08830738050200121301 PMID:16417850

Gander, M., Buchheim, A., Bock, A., Steppan, M., Sevecke, K., & Goth, K. (2020). Unresolved attachment mediates the relationship between childhood trauma and impaired personality functioning in adolescence. *Journal of Personality Disorders*, 34(2, Supplement B), 84–103. DOI:10.1521/pedi_2020_34_468 PMID:31990614

Gavrilova, M., Aslanova, M., Tarasova, K., & Zinchenko, Y. (2023). Russian version of BRIEF2 Teacher Forms: Validation study in typically developing children aged 5 to 7 years old. *Frontiers in Psychology*, 14, 1260107. DOI:10.3389/fpsyg.2023.1260107 PMID:38078211

Gawronski, B., & De Houwer, J. (2014). Implicit measures in social and personality psychology. *Handbook of research methods in social and personality psychology*, 2, 283-310.DOI:10.1007/978-3-319-08613-2_54-1

Gay, G. (2002). Preparing for culturally responsive teaching. *Journal of Teacher Education, 53*(2), 106-116. DOI:10.1177/0022487102053002003

Gazelle, H., & Druhen, M. J. (2009). Anxious solitude and peer exclusion predict social helplessness, upset affect, and vagal regulation in response to behavioral rejection by a friend. *Developmental Psychology*, 45(4), 1077–1096. DOI:10.1037/a0016165 PMID:19586181

Gentile, D. A., & Bushman, B. J. (2012). Reassessing media violence effects using a risk and resilience approach to understanding aggression. *Psychology of Popular Media Culture*, 1(3), 138–151. DOI:10.1037/a0028481

Gentil-Gutiérrez, A., Santamaría-Peláez, M., Mínguez-Mínguez, L. A., Fernández-Solana, J., González-Bernal, J. J., González-Santos, J., & Obregón-Cuesta, A. I. (2022). Executive Functions in Children and Adolescents with Autism Spectrum Disorder in Family and School Environment. *International Journal of Environmental Research and Public Health. International Journal of Environmental Research and Public Health*, 19(13), 7834. DOI:10.3390/ijerph19137834 PMID:35805490

Geoffroy, M.-C., Coté, S. M., Anne, I. H., Borge, A. I. H., Larouche, F., Jean, R., Séguin, J. R., & Rutter, M. (2007). Association between nonmaternal care in the first year of life and children's receptive language skills prior to school entry: The moderating role of socioeconomic status. *Journal of Child Psychology and Psychiatry, and Allied Disciplines*, 48(5), 490–497. DOI:10.1111/j.1469-7610.2006.01704.x PMID:17501730

Georgas, D. D., Paraskevopoulos, I. N., Bezevegis, H. G., & Giannitsas, N. D. (1997). *Greek version of Wechsler intelligence scale for children, WISC-III*. Ellinika Grammata.

Georgiades, S., Bishop, S. L., & Frazier, T. (2017). Editorial Perspective: Longitudinal research in autism–introducing the concept of 'chronogeneity'. *Journal of Child Psychology and Psychiatry, and Allied Disciplines*, 58(5), 634–636. DOI:10.1111/jcpp.12690 PMID:28414862

Geurts, H. M., Verte, S., Oosterlaan, J., Roeyers, H., & Sergeant, J. (2004). How specific are executive functioning deficits in attention deficit hyperactivity disorder and autism? *Journal of Child Psychology and Psychiatry, and Allied Disciplines*, 45(4), 836–854. DOI:10.1111/j.1469-7610.2004.00276.x PMID:15056314

Ghadampour, E., Shirazi, A., & Tehrani, M. A. (2016). Effectiveness of training of mindfulness-based stress reduction on psychological well-being of ADHD children's mothers. *Journal of Exceptional Children*, 16(3), 35–48.

Gharamaleki, S. N., Roshan, R., Pourabdol, S., Saravani, S., & Ghaedi, H. G. (2018). A Comparison of Frontal Lobe Function Between Students with Attention-Deficit Hyperactivity Disorder and Normal Students. *Zahedan Journal of Researches in Medical Sciences*, 20(4), e64198. DOI:10.5812/zjrms.64198

Ghirardi, L., Pettersson, E., Taylor, M. J., Freitag, C. M., Franke, B., Asherson, P., Larsson, H., & Kuja-Halkola, R. (2019). Genetic and environmental contribution to the overlap between ADHD and ASD trait dimensions in young adults: A twin study. *Psychological Medicine*, 49(10), 1713–1721. DOI:10.1017/S003329171800243X PMID:30191778

Giaouri, S., Alevriadou, A., & Lang, L. (2011). Ambiguous figures perception and theory of mind understanding in children with intellectual disabilities: An empirical study with some educational implications. *International Journal of Academic Research*, 3(1), 396–400.

Giaouri, S., Alevriadou, A., & Tsakiridou, E. (2010). Theory of mind abilities in children with Down syndrome and non-specific intellectual disabilities: An empirical study with some educational implications. *Procedia: Social and Behavioral Sciences*, 2(2), 3883–3887. DOI:10.1016/j.sbspro.2010.03.609

Gibson, D. (1991). Down syndrome and cognitive enhancement: Not like the others. In Marfo, K. (Ed.), *Early intervention in transition: Current perspectives in programs for handicapped children* (pp. 61–90). Praeger.

Gierk, B., Kohlmann, S., Kroenke, K., Spangenberg, L., Zenger, M., Brähler, E., & Löwe, B. (2014). The Somatic Symptom Scale-8 (SSS-8): A Brief Measure of Somatic Symptom Burden. *JAMA Internal Medicine*, 174(3), 399–407. DOI:10.1001/jamainternmed.2013.12179 PMID:24276929

Giles-Sims, J. (1998). The aftermath of partner violence. In Jasinski, J. L., & Williams, L. M. (Eds.), *Partner violence: A comprehensive review of 20 years of research* (pp. 44–72). Sage.

Gioia, G. A., Isquith, P. K., Guy, S. C., & Kenworthy, L. (2015). *Behavior Rating Inventory of Executive Function* (2nd ed.). PAR. https://www.parinc.com/Products/Pkey/24

Giordano, P. C., Soto, D. A., Manning, W. D., & Longmore, M. A. (2010). The characteristics of romantic relationships associated with teen dating violence. *Social Science Research*, 39(6), 863–874. DOI:10.1016/j.ssresearch.2010.03.009 PMID:21037934

Giovanni, A. (2023, May 31). Fava; Patients as Health Producers: The Psychosomatic Foundation of Lifestyle Medicine. *Psychotherapy and Psychosomatics*, 92(2), 81–86. DOI:10.1159/000529953 PMID:36958303

Glahn, D. C., Knowles, E. E. M., Mckay, D. R., Sprooten, E., Raventós, H., Blangero, J., Gottesman, I. I., & Almasy, L. (2014). Arguments for the sake of endophenotypes: Examining common misconceptions about the use of endophenotypes in psychiatric genetics. *American Journal of Medical Genetics. Part B, Neuropsychiatric Genetic. American Journal of Medical Genetics. Part B, Neuropsychiatric Genetics*, 165(2), 122–130. DOI:10.1002/ajmg.b.32221 PMID:24464604

Glozman, J. (2013). *Developmental neuropsychology.* Routledge/Taylor & Francis Group.

Goldbeck, L., & Ellerkamp, T. (2012). A randomized controlled trial of multimodal music therapy for children with anxiety disorders. .*Journal of Music Therapy*, 49(4), 395–413. DOI:10.1093/jmt/49.4.395 PMID:23705344

Goldberg, L., Stahl, S., & Castro, R. A. (2014). Yoga for pediatric ADHD: A pilot study. *Complementary Therapies in Clinical Practice, 20*(2), 123-126. https://doi.org/DOI:10.1016/j.ctcp.2014.01.003

Golomb, C., & Kuersten, R. (1996). On the transition from pretence play to reality: What are the rules of the game? *British Journal of Developmental Psychology*, 14(2), 203–217. DOI:10.1111/j.2044-835X.1996.tb00702.x

Goodall, C. (2020). Inclusion is a feeling, not a place: A qualitative study exploring autistic young people's conceptualisations of inclusion. *International Journal of Inclusive Education*, 24(12), 1285–1310. DOI:10.1080/13603116.2018.1523475

Goosby, B. J., Bellatorre, A., Walsemann, K. M., & Cheadle, J. E. (2013). Adolescent loneliness and health in early adulthood. *Sociological Inquiry*, 83(4), 505–536. DOI:10.1111/soin.12018 PMID:24187387

Gordon-Lipkin, E., Marvin, A. R., Law, J. K., & Lipkin, P. H. (2018). Anxiety and mood disorder in children with autism spectrum disorder and ADHD. *Pediatrics*, 141(4), e20171377. DOI:10.1542/peds.2017-1377 PMID:29602900

Gougoulis, K., & Karakatsani, D. (Eds.). (2008). *The Greek game. Routes in the history of* (1st ed.). MIET.

Gray, L., Hill, V., & Pellicano, E. (2023). "He's shouting so loud but nobody's hearing him": A multi-informant study of autistic pupils' experiences of school non-attendance and exclusion. *Autism & Developmental Language Impairments*, 8, 23969415231207816. DOI:10.1177/23969415231207816 PMID:37860824

Graziano, P. A., Reavis, R. D., Keane, S. P., & Calkins, S. D. (2007). The role of emotion regulation in children's early academic success. *Journal of School Psychology*, 45(1), 3–19. DOI:10.1016/j.jsp.2006.09.002 PMID:21179384

Green, A. (2002). *Key Ideas for a Contemporary Psychoanalysis. Misrecognition and Recognition of the Unconscious* [Trans. A. Weller]. Hove: Routledge, 2005.

Greenberg, T. M. (2014). Abnormal Illness behaviors. *Encyclopedia of the Neurological Sciences, 21*(1), 7-10. DOI:10.1016/B978-0-12-385157-4.01072-1

Greenman, P. S., Renzi, A., Monaco, S., Luciani, F., & Trani, M. D. (2024). How does trauma make you sick the role of attachment in explaining somatic symptoms of survivors of childhood trauma. *Health Care*, 12(2), 1–10. DOI:10.3390/healthcare12020203 PMID:38255090

Griffin, J. (2010). *The lonely society?* Social Welfare Foundation. https://www.bl.uk/collection-items/lonely-society

Griffin, G., Charron, D., & Al-Daccak, R. (2014). Post-traumatic stress disorder: Revisiting adrenergics, glucocorticoids, immune system effects and homeostasis. *Clinical & Translational Immunology*, 3(11), e27. DOI:10.1038/cti.2014.26 PMID:25505957

Grinker, R. R. (2007). *Unstrange minds: Remapping the world of autism.* Basic Books.

Guldberg, G., Wallace, S., Bradley, R., Perepa, P., Ellis, L., & MacLeod, A. (2021). *Investigation of the causes and implications of exclusion for autistic children and young people.* University of Birmingham. https://www.birmingham.ac.uk/documents/college-social-sciences/education/reports/causes-and-implications-of-exclusion-for-autistic-children-and-young-people.pdf

Gupta, M. K., Mohapatra, S., & Mahanta, P. K. (2022). Juvenile's Delinquent Behavior, Risk Factors, and Quantitative Assessment Approach: A Systematic Review. *Indian Journal of Community Medicine*, 47(4), 483–490. DOI:10.4103/ijcm.ijcm_1061_21 PMID:36742966

Habukawa, C., Nagamitsu, S., Koyanagi, K., Nishikii, Y., Yanagimoto, Y., Yoshida, S., Suzuki, Y., & Murakami, K. (2021). Early intervention for psychosomatic symptoms of adolescents in school checkup. *Pediatrics International*, 64(1), e15117. DOI:10.1111/ped.15117 PMID:35616207

Hackman, A. D., Farah, J. M., & Meaney, J. M. (2010). Socioeconomic status and the brain: Mechanistic insights from human and animal research. *Nature Reviews. Neuroscience*, 11(9), 651–659. DOI:10.1038/nrn2897 PMID:20725096

Haddad, F., Bourke, J., Wong, K., & Leonard, H. (2018). An investigation of the determinants of quality of life in adolescents and young adults with Down syndrome. *PLoS One*, 13(6), e0197394. DOI:10.1371/journal.pone.0197394 PMID:29897903

Hadders-Algra, M. (2022). *The developing brain: Challenges and opportunities to promote school readiness in young children at risk of neurodevelopmental disorders in low- and middle-income countries.*

Hadfield, K., Amos, M., Ungar, M., Gosselin, J., & Ganong, L. (2018). Do Changes to Family Structure Affect Child and Family Outcomes? A Systematic Review of the Instability Hypothesis. *Journal of Family Theory & Review*, 10(1), 87–110. DOI:10.1111/jftr.12243

Hagner, D., & Cooney, B. F. (2005). Building employer capacity to support employees with severe disabilities in the workplace. *Work, 25*(1), 111-120.

Hala, S., Chandler, M., & Fritz, A. S. (1991). Fledgling theories of mind: Deception as a marker of three-year-olds' understanding of false belief. *Child Development*, 62(1), 83–97. DOI:10.2307/1130706

Hallberg, U., Klingberg, G., Reichenberg, K., & Möller, A. (2008). Living at the edge of one's capability: Experiences of parents of teenage daughters diagnosed with ADHD. *International Journal of Qualitative Studies on Health and Well-being*, 3(1), 52–58. DOI:10.1080/17482620701705523

Hamadelseed, O., Chan, K. S. M., Wong, B. F. M., & Skutella, T. (2023). Distinct neuroanatomical and neuropsychological features of Down syndrome compared to related neurodevelopmental disorders: A systematic review. *Frontiers in Neuroscience*, 17, 1–26. DOI:10.3389/fnins.2023.1225228 PMID:37600012

Handen, B. L., Aman, M. G., Arnold, L. E., Hyman, S. L., Tumuluru, R. V., Lecavalier, L., Corbett-Dick, P., Pan, X., Hollway, J. A., Buchan-Page, K. A., Silverman, L. B., Brown, N. V., Rice, R. R.Jr, Hellings, J., Mruzek, D. W., McAuliffe-Bellin, S., Hurt, E. A., Ryan, M. M., Levato, L., & Smith, T. (2015). Atomoxetine, parent training, and their combination in children with autism spectrum disorder and attention-deficit/hyperactivity disorder. *Journal of the American Academy of Child and Adolescent Psychiatry*, 54(11), 905–915. DOI:10.1016/j.jaac.2015.08.013 PMID:26506581

Happe, F. (1999). Autism: Cognitive deficit or cognitive style? *Trends in Cognitive Sciences*, 3(6), 216–222. DOI:10.1016/S1364-6613(99)01318-2 PMID:10354574

Happé, F. G. E. (1995). The role of age and verbal ability in the theory of mind task performance of subjects with autism. *Child Development*, 66(3), 843–855. DOI:10.2307/1131954 PMID:7789204

Happe, F., & Firth, U. (2006, January). (1006). The weak central coherence account: Detailed focused cognitive style in Autism Spectrum Disorders. *Journal of Autism and Developmental Disorders*, 36(1), 5–25. DOI:10.1007/s10803-005-0039-0 PMID:16450045

Happé, F., & Vital, P. (2009). What aspects of autism predispose to talent? *Philosophical Transactions of the Royal Society of London. Series B, Biological Sciences*, 364(1522), 1369–1375. DOI:10.1098/rstb.2008.0332 PMID:19528019

Hapsari, I. I., Iskandarsyah, A., Joefiani, P., & Siregar, J. R. (2020). Parents' Perceptions of Subjective Well-Being in Children with ADHD. *Journal of Psychology and Instruction*, 4(2), 44–51. DOI:10.23887/jpai.v4i2.32437

Haris, T. (1995). *The Adventure of Assessment in Schools*. Kodika.

Harmony, T. (2009). *Handbook of clinical child neuropsychology* (3rd ed.). Springer.

Harnett, P. H., & Dawe, S. (2012). The contribution of mindfulness-based therapies for children and families and proposed conceptual integration. *Child and Adolescent Mental Health*, 17(4), 195–208. DOI:10.1111/j.1475-3588.2011.00643.x PMID:32847274

Harris, P. L., & Kavanaugh, R. D. (1993). Young children's understanding of pretense. *Monographs of the Society for Research in Child Development, 58*(1)[231], v–92. DOI:10.2307/1166074

Harris, P. L., Brown, E., Marriott, C., Whittall, S., & Harmer, S. (1991). Monsters, ghosts, and witches: Testing the limits of the fantasy-reality distinction in young children. *British Journal of Developmental Psychology*, 9(1), 105–123. DOI:10.1111/j.2044-835X.1991.tb00865.x

Hartmann, K., Hitz, K., & Guldimann, R. (2012). The potential of virtual reality for education and training. *Journal of Educational Technology & Society, 15*(2), 233-245.

Haugland, S. H., Dovran, A., Albaek, A. U., & Sivertsen, B. (2021). Adverse childhood experiences among 28,047 Norwegian adults from a general population. *Frontiers in Public Health*, 9(1), 1–8. DOI:10.3389/fpubh.2021.711344 PMID:34381754

Haworth, C. M., Wright, M. J., Luciano, M., Martin, N. G., de Geus, E. J., van Beijsterveldt, C. E. M., Bartels, M., Posthuma, D., Boomsma, D. I., Davis, O. S., Kovas, Y., Corley, R. P., Defries, J. C., Hewitt, J. K., Olson, R. K., Rhea, S. A., Wadsworth, S. J., Iacono, W. G., McGue, M., & Plomin, R. (2010). The heritability of general cognitive ability increases linearly from childhood to young adulthood. *Molecular Psychiatry*, 15(11), 1112–1120. DOI:10.1038/mp.2009.55 PMID:19488046

Hazer, L., & Gredebäck, G. (2023). The effects of war, displacement, and trauma on child development. *Humanities & Social Sciences Communications*, 10(909), 1–7. DOI:10.1057/s41599-023-02438-8

Hecht, P. M., Hudson, M., Connors, S. L., Tilley, M. R., Liu, X., & Beversdorf, D. Q. (2016). Maternal serotonin transporter genotype affects risk for ASD with exposure to prenatal stress. *Autism Research*, 9(11), 1151–1160. DOI:10.1002/aur.1629 PMID:27091118

Hehir, T., Schifter, L., Grindal, T., Ng, M., & Eidelman, H. (2016). *A summary of the evidence on inclusive education*. Abt Associates.

Heinrich, L. M., & Gullone, E. (2006). The clinical significance of loneliness: A literature review. *Clinical Psychology Review*, 26(6), 695–718. DOI:10.1016/j.cpr.2006.04.002 PMID:16952717

Hendricks, D. R. (2010). Employment and adults with autism spectrum disorders: Challengesand strategies for success. *Journal of Vocational Rehabilitation, 32*(2), 125-134. DOI:10.3233/JVR-2010-0502

Hervás, G., Cebolla, A., & Soler, J. (2016). Intervenciones psicológicas basadas en mindfulness y sus beneficios: Estado actual de la cuestión. *Clinica y Salud*, 27(3), 115–124. DOI:10.1016/j.clysa.2016.09.002

Hettler, S., & Johnston, L. M. (2009). Living peace: An exploration of experiential peace education, conflict resolution and violence prevention programs for youth. *Journal of Peace Education*, 6(1), 101–118. DOI:10.1080/17400200802658340

Heward, W. L. (2011). *Children with special needs. An introduction to Special Education*. Topos.

Hiemstra, W., De Castro, B. O., & Thomaes, S. (2018). Reducing Aggressive Children's Hostile Attributions: A Cognitive Bias Modification procedure. *Cognitive Therapy and Research*, 43(2), 387–398. DOI:10.1007/s10608-018-9958-x

Hill, E. L. (2004). Evaluating the theory of executive dysfunction in autism. *Developmental Review*, 24(2), 189–233. DOI:10.1016/j.dr.2004.01.001

Hill, E. L. (2004). Executive Dysfunction in autism. *Trends in Cognitive Sciences*, 8(1), 26–32. DOI:10.1016/j.tics.2003.11.003 PMID:14697400

Hill, E. L., & Frith, U. (2003). Understanding Autism: Insights from mind and brain. In Frith, U., & Hill, E. (Eds.), *Autism: Mind and brain* (pp. 1–19). Oxford University Press.

Hodapp, R. (1990). One road or many? Issues in the similar sequence hypothesis. In Hodapp, R., Burack, J., & Zigler, E. (Eds.), *Issues in the developmental approach to mental retardation* (pp. 49–70). Cambridge University Press. DOI:10.1017/CBO9780511582325.004

Hodapp, R., & Fidler, D. (2016). *International review of research in developmental disabilities*. Elsevier Academic Press.

Hoffmann, J. D., & Russ, S. W. (2016). Fostering pretend play skills and creativity in elementary school girls: A group play intervention. *Psychology of Aesthetics, Creativity, and the Arts*, 10(1), 114–125. DOI:10.1037/aca0000039

Hofmann, S. G., Asnaani, A., Vonk, I. J., Sawyer, A. T., & Fang, A. (2012). The efficacy of cognitive behavioral therapy: A review of meta-analyses. *Cognitive Therapy and Research*, 36(5), 427–440. DOI:10.1007/s10608-012-9476-1 PMID:23459093

Hollister Sandberg, E., & Spritz, L. B. (2010). *A Clinician's Guide to Normal Cognitive Development in Childhood*. Taylor & Francis.

Holman, D. H., Ports, K. A., Buchanan, N. D., Hawkins, N. A., Merrick, M. T., Metzler, M., & Trivers, K. F. (2016). The association between adverse childhood experiences and risk of cancer in adulthood: A systematic review of the literature. *Pediatrics*, 138(Supplement_1), S81–S91. DOI:10.1542/peds.2015-4268L PMID:27940981

Holmes, C. J., Kim-Spoon, J., & Deater-Deckard, K. (2016, January). Linking Executive Function and Peer Problems from Early Childhood Through Middle Adolescence. *Journal of Abnormal Child Psychology*, 44(1), 31–42. DOI:10.1007/s10802-015-0044-5 PMID:26096194

Hornby, G., & Witte, C. (2010). Parental involvement in inclusive education: Attitudes of parents of children with special educational needs. *European Journal of Special Needs Education, 25*(4), 345-358. DOI:10.1080/08856257.2010.513550

Hornor, G. (2005). Domestic violence and children. *Journal of Pediatric Health Care*, 19(4), 206–212. DOI:10.1016/j.pedhc.2005.02.002 PMID:16010259

Houghton, F., Rourke Scott, L., Moran Stritch, J., Larkin, H. K., & Heinz, L. (2024). Sexual, Domestic, and Gender-based Abuse: A collection of experience and opinion. *JGPOH*, 2023. DOI:10.61034/JGPOH-2024-2

Hours, C., Recasens, C., & Baleyte, J. M. (2022). ASD and ADHD comorbidity: What are we talking about? *Frontiers in Psychiatry*, 13, 837424. DOI:10.3389/fpsyt.2022.837424 PMID:35295773

Howlin, P., Goode, S., Hutton, J., & Rutter, M. (2009). Savant Skills in Autism: Psychometric Approaches and Parental Reports. *Philosophical Transactions of the Royal Society of London. Series B, Biological Sciences*, 364(1522), 1359–1367. https://www.jstor.org/stable/40485907. DOI:10.1098/rstb.2008.0328 PMID:19528018

Hughes, C., Russell, J., & Robbins, T. W. (1994). Evidence for executive dysfunction in autism. *Neuropsychologia, 32*(4), 477–492.

Hughes, C., Lecce, S., & Wilson, C. (2007). Do you know what I want? Preschoolers' talk about desires, thoughts, and feelings in their conversations with sibs and friends. *Cognition and Emotion*, 21(2), 330–350. DOI:10.1080/02699930600551691

Huizinga, M., Smidts, D. P., Baeyens, D., & Kan, K. (2023). The Dutch version of the Behavior Rating Inventory of Executive Function-2 (BRIEF-2). *Psychological Test Adaptation and Development*, 4(1), 97–115. DOI:10.1027/2698-1866/a000038

Huntington, D. D., & Bender, W. N. (1993). Adolescents with learning disabilities at risk? Emotional well-being, depression, suicide. *Journal of Learning Disabilities*, 26(3), 159–166. DOI:10.1177/002221949302600303 PMID:8486993

Hutchins, T. L., Prelock, P. A., Morris, H., Benner, J., LaVigne, T., & Hoza, B. (2016). Explicit vs. applied theory of mind competence: A comparison of typically developing males, males with ASD, and males with ADHD. *Research in Autism Spectrum Disorders*, 21, 94–108. DOI:10.1016/j.rasd.2015.10.004

Hu, Y., Cai, Y., Wang, R., Gan, Y., & He, N. (2023). The relationship between self-esteem and aggressive behavior among Chinese adolescents: A moderated chain mediation model. *Frontiers in Psychology*, 14, 1191134. DOI:10.3389/fpsyg.2023.1191134 PMID:37377697

Icekson, T., Begerano, O. D., Levinson, M., Savariego, J., & Margalit, M. (2021). Learning difficulties and loneliness in college and beyond: The mediating role of self-efficacy, proactive coping, and hope. *International Journal of Environmental Research and Public Health*, 18(19), 10508. DOI:10.3390/ijerph181910508 PMID:34639809

Irvin, M. (2017). *The Importance of Play in Early Childhood Education.* Northwestern College- Orange City.

Jacobs, B. A. (2010). Deterrence and deterrability. *Criminology*, 48(2), 417–441. DOI:10.1111/j.1745-9125.2010.00191.x

Jacobsen, S. K., & Zaatut, A. (2020). Quantity or Quality? Assessing the Role of Household Structure and Parent-Child Relationship in Juvenile Delinquency. *Deviant Behavior*, 43(1), 30–43. DOI:10.1080/01639625.2020.1774241

Jahromi, B. L., Gulsrud, A., & Kasari, C. (2008). Emotional competence in children with Down syndrome: Negativity and regulation. *American Journal of Mental Retardation*, 113(1), 32–43. DOI:10.1352/0895-8017(2008)113[32:ECICWD]2.0.CO;2 PMID:18173298

Jankowski, T., Bak, W., & Miciuk, Ł. (2021). Adaptive self-concept: Identifying the basic dimensions of self-beliefs. *Self and Identity*, 21(7), 739–774. DOI:10.1080/15298868.2021.1997796

Janzen, H. L., Obrzut, J. E., & Marusiak, C. W. (2004). Test Review: Roid, G. H. (2003). Stanford-Binet Intelligence Scales, fifth Edition (SB:V). Itasca, IL: Riverside Publishing. *Canadian Journal of School Psychology, 19*(1–2), 235–244. DOI:10.1177/082957350401900113

Jersild, A. T. (1943). Studies of children's fears. In Barker, R. G., Kounin, J. S., & Wright, H. F. (Eds.), *Child Behavior and Development*. McGraw-Hill. DOI:10.1037/10786-019

Joellenbeck, L. M., Russell, P. K., & Guze, S. B. (1999). Strategies to Protect the Health of Deployed U.S. Forces: Medical Surveillance, Record Keeping, and Risk Reduction. Institute of Medicine (US) Medical Follow-Up Agency, National Academies Press (US), USA. DOI:10.17226/9711

Johnson, C. N., & Harris, P. L. (1994). Magic: Special but not excluded. *British Journal of Developmental Psychology*, 12(1), 35–51. DOI:10.1111/j.2044-835X.1994.tb00617.x

Joseph, R. M., & Tager–Flusberg, H. E. L. E. N. (2004). The relationship of theory of mind and executive functions to symptom type and severity in children with autism. *Development and Psychopathology*, 16(1), 137–155. DOI:10.1017/S095457940404444X PMID:15115068

Joshi, G., Faraone, S. V., Wozniak, J., Tarko, L., Fried, R., Galdo, M., Furtak, S. L., & Biederman, J. (2017). Symptom Profile of ADHD in Youth With High Functioning Autism Spectrum Disorder: A Comparative Study in Psychiatrically Referred Populations. *Journal of Attention Disorders*, 21(10), 846–855. DOI:10.1177/1087054714543368 PMID:25085653

Juvonen, J., & Graham, S. (2014). Bullying in schools: The power of bullies and the plight of victims. *Annual Review of Psychology*, 65(1), 159–185. DOI:10.1146/annurev-psych-010213-115030 PMID:23937767

Kabat-Zinn, J. (2003). Mindfulness-based interventions in context: Past, present, and future. *Clinical Psychology: Science and Practice, 10*(2), 144-156. DOI:10.1093/clipsy/bpg016

Kabat-Zinn, J. (2013). *Full Catastrophe living: Using the wisdom of your body and mind to face stress, pain, and illness* (Revised and Updated ed.). New York, NY: Bantam.

Kabat-Zinn, J. (2003). Mindfulness-based interventions in context: Past, present, and future. *Clinical Psychology : a Publication of the Division of Clinical Psychology of the American Psychological Association*, 10(2), 144–156. DOI:10.1093/clipsy.bpg016

Kallivayalil, R. A., & Punnoose, V. P. (2010). Understanding and managing somatoform disorders: Making sense of non-sense. *Indian Journal of Psychiatry*, 52(7, 11), 240–245. DOI:10.4103/0019-5545.69239 PMID:21836685

Kalra, R., Gupta, M., & Sharma, P. (2023). Recent advancement in interventions for autism spectrum disorder: A review. *Journal of Neurorestoratology*, 11(3), 100068. DOI:10.1016/j.jnrt.2023.100068

Kamphaus, R. W., & Juechter, J. I. (2010). Stanford-Binet Intelligence scales. *The Corsini Encyclopedia of Psychology*, 1–2. DOI:10.1002/9780470479216.corpsy0941

Kanner, L. (1943). Autistic disturbances of affective contact. *Nervous Child*, 2(3), 217–250.

Kao, C. (2019). Development of Team Cohesion and Sustained Collaboration Skills with the Sport Education Model. *Sustainability (Basel)*, 11(8), 2348. DOI:10.3390/su11082348

Kapp, S. K., Gillespie-Lynch, K., Sherman, L. E., & Hutman, T. (2013). Deficit, difference, or both? Autism and neurodiversity. *Developmental Psychology*, 49(1), 59–71. DOI:10.1037/a0028353 PMID:22545843

Karr, J. E., Areshenkoff, C. N., Rast, P., Hofer, S. M., Iverson, G. L., & Garcia-Barrera, M. A. (2018). The unity and diversity of executive functions: A systematic review and re-analysis of latent variable studies. *Psychological Bulletin*, 144(11), 1147–1185. DOI:10.1037/bul0000160 PMID:30080055

Kasari, C., & Freeman, S. (2001). Task-related social behavior in children with Down syndrome. *American Journal of Mental Retardation*, 106(3), 253–264. DOI:10.1352/0895-8017(2001)106<0253:TRSBIC>2.0.CO;2 PMID:11389666

Katsarou, D. (2018). Emotional state differences of parents with children diagnosed with autism. *International Journal of Current Innovation Research*, 4(4), 1177–1183.

Katsarou, D., Nikolaou, E., & Stamatis, P. (2023). Is coteaching an effective way of including children with autism? The Greek parallel coteaching as an example: Issues and Concerns. In Efthymiou, E. (Ed.), *Inclusive Phygital Learning Approaches and Strategies For Students with Special Needs* (pp. 189–197). IGI Global. DOI:10.4018/978-1-6684-8504-0.ch009

Katsarou, D., & Zerva, E. (2024). Writing disorders in specific reading disorder (dyslexia) and attention deficit hyperactivity disorder: The clinical continuum between the two neurodevelopmental disorders. *Archives of Hellenic Medicine*, 41(3), 339–345.

Katsarou, E., & Tsafos, B. (2003). *From Research to Teaching: Educational action research*. Savvalas.

Kaur, K., & Pany, S. (2020). Executive function profiles of autism spectrum disorder using the executive function performance based tasks: A systematic review. *Journal of Critical Reviews*, 7(19), 8395–8403.

Ke, F., & Im, T. (2013). Virtual-reality-based social interaction training for children with high-functioning autism. *Journal of Educational Research, 106*(6), 441-451. DOI:10.1080/00220671.2013.832999

Keen, D., Webster, A., & Ridley, G. (2016). How well are children with autism spectrum disorder doing academically at school? An overview of the literature. *Autism*, 20(3), 276–294. DOI:10.1177/1362361315580962 PMID:25948598

Keith, T. Z., Kranzler, J. H., & Flanagan, D. P. (2001). What does the Cognitive Assessment System (CAS) measure? Joint Confirmatory Factor Analysis of the CAS and the Woodcock-Johnson Tests of Cognitive Ability (3rd Edition). *School Psychology Review, 30*(1), 89–119. DOI:10.1080/02796015.2001.12086102

Keles, F., & Idsoe, T. (2018). A meta-analysis of group cognitive behavioral therapy (CBT) for adolescents with depression. *Journal of Child Psychology and Psychiatry, 59*(3), 252-261. DOI:10.1111/jcpp.12818

Keng, S. L., Smoski, M. J., & Robins, C. J. (2011). Effects of mindfulness on psychological health: A review of empirical studies. *Clinical Psychology Review*, 31(6), 1041–1056. DOI:10.1016/j.cpr.2011.04.006 PMID:21802619

Kenworthy, L. E., Black, D. O., Wallace, G. L., Ahluvalia, T., Wagner, A. E., & Sirian, L. M. (2010). Disorganization: The forgotten executive dysfunction in high-functioning autism (HFA) spectrum disorders. *Developmental Neuropsychology*, 28(3), 809–827. DOI:10.1207/s15326942dn2803_4 PMID:16266250

Kenworthy, L., Yerys, B. E., Anthony, L. G., & Wallace, G. L. (2008). Understanding executive control in autism spectrum disorders in the lab and in the real world. *Neuropsychology Review*, 18(4), 320–338. DOI:10.1007/s11065-008-9077-7 PMID:18956239

Kerr, M., Stattin, H., Biesecker, G., & Ferrer-Wreder, L. (2003). Handbook of Psychology: Vol. 395–419. *Relationships with parents and peers in adolescence.*, DOI:10.1002/0471264385.wei0616

Keskin, D.B. (2019). Neoantigen vaccine generates intratumoral T cell responses in phase Ib glioblastoma trial. *Nature. Jan, 565*(7738), 234-239. .DOI:10.1038/s41586-018-0792-9

Khalfa, S., Bruneau, N., Rogé, B., Georgieff, N., Veuillet, E., Adrien, J. L., Barthélémy, C., & Collet, L. (2004, December). Increased perception of loudness in autism. *Hearing Research*, 198(1-2), 87–92. DOI:10.1016/j.heares.2004.07.006 PMID:15617227

King, M., & Bearman, P. (2009). Diagnostic change and the increased prevalence of autism. *International Journal of Epidemiology*, 38(5), 1224–1234. DOI:10.1093/ije/dyp261 PMID:19737791

Kirmayer, L. J., Robbins, J. M., & Paris, J. (1994). Somatoform disorders: Personality and the social matrix of somatic distress. *Journal of Abnormal Psychology*, 103(1), 125–136. DOI:10.1037/0021-843X.103.1.125 PMID:8040474

Kirsch, A. C., Huebner, A. R. S., Mehta, S. Q., Howie, F. R., Weaver, A. L., Myers, S. M., Voigt, R. G., & Katusic, S. K. (2020). Association of comorbid mood and anxiety disorders with autism spectrum disorder. *JAMA Pediatrics*, 174(1), 63. DOI:10.1001/jamapediatrics.2019.4368 PMID:31790555

Kitsaras, G. (2001). *Preschool Pedagogy*. GSAR Publishers.

Klassen, A. F., Miller, A., & Fine, S. (2004). Health-related quality of life in children and adolescents who have a diagnosis of attention-deficit/hyperactivity disorder. *Pediatrics*, 114(5), e541–e547. DOI:10.1542/peds.2004-0844 PMID:15520087

Kleszczewska, D., Mazur, J., Bucksch, J., Dzielska, A., Brindley, C., & Michalska, A. (2020). Active Transport to School May Reduce Psychosomatic Symptoms in School-Aged Children: Data from Nine Countries. *International Journal of Environmental Research and Public Health*, 17(23), 8709. DOI:10.3390/ijerph17238709 PMID:33255182

Knight, Z. G. (2017). A proposed model of psychodynamic psychotherapy linked to Erik Erikson's eight stages of psychosocial development. *Clinical Psychology & Psychotherapy. Clinical Psychology & Psychotherapy*, 24(5), 1047–1058. DOI:10.1002/cpp.2066 PMID:28124459

Kohn-Wood, L. P., & Hooper, L. M. (2014). Cultural competence in applied psychology: We are not there yet. *Journal of Clinical Psychology, 70*(9), 829-843. DOI:10.1002/jclp.22117

Kollins, S. H., Childress, A., Heusser, A. C., & Lutz, J. (2021). Effectiveness of a digital therapeutic as adjunct to treatment with medication in pediatric ADHD. *NPJ Digital Medicine*, 4(1), 58. DOI:10.1038/s41746-021-00429-0 PMID:33772095

Kong, J., Martire, L. M., Liu, Y., & Almeida, D. M. (2021). Effects of parental childhood abuse on daily stress processes in adulthood. *Journal of Interpersonal Violence*, 36(19-20), 9580–9599. DOI:10.1177/0886260519869068 PMID:31423882

Konnopka, A., Kaufmann, C., König, H. H., Heider, D., Wild, B., Szecsenyi, J., Herzog, W., Heinrich, S., & Schaefert, R. (2013). Association of costs with somatic symptom severity in patients with medically unexplained symptoms. *Journal of Psychosomatic Research*, 75(4), 370–375. DOI:10.1016/j.jpsychores.2013.08.011 PMID:24119945

Konrad, K., Herpertz, S. C., & Herpertz-Dahlmann, B. (2016). Early trauma: Long lasting, difficult to treat and transmitted to the next generation'. *Journal of Neural Transmission (Vienna, Austria)*, 123(9), 1033–1035. DOI:10.1007/s00702-016-1601-y PMID:27522500

Korbin, J. E. (1991). Cross-cultural perspectives and research directions for the 21st century. *Child Abuse & Neglect*, 15(1), 67–77. DOI:10.1016/0145-2134(91)90010-B PMID:2032129

Korhonen, T., Sihvola, E., Latvala, A., Dick, D. M., Pulkkinen, L., Nurnberger, J., Rose, R., & Kaprio, J. (2018). Early-onset tobacco use and suicide-related behavior–A prospective study from adolescence to young adulthood. *Addictive Behaviors*, 79(1), 32–38. DOI:10.1016/j.addbeh.2017.12.008 PMID:29245024

Kosmatos, K., & Martinis, M. (2021). Article 121. In: Charalabakis, A. *The New Criminal Code* (law N. 4609/2019), 991-1003.

Kotelnikova, Y., Olino, T. M., Mackrell, S. V., Jordan, P. L., & Hayden, E. P. (2013). Structure of observed temperament in middle childhood. *Journal of Research in Personality*, 47(5), 524–532. DOI:10.1016/j.jrp.2013.04.013 PMID:24293740

Kotsalidou, D. (2010). *Interdisciplinary work proposals for kindergarten and elementary school: Theory and practice*. Kastaniotis.

Kozlowski, A. M., Matson, J. L., & Belva, B. C. (2019). A review of social skills training and social skills interventions for children with autism spectrum disorders. *Behavior Modification, 36*(2), 317-335. https://doi.org/DOI:10.1177/0145445512443983

Krahé, B., & Busching, R. (2014). Interplay of normative beliefs and behavior in developmental patterns of physical and relational aggression in adolescence: A four-wave longitudinal study. *Frontiers in Psychology*, 5. DOI:10.3389/fpsyg.2014.01146 PMID:25360124

Kranzler, J. H., Floyd, R. G., Bray, M. A., & Demaray, M. K. (2020). Past, present, and future of research in school psychology: The biopsychosocial ecological model as an overarching framework. *School Psychology*, 35(6), 419–427. DOI:10.1037/spq0000401 PMID:33444055

Kratzer, L., Knefel, M., Haselgruber, A., Heinz, P., Schennach, R., & Karatzias, T. (2022). Co-occurrence of severe PTSD, somatic symptoms and dissociation in a large sample of childhood trauma inpatients: A network analysis. *European Archives of Psychiatry and Clinical Neuroscience*, 272(5), 897–908. DOI:10.1007/s00406-021-01342-z PMID:34635928

Kraus, J. (2000). Causes of Delinquency as Perceived by Juveniles. *International Journal of Offender Therapy and Comparative Criminology*, 79–86.

Kristen, S., & Sodian, B. (2014). Theory of mind (ToM) in early education: Developmental progression of early theory of mind skills, social developmental factors and the importance of ToM for learning. In Saracho, O. N. (Ed.), *Contemporary perspectives on research in theory of mind in early childhood education* (pp. 291–320). IAP Information Age Publishing.

Kroenke, K. (2014). A practical and evidence-based approach to common symptoms: A narrative review. *Annals of Internal Medicine*, 161(8), 579–586. DOI:10.7326/M14-0461 PMID:25329205

Kroenke, K., Spitzer, R. L., & Williams, J. B. W. (2002). The PHQ-15: Validity of a new measure for evaluating the severity of somatic symptoms. *Psychosomatic Medicine*, 64(2), 258–266. DOI:10.1097/00006842-200203000-00008 PMID:11914441

Kross E, Berman MG, Mischel W, Smith EE, & Wager TD. (2011). Social rejection shares somatosensory representations with physical pain. *Proc Natl Acad. Science 12, 108*(15), 6270-5.DOI:10.1073/pnas.1102693108

Kugler, B. B., Bloom, M., Kaercher, L. B., Truax, T. V., & Storch, E. A. (2012). Somatic symptoms in traumatized children and adolescents. *Child Psychiatry and Human Development*, 43(5), 661–673. DOI:10.1007/s10578-012-0289-y PMID:22395849

Kuhfuß, M., Maldei, T., Hetmanek, A., & Baumann, N. (2021). Somatic experiencing–effectiveness and key factors of a body-oriented trauma therapy: A scoping literature review. *European Journal of Psychotraumatology*, 12(1), 1–7. DOI:10.1080/2000 8198.2021.1929023 PMID:34912501

Kurahashi, M., & Reichert, E. (2020). How Mindful Parenting Can Support Caregivers In Managing Their Young Children With ADHD. *Journal of the American Academy of Child & Adolescent Psychiatry, 59*(10). DOI:10.1016/j.jaac.2020.07.458

Kurth, J. A., & Mastergeorge, A. M. (2010). Individual education plan goals and services for adolescents with autism: Impact of age and educational setting. *Journal of Special Education, 44*(3), 146-160. DOI:10.1177/0022466908329825

Kwan, C., Gitimoghaddam, M., & Collet, J.-P. (2020). Effects of social isolation and loneliness in children with neurodevelopmental disabilities: A scoping review. *Brain Sciences*, 10(11), 786. DOI:10.3390/brainsci10110786 PMID:33126519

Kyriazopoulou – Valinaki, P. (1997). Kindergarten. *Vlassi, 3*, 236.

Labella, M. H., & Masten, A. S. (2018). Family influences on the development of aggression and violence. *Current Opinion in Psychology*, 19, 11–16. DOI:10.1016/j. copsyc.2017.03.028 PMID:29279207

Lackaye, T., & Margalit, M. (2008). Self-efficacy, loneliness, effort, and hope: Developmental differences in the experiences of students with learning disabilities and their non-learning disabled peers at two age groups. Learning Disabilities. *Learning Disabilities (Weston, Mass.)*, 6(2), 1–20. https://files.eric.ed.gov/fulltext/EJ804508.pdf

Lam, Y. G. (2013). Re-examining the cognitive phenotype in autism: a study with young Chinese children. *Research in Developmental Disabilities, 34*(12), 4591-4598. DOI:10.1016/j.ridd.2013.09.039

Lam, I. K. Y., Hong, J., & Shum, K. K. M. (2024, July). Mediating role of emotion regulation between ADHD children's adjustment and parents' well-being. In *33rd International Congress of Psychology*, Prague.

Landi, N., Avery, T., Crowley, J. M., Wu, J., & Mayes, L. (2017). Prenatal Cocaine Exposure Impacts Language and Reading Into Late Adolescence: Behavioral and ERP Evidence. *Developmental Neuropsychology*, 42(6), 369–386. DOI:10.1080/8 7565641.2017.1362698 PMID:28949778

Landreth, G. L. (1991). *Play therapy: The art of the relationship*. Accelerated Development.

Lanfranchi, S., Cornoldi, C., & Vianello, R. (2015). Verbal and visuospatial working memory deficits in children with Down syndrome. *American journal of mental retardation. American Journal of Mental Retardation*, 109(6), 456–466. DOI:10.1352/0895-8017(2004)109<456:VAVWMD>2.0.CO;2 PMID:15471512

Lanjekar, P. D., Joshi, S. H., Lanjekar, P. D., & Wagh, V. (2022). The Effect of Parenting and the Parent-Child Relationship on a Child's Cognitive Development: A literature review. *Cureus*. DOI:10.7759/cureus.30574 PMID:36420245

Lappas, A. (Λάππας, A.) (2023). *Κακοποίηση Παιδιών από Κακοποιημένες Μητέρες*. Προφορική Ανακοίνωση στο Ινστιτούτο ΠροςΟψη. [Video]. Youtube. https://www .youtube.com/watch?v=ybIGqTKPN0Q

Latimer, J., Dowden, C., & Muise, D. (2005). The effectiveness of restorative justice practices: A meta-analysis. *The Prison Journal*, 85(2), 127–144. DOI:10.1177/0032885505276969

Latimer, J., & Kleinknecht, S. (2000). *The effects of restorative justice programming: A review of the empirical research*. Department of Justice Canada, Research and Statistics Division.

Laube, C., Lorenz, R., & Van Den Bos, W. (2020). Pubertal testosterone correlates with adolescent impatience and dorsal striatal activity. *Developmental Cognitive Neuroscience*, 42, 100749. DOI:10.1016/j.dcn.2019.100749 PMID:31942858

Laugeson, E. A., & Park, M. N. (2014). Using a CBT approach to teach social skills to adolescents with autism spectrum disorder and other social challenges: The PEERS® method. *Journal of Rational-Emotive & Cognitive-Behavior Therapy*, 32(1), 84–97. DOI:10.1007/s10942-014-0181-8

Laursen, B., & Veenstra, R. (2021). Toward understanding the functions of peer influence: A summary and synthesis of recent empirical research. *Journal of Research on Adolescence*, 31(4), 889–907. DOI:10.1111/jora.12606 PMID:34820944

Lawson, J., Baron-Cohen, S., & Wheelwright, S. (2004). Empathising and Systemising in Adults with and without Asperger Syndrome. *Journal of Autism and Developmental Disorders*, 34(3), 301–310. DOI:10.1023/B:JADD.0000029552.42724.1b PMID:15264498

Lebersfeld, J. B., Swanson, M., Clesi, C. D., & O'Kelley, S. E. (2021). Systematic Review and Meta-Analysis of the Clinical Utility of the ADOS-2 and the ADI-R in Diagnosing Autism Spectrum Disorders in Children. *Journal of Autism and Developmental Disorders*, 51(11), 4101–4114. DOI:10.1007/s10803-020-04839-z PMID:33475930

Leekam, S. R., & Perner, J. (1991). Does the autistic child have a metarepresentational deficit? *Cognition*, 40(3), 203–218. DOI:10.1016/0010-0277(91)90025-Y PMID:1786675

Lee, P. C., Niew, W. I., Yang, H. J., Chen, V. C. H., & Lin, K. C. (2012). A meta-analysis of behavioral parent training for children with attention deficit hyperactivity disorder. *Research in Developmental Disabilities*, 33(6), 2040–2049. DOI:10.1016/j.ridd.2012.05.011 PMID:22750360

Lehman, B. J., David, D. M., & Gruber, J. A. (2017). Rethinking the biopsychosocial model of health: Understanding health as a dynamic system. *Social and Personality Psychology Compass*, 11(8), e12328. DOI:10.1111/spc3.12328

Leitner, Y. (2014). The Co-Occurrence of Autism and Attention Deficit Hyperactivity Disorder in Children â€" What Do We Know? *Frontiers in Human Neuroscience*, 8. Advance online publication. DOI:10.3389/fnhum.2014.00268 PMID:24808851

Leonidou, C., Panayiotou, G., Bati, A., & Karekla, M. (2019). Coping with psychosomatic symptoms: The buffering role of psychological flexibility and impact on quality of life. *Journal of Health Psychology*, 24(2), 175–187. DOI:10.1177/1359105316666657 PMID:27596277

Leung, R. C., Vogan, V. M., Powell, T. L., Anagnostou, E., & Taylor, M. J. (2015). The role of executive functions in social impairment in Autism Spectrum Disorder. *Child Neuropsychology/Neuropsychology, Development, and Cognition. Section C. Child Neuropsychology*, 22(3), 336–344. DOI:10.1080/09297049.2015.1005066 PMID:25731979

Levi-Keren, M., Godeano-Barr, S., & Levinas, S. (2021). Mind the conflict: Empathy when coping with conflicts in the education sphere. *Cogent Education*, 9(1), 2013395. Advance online publication. DOI:10.1080/2331186X.2021.2013395

Lewis, P., Abbeduto, L., Murphy, M., Richmond, E., Giles, N., Bruno, L., & Schroeder, S. (2006). Cognitive, language and social skills of individuals with fragile X syndrome with and without autism. *Journal of Intellectual Disability Research*, 50(7), 532–545. DOI:10.1111/j.1365-2788.2006.00803.x PMID:16774638

Lezak, M. D., Howieson, D. B., Bigler, E. D., & Tranel, D. (2012). *Neuropsychological assessment* (5th ed.). Oxford University Press.

Li D., et al. (2021) Patterns of six behaviors and psychosomatic symptoms in adolescents: A six-province study in China. *Journal of Affective Disorders, 297*(2022), 593–601

Libisch, C. A., Marsiglia, F., Kulis, S., Cutrín, O., Gómez-Fraguela, J. A., & Ruiz, P. (2022). *The role of peer pressure in adolescents' risky behaviors.* Springer. DOI:10.1007/978-3-031-06908-6_8

Lindsay, S., Cagliostro, E., Alcorn, A., Srikanthan, D., & Mortaji, N. (2019). A systematic review of the benefits of assistive technology for individuals with autism spectrum disorders. *Disability and Rehabilitation: Assistive Technology, 14*(7), 345-357. https://doi.org/DOI:10.1080/17483107.2018.1465137

Lipowski, Z. J. (1987). Somatization: The experience and communication of psychological distress as somatic symptoms. *Psychotherapy and Psychosomatics*, 47(3-4), 160–167. DOI:10.1159/000288013 PMID:3333284

Liss, M., Fein, D., Allen, D., Dunn, M., Feinstein, C., Morris, R., Waterhouse, L., & Rapin, I. (2001). Executive functioning in high-functioning children with autism. *Journal of Child Psychology and Psychiatry, and Allied Disciplines*, 42(2), 261–270. DOI:10.1111/1469-7610.00717 PMID:11280422

Liu, J. (2011). Early health risk factors for violence: Conceptualization, evidence, and implications. *Aggression and Violent Behavior*, 16(1), 63–73. DOI:10.1016/j.avb.2010.12.003 PMID:21399727

Liu, L., Cohen, S., Schulz, M. S., & Waldinger, R. J. (2011). Sources of somatization: Exploring the roles of insecurity in relationships and styles of anger experience and expression. *Social Science & Medicine*, 73(9), 1436–1443. DOI:10.1016/j.socscimed.2011.07.034 PMID:21907475

Lo, H. H. M., Wong, S., Wong, J., Wong, S., & Yeung, J. (2016). The effect of a family-based mindfulness intervention on children with attention deficit and hyperactivity symptoms and their parents: Design and rationale for a randomized, controlled clinical trial (Study protocol). *BMC Psychiatry*, 16(1), 65. DOI:10.1186/s12888-016-0773-1 PMID:26980323

Lo, H. H., Wong, S. W., Wong, J. Y., Yeung, J. W., Snel, E., & Wong, S. Y. (2020). The effects of family-based mindfulness intervention on ADHD symptomology in young children and their parents: A randomized control trial. *Journal of Attention Disorders*, 24(5), 667–680. DOI:10.1177/1087054717743330 PMID:29185375

López Resa, P., & Moraleda Sepúlveda, E. (2024). Developmental Profile in Children Aged 3–6 Years: Down Syndrome vs. Autism Spectrum Disorder. *Behavioral Sciences (Basel, Switzerland)*, 14(5), 380. DOI:10.3390/bs14050380 PMID:38785871

Lopez, M. A. (2024). Scars unseen: the enduring effects of war on children's mental health. *Psychiatry Advisor*. https://www.psychiatryadvisor.com/features/psychological-effects-of-war-on-children/

Lopez, B. R., Lincoln, A. J., Ozonoff, S. J., & Lai, Z. (2005). Examining the Relationship between Executive Functions and Restricted, Repetitive Symptoms of Autistic Disorder. *Journal of Autism and Developmental Disorders*, 35(4), 445–460. DOI:10.1007/s10803-005-5035-x PMID:16134030

Lopez-Martinez, A. E., Serrano-Ibanez, E. R., Ruiz-Parraga, G. T., Gomez-Perez, L., Ramirez-Maestre, C., & Esteve, R. (2018). Physical health consequences of interpersonal trauma: A systematic review of the role of psychological variables. *Trauma, Violence & Abuse*, 19(3), 305–322. DOI:10.1177/1524838016659488 PMID:27456113

Lord, C., Brugha, T. S., Charman, T., Cusack, J., Dumas, G., Frazier, T., Jones, J. H. E., Jones, M. R., Pickles, A., State, W. M., Taylor, L. J., & Veenstra-VanderWeele, J. (2020). Autism spectrum disorder. *Nature Reviews. Disease Primers*, 6(1), 1–23. DOI:10.1038/s41572-019-0138-4 PMID:31949163

Lord, C., Risi, S., Lambrecht, L., Cook, E. H.Jr, Leventhal, B. L., DiLavore, P. C., Pickles, A., & Rutter, M. (2000). The autism diagnostic observation schedule-generic: A standard measure of social and communication deficits associated with the spectrum of autism. *Journal of Autism and Developmental Disorders*, 30(3), 205–223. DOI:10.1023/A:1005592401947 PMID:11055457

Lorusso, L., Galli, R., Libera, L., Gagliardi, C., Borgatti, R., & Hollebrandse, B. (2007). Indicators of theory of mind in narrative production: A comparison between individuals with genetic syndromes and typically developing children. *Clinical Linguistics & Phonetics*, 21(1), 37–53. DOI:10.1080/02699200600565871 PMID:17364616

Luckin, R., Holmes, W., Griffiths, M., & Forcier, L. B. (2016). *Intelligence unleashed: An argument for AI in education*. Pearson Education.

Lu, H., Chen, D., & Chou, A. (2022). The school environment and bullying victimization among seventh grades with autism spectrum disorder: A cohort study. *Child and Adolescent Psychiatry and Mental Health*, 16(22), 22. DOI:10.1186/s13034-022-00456-z PMID:35292070

Lunkenheimer, E., Ram, N., Skowron, E. A., & Yin, P. (2017, September). Harsh parenting, child behavior problems, and the dynamic coupling of parents' and children's positive behaviors. *Journal of Family Psychology*, 31(6), 689–698. DOI:10.1037/fam0000310 PMID:28333490

Lyall, K., Croen, L., Daniels, J., Fallin, M. D., Ladd-Acosta, C., Lee, B. K., Park, B. Y., Snyder, N. W., Schendel, D., Volk, H., Windham, G. C., & Newschaffer, C. (2017). The changing epidemiology of autism spectrum disorders. *Annual Review of Public Health*, 38(1), 81–102. DOI:10.1146/annurev-publhealth-031816-044318 PMID:28068486

Lynch, E. W., & Hanson, M. J. (2011). *Developing cross-cultural competence: A guide for working with children and their families*. Brookes Publishing.

Lynch, K. B., Geller, S. R., & Schmidt, M. G. (2004). Multi-Year Evaluation of the Effectiveness of a Resilience-Based Prevention Program for Young Children. *The Journal of Primary Prevention*, 24(3), 335–353. DOI:10.1023/B:JOPP.0000018052.12488.d1

Lynn Mulvey, K., Boswell, C., & Zheng, J. (2017). Causes and Consequences of Social Exclusion and Peer Rejection Among Children and Adolescents. *PubMed, 17*(3), 30100820. https://pubmed.ncbi.nlm.nih.gov/30100820/

Magnuson, K., & Berger, L. M. (2009). Family structure states and transitions: Associations with children's well-being during middle childhood. *Journal of Marriage and Family*, 71(3), 575–591. DOI:10.1111/j.1741-3737.2009.00620.x PMID:20228952

Makrygianni, M. K., Gena, A., Katoudi, S., & Galanis, P. (2018). The effectiveness of applied behavior analytic interventions for children with Autism Spectrum Disorder: A meta-analytic study. *Research in Autism Spectrum Disorders*, 51, 18–31. DOI:10.1016/j.rasd.2018.03.006

Malik, F., & Marwaha, R. (2022, September 18). *Developmental stages of social emotional development in children*. StatPearls - NCBI Bookshelf. https://www.ncbi.nlm.nih.gov/books/nbk534819/

Malik, F., & Marwaha, R. (2023, April 23). *Cognitive Development*. NCBI. https://www.ncbi.nlm.nih.gov/books/NBK537095/

Margalit, M. (2010). *Lonely children and adolescents: Self perceptions, social exclusion and hope*. Springer. DOI:10.1007/978-1-4419-6284-3

Margalit, M., & Al-Yagon, M. (2002). The loneliness experience of children with learning disabilities. In Wong, B. Y. L., & Donahue, M. L. (Eds.), *The social dimensions of learning disabilities: Essays in honor of Tanis Bryan* (pp. 53–75). Lawrence Erlbaum Associates Publishers.

Margari, F., Craig, F., Margari, L., Matera, E., Lamanna, A. L., Lecce, P. A., La Tegola, D., & Carabellese, F. (2015). Psychopathology, symptoms of attention-deficit/hyperactivity disorder, and risk factors in juvenile offenders. *Neuropsychiatric Disease and Treatment*, 11, 343–352. DOI:10.2147/NDT.S75942 PMID:25709458

Marshall, L. L. (1992). Development of the severity of violence against women scales. *Journal of Family Violence*, 7(2), 103–121. DOI:10.1007/BF00978700

Martel, M. M., Nikolas, M., Jernigan, K., Friderici, K., Waldman, I., & Nigg, J. T. (2011). The dopamine receptor D4 gene (DRD4) moderates family environmental effects on ADHD. *Journal of Abnormal Child Psychology*, 39(1), 1–10. DOI:10.1007/s10802-010-9439-5 PMID:20644990

Martin-Denham, S. (2022). Marginalization, autism and school exclusion: Caregivers' perspectives. *Support for Learning*, 37(1), 108–143. DOI:10.1111/1467-9604.12398

Martin, E. G., Klusek, J., Estigarribia, B., & Roberts, E. J. (2009). Language Characteristics of Individuals with Down Syndrome. *Topics in Language Disorders*, 29(2), 112–132. DOI:10.1097/TLD.0b013e3181a71fe1 PMID:20428477

Martin, L., Byrnes, M., McGarry, S., Rea, S., & Wood, F. (2017). Social challenges of visible scarring after severe burn: A qualitative analysis. Burns. *Burns*, 43(1), 76–83. DOI:10.1016/j.burns.2016.07.027 PMID:27576930

Marty, P. (1991). Mentalisation et psychosomatique. *Les Empécheurs de tourner en rond, Paris.*

Marty, P. (1980). L'ordre psychosomatique: les mouvements individuels de vie et de mort: Vol. 2. *Désorganisation et régression [The Psychosomatic Order: Individual Life and Death Movements, vol 2. Disorganization and Regression].* Payot.

Marty, P. (1990). *La psychosomatique de l'adulte[Adult Psychosomatics].* Presses Universitaires de France.

Marty, P. (1997). Psychothérapie psychanalytique des troubles psychosomatiques [Psychoanalytic Psychotherapy of Psychosomatic Disorders]. *Revue Française de Psychosomatique*, 16, 195–204.

Masarik, A. S., & Conger, R. D. (2017). Stress and child development: A review of the Family Stress Model. *Current Opinion in Psychology*, 13, 85–90. DOI:10.1016/j.copsyc.2016.05.008 PMID:28813301

Mash, E., & Barkley, R. (1998). Treatment of childhood disorders. New York: The Guilford Press MTA Cooperative Group. (1999). A 14-month randomized clinical trial of treatment strategies for Attention-Deficit/Hyperactivity Disorder. *Archives of General Psychiatry*, 56, 1073–1086.

Masi, A., DeMayo, M. M., Glozier, N., & Guastella, A. J. (2017). An overview of autism spectrum disorder, heterogeneity and treatment options. *Neuroscience Bulletin*, 33(2), 183–193. DOI:10.1007/s12264-017-0100-y PMID:28213805

Massullo, C., De Rossi, E., Carbone, G. A., Imperatori, C., Ardito, R. B., Adenzato, M., & Farina, B. (2023). Child maltreatment, abuse, and neglect: An umbrella review of their prevalence and definitions. *Clinical Neuropsychiatry: Journal of Treatment Evaluation*, 20(2), 72–99. PMID:37250758

Mathews, B., Pacella, R., Scott, J. G., Finkelhor, D., Meinck, F., Higgins, D. J., Erskine, H. E., Thomas, H. J., Lawrence, D. M., Haslam, D. M., Malacova, E., & Dunne, M. P. (2023). The prevalence of child maltreatment in Australia: Findings from a national survey. *The Medical Journal of Australia*, 218(1), 13–18. DOI:10.5694/mja2.51873 PMID:37004184

Matthews, N. L., Pollard, E., Ober-Reynolds, S., Kirwan, J., Malligo, A., & Smith, C. J. (2015). Revisiting Cognitive and Adaptive Functioning in Children and Adolescents with Autism Spectrum Disorder. *Journal of Autism and Developmental Disorders*, 45(1), 138–156. DOI:10.1007/s10803-014-2200-0 PMID:25117583

May, J., Osmond, K., & Billick, St. (2014). Juvenile Delinquency Treatment and Prevention: A Litterature Review. *The Psychiatric Quarterly*, 85(3), 295–301. DOI:10.1007/s11126-014-9296-4 PMID:24610601

Mazefsky, C. A., Herrington, J., Siegel, M., Scarpa, A., Maddox, B. B., Scahill, L., & White, S. W. (2013). The role of emotion regulation in autism spectrum Disorder. *Journal of the American Academy of Child and Adolescent Psychiatry*, 52(7), 679–688. DOI:10.1016/j.jaac.2013.05.006 PMID:23800481

Mcauley, T., Chen, S., Goos, L., Schachar, R., & Crosbie, J. (2010). Is the behavior rating inventory of executive function more strongly associated with measures of impairment or executive function? *Journal of the International Neuropsychological Society*, 16(3), 495–505. DOI:10.1017/S1355617710000093 PMID:20188014

McCartney, K., Dearing, E., Taylor, B. A., & Bub, K. L. (2007, September 1). Quality Child Care Supports the Achievement of Low-Income Children: Direct and Indirect Pathways Through Caregiving and the Home Environment. *Journal of Applied Developmental Psychology*, 28(5-6), 411–426. DOI:10.1016/j.appdev.2007.06.010 PMID:19578561

McCold, P., & Wachtel, B. (1998). *Restorative policing experiment: The Bethlehem Pennsylvania, Police Family Group Conferencing Project*. Community Service Foundation.

McConkey, R. (2019). The increasing prevalence of school pupils with ASD: Insights from Northern Ireland. *European Journal of Special Needs Education*, 35(3), 414–424. DOI:10.1080/08856257.2019.1683686

McCraty, R., & Childre, D. (2010). Coherence: Bridging personal, social, and global health. *Alternative Therapies in Health and Medicine*, 16(4), 10–24. PMID:20653292

McFarlane, A. C. (1992). Avoidance and intrusion in posttraumatic stress disorder. *The Journal of Nervous and Mental Disease*, 180(7), 439–445. DOI:10.1097/00005053-199207000-00006 PMID:1624925

McFarlane, A. C. (2010). The long-term costs of traumatic stress: Intertwined physical and psychological consequences. *World Psychiatry; Official Journal of the World Psychiatric Association (WPA)*, 9(1), 3–10. DOI:10.1002/j.2051-5545.2010.tb00254.x PMID:20148146

McHugh, M. C. (2005). Understanding gender and intimate partner abuse. *Sex Roles*, 52(11-12), 717–724. DOI:10.1007/s11199-005-4194-8

McLean, R. L., Harrison, A. J., Zimak, E., Joseph, R. M., & Morrow, E. M. (2014). Executive function in probands with autism with average IQ and their unaffected First-Degree relatives. *Journal of the American Academy of Child and Adolescent Psychiatry*, 53(9), 1001–1009. DOI:10.1016/j.jaac.2014.05.019 PMID:25151423

Mcleod, S. (2024, January 24) *Piaget's Theory And Stages Of Cognitive Development*. Simply Psychology. https://www.simplypsychology.org/piaget.html

McNiff, J. (1999). *Action Research: Principles and Practices*. Routledge.

McNiff, J., Lomax, P., & Whitehead, J. (2003). *You and your action research project*. Routledge Falmer.

McVey, A. J., Schiltz, H. K., Haendel, A. D., Dolan, B. K., Willar, K. S., Pleiss, S. S., Karst, J. S., Carlson, M., Krueger, W., Murphy, C. C., Casnar, C. L., Yund, B., & Van Hecke, A. V. (2018). Social difficulties in youth with autism with and without anxiety and ADHD symptoms. *Autism research: official journal of the International Society for Autism Research, 11*(12), 1679–1689. DOI:10.1002/aur.2039

Megari, K. (2013). Quality of life in chronic disease patients. *Health Psychology Research*, 1(3), 141–148. DOI:10.4081/hpr.2013.932 PMID:26973912

Megari, K., Frantzezou, C. K., Polyzopoulou, Z. A., & Tzouni, S. K. (2024). Neurocognitive features in childhood & adulthood in autism spectrum disorder: A Neurodiversity Approach. *International Journal of Developmental Neuroscience*, 1–29. DOI:10.1002/jdn.10356 PMID:38953464

Megari, K., Sofologi, M., Kougioumtzis, G., Thomaidou, E., Thomaidis, G., Katsarou, D., Yotsidi, V., & Theodoratou, M. (2024). Neurocognitive and psycho-emotional profile of children with disabilities. *Applied Neuropsychology. Child*, 4, 1–6. DOI:10.1080/21622965.2024.2304781 PMID:38574392

Mercader-Rubio, I., Ángel, N. G., Silva, S., & Brito-Costa, S. (2023). Levels of somatic anxiety, cognitive anxiety, and self-efficacy in university athletes from a Spanish public university and their relationship with basic psychological needs. *International Journal of Environmental Research and Public Health*, 20(5), 44–52. DOI:10.3390/ijerph20032415 PMID:36767781

Merchán-Naranjo, J., Boada, L., Del Rey-Mejías, Á., Mayoral, M., Llorente, C., Arango, C., & Parellada, M. (2016). La función ejecutiva está alterada en los trastornos del espectro autista, pero esta no correlaciona con la inteligencia. *Revista de Psiquiatría y Salud Mental*, 9(1), 39–50. DOI:10.1016/j.rpsm.2015.10.005 PMID:26724269

Merrill, E., Goodwwyn, E., & Gooding, H. (1996). Mental Retardation and the Acquisition of Automatic Processing. *American Journal of Mental Retardation*, 101, 49–62. PMID:8827251

Merry, S. N., Hetrick, S. E., Cox, G. R., Brudevold-Iversen, T., Bir, J. J., & McDowell, H. (2011). The effectiveness of school-based mental health services for elementary-aged children: A meta-analysis. *Journal of the American Academy of Child & Adolescent Psychiatry, 50*(9), 865-878. DOI:10.1016/j.jaac.2011.05.003

Messer, D. J., Henry, L. A., & Danielsson, H. (2021). Children with intellectual and developmental disabilities: Issues about matching, recruitment, and group comparisons. *Manuscript.*

Meyer, A., Rose, D. H., & Gordon, D. (2014). *Universal design for learning: Theory and practice.* CAST Professional Publishing.

Meyer, J. A., & Minshew, N. J. (2002). An Update on Neurocognitive Profiles in Asperger Syndrome and High- Functioning Autism. *Focus on Autism and Other Developmental Disabilities*, 17(3), 152–160. DOI:10.1177/10883576020170030501

Milton, D. (2012). On the ontological status of autism: The 'double empathy problem'. *Disability & Society*, 27(6), 883–887. DOI:10.1080/09687599.2012.710008

Milton, D., & Ryan, S. (Eds.). (2023). *The routledge international handbook of critical autism studies*. Routledge.

Minshew, N. G., & Goldstein, G. (2001). The Pattern of Intact and Impaired Memory Functions in Autism. *Journal of Child Psychology and Psychiatry, and Allied Disciplines*, 42(8), 1095–1101. DOI:10.1111/1469-7610.00808 PMID:11806691

Mirzaei, M., Ardekani, S. M. Y., Mirzaei, M., & Dehghani, A. (2019). Prevalence of depression, anxiety and stress among adult population: Results of Yazd health study. *Iranian Journal of Psychiatry*, 14(2), 137–146. https://pubmed.ncbi.nlm.nih.gov/31440295/. DOI:10.18502/ijps.v14i2.993 PMID:31440295

Mitchell, L. L., Lodi-Smith, J., Baranski, E. N., & Whitbourne, S. K. (2021). Implications of identity resolution in emerging adulthood for intimacy, generativity, and integrity across the adult lifespan. *Psychology and Aging*, 36(5), 545–556. DOI:10.1037/pag0000537 PMID:34197138

Moen, Ø. & Hedelin, B. & Hall-Lord, M. (2016). Family Functioning, Psychological Distress, and Well-Being in Parents with a Child Having ADHD. *SAGE Open*. 6. 1-10.1177/2158244015626767.

Moen, Ø. L., Hall-Lord, M. L., & Hedelin, B. (2011). Contending and adapting every day: Norwegian parents' lived experience of having a child with ADHD. *Journal of Family Nursing*, 17(4), 441–462. DOI:10.1177/1074840711423924 PMID:22084482

Moen, Ø. L., Hall-Lord, M. L., & Hedelin, B. (2014). Living in a family with a child with attention deficit hyperactivity disorder: A phenomenographic study. *Journal of Clinical Nursing*, 23(21-22), 3166–3176. DOI:10.1111/jocn.12559 PMID:25453121

Mollon, J., Knowles, E. E. M., Mathias, S. R., Gur, R., Peralta, J. M., Weiner, D. J., Robinson, E. B., Gur, R. E., Blangero, J., Almasy, L., & Glahn, D. C. (2021). Genetic influence on cognitive development between childhood and adulthood. *Molecular Psychiatry*, 26(2), 656–665. DOI:10.1038/s41380-018-0277-0 PMID:30644433

Montazeri A, Harirchi AM, Shariati M, Garmaroudi G, Ebadi M, Fateh A. (2003) The 12-item General Health Questionnaire (GHQ-12): translation and validation study of the Iranian version. *Health Qual Life Outcomes*. BMC. .DOI:10.1186/1477-7525-1-66

Montero, J. (2022). Developing empathy through design thinking in elementary art education. *The International Journal of Art & Design Education. International Journal of Art & Design Education*, 42(1), 155–171. DOI:10.1111/jade.12445

Moorfoot, N., Leung, R. K., Toumbourou, J. W., & Catalano, R. F. (2015). The longitudinal effects of adolescent volunteering on secondary school completion and adult volunteering. *International Journal of Developmental Science*, 9(3,4), 115–123. DOI:10.3233/DEV-140148 PMID:27458548

Morina, N., Schnyder, U., Klaghofer, R., Müller, J., & Martin-Soelch, C. (2018). Trauma exposure and the mediating role of posttraumatic stress on somatic symptoms in civilian war victims. *BMC Psychiatry*, 18(92), 1–7. DOI:10.1186/s12888-018-1680-4 PMID:29631551

Mottron, L., Dawson, M., & Soulières, I. (2009). Enhanced perception in savant syndrome: Patterns, structure and creativity. *Philosophical Transactions of the Royal Society of London. Series B, Biological Sciences*, 364(1522), 1385–1391. DOI:10.1098/rstb.2008.0333 PMID:19528021

Mottron, L., Dawson, M., Soulieres, I., Hubert, B., & Burack, J. (2006). Enhanced perceptual functioning in autism: An update, and eight principles of autistic perception. *Journal of Autism and Developmental Disorders*, 36(1), 27–43. DOI:10.1007/s10803-005-0040-7 PMID:16453071

Mousavi, S., Pahlavanzadeh, S., & Maghsoudi, J. (2019). Evaluating the effect of a need-based program for caregivers on the stress, anxiety, depression, and the burden of care in families of children with attention deficit-hyperactive disorder. *Iranian Journal of Nursing and Midwifery Research*, 24(2), 96–101. DOI:10.4103/ijnmr.IJNMR_11_17 PMID:30820219

Mrug, S., Madan, A., & Windle, M. (2015). Emotional desensitization to violence contributes to adolescents' violent behavior. *Journal of Abnormal Child Psychology*, 44(1), 75–86. DOI:10.1007/s10802-015-9986-x PMID:25684447

MTA Cooperative Group. (2004). National institute of mental health multimodal treatment study of ADHD follow-up: 24-month outcomes of treatment strategies for Attention-Deficit/Hyperactivity Disorder. *Pediatrics*, 113(4), 754–761. DOI:10.1542/peds.113.4.754 PMID:15060224

Mueller, A. K., Fuermaier, A. B., Koerts, J., & Tucha, L. (2012). Stigma in attention deficit hyperactivity disorder. *Attention Deficit and Hyperactivity Disorders*, 4(3), 101–114. DOI:10.1007/s12402-012-0085-3 PMID:22773377

Mulligan, A., Anney, R., Butler, L., O'Regan, M., Richardson, T., Tulewicz, E. M., Fitzgerald, M., & Gill, M. (2011). Home environment: Association with hyperactivity/impulsivity in children with ADHD and their non-ADHD siblings. *Child: Care, Health and Development*, 39(2), 202–212. DOI:10.1111/j.1365-2214.2011.01345.x PMID:22168816

Muñoz-Silva, A., Lago-Urbano, R., Sanchez-Garcia, M., & Carmona-Márquez, J. (2017). Child/adolescent's ADHD and parenting stress: The mediating role of family impact and conduct problems. *Frontiers in Psychology*, 8, 300021. DOI:10.3389/fpsyg.2017.02252 PMID:29312090

Muris, P., & Ollendick, T. H. (2005). The role of Temperament in the etiology of Child Psychopathology. *Clinical Child and Family Psychology Review*, 8(4), 271–289. DOI:10.1007/s10567-005-8809-y PMID:16362256

Murray-Close, D., Ostrov, J. M., Nelson, D. A., Crick, N. R., & Coccaro, E. F. (2010). Proactive, reactive, and romantic relational aggression in adulthood: Measurement, predictive validity, gender differences, and association with Intermittent Explosive Disorder. *Journal of Psychiatric Research*, 44(6), 393–404. DOI:10.1016/j.jpsychires.2009.09.005 PMID:19822329

Musetti, A., Eboli, G., Cavallini, F., & Corsano, P. (2019). Social relationships, self-esteem, and loneliness in adolescents with learning disabilities. *Clinical Neuropsychiatry, 16*(4), 165–172. https://doi.org/PMID: 34908952.

Mwangangi, R. M. (2019). The Role of Family in Dealing with Juvenile Delinquency. *Journal of Social Sciences*, 7, 52–63.

Nader, K. (2012). School shootings and other youth problems: The need for early preventive interventions. In K. Nader (Ed.), *School rampage shootings and other youth disturbances: Early preventative interventions* (pp. 3–32). Routledge/Taylor & Francis Group.

Nation. (2021). India saw 31 kids die by suicide every day in 2020; experts say COVID upped trauma. *Daccan Chronicle*. https://www.deccanchronicle.com/nation/in-other-news/311021/india-saw-31-kids-die-by-suicide-every-day-in-2020-experts-say-covid.html

National Crime Records Bureau. (2020). *Crime in India, 2020.* NCRB. https://ruralindiaonline.org/en/library/resource/crime-in-india-2020-volume-iii/

Nayla, M. R. (2024). Factors Influencing The Subjective Well-Being Of Mothers Who Have Hyperactive Children. *JHSS*, 8(1), 216–220.

Neff, P. E. (2010). Fathering an ADHD Child: An Examination of Paternal Well-being and Social Support*. *Sociological Inquiry*, 80(4), 531–553. DOI:10.1111/j.1475-682X.2010.00348.x PMID:20879176

Nevo, D. (2001). School evaluation: Internal or external? *Studies in Educational Evaluation*, 27(2), 95–106. DOI:10.1016/S0191-491X(01)00016-5

Nicolaidis, C., Raymaker, D., Kapp, S. K., Baggs, A., Ashkenazy, E., McDonald, K., Weiner, M., Maslak, J., Hunter, M., & Joyce, A. (2019). The AASPIRE practice-based guidelines for the inclusion of autistic adults in research as co-researchers and study participants. *Autism*, 23(8), 2007–2019. DOI:10.1177/1362361319830523 PMID:30939892

NIDCD (National Institute on Deafness and Other Communication Disorders). (2020). *Autism Spectrum Disorder: Communication Problems in Children NIH Pub. No. 97–4315*. NIDCD.

Niemeyer, M., & Shichor, D. (1996). A preliminary study of a large victim/offender reconciliation program. *Federal Probation*, 60, 30–34.

Nijhof, S. L., Vinkers, C. H., Van Geelen, S. M., Duijff, S. N., Achterberg, E. J. M., Van der Net, J., Veltkamp, R. C., Grootenhuis, M. A., van de Putte, E. M., Hillegers, M. H. J., van der Brug, A. W., Wierenga, C. J., Benders, M. J. N. L., Engels, R. C. M. E., van der Ent, C. K., Vanderschuren, L. J. M. J., & Lesscher, H. M. B. (2018). Healthy play, better coping: The importance of play for the development of children in health and disease. *Neuroscience and Biobehavioral Reviews*, 95(September), 421–429. DOI:10.1016/j.neubiorev.2018.09.024 PMID:30273634

Ningrum, I. T. K. (2024). Legal Political Review of The Protection of Sexual Violence Victims In the Perspective of Law Number 12 of 2022 Concerning Sexual Violence Crimes. *Journal Equitable*, 9(2), 156–168.

Nisar, M., Ullah, S., Ali, M., & Alam, S. (2015). Juvenile Delinquency: The Influence of Family, Peer and Economic Factors of Juvenile Delinquents. *Applied Scientific Research*, 9(1), 37–48.

Nistor, G., & Dumitru, C.-L. (2021). Preventing school exclusion of students with autism spectrum disorder (ASD) through reducing discrimination: Sustainable integration through contact-based education sessions. *Sustainability (Basel)*, 13(13), 7056. DOI:10.3390/su13137056

Noble, K. G., McCandliss, B. D., & Farah, M. J. (2007). Socioeconomic gradients predict individual differences in neurocognitive abilities. *Developmental Science*, 10(4), 464–480. DOI:10.1111/j.1467-7687.2007.00600.x PMID:17552936

Noggle, J. J., Steiner, N. J., Minami, T., & Khalsa, S. B. (2012). Benefits of yoga for psychosocial well-being in a US high school curriculum: A preliminary randomized controlled trial. *Journal of Developmental & Behavioral Pediatrics, 33*(3), 193-201. DOI:10.1097/DBP.0b013e31824afdc4

North, C. S. (2002). Somatization in survivors of catastrophic trauma: A methodological review. *Environmental Health Perspectives*, 4(4, suppl 4), 637–640. DOI:10.1289/ehp.02110s4637 PMID:12194899

Nugent, W., Williams, M., & Umbreit, M. (2003). Participation in victim-offender mediation and the prevalence and severity of subsequent delinquent behavior: A meta-analysis. *Utah Law Review*, 137(1), 137–166.

Nugent, W., Williams, M., & Umbreit, M. (2004). Participation in victim-offender mediation and the prevalence of subsequent delinquent behavior: A meta-analysis. *Research on Social Work Practice*, 14(6), 408–416. DOI:10.1177/1049731504265831

Nuri, C., Akçamete, G., & Direktör, C. (2019). The Quality Of Life And Stress Levels In Parents Of Children With Attention Deficit Hyperactivity Disorder. *European Journal Of Special Education Research, 4*(3).

Oginyi, C., Nwoye, E., Ude, U., & Okeke, N. (2024). Childhood sexual abuse among undergraduates: Personality trait, substance abuse, and loneliness as predictor variables. *The Japanese Psychological Research*, 48(2), 123–136. https://ebsu-jssh.com/index.php/EBSUJSSH/article/view/148

Ogundele, O. M. (2018). Behavioural and emotional disorders in childhood: A brief overview for paediatricians. *World Journal of Clinical Pediatrics*, 7(1), 9–26. DOI:10.5409/wjcp.v7.i1.9 PMID:29456928

Oliver, M. (1990). *The politics of disablement*. Macmillan. DOI:10.1007/978-1-349-20895-1

Operto, F. F., Smirni, D., Scuoppo, C., Padovano, C., Vivenzio, V., Quatrosi, G., Carotenuto, M., Precenzano, F., & Pastorino, M. G. G. (2021). Neuropsychological Profile, Emotional/Behavioral Problems, and Parental Stress in Children with Neurodevelopmental Disorders. *Brain Sciences*, 11(5), 584–594. DOI:10.3390/brainsci11050584 PMID:33946388

Ornoy, A., Weinstein-Fudim, L., & Ergaz, Z. (2015). Prenatal factors associated with autism spectrum disorder (ASD). *Reproductive Toxicology (Elmsford, N.Y.)*, 56, 155–169. DOI:10.1016/j.reprotox.2015.05.007 PMID:26021712

Ozonoff, S., Pennington, B. F., & Rogers, S. I. (1991). Executive function deficits in high-functioning autistic children: Relationship to theory of mind. *Journal of Child Psychology and Psychiatry, and Allied Disciplines*, 32(7), 1081–1105. DOI:10.1111/j.1469-7610.1991.tb00351.x PMID:1787138

Pane, J. F., Griffin, B. A., McCaffrey, D. F., & Karam, R. (2017). Effectiveness of cognitive tutor algebra I at scale. *Educational Evaluation and Policy Analysis, 36*(2), 127-144. DOI:10.3102/0162373713507480

Pantazis, S. (2004). *Pedagogy and play - a target object of the kindergarten*. Gutenberg.

Papaeliou, F. C., Fryssira, H., Kodakos, A., Kaila, M., Benaveli, E., Michaelides, K., Stroggilos, V., Vrettopoulou, M., & Polemikos, N. (2011). Nonverbal communication, play, and language in Greek young children with Williams syndrome. *Child Neuropsychology*, 17(3), 225–241. DOI:10.1080/09297049.2010.524151 PMID:21229406

Papoudi, D., Jørgensen, C. R., Guldberg, K., & Meadan, H. (2021). Perceptions, experiences, and needs of parents of culturally and linguistically diverse children with autism: A scoping review. *Review Journal of Autism and Developmental Disorders*, 8(2), 195–212. DOI:10.1007/s40489-020-00210-1

Parhoon, K., Moradi, A., Alizadeh, H., Parhoon, H., Sadaphal, D. P., & Coolidge, F. L. (2021). *Psychometric properties of the behavior rating inventory of executive function,* second edition (BRIEF2) in a sample of children with ADHD in Iran. *Child Neuropsychology/Neuropsychology, Development, and Cognition. Section C, Child Neuropsychology, 28*(4), 427–436. DOI:10.1080/09297049.2021.1975669

Parker, R., & Thomsen, B. S. (2019). *Learning through play at school: A study of playful integrated pedagogies that foster children's holistic skills development in the primary school classroom.* Billund: LEGOFoundation.

Park, J., Bouck, E. C., & Duenas, A. (2020). Using video modeling to teach social skills for employment to youth with intellectual disability. *Career Development and Transition for Exceptional Individuals*, 43(1), 40–52. DOI:10.1177/2165143418810671

Park, N. (2004). The Role of Subjective Well-Being in Positive Youth Development. *The Annals of the American Academy of Political and Social Science*, 2004(591), 25–39. DOI:10.1177/0002716203260078

Patrick-Hoffman, P. (1982). *Psychological abuse of women by spouses and live-in lovers.* [Unpublished doctoral dissertation, Union for Experimenting Colleges and Universities].

Patterson, G. R., & Reid, J. B. (1973). Intervention for families of aggressive boys: A replication study. *Behaviour Research and Therapy*, 11(4), 383–394. DOI:10.1016/0005-7967(73)90096-X PMID:4777636

Paulra, S. J. P. V., Chinchai, S., Munkhetvit, P., & Sriphetcharawut, S. (2024). The development and content validity of the emotional recognition memory training program (ERMTP) for children with autism spectrum disorder: A trial phase. *Journal of Associated Medical Sciences*, 57(1), 177–189. DOI:10.12982/JAMS.2024.020

Pavlacic, J. M., Kellum, K. K., & Schulenberg, St. E. (2021). Advocating for the Use of Restorative Justice Practices: Examining the Overlap between Restorative Justice and Behavior Analysis. *Behavior Analysis in Practice*, 1–10. PMID:34457213

Peasgood, T., Bhardwaj, A., Biggs, K., Brazier, J. E., Coghill, D., Cooper, C. L., Daley, D., De Silva, C., Harpin, V., Hodgkins, P., Nadkarni, A., Setyawan, J., & Sonuga-Barke, E. J. (2016). The impact of ADHD on the health and well-being of ADHD children and their siblings. *European Child & Adolescent Psychiatry*, 25(11), 1217–1231. DOI:10.1007/s00787-016-0841-6 PMID:27037707

Pelham, W. E.Jr, Wheeler, T., & Chronis, A. (1998). Empirically supported psycho-social treatments for attention deficit hyperactivity disorder. *Journal of Clinical Child Psychology*, 27(2), 190–205. DOI:10.1207/s15374424jccp2702_6 PMID:9648036

Pelham, W., Burrows-MacLean, L., Gnagy, E., Fabiano, G., Coles, E., Tresco, K., Wymbs, B., Wienke, A., Walker, K., & Hoffman, M. (2005). Transdermal methylphenidate, behavioral, and combined treatment for children with ADHD. *Experimental and Clinical Psychopharmacology*, 13(2), 111–126. DOI:10.1037/1064-1297.13.2.111 PMID:15943544

Pellicano, E. (2012). The Development of Executive Function in Autism. *Autism Research and Treatment*, 146132, 1–8. DOI:10.1155/2012/146132 PMID:22934168

Pellicano, E., & Stears, M. (2011). Bridging autism, science and society: Moving toward an ethically informed approach to autism research. *Autism Research*, 4(4), 271–282. DOI:10.1002/aur.201 PMID:21567986

Pennant, M. E., Loucas, C. E., Whittington, C., Creswell, C., Fonagy, P., & Fuggle, P. (2015). Computerised therapies for anxiety and depression in children and young people: A systematic review and meta-analysis. *Behaviour Research and Therapy, 67*, 1-18. DOI:10.1016/j.brat.2015.01.009

Perepa, P., Wallace, S., & Guldberg, G. (2023). *The experiences of marginalized families with autistic children*. University of Birmingham., https://www.birmingham.ac.uk/documents/college-social-sciences/education/publications/marginalised-families-with-autistic-children.pdf.pdf

Perry-Parrish, C., Copeland-Linder, N., Webb, L., Shields, A. H., & Sibinga, E. M. (2016). Improving self-regulation in adolescents: Current evidence for the role of mindfulness-based cognitive therapy. *Adolescent Health, Medicine and Therapeutics*, 7, 101–108. DOI:10.2147/AHMT.S65820 PMID:27695378

Persico, A. M., Ricciardello, A., Lamberti, M., Turriziani, L., Cucinotta, F., Brogna, C., Vitiello, B., & Arango, C. (2021). The pediatric psychopharmacology of autism spectrum disorder: A systematic review - Part I: The past and the present. *Progress in Neuro-Psychopharmacology & Biological Psychiatry*, 110, 110326. DOI:10.1016/j.pnpbp.2021.110326 PMID:33857522

Peters, K., & Jackson, D. (2009). Mothers' experiences of parenting a child with attention deficit hyperactivity disorder. *Journal of Advanced Nursing*, 65(1), 62–71. DOI:10.1111/j.1365-2648.2008.04853.x PMID:19120583

Petkanopoulou, M. (2017). *The improvised board game as a "supporting tool" for teaching in preschool age"*, [Master thesis, University of Western Macedonia]. https://dspace.uowm.gr/xmlui/bitstream/handle/123456789/919/Maria%20Petkanopoulou.pdf?sequence=1&isAllowed=y

Piaget, J. (1929). *The Child's Conception of the World*. Routledge & Kegan Paul.

Piaget, J. (1936). *Origins of intelligence in the child*. Routledge & Kegan Paul.

Piaget, J. (1952). *The origins of intelligence in children*. W W Norton & Co., DOI:10.1037/11494-000

Picard, R. W., Vyzas, E., & Healey, J. (2016). Toward machine emotional intelligence: Analysis of affective physiological state. *IEEE Transactions on Pattern Analysis and Machine Intelligence, 23*(10), 1175-1191. DOI:10.1109/34.954607

Pinder-Amaker, S. (2014). Identifying the unmet needs of college students on the autism spectrum. *Harvard Review of Psychiatry*, 22(2), 125–137. DOI:10.1097/HRP.0000000000000032 PMID:24614767

Pitcairn, T., & Wishart, J. (1994). Reactions of young children with Down' syndrome to an impossible task. *British Journal of Developmental Psychology*, 12(4), 485–489. DOI:10.1111/j.2044-835X.1994.tb00649.x

Pollak, S. D., Cicchetti, D., Hornung, K., & Reed, A. (2000). Recognizing Emotion in Faces: Developmental Effects of Child Abuse and Neglect. *Developmental Psychology*, 36(5), 679–688. DOI:10.1037/0012-1649.36.5.679 PMID:10976606

Pollak, S. D., & Sinha, P. (2002). Effects of early experience on children's recognition of facial displays of emotion. *Developmental Psychology*, 38(5), 784–791. DOI:10.1037/0012-1649.38.5.784 PMID:12220055

Pooragha, F., Kafi, S. M., & Sotodeh, S. O. (2013). Comparing response inhibition and flexibility for two components of executive functioning in children with autism spectrum disorder and normal children. *Iranian Journal of Pediatrics*, 23(3), 309. PMID:23795254

Powell, D. R., Son, S. H., File, N., & San Juan, R. R. (2010). Parent–school relationships and children's academic and social outcomes in public school pre-kindergarten. *Journal of School Psychology*, 48(4), 269–292. DOI:10.1016/j.jsp.2010.03.002 PMID:20609850

Precate, B., & Yiotakos, O. (2006). *Σεξουαλική κακοποίηση: Μυστικό; Όχι πια*. Ελληνικά Γράμματα.

Priestley, M. (1998). Constructions and creations: Idealism, materialism and disability theory. *Disability & Society*, 13(1), 75–94. DOI:10.1080/09687599826920

Prioreschi, A., Wrottesley, S. V., Slemming, W., Cohen, E., & Norris, S. A. (2020). A qualitative study reporting maternal perceptions of the importance of play for healthy growth and development in the first two years of life. *BMC Pediatrics*, 20(1), 1–11. DOI:10.1186/s12887-020-02321-4 PMID:32907550

Psoma, M., & Vlahos, F. (2018). Neurocognitive Approaches to Autism Spectrum Disorders. In Vlachos, F. (Ed.), *Brain, learning and special education* (pp. 395–425). Gutenberg.

Pujol, J., Soriano-Mas, C., Ortiz, H., & Galles, S. N. (2006). Myelination of language-related areas in the developing brain. *Neurology*, 66(3), 339–343. DOI:10.1212/01.wnl.0000201049.66073.8d PMID:16476931

Pulina, F., Vianello, R., & Lanfranchi, S. (2019). Cognitive profiles in individuals with Down syndrome. In Lanfranchi, S. (Ed.), *International review of research in developmental disabilities: State of the art of research on Down syndrome* (pp. 67–92). Elsevier Academic Press. DOI:10.1016/bs.irrdd.2019.06.002

Puri, B. K., & Theodoratou, M. (2023). The efficacy of psychoeducation in managing low back pain: A systematic review. *Psychiatrike = Psychiatriki, 34*(3), 231–242. DOI:10.22365/jpsych.2022.104

Purper-Ouakil, D., Ramoz, N., Lepagnol-Bestel, A. M., & Simonneau, M. (2011). Neurobiology of attention deficit/hyperactivity disorder. *Pediatric Research*, 69(5 Part 2), 69–76. DOI:10.1203/PDR.0b013e318212b40f PMID:21289544

Purpura, D., Baroody, A., Eiland, M., & Reid, E. (2016). Fostering first graders' reasoning strategies with basic sums: The value of guided instruction. *The Elementary School Journal*, 117(1), 72–100. DOI:10.1086/687809

Raburu, P. A. (2015). The Self- Who Am I?: Children's Identity and Development through Early Childhood Education. *Journal of Educational and Social Research*. DOI:10.5901/jesr.2015.v5n1p95

Ralli, A. M., Alexandri, M., & Sofologi, M. (2024). Language, Socio-Emotional Skills, and School Performance of Children and Adolescents With Developmental Language Disorder According to Parents' Perceptions. In *Childhood Developmental Language Disorders: Role of Inclusion, Families, and Professionals* (pp. 85-101). IGI Global.

Ramani, G. B., & Brownell, C. A. (2014). Preschoolers' cooperative problem solving: Integrating play and problem solving. *Journal of Early Childhood Research*, 12(1), 92–108. DOI:10.1177/1476718X13498337

Ranjan, R., & Pradhan, K. R. (2022). Social Interaction Skills Development in Children with ASD: A Group-Based Comparative Study. *International Journal of Science and Healthcare Research*, 7(2), 450–456. DOI:10.52403/ijshr.20220463

Rathinabalan, I., & Naaraayan, S. A. (2017). Effect of family factors on juvenile delinquency. *International Journal of Contemporary Pediatrics*, 4(6), 2079–2082. DOI:10.18203/2349-3291.ijcp20174735

Reavley, N. J., & Jorm, A. F. (2015). The quality of mental health literacy in Australia: A national review. *BMC Public Health, 15*(1), 994. https://doi.org/DOI:10.1186/s12889-015-2333-9

Renzi, A., Lionetti, F., Bruni, O., Parisi, P., & Galli, F. (2024). Somatization in children and adolescents with headache: The role of attachment to parents. *Current Psychology (New Brunswick, N.J.)*, 43(1), 14358–14366. DOI:10.1007/s12144-023-05466-4

Research Units on Pediatric Psychopharmacology (RUPP) Autism Network. (2005). Randomized, controlled, crossover trial of methylphenidate in pervasive developmental disorders with hyperactivity. *Archives of General Psychiatry*, 62(11), 1266–1274. DOI:10.1001/archpsyc.62.11.1266 PMID:16275814

Richards, K., Austin, A., Allen, K., & Schmidt, U. (2019). Early intervention services for non-psychotic mental health disorders: A scoping review protocol. *BMJ Open*, 9(12), e033656. DOI:10.1136/bmjopen-2019-033656 PMID:31811012

Richman, S. (2001). *Raising a Child with Autism: A Guide to Applied Behavior Analysis for Parents*. Jessica Kingsley Publishers.

Rief, S. F. (2005). *How to reach and teach children with ADD/ADHD: Practical Techniques, strategies and interventions* (2nd ed.). Jossey-Bass.

Roberts, J. M., & Simpson, K. (2016). A review of research into stakeholder perspectives on inclusion of students with autism in mainstream schools. *International Journal of Inclusive Education, 20*(10), 1084-1096. DOI:10.1080/13603116.2016.1145267

Roberts, E. J., Price, J., & Malkin, C. (2007). Language and communication development in Down syndrome. *Mental Retardation and Developmental Disabilities Research Reviews*, 13(1), 26–35. DOI:10.1002/mrdd.20136 PMID:17326116

Robinson, S., Goddard, L., Dritschel, B., Wisley, M., & Howlin, P. (2009). Executive functions in children with Autism Spectrum Disorders. *Brain and Cognition*, 71(3), 362–368. DOI:10.1016/j.bandc.2009.06.007 PMID:19628325

Rodrigo, M. J., Máiquez, M. L., García, M., Mendoza, R., Rubio, A., Martínez, A., & Martín, J. C. (2004). Relaciones padres-hijos y estilos de vida en la adolescencia. *Psicothema*, 16, 203–210.

Rodriguez, M. A., Bauer, H. M., McLoughlin, E., & Grumbach, K. (1999). Screening and Intervention for Intimate Partner Abuse: Practices and Attitudes of Primary Care Physicians. *Journal of the American Medical Association*, 282(5), 468–474. DOI:10.1001/jama.282.5.468 PMID:10442663

Roelofs, K., Spinhoven, P., Sandijck, P., Moene, F. C., & Hoogduin, K. A. (2005). The impact of early trauma and recent life-events on symptom severity in patients with conversion disorder. *The Journal of Nervous and Mental Disease*, 193(8), 508–514. DOI:10.1097/01.nmd.0000172472.60197.4d PMID:16082294

Rohlf, H. L., & Krahé, B. (2015). Assessing anger regulation in middle childhood: Development and validation of a behavioral observation measure. *Frontiers in Psychology*, 6. DOI:10.3389/fpsyg.2015.00453 PMID:25964767

Roid, G. H., & Barram, R. A. (2004). *Essentials of Stanford-Binet Intelligence Scales (SB5) assessment*. John Wiley & Sons.

Rommelse, N., Langerak, I., Van Der Meer, J., De Bruijn, Y., Staal, W., Oerlemans, A., & Buitelaar, J. (2015). Intelligence May Moderate the Cognitive Profile of Patients with ASD. *PLoS One*, 10(10), e0138698. DOI:10.1371/journal.pone.0138698 PMID:26444877

Rommelse, N., Visser, J., & Hartman, C. (2018). Differentiating between ADHD and ASD in childhood: Some directions for practitioners. *European Child & Adolescent Psychiatry*, 27(6), 679–681. DOI:10.1007/s00787-018-1165-5 PMID:29754280

Ronald, A., Pennell, C. E., & Whitehouse, A. J. O. (2011). Prenatal Maternal Stress Associated with ADHD and Autistic Traits in early Childhood. *Frontiers in Psychology*, 1. DOI:10.3389/fpsyg.2010.00223 PMID:21833278

Rosenqvist, J., Lahti-Nuuttila, P., Urgesi, C., Holdnack, A. J., Kemp, S. L., & Laasonen, M. (2017). Neurocognitive Functions in 3- to 15-Year-Old Children: An International Comparison. *Journal of the International Neuropsychological Society*, 23(4), 1–14. DOI:10.1017/S1355617716001193 PMID:28143627

Rothbart, M. K., & Bates, J. E. (2007). Temperament. In Eisenberg, N., Damon, W., & Lerner, R. M. (Eds.), *Social, emotional, and personality development* (6th ed., pp. 99–166). Handbook of child psychology. John Wiley & Sons, Inc.

Roy, S. (1993). Two types of juvenile restitution programs in two Midwestern counties: A comparative study. *Federal Probation*, 57, 48–53.

Rozin, P., Millman, L., & Nemeroff, C. (1986). Operation of the laws of sympathetic magic in disgust and other domains. *Journal of Personality and Social Psychology*, 50(4), 703–712. DOI:10.1037/0022-3514.50.4.703

Rubin, K. H., Coplan, R. J., & Bowker, J. C. (2009). Social withdrawal in childhood. *Annual Review of Psychology*, 60(1), 141–171. DOI:10.1146/annurev.psych.60.110707.163642 PMID:18851686

Rueger, S. Y., Malecki, C. K., Pyun, Y., Aycock, C., & Coyle, S. (2016). A meta-analytic review of the association between perceived social support and depression in childhood and adolescence. . *Psychological Bulletin*, 142(10), 1017–1067. DOI:10.1037/bul0000058 PMID:27504934

Russo, N. F., & Pirlott, A. (2006). Gender-based violence: Concepts, methods, and findings. In Denmark, F. L., Krauss, H. H., Halpern, E., & Sechzer, J. A. (Eds.), *Violence and exploitation against women and girls* (pp. 178–205). Blackwell Publishing.

Rutter, M., LeCouteur, A., & Lord, C. (2003). *Autism Diagnostic Interview-Revised (ADI-R)*. Western Psychological Services.

Ryff, C. D. (2013). Psychological well-being revisited: Advances in the science and practice of eudaimonia. *Psychotherapy and Psychosomatics*, 83(1), 10–28. DOI:10.1159/000353263 PMID:24281296

Sachs-Ericsson, N., Kendall-Tackett, K., & Hernandez, A. (2007). Childhood abuse, chronic pain, and depression in the National Comorbidity survey. *Child Abuse & Neglect*, 31(5), 531–547. DOI:10.1016/j.chiabu.2006.12.007 PMID:17537506

Sadeghi, S., Dolatshahi, B., Pourshahbaz, A., Zarei, M., & Kami, M. (2017). Relationship between traumatic experiences and somatic symptoms severity in students. *Practice in Clinical Psychology*, 5(3), 211–216. https://jpcp.uswr.ac.ir/article-1-465-en.html. DOI:10.18869/acadpub.jpcp.5.3.211

Sadock, B. J., & Sadock, V. A. (2014). *Synopsis of Psychiatry: Behavioural Sciences/ Clinical Psychiatry.* NIH.

Salgado, C., Martín Antón, L., & Carbonero, M. (2020). Impact of a Mindfulness and Self-Care Program on the Psychological Flexibility and Well-Being of Parents with Children Diagnosed with ADHD. *Sustainability (Basel)*, 12(18), 7487. DOI:10.3390/su12187487

Salimpoor, V. N., & Desrocher, M. (2006). Increasing the Utility of EF Assessment of Executive Function in Children. *Developmental Disabilities Bulletin*, 34, 15–42.

Salmon, P., Skaife, K., & Rhodes, J. (2003). Abuse, dissociation, and somatization in irritable bowel syndrome: Towards an explanatory model. *Journal of Behavioral Medicine*, 26(1), 1–18. DOI:10.1023/A:1021718304633 PMID:12690943

Sameroff, A. (2010). A unified theory of development: A dialectic integration of nature and nurture. *Child Development*, 81(1), 6–22. DOI:10.1111/j.1467-8624.2009.01378.x PMID:20331651

Sandbank, M., Bottema-Beutel, K., Crowley, S., Cassidy, M., Dunham, K., Feldman, J., Crank, J., Albarran, S., Raj, S., Mahbub, P., & Woynaroski, T. (2020). Project AIM. *Psychological Bulletin*, 146(1), 1–29. DOI:10.1037/bul0000215 PMID:31763860

Santiago-Rivera, A. L., Altarriba, J., Poll, N., Gonzalez-Miller, N., & Cragun, C. (2002). Therapists' views on working with bilingual Spanish-English speaking clients: A qualitative investigation. *Professional Psychology: Research and Practice, 33*(5), 435-442.

Sardesai, A., Muneshwar, K. N., Bhardwaj, M., & Goel, D. B. (2023). The importance of early diagnosis of somatic symptom disorder: A case report. *Cureus*, 15(9), 1–17. DOI:10.7759/cureus.44554 PMID:37790046

Sayal, K., Prasad, V., Daley, D., Ford, T., & Coghill, D. (2018). ADHD in children and young people: Prevalence, care pathways, and service provision. *The Lancet. Psychiatry*, 5(2), 175–186. DOI:10.1016/S2215-0366(17)30167-0 PMID:29033005

Schepers, D. (2016). Causes of the causes of juvenile delinquency: Social disadvantages in the context of Situational Action Theory. *European Journal of Criminology*, 1–17.

Schiff, R., & Joshi, R. M. (2016). *Interventions in learning disabilities: A handbook on systematic training programs for individuals with learning disabilities*. Springer. DOI:10.1007/978-3-319-31235-4

SchoolsWeb. (2022). *General learning difficulties*. SchoolsWeb. https://schoolsweb .buckscc.gov.uk/ send-and-inclusion/sen-support-toolkit/supporting-presenting-needs/cognition-a n d-learning/general-learning-difficulties/

Schrank, F. A., & Wendling, B. J. (2018). The Woodcock–Johnson IV: Tests of cognitive abilities, tests of oral language, tests of achievement. In Flanagan, D. P., & McDonough, E. M. (Eds.), *Contemporary intellectual assessment: Theories, tests, and issues* (4th ed., pp. 383–451). The Guilford Press.

Schur, L. A., Kruse, D., Blanck, P., & Blanck, P. (2014). *People with disabilities: Sidelined or mainstreamed?* Cambridge University Press.

Scott, K. E., & Graham, J. A. (2015). Service-Learning. *Journal of Experiential Education*, 38(4), 354–372. DOI:10.1177/1053825915592889

Scott, M., Falkmer, M., Girdler, S., & Falkmer, T. (2017). Viewpoints on factors for successful employment for adults with autism spectrum disorder. *PLoS One*, 12(12), e0187936.

Sedgewick, F., Hill, V., Yates, R., Pickering, L., & Pellicano, E. (2016). Gender differences in the social motivation and friendship experiences of autistic and non-autistic adolescents. *Journal of Autism and Developmental Disorders*, 46(4), 1297–1306. DOI:10.1007/s10803-015-2669-1 PMID:26695137

Sedikides, C., & Gregg, A. P. (2003). Portraits of the self. In Hogg, M., & Cooper, J. (Eds.), *The SAGE Handbook of Social Psychology* (pp. 110–138). SAGE Publications. DOI:10.4135/9781848608221.n5

Seligman, M. E. P., Parks, A. C., & Steen, T. (2004). A balanced psychology and a full life. *Philosophical Transactions of the Royal Society of London. Series B, Biological Sciences*, 359(1449), 1379–1381. DOI:10.1098/rstb.2004.1513 PMID:15347529

Selye, H. (1994). *Stress sans détresse*. La Presse.

Sentenac, M., Arnaud, C., Gavin, A., Molcho, M., Gabhainn, S. N., & Godeau, E. (2012). Peer victimization among school-aged children with chronic conditions. *Epidemiologic Reviews*, 34(1), 120–128. DOI:10.1093/epirev/mxr024 PMID:22130095

Shahzad, S., & Yasmin, S. (2015). Aggression as risk for delinquency and substance abuse in adolescents. *International Journal of Prevention and Treatment*, 1(3–4), 106. DOI:10.4038/ijptsud.v1i3-4.7842

Shapiro, S. L., Carlson, L., Astin, J., & Freedman, B. (2006). Mechanisms of mindfulness. *Journal of Clinical Psychology*, 62(3), 373–386. DOI:10.1002/jclp.20237 PMID:16385481

Sharma, A. E., Willard-Grace, R., Hessler, D., Bodenheimer, T., & Thom, D. H. (2016). What happens after health coaching? observational study 1 year following a randomized controlled trial. *Annals of Family Medicine*, 14(3), 200–207. DOI:10.1370/afm.1924 PMID:27184989

Sharma, A., & Tanwar, P. (2024). Model for autism disorder detection using deep learning. *IAES International Journal of Artificial Intelligence*, 13(1), 391. DOI:10.11591/ijai.v13.i1.pp391-398

Sharma, S. R., Gonda, X., & Tarazi, F. I. (2018). Autism Spectrum Disorder: Classification, diagnosis and therapy. *Pharmacology & Therapeutics*, 190, 91–104. DOI:10.1016/j.pharmthera.2018.05.007 PMID:29763648

Sharma, S., & Agarwala, S. (2015). Self-esteem and collective self-esteem among adolescents: An interventional approach. *Psychological Thought*, 8(1), 105–113. DOI:10.5964/psyct.v8i1.121

Sharon, T., & Woolley, J. D. (2004). Do monsters dream? Young children's understanding of the fantasy/reality distinction. *British Journal of Developmental Psychology*, 22(2), 293–310. DOI:10.1348/026151004323044627

Shaw, P., Stringaris, A., Nigg, J., & Leibenluft, E. (2014). Emotion dysregulation in attention deficit hyperactivity disorder. *The American Journal of Psychiatry*, 171(3), 276–293. DOI:10.1176/appi.ajp.2013.13070966 PMID:24480998

Sheehan, D. V., Lecrubier, Y., Sheehan, K. H., Amorim, P., Janavs, J., Weiller, E., Hergueta, T., Baker, R., & Dunbar, G. C. (1998). The Mini-International Neuropsychiatric Interview (M.I.N.I.): The development and validation of a structured diagnostic psychiatric interview for DSM-IV and ICD-10. *The Journal of Clinical Psychiatry*, 59(Suppl 20), 22–33. PMID:9881538

Sheffler, J. L., Stanley, I., & Sachs-Ericsson, N. (2020). Chpt. 4 - ACEs and mental health outcomes. In: Asmundson GJG, Afifi TO, (eds.) *Adverse childhood experiences*. Academic Press.

Sherin, J. E., & Nemeroff, C. B. (2011). Post-traumatic stress disorder: The neurobiological impact of psychological trauma. *Dialogues in Clinical Neuroscience*, 13(3), 263–278. DOI:10.31887/DCNS.2011.13.2/jsherin PMID:22034143

Shimabukuro, S., Daley, D., Thompson, M. J., Laver-Bradbury, C., Nakanishi, E., & Tripp, G. (2017). Supporting Japanese mothers of children with ADHD: Cultural adaptation of the new Forest parent training Programme. *The Japanese Psychological Research*, 59(1), 35–48. DOI:10.1111/jpr.12140

Shimabukuro, S., Oshio, T., Endo, T., Harada, S., Yamashita, Y., Tomoda, A., Guo, B., Goto, Y., Ishii, A., Izumi, M., Nakahara, Y., Yamamoto, K., Daley, D., & Tripp, G. (2024). A pragmatic randomised controlled trial of the effectiveness and cost-effectiveness of Well Parent Japan in routine care in Japan: The training and nurturing support for mothers (TRANSFORM) study. *Journal of Child Psychology and Psychiatry, and Allied Disciplines*, jcpp.14007. DOI:10.1111/jcpp.14007 PMID:38831654

Shinde, S., Weiss, H. A., Khandeparkar, P., Pereira, B., Sharma, A., Gupta, R., & Patel, V. (2018). A multicomponent school-based intervention to reduce aggression, mental health problems, and improve psychosocial functioning among adolescents in India: A cluster-randomised controlled trial. . *Lancet*, 392(10154), 577–589. DOI:10.1016/S0140-6736(18)31617-5

Sibinga, E. M., Webb, L., Ghazarian, S. R., & Ellen, J. M. (2016). School-based mindfulness instruction: An RCT. *Pediatrics, 137*(1), e20152532. DOI:10.1542/peds.2015-2532

Sibley, M. H., Swanson, J. M., Arnold, L. E., Hechtman, L. T., Owens, E. B., Stehli, A., Abikoff, H., Hinshaw, S. P., Molina, B. S. G., Mitchell, J. T., Jensen, P. S., Howard, A. L., Lakes, K. D., & Pelham, W. E.MTA Cooperative Group. (2017). Defining ADHD symptom persistence in adulthood: Optimizing sensitivity and specificity. *Journal of Child Psychology and Psychiatry, and Allied Disciplines*, 58(6), 655–662. DOI:10.1111/jcpp.12620 PMID:27642116

Siebelink, N. M., Bögels, S. M., Speckens, A. E., Dammers, J. T., Wolfers, T., Buitelaar, J. K., & Greven, C. U. (2022). A randomised controlled trial (Mind-Champ) of a mindfulness-based intervention for children with ADHD and their parents. *Journal of Child Psychology and Psychiatry, and Allied Disciplines*, 63(2), 165–177. DOI:10.1111/jcpp.13430 PMID:34030214

Siffredi, V., Liverani, M. C., Hüppi, P. S., Freitas, L. G., De Albuquerque, J., Gimbert, F., & Borradori Tolsa, C. (2021). The effect of a mindfulness- based intervention on executive, behavioural and socio-emotional competencies in very preterm young adolescents. *Scientific Reports*, 11(1), 1–12. DOI:10.1038/s41598-021-98608-2 PMID:34615893

Silberman, S. (2015). *NeuroTribes: The legacy of autism and the future of neuro-diversity*. Avery.

Singer, J. (2017). *Neurodiversity: The birth of an idea*. Singer Books.

Singh, A. K., Kumar, S., & Jyoti, B. (2022). Impact of the COVID-19 on food security and sustainable development goals in India: Evidence from existing literature. *GNOSI: AnInterdisciplinary Journal of Human Theory and Praxis*5(2), 94-109. http://gnosijournal.com/index.php/gnosi/article/view/196/225

Singh, A. K., & Singh, B. J. (2020). Assessing the infectious diseases of students in different weather seasons in DIT University Dehradun, Uttarakhand (India). *Asian Journal of Multidimensional Research*, 9(3), 34–48. DOI:10.5958/2278-4853.2020.00055.5

Siouti, Z., Kougioumtzis, G. A., Kaltsouda, A., & Theodoratou, M. (2023). The role of support networks for children and adolescents with language developmental problems. In Katsarou, D. (Ed.), *Childhood Developmental Language Disorders* (pp. 149–158). IGI Global. DOI:10.4018/979-8-3693-1982-6.ch010

Siouti, Z., Kougioumtzis, G. A., Kaltsouda, A., Theodoratou, M., Yotsidi, V., & Mitraras, A. (2024). Stress Management, Clinical Interventions, and Social Support of Students With Learning Disabilities. In Sofologi, M., Kougioumtzis, G., & Koundourou, C. (Eds.), *Perspectives of Cognitive, Psychosocial, and Learning Difficulties From Childhood to Adulthood: Practical Counseling Strategies*. IGI Global. DOI:10.4018/978-1-6684-8203

Slonim, D. A., Shefler, G., Slonim, N., & Tishby, O. (2013). Adolescents in psychodynamic psychotherapy: Changes in internal representations of relationships with parents. *Psychotherapy Research*, 23(2), 201–217. DOI:10.1080/10503307.2 013.765998 PMID:23577626

Smadja, C. (2007). L'impératif de retour au calme [The Imperative of Restoring a State of Calm]. *Revue Française de Psychosomatique*, 32(32), 71–79. DOI:10.3917/rfps.032.0071

Smith, J. D., Dishion, T. J., Shaw, D. S., Wilson, M. N., Winter, C. C., & Patterson, G. R. (2014). Coercive family process and early-onset conduct problems from age 2 to school entry. *Development and Psychopathology*, 26(4pt1), 917–932. DOI:10.1017/S0954579414000169 PMID:24690305

Smith, S. S. (2013). The influence of stress at puberty on mood and learning: Role of the $\alpha_4\beta\delta$ GABA$_A$ receptor. *Neuroscience*, 249, 192–213. DOI:10.1016/j.neuroscience.2012.09.065 PMID:23079628

Sobański, J. A., Klasa, K., Mielimąka, M., Rutkowski, K., Dembińska, E., Müldner-Nieckowski, Ł., & Popiołek, L. (2015). The crossroads of gastroenterology and psychiatry – what benefits can psychiatry provide for the treatment of patients suffering from gastrointestinal symptoms. *Gastroenterology Research*, 4, 222–228.

Sobel, D., & Lillard, A. (2001). The impact of fantasy and action on young children's understanding of presence. *British Journal of Developmental Psychology*, 19(1), 85–98. DOI:10.1348/026151001165976

Sofologi, M., Markou, E., Kougioumtzis, G. A., Kamari, A., Theofyllidis, A., & Bonti, E. (2020). Emphasizing on the Neurobiological Basis of Autism Spectrum Disorder: A Closer look to a Different Brain. *Dual Diagnosis Open Access, 5*(1, 2). http://hdl.handle.net/11728/12137

Sofologi, M., Pliogou, V., Bonti, E., Efstratopoulou, M., Kougioumtzis, G. A., Papatzikis, E., Ntritsos, G., Moraitou, D., & Papantoniou, G. (2022). An investigation of working memory profile and fluid intelligence in children with neurodevelopmental difficulties. *Frontiers in Psychology, 6657*. DOI:10.3389/fpsyg.2021.773732

Solloway, M. R., Taylor, S. L., Shekelle, P. G., Miake-Lye, I. M., Beroes, J. M., & Shanman, R. M. (2020). An evidence map of mindfulness. *Systematic Reviews*, 9(1), 67. PMID:32228696

Sommariva, G., Zilli, T., Crescentini, C., Marini, A., Pilotto, C., Venchiarutti, M., Gortan, J. A., Fabbro, F., & Cogo, P. (2020). Toward a characterization of language development in children with congenital heart disease: A pilot study. *Child Neuropsychology*, 26(1), 1–14. DOI:10.1080/09297049.2019.1617261 PMID:31120368

Song, C., Benin, M., & Glick, J. (2012). Dropping Out of High School: The Effects of Family Structure and Family Transitions. *Journal of Divorce & Remarriage*, 53(1), 18–33. DOI:10.1080/10502556.2012.635964

Song, J., Volling, B. L., Lane, J. D., & Wellman, H. M. (2016). Aggression, Sibling Antagonism, and Theory of Mind during the first Year of Siblinghood: A Developmental cascade model. *Child Development*, 87(4), 1250–1263. DOI:10.1111/cdev.12530 PMID:27096923

Sonuga-Barke, E. J. (2003). The dual pathway model of ADHD: An elaboration of neuro-developmental characteristics. *Neuroscience and Biobehavioral Reviews*, 27(7), 593–604. DOI:10.1016/j.neubiorev.2003.08.005 PMID:14624804

Sonuga-Barke, E. J., Daley, D., Thompson, M., Laver-Bradbury, C., & Weeks, A. (2001). Parent-based therapies for preschool attention-deficit/hyperactivity disorder: A randomized, controlled trial with a community sample. *Journal of the American Academy of Child and Adolescent Psychiatry*, 40(4), 402–408. DOI:10.1097/00004583-200104000-00008 PMID:11314565

Sonuga-Barke, E., Bitsakou, P., & Thompson, M. (2010). Beyond the dual pathway model: Evidence for the dissociation of timing, inhibitory, and delay-related impairments in attention-deficit/hyperactivity disorder. *Journal of the American Academy of Child and Adolescent Psychiatry*, 49(4), 345–355. DOI:10.1097/00004583-201004000-00009 PMID:20410727

Sørensen, T., & Næss, S. (1996). To measure quality of life: Relevance and use in the psychiatric domain. *Nordic Journal of Psychiatry*, 50(sup37, Suppl. 37), 29–39. DOI:10.3109/08039489609099728

Sosa, M., Bragado, P., & Aguirre-Ghiso, J. (2014). Mechanisms of disseminated cancer cell dormancy: An awakening field'. *Nature Reviews. Cancer*, 14(9), 611–622. DOI:10.1038/nrc3793 PMID:25118602

Speckens, A. E., Spinhoven, P., Sloekers, P. P., Bolk, J. H., & van Hemert, A. M. (1996). A validation study of the Whitely Index, the illness attitude scales, and the somatosensory amplification scale in general medical and general practice patients. *Journal of Psychosomatic Research*, 40(1), 95–104. DOI:10.1016/0022-3999(95)00561-7 PMID:8730649

Sperling, E. L., Hulett, J. M., Sherwin, L. B., Thompson, S., & Betterncourt, B. A. (2023). Prevalence, characteristics and measurement of somatic symptoms related to mental health in medical students: A scoping review. *Annals of Medicine*, 55(2), 1–13. DOI:10.1080/07853890.2023.2242781 PMID:37552776

Spironelli, C., Penolazzi, B., & Angrilli, A. (2010). Gender Differences in Reading in School-Aged Children: An Early ERP Study. *Developmental Neuropsychology*, 35(4), 357–375. DOI:10.1080/87565641.2010.480913 PMID:20614355

Steele, S.D., Minshew, N.J., Luna, B. & Sweeney, J.A. (2007). Spatial working memory deficits in autism. *Journal of Autism and Developmental Disorders, 37.* DOI:10.1007/s10803-006-0202-2

Stewart, S.H. & Watt, M.C. (2000). Illness Attitudes Scale dimensions and their associations with anxiety-related constructs in a nonclinical sample. *Behav Res Ther., 38*(1), 83-99. . PMID: 10645026.DOI:10.1016/S0005-7967(98)00207-1

Stiggins, R. J. (2002). Assessment crisis: The absence of assessment for learning. *Phi Delta Kappan*, 83(10), 758–765. DOI:10.1177/003172170208301010

Stigler, K. A. (2014). Psychopharmacologic Management of Serious Behavioral disturbance in ASD. *Child and Adolescent Psychiatric Clinics of North America*, 23(1), 73–82. DOI:10.1016/j.chc.2013.07.005 PMID:24231168

Straub, L., Bateman, T. B., Hernandez-Diaz, S., York, C., Lester, B., Wisner, L. K., McDougle, J. C., Pennell, B. P., Gray, J. K., Zhu, Y., Suarez, A. E., Mogun, H., & Huybrechts, F. K. (2022). Neurodevelopmental Disorders Among Publicly or Privately Insured Children in the United States. *JAMA Psychiatry*, 79(3), 232–242. DOI:10.1001/jamapsychiatry.2021.3815 PMID:34985527

Street, A. E., & Arias, I. (2001). Psychological abuse and posttraumatic stress disorder in battered women: Examining the role of shame and guilt. *Violence and Victims*, 16(1), 65–78. DOI:10.1891/0886-6708.16.1.65 PMID:11281225

Stromer, R., Kimball, J. W., Kinney, E. M., & Taylor, B. A. (2006). Activity schedules, computer technology, and teaching children with autism spectrum disorders. *Focus on Autism and Other Developmental Disabilities, 21*(1). DOI:10.1177/108 83576060210010301

Sullivan, K., Zaitchik, D., & Tager-Flusberg, H. (1994). Preschoolers can attribute second-order beliefs. *Developmental Psychology*, 30(3), 395–402. DOI:10.1037/0012-1649.30.3.395

Swanson, J. M., Wigal, T., & Lakes, K. (2009). DSM-V and the future diagnosis of attention-deficit/hyperactivity disorder. *Current Psychiatry Reports*, 11(5), 399–406. DOI:10.1007/s11920-009-0060-7 PMID:19785982

Tager-Flusberg, H., & Sullivan, K. (2000). A componential view of theory of mind: Evidence from Williams syndrome. *Cognition*, 76(1), 59–89. DOI:10.1016/S0010-0277(00)00069-X PMID:10822043

Tan, L. B., & Martin, G. (2016). Taming the adolescent mind: Preliminary development of a mindfulness-based psychological intervention for adolescents with clinical heterogeneity. *Cognitive and Behavioral Practice, 23*(3), 370-380. DOI:10.1016/j.cbpra.2015.09.006

Tarabia, E., & Abu-Rabia, S. (2016). Social competency, sense of loneliness and self-image among reading disabled (RD) Arab adolescents. *Creative Education*, 7(9), 1292–1313. DOI:10.4236/ce.2016.79135

Tarkhanova, P. M., & Kholmogorova, A. B. (2011) Sotsial'nye i psikhologicheskie faktory fizicheskogo perfektionizma i unsatisfactoriness svoi telyu [Social and psychological factors of physical perfectionism and dissatisfaction with one's body]. *-PsyJournals.RU, (5),* 52-60.

Tarsha, M. S., & Narvaez, D. (2019). Early life experience and aggression. *Peace Review*, 31(1), 14–23. DOI:10.1080/10402659.2019.1613591

Tasiou, K., & Nikolaou, E. N. (2024). A Family's Experiences of Raising a Child Diagnosed With ADHD: Family Functioning and Organization, Sources of Support and Quality of Life–A Case Study. In *Childhood Developmental Language Disorders: Role of Inclusion, Families, and Professionals* (pp. 116-133). IGI Global.

Tasiou, K., & Nikolaou, E. N. (2023). Psychological resilience of families of children with Attention Deficit Hyperactivity Disorder. In *New trends and approaches in child and adult psychopathology and mental health* (pp. 99–121). Gutenberg.

Tavara, L. (2006). Sexual Abuse. *Best Practice & Research Clinical Obstetrics and Gynaecology, 20,* 3, 395e408. http://www.sciencedirect.comDOI:10.1016/j.bpobgyn.2006.01.011

Teixeira, A. L., Barbosa, I. G., Diniz, B. S., & Kummer, A. (2010). Circulating levels of brain-derived neurotrophic factor: Correlation with mood, cognition, and motor function. *Biomarkers in Medicine*, 4(6), 871–887. DOI:10.2217/bmm.10.111 PMID:21133708

Thabrew, H., de Sylva, S., & Romans, S. E. (2012). Evaluating childhood adversity. *Advances in Psychosomatic Medicine*, 32, 35–57. DOI:10.1159/000330002 PMID:22056897

The MTA Cooperative Group. (1999). A 14-month randomized clinical trial of treatment strategies for attention-deficit/hyperactivity disorder. *Archives of General Psychiatry*, 56(12), 1073–1086. DOI:10.1001/archpsyc.56.12.1073 PMID:10591283

Theodoratou, M., Farmakopoulou, I., & Gkintoni, E. (2023). ADHD, Comorbidities, and Multimodal Treatment: Case Study Vignette. *Perspectives of Cognitive, Psychosocial, and Learning Difficulties From Childhood to Adulthood: Practical Counseling Strategies*, 245-278. IGI Global.

Theodoratou, M., & Farmakopoulou, I. (2021). Comorbidity Issues between Autism Spectrum Disorders and Internet Addiction. Diagnosis and Treatment Implications. *EC Neurology*, 13, 10–17.

Theodoratou, M., Gkintoni, E., & Farmakopoulou, I. (2023). Executive Functions and Quality of Life in Neurodevelopmental Spectrum. An Outline. *Technium Social Sciences Journal*, 39(1), 430–439. DOI:10.47577/tssj.v39i1.8231

Theodoratou, M., Kougioumtzis, G. A., Kaltsouda, A., Katsarou, D., Siouti, Z., Sofologi, M., Tsitsas, G., & Flora, K. (2023). Neuropsychological Aspects and Interventions for Internet Addiction in Adolescents with Asperger's Syndrome-Narrative Review. *Neurology & Neuroscience*, 4(3), 1–9. DOI:10.33425/2692-7918.1052

Theodoratou, M., Ralli, M., Mylonaki, T., & Bekou, H. (2024). Screening for ADHD Traits in University Students: Prevalence, Traits and Departmental Variations. *Journal of Behavioral Sciences*, 34(1).

Theule, J., Wiener, J., Tannock, R., & Jenkins, J. M. (2013). Parenting stress in families of children with ADHD: A meta-analysis. *Journal of Emotional and Behavioral Disorders*, 21(1), 3–17. DOI:10.1177/1063426610387433

Thirion-Marissiaux, A., & Nader-Grosbois, N. (2008). Theory of mind "beliefs", developmental characteristics and social understanding in children and adolescents with intellectual disabilities. *Research in Developmental Disabilities*, 29(6), 547–566. DOI:10.1016/j.ridd.2007.09.004 PMID:18023323

Thomas, C., & Woods, H. (2008). The medical model of disability: A sociological critique. *Disability & Society*, 23(2), 209–222.

Thompson, M. P., Kingree, J. B., & Lamis, D. (2019). Associations of adverse childhood experiences and suicidal behaviors in adulthood in a U.S. nationally representative sample. *Child: Care, Health and Development*, 45(1), 121–128. DOI:10.1111/cch.12617 PMID:30175459

Thomson, J. K. (2002). Measuring Body image attitudes among adolescents and adults / J.K. Thomson, P. Van den Berg. In Cash, T. F., & Pruzinsky, T. (Eds.), *Body Image: A Handbook of Theory, Research and Clinical Practice* (pp. 142–153). The Gilford Press.

Thomson, K., Randall, E., Ibeziako, P., & Bujoreanu, I. S. (2014). Somatoform disorders and trauma in medically-admitted children, adolescents, and young adults: Prevalence rates and psychosocial characteristics. *Psychosomatics*, 55(6), 630–639. DOI:10.1016/j.psym.2014.05.006 PMID:25262040

Thümmler, R., Engel, E.-M., & Bartz, J. (2022). Strengthening Emotional Development and Emotion Regulation in Childhood—As a Key Task in Early Childhood Education. *International Journal of Environmental Research and Public Health*, 19(7), 3978. DOI:10.3390/ijerph19073978 PMID:35409661

Timimi, S., Gardner, N., & McCabe, B. (2010). *The myth of autism: Medicalising men's and boys' social and emotional competence*. Palgrave Macmillan. DOI:10.1007/978-1-137-05773-0

Toto, A. G., & Limone, P. (2021). *The effect of motor development in adolescence on cognition: A cumulative literature review. Autumn Conferences of Sports Science.* Costa Blanca Sports Science Events., DOI:10.14198/jhse.2021.16.Proc2.51

Treacy, L., Tripp, G., & Baird, A. (2005). Parent stress management training for attention-deficit/hyperactivity disorder. *Behavior Therapy*, 36(3), 223–233. DOI:10.1016/S0005-7894(05)80071-1

Treffert, D. (1009). The savant syndrome: an extraordinary condition. A synopsis: Past, Present, Future. *Philosophical Transactions of the Royal Society V, 364*, 1351-1357. DOI:10.1098/rstb.2008.0326

Trivedi, M. H. (2004). The link between depression and physical symptoms. *Primary Care Companion to the Journal of Clinical Psychiatry*, 6(1), 12. https://www.ncbi.nlm.nih.gov/pmc/articles/PMC486942/ PMID:16001092

Troyb, E., Orinstein, A., Tyson, K., Helt, M., Eigsti, I., Stevens, M., & Fein, D. (2014). Academic abilities in children and adolescents with a history of autism spectrum disorders who have achieved optimal outcomes. *Autism*, 18(3), 233–243. DOI:10.1177/1362361312473519 PMID:24096312

Tsakiridou, E., & Alevriadou, A. (2017). A challenging approach concerning the cognitive strategies in problem solving situations by boys with and without intellectual disabilities using Markov chains. In Colombus, A. (Ed.), *Advances in Psychology Research* (Vol. 127). Nova Press.

Tschida, J. E., & Yerys, B. E. (2021). Real-world executive functioning for autistic children in school and home settings. *Autism*, 26(5), 1095–1107. DOI:10.1177/13623613211041189 PMID:34465230

Tseng, H. M., Henderson, A., Chow, M. K. S., & Yao, C. (2004). Relationship between motor proficiency, attention, impulse, and activity in children with ADHD. *Developmental Medicine and Child Neurology*, 46(6), 381–388. DOI:10.1017/S0012162204000623 PMID:15174529

Tuckman, B. W., & Monetti, D. M. (2011). *Educational psychology* [International ed.]. Wadsworth Cengage Learning.

Tukhtaeva D.A. & Lukovtseva Z.V. (2024). Psychological Characteristics of Adults Who Have Experienced Sexual Violence in Childhood or Adolescence. Psikhologiya i pravo = *Psychology and Law, 14,* 1, 33–52. DOI:10.17759/psylaw.2024140103

Tura, H., & Licoze, A. (2019). Women's experience of intimate partner violence and uptake of antenatal care in sofala, mozambique. *PLoS One*, 14(5), e0217407. DOI:10.1371/journal.pone.0217407 PMID:31125370

Turnock, A., Langley, K., & Jones, C. (2022). Understanding stigma in autism: A narrative review and theoretical model. *Autism in Adulthood: Challenges and Management*, 4(1), 76–91. DOI:10.1089/aut.2021.0005 PMID:36605561

Tuvblad, C., & Beaver, K. M. (2013). Genetic and environmental influences on antisocial behavior. *Journal of Criminal Justice*, 41(5), 273–276. DOI:10.1016/j.jcrimjus.2013.07.007 PMID:24526799

Uddin, L. Q. (2022, December). Exceptional abilities in autism: Theories and open questions. *Current Directions in Psychological Science*, 31(6), 509–517. DOI:10.1177/09637214221113760 PMID:36776583

UN. (2015). *Sustainable Development Goal 4*. United Nations. https://www.un.org/sustainabledevelopment/education/

UNESCO. (1994). *The Salamanca Statement and framework for action on special needs*. UNESCO. https://unesdoc.unesco.org/ark:/48223/pf0000098427

UNESCO. (2005). *Guidelines for inclusion*. UNESCO.

UPIAS. (1976). *Fundamental Principles of Disability*. Union of the Physically Impaired Against Segregation.

Utley, A., & Garza, Y. (2011). The therapeutic use of journaling with adolescents. . *Journal of Creativity in Mental Health*, 6(1), 29–41. DOI:10.1080/15401383.2011.557312

Vago, D. R., & Silbersweig, D. A. (2012). Self-awareness, self-regulation, and self-transcendence (S-ART): A framework for understanding the neurobiological mechanisms of mindfulness. *Frontiers in Human Neuroscience*, 6, 296. DOI:10.3389/fnhum.2012.00296 PMID:23112770

Vaidya, J. C. (2012). Neurodevelopmental Abnormalities in ADHD. *Current Topics in Behavioral Neurosciences*, 9, 49–66. DOI:10.1007/7854_2011_138 PMID:21541845

Van der Molen, M. J., Van Luit, J. E., Jongmans, M. J., & Van der Molen, M. W. (2007). Verbal working memory in children with mild intellectual disabilities. *Journal of Intellectual Disability Research*, 51(2), 162–169. DOI:10.1111/j.1365-2788.2006.00863.x PMID:17217480

Van der Oord, S., Bögels, S. M., & Peijnenburg, D. (2012). The effectiveness of mindfulness training for children with ADHD and mindful parenting for their parents. *Journal of Child and Family Studies*, 21(1), 139–147. DOI:10.1007/s10826-011-9457-0 PMID:22347788

Van Eylen, L., Boets, B., Steyaert, J., Wagemans, J., & Noens, I. (2015). Executive functioning in autism spectrum disorders: Influence of task and sample characteristics and relation to symptom severity. *European Child & Adolescent Psychiatry*, 24(11), 1399–1417. DOI:10.1007/s00787-015-0689-1 PMID:25697266

Velarde, M., & Cárdenas, A. (2022). Trastornos del espectro autista y trastornos por déficit de atención con hiperactividad: Desafíos en el diagnóstico y tratamiento [Autism spectrum disorder and attention-deficit/hyperactivity disorder: Challenge in diagnosis and treatment]. *Medicina*, 82(Suppl 3), 67–70. PMID:36054861

Vergidis, D. (2003). The contribution of assessment to the implementation of integrated adult education programs. In Vergidis, D. (Ed.), *Adult Education. Contribution to the specialization of executives and trainers*. Greek Letters.

Vesterling, C. (2023) Epidemiology of Somatoform Symptoms and Disorders in Childhood and Adolescence: A Systematic Review and Meta-Analysis. *Health & Social Care in the Community*. DOI:10.1155/2023/6242678

Vesterling, C., & Koglin, U. (2020). The relationship between attachment and somatoform symptoms in children and adolescents: A systematic review and meta-analysis. *Journal of Psychosomatic Research*, 130, 109932. DOI:10.1016/j.jpsychores.2020.109932 PMID:31981896

Vitomska, M. V. (2021). Modern Approaches to Occupational Therapy of Children with Authistic Spectric Disorders. *Ukraïns kij Žurnal Medicini. Bìologiï Ta Sportu*, 6(2), 7–12. DOI:10.26693/jmbs06.02.007

Vlachakis, I., & Kougioumtzis, G. A. (2016). ADHD and Teachers' Counseling. *Journal of Regional Socio-Economic Issues, 6*(2).

Vogan, V. M., Leung, R. C., Safar, K., Martinussen, R., Smith, M. L., & Taylor, M. J. (2018). Longitudinal examination of everyday executive functioning in children with ASD: Relations with social, emotional, and behavioral functioning over time. *Frontiers in Psychology*, 9, 1774. DOI:10.3389/fpsyg.2018.01774 PMID:30364134

Vogt, E. M., & Heffelfinger, A. (2024). Pediatric assessment. In Parsons, M. W., & Braun, M. M. (Eds.), *Clinical neuropsychology: A pocket handbook for assessment* (4th ed., pp. 44–71). American Psychological Association., DOI:10.1037/0000383-003

Voronova, N. M., Korneev, A. A., & Akhutina, V. T. (2015). Longitudinal Study of the Development of Higher Mental Functions in Primary School Children. *Journal of Russian & East European Psychology*, 52(3), 16–35. DOI:10.1080/10610405.2015.1175833

Vygotsky, L. (1978). *Mind in Society: The Development of Higher Psychological Processes*. Harvard University Press.

Wagner, M., Newman, L., Cameto, R., Levine, P., Marder, C., & Malouf, D. (2007). *Perceptions and expectations of youth with disabilities. A special topic report of findings from the National Longitudinal Transition Study-2 (NLTS2) (NCSER 2007-3006)*. SRI International.

Waitzkin, H., & Magana, H. (1997). The black box in somatization: Unexplained physical symptoms, culture, and narratives of trauma. *Social Science & Medicine*, 45(6), 811–825. DOI:10.1016/S0277-9536(96)00422-4 PMID:9255914

Wakabayashi, A., Baron-Cohen, S., Wheelright, S., Goldenfeld, N., Delaney, J., Fine, D., Smith, R., & Weil, L. (2006). Development of short forms of the Empathy Quotient (EQ-Short) and the Systemizing Quotient (SQ-Short). *Personality and Individual Differences*, 41(5), 929–940. DOI:10.1016/j.paid.2006.03.017

Waldinger, R. J., Schulz, M. S., Barsky, A. J., & Ahern, D. K. (2006). Mapping the road from childhood trauma to adult somatization: The role of attachment. *Psychosomatic Medicine*, 68(1), 129–135. DOI:10.1097/01.psy.0000195834.37094.a4 PMID:16449423

Walker, N. (2021). *Neurodiversity: Some basic terms & definitions*. Autistic Self Advocacy Network.

Walkup, J. T., Albano, A. M., Piacentini, J., Birmaher, B., Compton, S. N., Sherrill, J. T., Ginsburg, G. S., Rynn, M. A., McCracken, J., Waslick, B., Iyengar, S., & March, J. S. (2008). Cognitive behavioral therapy, sertraline, or a combination in childhood anxiety. *The New England Journal of Medicine, 359*(26), 2753-2766. DOI:10.1056/NEJMoa0804633

Waller, G., Hamilton, K., Elliott, P., Lewendon, J., Stopa, L., Waters, A., Kennedy, F., Lee, G., Pearson, D., Kennerey, H., Hargreaves, I., Bashford, V., & Chalkley, J. (2001). Somatoform dissociation, psychological dissociation, and specific forms of trauma. *Journal of Trauma & Dissociation*, 1(4), 81–98. DOI:10.1300/J229v01n04_05

Wechsler, D. (2003). Wechsler Intelligence Scale for Children, *Fourth Edition (WISC-IV)* [Database record]. APA PsycTests. DOI:10.1037/t15174-000

Wechsler, D. (1974). *Selected papers of David Wechsler*. Academic Press.

Wehmeyer, M., Buntinx, W., Lachapelle, Y., Luckasson, R., Schalock, R., Verdugo, M., Borthwick-Duffy, S., Bradley, V., Craig, E. M., Coulter, D. L., Gomez, S. C., Reeve, A., Shogren, K. A., Snell, M. E., Spreat, S., Tassé, M. J., Thompson, J. R., & Yeager, M. H. (2008). The intellectual disability. Construct and its relation to human functioning. *Intellectual and Developmental Disabilities*, 46(4), 311–318. DOI:10.1352/1934-9556(2008)46[311:TIDCAI]2.0.CO;2 PMID:18671445

Weil, L. G., Fleming, S. M., Dumontheil, I., Kilford, E. J., Weil, R. S., Rees, G., Dolan, R. J., & Blakemore, S. (2013). The development of metacognitive ability in adolescence. *Consciousness and Cognition*, 22(1), 264–271. DOI:10.1016/j.concog.2013.01.004 PMID:23376348

Weisz, J. R. (1979). Perceived control and learned helplessness among retarded and nonretarded children: A developmental analysis. *Developmental Psychology*, 15(3), 311–319. DOI:10.1037/0012-1649.15.3.311

Welker, K. M., Norman, R. E., Goetz, S., Moreau, B. J., Kitayama, S., & Carré, J. M. (2017). Preliminary evidence that testosterone's association with aggression depends on self-construal. *Hormones and Behavior*, 92, 117–127. DOI:10.1016/j.yhbeh.2016.10.014 PMID:27816624

Wellman, H. M., & Estes, D. (1986). Early understanding of mental entities: A reexamination of childhood realism. *Child Development*, 57(4), 910–923. DOI:10.2307/1130367 PMID:3757609

Wheelright, S., Baron-Cohen, S., Goldenfeld, N., Delaney, J., Fine, D., Smith, R., Weil, L., & Wakabayashi, A. (2006). Predicting Autism Spectrum Quotient (AQ) from the Systemizing Quotient-Revised (SQ-R) and Empathy Quotient (EQ). *Brain Research*, 1079(1), 47–56. DOI:10.1016/j.brainres.2006.01.012 PMID:16473340

Whitebread, D., Basilio, M., Kuvalja, M., & Verma, M. (2012). *The Importance of Play*. Toy Industries of Europe.

Whitebread, D., & O'Sullivan, L. (2012). Preschool children's social pretend play: Supporting the development of metacommunication, metacognition and self regulation. *International Journal of Play*, 1(2), 197–213. DOI:10.1080/21594937.2012.693384

WHO. (2021). *Violence against women Prevalence Estimates 2018. Violence Global, regional and national prevalence estimates for intimate partner violence against women and global and regional prevalence estimates for non-partner sexual violence against women*. World Health Organisation.

Wikström, P.-O. (2006). Individuals, settings, and acts of crime: Situational mechanisms and the explanation of crime. In Wikström, P.-O., & Sampson, R. J. (Eds.), *The Explanation of Crime* (pp. 61–108). Cambridge University Press. DOI:10.1017/CBO9780511489341.004

Wikström, P.-O. (2009). Crime propensity, criminogenic exposure and crime involvement in early to mid-adolescence. *Monatsschrift fur Kriminologie und Strafrechtsreform*, 92(2-3), 253–266. DOI:10.1515/mks-2009-922-312

Wikström, P.-O., Oberwittler, D., Treiber, K., & Hardie, B. (2012). *Breaking Rules. The Social and Situational Dynamics of Young People's Urban Crime*. Oxford University Press.

Williams, D. (1996). *Autism: An inside-out approach*. Jessica Kingsley Publishers.

Williams, D. L., Goldstein, G., Carpenter, P. A., & Minshew, N. J. (2005). Verbal and spatial working memory in autism. *Journal of Autism and Developmental Disorders*, 35(6), 747–756. DOI:10.1007/s10803-005-0021-x PMID:16267641

Williams, G. L. (2021). Theory of autistic mind: A renewed relevance theoretic perspective on so-called autistic pragmatic "impairment.". *Journal of Pragmatics*, 180, 121–130. DOI:10.1016/j.pragma.2021.04.032

Wilson, A. C. (2024). Cognitive Profile in Autism and ADHD: A Meta-Analysis of Performance on the WAIS-IV and WISC-V. *Archives of Clinical Neuropsychology*, 39(4), 498–515. DOI:10.1093/arclin/acad073 PMID:37779387

Winstok, Z., & Sowan-Basheer, W. (2015). Does psychological violence contribute to partner violence research? A historical, conceptual and critical review. *Aggression and Violent Behavior*, 21, 5–16. DOI:10.1016/j.avb.2015.01.003

Wise, T. N. (2014). Psychosomatics: Past, present and future. *Psychotherapy and Psychosomatics*, 83(2), 65–69. DOI:10.1159/000356518 PMID:24457983

Wolff, N., Stroth, S., Kamp-Becker, I., Roepke, S., & Roessner, V. (2022). Autism spectrum disorder and IQ – a complex interplay. *Frontiers in Psychiatry*, 13, 856084. DOI:10.3389/fpsyt.2022.856084 PMID:35509885

Wolraich, M., Lambert, W., Doffing, M., Bickman, L., Simmons, T., & Worley, K. (2003). Psychometric Properties of the Vanderbilt ADHD Diagnostic Parent Rating Scale in a Referred Population. *Journal of Pediatric Psychology*, 28(8), 559–568. DOI:10.1093/jpepsy/jsg046 PMID:14602846

Wong, W. C. W., Leung, P. W. S., Tang, C. S. K., Chen, W. Q., Lee, A., & Ling, D. C. (2009). To unfold a hidden epidemic: Prevalence of child maltreatment and its health implications among high school students in Guangzhou, China. *Child Abuse & Neglect*, 33(1), 441–450. DOI:10.1016/j.chiabu.2008.02.010 PMID:19586660

Wood, J. J., Drahota, A., Sze, K., Har, K., Chiu, A., & Langer, D. A. (2009). Cognitive behavioral therapy for anxiety in children with autism spectrum disorders: A randomized, controlled trial. *Journal of Child Psychology and Psychiatry, and Allied Disciplines*, 50(3), 224–234. DOI:10.1111/j.1469-7610.2008.01948.x PMID:19309326

Woods, R. (2017). Exploring how the social model of disability can be re-invigorated for autism: In response to Jonathan Levitt. *Disability & Society*, 32(7), 1090–1095. DOI:10.1080/09687599.2017.1328157

Woolley, J. D. (1997). Thinking about fantasy: Are children fundamentally different thinkers and believers from adults? *Child Development*, 68(6), 991–1011. DOI:10.2307/1132282 PMID:9418217

Woolley, J. D. (2000). The development of beliefs about mental-physical causality in imagination, magic, and religion. In Rosengren, K., Johnson, C., & Harris, P. (Eds.), *Imagining the impossible: Magical, scientific, and religious thinking in children*. Cambridge University Press. DOI:10.1017/CBO9780511571381.005

Woolley, J. D., & Ghossainy, M. E. (2013). Revisiting the fantasy-reality distinction: Children as naïve skeptics. *Child Development*, 84(5), 1496–1510. DOI:10.1111/cdev.12081 PMID:23496765

Woolley, J. D., & Phelps, K. E. (1994). Young children's practical reasoning about imagination. *British Journal of Developmental Psychology*, 12(1), 53–67. DOI:10.1111/j.2044-835X.1994.tb00618.x

Woolley, J. D., & Wellman, H. M. (1990). Young children's understanding of realities, nonrealities, and appearances. *Child Development*, 61(4), 946–961. DOI:10.2307/1130867 PMID:2209198

Woolley, J. D., & Wellman, H. M. (1992). Children's conceptions of dreams. *Cognitive Development*, 7(3), 365–380. DOI:10.1016/0885-2014(92)90022-J

World Health Organization. (2014). *Health for the World's Adolescents: A Second Chance in the Second Decade: Summary (Internet)*. WHO Press.

World Health Organization. (2023). A focus on adolescent mental health and well-being in Europe, central Asia and Canada. *Health Behaviour in School-aged Children international report from the 2021/2022 survey*. WHO.

World Health Organization. (2023). *Disability*. WHO. https://www.who.int/news-room/fact-sheets/detail/disability

Xiao, S. (2023). Development of Emotional Autonomy of Adolescents in the Context of Family Relations and Academic Performance in Middle School. *Polish Psychological Bulletin*, 54(1), 58–64. DOI:10.24425/ppb.2023.144884

Xochellis, P. (2005). *Education in the modern world*. Typothito.

Xu, Y. (2010). Children's social play sequence: Parten's classic theory revisited'. *Early Child Development and Care*, 180(4), 489–498. DOI:10.1080/03004430802090430

Yáñez-Téllez, G., Romero-Romero, H., Rivera-García, L., Prieto-Corona, L., Bernal-Hernandez, J., Marosi-Holczberger, E., Guerrero-Juárez, V., Rodríguez-Camacho, M., & Silva-Pereyra, F. J. (2012). Cognitive and executive functions in ADHD. *Actas Españolas de Psiquiatría*, 40(6), 293–298. PMID:23165410

Yasunobe, Y., Akasaka, H., Yamamoto, K., Onishi, Y., Minami, T., Yoshida, S., & Rakugi, H. (2023). The relationship between changes in exercise habits and psychosomatic activities in older hypertensive patients during the COVID-19 pandemic. *Hypertension Research*, 46(1), 208–213. DOI:10.1038/s41440-022-01043-7 PMID:36229528

Yazejian, N., Bryant, D., Freel, K., Burchinal, M., & the Educare Learning Network (ELN) Investigative Team. (2015). High-quality early education: Age of entry and time in care differences in student outcomes for English-only and dual language learners. *Early Childhood Research Quarterly, 32,* 23-39. . ecresq.2015.02.002). DOI:10.1016/j

Yen, S. C., & Spa, J. M. (2000). Children's Temperament and Behavior in Montessori and Contructivist Early Childhood Programms. *Early Education and Development*, 11(2), 171–186. DOI:10.1207/s15566935eed1102_3

Yirmiya, N., Erel, O., Shaked, M., & Solomonica-Levi, D. (1998). Meta-analysis comparing theory of mind abilities of individuals with autism, individuals with mental retardation, and normally developing individuals. *Psychological Bulletin*, 124(3), 283–307. DOI:10.1037/0033-2909.124.3.283 PMID:9849110

Yirmiya, N., & Shulman, C. (1996). Seriation, conservation, and theory of mind abilities in individuals with autism, individuals with mental retardation, and normally developing children. *Child Development*, 67(5), 2045–2059. DOI:10.2307/1131608 PMID:9022228

Yirmiya, N., Solomonica-Levi, D., Shulman, C., & Pilowsky, T. (1996). Theory of mind abilities in individuals with autism, Down syndrome, and mental retardation of unknown etiology: The role of age and intelligence. *Journal of Child Psychology and Psychiatry, and Allied Disciplines*, 37(8), 1003–1014. DOI:10.1111/j.1469-7610.1996.tb01497.x PMID:9119934

Yoshikawa, H., Weiland, C., Brooks-Gunn, J., Burchinal, M. R., Espinosa, L. M., Gormley, W. T., Ludwig, J., Magnuson, K., Phillips, D., & Zaslow, M. J. (2013). *Investing in our future: The evidence base on preschool education.* Society for Research in Child Development.

Young, S., Hollingdale, J., Absoud, M., Bolton, P., Branney, P., Colley, W., Craze, E., Dave, M., Deeley, Q., Farrag, E., Gudjonsson, G., Hill, P., Liang, H. L., Murphy, C., Mackintosh, P., Murin, M., O'Regan, F., Ougrin, D., Rios, P., & Woodhouse, E. (2020). Guidance for identification and treatment of individuals with attention deficit/hyperactivity disorder and autism spectrum disorder based upon expert consensus. *BMC Medicine*, 18(1), 146. DOI:10.1186/s12916-020-01585-y PMID:32448170

You, X.-R., Gong, X.-R., Guo, M.-R., & Ma, B.-X. (2024). Cognitive behavioural therapy to improve social skills in children and adolescents with autism spectrum disorder: A meta-analysis of randomised controlled trials. [Αρχή φόρμας]. *Journal of Affective Disorders*, 344, 8–17. DOI:10.1016/j.jad.2023.10.008 PMID:37802322

Yuan, J. J., Zhao, Y. N., Lan, X. Y., Zhang, Y., & Zhang, R. (2024). Prenatal, perinatal and parental risk factors for autism spectrum disorder in China: A case-control study. *BMC Psychiatry*, 24(1), 219. DOI:10.1186/s12888-024-05643-0 PMID:38509469

Yu, G., Zhang, Y., & Yan, R. (2005). Loneliness, peer acceptance, and family functioning of Chinese children with learning disabilities: Characteristics and relationships. *Psychology in the Schools*, 42(3), 325–331. DOI:10.1002/pits.20083

Zagaria, T., Antonucci, G., Buono, S., Recupero, M., & Zoccolotti, P. (2021). Executive Functions and Attention Processes in Adolescents and Young Adults with Intellectual Disability. *Brain Sciences*, 11(1), 42. DOI:10.3390/brainsci11010042 PMID:33401550

Zelazo, P. D., Burack, J. A., Benedetto, E., & Frye, D. (1996). Theory of mind and rule use in individuals with Down's syndrome: A test of the uniqueness and specificity claims. *Journal of Child Psychology and Psychiatry, and Allied Disciplines*, 37(4), 479–484. DOI:10.1111/j.1469-7610.1996.tb01429.x PMID:8735448

Zeng, S., Hu, X., Zhao, H., & Stone-MacDonald, A. K. (2020). Examining the relationships of parental stress, family support and family quality of life: A structural equation modeling approach. *Research in Developmental Disabilities*, 96, 103523. DOI:10.1016/j.ridd.2019.103523 PMID:31785472

Zhang, Y., & Qin, P. (2023). Comprehensive Review: Understanding Adolescent Identity. *Studies in Psychological Science*, 1(2), 17–31. DOI:10.56397/SPS.2023.09.02

Zilanawala, A., & Pilkauskas, N. V. (2012). Material hardship and child socioemotional behaviors: Differences by types of hardship, timing, and duration. *Children and Youth Services Review*, 34(4), 814–825. DOI:10.1016/j.childyouth.2012.01.008 PMID:22408284

Zoogman, S., Goldberg, S. B., Hoyt, W. T., & Miller, L. (2015). Mindfulness interventions with youth: A meta-analysis. . *Mindfulness*, 6(2), 290–302. DOI:10.1007/s12671-013-0260-4

About the Contributors

Maria Sofologi is an Adjunct Assistant Professor, Department of Early Childhood Studies at the University of Ioannina in Greece. Her postdoctoral research is associated with the evaluation and identification of gifted and talented children and their cognitive performance. She holds a Ph.D. in Cognitive Psychology from the Aristotle University of Thessaloniki. She also holds a Master of Science degree in Cognitive Psychology from the Aristotle University of Thessaloniki. Her research interests are focused on cognitive profiles of typical and atypically developing children, in special Education filed, and evaluation and identification of giftedness.

Dimitra Katsarou is an Assistant Professor of Developmental Psychopathology and Language Disorders at the Department of Preschool Education Sciences and Educational Design of the University of the Aegean. She studied Philology at the Department of Philology of the School of Philosophy of the Aristotle University of Thessaloniki. She holds three postgraduate degrees (MSc Sports and Exercise Psychology- University of Thessaly, Med Adult Education- Hellenic Open University, MA Education: Special Education- University of Nicosia) and Ph.D. of the Special Education Department of the University of Thessaly. She is a certified adult educator and College teacher and has worked as a special education philologist in public high schools and second chance schools and has developed differentiated material for people with intellectual disabilities. She has worked as an adult educator in private and public Vocational Training Centers, as a teacher in Second Chance Schools, in Lifelong Learning Centers, in Vocational Training Institutes, in the Youth and Lifelong Learning Institute, in the School of Probationary Police and in Private Colleges. She has participated in research projects funded by the University of Thessaly, the National Technical University of Athens, the European Union and the Information Society. She has conducted her postdoctoral research co-financed by six universities in the European Union. She speaks four foreign languages (English, French, Italian, Spanish) as well as Greek Sign Language, writes and reads in the Braille System. She has 29 scholarly publications in influential peer-reviewed journals and more than 100 conference presentations, she has written eleven children's fairy tales and three theatrical plays. She has authored a monograph, four co- editing books, and three editing books in Greek language, as well as participating in several chapters in other scientific publications. She is academically responsible for education, training and education programs of Greek and international organizations and participates as a key researcher in Greek and international research programs, such as Erasmus Plus, Alliance edu, Cost. eu, Erasmus Sport. In parallel with the University of the Aegean, she has worked as adjunct faculty at the University of Nicosia, the University of Thessaly, the Aristotle University of Thessaloniki, the Hellenic Open University, the Neapolis University of Paphos and Frederick University. Her research interests focus on the special education of children with intellectual disabilities, neurolinguistics, cognitive processes, autism, developmental psychopathology, speech and language development, genetic syndromes and intergenerational activities.

Efthymia Efthymiou's research focuses on inclusive teaching practices, classroom discourse, and creating educational environments that support the inclusion of all students, including those with special needs. Her work centers on understanding the perspectives of various stakeholders, such as teachers and children with special needs, to develop more inclusive educational systems. She explores the role of both physical and psychological environments in shaping attitudes, positioning, and inclusion. Her research aims to identify and overcome barriers to inclusive education, with emphasis on leveraging technology-based teaching practices to address digital exclusion and promote inclusive teaching methods. In addition to her research efforts, Dr. Efthymia actively contributes to the advancement of inclusive education through her workshops and seminars conducted for teachers and principals in federal schools within the UAE. She recognizes the urgent need to equip educators with the necessary tools and knowledge to foster inclusive learning environments, ensuring that all students have equal opportunities for education and growth.

***

Sana Butti Al Maktoum is an Assistant Professor in the Department of Language Studies at Zayed University, Dubai campus. She has a bachelor's degree in English Language and Literature and a Master's in Special and Inclusive Education from the British University in Dubai. She pursued her doctorate in Curriculum and Instruction – English language track and has been an active researcher in various inter-institutional projects with United Arab Emirates University and the University College of London, among others.

Anastasia Alevriadou is Professor of Psychology of Special Education at the Aristotle University of Thessaloniki– Greece. She has published more than 150 articles in Greek and international journals, 5 books and 6 chapters in American books on these issues, and many conference proceedings. She has also participated in many European and International conferences. She is a member of many Greeks and International Associations of Psychology and Special Education. Fulbright Scholar in psychology/special education in 2019, Nisonger Center of Developmental Disabilities, OSU, USA. Visiting Professor in USA, Czech Republic and Cyprus.

Georgia Andreou is a Professor in Neurolinguistics/Psycholinguistics and Director of the Laboratory of Bilingual Education at the Department of Special Education, University of Thessaly, Greece. She is also the Director of the Postgraduate Program of Studies (Masters in Special Education) "Special Education and Training of People with Oral and Written Speech Problems" (joint with the Hellenic Open University). She is the writer of one book, 17 chapters in books and of more than 150 articles published in international Journals and Proceedings. She has more than 1.960 citations (h-index 26, i10-index 48, according to google scholar) and she is also member of the Editorial Board of 11 international Journals and guest Editor of the International Journal of Disability, Development and Education. She has been an invited speaker at Universities in Australia and USA (Flinders University, University of Sydney, University of Queensland, University of Massachusetts, San Fransisco State University, California State University, Chapman University, International University of Florida, University of Alabama). Her research interests include among others, bilingualism/multilingualism, language/communication and cognitive development in typical population and in individuals with developmental disorders.

Marios Argyrides is an Associate Professor in the Department of Psychology at Neapolis University and a Licensed Psychologist in Cyprus. He received a PhD in 2006 in Counseling Psychology from Tennessee State University and an MSc in 2002 in Applied Psychology from the University of South Alabama. He has worked as an intern at different counseling centers of universities including the University of South Alabama, Tennessee State University and Vanderbilt University. He completed his Pre-Doctoral Internship at Florida State University. He has worked as an instructor at Tennessee State University and as a visiting lecturer at public and private universities in Cyprus. He is an Associate Scientist in several research teams in the USA and in COST and Erasmus+ projects in Europe as well as the Director of the Eating and Appearance Research Laboratory (EARL) at Neapolis University. He has published several articles and specialized books whilst also presenting at international conferences. He is the Editor-in-Chief of the European Journal of Counseling Psychology. He is also a professional member of the Cyprus Psychological Association and the American Psychological Association. Finally, he is the consulting psychologist of the non-profit organization MediCleft that supports patients with Cleft and Craniofacial abnormalities.

Vasiliki Aslanoglou has a bachelor degree from the Faculty of Philosophy, Pedagogy and Psychology of the National and Kapodistrian University of Athens in the field of psychology and a Master's Degree in the field of "Organization and Administration of Education" from the Department of Primary Education of the University of Thessaly. She is also a PhD holder (thesis title: Written language skills in children with Developmental Language Disorder) from the Department of Special Education of the University of Thessaly. Her research interests include among others language development in typical population and in individuals with developmental disorders, such as Developmental Language Disorder.

Panagiota Athanasiadou has a Bachelor's Degree from the Faculty of English Studies of the National and Kapodistrian University of Athens and a Master's Degree in the field of "Education Sciences: Special Education for People with Oral and Written Language Difficulties" from the University of Thessaly and the Hellenic Open University (joint postgraduate program). She is a PhD candidate at the Department of Special Education, University of Thessaly. Her research interests include second/foreign language learning and differentiated assessment of individuals with Learning Disabilities.

Beazidou Eleftheria PhD Assistant Professor, works as Assistant Professor at the Department of Special Education of the University of Thessaly, Greece. Her undergraduate and postgraduate studies concern the field of pedagogy and her main research interest focus on supporting children's growth and wellbeing. She has published many articles in international journals and proceedings of international conferences.

Vana Chiou is member of the Laboratory Teaching Staff at the Department of Geography, University of the Aegean (Greece) in Educational Psychology. Her research interests include contemporary methods of teaching, didactics in teaching geography, teacher training, and inclusion in education. She is co-editor of the book series "Voices from the Classroom" (Waxman publications). Her published work includes editing books, chapters in books, and articles in Greek and international journals. She is a participant in and co-coordinator of different European projects.

Andri Christodoulou is the Director of the Counseling Center for Research and Psychological Services (SKEPSI) and a Lecturer in Clinical Psychology in the graduate Counseling Psychology program at Neapolis University of Pafos (NUP). She is also a practicing Registered Clinical Psychologist with a specialization in children and adolescents. She holds a Doctorate degree in Clinical-Child Psychology and a Master's degree in School Psychology from Pace University, and a Master's degree in Experimental Psychology from the C.W. Post Campus of Long Island University in New York, USA. Her interests include the study of family dynamics, ego development, trauma, defense structure, attachment, and working alliance as seen by the patient and therapist. She is also researching aggression, delinquency, and victimization, and works on developing and applying prevention and intervention programs that aim to cultivate and improve the socio-emotional skills of children and adolescents.

Pineio Christodoulou is a graduate of the Pedagogical Department of Kindergarten Teachers of the School of Humanities and Social Sciences of the University of Patras, Greece. She holds a master's and doctoral degree in Special Education. She was a scholarship holder of I.K.Y. at undergraduate, postgraduate and doctoral level. She has taught in primary, secondary and tertiary education. She is a kindergarten teacher at 23 Kindergarten in Agrinio and also teaches in the postgraduate program of Special Education at the University of Nicosia in Cyprus. She participated as a delegate, but also as a speaker at Greek and international scientific conferences. Publishes articles in reputable Greek and international scientific journals. She is the co-author of a book. She has been a reviewer of articles in Greek and international scientific journals, as well as conference presentations. She has attended many specialization seminars in Special Education. She is a certified instructor in adult education in non-formal education.

Ifigeneia Dosi is an Assistant Processor in Linguistics at Democritus University of Thrace (Department of Greek Philology). She holds a PhD from the Department of Greek Philology (Aristotle University of Thessaloniki). Her doctoral thesis investigated the interrelation of grammatical & lexical aspect and cognitive abilities in bilingual children. She received an individual IKY fellowship for her postdoctoral research on Developmental Language Disorder. She has also participated in several research projects and she has published her work on international journal and conferences. She has considerable teaching experience and participation in training programs for educators who work with refugees and heritage speakers. Finally, her research interests include language development of bilinguals in interrelation with cognitive abilities and contextual factors in (a)typical development.

Ifigeneia Dosi, Assistant Professor of Applied Linguistics at Democritus University of Thrace, works on bilingual language development. She was awarded an IKY scholarship for her research on word definition strategies in children with language disorders. With a focus on bilingual children's language and cognitive development, she has published in high-impact scientific journals. Additionally, she has provided training for educators working with refugees and heritage speakers. Her research interests center on studying the language development of bilingual children, examining the interplay of cognitive and environmental factors in both typical and atypical development.

Vasiliki Folia earned her graduate degree from the Department of Psychology at Aristotle University of Thessaloniki and holds a MSc degree in Cognitive Neuroscience from Radboud University, The Netherlands. Her PhD, completed at Karolinska Institutet, Department of Clinical Cognitive Neuroscience, Sweden, focused on Implicit Learning of Artificial Grammars/Syntax via neuroimaging and neurophysiological methods (fMRI, EEG and rTMS). Following her doctoral studies, Dr. Folia taught at the Amsterdam University of Applied Sciences (AUAS), as an Assistant Pofessor from 2009 to 2012; and as an Associate Professor from 2013 to 2018. She also served as a Research Chair from 2016 to 2018. She joined the Department of Psychology in Aristotle University in 2021. Her primary research interests lie in the field of neuropsychology of language, both in healthy and clinical populations. Specifically, her work revolves around investigating neural language mechanisms, serial language processing, implicit learning and other cognitive functions that contribute to syntactic and linguistic ability. To achieve these objectives, she employs a combination of behavioral/neuropsychological, neurophysiological, and neuroimaging methods.

Theodoros Goutoglou is a fourth-year undergraduate psychology student at Neapolis University Pafos. He is keen on both research and applied psychology. His primary research interests include developmental and cognitive psychology, focusing on nutrition and body image, children and adolescents, delinquent behavior, abuse, and migration. During the academic year 2023-2024, Mr. Goutoglou served as President of the Neapolis University Psychology Club, where he actively organized and implemented various activities. Since February 2023, he has worked as the Secretary to the Director at the Counselling Centre for Research and Psychological Services (SKEPSI). Additionally, Mr. Goutoglou has contributed as a research assistant to various research projects.

Georgios A. Kougioumtzis is an Associate Professor in the Department of Turkish Studies and Modern Asian Studies, at National and Kapodistrian University of Athens, Greece, in the field of Counseling, ICT, and Teaching Methodology; a Visiting Professor in the School of Psychology, at Neapolis University Pafos, Cyprus, in the field of Counseling / Educational Psychology, and Specific Learning Difficulties, and a Visiting Academic in the School of Social Sciences, at Hellenic Open University, Patras, Greece, in the field of Psychology / Counseling. He holds a Ph.D. in Pedagogics, Teaching Methodology, and Counseling / Teacher Mentoring, from the Department of Philosophy, Pedagogy, and Psychology - National and Kapodistrian University of Athens. He has published 12 books by IGI Global (USA) and Grigori Publications (Greece) in the fields of Educational Psychology, Counseling Psychology, Specific Learning Difficulties, and Teaching Methodology and ICT, and over than two hundred (200) papers. He is married and the father of three daughters.

Eleni Kouki is an elementary school teacher, and she is currently pursuing her PhD in Applied Linguistics at Democritus University of Thrace. Her research focuses on the interplay of lexical development, working memory and contextual factors in bilingual/multilingual children within minority educational communities. She is also interested in implementing intervention programs aimed at fostering language development, addressing learning challenges, and promoting inclusion.

Panagiota Koutsimani is a Cognitive Neuropsychologist. Her main interests include the examination of the factors that affect the cognitive performance of both underage and adult populations, such as chronic stress and brain injuries. Panagiota Koutsimani is also doing research in clinical neuropsychology. Currently, she is a post-doctoral researcher on the School of Psychology at the Aristotle University of Thessaloniki where she examines the sleep trajectories of older individuals and the consequent onset of mild cognitive impairment and dementia. She also works as an Adjunct Lecturer on the School of Psychology at the University of Western Macedonia. She has published her research in scientific journals and she has presented her research work in conferences. Her PhD thesis has received the "Maria Nasiakou" award from the Hellenic Psychological Society. She is a member of the Hellenic Psychological Society and the Hellenic Neuropsychological Society, and is also Treasurer of the Hellenic Neuropsychological Society.

Vasiliki Lymperopoulou is a bachelor degree holder from the Department of Primary Education, University of Patras and has a Master's degree in Special Education: "Special Education and Training of People with Oral and Written Speech Problems" from the Hellenic Open University and the University of Thessaly (joint postgraduate program). She is a PhD candidate at the Department of Special Education, University of Thessaly. Her research interests include language development in individuals with developmental disorders, specifically Developmental Language Disorder and Autism Spectrum Disorder.

Afroditi Malisiova is an EFL teacher and a Ph.D. candidate in the Department of Psychology at Aristotle University of Thessaloniki, Greece. She holds a degree in English Language and Literature from the Aristotle University of Thessaloniki, a Master's degree in Teaching English as a Foreign Language (TEFL) from the Hellenic Open University, and a Master of Science in Educational Psychology from the University of Neapolis, Pafos. Since 2005, she has been working as an English language teacher in both the private and state sectors of Greek primary and secondary schools. Her research interests lie in the fields of teaching English as a foreign language, cognitive psychology, special education, and intercultural education.

Kalliopi Megari is a Postdoctoral researcher of Aristotle University of Thessaloniki, Greece, Academic Director of MSc in Clinical Psychology and Clinical supervisor at City College, University of York, Europe Campus. She is Adjunct lecturer at University of Western Macedonia in Florina, Greece. Dr. Megari is a psychologist with a history of working in the hospital & health care industry, skilled in Clinical Neuropsychology, Clinical Research, Medical Education, Psychological Assessment and Learning Disabilities. She works both in clinical and in research practice and she provides strong professional healthcare services, graduated from Aristotle University of Thessaloniki, and attended further education from Department of Educational and Social Policy, University of Macedonia, in people with special needs and disabilities. She holds undergraduate degrees in Nursing and Psychology, as well as a Master's and a PhD in Neuropsychology from Aristotle University of Thessaloniki. She has some years of occupational and research experience working with patients who have neurological, psychiatric, and cognitive disorders, as well as chronic disease patients suffering from cancer and cardiovascular diseases. She is the head of the Centre of creative activities of children and adults with disabilities and she also works as a counseling psychologist in Prison, Diavata Thessaloniki, at the school of second chance. She was the Global Engagement Representative of SLC International Neuropsychological Society from 2018-2021 and she was a research fellow in the Department of Cardiovascular Surgery in AHEPA Hospital. Currently she is a Global Membership Committee member of International Neuropsychological Society and leader of Rehabilitation of COVID-19 patients working group of NeuroCOVID International Neuropsychology Taskforce SIG. In addition, she is the General Secretary of the board of directors of Hellenic Neuropsychological Society and Ethics Committee president of Hellenic Neuropsychological Society. Since 2021, she is a member of PIAC Community Outreach Subcommittee of AMERICAN PSYCHOLOGICAL ASSOCIATION Membership and a member of Engagement Committee of American Group Psychotherapy Association (AGPA). Her work has earned her many prestigious international awards and was an Ambassador of National Academy of Neuropsychology (NAN), USA Leadership and Ambassador Development Program (2022-23). She has given lectures at Aristotle University of Thessaloniki, University of Warsaw and Norwegian University of Science and Technology in Oslo. She is committed to leadership skills and issues on equity, diversity, and inclusion as her clinical and research work states.

Amani Mohamed is a dedicated educator with extensive expertise in K-12 and higher education in the United Arab Emirates. She holds a Bachelor's degree in Economics and Social Studies and a Master's in Leadership, Management, and Policy in Education from the British University in Dubai. Dr. Mohamed earned her PhD in Special Education from the United Arab Emirates University (UAEU). Her expertise spans special education, inclusive education, assessment, curriculum development, Arabic language instruction, teaching, and educational leadership. Additionally, Dr. Mohamed has been involved in collaborative research between UAEU and University College London (UCL), contributing to one of the largest studies on special education and cultural practices in the UAE.

Marilena Mousoulidou is an Assistant Professor of Cognitive Psychology in the Department of Psychology at Neapolis University Pafos. She obtained her PhD in Cognitive Psychology from the University of Leicester (UK) and her BSc in Psychology from the University of Derby (UK). Marilena Mousoulidou's primary research interest concerns examining the impact of reading on a person's attitudes, decisions, beliefs, emotions, and well-being. She is also researching aggression, delinquency, and victimization, and she works on developing and applying prevention and intervention programs that aim to cultivate and improve the socio-emotional skills of children and adolescents. She has provided dozens of invited seminars and training to primary and secondary education teachers regarding delinquency and aggression in the school setting. She has published articles in peer-reviewed journals and participates in COST and Erasmus+ research programs in Europe.

Eleni Nikolaou is an Assistant Professor at the Department of Sciences of Preschool Education and Educational Design, University of the Aegean. She has been teaching at the University of the Aegean since 2006. She has worked for almost fifteen consecutive years in a counseling and mental health service for children, adolescents and their families in Rhodes, Greece. During her career she has given a lot of lectures in schools regarding mental health issues and she has been participated in professional development training courses for teachers. She holds a Ph.D. from the Department of Preschool Education and Educational Design, University of the Aegean (2005). She completed her postgraduate studies at City University, London (M.Sc. in Counseling Psychology, 1999). She holds a Bachelor's Degree in Psychology from the University of Crete (1996). She has numerous publications in reputable journals, books and conference proceedings.

Eleonora Papaleontiou - Louca is an associate professor in Psychology at the European University Cyprus, Department of Social and Behavioral Sciences. She has a B.Ed. degree (Cyprus & Greece), an M.A. in Education (University of Reading, U.K.) and a PhD in Developmental / Cognitive and Educational Psychology (Cardiff University, U.K.). She is also a PhD candidate in Psychology of Religion, at the Kapodistrian University of Athens. She has published many articles in Greek and international journals and has also published 6 books: 2 books on "Children's and Adolescents' Mental Health" (Armos pl/hers), "Current Trends in Preschool Curriculum" Tipothito pl/hers, Getting Out of the Woods: A Guide for the Creative Path – Fostering Creativity in Universities (Group Project publishes by EUC Research Center), "Metacognition and Theory of Mind", Cambridge Scholars Publications and "Metacognition: Theory and Practice" Thymari Publications, Greece. Dr E. Louca has also given hundreds of lectures to parents and specialized groups on psychological topics and children's upbringing issues. She presents her radio program on topics of psychology and education (The Soul's Paths).

Asterios Patsiaouras has been teaching undergraduate and post-graduate courses on subjects relevant to sport psychology. He is a Section Editor for the scientific journal of Physical Education and Sports (www.pepfa.gr). Dr. Patsiaouras has published widely on physical education, sport psychology, and high level performance, mainly in Volleyball. His work has been recognized through distinguished invitations from international organizations served as a Supervisor in CEV and BVA responsible, as a president of game Jury, for international volleyball matches. He was Board member of the Development Committee in the Hellenic Volleyball Federation. Nowadays, he is elected vice President of Hellenic Volleyball Coaches Association (seppe.com.gr) and he is elected President of the Volleyball Union in Central Greece (espekel.com). Since 2015 he is an Expert Consultant for IKY and the Erasmus+KA2 projects in field of Universities and Sports and as a Evaluator for the Research Promotion Foundation's IRIS, (RPF) for Cyprus (IRID: 49880). His citation index is >1343 with an h-index of 15, i10 index=19

Aastha Singh is currently pursuing Bachelors in psychology honours at Graphic Era (Deemed to be) University. As a bachelor's student, she developed an interest in research and is keen to explore and contribute to the field of psychological sciences. Her research started with exploring various subjects and analysing data.

Ajay K. Singh is working as an Associate Professor (Research) in the Department of Humanities and Social Science, Graphic Era (Deemed to be University) Dehradun. He has worked as Assistant Professor (Economics) in the School of Liberal Arts & Management, DIT University Dehradun for 6 years. He did Post-Doctorate Research with EDI of India, Ahmedabad, Gujarat (India). He received MPhil (Economics) from DAVV Indore (India), and PhD (Economics) from IIT Indore (India. He has published several research papers in the diversified area such as climate change, agricultural productivity, assessment of food security; estimation of GFSI, development of environmental sustainability index (ESI) and its association with socio-economic indicators; measurement and determinants of entrepreneurship ecosystem, and dimension of sustainable development and its interlinkages with economic development.

Ravindra Singh has completed his Ph.D. from Banaras Hindu University (Institute of Eminence). Currently, he is working as an Assistant Professor of Psychology at Graphic Era Deemed to be University, Dehradun. Earlier he was Indian Youth Ambassador at BRICS. Beijing China 2017 during the Indian delegation. Dr. Singh has also worked as a Junior Project Fellow, on a funded project, in New Delhi in 2018. He worked as a Former Teaching Assistant at IIT, BHU. Recently he was the Youth Member at G20 Youth for India's G-20 Presidency. He served as an Independent Reviewer in Frontiers in Psychology Journal and a Member at APA, International Affiliate, Washington DC, and a member of the prestigious National Academy of Psychology, (NAOP) India. He has 7 Years of teaching experience and supervising 3 PhD candidates along with many posts' graduate thesis supervision.

Zoi Siouti (PhDc) is a Clinical and Counseling Psychologist for children, adolescents and adults, specializing in Cognitive Behavioral Therapy (CBT), Eye Movement Desensitization and Reprocessing (EMDR) and Acceptance and Commitment Therapy (ACT). She has studied Psychology at the University of Crete and holds five postgraduate degrees. Mrs Siouti has conducted research and participated in Psychology Conferences as well as she has worked as a Psychologist in Public and Private institutions. At the moment Mrs Siouti works as an external scientific associate – Psychologist at the Department of Clinical and Translational Research in Endocrinology of the Medical School (University of Athens) and maintains a private practice in Attica.

Kyriaki Tasiou is a teacher and works for the last 14 years at a primary school as a special education teacher. She holds a Master's degree on the topic: "Gender and New Educational and Working Environments in the Information Society" of the T.E.P.A.E.S.-University of the Aegean and Master's degree with the title: "Sciences of Education: Special Education and Education of Persons with Problems of Oral and Written Communication" of the Inter-University MSc of the EAP with the University of Thessaly. She has been trained in Greek Sign Language. She is a PhD candidate at the T.E.P.A.E.S of the University of the Aegean.

Maria Theodoratou-Bekou, Ph.D., is a Clinical Psychologist holding a doctorate in Clinical Psychology from the National and Kapodistrian University of Athens, Greece. Her academic journey commenced with a Bachelor's degree in Philosophy, Pedagogy, and Psychology from the University of Athens, followed by an additional Bachelor's degree in Psychology obtained in France. She furthered her education with a successful completion of a Master's degree in Clinical Psychology and Psychopathology at the University of Aix-Marseille I, Provence, France. With over 25 years of extensive experience, Maria has shared her expertise by serving as an Adjunct Lecturer in psychology at the Hellenic Open University, Greece, and Neapolis University of Pafos, Cyprus, since 2017. Her professional repertoire also includes work as a psychologist in the private sector. Despite her demanding professional commitments, Maria maintains a balanced life as a dedicated spouse and mother to two students.

Assimina Tsibidaki is an Associate Professor of Special Education in the Department of Primary Education at the University of the Aegean (Greece). Her research interests focus on the following areas: Students with special educational needs and disabilities (SEND), families raising a child with SEND, home-school collaboration, social support networks, technology and inclusive education, disability in children's literature and cinema. Her published work includes two books, editing and articles in Greece and abroad, as well as various participations in Greek and international conferences

Esther Vicente Manzanedo is completing her PhD at the University of East Anglia. Her current project focuses on foreign language aptitude in multilingual children, and how it presents itself at different ages. She is also interested in the role of working memory, its relationship with aptitude, and how different aspects of working memory (phonological/executive) gain relevance at early or late stages of the second language acquisition process. Her research interests lay in the intersectionallity between Applied Lingusitics, Psycholinguistics, and Language Learning (Education), especially in relation to Individual Differences.

Filippos Vlachos is a Professor of Educational Neuroscience and Developmental Disorders at the University of Thessaly, Greece, where he has taught and conducted research since 1997. He is the author of the book Handedness: Myths and Reality (in Greek), editor of the book Brain, Learning & Special Education (in Greek) and co-editor in three more scientific editions. He has published more than 160 articles in referred national & international journals, book chapters and congress proceedings, with more than 1500 known citations. His research interests include the investigation of the neural mechanisms of reading, numerical cognition, attention and their attendant difficulties including learning difficulties and other developmental disorders as they relate to education, as well as the relationship between brain laterality and cognitive abilities.

Index

T

theory of mind 30, 40, 142, 146, 149, 152, 154, 155, 157, 159, 249, 250, 252, 253, 254, 255, 258, 259, 262, 264, 265, 266, 267, 269, 270, 271

treatment 27, 35, 42, 49, 50, 52, 57, 61, 62, 63, 66, 70, 87, 137, 142, 145, 150, 153, 154, 163, 164, 165, 167, 175, 176, 180, 203, 212, 213, 214, 220, 221, 222, 223, 224, 227, 228, 232, 236, 239, 240, 241, 243, 244, 277, 285, 305, 311, 312, 314, 317, 320

typical children 23, 24, 26, 28, 32

W

weak central cohesion 149

well-being 2, 3, 9, 10, 12, 13, 14, 15, 16, 27, 45, 46, 55, 56, 57, 60, 61, 62, 67, 69, 70, 71, 76, 77, 78, 79, 80, 81, 82, 84, 87, 88, 92, 118, 168, 188, 212, 221, 222, 229, 230, 231, 232, 233, 234, 235, 236, 237, 238, 239, 240, 241, 242, 243, 244, 245, 283, 299, 315, 320

working memory 27, 29, 36, 147, 150, 153, 159, 160, 179, 181, 182, 183, 189, 192, 193, 194, 195, 196, 197, 198, 199, 200, 226, 234, 254, 266, 268, 270

Milton Keynes UK
Ingram Content Group UK Ltd.
UKHW051829230924
448765UK00009B/192